Heavenly wisdom

Heavenly wisdom

Proverbs simply explained

Gary Brady

 **EVANGELICAL PRESS**

EVANGELICAL PRESS
Faverdale North Industrial Estate, Darlington, DL3 0PH, England

Evangelical Press USA
P. O. Box 825, Webster, New York 14580, USA

e-mail: sales@evangelicalpress.org

web: http://www.evangelicalpress.org

First published 2003

British Library Cataloguing in Publication Data available

ISBN 0 85234 543 7

Printed and bound in Great Britain by Creative Print & Design Wales,
Ebbw Vale

To the memory of my mother, now in heaven,
who taught me my first proverbs;
and to my father,
who taught me in his house
when I was a boy and still tender,
while I was still my mother's only child.

i fy mechgyn Rhodri, Dylan, Dewi, Gwïon ac Owain
*Yr awr hon, O blant, gwrandewch arnaf fi, ac na ymadewch
â geiriau fy ngenau*

Contents

Vocabulary (10:1-22:16)

More vocabulary (22:17 – 29:27)

Final lessons (30:1 – 31:31)

Acknowledgements

In producing a volume of this sort, one draws on many resources, both directly and indirectly. Sometimes one is conscious of this, sometimes not. Here I simply wish to acknowledge some of the many to whom I believe I am most directly indebted.

As a student in my twenties, I listened to Philip H. Eveson's lectures on Proverbs. At this remove it is difficult to calculate the extent of their impact on my thinking, but it has undoubtedly been significant.

It has been my privilege to pastor Childs Hill Baptist Church, 'man and boy', since 1983. These have been demanding but happy years of constant change. The core of the book was prepared originally for that congregation. Some have heard much of this material twice over, first on Sunday evenings and later at midweek meetings. I am thankful for various contributions. Cliff and Rick in particular (usually from opposite ends of the spectrum) have sharpened my exegesis at certain points.

I am also indebted to my sisters-in-law and their husbands, Catrin and Ian and Fflur and Glyn, for their kindness in reading drafts of the early chapters and for their enthusiasm and comments.

Thanks also to Gwydion and Catrin Lewis, to Derek Lewis, to Andrew Shrimpton and to my father-in-law Geoff Thomas and the Evangelical Library in London for the loan of relevant books.

I am very thankful to David Clark, Anthony Gosling, Anne Williamson and all at Evangelical Press. Their enthusiasm, efficiency and patience have been a great encouragement.

I was slightly embarrassed a few years ago when in response to the telephone company's offer of reduced charges on calls to my 'best friend' I nominated my computer! Various aspects of computer technology have been harnessed for the execution of this project, including the resources of the world-wide web; Larry Pierce's *On-line Bible*; various *Ages Software* CDs; the whole *Word for Windows* word-processing package and, occasionally, music from Jan Akkerman and others on the *Yamaha 32*. The equipment used was paid for by the trustees of *Grace Magazine*, which I edited for much of the time that I was working on this commentary. I am very grateful to them.

My real best friend is my wife Eleri, who possesses the divine characteristic of knowing all about me and yet still loving me. Without her wisdom, patience, encouragement, understanding and love this book would never have seen the light of day. *Diolch yn fawr, fy nghariad!* Many women have done noble things, but you surpass them all.

Preface

In the course of preparing this commentary I found myself thumbing through a beautiful old Passmore and Alabaster edition of C. H. Spurgeon's wonderful *Salt Cellars*. There I happened on a salutary proverb for anyone who invests time in Solomon's proverbs. It reads: 'Solomon made a Book of Proverbs but a Book of Proverbs won't make a Solomon.'

In one way I would like to say, 'Read this commentary and you will be wise.' However, having studied the book of Proverbs I know by experience that wisdom does not come in that simplistic fashion. Reading the book of Proverbs itself will not guarantee you wisdom. It was God who made Solomon wise and he alone can make you wise. However, in his providence, close attention to the proverbs can certainly be one of the things that he uses to give you wisdom. It is my prayer that this will be the case.

Before you begin to read, let me say a few things about this commentary that may help you to get the most out of it.

1. It is an 'interactive' commentary

The commentary is intended as much to be read as to be consulted. It is possible to look up what it says on individual verses in most cases but it is intended to be read chapter by chapter, page by page. I have sought throughout to interact with the reader in the way that preaching and good books do, but that commentaries often do not.

2. It is a devotional commentary

The chief aim of this commentary is to draw you nearer to God, not to explain every jot and tittle of the book of Proverbs. The concern throughout has been to discover the thrust of the verses expounded rather than to give a meticulous account of the various possible expositions. I have relied largely on the NIV text, although other texts have been consulted.

3. It is a practical commentary

True wisdom, as you will see, is a very practical thing. The purpose of this commentary is also to provide a practical tool that will enable the reader to put into practice what is written in Proverbs. Therefore, there are no endnotes, nor any careful attempt to trace back to their source ideas presented here. This is not because of any desire to deny due credit to the work of others but in order to concentrate attention on the main thing — practical godliness.

4. It is a Christian commentary

This may seem an odd thing to say about an evangelical commentary, but it is intended to underline that throughout the book I have been eager to trace the verses, as far as possible, back to our Saviour Christ. 'What does this teach us about him?' has been a constant question. Too often commentators confine themselves to moral and common-sense observations from Proverbs. It has been my concern throughout to discover spiritual applications. Some may feel that sometimes I have missed a route to Christ, and at others that a route to Christ has been pursued that involves jumping over hedges and running through fields, rather than sticking to the main road. If that is the case, I regret it. However, I have endeavoured to deal with the Scriptures faithfully and bring glory to Christ.

Gary Brady,
Childs Hill,
November 2003

Heavenly wisdom

The grammar and vocabulary of heavenly wisdom

The grammar
(Proverbs 1:1 – 9:18)

1.
How to be wise — lesson one

Please read Proverbs 1:1-7

Do you want to be wise? Do you want to be skilful, shrewd and practically able? Do you want to be intelligent, witty, informed, knowledgeable? Do you want success? The purpose of this book is to show you how.

'Sounds like a dodgy newspaper advertisement to me,' you say. Maybe you are instinctively cautious. Caution is good. Remember how the serpent spoke to Eve in the garden. Despite his grand claims, that episode led, not to wisdom, but to woe. Like Eve, we all want to be wise but, if we have any experience at all, we have learned to be cautious about amazing offers that promise the earth. 'Once bitten, twice shy,' says an English proverb. Proverbs itself encourages due caution: 'A simple man believes anything, but a prudent man gives thought to his steps' (14:15); 'The prudent see danger and take refuge, but the simple keep going and suffer for it' (27:12).

There are plenty of gullible people out there — immature, inexperienced and naïve souls who can easily be taken advantage of. There are plenty of frauds, scams and swindles too, waiting to catch the next unwary customer. A few years ago companies were offering to fly people across the Atlantic for free. The catch? You agree to pay for your stay in an expensive hotel while over there! Every weekend the glossy magazine supplements with the newspapers are full of advertisements for books and CDs at knock-down prices. But do read the small print explaining what it is you are committing yourself to before you sign up!

It is right to be cautious, but in this book I want us to focus on a book that is 'God-breathed'. It is the very Word of God. Proverbs is a book that, like the sixty-five others that make up Holy Scripture, is 'useful for teaching, rebuking, correcting and training in righteousness' (2 Tim. 3:16). An Old Testament book, it is quoted several times in the New Testament (see Rom. 2:6, quoting Prov. 24:12; Rom. 12:20, quoting Prov. 25:21-22; Heb. 12:5-6, quoting Prov. 3:11-12; Heb. 12:13, quoting Prov. 4:26; James 4:6, quoting Prov.3:34; 1 Peter 4:18, quoting Prov. 11:31; 1 Peter 5:5, quoting Prov. 3:34; 2 Peter 2:22, quoting Prov. 26:11).

It is usually grouped with the 'Wisdom Literature'. This also includes several psalms and especially Job and Ecclesiastes. The latter two books, as a modern writer puts it, deal with questions of 'Why?' and 'How?' They are somewhat 'speculative'. Proverbs, on the other hand, deals with the more basic questions that ask, 'What...?' It is intensely practical. Here is, in Derek Kidner's words, 'truth in street clothes'. It deals with everyday subjects such as laziness, pride, handling money and telling lies. Here we meet familiar folk such as the bargain-hunter (20:14), the neighbour you see too much of (25:17), the practical joker (26:19) and the 'morning person' who forgets that others take a while to surface (27:14).

Wisdom Literature is striking. Although it refers to 'the LORD', the covenant God of Israel, it is nevertheless willing to put the matter of Mosaic laws and ceremonies largely to one side and communicate in a way more readily understood by those without that background. It endeavours to show, not so much the sinfulness of sin, but the folly of it and deals much in what we may term 'sanctified common sense'. This makes it of perennial interest to people of all cultures. It is an ideal way into Scripture for those unwilling to approach from other angles. The nineteenth-century commentator Charles Bridges put it this way: of all Old Testament books it 'is the one which we may think of as most distinctively educational'. This is its tone. A teacher speaks to his student, an old man to a young man and, chiefly, a father to his son.

Having said this, we should recognize that the book is fully in line with what is found in the law of Moses. As with the prophets, what is laid down in Deuteronomy is always in the background and 'the LORD' is referred to directly some ninety times. In Deuteronomy 4:5-6 Moses says, 'See, I have taught you decrees and laws as the LORD my God commanded me, so that you may follow them in the land you are entering to take possession of it. Observe them carefully, for this will show your wisdom and understanding to the nations, who will hear about all these decrees and say, "Surely this great nation is a wise and understanding people."' Sadly, near the end of the book the Lord has to say:

> They are a nation without sense,
>   there is no discernment in them.
> If only they were wise and would understand this
>   and discern what their end will be!
>
> (Deut. 32:28-29).

The wisdom of Proverbs is there to remedy that potentially fatal tendency in the professing people of God.

'The proverbs'

A 'proverb' was originally a comparison or simile, such as, 'Like a gold ring in a pig's snout is a beautiful woman who shows no discretion' (Prov. 11:22). It could be any length and was, in some ways, more like a parable than a proverb as we think of it today. The word came to refer to any wise saying, maxim or observation — anything from a mere wisecrack to true wisdom from on high. Proverbs are words 'aptly spoken ... like apples of gold in settings of silver' (25:11). They act individually as 'goads', together as 'firmly embedded nails' and in Proverbs, as in Ecclesiastes, are ultimately 'given by one Shepherd' (Eccles. 12:11). The book is full of terse, memorable proverbs. Hence its official and popular name.

Where did the proverbs come from? Firstly and chiefly, they are **'the proverbs of Solomon'** (1:1). The book of Ecclesiastes also has a strong connection with that name. Ecclesiastes 12:9 speaks of 'the Teacher' imparting 'knowledge to the people'. It says, 'He pondered and searched out and set in order many proverbs.' Perhaps that explains what happened here. Some proverbs are the result of Solomon's own pondering; others he searched out from various sources. He and, later, others then set these in order to form the book we have today.

'... of Solomon'

A strong argument for paying attention to what we find in the book is the person of its chief author, **'Solomon son of David, king of Israel'**. In fact, here are a number of arguments.

1. These are the words of a king

Solomon ruled about 961-922 B.C., succeeding his father David as king of all Israel. Few kings write books, but surely someone who has ruled over a nation has insights to share.

2. These are the words of a king of Israel, God's chosen nation

Jeremiah 18:18 and other verses reveal that Israel had a place not only for 'the teaching of the law by the priest' and 'the word from the prophets', but also 'counsel from the wise'. God sent his ancient people, not only prophets and teachers, but also wise men. Even before Solomon, a wisdom tradition already existed in Israel. David's court had a place for wise counsellors such as his uncle, Jonathan, 'a counsellor, a man of insight and a scribe', and Ahithophel and Hushai (1 Chr. 27:32,33), who seem to have acted in an official capacity. We also read of the wise woman of Tekoa and of another from Abel, a town with a long reputation for wisdom (2 Sam. 14:2; 20:16). 1 Kings 4:31 refers to other wise men of Solomon's day: 'Ethan the Ezrahite ... Heman, Calcol and Darda, the sons of Mahol'.

Established cultures generate their own wisdom, often in the form, firstly of single proverbs, and then, later, of collections. Because they are brief and memorable, proverbs are an excellent means of retaining compact and portable nuggets of accumulated wisdom. To carry £100 sterling in silver coins is to bear a considerable weight, but five £20 notes are so light that even a child can carry them easily. A small expensive diamond in a pocket may be worth more than a truckload of steel. That illustrates the advantage that proverbs give.

Israel's neighbours also esteemed wisdom and there are examples of it in ancient Egyptian, Babylonian, Phoenician and other literatures. 'Solomon's wisdom was greater than the wisdom of all the men of the East, and greater than all the wisdom of Egypt' (1 Kings 4:30). It seems that on occasion Scripture makes use of such wisdom from other cultures in modified form. God's people, inevitably, received superior wisdom. Their wisdom came, ultimately, from heaven itself.

3. These are the words of a great king of Israel

Solomon was the greatest king Israel ever had. He was one of the greatest kings who ever lived. The description of the splendour of his reign in 1 Kings 10 is full of superlatives. He was 'greater in riches ... than all the other kings of the earth'.

4. These are the words of the son of great King David, a
man after God's own heart

David's son and heir, wrote the early nineteenth-century com-
mentator George Lawson, 'enjoyed all the advantages to be expected from the instructions and the example, the prayers and the blessings, of so good a father'. Solomon was both a prophet and the son of a prophet.

5. These are the words of the wisest man who ever lived

We know from 1 Kings how, on becoming king, Solomon was conscious of his unworthiness and so asked God for wisdom. God always 'gives generously to all without finding fault' (James 1:5) and Solomon became the wisest man ever. His wisdom was typified in his famous judgement, early in his reign, between two prostitutes who came to him seeking justice (1 Kings 3:16-28). Both women had given birth to babies and were living together under the same roof. One night, one of them had rolled onto her baby, suffocating it, and it had died. She had then gone to the other bed, put the dead baby next to the other woman and taken her baby. This had led to a dispute over who truly was mother to the surviving baby.

'The living one is my son; the dead one is yours,' says the one.

'No!' replies the other. 'The dead one is yours; the living one is mine.'

'My son is alive and your son is dead.'

'No! Your son is dead and mine is alive.'

And so it went on, until Solomon hit on the surprising expedient of calling for a sword to cut the surviving child in two!

That soon revealed the true mother as she pleaded that he spare the life of her dear little one even if it meant her losing custody of the baby. 'When all Israel heard the verdict the king had given, they held the king in awe, because they saw that he had wisdom from God to administer justice' (1 Kings 3:28).

1 Kings 4:29-34 speaks of Solomon's wisdom and fame and of his 3,000 proverbs and 1,005 songs. Clearly, only a selection has been preserved in the book before us. Maybe the other songs and proverbs dealt with 'plant life ... animals and birds, reptiles and fish', and so were not preserved. Bridges and others suggest this and underline the purpose of Scripture, which is 'not to teach philosophy but religion; not to make men of science, but men of sound godliness'. On the other hand, several proverbs grow out of an observation of nature. There are references to flora ('a green leaf', 11:28; 'thorns' and 'weeds', 24:31; 'a thornbush', 26:9; 'a fig tree', 27:18; 'grain', 27:22; 'hay' and 'grass', 27:25; 'crops', 28:3); to fauna (' a gazelle,' 'a bird' and 'the ant', 6:5,6; 'a bear', 17:12; 'a lion', 19:12; 'an eagle', 23:5; 'a snake' and 'a viper', 23:32; 'a fluttering sparrow' and 'a darting swallow', 26:2; 'the horse' and 'the donkey', 26:3; 'a dog', 26: 11; 'a bird that strays from its nest', 27:8; 'flocks' and 'herds', 27:23; 'lambs' and 'goats', 27:26; 'the leech', 30:15; 'ants', 'conies', 'locusts' and 'a lizard', 30:26-28; 'a strutting cock', 30:31); and to meteorology ('a storm' and 'a whirlwind', 1:27; 'the clouds' that 'drop the dew', 3:20; 8:28; snow, 25:13; 'a north wind' that 'brings rain', 25:23).

'God gave Solomon wisdom and very great insight, and a breadth of understanding as measureless as the sand on the seashore. Solomon's wisdom was greater than the wisdom of all the men of the East, and greater than all the wisdom of Egypt. He was wiser than any other man... And his fame spread to all the surrounding nations' (1 Kings 4:29-31).

Hiram, King of Tyre, observed that the Lord had 'given
King David a wise son, endowed with intelligence and discernment' (2 Chr. 2:12). In 1 Kings 10, we have an unembel-
lished account of the Queen of Sheba's visit and her amaze-
ment at his wisdom and splendour. 1 Kings 4:34 tells us that
'Men of all nations came to listen to Solomon's wisdom, sent
by all the kings of the world, who had heard of his wisdom.'

6. These are the words of God himself

They come through men, of course, but form part of Scripture. God had his hand on Solomon as he sorted, sifted and
recorded these proverbs, gathered from diverse sources, so
that we have here inspired, God-breathed words of life that
are able to 'make wise to salvation'. As one writer puts it, the
Spirit used 'Solomon like a magpie to snatch up sparkling treasures of wisdom' wherever he found them.

Not all the proverbs are Solomon's, any more than all the
psalms are David's. He is, however, the principal author. Other
authors (Lemuel and Agur) and compilers (Hezekiah) are
mentioned and the final section is anonymous. There are also
collected 'sayings of the wise'. We cannot be sure when the
whole book was assembled. It seems likely that it reached its
present form in the time of another wise king, King Hezekiah,
but it may have been later still.

The introduction

The book of Proverbs is not simply an anthology of proverbs.
First, in chapters 1-9, we have an important introduction. Here
is instruction on how to make proper use of the proverbs found
in the sections that follow. After the opening verses, we can

divide the text into a series of some ten fatherly talks, followed by an appeal from wisdom itself and a conclusion in chapter 9. John H. Sket and others have worked to show how carefully structured these chapters are, 'utilizing certain common features of the Israelite literary traditions', especially symmetry and inclusion. Some of the detail is difficult but this observation is undoubtedly true and we shall seek to note such features where appropriate.

It is sometimes tempting to skip introductions in books or similar materials. Wading through every word of a manual for a computer or some other piece of equipment before using it can seem tedious, even pointless. However, experience teaches us that making efforts to master introductory materials early on can often save time in the long run.

> If the axe is dull
>   and its edge unsharpened,
> more strength is needed
>
> (Eccles. 10:10).

Time spent in preparation is not time wasted. One of the later proverbs warns: 'Like a lame man's legs that hang limp is a proverb in the mouth of a fool' (26:7). Worse still, it can be like 'a thornbush in a drunkard's hand' (26:9). We need to master wise ways before we start giving wise advice.

Over the years, I have attempted to learn different languages. I remember in school receiving textbooks for French, German and Latin. Each time my attention was drawn first to the ends of these books, where the vocabulary lists were. Learning vocabulary always seemed to me the most interesting, easy and worthwhile component. However, I have learned that proficiency in vocabulary without a proper understanding of the grammar found at the front of the textbook makes communication in any language rather difficult. A lack of early application here may mean never speaking the new language with any great facility. Proverbs 1-9, we may say, gives us the 'grammar', the proper context, in order for us to make use of the extensive vocabulary provided at the end of the book. It is, therefore, well worth our attention. Proverbs is here to provide a course of education in how to live a life of wisdom. Time spent mastering its initial lessons, before moving on to the wisdom of the proverbs proper, is not time wasted. Remember, *all Scripture* 'is useful'. It is *all* there to make us 'wise to salvation'.

Five purposes

Right at the beginning, Solomon lists five purposes for the book. Before you can look for a thing, you must have some idea of what it is you are looking for. These descriptions overlap, but together they give a good idea of the book's purpose. They give an insight into the many colours that make up the rainbow of wisdom. As David Hubbard puts it, this paragraph is 'chock full of meaty morsels ... that ... whet the appetite of even the most casual reader'.

1. For attaining wisdom and discipline (1:2)

The chief use of the book is in order to know or gain wisdom, or *skill*. In Job 28, Job reflects on how hard wisdom is to obtain. Silver and gold are difficult enough to mine from the ground, but wisdom is rarer and even more difficult to extract:

But where can wisdom be found?
   Where does understanding dwell? ...
   it cannot be found in the land of the living...

It cannot be bought with the finest gold,
    nor can its price be weighed in silver…
Neither gold nor crystal can compare with it,
    nor can it be had for jewels of gold.
Coral and jasper are not worthy of mention;
    the price of wisdom is beyond rubies…
It is hidden from the eyes of every living thing,
    concealed even from the birds of the air…
God understands the way to it
    and he alone knows where it dwells
                    (Job 28:12-18,21,23).

The use here of the word **'discipline'**, or' instruction', or 'correction', confirms that wisdom is hard-won. Like mining for precious metal or stones, wisdom does not come without effort on the part of the one who would gain it. Wisdom is a matter of character and discipleship as much as of intelligence or use of the mind. This is something to which old fairy tales sometimes allude, as do more modern stories about practitioners of ancient martial arts who gain mental strength through rigorous physical discipline. Modern sportsmen have realized that success in their chosen field is a matter of mental as well as physical training. This has been marked by the advent of the sports psychologist.

The same discipline required to achieve a physical peak is also necessary to gain the mental and spiritual prowess that characterizes true heavenly wisdom. From time to time newspaper headlines hail a previous unknown as an 'overnight success'. We soon discover, however, that the success has been anything but 'overnight'. Rather, it is usually the result of years of struggle and effort. So it is with wisdom. Even Solomon, who received a dramatic, overnight and miraculous donation of wisdom, knew this. The very fact that, paradoxically, he had the wisdom to ask God for wisdom, and not for riches or long life, shows that God had already given him a measure of insight before he prayed. It reminds us of the later promise: 'Before they call I will answer; while they are still speaking I will hear' (Isa. 65:24). By God's grace, wisdom and discipline are attainable. Cry to God for them.

2. For understanding words of insight (1:2)

This book is here to show, or teach, us how to be *discerning*, how to understand **'words of insight'** or gain insights into words of understanding. I used to love to watch a man called Arthur Negus talking about antiques on the television. He would take an ornament, turn it over a few times, then tell you when and where it was made, and sometimes even who made it. He could tell the genuine article from a fake, too. An authority on precious metals or stones possesses similar abilities. He can discern genuine from counterfeit. A long-serving bank teller picks up what looks like a £20 note. 'A forgery,' he says. He can tell by touch alone. These are discerning people. They have learned to distinguish things that differ. This quality is one we all need to develop. According to Hebrews 5:14, mature Christians have 'trained themselves to distinguish good from evil'. Obviously experience is important here, but the book of Proverbs can be a great help to us in the maturing process. It will also deliver us from the superficial approach so common in our age of 'spin', where image is often made to count for more than substance.

3. For acquiring a displined and prudent life, doing what is just and right and fair (1:3)

True wisdom is very practical. It involves good sense. It encompasses not only discipline but also careful thought, insight or prudence. You will find the same word in Isaiah 52:13 referring to Christ: 'See, my servant will act wisely.' We see such wisdom not only in Christ but also, to a lesser degree, in all who follow him. The effect of this practical wisdom is always moral renovation — what is right and just and fair, or *justice, judgement and equity*, will characterize the truly wise in all their dealings. A man who thinks he is wise but is unfair or immoral needs to think again. Paul Johnson's book *The Intellectuals* is a disturbing exposé of how men such as Hemingway, Ibsen, Marx, Shelley, Rousseau and Bertrand Russell, despite undoubted brilliance, proved moral disasters in their private lives. All the way through Proverbs, the interconnection between true wisdom and righteousness is emphasized. What is wrong and unfair often springs from ill-discipline and imprudence.

4. For giving prudence to the simple, knowledge and discretion to the young (1:4-5)

Those who are **'simple'** are not the mentally deficient but the immature and untaught. Literally, they are 'open' — ready to receive impressions, good or bad. Often they are young, though not always. **'Prudence'** here is a rare word meaning shrewdness or subtlety; **'knowledge'** refers not just to head knowledge but to knowing God himself and all that flows from it; **'discretion'** is the power to form plans, devise, formulate.

Verse 5 goes on to refer to **'learning'** and **'guidance'**. The emphasis is on receiving — receiving knowledge or counsel. 'Guidance' or 'counsel' is another rare word. It may literally be 'the ropes' — in other words, learning how to live day by day, how to steer a right course on life's dangerous seas.

All this can be yours, however much you lack at present. Many look for such things but never find them. They remain foolish, ignorant, clueless, aimless. But here are the answers.

Here is the solution. Here is true wisdom. It is particularly encouraging that it is put in the way that it is. University courses often require a great many qualifications before you can even start but here, even if you know nothing at all, there is hope. For other courses there may be age-barriers, but Proverbs is especially for the young who have so much to learn. Much of the book deliberately aims at young people. At the entrance to Plato's school, we are told, there was a notice which said, 'Let no one who is not a geometrician enter.' Over the entrance to Solomon's school we read, 'Let the simple, ignorant, foolish and immature come in.'

But this instruction is not only for the young and the simple. Verse 5 says, **'Let the wise listen and add to their learning, and let the discerning get guidance.'** There is plenty here for those who believe they are already wise and discerning. We all have more to learn. It is an important part of wisdom to realize this. However far you have come, you have not advanced so far that this book cannot teach you something. Here is wisdom for the youngest Sunday school child, the most profound theologian and all of us in between.

5. For understanding proverbs and parables, the sayings and riddles of the wise (1:6)

Finally, this book is here to set you thinking. It aims to get under your skin. Most of our thoughts are shallow. People avoid big questions, the hard ones. Few want to talk purposefully about God, death, the soul, or the meaning of life. True wisdom is not like that. True wisdom tackles such questions. It goes to the heart of the matter. Here is a book that will instil in you the habit of mind that thinks in a deeper, more profound way. It will help you with **'proverbs and parables'**, or 'satires' or enigmas — sayings that slip away — and also with '**sayings and riddles** [or hard questions] **of the wise**'. The wisdom here is practical but it opens up great vistas yet unseen.

The first lesson

So, do you want to be wise? Do you want to be well instructed, discerning, morally upright, shrewd, aware of how to live, able to understand difficult things? Enquire within. Here is true wisdom. For here, as throughout Scripture, we see the Messiah Jesus. Especially we see him in Proverbs as the one greater than Solomon 'who has become for us' who believe 'wisdom from God' (1 Cor. 1:30). Christ, and especially his death on the cross, seems foolish to the world, but 'The foolishness of God is wiser than man's wisdom' (1 Cor. 1:25). If you cannot see it, ask God to open your eyes. Here is an excellent place to begin to learn about Christ and about wisdom. It is clear that Jesus knew this book well. Often his sayings and parables and other teachings parallel and reflect things found here. It is said that as the Psalms give us Jesus singing the law, so the Proverbs give us him meditating on it. Truly to understand him, we must get to grips with Proverbs. Truly to be wise, we must get to grips with Christ.

So we come to lesson number one in wisdom. It is Proverbs 1:7 and our first proverb proper. It governs all the rest. It is well balanced and memorable: '**The fear of the LORD is the beginning of knowledge**' *(positive)*, '**but fools despise wisdom and discipline**' *(negative)*.

We find similar statements elsewhere in the Wisdom Literature. Proverbs 9:10 and 15:33 repeat what is here: 'The fear of the LORD is the beginning of wisdom, and knowledge of the Holy One is understanding'; 'The fear of the LORD teaches a man wisdom' (see also 1:29; 2:5; 3:7; 8:13). Solomon's own father wrote, 'The fear of the LORD is the beginning of wisdom' (Ps. 111:10), and 'Blessed is the man who fears the LORD' (Ps. 112:1). In Job 28:28 we read, 'The fear of the Lord — that is wisdom, and to shun evil is understanding.' Interestingly, just as Proverbs — a book of instruction — begins with this topic, so Ecclesiastes — a more 'speculative book' — ends with it:

> Now all has been heard;
>> here is the conclusion of the matter:
> Fear God and keep his commandments,
>> for this is the whole duty of man
>>>>> (Eccles. 12:13).

In Revelation 14:7 the eternal gospel is summed up in the words: 'Fear God and give him glory.'

Here is the **'beginning'** of wisdom, the first and controlling principle — not stage one, to be left behind at some point, but the foundation on which to build.

'The LORD' is, of course, the covenant God, the true and only triune God revealed in Scripture.

To this God the wise show **'fear'**. We ought to fear him as creatures because *he is our Creator*. We ought to fear him as sinners because *he is holy and we are steeped in sin*.

Fear can, of course, have a bad sense (a phobia) or a good one (necessary alarm or concern). There are also gradations:

1. There is *servile fear*, that of slave to master. Certainly, God has all power.

2. It is also certainly right to *fear God and his power* to throw you into hell (see Matt. 10:28). This is a basic fear, one that demons know.

3. More importantly, there is a fear and *reverence for the majesty and splendour of God*. Job 37:22-24 speaks about this.

4. Highest of all is *filial fear*, that of a son to his father. The New Testament makes this clear, but the Old Testament anticipates it. Such fear is also described as 'hope ... in his unfailing love' (Ps. 33:18).

In a treatise on the subject John Bunyan lists different kinds of fear of God. He speaks of:

1. A fear arising 'from the light of nature'.
2. A fear arising 'from some of his dispensations to men'.
3. A temporary fear that is 'good and godly, but only for a time'.
4. Fear that comes through adoption.

He gives five reasons for this childlike fear of God: firstly, that God himself considers it right; secondly, that he is omnipotent; thirdly, that he is omnipresent; fourthly, that he is holy; and, fifthly, that he is good.

This fear of the Lord is vital

Without it, there is no wisdom or knowledge and without these, there is no life: '... the eyes of the LORD are on those who fear him ... to deliver them from death and keep them alive in famine' (Ps. 33:18-19). Proverbially, fear of the Lord 'adds length to life' (Prov. 10:27) and is 'a fountain of life' (14:27). It brings 'wealth and honour' (22:4). Through it, 'a man avoids evil' (16:6). God 'fulfils the desires of those who fear him' (Ps. 145:19).
But how does this fear express itself?

In faithful obedience to God's holy law.
In loyal service to God and God alone.
In true worship of God and God alone.

We can put the reasoning this way: you will find true wisdom only in Christ. Isaiah 11:1-3 tells us that 'a shoot ... from the stump of Jesse ... a Branch' which bears fruit is the Anointed One, Messiah, or Christ. His anointing was with the Spirit:

> ... the Spirit of wisdom and of understanding,
> the Spirit of counsel and of power,
> the Spirit of knowledge and of the fear of the LORD.

His delight, therefore, was 'the fear of the LORD'. The way to Christ begins with, and goes on with, the fear of the Lord. Malachi also bears witness to this. It is for 'you who revere [fear] my name' that 'the sun of righteousness will rise with healing in its wings' (Mal. 4:2).

Similarly, the Bible makes clear that salvation is through Christ alone. That salvation 'is near those who fear him' (Ps. 85:9). A 'rich store of salvation and wisdom and knowledge' is found in Christ alone, and 'the fear of the LORD is the key to this treasure' (Isa. 33:6). Real knowledge is knowledge of a person — knowledge of Christ.

Do you fear the Lord? Do you seek to obey, serve and worship him? Or are you despising true wisdom and discipline? In this connection, Bunyan warns against having a heart that is hard, prayerless, superficial or careless, covetous, unbelieving, forgetful, ungrateful, proud or critical, envious, or unwilling to respond to good desires. To seek anything else but true godly fear is to go the way of foolishness. It is to reject the true wisdom found only in Christ. The first step on a journey is most important. If you go wrong here, you may never reach your destination. Start correctly on the road to wisdom and fear the Lord now and always. There is no true wisdom without it.

2.
A first fatherly talk begun:
A warning against sin — seducer and slayer of souls

Please read Proverbs 1:8-19

At the end of the road from where I sit, there is a public park. Older locals call it the 'rec' (short for 'recreation ground'). As well as tennis courts and swings, it has a bowling green and some of our more elderly neighbours love to use this in the summer months. Bowls is a deceptively simple game. You just roll your bowling ball so that it stops as near as possible to the 'jack', the little white ball at the end of the green. But what may not be immediately obvious is that each bowling ball has a bias. They say that the earliest games were played using wooden balls from the ends of the balustrades on the staircase of some large country manor house. These were not perfectly spherical and so had a similar bias. Whether or not that is true, anyone playing the game today must take into account the ball's bias if he or she is going to be a proficient player.

In a similar way it is no use someone reading Proverbs 1:7 and saying, 'Well that's easy. All I need to do is fear the Lord and all will be well. As long as I'm basically religious, wisdom, and all it brings, is bound to follow.' That is a little like saying, 'I'm a good swimmer, so it's okay for me to go into the water and swim,' without taking into account possible eddies and currents, whirlpools and rip tides that can carry away the strongest of swimmers.

Before any of us can make progress in wisdom, or the fear of the Lord that precedes it, we must take into account the fact of sin. Sin, which the Bible defines as lawlessness (1 John 3:4), is the great enemy of all that is wise, all that is righteous. It instinctively opposes any desire to fear the Lord. Sin is a great enemy, and it is part of true wisdom to recognize this. This is why the section, Proverbs 1:8 – 9:18, begins and ends by facing its enticements (see 1:8-19; 9:13-18).

Like many enemies, sin works on more than one front. It uses seduction and destruction, temptation and death. Before the outbreak of open hostilities that we call the Second World War, the German *Führer*, Adolph Hitler, was already hard at work preparing for his intended domination of Europe. Even after September 1939, he continued to work subtly and secretly in what has been termed the 'phoney war', prior to his invasion of Norway in 1940. In any war there will be both open hostility and the much more subtle work of propaganda, espionage and infiltration, all aimed at luring in the unsuspecting. It is frightening to think of sin advancing on both these fronts. However, God has provided bastions, or defences, against its advance. It is again part of wisdom to make use of these bastions.

The bastions against sin (1:8-9)

All of us have, or have had, parents or guardians. You may know who your natural parents were, or you may not. They may have been good parents, bad parents or indifferent. They may have brought you up, or maybe someone else did. Perhaps you had only one parent. Whatever our story, we all had someone to bring us up. God put these people there to be, to a greater or lesser extent, bastions against sin.

Other authorities have also had a significant role in our upbringing. Teachers, preachers, youth workers, policemen, the various rules and laws that have been imposed on us — they have all played a part. Again, these may have been good, bad or indifferent, but they were all intended as bastions against sin.

Because this is a fallen world, none of these authorities will have been perfect, any more than our response to their good intentions has been all that it should have been. However, to some extent we all accept that there is a difference between right and wrong and many have urged us to follow the good and reject the bad. For the most part, we are utterly without excuse for our sins.

God has raised up parents and similar authority figures in order to halt the march of sin and to lead men and women to true wisdom, to the Lord Jesus Christ. You may not have had Christian parents. Those who brought you up may have left a great deal to be desired. However, in Proverbs 1:8-9 God speaks to you and he says:

> **Listen, my son, to your father's instruction**
> **and do not forsake your mother's teaching.**
> **They will be a garland to grace your head**
> **and a chain to adorn your neck.**

The purpose of Proverbs is a fatherly and motherly one, a parental one. This is only the first of more than a dozen places in the first eight chapters where it speaks like this (see 1:10,15; 2:1; 3:1,11,21; 4:1,10,20; 5:1,7; 6:1,3,20; 7:1,24; 8:32 for other references to 'my son(s)'). Usually, as here, there is an accompanying exhortation to 'listen' and not to 'forsake' the teaching. The message is: 'Accept my words and store up my commands; keep my commands' (see the references already quoted). Do not reject faithful instruction and teaching. Do not reject wisdom. Do not reject the Saviour who is wisdom personified and who left us his example by obeying and honouring his parents and showing respect to other authorities.

These words will be a great blessing to you if you will only 'listen'. How vital listening is! (See, for example, 1:5; 4:1,10,20; 13:1; 19:20).

The book speaks tenderly and authoritatively to guide and help you. Do not reject it. When travelling on an unknown road you need to follow the signs with care. Be sure you are on the right road. Avoid going down one-way streets the wrong way. Keep to the correct side of the road. Make sure you do not miss your turning. The signs are there to help you. In this book, you will see the signs you need to follow to arrive home. If you wander in the mountains it is easy to get lost, but with a reliable mountain guide to lead you, all will be well. The writer of Proverbs speaks to you like that — like a faithful, experienced mountain guide. Do not despise him or reject his authority. If you will only listen, there will certainly be blessing.

The attractions of sin (1:10-14)

As we have said, we cannot be simplistic when it comes to wisdom. Although God has set up these authority figures, these bastions against sin, by nature we find submission to authority unattractive. Why else would young boys find pirates, smugglers and outlaws so attractive, or older children be so fascinated with popular entertainers who promote rebellious attitudes? Constitutionally, we do not want to obey our parents, listen to our teachers, or accept what preachers say. Sin often seems far more attractive to us than wisdom's garlands. The chain of grace seems heavy and the rewards of sin so attractive. Sin entices. It allures, coaxes, charms. It tempts so powerfully at times. It is personified in 1:10-14. **'Sinners'** here means 'confirmed sinners'. We are all sinners, but here we are thinking of those for whom sin is a settled way of life.

1. Sin speaks so affably, so convivially, so genially

How agreeable and attractive it sounds! **'Come along with us'** it says; **'throw in your lot with us'** (1:11,14). There is a great deal of apparent friendliness on the broad road to destruction. What camaraderie! What bonhomie! 'We're all the same,' it argues. 'We all believe in the same God and we're all going to the same place in the end, so let's not argue or squabble. Let's be friends. Let's try to help each other. Come and join us.'

2. Sin offers excitement, easy pickings and power

Here the figure is that of a gang of highway robbers:

> **Let's lie in wait for someone's blood,**
> **let's waylay some harmless soul;**
> **let's swallow them alive, like the grave,**
> **and whole, like those who go down to the pit...**
> (1:11-12).

'Let's beat someone up'; 'Let's go joyriding'; 'Let's burgle a house'; 'Let's mock a stranger'; 'Let's talk about Suzy.' Sin can sound so strong, so straightforward, yet the moment we stop to think about what it proposes, the horror of it should fill us with terror. Yes, it all sounds exciting and easy, but what about the harmless souls who get hurt? What about the bloodshed, the killing, the embarrassment, the lost reputation? Wake up to what sin is actually proposing.

3. It offers us the world

> **We will get all sorts of valuable things**
> **and fill our houses with plunder;**

> **throw in your lot with us,**
> **and we will share a common purse**
>
> (1:13-14).

Sin, it seems, is generous. It will share all its ill-gotten gains with you. 'Here's the way to riches and fortune,' it cries.

This is how sin makes its appeal. Think of some concrete examples:

> *Alcohol and drug abuse.* Many will tell you that this is an exciting, manly, enjoyable, popular world. But think what untold harm it causes.
>
> *Dishonesty and petty crime.* Again this is presented as harmless, a means of gain, but it has proved the first step on the road to eternal ruin for many.
>
> *Gambling.* Increasingly attempts are made to present gambling as an easy route to riches, a respectable way to enjoy our hard-earned cash, and even to see the end of our financial problems for ever. What misery it unleashes, however, in so many instances! Dissatisfaction, unrest and poverty often trail in its wake.
>
> *Sexual immorality.* 'Everybody's doing it. It's just a cheap thrill. What harm can it do?' Broken homes, fortunes squandered, the endless unhappiness of perverted desire, the death of babies in the womb — all testify to the harm such sins can cause.

These are obvious examples. By the very nature of things, however, sin will entice us in more subtle ways at times. The media, our peers, sometimes even family and friends, or fellow believers — sin will enlist any available ally in its cause.

The admonitions against sin (1:10,15)

What does God say about such enticements? His Word is clear: **'Do not give in to them'** (1:10); **'My son, do not go along with them, do not set foot on their paths'** (1:15). These are the first of several 'Do not ...' commands in the book. 'Fight, struggle, resist!' — that is the message. They say, 'Come,' but you must not go with them. Think of Christ in the desert rebuffing Satan's temptations. Follow his example and resist the devil. We must get off the broad road. Do not take one more step on it. By God's grace, escape the slippery slope that leads down to hell.

Solomon sets out the downward steps to disaster clearly for us here. It all starts with being in the wrong crowd. Together men plan evil deeds and then carry them out. In no time at all you are in the habit of doing evil deeds. 'My son, do not go along with them, do not set foot on their paths.' Do not even begin on this perilous road. 'Do not be misled. "Bad company corrupts good character"' (1 Cor. 15:33).

> Therefore come out from them
> and be separate,
> says the Lord.
> Touch no unclean thing,
> and I will receive you.
>
> (2 Cor. 6:17).

Be like the psalmist who said:

> I do not sit with deceitful men,
> nor do I consort with hypocrites;
> I abhor the assembly of evildoers
> and refuse to sit with the wicked
>
> (Ps. 26:4-5).

Take care over who you spend your time with, whether you meet them in the flesh, or on paper, or by electronic means. Choose your friends with care. 'Do not love the world or anything in the world. If anyone loves the world, the love of the Father is not in him' (1 John 2:15). We must all recognize the power of peer-group pressure, especially on the young. Parents need to know not only where their children are going, and for how long, but also who else will be there.

The moment anyone begins to plan evil deeds he or she is already on the road to sin. This comes out in the Sermon on the Mount. The command not to murder prohibits all forms of hatred, not just murder. Similarly, the command against adultery also prohibits the look of lust that precedes immorality. We must not be like those who, Jeremiah says, 'greatly love to wander; they do not restrain their feet' (Jer. 14:10). We must pray with Charles Wesley to learn to 'tremble at the approach of sin'.

Not every wicked thought becomes a wicked deed, but there is always that potential. How quickly buffoonery turns to blasphemy, coveting to cheating, robbery to rape! That is what the devil aims at when he tempts. Those who practise evil must expect God's judgements.

When we are in the habit of doing evil (and how easily bad habits form!), it is all that much harder to break out from it. Sometimes to transgress a command takes a great struggle the first time, but the second time it is often much easier. We can become so used to sinning that we are not even aware that something is sin. God has made us creatures of habit. This is a blessing if we are in the habit of doing good, yet so often we fall into bad habits. Remember Jeremiah 13:23:

> Can the Ethiopian change his skin
>   or the leopard its spots?
> Neither can you do good
>   who are accustomed to doing evil.

The destination of sin (1:15-19)

Some react to such reasoning by saying, 'Why should I turn from sin?' The answer is to be found in 1:15-19. To follow the crowd is to **'rush'** with them **'into sin'**. It is to join those who **'are swift to shed blood'**.

The root of the word used for **'sin'** is one meaning 'to crush, to break, to wreck or ruin'. Such ways are ruinous. They spoil. They lead to bloodshed. Again the reaction may be: 'So what? What if I harm others? As long as I'm all right, what do I care?' We find the answer in the verses that follow.

Verse 17 is, technically, the first proverb in the book, although, as we have already seen, verse 7 is really a proverb. **'How useless to spread a net in full view of all the birds!'** Commentators disagree widely as to the point Solomon is making. Part of the disagreement is over whether the birds are alarmed to see the trap. Certainly, the picture is that of a man laying a snare to catch birds. Perhaps we would do best to see this as the point. When you do such a thing, it is foolish to let the birds see what you are up to. The reasoning is then that, as birds instinctively fly away when they see a man laying a snare, so sinners should avoid the obvious trap!

The trap is explained in verses 18:19:

> **These men lie in wait for their own blood;**
> **they waylay only themselves!**
> **Such is the end of all who go after ill-gotten gain;**
> **it takes away the lives of those who get it.**

It is a trap that backfires on its perpetrator. Men who act in the ways outlined above only harm themselves. They shoot themselves in the foot.

> He who digs a hole and scoops it out
> falls into the pit he has made.

> The trouble he causes recoils on himself;
> his violence comes down on his own head
>
> (Ps. 7:15-16).

Those 'who go after ill-gotten gain' will lose their lives in the end. Think of Elisha's servant Gehazi. His greed led to his contracting leprosy (2 Kings 5). Think of the book of Esther and Haman hanging on the gallows he had constructed for Mordecai.

Those who remain on the broad road are headed for destruction. Even in everyday life, we see things backfire on people. A child tries to get another into trouble but ends up being told off himself. Another tries to hit someone and in the process hurts himself. Thieves steal a truckload of oil drums that contain deadly poison. I remember reading of a former rugby player who, having spent the day drinking, attacked his wife. In his effort to punch her, he missed completely, put his hand through some glass and severed a main artery. He died shortly afterwards.

From time to time, we hear of terrorist bomb-makers blowing themselves up. I remember meeting a man who blew his own hands off in just that way. Perillus of Athens is the great example from classical times. He apparently invented an execution device shaped like a bull for the evil King Phalaris of Agrigentum. Whom did Phalaris choose as the first victim? You guessed it — Perillus himself! Although justice is not always so well-proportioned in this life, we recognize the equity in such outcomes. They are reminders that God will one day deal justly with all who sin against him.

The benediction of escape from sin (1:9)

At the beginning of Ephesians 6 Paul says, 'Children, obey your parents in the Lord, for this is right. "Honour your father and mother" — which is the first commandment with a promise — "that it may go well with you and that you may enjoy long life on the earth." '

As with the fifth command, a promise accompanies the directions in these verses. We must not miss it. This teaching will become **'a garland to grace your head and a chain to adorn your neck'** (1:9). Like a general returning home from victory, you will be wreathed in flowers. Like a person holding high office, you will be invested with **'a chain to adorn your neck'**. People may talk of others beating them over the head with religion. They may feel that Christianity drags them down like a heavy chain. The truth is, however, that faithful instruction leads to victory and power — victory over sin and power to do good. In the words of the first psalm:

> Blessed is the man
> who does not walk in the counsel of the wicked
> or stand in the way of sinners
> or sit in the seat of mockers.

The victory will be complete when the believer enters heaven itself. This is the eternal life found at the end of the narrow road. But how does one get off the broad road and on to the narrow one? How does one resist its pull and make use of the bastions we have here? Jesus tells us that there is a narrow gate leading onto the narrow road, but that few even find it. Without grace from God to find the way and to be converted there is no hope of escape for any of us from the cruel clutches of sin. But if we look to the Lord there is hope. What glory awaits all who do!

3.
A first fatherly talk concluded: An open invitation

Please read Proverbs 1:20-33

It was the last and greatest day of the Feast of Tabernacles in the holy city of Jerusalem. Large numbers of Jews and God-fearers had gathered together from all the many places to which the Jews had been scattered. We do not know exactly all the rituals that went on at that time. We are told, however, that it was then that Jesus of Nazareth stood up and cried out in a loud voice: 'If anyone is thirsty, let him come to me and drink. Whoever believes in me, as the Scripture has said, streams of living water will flow from within him' (John 7:37-39).

The apostle John explains that this was a reference to the Holy Spirit who was to be poured out, following Christ's death, resurrection and ascension, on the great Day of Pentecost, as described in Acts 2. The closing verses of Proverbs 1 foreshadow the announcement that Jesus made on that occasion.

The book of Proverbs is incontrovertibly about wisdom. It is about how to be wise. It is important to remember that, ultimately, wisdom is not something abstract but personal. As in later passages, Wisdom is here personified and depicted as crying aloud in the streets. There are very personal references to 'my rebuke', 'my heart', 'my thoughts', 'my hand', 'my advice', to being rejected and to Wisdom laughing and mocking. David Atkinson argues that the personification is not merely a literary device, but a reflection of the essential nature of biblical wisdom, as wisdom is for living by. It cannot be known until it is lived out.

So here is the message of Wisdom. It is an expansion of verses 8 and 9 and the antithesis of the invitation from the gang in verses 8-19 and the adulteress in 2:16-19.

Each prophet and apostle of God, before Christ and after, has been sent in the wisdom of God, and brings God's wisdom to this world. 'God in his wisdom said, "I will send them prophets and apostles, some of whom they will kill and others they will persecute"' (Luke 11:49). 'Therefore I am sending you prophets and wise men and teachers...' (Matt. 23:34). At the apex is the coming from heaven of the one 'greater than Solomon' (Luke 11:31), the true Wisdom of God (see 1 Cor. 1:24). Jesus closely identifies himself and his ministry with God's wisdom when he says that 'Wisdom is proved right by all her children' (Luke 7:35; cf. Matt. 11:19). He is the one 'in whom are hidden all the treasures of wisdom and knowledge' (Col. 2:3).

The fact that Wisdom here is feminine is not a problem. Jesus spoke of himself as being like a mother hen longing to gather her chicks. He is both the Bridegroom and, in this book, a tender Bride to be won. To be truly wise we must listen to Christ. We must receive him. To find Christ, or to be found by him, is to find wisdom. Every part of the Bible points us to Christ in one way or another. In Proverbs 1:20-33 Christ speaks as Wisdom. He urges all who are simple to respond to him. Here is an open invitation to all in five parts.

The appeal (1:20-21)

1. It is open

Unlike the sinners of verses 8-19, Christ makes his appeal openly. Wisdom is referred to here in the plural, a plural of excellence. Wisdom has many sides.

'**Wisdom calls aloud ... raises her voice ... she cries out...**' There is a sense in which Wisdom — that is, Christ — is hidden away and does not call out in the streets ('He will not quarrel or cry out; no one will hear his voice in the streets' — Matt. 12:19, quoting Isa. 42). There is nothing harsh or self-promoting about him. On the other hand, when on earth Jesus himself stressed that 'I have spoken openly to the world... I always taught in synagogues or at the temple, where all the Jews come together. I said nothing in secret' (John 18:20).

As Matthew Henry comments, 'Truth seeks not corners, nor is virtue ashamed of itself.' Christ is always open and frank in his approach. As he speaks in John 7 (and, for example, in Isa. 55:1-3), so he speaks here.

2. It is indiscriminate

The crying out takes place '**in the street ... in the public squares, at the head of the noisy streets ... in the gateways of the city**', not tucked away in some quiet corner. True gospel preaching is not confined to certain select groups or to certain clearly defined places. When governments pass laws that make such restrictions, or when tradition dictates a similar policy, we must tactfully resist such laws and traditions. Like the early Methodists who preached in the fields, though forbidden to do so, or Russian and Chinese believers of more recent times who refused to confine their preaching to the four walls of a building, we must recognize that Christ, and his message, is to be preached wherever there is hope of people hearing: in the worlds of education, of commerce, of politics — wherever there is community interaction. Like the sower of the parable, Jesus scatters his seed widely, and so must his followers. Gospel preachers should cast their bread on the waters, give portions to seven or eight and never be weary in sowing the good seed (see Eccles. 11:1-6). Out into the streets and alleys and the roads and country lanes — this must be the policy (see Luke 14). Christ is for the 'man in the street,' not a supposed elite of any sort. He is, to borrow a term from the language of film classification, 'suitable for all'. We must preach Christ promiscuously, indiscriminately. We must do whatever is necessary to proclaim the message to all. The idea of a church out of touch, out of contact with society, is alien to true wisdom.

Christ is calling to all. Christ is calling to you. Be wise and listen.

The rebuke (1:22)

Even when we declare the gospel with the abandon it merits, there is often no great movement to Christ. Sometimes, it seems, the more effort we make, the less successful we are. Why? Part of the reason is that Jesus here comes firstly with a rebuke. If you ask people whether they want to see more police-men on the streets, most will say 'Yes'. However, if it means they are more likely to be fined for speeding, parking offences, or other petty infringements of which even otherwise upright citizens may be guilty, then the reaction is rather different. And so when you speak to people, of many faiths and none, there is often a warm reaction to Christ at first. However, few want to heed his rebukes. They want the sowing without the ploughing and harrowing. They want to be made fit vessels without the kneading of the clay. They want to be in the kitchen, but not if it is hot.

Christ's rebuke is implicit at first, in the names he uses to address his audience. He speaks to three sorts of fool. He describes three increasingly foolish types of people.

1. Simple ones. The **'simple ones'** are those who are naïve, lacking moral direction, and so open to evil. We are slow to recognize a portrait of ourselves in such a description, but this is what we are like by nature.

2. Mockers. By nature, we do not believe in the power of prayer, the goodness of God, or the importance of hearing his Word. If not outwardly, then inwardly we are tempted to mock these things.

3. Fools. The reference, as throughout the book, is not so much to lack of mental skill, but to moral deficiency. By nature, we love evil; we hate the knowledge of the truth.

The message itself is more explicit. Christ calls on us to abandon our *love of simple ways*, our *delight in mockery* and our *hatred of knowledge*.

'How long,' he says, **'will you ... love [such] ways?'** This implies a great desire for change. The Lord longs that such people would repent. It is a call to repentance, to respond and turn to him. We must turn from our foolish, mocking, simple ways. What makes this so hard is that we love these wicked and sinful ways as much as we do.

Christ urges you to repent. Be wise and turn from all your sins.

The offer (1:23)

We can trace nearly all our troubles to our failure to respond to Christ's rebukes. If only we would listen! He says plainly:

If you had responded to my rebuke,
I would have poured out my heart to you
and made my thoughts known to you

(1:23).

If we had listened, God would have poured every drop of wisdom into our laps. Literally, he says, 'I would have poured out *my Spirit...*' This takes us forward again to John 7. See what Christ offers — the very Spirit of God, the Holy Spirit himself. We can also take verse 23 as a direct command to turn, with promises to follow. Whether stated or implied, the need to turn to the Lord is clear.

Athletes who want to win are willing to make great sacrifices in their training. Or think of the way most raw recruits for the army submit to being bawled at by the sergeant major and are willing to be humiliated. Such people are content to undergo these strict regimes because they know it will be for their good in the end. Can we not learn from them and heed Christ's rebuke to our simplicity, mockery and foolishness? Often it is the bitterest medicine that does the most good. 'Accept my rebuke,' says Jesus, 'and I will give you the most precious thing there is — to have God himself living in you.' This is not to suggest that we can earn our salvation, of course, but to highlight the way Jesus works when he draws near. What he requires is that you respond to his 'rebuke'. Then you will have his 'heart' poured out to you and his 'thoughts' made known to you.

First comes the rebuke, but with it comes the hope of something far better. Think of how stern Jesus was towards the rich young ruler. But he leaves the door wide open. If the man will only abandon his wealth and his love of money, he may follow Jesus and be his disciple (see Matt. 19:16-22). Think of the Syro-Phoenician woman and Jesus' similarly hard exterior. She accepted the rebuke but still looked to Jesus for healing for her daughter (see Matt. 15:21-28). Here is the pattern, then, in coming to Jesus. See beyond his rebukes to his good intentions for all who truly trust in him.

Christ is willing to give you the Holy Spirit and everything else you need. Wisely go to him.

The warning (1:24-32)

Sadly, many make the wrong response. They reject Christ when he calls and will not take his outstretched hand. They ignore his advice and refuse to accept it. They do not embrace his rebuke; they rather spurn it. They hate knowledge and will not revere the Lord. Jesus came to 'his own', but they 'did not receive him' (John 1:11). What a rejection it was! They made him an outsider, an outcast and stranger. In the words of Samuel Crossman's seventeenth-century hymn:

> He came from his blest throne
> Salvation to bestow;
> But men made strange, and none
> The longed-for Christ would know.

In an advertising campaign on the London Underground some years ago, a rather tragic picture was used to portray the plight of those with impaired vision. A poster featured a blind man being disregarded and no one helping him. The picture here in Proverbs 1 is even more tragic. Wisdom says:

> ... you rejected me when I called
> and no one gave heed when I stretched out my
> hand,
> ... you ignored all my advice
> and would not accept my rebuke
>
> (1:24-25).

Jesus is offering all the help men could ever need, but they disregard him; they ignore him; they shun and reject him: 'O Jerusalem, Jerusalem, you who kill the prophets and stone those sent to you, how often I have longed to gather your children together, as a hen gathers her chicks under her wings, but you were not willing' (Matt. 23:37).

It takes a degree of humility to accept help from someone else. Some of us are better at this than others. We all need help of one sort or another. Without Christ and his wisdom, there is no hope for anyone. In verse 26 he warns, **'I in turn will laugh at your disaster; I will mock when calamity overtakes you.'** Just as people would mock Christ when he hung on the cross, so he warns of a day when he will mock those who reject him. It reminds us of the passages in the Psalms which tell us, 'The One enthroned in heaven laughs; the Lord scoffs at' those who oppose him (Ps. 2:4), and 'The Lord laughs at the wicked, for he knows their day is coming' (Ps. 37:13). He is filled with compassion towards sinners and takes no delight in the death of the wicked, but when he is thoroughly rejected, he exults in bringing down such rebels.

Christ goes on to speak of the coming disaster for those who refuse to repent.

The coming disaster

Wisdom incarnate speaks of **'calamity'** which **'overtakes ... like a storm'**, **'disaster'** which **'sweeps over ... like a**

whirlwind' and of **'distress and trouble'** which will **'over-whelm'** her hearers (1:27). This reminds us of Jesus' warning at the end of the Sermon on the Mount (Matt. 7:24-27). The foolish man is the one who built his house on sand. All was well for a while, but when the storms came, his house fell flat.

Using different figures, Wisdom speaks of fools who **'will eat the fruit of their ways'** and **'their schemes'** (see Matt. 7:15-20), and of the inevitable death and destruction awaiting wayward simpletons and complacent fools (1:31-32). It is easy to pretend we are wise when all is well, but when testing and judgement come, it is a different story. Soon the Final Judgement will be here. Will you stand on that day? All who are found wanting at that time will be consigned to the everlasting flames of hell.

Christ's response at that time

'Then they will call to me but I will not answer; they will look for me but will not find me' (1:28). Again our minds go to the 'Sermon on the Mount' and to those of whom Jesus speaks who will cry, 'Lord, Lord!' but to whom he will reply, 'I never knew you.'

Or think of Luke 13:24-28, where Jesus says, 'Make every effort to enter through the narrow door, because many, I tell you, will try to enter and will not be able to. Once the owner of the house gets up and closes the door, you will stand outside knocking and pleading, "Sir, open the door for us." But he will answer, "I don't know you or where you come from." Then you will say, "We ate and drank with you, and you taught in our streets." But he will reply, "I don't know you or where you come from. Away from me, all you evildoers!" There will be weeping there, and gnashing of teeth, when you see Abraham, Isaac and Jacob and all the prophets in the kingdom of God, but you yourselves thrown out.'

This is not vindictiveness but a graphic representation of the true situation. When a sign on a train says, 'No smoking — fine £50', it is not simply there to frighten people off from breaking the rules. Rather it is a statement of what will actually happen if they break that regulation. So it is with anyone who refuses to listen to Christ. These warnings are real.

The fairness of it all

If you hate **'knowledge'** and choose not to **'fear the LORD'** (the two go together), if you will **'not accept'** Christ's **'advice'** and spurn his **'rebuke'**, you will suffer for it. **'Waywardness'**, or 'backsliding', kills and **'complacency'** destroys. If you sow cheap seeds or buy inferior products, do not be surprised if you reap a poor crop, or soon find you are disappointed with your purchases. If children are badly treated, they are likely to come to harm as they grow up. It is a biblical and experiential fact that a man reaps what he sows (see Gal. 6:7-8). Are you wayward, wandering from Christ? Are you complacent about your future? There is great danger, and you will surely perish if you do not repent today. A sign saying 'Danger!' at the edge of a cliff is there for a good reason. When a sign says, 'Danger — quicksand', the wise man will take notice of it. Dare you be complacent?

Are you guilty of ignoring Christ's appeal and rebuke and offer? Do not be so foolish.

The summarizing promise (1:33)

The emphasis has been somewhat negative but, finally, look at the great blessing promised in the last verse of the chapter. Together with verse 32 it encapsulates the teaching of this section and introduces a theme that goes on throughout chapters 1-9 — that of avoiding death by avoiding foolishness and finding life by finding wisdom. We must choose which way to go.

This is the first of seven summarizing sections (see 2:21-22; 3:33-35; 4:18-19; 5:21-23; 8:35-36; 9:12), most of them making use of contrast.

Warning

On one hand, there is the warning: **'For the waywardness of the simple will kill them, and the complacency of fools will destroy them.'**

Promise

On the other hand, there is a promise for those who make the right response. What is the right response? **'But whoever listens to me will live in safety and be at ease without fear of harm.'** What a great promise! Its only condition is that we *listen*. This is emphasized frequently in Proverbs 1-9. As Jesus said more than once during his earthly ministry, 'He who has ears to listen, let him hear.' To listen, to hear with hearing ears, is to obey. Love knowledge; fear the Lord; accept his advice and rebuke; show the obedience of faith. Call to the Lord now while there is time. Do not wander away or be complacent about your eternal state.

All who trust in Christ can be sure of safety, contentment and freedom from eternal harm. In the arms of Jesus, you will be safe. If you build on the Rock you will remain firm. With Christ's protection, you can survive every avalanche. No one can pluck those who truly trust in him from his hand. You can know safety, certainty and enjoyment simply by trusting in him. His yoke is easy and his burden is light.

Christ promises to bless you if you listen to him. Be wise and listen.

4.
A second fatherly talk: Seek and you will find

Please read Proverbs 2:1-22

Do you like adventure stories? Do you like stories that describe a journey to find lost treasure? Think of books such as *Treasure Island* or *King Solomon's Mines.* They begin by describing the gathering of the party, or parties, of travellers and the preparations for the journey. Then comes the journey itself and the dicing with danger and death en route. Finally, there is the account of the discovery of the treasure itself. Such books are always popular.

Often adventure stories for children deliberately begin with a description of children in the most ordinary of circumstances. Think of Lewis Carroll's *Alice in Wonderland,* or C. S. Lewis's characters before they slip from the everyday world into Narnia. Perhaps you have often told yourself that such things do not happen in real life, so it is pointless dreaming about them. Or perhaps you have not quite given up such thoughts. Maybe you collect stamps, postcards, books or records and sometimes dream of finding an extremely rare example that will bring you a fortune. Many pursue other sports, hobbies and careers with related thoughts. Some literally go out searching for buried treasure with metal detectors. Others engage in various forms of escapism — ranging from those which are harmless to those which are far from it — as they look for excitement.

Books, films and computer games provide vicarious adventure for an hour or two, but where can you find true adventure? A booklet appeared some years ago entitled *Dying — The greatest adventure of my life.* By a Christian called James Casson, it was written in the closing months of his life when he knew he would soon die from cancer. The title is a striking one. It reminds us that the real adventure we all have to face is that of our own life and death. As John Lennon wryly observed in song, we are slow to discover that 'Life is what happens to you while you're busy making other plans.'

A good adventure book that we all ought to read is *Pilgrim's Progress* by John Bunyan. It tells of the epic journey of Christian from the City of Destruction to the Celestial City. What makes it so exciting is that it is a description of the Christian life. Perhaps some of the saddest people on earth are those who are 'looking for adventure'. They have failed to see that there is enough adventure to be had simply in living and dying where they are, if only they properly understood the purpose of life.

Do you know where you will find the most exciting place in your locality on a Sunday morning? It is probably in your nearest evangelical church. It may not seem that way, but if it is a church that believes and preaches the truth, it is so. No form or place of entertainment can begin to compete. All the ingredients are there:

> *The treasure.* Nothing can compare with the gift of eternal life in the glory of heaven. It is to be sought for 'as for silver' and 'as for hidden treasure' (2:4).
> *The journey.* These verses provide a welcome stop on the way. They provide fortification for the remaining journey. The journey metaphor is in the background

throughout verses 7-20: 'those whose walk is blameless ... the course of the just ... the way of his faithful ones ... every good path ... the ways of wicked men ... who leave the straight paths to walk in dark ways ... whose paths are crooked ... who are devious in their ways ... who has left the partner [literally "guide"] of her youth ... her house leads down to death ... her paths to the spirits of the dead. None who go to her return or attain the paths of life ... you will walk in the ways of good men and keep to the paths of the righteous.'

The opposition of enemies — the devil and all his helpers. This includes 'wicked men' and 'the adulteress'.

With these come mystery, suspense, thrills and spills galore.

But you may be reading this and have no idea of what I am talking about. You have not even taken a first tentative step on the road to the Celestial City. The purpose of this chapter, a consideration of Proverbs 2, is to urge those who have never begun this journey to set out on it today, and to encourage those who have begun to press on to the journey's end.

The call to seek and to find wisdom

What to seek

In Proverbs 2:1 we are back in the quiet of the home, as it were, and once again a father speaks, as to his only son, encouraging him to **'accept'** his **'words'** and **'store up'** his **'commands within'** himself. Once more, his subject is wisdom and, as we have already said, that ultimately means Jesus himself. We must accept Jesus' words, his commands. We must seek the wisdom, understanding and insight that come from him. Too many throw their lives away seeking health, wealth, fame and all this world claims to offer. But what we need is God's Word and Wisdom, his Christ.

How to seek

First notice the 'ifs' in verses 1, 3 and 4.

Believe God's Word (2:1-2)

This is made plain here. **'*If* you accept my words,'** says Wisdom, **'*if* you ... store up my commands...'** (2:1). Acceptance is required, not criticism or rejection. We must say, 'Speak, Lord, for your servant is listening.' In the parable of the sower, the good soil receives the good seed of the Word and produces fruit. 'Let the Word of Christ dwell in you richly,' says Paul in Colossians 3:16.

We must not only receive the Word, but retain it too. Like the psalmist we should hide God's Word in our hearts (Ps. 119:11). Think of how Jacob pondered the dreams of his son Joseph, and how Mary kept in her heart her memories of what happened to Jesus as a baby. We should do the same kind of thing.

Proverbs 2:2 talks about **'turning your ear to wisdom and applying your heart to understanding'**. Our listening must be diligent and wholehearted. We must engage our ears and our hearts. The **'heart'** in Hebrew thought, scholars say, is the seat of reason and will, not of the emotions. Too many only appear to be listening, or are only half-listening. This is the first of several references to the need for wisdom to enter our hearts (see especially 3:1,3,5; 4:4,21,23).

Pray to God (2:3)

Someone who is genuinely seeking the wisdom of God will not only be engaged in the passive act of listening, but also in the active pursuit of God in prayer: **'If you call out for insight and cry aloud for understanding ... then you will understand...'** (2:3,5). Like newborn babies crying for their mother's milk, so we should cry out for the Word (see 1 Peter 2:2). Solomon, of course, knew by experience that if you ask God for wisdom he will give it. James reminds us of this fact: 'If any of you lacks wisdom, he should ask God, who gives generously to all without finding fault, and it will be given to him' (James 1:5).

Search intently (2:4)

Are you looking for wisdom **'as for silver'** and searching for it **'as for hidden treasure'**? Are you calling out to God to show you this precious but hidden thing? Are you crying aloud to him? *If* you do, God will teach you to fear him and to know him. As he leads the gold-miner to the treasure that he himself has hidden in the ground, so he leads those who seek him earnestly to fear him and know him. Sadly, some are simply too lazy to seek the Lord, although he is not far from any one of us. This connection between wisdom and treasure occurs again in several other places (e.g., 3:14; 8:10-11,19).

The promise of success to those who seek and find wisdom

Some never see the point of seeking God and so never begin. Some see the point but give up seeking due to discouragement. Some are even now seeking God but are often tempted to give up.

What a help it is to all such people to remember the success promised here to those who truly seek the Lord! There is some exhilaration in seeking, of course. The thrill of the chase is generally recognized. But even an angler or a huntsman would be rather discouraged if he *never* caught anything. No, the finding is the thing. 'The end of a matter is better than its beginning' (Eccles. 7:8). We must keep the object of true seeking in mind. This chapter will help us.

The promises

Those who seek and find wisdom receive good things. Note the 'thens' in verses 5 and 9.

The promise of finding God (2:5-8)

Verse 5 speaks of the greatest reward: '***Then* you will understand the fear of the LORD**', which is necessary to true wisdom (as 1:7 teaches) '**... and find the knowledge of God**' to which that fear leads. That is the purpose of reading the Word and praying. Do you desire this? Remember there is no wisdom without it. By nature, none of us desires it as we should but, to paraphrase Augustine, God made our hearts for himself and they are inevitably restless until God enters them. To put it in modern terms, there is a God-shaped vacuum at the centre of our being that Christ alone can fill. Without the Spirit of Christ stirring us to fear the Lord in obedience and to know and love him, we have nothing.

The promise of finding the right way (2:9-11)

Once you know God, other things fall into place. Guidance can be a problem for all of us, Christian or not — knowing how to live, what to do and what not to do. Unless we know God, we shall never properly **'understand what is right and just and fair'** (2:9). Many who claim they know such things do not in reality. Ultimately, it is only when we understand what happened to Christ on the cross, dying in the place of sinners, that we really understand. As Paul observes, 'The

spiritual man makes judgements about all things … we have
the mind of Christ' (1 Cor. 2:15-16). If we are believers, we
also know **'every good path'**, at least in principle, as verse 9
makes clear. The Good Shepherd leads his flock 'in paths of
righteousness for his name's sake' (Ps. 23:3).

The arguments

There are two reasons why we can be sure that God will honour
these promises.

The Lord has wisdom to give (2:6)

All other so-called wisdom is either derivative or counterfeit.
As with anything valuable, there are many imitations. Some
are very poor ones indeed. Repeatedly men have set up rival
systems with their own book, their own rituals, their own fig-
urehead. Perhaps the various versions of communism and
fascism in the twentieth century are the most obvious examples
in modern times. Yet, as verse 6 says (referring to 'the LORD'
for the first time, apart from the phrase 'the fear of the LORD'),
it is **'the LORD'** who **'gives wisdom, and from his mouth
come knowledge and understanding'**. You will not find it
elsewhere. Not only does all wisdom belong to the Lord, but
he also 'gives' that wisdom to those who seek it. He has already given it in his Word, the Bible, and it is by his Spirit that
he imparts understanding of that Word.

The Lord reserves his blessings for his holy people (2:7-8)

God reserves his blessings for those who are **'upright'**, **'whose
walk is blameless'**, **'just'** and **'faithful'** in Christ. These are
the ones for whom **'he holds victory in store'** and **'is a shield'**,
whose course of life **'he guards'** and whose way **'he protects'**

(2:7,8). The word translated **'victory'** is really a wisdom word meaning 'sound sense' or 'effectiveness' (it is translated 'sound judgement' in 3:21; 8:14 and 18:1, the other places where it appears in the book). This is the sort of victory ahead for God's people. No holiness, no blessing. However, if we are living holy lives in Christ, there is every hope for us.

The summary

Verses 10 and 11 conclude the first half of the chapter. Here is a great promise for the man who finds the truth:

> **For wisdom will enter your heart,**
>   **and knowledge will be pleasant to your soul.**
> **Discretion will protect you,**
>   **and understanding will guard you.**

Heavenly wisdom and knowledge, God-given discretion and understanding — like two guard dogs — will be there. These are both pleasant to the soul in themselves and will protect you from the many attacks of the Evil One. Here is safety and joy. To put it in terms of the first question of the *Shorter Catechism*, the man who glorifies God will also enjoy him for ever.

The emphasis in the subsequent verses is on protection.

Why blessings will follow those who successfully seek and find wisdom

They find protection from those who follow wicked principles (2:12-15)

Does the wickedness of the world frighten you sometimes? Think of the power of terrorists to commit atrocities, more or less at will. Think of murder and rape happening sometimes on quiet street-corners or down secluded lanes. The blessing promised here is that, if you heed it, **'Wisdom will save you from the ways of wicked men'** (2:12). Think of how **'perverse'** people can be (2:12). Think how far they wander from **'straight paths to walk in dark ways'** (2:13). Think how they even **'delight in doing wrong and rejoice in the perverseness of evil'** (2:14). How **'crooked'** their **'paths'** and how **'devious'** their **'ways'** at times! (2:15). It is a minefield. We all need heavenly wisdom. Do we honestly think we shall survive out there otherwise?

Not only is there the danger that such people will hurt us, but also that we may become increasingly like them. If we are to believe what we see in television dramas, some policemen become so like the people they are trying to catch that they are indistinguishable from them. The same danger confronts us all in this world. Does it horrify you sometimes to realize how perverse and devious your thinking can be?

They find salvation from those who follow wicked ways
(2:16-19)

We can often spot the wicked. However, sometimes they approach us in less obvious, more subtle, ways. Here the blessing promised is that Christ, who is wisdom, **'will save you also from the adulteress'** (literally, 'the strange woman'), **'from the wayward wife'** (literally, 'the foreigner') **'with her seductive words'** (2:16). She is described as one **'who has left the partner'** (literally, 'guide') **'of her youth'** and disregarded her wedding vows — she has **'ignored'**, or forgotten, **'the covenant she made before God'** (2:17).

The figure used, then, is that of the adulteress, someone whom we shall meet again several times. She is strange, foreign — not in a regular relationship within the community.

The word 'exotic' is still sometimes used in English in this way.

Sexual immorality is one of the more obvious ways by which Satan seeks to lure believers to destruction, but it is by no means the only one. Rather the adulteress symbolizes this barren world and its efforts to seduce us from the way of truth. We must remember where the paths to her house ultimately lead: **'For her house leads down to death and her paths to the spirits of the dead'** (2:18). The fact is that **'None who go to her return or attain the paths of life'** (2:19). There are all kinds of offers of supposed pleasure out there, but they lead in the end to death — both spiritual and physical. Think how adultery and fornication so easily lead to the misery of broken homes, to addictions to pornography, to all sorts of sexual perversions. Think how worldly ways and a host of subtle heresies vie to lead us away from life in Christ. How will you escape? If you do not find wisdom, you are doomed. That wisdom is found only in Christ.

They find good and righteous ways (2:20)

Verse 20 gives the positive side: **'Thus you will walk in the ways of good men and keep to the paths of the righteous.'** Do you not long for this? It can come to you only through Christ. He is the only one who can justify you so that you are legally righteous, and the only one who can sanctify you so that you are actually good.

Why blessings will follow those who successfully seek and find wisdom

Finally, we consider why such blessings come only to those who find Christ. It may not be clear to you. Many people honestly wonder why they cannot be good without being religious. This was one of the great hopes of many in the twentieth century — religion without God; Christianity without Christ. Yet it is impossible. There is an intimate and indissoluble connection between true wisdom and true morality, between right doctrine and right practice, between loving God and loving your neighbour, between Jesus Christ and true holiness.

True wisdom is found only in the Lord

As we learned in verse 6, 'The LORD gives wisdom, and from his mouth come knowledge and understanding.' You will not find it elsewhere.

The Lord reserves his blessings for his holy people

God reserves his blessings for those who are upright, whose walk is blameless, just and faithful in Christ. Verses 21 and 22 underline this:

For the upright will live in the land,
and the blameless will remain in it;
but the wicked will be cut off from the land,
and the unfaithful will be torn from it.

Without wisdom, it is impossible to be holy

The blessing comes through holiness, but without wisdom we never shall be holy. Remember verses 9-11. It is when we accept what Scripture says that we 'understand what is right and just and fair — every good path'. It is then that 'wisdom will enter your heart, and knowledge will be pleasant to your soul'. It is then that 'discretion will protect you, and understanding

will guard you'. Until wisdom comes, there can be no blessing. So many make a false connection. They rightly say, 'God
"holds victory in store for the upright, he is a shield to those
whose walk is blameless, for he guards the course of the just
and protects the way of his faithful ones," so I will try to be
holy in my own strength.' But that is impossible. Left to ourselves we are soon sucked into the wickedness and spiritual
adultery all around. How can we escape? That is wisdom. That
is what we need in our hearts. The New Testament makes it
even clearer. There we learn of the coming of Jesus Christ and
the apparent foolishness of his death on the cross. That death
is true wisdom, however, for there he died in the place of sinners, so that all who trust in him may find forgiveness.

So remember, the way to holiness is the way of wisdom:

> My son, if you accept my words
>   and store up my commands within you,
> turning your ear to wisdom
>   and applying your heart to understanding…
> Then you will understand what is right and just
>   and fair — every good path.
> For wisdom will enter your heart,
>   and knowledge will be pleasant to your soul.
> Discretion will protect you,
>   and understanding will guard you
>
>   (2:1-2,9-10).

Make the right choice.

The summary to the chapter

Just as there is a conclusion at the end of the first half of this
chapter, so there is at the end of the second half. Further, as at

the end of Proverbs 1, so here we have a summarizing pair of verses contrasting promise and warning that sum up the section. Again, the theme of life and death, introduced in verse 18, is there, but in a different form.

Positively

The promise is that heaven is reserved for the holy: **'For the upright will live in the land, and the blameless will remain in it'** (2:21). **'The land'** probably does not refer to the promised land, but is making use of an agrarian metaphor. The upright grow in the field; the blameless flourish there.

Negatively

The warning is that there is no heaven for those who are not holy: **'… but the wicked will be cut off from the land, and the unfaithful will be torn from it'** (2:22). Like so many weeds and thorns, they will be cut down and rooted out for their wickedness.

So accept Christ's words. Store them up in your heart. Call out for insight and cry aloud for understanding. Look for him as for silver and search for him as for hidden treasure — then you will understand the fear of the Lord and find the knowledge of God, which, of course, is the key to true wisdom.

5.
A third fatherly talk:
Five great promises

Please read Proverbs 3:1-10

Standing, standing,
Standing on the promises of God my Saviour,
Standing, standing,
Standing on the promises of God...

I remember singing those words when I was younger. They come from a nineteenth-century hymn included in the old Sankey hymn book and written by an American Methodist called R. Kelso Carter. The verse goes on:

Standing on the promises that cannot fail
When the storms of doubt and fear assail,
By the living Word of God I shall prevail,
Standing on the promises of God.

There is no better place to stand than on the promises of God found in his Word. As one writer put it, 'You cannot starve a man who's feeding on the promises of God.'

The Bible is a book full of wonderful promises. That is one reason why it is such a precious book. Its promises are not empty ones either. Every promise God makes will hold good. They are all 'Yes' and 'Amen' in Christ. God's Word cannot fail.

Do you know any of the promises found in God's Word? Are you building your life on them? Here in Proverbs 3:1-10 the writer again speaks to 'my son'. This time he begins with the five great promises that we are going to look at here.

Like many of God's promises to his children, they have conditions attached to them. God is under no obligation to give us reasons why we should obey him, but he often does. We can see these promises as conditional promises. An example of an unconditional promise would be a man saying to his teenage son, 'Leon, I will give you £5.' An example of a conditional promise would be if he said, 'I will give you £5 if you wash my car,' or 'I will give you £5, Leon, if you do well in your mathematics examination.' Often God ties his promises to certain commands and we cannot expect to see his promises fulfilled if we refuse to obey him. This is not to suggest that God's blessings can be earned in the absolute sense. Rather, it is to underline that it is as we approach him in faith and do what he desires that he blesses us. Calvin put it like this: 'As God gives himself to us in promises, we must give ourselves to him in duties.'

It is important to remember, too, as always in Proverbs, that what is promised here in material terms may not always come in that form to each individual. However, the spiritual reality that lies behind wonderful things such as long life, a good name, good health and overflowing barns will certainly come to all who, through Christ, fulfil the conditions laid down here.

The promise of life and prosperity (3:1-2)

The promise

In verse 2, there is the promise of long life and of prosperity: **'for they will prolong your life many years and bring you**

prosperity'. The promise of long life is prominent throughout this book. For example, 'Long life is in [Wisdom's] right
hand; in her left hand are riches and honour' (3:16; cf. 4:10;
9:11).

Literally, the second part of the promise is that of 'peace'.
The Hebrew word *shalom* means far more than the mere absence of war. It has a much fuller import.

So the promise here is of life. That is foundational; there is
nothing without that. With it comes the promise of peace. A
long life is useless of itself, a curse as much as a blessing, if we
have no peace. We need both life and the power to enjoy it.

Jesus makes many similar promises in the New Testament.
He speaks of himself as 'the bread of life', 'the resurrection
and the life' and 'the way, the truth and the life' (John 6:35;
11:25; 14:6). 'I have come that they may have life and have it
to the full,' he says (John 10:10). He is the one who has 'the
words of eternal life' (John 6:68). The angels spoke of the
'peace' on earth he would bring at his birth (Luke 2:14), and
he himself often had the word 'peace' on his lips. 'Peace I
leave with you,' he says to his disciples; 'my peace I give you.
I do not give to you as the world gives' (John 14:27).

The condition

How does such peace come to individuals? Verse 1 reminds
us of the importance of God's Word. It is by remembering
what it teaches and storing it in the heart that life and prosperity come: **'My son, do not forget my teaching, but keep my
commands in your heart.'** As in the previous chapters, a
father addresses his son and again his first concern is concen-
tration (cf. 1:8,10,15; 2:1). We too need to read, mark, learn
and inwardly digest the Scriptures.

Negatively, we must 'not forget'. *Positively,* we must remember, or keep in our hearts, God's law, his commands.

In John 17 the Lord Jesus says of his disciples, 'I gave them the words you gave me and they accepted them.' He revealed God to them, to those given to him by the Father and, he says, 'They have obeyed your word.' Earlier in John's Gospel, Jesus had condemned others who were ready to kill him. Unlike the disciples, they had no room for God's Word in their hearts (John 8:37). It was not that they did not diligently study the Scriptures — they did (John 5:39), but they never saw that those Scriptures speak of Christ. It is only as we meditate with this in mind that we shall know the life and prosperity revealed in Scripture.

Remember what is said of the blessed man, the man who is 'like a tree planted by streams of water, which yields its fruit in season and whose leaf does not wither', the one who prospers in all he does. 'His delight is in the law of the LORD'; he 'meditates day and night' on God's Word (Ps. 1:1-3). Like Joshua, you must 'not let this Book of the Law depart from your mouth; [but] meditate on it day and night, so that you may be careful to do everything written in it. Then you will be prosperous and successful' (Josh. 1:8).

To find God's blessing we do not need to go up to heaven, as it were, or to the other side of the world. 'No, the word is very near you; it is in your mouth and in your heart so that you may obey it' (Deut. 30:14). In the Bible itself 'life and prosperity' and 'death and destruction' are set before us (see Deut. 30:15). If we take seriously what it says we will choose the life and peace it offers. Like those mentioned in Revelation 22:14, we will wash our robes that we 'may have the right to the tree of life and may go through the gates into the city' of God.

When Paul says, 'Let the peace of Christ rule in your hearts,' he immediately follows it by saying, 'Let the word of Christ dwell in you richly'(Col. 3:15,16). The two are intimately connected. In Isaiah 55:10-11 the illustration is used of rain and snow coming down and 'making [the earth] bud and flourish, so that it yields seed for the sower and bread for the eater'. In the same way, as we read and meditate on God's Word it accomplishes God's purposes in our hearts. We know eternal life and spiritual prosperity. Psalm 119:93 is relevant here too: 'I will never forget your precepts, for by them you have preserved my life.'

We need to immerse ourselves in the Word of God. We need to be like John Bunyan, of whose works Spurgeon once said, 'Prick him anywhere and his blood is bibline.' 'Man does not live on bread alone,' remember, 'but on every word that comes from the mouth of God' (Matt. 4:4) Without the water of the Word, we shall grow dry and cracked. We shall become dehydrated in the desert of this world and we shall die. However, if we look to the teaching and commands found in the Word we shall know life and prosperity.

The promise of reputation and success (3:3-4)

The promise

Dr Samuel Mudd was the man who treated the injured assassin of American president, Abraham Lincoln. Many felt that this act of kindness was a treacherous deed and, as the saying goes, 'His name was mud'! Proverbs 22:1 reminds us that 'A good name is more desirable than great riches; to be esteemed is better than silver or gold.' To have a good reputation is a great asset and something we should desire.

It is true that Jesus said, 'Woe to you when *all* men speak well of you, for that is how their fathers treated the false prophets' (Luke 6:26), but to have a good name with *many* is both desirable and right.

In Romans 12:17 Paul reminds Christians that they should be concerned about what men think of them as well as what God thinks. A little later he commends those who are 'pleasing to God and approved by men' (Rom. 14:18). A good reputation was a characteristic of godly men such as Joseph (Gen. 39:2-6,21-23). Jesus himself, like Samuel, we are told, from a child 'grew in wisdom and stature, and in favour with God and men' (Luke 2:52; cf. 1 Sam 2:26). He had a good reputation both with men and with God. Here the promise is of winning **'favour and a good name in the sight of God and man'** (3:4). We need both.

The condition

How did Joseph, Samuel and Jesus grow in favour with God and men? How can we? The answer is here in verse 3:

> **Let love and faithfulness never leave you;**
> **bind them around your neck,**
> **write them on the tablet of your heart.**

'Love and faithfulness', or 'mercy and truth' — these are the key elements. The instruction and teaching in this book are designed to be 'a garland to grace your head and a chain to adorn your neck' (1:9). If we are wise, we will bind the love and faithfulness commended around our necks. Fashions in tattooing and in jewellery change from year to year. This is the message to have tattooed on your heart: 'Love and faithfulness'. This is the necklace to obtain: 'Mercy and truth'.

On our part, there must be love to God and faithfulness to him. We must speak the truth in love (Eph. 4:25). We remember, however, that 'Love comes from God,' and 'Everyone who loves has been born of God and knows God' (1 John

4:7). In fact, 'Whoever does not love does not know God, because God is love. This is how God showed his love among us: he sent his one and only Son into the world that we might live through him. This is love: not that we loved God, but that he loved us and sent his Son as an atoning sacrifice for our sins' (1 John 4:8-10).

Simply wearing a cross around your neck or putting a text on the wall cannot do it. Rather, we must commit ourselves to Christ who died and devote ourselves to the true and living God. By nature, we do not have a good name. However, just as a good name can sometimes be acquired by marrying into the right family, so through Christ we can be adopted into his family and gain the worthy name of Christian.

The promise of guidance and blessing (3:5-6)

These verses are well known. Christians often quote them. They are very similar to the proverb which says, 'Commit to the LORD whatever you do, and your plans will succeed' (16:3). Some forget that these are proverbs and cannot bear the weight that they want them to bear. They do not say, 'Trust in the Lord and not yourself, and everything will turn out just as you hope without so much as a hitch'! We need to keep in mind everything else Scripture tells us before we jump to such a conclusion.

The promise

I live at the edge of the London Borough of Barnet where it adjoins the borough of Brent. Brent's eastern margin is the Edgware Road. That road follows the lines of the old Roman road from London to St Albans (Verulamium) and on to Wroxeter (Viroconium). Known as Watling Street (from the Anglo-Saxon name for St Albans, Waetlingaceaster), it was one of the great arterial roads of Roman and post-Roman Britain. The name has been used to refer to the whole road since the ninth century. In all, the Romans built 50,000 miles of hard-surfaced highway, primarily for military reasons. Not all of these roads are straight, but most are. They are famous for their straightness. There is nothing like a straight road. It is always easier to get along when there are no turns to negotiate. Here the wonderful promise is: '**... and he will make your paths straight**'. We could translate it as: 'He will direct your paths.' That is the meaning. It is a promise of guidance, of entrance onto the narrow road that leads to life, and of God's leading all the way to heaven. One of the beauties of the Christian life is that although it is not always easy, it is generally straightforward. There are difficult questions of guidance, but we are more often asking for strength to do the right thing than for wisdom to know what it is.

The condition

In Hebrew verse 5 is arranged in a chiasmus:

> Trust
>
>   in the LORD with all your heart.
>
> And on your own understanding,
>
>   lean not.

There are three elements in the condition.

Concentration

'**Trust in the LORD with all your heart.**' Firstly, there must be faith. This is basic, the key to every promise. It is more than believing God's Word. It is putting your trust in a person, in God himself.

'Believe in the Lord Jesus, and you will be saved — you and your household' (Acts 16:31). 'Do not let your hearts be troubled. Trust in God; trust also in me' (John 14:1). 'Yet to all who received him, to those who believed in his name, he gave the right to become children of God' (John 1:12). 'Whoever believes in him shall not perish but have eternal life' (John 3:16). 'I tell you the truth, whoever hears my word and believes him who sent me has eternal life and will not be condemned; he has crossed over from death to life' (John 5:24).

It is required that we do this in a sincere and wholehearted way — **'with all your heart'**. In the same way as we are to love God, so we are to trust in him.

Correction

'And lean not on your own understanding.' Lean on Christ, not on yourself or on your own understanding. By nature we are 'darkened in [our] understanding and separated from the life of God'. There is 'ignorance' in us 'due to the hardening of [our] hearts' (Eph. 4:18).

> Cursed is the one who trusts in man,
>   who depends on flesh for his strength
>   and whose heart turns away from the LORD.
> He will be like a bush in the wastelands;
>   he will not see prosperity when it comes.
> He will dwell in the parched places of the desert,
>   in a salt land where no one lives.
> But blessed is the man who trusts in the LORD,
>   whose confidence is in him.
> He will be like a tree planted by the water
>   that sends out its roots by the stream.
> It does not fear when heat comes;
>   its leaves are always green.

It has no worries in a year of drought
and never fails to bear fruit.
The heart is deceitful above all things and beyond cure.
Who can understand it?

(Jer. 17:5-9).

Look only to Christ, never to self.

Consistency

'**In all your ways acknowledge him.**' Whether small or great, look to him 'in all your ways'. Jesus does not say that we *must* not serve God and Mammon, but that we *cannot.* The idea of a compartmentalized life cannot work as far as the gospel is concerned. If you try to cultivate only part of your garden and leave the rest, the weeds will soon invade the part you have set aside. Is there a part of your life that you are trying to keep for yourself? Are you guilty of compartmentalizing? Are you trying to be one thing on Sunday and another on Monday morning, or Saturday afternoon?

The promise of health and strength (3:7-8)

The promise

In verse 8 we read, '**This will bring health to your body and nourishment to your bones.**' Here, as in verse 2, is a very concrete promise of health to your body (literally, 'your navel') and strength (or 'marrow') to your bones. The gospel is good for body and soul: '… godliness has value for all things, holding promise for both the present life and the life to come' (1 Tim. 4:8). However, it is true that Christians become ill and die, although they may be full of faith and the Holy Spirit.

Nevertheless, every believer can know both great spiritual health in this life and resurrection to eternal life in the one to come. We shall say more about this below.

The condition

The condition for this promise is found in the previous verse: **'Do not be wise in your own eyes; fear the LORD and shun evil.'** Again, there is a threefold prescription: humility, homage and holiness.

Humility

'Do not be wise in your own eyes.' This is one of the first steps on the road to wisdom. Too often, our attitude is far more like that of Kenneth Grahame's fictional Mr Toad. He sang:

> The clever men at Oxford
> Know all there is to be knowed,
> But they none of them know one half as much
> As intelligent Mr Toad.

There is a sense in which the way to heaven is downward rather than upward.

Homage

'Fear the LORD.' We keep coming back to this theme of reverence. This is where wisdom begins. It is what Calvin called 'the root and origin of all righteousness', and what Professor John Murray called 'the soul of piety'. American preacher Al Martin once identified its three essential ingredients as:

1. A correct concept of the character of God — God is exactly who the Bible says he is.

2. A pervasive sense of the presence of God — he is always present.

3. A constant awareness of our obligation to God — we must always obey him.

Holiness

'And shun evil.' These three ideas follow fast on the heels of one another. True humility leads to the fear of God, and true fear leads to a turning from every evil. The Amish people and other similar groups practise what they call 'shunning' as a means of dealing with backsliders and apostates. If such a group shuns you, they will not so much as speak to you. Whatever we may think of such a practice, we must certainly shun all that is evil with the same vigour.

A problem

So what about people who fear the Lord and shun evil, yet still fall ill? Are they all hypocrites? Not necessarily. This is the problem that another wisdom book, the book of Job, tackles head-on. There is no question that Job feared God and shunned evil. The very first verse of the book says, 'In the land of Uz there lived a man whose name was Job. This man was blameless and upright; he feared God and shunned evil.' Nevertheless, he suffered appallingly. What we find in that book should warn us against taking a verse like this and assuming it can be applied universally. That was the great mistake of Job's so-called 'comforters'. If things were that simple, then no one would ever have doubts or perplexities.

There are many reasons why God allows people to suffer. Sometimes it is because they fail to fear the Lord and shun evil. At other times, even though they are truly godly, they still fall ill and even die. In this life, we can never be sure exactly why a person is suffering, but we do know, for example, that God disciplines his children. This very theme is taken up in this same chapter of Proverbs, from verse 11. We also know from Job that God's outlook and purpose are higher than ours and we need to recognize that there are many things about his rule over this world that we do not, and cannot, now understand.

The promise of wealth and abundance (3:9-10)

The promise

In verses 9 and 10, we have our fifth promise. This promise is also well known. Again, we are wise not to be too literalistic about it, although even the New Testament contains a similar promise: ' "I tell you the truth," Jesus replied, "no one who has left home or brothers or sisters or mother or father or children or fields for me and the gospel will fail to receive a hundred times as much in this present age (homes, brothers, sisters, mothers, children and fields — and with them, persecutions) and in the age to come, eternal life" ' (Mark 10:29-30).

Here in Proverbs 3:10 the promise is: '**... then your barns will be filled to overflowing, and your vats will brim over with new wine.**' I suppose the modern urban equivalent would be a bank account in credit and the car paid for.

The condition

The condition concerns our giving: '**Honour the LORD with your wealth, with the first-fruits of all your crops**' (3:9). A similar point is made in several proverbs, such as, 'A generous man will prosper; he who refreshes others will himself be refreshed' (11:25; cf. 19:17; 22:9; 28:27). Malachi 3:10 breathes the same spirit: ' "Bring the whole tithe into the storehouse, that there may be food in my house. Test me in this," says the LORD Almighty, "and see if I will not throw open the floodgates of heaven and pour out so much blessing that you will not have room enough for it." '

To raise the subject of giving here may seem incongruous to some, but it is a matter of 'putting your money where your mouth is'. If you are a genuine believer then it will affect your finances. You will want to go further than simply putting your small change in the offering plate when it comes around on a Sunday morning. You will want to think through what you give to the Lord's work and you will want to be eager and generous.

Under the law, certain gifts were required, including firstfruits from the crops. Under the new covenant, things are less regimented, but the principles of putting God first and giving generously remain. Paul writes to the Corinthians and he says, 'On the first day of every week, each one of you should set aside a sum of money in keeping with his income, saving it up, so that when I come no collections will have to be made' (1 Cor. 16:2). Later he tells them, 'Remember this: Whoever sows sparingly will also reap sparingly, and whoever sows generously will also reap generously. Each man should give what he has decided in his heart to give, not reluctantly or under compulsion, for God loves a cheerful giver' (2 Cor. 9:6-7).

John Bunyan wrote somewhere:

A man there was, some call him mad;
The more he gave away, the more he had.

Here, then, are five wonderful promises of blessing — promises of life, of honour, of vigour, of guidance and success, and of prosperity. Through Christ they can be yours if you treasure up God's Word, faithfully love, trust in the Lord, fear him and shun evil, and honour him with your wealth. If we take God at his Word, we shall be blessed abundantly.

6.
A fourth fatherly talk:
A warning, an encouragement, something to think about

Please read Proverbs 3:11-20

Think about what it is like learning to do something new —
clicking your fingers, riding a bicycle, driving a car, skiing,
learning a musical instrument. Some years ago I decided to
teach myself to play the descant recorder. There were some
hindrances, some difficulties, but as I persevered, I was able
to learn to play the instrument to my own satisfaction. Flushed
with success, I then took up the treble recorder. Having mastered the one, I should have been able to master the other —
but I never have.

Inevitably, in any such enterprise there are two possible
outcomes: success despite difficulty, or failure despite effort.
Another element here is the relative importance of the task we
are seeking to master. If you have never mastered the yo-yo,
or the clarinet, or knitting, it probably does not matter too
much. However, if it is reading and writing, or driving the
children to school, or conducting a medical test correctly, we
want to get it absolutely right. To a certain extent, we can
look at becoming a Christian and living the Christian life in
similar terms.

We need to see that *it is not easy.* There are hindrances and
difficulties. Jesus talks about it being 'easier for a camel to go

through the eye of a needle' than for a rich man to enter God's kingdom. He talks, too, of a narrow gate and a narrow road to eternal life. Paul says in Acts 14 that we must go through many hardships to enter the kingdom of God.

We need to see, however, *what a great thing it is to be a Christian*. There is nothing better. It is the difference between glory and disgrace, life and death, heaven and hell. It is a glorious life.

The profound element is that, because it is a matter of life and death, it affects every single part of our lives. Whether you are a Christian is not on the same level as whether you can play the piano, or even whether you can read and write. Its implications are far, far greater.

One can present the gospel in a variety of ways. Here in Proverbs it is in terms of wisdom — how to be wise. The New Testament reveals clearly that Jesus Christ is Wisdom personified. As the light of the sun shines into every place, so the wisdom of the Son has gone out and enlightens all sorts of people. All of Scripture is about Jesus Christ. That is true of Proverbs, just as much as the rest of the Bible.

Proverbs 3 opens with five commands, each with a promise attached. By means of wholehearted commitment to Christ, humility and godly living, we may know life, success, health and prosperity. Following this, in verses 11-20, we have something of a hymn of praise to wisdom. Verses 11 and 12 are transitional and contain a warning. As in the previous verses, there is a command, but this time accompanied by a word of encouragement, rather than a promise. This leads to a change of pace before the commands resume. With the warning, then, there is both an encouragement and something for us to consider.

A warning (3:11-12)

The book continues to talk as father to son and says, **'My son, do not despise the L**O**RD's discipline and do not resent his rebuke.'** Some people think that wisdom is just a matter of enthusiasm, or that you can simply volunteer to be a Christian. But being wise, or being a Christian, is not quite as easy as it may seem. It is a matter of obedience, of self-denial, of temptation and trial and persecution, of bearing the cross daily. To become a Christian is to become a child of God, and that means to come under his discipline. It means that at times he will rebuke you when you step out of line. In the light of this, we are open to two possible dangers.

Despising discipline

On the one hand, there is the danger of despising and rejecting the Lord's discipline, in the sense of making light of it and failing to see his hand in it all.

Resentment

On the other hand, we can so shrink from such disciplines that we become discouraged and either never come to Christ or, having apparently come, begin to drift away. In Proverbs 15:10 we read, 'Stern discipline awaits him who leaves the path; he who hates correction will die.' Accepting discipline is one of the things that the book often commends.

The Roman philosopher Seneca was perhaps nearing the right balance when he said that it was inhuman not to feel setbacks, and yet unmanly not to bear them.

It is important not to overlook the phrase, **'My son'**, here and especially the words in verse 12: **'... because the L**O**RD**

disciplines those he loves, as a father the son he delights in'. This is why when, in Hebrews 12, the writer quotes these verses he can speak of them as a 'word of encouragement'. It is encouraging because it 'addresses you as sons'. Even the Bible's warnings are there to encourage us! It is clear from Hebrews 12 that believers are to 'endure hardship as discipline'. It is a proof that 'God is treating you as sons. For what son is not disciplined by his father?' The writer of Hebrews goes as far as to say that 'If you are not disciplined (and everyone undergoes discipline), then you are illegitimate children and not true sons' (v. 8). He takes the analogy of human fatherhood: 'Moreover, we have all had human fathers who disciplined us and we respected them for it. How much more should we submit to the Father of our spirits and live! Our fathers disciplined us for a little while as they thought best; but God disciplines us for our good, that we may share in his holiness' (vv. 9-10). He adds that 'No discipline seems pleasant at the time, but painful. Later on, however, it produces a harvest of righteousness and peace for those who have been trained by it' (v. 11).

On occasion, when I was a child, my parents would beat me with a wooden spoon. When I was quite young they would sometimes make me go to bed while it was still light and other children were playing outside. They would not let me play in the street on Sundays. When I was fourteen they refused to let me go to a pop concert. Such disciplines were often unpleasant at the time but I am not really sorry for them now. I see how they helped me to be a better person. Many readers could say similar things. We need this same perspective on the troubles and setbacks that mark our efforts to live Christian lives. The Puritan Thomas Brooks wrote that God would not rub so hard, were it not to fetch out the dirt and spots in his people. C. S. Lewis takes up the rubbing idea in a different way and notes how an artist making a quick sketch will be rapid and there will be no rubbing out. However, when he is working on a masterpiece it will take a long time and there will be many rubbings out. Believers are God's masterpieces ('created in Christ Jesus to do good works,' Eph. 2:10) and they have to endure many 'rubbings out' before the work is complete.

An encouragement (3:13-18)

Having laid down this warning, it is very important that we underline the fact that there is nothing better than to find wisdom — that is, to know Christ, to trust in him and what he has done. Breaking from the series of commands in chapter 3, a double argument follows: an encouraging and practical beatitude (3:13-18), and then a thought-provoking theological affirmation (3:19-20).

The beatitude is the first of five in Proverbs 1-9 (see 3:18,33; 8:32,34 for the others). **'Blessed is the man who finds wisdom, the man who gains understanding.'** The words **'finds'** and **'gains'** (a rare word meaning 'to obtain' or 'draw out') are important. We are not born with wisdom. We have to find, or encounter, it. We need to obtain it.

In general, the great thing that finding wisdom gives is God's blessing. Admittedly, Ecclesiastes 1:18 says that 'With much wisdom comes much sorrow; the more knowledge, the more grief,' but this is referring to mere worldly wisdom. God reserves a profound happiness, or contentment, for the one who finds him and his wisdom. This message is underlined repeatedly in Scripture. For example, 'Blessed are all who take refuge in him' (Ps. 2:12); 'Blessed is the man who takes refuge in him' (Ps. 34:8); 'Blessed is the man who makes the LORD his trust' (Ps. 40:4); 'O LORD Almighty, blessed is the man who trusts in you' (Ps. 84:12). The beatitudes at the start of the

Sermon on the Mount say the same thing. Remember Jesus' words to his disciples when he said, 'Blessed are the eyes that see what you see. For I tell you that many prophets and kings wanted to see what you see but did not see it, and to hear what you hear but did not hear it' (Luke 10:23-24).

To know Christ, the Wisdom of God, is something incomparable:

> **For she is more profitable than silver**
>   **and yields better returns than gold.**
> **She is more precious than rubies;**
> [perhaps precious red coral is intended, or pearls]
>   **nothing you desire can compare with her**
>   (3:14-15).

This follows on from 2:4. Think of all that this world has to offer, symbolized in the craftsmanship of silver ornaments, the buying power of gold, or the beauty of precious gems. Is there anything that is more worth having than this? Wealth? Fame? Power? Health? None of these begins to compare. C H Spurgeon rightly said that 'The slightest fragment of truth is more valuable than a diamond... You are so much the richer by every truth you know; you will be so much the poorer by every truth you forget.' In the words of Jesus himself, 'What good will it be for a man if he gains the whole world, yet forfeits his soul? Or what can a man give in exchange for his soul?' (Matt. 16:26).

Look at the rewards which are enumerated in verses 16 and 17 before the inclusive benediction which concludes the passage: **'She is a tree of life to those who embrace her; those who lay hold of her will be blessed'** (3:18). The book uses the 'tree of life' image three more times (11:30; 13:12, 15:4). The tree of life is mentioned in Genesis and Revelation, and in Psalm 1 the blessed man is said to thrive like a tree. The idea is the sustaining of life, as with fruit from a tree. Of course, the promises here are not absolute and unqualified, but they make clear the quality of life the wise man, the believer, can expect. Life is one of the great blessings promised in this book. Wisdom comes with her hands full of good things, some of which have already been intimated in 3:1-10:

> **Long life is in her right hand;**
> **in her left hand are riches and honour.**
> **Her ways are pleasant ways,**
> **and all her paths are peace**
>
> (3:16-17).

This all seems rather at odds with what has been said by way of warning. There is no contradiction, however, only paradox. Believers may know opposition from without, but they also know peace within. There may be many troubles on the road to heaven, but it is still pleasant to travel it. A believer may be poor in terms of this world's goods, but he has the riches of eternal life. Even the youngest martyr has an everlasting future ahead. The apostle Paul was keenly aware of paradoxes of this sort. He says of himself, 'We are hard pressed on every side, but not crushed; perplexed, but not in despair; persecuted, but not abandoned; struck down, but not destroyed'; '...dying, and yet we live on; beaten, and yet not killed; sorrowful, yet always rejoicing; poor, yet making many rich; having nothing, and yet possessing everything' (2 Cor. 4:8-9; 6:9-10).

Preaching on verse 16, the Puritan Thomas Adams noted that riches and honour are God's gifts. We cannot assume, however, that because we are rich this is a sign of God's favour, as wealth and honour are also found in evil men. He quotes Augustine as saying that riches are given to good men so that they will not be thought of as evil, but also to evil men that they may not be thought of as the best good. Adams sees significance in these gifts being in the *left* hand here. Eternal life (the gift of the right hand) is the first thing, the chief thing, to seek. We must also note that God gives with both hands, signifying his bountiful generosity. There is no better life on earth than that of a Christian, and with it comes everlasting life in heaven. God barred Adam and Eve from eating from the tree of life but now, through Christ, he has opened up the way afresh.

Jesus spoke of 'the kingdom of heaven' as being like a man digging in a field and finding treasure there. 'In his joy' the man 'went and sold all he had and bought that field' (Matt. 13:44). Similarly, there was 'a merchant looking for fine pearls. When he found one of great value, he went away and sold everything he had and bought it' (Matt. 13:45-46). To be a Christian will cost all that you have, but the price is not too great.

As Paul observed, 'I consider everything a loss compared to the surpassing greatness of knowing Christ Jesus my Lord, for whose sake I have lost all things. I consider them rubbish, that I may gain Christ and be found in him, not having a righteousness of my own that comes from the law, but that which is through faith in Christ — the righteousness that comes from God and is by faith. I want to know Christ and the power of his resurrection and the fellowship of sharing in his sufferings, becoming like him in his death, and so, somehow, to attain to the resurrection from the dead' (Phil. 3:8-11). Can you identify with that? Are you an overcomer like Paul?

Remember 'what the Spirit says to the churches': 'To him who overcomes, I will give the right to eat from the tree of life, which is in the paradise of God.' There in paradise, 'On each side of the river stood the tree of life, bearing twelve crops of fruit, yielding its fruit every month... Blessed are those who wash their robes, that they may have the right to the tree of life...' (Rev. 2:7; 22:2,14).

Something to think about (3:19-20)

Finally, we are left with something to consider, concerning God's Christ, God's wisdom. Think about creation — the earth, the sky, the sea. Where did it all come from? Evolutionary theories will tell you that it came from nowhere. But, although you may still resist the idea, you know that God created it all. How did he do it?

Genesis 1 tells us that God spoke. It was by his Word that he created the heavens and the earth. Who is this Word? John tells us plainly: 'In the beginning was the Word, and the Word was with God, and the Word was God. He was with God in the beginning. Through him all things were made; without him nothing was made that has been made… The Word became flesh and made his dwelling among us. We have seen his glory, the glory of the One and Only, who came from the Father, full of grace and truth' (John 1:1-3,14).

Here, in verses 19 and 20, 'the Word' is referred to as wisdom, understanding or knowledge:

By wisdom the Lord laid the earth's foundations,
  by understanding he set the heavens in place;
by his knowledge the deeps were divided,
  and the clouds let drop the dew.

This is similar to God's argument in Job 38-41.

Think of *earth's foundations* — the earth itself and its gravity. Think of *the heavens* — the sky, the stars, the planets, the sun and moon, the galaxies. Think of *the deeps* — the oceans, seas and rivers divided by the land. Think of *rain and dew* — things growing in this atmosphere. How was it all created? It was created by or through Christ.

We return to this subject in Proverbs 8, but for now just think about it. If God created the world through Jesus Christ, surely no trouble we may have to face will be too much for him. He has it all under control. You cannot come to know anyone greater. Think what he might bring about in your life if it is given over to serving him. When it speaks in Hebrews 1:3 of Christ 'sustaining all things', it refers not only to creation but to everything else as well.

This is the message, then: come to Christ and find wisdom. Belonging to him is not easy, but it is an incomparable honour. You will never regret coming to him.

7.
A fifth fatherly talk begun: Holding on in faith; letting go in repentance

Please read Proverbs 3:21-32

Sir James Simpson, the Victorian medical scientist and the discoverer of chloroform, was a fine Christian believer. He was once asked in a public meeting what had been his greatest discovery. He answered that his greatest discovery had been that he had a Saviour. The reported response of neo-orthodox theologian Karl Barth to a similar question strikes the same note. Asked about the greatest thing he had discovered in the Bible, he quoted the children's hymn: 'Jesus loves me, this I know, for the Bible tells me so.' The admired Christian thinker Dr Francis Schaeffer claimed the same song as his own favourite.

Consciously or unconsciously, these gifted men were paying testimony to the fact that the Christian gospel revealed in Scripture, though extremely profound, is essentially very simple. It is so deep that all eternity will not be time enough to sound it, yet it is so simple that a child can understand it.

At its most simple, God requires of us just two things — to repent and to believe. He simply demands that we put our trust in the Lord Jesus Christ and turn away from all our sins. To a child you might say, 'Be sorry for the wrong things you do; stop doing them and give yourself to Jesus.' The message is not complex. It is not hard to grasp. It is very simple indeed. We could sum up: 'Love Christ and hate what is evil,' or 'Lean on Christ and forsake all wrongdoing.' Although it may not be immediately obvious, exactly the same message is found here in Proverbs 3:21-32.

In verse 21 the fatherly exhortation to seek and find wisdom becomes a call to retain it once you have found it: **'My son, preserve sound judgement and discernment, do not let them out of your sight.'** In New Testament terms, this is a call to continued faith. In 1 Timothy 1:19 Paul urges Timothy to keep 'holding on to faith'. Not to do so is to risk making shipwreck of the faith. To hold on to 'sound judgement and discernment' is to hold on to faith in Christ, the true wisdom and insight that comes from God alone. If you do that, you will be rewarded. The rewards for such faith are spoken about in verses 22-26.

Then in the last verse in this section we are told, **'The LORD detests a perverse man but takes the upright into his confidence'** (3:32). Later in Proverbs we learn of a variety of things that the Lord detests, but here we are being reminded that he wants uprightness, not perversity. In New Testament terms, this is a call to continual repentance. 1 Timothy 1:19, which we quoted earlier, actually speaks about 'holding on to faith and a good conscience'. Rejecting either means making shipwreck of the faith. God detests the perverse, but shares his mind with the upright. Examples of perversity are given in verses 27-31.

So here are blessings for those who have faith and hold on to it, those who 'preserve sound judgement and discernment', and a call to repentance as we remember that the Lord detests the perverse who refuse to repent and that we must therefore hold on to a good conscience. We shall examine this in more detail below.

Five blessings that come through faith (3:21-26)

What is true faith? We know from the New Testament that it is to trust only in the Lord Jesus Christ as he is revealed in Scripture. It is to rely on him and on what he has done, and on this alone, for forgiveness of sins. This is sound wisdom. Only the man or woman who grasps the cross and what it means is truly wise and truly blessed. Such a person does two things:

> *He preserves* such knowledge. Have you ever made jam? Or have you seen it being made? You take fruit, some strawberries, or blackberries, or raspberries, or whatever, and instead of just leaving them to rot, you boil them with sugar to preserve them and then bottle the jam tightly so that it can be enjoyed in the months to come. If we have true knowledge we shall want to preserve it as best we can, making sure we lose none of it.
>
> *He does not let it out of his sight.* When a child is very naughty, you know you cannot let him out of your sight for a minute. If you have a particular interest in a horse in a race, you will not want to let it out of your sight throughout the race. That is why people take their binoculars to the races. Sometimes the police and similar authorities are involved in surveillance work. It is important that they do not let the subject out of their sight even for a moment. If we really have the truth, we shall keep it before us always.

Are you keeping the good news of the death and resurrection of Christ for sinners in your mind? In verses 22-26 at least five very desirable blessings are promised to those who do such a thing.

1. Life and loveliness

'They will be life for you, an ornament to grace your neck' (3:22). This is a familiar thought in Proverbs (cf. 1:9). As sinners, we are dead by nature, but through faith in Christ we can know life for our souls. By **'life'** is meant not mere existence, but life in all its abundance. (In John 10:10 Jesus talks about having come so that his followers 'may have life, and have it to the full'.) It is a beautiful life, a lovely life. Think of the difference between a beautiful and ornate necklace — a symbol of life, joy and beauty — and life without Christ, which, by contrast, is ugly and bare, joyless and dead. We need to discern that life is found only in the Lord Jesus.

2. Safety and stability

'Then you will go on your way in safety, and your foot will not stumble' (3:23). This is again a thought found elsewhere in Proverbs and also in Psalms 37 and 121. Outside of Christ, there is danger at every point. There is evil all around us, as we know. The danger of stumbling into hell is a constant one, but Christ can keep you safe and keep you from falling if you look to him. He is both the light along the way and the way itself (see John 8:12; 14:6).

3. Confidence and composure

'When you lie down, you will not be afraid; when you lie down, your sleep will be sweet' (3:24). How well do you sleep? Insomnia is a terrible thing. We vary in the way we are made, of course, but sleep is a gift from God for his loved ones (see Ps. 127:2). Not everyone finds it easy to receive that gift by any means. Sometimes noisy neighbours or physical pain keep people awake, but there can also be less obvious causes of sleeplessness. For example, some cannot sleep because they are too afraid to lie down and slumber. Others find their conscience keeping them awake in the quiet of the night.

Ideally, the true Christian should not have problems with these distractions. He should be both free from fear and confident, because if he is trusting in Christ he has been saved from hell and judgement. Remember Peter in Acts 12. Although he was in prison and was likely to die the next day, when the angel came to rescue him, he found the apostle fast asleep and had to dig him in the ribs to get him to wake up!

Psalms 3, 4 and 121 are also relevant here. With the psalmist we should be able to say:

Though an army besiege me,
   my heart will not fear;
though war break out against me,
   even then will I be confident

(Ps. 27:3).

The Christian has a conscience that has been cleansed by the blood of Christ and so he can be composed even in the most testing circumstances. John speaks of this in his first epistle: 'This then is how we know that we belong to the truth, and how we set our hearts at rest in his presence whenever our hearts condemn us. For God is greater than our hearts, and he knows everything. Dear friends, if our hearts do not condemn us, we have confidence before God' (1 John 3:19-21).

4. Certainty and conviction

'Have no fear of sudden disaster or of the ruin that overtakes the wicked' (3:25). This follows. Judgement Day is coming for the wicked, but it is a day that the true believer can face with confidence, certain that all will be well. To the unbeliever wisdom says:

> Since you ignored all my advice
>   and would not accept my rebuke,
> I in turn will laugh at your disaster;
>   I will mock when calamity overtakes you —
> when calamity overtakes you like a storm,
>   when disaster sweeps over you like a whirlwind,
>   when distress and trouble overwhelm you.
> Then they will call to me but I will not answer;
>   they will look for me but will not find me
>
> (1:25-28).

However, for the believer there are no such fears.

5. Peace and perseverance

'For the Lord will be your confidence and will keep your foot from being snared' (3:26). The believer can be absolutely confident in God. He is at peace with him. With Job he can say, 'Though he slay me, yet will I hope in him' (Job 13:15). This is part of the fruit of faith. It is like the peace and confidence a small child has when he is holding daddy's hand. There are mantraps everywhere to catch the unwary, all sorts of gins and snares in this world, but the one who truly believes will be kept safe to the end. He will persevere. As we read in the next chapter, 'The path of the righteous is like the first gleam of dawn, shining ever brighter till the full light of day' (4:18). What was said of the Philippians can be said of all believers: 'He who began a good work in you will carry it on to completion until the day of Christ Jesus' (Phil. 1:6).

So faith is the first thing. But then there is her twin sister, as one of the Puritans used to put it, repentance.

Five sorts of things from which to repent (3:27-32)

There are several elements in true repentance. For example, it includes not only being sorry for sin, but also turning from it. In verses 27-31 we have five specific examples of the sorts of sin from which you must turn if you truly repent. Each verse is a negative command and begins, 'Do not...' These verses serve as a negative counterpart not only to verses 21-26, but also to the opening verses of the chapter. They help us to see something of what true repentance really involves. In each case, there is a double sin involved. Repentance means turning from five things.

1. Carelessness and complacency

'Do not withhold good from those who deserve it, when it is in your power to act' (3:27). Obviously we think first of the negative side of repentance, but there is a positive side too. It not only involves abandoning uncaring attitudes, but also adopting caring ones. Complacency must go. 'As we have opportunity, let us do good to all people' (Gal. 6:10).

For example, think of someone in need or in trouble, largely or wholly through no fault of their own — an unemployed man struggling to provide for his family; a child who is being physically or sexually abused; a lonely old woman with no family; someone who has fallen and hurt himself; an unwanted baby — born or unborn. Is there something you can do to help this person, without neglecting other duties? Not to do anything is carelessness and complacency. It is a sin.

To be a true Christian you must repent. True repentance includes forsaking all uncaring and complacent attitudes. We must not neglect those in need.

2. Play-acting and procrastination

Do not say to your neighbour,
'Come back later; I'll give it tomorrow' —
when you now have it with you

(3:28).

The double sin here is being hypocritical and procrastinating — that is, putting on an act and pretending that you want to help, but constantly putting off actually doing anything about it.

Is there a situation where you have something extra that is worth having — food, clothing, shelter, money, etc.? You have a neighbour who needs it — not someone who simply wants it, but who needs it. The question of who is my neighbour was settled once and for all by Jesus in his parable of the Good Samaritan (see Luke 10). It can be anyone you know of. If you refuse to give them what they need, pretending that you are going to give it to them later, and then do not, that is the sin of hypocrisy and procrastination.

There is a song on a slightly different subject by the contemporary American singer and song writer Tracey Chapman that asks:

If not now, then when?
If not today then why make your promises?
A love declared for days to come is as good as none.

She goes on to argue that today is the day; now is the moment. That is how we must live.

To be a true Christian you must repent. True repentance includes forsaking all hypocrisy and procrastination, especially in the area of helping our neighbours.

3. Plotting and breaking peace

'Do not plot harm against your neighbour, who lives trustfully near you' (3:29). Here the picture is of a neighbour — that is, anyone we come into contact with. What happens is that there is, firstly, a plot to do something harmful against him — to hurt him physically, mentally or spiritually, to take from him or bring him down; and, secondly, an aggravation of the sin — the fact that your neighbour trusted you to do him good, not harm.

Here again we are talking about sin — namely an unwillingness to live at peace with your neighbour. Paul tells us, 'If it is possible, as far as it depends on you, live at peace with everyone' (Rom. 12:18). If we exploit our neighbours and plot against them, it is a sin.

To be a true Christian you must repent. True repentance includes forsaking all plotting and scheming against, and taking advantage of, others, destroying their peace.

4. Slander and slyness

'Do not accuse a man for no reason — when he has done you no harm' (3:30). Here we come to slander, defamation, libel, or false accusation. From time to time newspapers are taken to the courts for libelling people. Sometimes they are found guilty; sometimes they are not. We certainly must take care over what we say or write about others. Here we have, firstly, a case of falsely accusing someone of doing wrong; and, secondly, an aggravation of the sin — the fact that this is not even revenge, but a sly, unprovoked attack. Are we also guilty of such things? Remember how Naboth died because those who had been bribed by Jezebel falsely accused him.

To be a true Christian you must repent. True repentance includes forsaking all acts of slander and slyness.

5. *Desiring or doing what is violent*

'Do not envy a violent man or choose any of his ways' (3:31). Envying the violent is also a sin to be repented of, as is any act of violence. The two sins here are: firstly, envying a violent man — wishing you could be like him and live as he does; and, secondly, copying him and actually doing similar violent things.

Later in Proverbs we are told:

> Do not envy wicked men,
>   do not desire their company;
> for their hearts plot violence,
>   and their lips talk about making trouble
>
> (24:1-2).

This was a sin into which Asaph began to fall. He tells us about it and how he escaped in Psalm 73.

To be a true Christian you must repent. True repentance includes forsaking all desire to do, or doing, what is violent.

A summary (3:32)

'Without holiness no one will see the Lord' (Heb. 12:14), and **'The LORD detests a perverse man but takes the upright into his confidence.'** We cannot be saved by what we do, but if we are to be intimate with the Lord and know his pleasure there must be a definite break with unkindness, malice, evil scheming, slander and envy.

'You must rid yourselves of all such things as these: anger, rage, malice, slander and filthy language from your lips' (Col. 3:8). 'Rid yourselves of all malice and all deceit, hypocrisy, envy, and slander of every kind' (1 Peter 2:1).

We must all hold on to Christ in faith and let go of sin in repentance.

8.
A fifth fatherly talk concluded: The Lord's curse; the Lord's blessing

Please read Proverbs 3:33-35

The greatest thing in all the world is to know God's blessing. Nothing can beat being under his smile and knowing his favour. To hear his, 'Come, you who are blessed by my Father; take your inheritance, the kingdom prepared for you since the creation of the world,' is the greatest thing anyone can possibly look forward to.

It is meant as a kindness when people say, 'Bless you'. I suffer from hay fever and so at a certain time of the year people are often saying it to me. Sometimes they are complete strangers! Of course, by itself, a human blessing can no more improve things than a gypsy curse can make them worse. But if God blesses you then it will make all the difference. Forgiveness, strength, protection, hope, life, heaven — all these and more are yours if God blesses you.

Alternatively, the worst thing in all the world is to know God's curse. Nothing can be worse than his frown, his displeasure. If he says to you at the end, 'Depart from me, you who are cursed, into the eternal fire prepared for the devil and his angels,' then you are finished. If God curses you, you are damned. There is no hope. A gypsy curse may bother some people, but it has no power in itself to do harm. 'Like a fluttering sparrow or a darting swallow, an undeserved curse does not come to rest' (26:2). But if God curses you, you are doomed. No talisman can protect you from that. No amulet or charm can preserve you. There is no strength, no protection, no hope. You are bound for hell.

This is a vital question, then, to which we must all know the answer. It is a covenant question. Am I under God's covenant protection, or am I not? Am I under his curse, or under his blessing? It is not enough to be guided by our feelings about this, or to follow merely human ideas about the subject. Rather, we need to know for certain whom God curses and whom he blesses. Some say, 'I don't care if I'm blessed or damned. It makes no difference to me.' As we shall see, to speak like that is a great mistake.

Here at the end of Proverbs 3 we have a brief epilogue, a little bit of 'vocabulary' amid the 'grammar'. Here is a foretaste of the proverbs proper. These verses are full of contrasts and teach us something of what it really means to be either under God's curse, or under his blessing. Verse 34 is quoted twice in the New Testament, in James 4:6 and in 1 Peter 5:5. Several later proverbs deal with this same subject.

Whom does the Lord curse?

In Proverbs 3:33-35 we have the third of our summaries. Once more, it is presented in the form of a contrast — indeed, it contains three contrasting proverbs. The first two begin negatively and end positively. The third begins positively but ends negatively. The purpose of each is to encourage righteousness and discourage wickedness by reference to the Lord, a pattern that begins with verse 32. So, negatively, we are told very plainly three things about just who it is that the Lord, who 'detests a perverse man', curses: **'The LORD's curse is on the house of the wicked... He mocks proud mockers ... fools he holds up to shame.'** This leaves us with three obvious and important questions that we all need to ask ourselves: 'Am I wicked? Am I proud? Am I a fool?'

If your honest answer to one or more of those questions is 'Yes', then you are under God's curse and heading for shame.

1. Am I wicked?

To be wicked is to be guilty before God. It is to have broken his law. It is to be guilty, for example, of the sins spoken of in verses 27-31. These are:

> withholding good from those who deserve it when you
>   can help;
> failing to help people in genuine need by pretending you
>   are unable to;
> plotting harm against your unsuspecting neighbour;
> accusing a man for no reason;
> envying a violent man or copying his violence.

To be wicked is to disobey the Ten Commandments in thought, word or deed, either in an active or a passive way. So, for example, if, on the one hand, I think hateful thoughts, speak hateful words or do a hateful deed or if, on the other, I fail to think loving thoughts, say loving things or do loving deeds, then I am guilty of wickedness. Have you failed to put God first in all things? Have you failed to love your neighbour as yourself? Then you are wicked and by nature you are under God's curse. You may have many things that arouse the envy of others, but if you are cursed, not one of those things is worth having.

2. Am I proud?

How you react to the previous question will probably give the clue as to how you answer this one. If you react to accusations of wickedness with denials, loudly asserting yourself and your abilities, then there is something wrong. Do you believe you can save yourself? Do you think you can make yourself right before God without any help? That is pride.

There are different sorts of pride — pride of face, of race, of place, of pace, even of grace — but they all centre on self and they are all under God's curse. The Bible speaks repeatedly against human pride in every shape or form. Charles Bridges says, 'On no point is the mind of God more fully declared than against pride.' We have already noted that verse 34 is quoted in James and 1 Peter in the midst of passages encouraging humility. Here are a couple of Old Testament examples: 'Though the LORD is on high, he looks upon the lowly, but the proud he knows from afar' (Ps.138:6); God says:

I live in a high and holy place,
    but also with him who is contrite and lowly in spirit,
to revive the spirit of the lowly
    and to revive the heart of the contrite

(Isa. 57:15).

Think of Babel, Pharaoh, Haman and Herod and you will be in no doubt about God's attitude to pride.

Augustine famously once noted the three chief marks of a man who is learning God's ways: firstly, humility; secondly, humility; thirdly, humility.

A farmer and his young son were in the field on one occasion discussing which of the barley looked the best. The boy liked the stalks of barley that stood upright like soldiers in a line. However, his father, knowing better, preferred the barley stalks that were bent over, their full heads much nearer the ground. It is the genuinely humble man who is the truly blessed man.

3. Am I a fool?

Again, our instinct is to say 'No'. We are not talking about mental ability, however. The fool is obstinate. He automatically says 'No' to such a question and never thinks about it. Yet part of the beginning of wisdom is to see that you are a fool. 'Do you see a man wise in his own eyes?' we read in 26:12. 'There is more hope for a fool than for him.' Have you ever grasped how little you know? Have you ever realized how needy you are? Are you aware of how prone you are to wander away from what is good and right? Have you never seen yourself as your own worst enemy? If not, what a fool you are! You are under God's curse.

Whom does the Lord bless?

So how can you know God's blessing? Obviously, the first thing is to escape his curse, and so we must turn from all wickedness, pride and foolishness. Positively, we are told very plainly three things about who it is that the Lord, who 'takes the upright into his confidence', blesses: **'... he blesses the home of the righteous ... gives grace to the humble. The wise inherit honour...'** This leaves us with three further obvious and important questions that we all need to ask ourselves: 'How can I be righteous? How can I be humble? How can I be wise?' This is the direction in which our thoughts should head.

1. How can I be righteous?

Righteousness is a matter of wholeheartedly loving God and loving our neighbour as ourselves. It is seeking to do the very opposite of the wicked things we have just been speaking about. However, if you have ever tried to be righteous you will know that it is not possible to do so fully. Remember how Jesus said, 'Unless your righteousness surpasses that of the Pharisees and the teachers of the law, you will certainly not enter the kingdom of heaven' (Matt. 5:20). The Pharisees and the teachers of the law prided themselves on their fastidiousness in legalistic righteousness. Their name was a byword for it. So how could anyone surpass them?

This is the glory of the gospel: 'In the gospel a righteousness from God is revealed' (Rom. 1:17). Jesus Christ is the only truly righteous one. He alone has inherent righteousness. He was 'holy, blameless, pure, set apart from sinners' (Heb. 7:26). He lived a perfect and holy life and then died bearing in his own body the penalty for wickedness. Because of what he has done on behalf of his people, when they trust in him, they receive his righteousness. It is imputed to them and they are justified through their faith, which is a gift from God. By this means, they escape from wickedness and death. This is the only way to true righteousness. There is no other. It is the only way out from under the curse. Paul speaks about it in Galatians 3:10-14, where he explains that there is no way to be forgiven by obeying the law. Rather, 'Christ redeemed [believers] from the curse of the law by becoming a curse for [them].' The apostle quotes the verse from Deuteronomy which says, 'Cursed is everyone who is hung on a tree' (Deut. 21:23), to prove that Christ was cursed. It is by this means that God redeems his people, Jews and Gentiles alike. If you want to be righteous you must trust in the Lord Jesus Christ.

2. How can I be humble?

Along with true righteousness comes real humility. Bishop J. C. Ryle called humility the surest mark of conversion, the first letter in the alphabet of Christianity. It really is basic. When you realize that forgiveness and every other blessing cannot be earned, but that they come from Christ himself as a gift, then humility must follow. However, it is not easy to say, 'Yes, I am a hopeless sinner.' Drunkards are often encouraged to confess publicly, 'I am an alcoholic,' and admit that they need the help of a higher power than themselves to overcome their problems. This is seen as the first step to some sort of cure. It is not easy to admit that you are in a hopeless state, but it is recognized as a vital step. The very first step in any healing process is usually to realize that you are ill. Similarly, until we see that we are in sin's grip and have no way of extricating ourselves, there is no hope for us at all. We need to bow down before God and confess our total inability to save ourselves. Humility is not an inferiority complex, but a matter of honesty. To be humble is to realize your own weakness and sin and the greatness and glory of God.

'God opposes the proud but gives grace to the humble,' say James and Peter. It is 'the meek' who 'inherit the earth', says Jesus, reflecting Psalm 37:11. The proud are brought down. 'Better to be a humble worm than a proud angel,' wrote one Puritan. Two simple prayers that almost anyone can pray are: 'Lord, show me myself,' and 'Lord show me yourself.' If you sincerely pray those two prayers you will learn how to be humble and your whole life will be transformed.

3. How can I be wise?

This is the theme of this whole book of Proverbs, of course. We are concerned here not with sophistication, with worldly wisdom, but with true heavenly wisdom. Are you wise enough to see that a holy and perfect God will demand holiness and perfection from the creatures he has made? Are you also wise enough to see that he himself provides the necessary holiness and perfection? Having seen that, are you finally wise enough to see that it is through Christ and his humiliating death on the cross that God provides salvation to his people, to all who trust in the Saviour? The message of the cross is foolishness to unbelievers, but in fact it is the wisdom of God, for God's foolishness is wiser than man's wisdom. It is on God's power that we must rely, not on man's so-called wisdom.

What is his curse or his blessing like?

Do you realize *what it means to be under God's curse* — to be bound by him, shut up and hemmed in by his mighty hand? Once he lifts his hand against you, there is no escape. You are shut up in the dark dungeon of death and hell for ever. That is the end that awaits the wicked, proud and foolish of this world. God's curse remains on them. He will mock them as they once mocked him. He will hold them up to shame. It is easy to laugh at hell now, but the last laugh will be his. 'He who laughs last laughs loudest.' Psalm 2 speaks of how 'the One enthroned in heaven laughs', of how 'the Lord scoffs' at those who oppose his Christ. He then deals with them. How you will hate yourself then! How ashamed of yourself you will be! But it does not have to be like that. If we humbly come to Christ for righteousness and wisdom and put our trust in him now, then all will be well.

Do not forget *how great God's blessing is*. Essentially, to be blessed means to be contented in God. He alone can give true joy, peace, life and assurance of those blessings. There is nothing better. It is something that affects the believer and all his family. His blessing is to be humbly received through grace. 'Grace' is a wonderful word. It means love freely given. God's grace guarantees his favour and forgiveness. It also means heaven itself at last. That is the last and greatest honour for the true child of God. All this is his inheritance, an inheritance greater than any human one. If someone left you a billion pounds in his will, it could not be better than the gift of being blessed by God. The day is fast approaching when 'Multitudes who sleep in the dust of the earth will awake: some to everlasting life, others to shame and everlasting contempt.' At that time, 'Those who are wise will shine like the brightness of the heavens, and those who lead many to righteousness, like the stars for ever and ever' (Dan. 12:2,3).

The challenge

It must have been a very solemn moment when, following success at Ai, Joshua and the people gathered between Mount Ebal and Mount Gerizim, as Moses had commanded, and heard the law of the Lord, and especially its blessings and curses. We read that 'All Israel, aliens and citizens alike ... were standing on both sides of the ark of the covenant of the LORD, facing those who carried it — the priests, who were Levites. Half of the people stood in front of Mount Gerizim and half of them in front of Mount Ebal, as Moses the servant of the LORD had formerly commanded... Afterwards, Joshua read all the words of the law — the blessings and the curses — just as it is written in the Book of the Law' (Josh. 8:33-34).

That is what we have been doing in this chapter, standing in the valley and hearing the Lord's curses and blessings. Like Moses, I want to plead with you. In Deuteronomy he says to the people, 'See, I am setting before you today a blessing and a curse — the blessing if you obey ... the curse if you disobey'

(Deut. 11:26-28). Or as he says later, 'See, I set before you today life and prosperity, death and destruction' (Deut. 30:15). These are the alternatives I am setting before you here.

If you find righteousness, humility and wisdom, 'then you will live and increase, and the LORD your God will bless you... But if your heart turns away and you are not obedient', but are drawn to wickedness, pride and foolishness, 'I declare to you this day that you will certainly be destroyed... This day I call heaven and earth as witnesses against you that I have set before you life and death, blessings and curses. Now choose life, so that you and your children may live and that you may love the LORD your God, listen to his voice, and hold fast to him' (Deut. 30:16-20).

The Lord will truly bless you if you will simply look to him.

9.
A sixth fatherly talk begun: Wisdom is supreme, so get wisdom

Please read Proverbs 4:1-17

In a poignant song from the sixties called 'Some day never comes', John Fogerty sang that the first thing he remembered was 'asking papa "Why?"' There were many things he did not know. He tells us that

> Daddy always smiled and took me by the hand,
> saying, 'Some day you'll understand.'

Sadly, as the song title suggests, 'Some day' never came and the father left home. In turn, the son found history repeating itself with his own son. Nevertheless, the picture of a father at least trying to help his son to understand is attractive. Many a boy would give his eye teeth just to have a father to talk to.

Here in Proverbs 4 once again we have, not only a father who is willing to take time to talk to his son, but one who has more than mere platitudes to share. The sixth fatherly speech, which begins with these verses, parallels the second speech in Proverbs 2, which also speaks of the benefits of wisdom. Although the reference in this passage is more autobiographical than previously, this is the first of four occasions on which the plural **'sons'** is used (see 5:7; 7:24; 8:32). This stresses that the message is for a wider audience.

As on previous occasions, the first exhortation is to **'Listen ... to a father's instruction; pay attention and gain understanding'** and not to **'forsake'** this **'teaching'** (cf. 1:8). The father can remember the time when his own father would take him aside and speak to him, even though he was very young:

> **When I was a boy in my father's house,**
> **still tender, and an only child of my mother,**
> **he taught me ...**
>
> (4:3-4).

I can remember my own father sometimes passing on, not only his own wisdom but things that he had received directly from his father. Although some of it was quite mundane (such as, 'Always leave the table wanting more,' or, 'Never try to catch a falling glass') there was something powerful about such double-strength testimony.

If you have learned anything good from your parents, or from whoever brought you up, or from others who had a big influence on you when you were young, then give thanks to God. If they passed on the gospel to you, you should be even more thankful. You have a sacred duty to pass on what you have received from them to the next generation. Like a good rugby player, you must not drop the ball but pass it on to the next man, running to the 'try line' all the while.

Perhaps you have no cherished childhood memories of a parent passing on good advice. Do not despair. His name is not mentioned here, but it is God himself who speaks to you, and he speaks as a Father to his child. 'Listen,' he says to you, 'here are three vital pieces of advice which you need to hear.'

What you need

In so many areas of life half the battle is to know what is required. When you sit an examination it greatly helps to know what topics you are likely to be asked about. When you are out shopping, a little list can make things so much easier. One of the biggest problems that most people have is that they have no more than the vaguest ideas about what God requires from them. They have little notion of how to please him at all. They do not know why they are here on earth. They have no idea what the purpose of life might be. What such people need is wisdom. **'Wisdom is supreme; therefore get wisdom'** (4:7). This is 'the principal thing', as the AV puts it. They do not need fame, or more money, or greater talent, but wisdom. What we all need, supremely, is wisdom. It is referred to here in several ways:

1. **'Wisdom'** (4:5,6,7);
2. **'the way of wisdom'** (4:11) — it is a practical thing;
3. **'understanding'** (4:1,5,7) — insight, discernment, making sense of life;
4. **'instruction'** (4:1,13) — discipline or training;
5. **'sound learning'** (4:2);
6. **'teaching'** (4:2);
7. **'words'** (4:4,5; cf. 4:10)
8. **'commands'** (4:4) — wisdom is not something nebulous, but very definite.

What do we all need? Wisdom from God. We need wisdom to know how to live and how to make sense of life. True wisdom gives us definite truths to live by and teaches us to be obedient.

This is fleshed out most clearly in the New Testament. Put quite simply, the purpose of life is to live for the glory of the God who made us. No one does that by nature, and so we deserve the judgement of hell. However, in his mercy God has provided a way out, a way of wisdom ('the way') in the gospel of Jesus Christ. He himself has provided a way back to God by means of his perfect life and his atoning death. This is the teaching, the words, the understanding, or sound learning, that we need. It is the obedience of faith to the command to trust in Christ, God's wisdom, that we need.

Why you need it

We must not go too quickly. It is important to understand *why* we need to trust in Christ and walk the way of wisdom. Often it is not until we see how necessary a thing is that we have any desire for it. Babies and toddlers have little use for coins and bank-notes in their hands, or labour-saving gadgets for tasks around the house. Sometimes schoolchildren are bored with their lessons chiefly because they seem so irrelevant. The reason why so many people have no desire for heavenly wisdom is that they cannot see any use for it. They do not realize what good it would bring to their lives.

What is the good it will bring? We can sum it up in one word — life! Those who come to Christ, who come to understand divine wisdom, find life, and nothing less than that:

> **Lay hold of my words with all your heart;**
> **keep my commands and you will live...**
> **Listen, my son, accept what I say,**
> [this repeated instruction is fundamental; see 1:8]
> **and the years of your life will be many...**

**Hold on to instruction, do not let it go;
   guard it well, for it is your life**
            (4:4,10,13; cf. 1:3,33; 2:19-21; 3:2,16-22).

By nature we are all spiritually dead. We are lifeless, hope-less, godless and headed for everlasting death. But when you find wisdom you find life.

William Arnot illustrates with a story of an American ship in open sea that was attacked by a whale and began to sink. The sailors manned the lifeboats and filled them with provisions. Then two men returned to the sinking vessel to rescue some-thing else just before it went down. Their prize was nearly lost in the downward swirl but they were able to bring it safely to a lifeboat. What was it that was so important they were will-ing to risk their lives for it? It was the ship's compass. Without it they might have drifted to their deaths. It was life to them, just as wisdom is life to all of us. We are sunk without it.

More specifically, here are some of the blessings wisdom will bring:

Protection (4:6)

'Do not forsake wisdom, and she will protect you; love her, and she will watch over you.' Here we have two com-mands, one negative and one positive, each with a promise — promises of a protecting hand and eye. Wisdom is both a shel-ter and a guard. These promises are also found in Proverbs 2:8,11.

Exaltation (4:8-9)

'Esteem her, and she will exalt you; embrace her, and she will honour you' (more literally, 'Esteem her and she will exalt you; she will honour you if you embrace her'). **'She will set a garland of grace on your head and present you with a crown of splendour.'** Heaven is the prospect of all who find such wisdom. Here the garland of 1:9 is supplemented by **'a crown of splendour'** which points to the triple diadem of the New Testament:

> 1. 'The crown of righteousness, which the Lord, the righteous Judge, will award … to all who have longed for his appearing' (2 Tim. 4:8).
> 2. 'The crown of life that God has promised to those who love him' (James 1:12).
> 3. 'The crown of glory that will never fade away' (1 Peter 5:4).

Direction (4:11)

The offer, **'I guide you in the way of wisdom and lead you along straight paths,'** becomes a way of life when it is accepted.

Stabilization (4:12)

'When you walk, your steps will not be hampered; when you run, you will not stumble.' Where there are hills and rocks it is easy to stumble and trip. Following the theme of the journey from the previous verse, the promise here is of stability regardless of terrain.

If we lack heavenly wisdom, we are under a curse and in constant danger. We shall be dragged down, denigrated and dishonoured. There will be no glory, no heaven. You will be continually falling into the bottomless pit.

How to get what you need

Knowing what you need and why you need it is very important, but with that there must be an understanding of how to
get it. It is easy to want a million pounds and think how you
would use it to improve your life, but how are you going to
get it? If you have no answer to that question, of what use are
your desires and plans?

So how can you get wisdom? It is not inherited from parents. People do not suddenly wake up and find they have somehow caught it, like chickenpox. You cannot buy it or earn it
either. So how do you obtain wisdom? Much depends on attitude. What makes it difficult is that you need two basic elements and these two can seem contradictory. On the one hand,
you need actively to seek wisdom, seeing this as absolutely
vital. On the other hand, you also need to recognize that wisdom is a gift that comes from God. There also needs to be a
firm rejection of all other ways.

Actively seek wisdom

'Listen ... pay attention' (4:1). Give it your full attention.
Concentrate. Read God's Word, study it, hear it expounded
and preached.

'Do not forsake my teaching' (4:2) Wisdom is like a wife
whom you must not leave, a sentry-post that you must not
abandon.

**'Lay hold of my words with all of your heart... Get
wisdom, get understanding'** (4:4,5). Do not simply admire
wisdom, but get it for yourself. Like a professional wrestler,
pin it to the ground. Verse 4 is similar to 3:5. Perhaps Solomon was thinking here of his father's words preserved in
1 Chronicles 28:9: 'And you, my son Solomon, acknowledge
the God of your father, and serve him with wholehearted devotion and with a willing mind.'

We also remember that Jesus said, 'Make every effort to enter through the narrow door, because many, I tell you, will try to enter and will not be able to' (Luke 13:24).

'Keep my commands ... love her ... esteem her ... embrace her' (4:4,6,8). It cannot be a merely cerebral thing, merely intellectual. As you would love, esteem and embrace a loved one, so you must be passionate, devoted, committed, dedicated to wisdom. Love the Lord Jesus Christ and be devoted to him. Prize him above all else.

'Listen ... accept' (4:10). As you would accept any good gift, accept wisdom. If you come to the Word with a critical spirit and remain unwilling to accept it you will never be wise.

'Do not forget my words or swerve from them... Do not forsake wisdom... Hold on to instruction, do not let it go; guard it well' (4:5,6,13). Negatively, do not forget wisdom, or swerve from it, or lose hold of it. Positively, hold on to it and guard it well. Store up every precious bit. Hoard it.

See that gaining wisdom is absolutely vital

'Wisdom is supreme; therefore get wisdom. Though it cost all you have, get understanding' (4:7). The NRSV renders this, 'Whatever else you get, get insight' and the NASB: 'With all your acquiring, get understanding.' Have you seen how crucial it is to gain heaven's wisdom in Christ? Remember Jesus' parables of the pearl merchant and the man who finds treasure in a field: 'The kingdom of heaven is like treasure hidden in a field. When a man found it, he hid it again, and then in his joy went and sold all he had and bought that field. Again, the kingdom of heaven is like a merchant looking for fine pearls. When he found one of great value, he went away and sold everything he had and bought it' (Matt. 13:44-46).

Recognize that wisdom is nevertheless a gift

But how did the man come across the treasure in the first
place? How did the merchant come to see the pearl of great
price? It was the providence of God. And so we must remember that true wisdom is the gift of God. It is all of grace. Christ,
faith and everything else we need are only ours by grace. Speaking of this wisdom, the father says, **'I give you sound learning'** (4:2). It is something *taught.* **'I guide you in the way of
wisdom and lead you along straight paths,'** he says (4:11).
To gain wisdom we must realize our absolute dependence on
God.

Firmly reject all other ways

Finally, there is the negative note found in verses 14-17. From
verse 11 onwards, a travelling metaphor is again introduced
(see Prov. 2). It continues in verses 12-15 and recurs in verses
18-19 and 25-27. Life is a journey with a right path and a
good destination. Words and phrases such as **'guide'**, **'way'**,
'lead', **'paths'**, **'walk'**, **'steps'**, **'run'**, **'stumble'**, **'set foot
on the path'**, **'travel'**, **'turn from'** and **'go on your way'** all
occur, some of them more than once. Here are the roots, no
doubt, of what Jesus has to say in Matthew 7 about the narrow and broad roads, one leading to eternal life and the other
to destruction. This is a favourite metaphor to describe the
Christian life. Paul often speaks of the Christian life as the
Christian walk (see Eph. 2:10; 4:1,17; 5:2,8,15, AV).

Negative warnings follow the positive promises of verses
11 and 12 and the commands of verse 13. We are told:

**Do not set foot on the path of the wicked
or walk in the way of evil men.**

Avoid it, do not travel on it;
turn from it and go on your way

(4:14-15).

We must not even think about going in the way of evil. Some Americans like to use the emphatic negative: 'Don't even think about it.' We must not even think about going in any direction but the right one. The priest and the Levite were condemned for passing by on the other side, to the neglect of the man fallen among thieves, but when we are dealing with the path of the wicked it is perfectly right to pass it by.

Speaking of the wicked, he says:

For they cannot sleep till they do evil;
they are robbed of slumber till they make some-
one fall.
They eat the bread of wickedness
and drink the wine of violence

(4:16-17).

There are wicked people in this world. Some are so wicked that they eat, drink and sleep wickedness, or stay up half the night pursuing wicked schemes. They are not ready for bed until they have done something evil. The psalmist speaks of such a one:

Even on his bed he plots evil;
he commits himself to a sinful course
and does not reject what is wrong

(Ps. 36:4).

If we are to escape from them and from being like them we must not only put faith in Christ, but also turn back from every evil path.

A story is told of an early Christian trying to drive an evil spirit out of a man and asking the spirit how he dared be so shameless as to enter a professing Christian. The spirit is said to have answered, 'I didn't go to church after him; he came after me at the drama.' Too often men are found pursuing the wrong paths. Do not be like that. Turn from the broad road that leads to destruction and follow Christ who himself is the way, the truth and the life.

Preaching at the Metropolitan Tabernacle in 1878 on Proverbs 4:13, C. H. Spurgeon exhorted his hearers 'to hold fast'. He said, 'Even a touch of the hem of Christ's garment causeth healing to come to us, but if we want the full riches which are treasured up in Christ, we must not only touch but take hold; and if we would know from day to day to the very uttermost all the fulness of his grace, we must take fast hold, and so maintain a constant and close connection between our souls and the eternal fountain of life. It were well to give such a grip as a man gives to a plank when he seizes hold upon it for his very life — that is a fast hold indeed.'

10.
A sixth fatherly talk concluded: Increasing light or deepest darkness? Time for a check-up

Please read Proverbs 4:18-27

We begin by thinking about two contrasting things:

1. *Light.* Think of the first gleam of daylight, just as the sun begins to rise. Then picture the dawn as it slowly brings light to the sleeping town until the rays and warmth of the sun glance on everything. Think of the heat increasing as the morning goes on until the sun is at the very highest point in a cloudless sky.

2. *Darkness.* Many of us do not know what darkness really is. If, like me, you live in a city, there are so many sources of light that real darkness is unusual. Astronomers actually talk about 'light pollution' spoiling our views of the heavens. A few years ago, we had a family holiday in a cottage in the wilds of North Wales. One thing that struck my wife and me was how very dark it can be at night in such a place, if there is no moonlight. In pitch darkness, even after your eyes have adjusted, you cannot see your hand in front of your face.

These pictures provide us with a vivid contrast between the believer and the unbeliever. They are found in Proverbs 4:18-19 in a sort of double metaphor. In some ways these verses belong more with what has gone before than with what follows. They summarize 4:1-17 (see 1:32-33; 2:21-22; 3:33-35). However, they also prepare us for the final section of the chapter (4:20-27).

The metaphor of life as a journey begins back in verses 10-15 and is taken up again here as **'the path of the righteous'** is compared with **'the way of the wicked'**. However, the imagery of a journey is itself likened to, on one hand, **'the first gleam of dawn, shining ever brighter till the full light of day'**, and, on the other, to **'deep darkness'** that makes the wicked stumble in confusion. The Lord Jesus takes up the theme of light and darkness when he says, 'I am the light of the world. Whoever follows me will never walk in darkness, but will have the light of life' (John 8:12). The unbeliever is walking in darkness, but the believer has 'the light of life'. Paul says to believers, 'You were once darkness, but now you are light in the Lord. Live [literally "walk"] as children of light' (Eph. 5:8).

There is, then, what the twentieth-century Dutch American theologian R. B. Kuiper called 'a radical antithesis between the regenerate and the unregenerate'. In layman's terms, the difference between the true Christian and the unbeliever is enormous. It is like the difference between darkness and light. Further, as life progresses, the light or the darkness increases.

The route of the righteous (4:18)

The picture of light increasing, like dawn turning to the full light of day, suggests several things.

1. Sagacity

Darkness is often used in Scripture as a picture of ignorance. Light, then, is redolent of knowledge, wisdom, sagacity. When a man says he is agnostic about something, he is saying that he does not know. The overthrow of agnosticism can be pictured as the shining of light into the darkness of ignorance and unbelief. Truth, like a sudden light shining on your eyeballs when you have been in the darkness of sleep, can be painful at first but gradually, as you wake up, you grow accustomed to the light. We need to shine the torch of truth into the eyes of slumbering sinners and wake them up to their dangers. We need to bring men and women out into the glorious sunshine of God's kingdom of light by declaring the truth found in God's Word.

2. Sanctity

Holiness is referred to in Scripture as 'walking in the light': 'Come, O house of Jacob, let us walk in the light of the LORD' (Isa. 2:5). 'God is light; in him there is no darkness at all. If we claim to have fellowship with him yet walk in the darkness, we lie and do not live by the truth. But if we walk in the light, as he is in the light, we have fellowship with one another, and the blood of Jesus, his Son, purifies us from all sin' (1 John 1:5-7).

Note that 'The fruit of the light consists in all goodness, righteousness and truth' (Eph. 5:9). Christian armour is 'the armour of light' and is worn by 'sons of the light and sons of the day' who 'do not belong to the night or to the darkness' but live righteous lives (see 1 Thess. 5:5; Rom. 13:12-14; Eph. 6).

3. Sincerity

It is when we bring things into the light that their true state is seen. I remember buying clothing or material with my mother as a boy. She would often ask to see the product in natural daylight to ascertain its exact colour and quality. It is the light that reveals the true situation. We need to be exposed to the light of God's Word. The nearer we come to the light, the better we see our true state.

4. Safety

The daytime speaks also of safety, of being seen, of not being lost any more. The only safe place to be is in God's kingdom of light. In the darkness men stumble and fall, but in the light they can see where they are going. Salvation is found on the bright, narrow road to life.

5. Sureness that increases

We speak of hope as 'light at the end of the tunnel'. Here hope increases day by day as the journey progresses and our destination nears. The righteous are filled with assurance and expectancy. We are more and more certain about what lies ahead.

6. Steps forward

Here is the idea of going forward into ever-increasing light. The Christian life is marked by progress. The believer goes from faith to faith, from grace to grace, from glory to glory until the full light of day in heaven: 'And we, who with unveiled faces all reflect the Lord's glory, are being transformed into his likeness with ever-increasing glory, which comes from the Lord, who is the Spirit' (2 Cor. 3:18).

7. Spiritual life

The idea of light is often connected with life in the Bible, for obvious reasons. Without light, there is usually no life. Plants intuitively climb to where the light is. The Bible uses the phrase 'the light of life' (e.g., John 8:12). The psalmist says, 'For with you is the fountain of life; in your light we see light' (Ps. 36:9). Elsewhere he writes:

> You have delivered me from death
>   and my feet from stumbling,
> that I may walk before God
>   in the light of life
>
> (Ps. 56:13).

8. The splendour of heaven

For the Christian **'the full light of day'** is firstly the New Testament era anticipated in the Old Testament Scriptures. Personally, it is to enter heaven after death. Ultimately, it is the final consummation of all things, when God will have put everything under Christ's feet and will hand over the kingdom to his Father. Then we who believe will reign with Christ for ever. Daniel describes it: 'Those who are wise will shine like the brightness of the heavens, and those who lead many to righteousness, like the stars for ever and ever' (Dan. 12:3).

Revelation speaks of heaven itself in these terms: 'The city does not need the sun or the moon to shine on it, for the glory of God gives it light, and the Lamb is its lamp... There will be no more night. They will not need the light of a lamp or the light of the sun, for the Lord God will give them light' (Rev. 21:23; 22:5).

The way of the wicked (4:19)

How different is the situation of the wicked! Their way is marked by a deep darkness that is never dispelled. This points to a number of factors.

1. Dullness and ignorance

I remember one winter, as a teenager, having to go through a dark hall in our local chapel. Not wanting to draw the attention of anyone in the house nearby, I decided not to switch on the light. As I put my hands out to feel my way, I suddenly felt something very strange blocking my path. It was not warm to the touch, but it seemed almost alive. I froze, filled with fear. I could not think what it might be. I decided to switch the light on just for a second to see what it was. What was it? A Christmas tree! As we have seen, light and darkness are metaphors for, on the one hand, sagacity, knowledge or enlightenment and, on the other, dullness, ignorance or obscurity. The wicked are ignorant of God and so of themselves and of this world. They are dull-witted. They often bump into things and stumble, as it were, but they do not know why because they are in ignorance.

2. Deception

In the dark it easy to be deceived. Is that a stool over there, or is it someone crouching low, waiting to attack? Our eyes can, of course, deceive us in daylight, but this is even more likely in the dark. As a boy, I remember coming in from playing on winter evenings and being amazed at how dirty my clothes had become. The darkness had concealed the dirt until the light revealed the truth. Paul warns Timothy of 'evil men and impostors' who 'go from bad to worse, deceiving and being deceived' (2 Tim. 3:13).

3. Depravity

Darkness is a picture of wickedness itself, of depravity. Paul speaks of 'righteousness and wickedness' having as little in common as 'light' and 'darkness', or 'Christ' and 'Belial' (2 Cor. 6:14,15). He warns against 'the fruitless deeds of darkness' which we must avoid, yet 'expose' (Eph. 5:11). He speaks of the need to 'put aside the deeds of darkness', which include such things as 'orgies and drunkenness ... sexual immorality and debauchery ... dissension and jealousy' (Rom. 13:12,13).

4. Danger

We associate darkness with trouble and danger. Crimes often happen under the cover of darkness. It is much worse to be lost in the dark than in the daylight. How easy to stumble and fall then!

5. Degeneration

The idea of **'deep darkness'** suggests the very opposite of stepping forward, of velocity or progress. Rather it suggests stagnation and even degeneration. The wicked are headed for death, and the nearer they come to it, the more meaningless, the more empty, their life is. Their sorrows will only increase.

6. Despair

Despair, the very opposite of expectancy and hope, is symbolized by darkness. Gloominess, despondency and sadness are dark emotions. There is no hope for the wicked. God says to the wicked:

> Give glory to the LORD your God
>   before he brings the darkness,
> before your feet stumble
>   on the darkening hills.
> You hope for light,

> but he will turn it to thick darkness
> and change it to deep gloom
>
> > (Jer. 13:16).

7. *Death*

Degeneration leads eventually to the darkness and gloom of death. John the Baptist's father Zechariah refers to 'those living in darkness and in the shadow of death' (Luke 1:79).

8. *Damnation*

Jesus spoke of hell as a place 'outside', a place of 'darkness, where there will be weeping and gnashing of teeth' (Matt. 22:13). Peter and Jude say of false teachers that 'Blackest darkness is reserved for them' (2 Peter 2:17; Jude 13). The broad road leads to destruction.

Have you seen the light? Or are you still in the darkness of sin? Have you come 'out of darkness into his wonderful light'? (1 Peter 2:9). Have you been 'rescued … from the dominion of darkness and brought … into the kingdom of the Son he loves'? (Col. 1:13). We need the daystar to dawn in our hearts and to escape the darkness of hell. Life will remain utterly confusing otherwise. The Sun of Righteousness has risen with healing in his wings. Look to him and be healed. In the words of Isaiah we say to believers:

> Arise, shine, for your light has come,
> > and the glory of the LORD rises upon you.
> See, darkness covers the earth
> > and thick darkness is over the peoples,
> but the LORD rises upon you
> > and his glory appears over you
>
> > (Isa. 60:1-2).

Time for a check-up (4:20-27)

When did you last have a medical check-up? Some of us have not had one for years. My last proper one was just before I commenced a teacher-training course. That was many moons ago. I do try to keep my eye on things, however, of course.

For an older generation, in Britain at least, the word 'medical' immediately brings to mind the phrase 'army medical'. Armies are keen to have a fit fighting force as, even today, it is the best way of ensuring that units are able to move into position quickly. Traditionally, marching has been the method for achieving this. In Proverbs 4:20-27 we have direct references to ears, mouth, eyes and feet. Careful meditation on what the verses say can be a means of helping us to carry out a spiritual check-up on ourselves so that we may know whether we are fit to march in the army of Christ. Even if we seldom have medical check-ups on our bodies, we certainly ought to make it our practice to give our souls a regular check-up.

1. Your ears

'My son, pay attention to what I say; listen closely to my words' (4:20). 'Bend your ear to listen,' says the father to his son. Apparent hearing defects can sometimes be put down to a failure to concentrate, or to put ourselves in the best position to hear. Spiritually speaking, we are all deaf by nature, but if Christ unstops our ears we shall be able to hear the message of life. If we have ears to hear, we must listen to the message. We must listen closely to the words of God. Are we listening properly? Are our ears working? Are they attentive? Are they open to hear the command to march?

2. Your mind

Are you a fan of television quiz shows? Some of them can be
quite excruciating, but they are always trying to come up with
something new and some can be interesting. In Britain from
1976 to 1995 a programme called *The Krypton Factor* ran on
ITV. Besides the usual general knowledge questions, contestants were required to complete an army assault course and to
use their minds to answer observational questions and solve
IQ puzzles. They wanted to see if contestants could think as
well as remembering facts. I believe 'Think!' is still the motto
of the multi-national computer company IBM. Thinking is so
important. Hence the emphasis on words in verse 20 and the
command: **'Do not let them out of your sight, keep them
within your heart'** (4:21: cf. 4:1,4-5,10,13).

I remember some years ago buying a video recorder. The
price had been reduced because the instruction book was missing. How relieved I was when I found some written instructions under the lid! Without those, how difficult it might have
been to know how to use it! The Bible is something of a user's
manual for life. Bearing in mind the journey metaphor, we can
think of it too as a map guiding us to heaven. If we neglect to
inform our minds with it, they will suffer. It requires our constant, deep and close attention. We cannot be healthy, or stay
alive, otherwise. In particular, we must endeavour to remember what it says. Of course, reading or memorizing a book will
not make you healthy in and of itself either in the physical or
the spiritual sense. Armchair sports fans are not famous for
their healthy physique, and mere Bible knowledge never saved
anyone.

Today we can read all about far-away places without ever
visiting them. However, reading about them can prepare us
for going to those places, just as the Bible will give us all we
need to know for life and godliness. Peter underlines the

reliability of Scripture when he says, 'We did not follow cleverly invented stories when we told you about the power and coming of our Lord Jesus Christ, but we were eye-witnesses of his majesty... And we have the word of the prophets made more certain, and you will do well to pay attention to it, as to a light shining in a dark place, until the day dawns and the morning star rises in your hearts... For prophecy never had its origin in the will of man, but men spoke from God as they were carried along by the Holy Spirit' (2 Peter 1:16-21).

Is your mind a biblically informed one? If so, it will affect everything. Verse 22 declares that these words **'are life to those who find them and health to a man's whole body'**, an oft-repeated promise in various forms.

3. Your heart

What will familiarity with the message of the Bible do? More than anything else, it will help you obey the command: **'Above all else, guard your heart, for it is the wellspring of life'** (4:23). John H. Sket points out that this verse parallels verse 13, where we read, 'Hold on to instruction, do not let it go; guard it well, for it is your life.' In any medical examination, the heart is important because no one can be healthy if his heart is in a poor condition. The heart is a vital organ. The same is true spiritually. Jesus explains that it is 'out of the heart' that troubles come — 'evil thoughts, murder, adultery, sexual immorality, theft, false testimony, slander' (Matt. 15:19). If the heart is wrong, nothing else can be right. It is absolute madness to neglect your heart.

Puritan John Flavel penned a little work on this verse that begins: 'The heart of man is the worst part before it is regenerated, and the best afterward; it is the seat of principles and the foundation of actions. The eye of God is, and the eye of man ought to be, principally fixed on it.' He goes on to say that the text contains an exhortation and a reason or motive. The duty laid down is to guard one's soul. To keep or **'guard'** it is to diligently and constantly use 'all holy means to preserve the soul from sin and maintain its sweet and free communion with God'. The duty is ours, but the power is God's. Flavel takes **'above all else'** (AV, 'with all diligence') as a call to diligence. The Hebrew simply repeats the call to 'guard' one's heart. The reason for the duty is that the heart is like the mainspring in a watch, or the money supply for a business. Everything else hangs on it. And so Flavel concludes that the keeping and right managing of the heart, in every condition, is one great business of a Christian's life.

Our hearts are like musical instruments that easily go out of tune and often need retuning. We need to examine our hearts, to humble ourselves over their frequent disorder, to pray for purification, to make fresh resolves, to promote a holy jealousy for them within, and always remember that the Lord is watching. This is hard work, constant work and important work, but God's glory, sincere faith, a beautiful life, real peace, improved graces and stability in the face of temptation depend on it.

In a sermon on the same text called 'The Great Reservoir', Spurgeon imagines the foolishness of a water company changing pipes and taps when all the while the real problem is that the reservoir itself is poisoned. Yet, just as in the physical realm, many neglect their hearts. Jesus asks, 'What good will it be for a man if he gains the whole world, yet forfeits his soul? Or what can a man give in exchange for his soul?' (Matt. 16:26). Are you ignoring your heart or soul? Christ sees into it and knows all about it. Is it a heart of flesh, or a heart of stone? Is there faith in your heart? Jesus warns, 'Not everyone who says to me, "Lord, Lord," will enter the kingdom of heaven, but only he who does the will of my Father who is in heaven' (Matt. 7:21). It is those who do God's will who are saved. If our hearts are right, we can do God's will. 'Every good tree bears good fruit, but a bad tree bears bad fruit. A good tree cannot bear bad fruit, and a bad tree cannot bear good fruit' (Matt. 7:17-18).

4. Your mouth

A real change of heart will affect the whole of one's life. This is often seen first in the way a person speaks. What you say is a vital matter. Jesus takes up the tree-and-fruit image of the Sermon on the Mount when confronting the Pharisees: 'Make a tree good and its fruit will be good, or make a tree bad and its fruit will be bad, for a tree is recognized by its fruit.' He goes on: 'You brood of vipers, how can you who are evil say anything good? For out of the overflow of the heart the mouth speaks. The good man brings good things out of the good stored up in him, and the evil man brings evil things out of the evil stored up in him. But I tell you that men will have to give account on the day of judgement for every careless word they have spoken. For by your words you will be acquitted, and by your words you will be condemned' (Matt.12:33-37).

'Put away perversity from your mouth; keep corrupt talk far from your lips' (4:24). We seem to have forgotten the journey metaphor here, but the word **'perversity'** is actually the one for 'crooked paths'. Our mouths can lead us into places where we ought not to go. Do you grumble and moan, gossip or slander, speak hatefully or curse others, lie and misrepresent facts? How unhealthy! You are walking in darkness when you go down such paths.

5. Your eyes

Next, think about what you look at (we have already had a hint about this in verse 21). Looking straight ahead is the obvious thing to do on a straight and narrow road. Your eyes should be fixed on Christ. He says, 'The eye is the lamp of the body. If your eyes are good, your whole body will be full of light. But if your eyes are bad, your whole body will be full of darkness. If then the light within you is darkness, how great is that darkness!' (Matt. 6:22-23). Verse 25 is similar: **'Let your eyes look straight ahead, fix your gaze directly before you.'** It is practically impossible to walk straight with your eyes closed. Those who do not look to Christ are in the dark.

Certain sights are bad for the eyes and will do damage to your eyesight. Once again, this is true spiritually as well as physically. David said, 'I will set before my eyes no vile thing' (Ps. 101:3); 'Turn my eyes away from worthless things' (Ps.119:37); and Job revealed that 'I made a covenant with my eyes not to look lustfully at a girl' (Job 31:1). The godly man 'shuts his eyes against contemplating evil' (Isa. 33:15) and takes care not to give in to 'the lust of his eyes' (1 John 2:16). He knows when to switch off the television, close the book, keep his eyes lowered, or turn the other way.

6. Your feet

Finally, we come to the feet. Here we are concerned chiefly with *where* you go. We all ought to follow in Christ's foot-steps: 'Christ suffered for you, leaving you an example, that you should follow in his steps' (1 Peter 2:21); 'Whoever claims to live in him must walk as Jesus did' (1 John 2:6). That does not mean a trip to Israel, but obedience to the injunctions in verses 26 and 27:

> **Make level paths for your feet**
> **and take only ways that are firm.**
> **Do not swerve to the right or the left;**
> **keep your foot from evil.**

The last part of this exhortation is similar to Proverbs 1:15. The command to 'make level paths for your feet' is quoted in the New Testament (Heb. 12:13). Are you living a life of obedience? If not, you are still stumbling around in the dark and you will fall before much longer: 'Be very careful, then, how you live [literally, "walk"] — not as unwise but as wise, making the most of every opportunity, because the days are evil. Therefore do not be foolish, but understand what the Lord's will is' (Eph. 5:15-17).

If you are stumbling about in the dark, if you are in bad health spiritually and making no progress towards heaven, there is only one answer. Come out of the dark, off the broad road and onto the narrow road where the life-giving light found only in Jesus Christ shines. The trouble is that, as we have seen, coming into the light when you have been in the dark for some time can be difficult. We shrink from it: 'This is the verdict: Light has come into the world, but men loved darkness instead of light because their deeds were evil. Everyone who does evil hates the light, and will not come into the light for fear that his deeds will be exposed. But whoever lives by the truth comes into the light, so that it may be seen plainly that what he has done has been done through God' (John 3:19-21).

Once we have come into the light, however, we can see clearly to pursue the heavenward journey so well signposted for us here by one who has already made the journey himself. You should heed the words of Quaker Bernard Barton and 'Walk in the light'. Yours will then be 'a path, though thorny, bright; for God by grace, shall dwell in thee and God himself is light'. Join with medieval Italian writer Bianco da Siena in saying to God:

Let thy glorious light
Shine ever on my sight,

And clothe me round,
The while my path illuming.

Pray with Bishop William Walsham How:

Light of light! Shine o'er us, on our pilgrim way;
Go thou still before us to the endless day.

11.
A seventh fatherly talk:
How to make a right moral choice

Please read Proverbs 5:1-23

At a certain age children love to play at guessing which hand holds the sweet. The prospect of getting the choice right is appealing. Some adults subscribe to consumer magazines such as *Which?* They are eager to find out the salient facts which will help them to make an informed choice concerning their new washing machine, motor car or insurance policy. Life is full of choices. Some are relatively unimportant: 'Which flavour ice cream shall I choose? What colour shall we paint the back bedroom?' Many are very important: 'What job shall I apply for? Shall I marry this man? What shall I believe about life after death?' We are making choices all the time — to carry on reading or not; to do something about what this chapter says or not. Decisions, decisions, decisions — all the time. Napoleon once observed that there is nothing more difficult than making a decision. To be able to decide, therefore, is a most precious thing.

Making a decision is especially difficult when we are faced by a momentous choice that we know may affect the rest of our lives. There are many big issues that have all sorts of implications, depending on which side we come down. Do I believe in God? Do I accept that he created this world in six days? Does life have any meaning? Is the Bible God's Word? What do I believe about Jesus of Nazareth? The way we answer such questions, and others like them, will have major ramifications. How to decide about such things is very important. We must make informed decisions as far as we can. We should aim to be wise in our choices. We want to make sound judgements.

In this chapter we consider these issues. However, we are not simply concerned with *what* to choose but with *how* to choose. Proverbs 5 is the first in a series of warnings against pitfalls, especially using the figure of the adulterous woman. According to John H. Stek, whereas the chief purpose of chapters 2-4 was positive — to commend wisdom — that of chapters 5-7 is negative — to warn against going astray.

Some people find a ready-packaged religion to their liking. Rather than doing the hard work of thinking things through, they prefer to have a ready-made, 'off-the-peg' belief system that will save them the effort of thinking things through for themselves. There are cults and religions that cater for that mentality. They are happy to 'nanny' you all the way through. 'Leave your brain by the door as you come in,' they announce, as it were, and proceed to tell you what to believe about every jot and tittle of your whole life. The Bible does not really encourage that sort of thing. Rather, each individual is responsible before God for his or her choices. God is sovereign and although, on one hand, he does determine all things, Christianity does not teach a robotic determinism in which we are simply required to drift through life without much thought. That is why the matter of how to choose, or how to make a decision, is so important. All around us people are making decisions, many of them bad ones. We want to avoid doing the same. If we follow the guidelines below, we shall avoid some of the more obvious pitfalls.

Take care and be discerning (5:1-6)

This almost goes without saying. Even some advertisers to-day are learning to pitch their appeal, so they say, to the more discerning customer. Four principles arise in this chapter regarding discernment.

1. Discernment is something that you learn

We are not born with it. Obviously we differ in make-up and upbringing and some people acquire it quicker than others, but discernment is learned. We all begin by supposing the sweet must be in the hand that dad offers first. We begin by assuming that the most popular, or the cheapest, or the best-presented product must be best for us. I remember as a boy learning a lesson from my mother about watching the greengrocer. I had come home with a bag of potatoes that had been weighed out for me and that included two or three small stones! In the days before 'sell-by dates' my mother, like many another, tended to squeeze the bread and fruit before purchasing it and would not always take what was at the front of the supermarket shelf. Discernment is learned.

Proverbs 5 begins, once more, with a father speaking to his son:

My son, pay attention to my wisdom,
listen well to my words of insight,
that you may maintain discretion
and your lips may preserve knowledge

(5:1-2).

We have been exhorted several times to listen to the father. If we do not **'pay attention'** and **'listen'**, any discretion we may have picked up will be lost. We have noted in an earlier chapter how jewellers learn to have an eye for whether a gem is genuine and how bank-tellers can spot counterfeit notes by feel alone. We refer once again to Hebrews 5:14, which speaks of those 'who by constant use have trained themselves to distinguish good from evil'. This is a mark of spiritual maturity.

2. Realize that there are deceivers about

From an early age we have to teach children to take care if strangers approach them offering sweets, or a ride in the car. As we grow up we realize more and more what deceivers there are about. The adulteress symbolizes the many who want to lead us down a crooked path. There are all sorts of shifty people around, liars and deceivers who will lead us into trouble. Jesus says, 'Watch out for false prophets. They come to you in sheep's clothing, but inwardly they are ferocious wolves' (Matt. 7:15).

3. Not all that glitters is gold

Do not judge a book by its cover. Things are never quite the way they seem. It is too easy to make a superficial judgement. We must avoid doing that. How sweet, how soothing a thing may seem but, like a gullible fish, we can soon be taken in hook, line and sinker. Here the father warns:

For the lips of an adulteress drip honey,
**   and her speech is smoother than oil;**
but in the end she is bitter as gall,
**   sharp as a double-edged sword**

(5:3-4).

Like the bee, she has honey in her mouth but a sting in her tail. Yes, she has glossy lips and knows the words to get your pulse racing, but where will it end? That pornographic image seems so alluring; the promise of wealth or fame seems so seductive. The beer commercials and the lies about drugs and life in the fast lane are the same. But such things cannot ultimately satisfy the real longings of our hearts. Others promise you intellectual and ethical freedom once you loose your moral and biblical shackles. These are only more lies intended to deceive the unwary.

4. Look at things in the long term

'He who laughs last laughs longest.' Children find this particularly difficult. Christmas and birthdays seem to take so long to come around. They want things now, not tomorrow. Some adults think like that too. They are constantly thinking only in the short term. They fail to realize that although sin may give pleasure for a season, **'In the end she is bitter as gall, sharp as a double-edged sword.'** Spurgeon compares that **'in the end'** to a lamp lit in the brothel by the wise man, or to Ithuriel's spear, in Milton, that by a touch could reveal Satan's presence. There is an application here both to this life and the one to come.

In this world

Adultery is likely to lead to divorce. It always means financial loss. Unhappiness to you and your children is highly likely. Angry husbands sometimes take revenge. This points us to where lust for this world leads. With several other things, the likely result is perhaps just as obvious — misusing drugs, overindulging in alcohol, tobacco, or sugar and fat for that matter. However, the devil has a thousand means of seducing the unwary into betraying wisdom and falling into spiritual adultery. A life of sin may sound attractive to some, but something that involves turning your back on Christ can never bring joy.

> **Her feet go down to death;**
> **her steps lead straight to the grave.**
> **She gives no thought to the way of life;**
> **her paths are crooked, but she knows it not**
> (5:5-6).

Here we are back to the travel metaphor used in chapters 2, 3 and 4. Forget the adulteress's mouth and look at her feet — see where they are headed! Staying with the figure, what disease will she pass on to you? What will her husband do to you? Even if you stay together, where will that lead? Rebellion against God leads to hell. Unbelief ends in damnation. She is not interested in Christ, in the all-important **'way of life'**. She does not realize it herself, but all her paths are crooked and lead to hell (cf. 6:23).

Take care to avoid what is evil (5:7-14,22-23)

This chapter is couched in terms of a warning against adultery. Solomon knew all about this particular pitfall. Although the picture used is that of illicit physical union, illicit spiritual union is in mind. For Solomon the two went hand in hand. His many pagan wives led him astray. Throughout the Bible the relationship between God and his people is put in terms of a covenant of marriage. The image of Christ the Bridegroom and his church the Bride is potent. Here it is the believer and his bride Wisdom. A right relationship with God is possible only by means of faith in Christ. Anything else is spiritual fornication or adultery. Christ is freely offered to all. All who do come to him are blessed with great joy, deliverance from trouble, safety, confidence, clear purpose and eternal life. To go any other way can only mean misery and suffering. Those who want to please God will avoid adultery of any sort.

'**Now then, my sons**' (again it is plural as in 4:1), the passage begins again, as the father gives commands that are positive and negative:

> **...listen to me;**
> **do not turn aside from what I say.**
> **Keep to a path far from her,**
> **do not go near the door of her house**
>
> (5:7-8).

The Lord Jesus makes clear that avoiding adultery is a matter of keeping the mind pure (see Matt. 5:27-30). To do this you may have to change many habits. It may mean changing your television-viewing patterns, the newspaper you read, your friends, your job. Whatever it may cost, you must not fall into adultery — physical, mental or spiritual. In this chapter, we see at least six reasons why you need to work at this and what will happen to you if you do not.

1. You will waste your life

In this life we all have only so much '**strength**', so many '**years**', so much '**wealth**'. It is important that you do not waste '**your best strength**', but use it for the Lord. Dancing and sport may have their place, but take care. Do not waste your wealth on prostitutes or pornography, drink or drugs, gambling or goods that you really do not need. Use what wealth you have for the kingdom. What are you toiling for? Are you living for yourself, or are you truly toiling in the kingdom? Do not serve '**one who is cruel**', or let '**strangers feast on your wealth**' (see 5:9-10). There are enough rich pimps, pornographers and pushers, bookmakers, bingo-hall owners and brewers. Why put more money in their pockets? They will have no sympathy if you go under.

2. You will die a sorry person

If you do go that way then, **'At the end of your life you will groan, when your flesh and body are spent'** (5:11). Possibly the writer has in mind sexually transmitted disease and its consequences. It is, however, more likely that he is referring in a general manner to the way a wasted life brings its own burden. The story is disputed, but it has been said that when on his deathbed American author and infidel Tom Paine deeply regretted publishing his *Age of Reason*. He was afraid to be alone and died in despair feeling he had been used as an agent of the devil. Whether he did have such feelings or not, it was too late to groan then. We must not make such a mistake.

3. You will be haunted by regrets

Verses 12-13 contain a similar warning:

> **You will say, 'How I hated discipline!**
> **How my heart spurned correction!**
> **I would not obey my teachers**
> **or listen to my instructors...'**

We all have regrets in this life. We sometimes have to say we have been fools and have missed real opportunities. It may be that some who are reading this very chapter could still go far astray because they refuse to listen. May such regrets not haunt you. The 'pleasures of sin' are only 'for a short time' (Heb. 11:25).

4. You will be filled with shame and sorrow

The speech goes on: **'I have come to the brink of utter ruin in the midst of the whole assembly'** (5:14). Here we think of the shame and disgrace that come on those who stray from the right path. What shame and sorrow, disgrace and disaster will be yours if you do not listen!

5. You will be trapped by your sins

Later, there are some summarizing statements where the travel metaphor is taken up again. We read, **'The evil deeds of a wicked man ensnare him; the cords of his sin hold him fast'** (5:22). Adulterers and other sinners do not intend to end up trapped, any more than a fish biting a hook intends to be caught. The devil lays his traps, however, and the wicked are ensnared.

6. You will die

Finally, we all need to be clear that if we reject discipline we shall die: **'He will die for lack of discipline, led astray by his own great folly'** (5:23). I remember meeting a man who had already lost two limbs because of his smoking habit. The doctors warned him that he would die if he did not stop; yet he went on smoking. There are many examples of such folly. Do not be led astray by such foolish ways.

In his 1981 song 'Heart of mine', Bob Dylan speaks to his tempted heart and says:

Heart of mine, be still,
You can play with fire but you'll get the bill.

Don't let her know, don't let her know that you love
   her.
Don't be a fool, don't be blind.

When such temptations come to us, we need to speak to our
hearts in similar terms.

Take care and choose what is good (5:15-21)

Finally, let us be positive. Verses 15-21 extol the superiority
of marriage over fornication and adultery. This is a call both to
faithfulness within the marriage bond and more generally in
our relationships with one another, and especially with Christ.
Why be faithful to one man or one woman, 'till death do us
part'? Why trust only in Christ? At least four reasons are given
here.

1. Here is someone you can depend on

The call is to **'Drink water from your own cistern, running
water from your own well'** (5:15). What makes us think that
water from another well will be sweeter? To have a faithful
spouse is far better than going to a prostitute or being with an
adulteress. The prostitute will not want you if you have no
money. The adulteress will not want you when you have lost
your fame or fortune or fine looks. What good are such people
when you are on your deathbed? This is true in the realm of
spiritual adultery too. A good wife or husband is dependable.
This points us to the dependability of wisdom and ultimately
of the Saviour himself. You can rely on the Saviour: 'Come to
me, all you who are weary and burdened,' he says, 'and I will
give you rest' (Matt. 11:28).

2. Here there is no waste

In the street where I grew up there is a section of pavement that is always wet, even on the driest days. It is a hilly area and there must be an underground stream there. Only a trickle is produced, but hundreds of gallons must have poured out since I was born. Occasionally people have slipped on the wet pavement but I know of no good that all that water has ever done. Physical and spiritual adultery is wasteful. The writer here asks, **'Should your springs overflow in the streets, your streams of water in the public squares?'** (5:16). In a part of the world where water is a precious and scarce resource, is there any sense in taking it and pouring it out in the streets? The implied answer is 'No'. It is only as we obey God and are true to wisdom, remaining devoted to Christ, that we are of any real use to God. Do not give your best to strangers. Do not waste your life in sin and false religion.

3. Here is something beautiful

To be in covenant with Christ is something beautiful. It is reflected in the marriage bond, an institution that even many who are not Christians appreciate. Indeed, recent years have seen some state governments get into a tangle in their policies knowing that stable marriages can only do the country good, but not wanting to offend an anti-Christian minority. Here the wish for the man is that his **'fountain'** — pointing to wisdom as the source of much good — **'be blessed'**. The man rejoices in the wife he married when young, God's wisdom. She is pictured as **'a loving doe, a graceful deer'** — a docile, trusting creature who looks to her husband for good. **'May her breasts satisfy you always, may you ever be captivated by her love'** (5:19). In a day when breasts are used to attract attention from every direction, this is a text perhaps for the married man to keep in mind. Its point, however, is to inculcate devotion to wisdom. **'Why be captivated, my son, by an adulteress? Why embrace the bosom of another man's wife?'** (5:20). That is the unanswerable question. Adultery of any sort is inexcusable. Why should a married man look elsewhere? To quote 'Heart of mine' again:

> Heart of mine, go back home,
> You got no reason to wander, you got no reason to roam.
> Don't let her see, don't let her see that you need her.
> Don't put yourself over the line,
> Heart of mine.

And if we have found Christ satisfying our needs then why try the broken cisterns again? In him alone are found love and life and lasting joy.

God is watching

The final consideration is in the summary which closes the chapter:

> **For a man's ways are in full view of the LORD,**
> **and he examines all his paths.**
> **The evil deeds of a wicked man ensnare him;**
> **the cords of his sin hold him fast.**
> **He will die for lack of discipline,**
> **led astray by his own great folly**
>
> (5:21-23).

Life is a journey. God is watching over us every step of the way. Hebrews 4:13 reminds us that 'Nothing in all creation is hidden from God's sight. Everything is uncovered and laid bare before the eyes of him to whom we must give account.'

Do not deviate from the path of righteousness. Do not let your eye settle on the adulteress for a moment. Be devoted to your wife. Be devoted to Jesus. Look ever to him; he will carry you through. He knows the sacrifices you make to remain true to him. Evil deeds ensnare; sin spoils; lack of discipline destroys and folly takes you far from the Father.

Heart of mine, so malicious and so full of guile,
Give you an inch and you'll take a mile.
Don't let yourself fall, don't let yourself stumble.
If you can't do the time, don't do the crime,
Heart of mine.

12.
An eighth fatherly talk begun: Three routes to hell and how to avoid them

Please read Proverbs 6:1-15

We begin by thinking about hell. There is certainly such a place.

How do I know? God speaks about it in the Bible.

Where does the Bible speak about it? In many places, not just one. Jesus spoke of it several times.

What is it like? It was made for the devil and the other fallen angels. It is described as a place of outer darkness and unquenchable fire. It is a place of suffering and torment, of agony and anguish. The misery there goes on for ever and ever.

Who will be there through eternity? Not only the devil and his demons, but all who follow them — all who refuse to put their trust in Jesus Christ.

Many choose to deny such truths, or seek to temper them, or simply ignore them. Some even mock. However, hell is a real place and we all need to take great care that we do not end up there. Watch out! It is a place to which many are headed. Take heed of such a warning. It is a danger we all face.

There are many ways to end up in hell. Jesus speaks about the broad road that leads to destruction. Some go by way of atheism and agnosticism; others are very religious. The latter may follow one of the established religions, or a cult, or some other heretical group. They may come up with their own religion. There are many roads to hell.

In Proverbs 6:1-19 we take a break from the theme of adultery. We shall look at 6:16-19 in the next chapter. Here we consider 6:1-15. These verses begin by describing a fearful condition and then explain how to escape. They do not mention hell directly, but they do talk of being trapped, of poverty and of disaster and destruction. Hell looms in just the same way — closing on its victims like a trap; it is the worst sort of poverty and the ultimate disaster. Here three routes to hell are described and how to escape them. Let us consider the routes and how to avoid going down them.

The route of unhelpful alliances (6:1-5)

Thales of Miletus was, traditionally, the last of the seven sages of Greece and his aphorism was: 'He who hates suretyship is sure.' An apparently similar thought is found in Proverbs: 'He who puts up security for another will surely suffer, but whoever refuses to strike hands in pledge is safe' (11:15; cf. 17:18; 22:26). Here in verses 1-5, on much the same lines, the father is again warning his son:

> **My son, if you have put up security for your neighbour,**
> **if you have struck hands in pledge for another,**
> **if you have been trapped by what you said,**
> **ensnared by the words of your mouth...**
>
> (6:1-2).

Bearing in mind the Bible's advocacy of kindness and compassion, it would seem most likely that, as with the adulteress, we should take this as a picture warning us of ways in which we are likely to lose out spiritually. The scene envisaged would appear to involve the son, his neighbour and the man who lends the neighbour money. The neighbour has nothing to offer as security for the loan and so he has persuaded the son to act as surety, or co-signer, to put up security on his behalf.

On a moral level such a warning has something to teach us about the whole area of personal commitments, covenants and contracts, pledges, promises, vows and alliances. You have shaken hands on the deal. Afterwards you discover your partner has been declared bankrupt four times. The CD club looked attractive when you saw the advertisement, but now they want to know why you have only bought one CD in twelve months instead of six. Signing on for twelve years in the navy seemed like a good idea the day you turned eighteen, but now you have your doubts — and so does your wife. However wise we endeavour to be, we can all too easily and from the best of motives make foolish commitments. I write as one who is often approached by people in need. As careful as I am, I still managed to give a significant sum to some men who purported to be stranded Italian businessmen, accepting what I thought were three leather jackets as collateral. I was also conned into parting with £70 to help a man claiming to be a runaway monk. If these verses had been running through my head, I might have acted differently. Think twice before lending money, signing a contract or undertaking to do something.

But there is a more spiritual application. Jesus says, 'Suppose one of you wants to build a tower. Will he not first sit down and estimate the cost to see if he has enough money to complete it? For if he lays the foundation and is not able to finish it, everyone who sees it will ridicule him, saying, "This fellow began to build and was not able to finish." Or suppose a king is about to go to war against another king. Will he not first sit down and consider whether he is able with ten thousand men to oppose the one coming against him with twenty thousand? If he is not able, he will send a delegation while the other is still a long way off and will ask for terms of peace' (Luke 14:28-32). He is speaking about putting faith in him. It raises the question of who it is you are making alliances with. Many are allied to false religions, to evil companions and to the devil himself.

Now the question arises: 'But what if I find I am in such an alliance?' Then you are trapped. You are in a situation that is, humanly speaking, irrecoverable. This is the position of many, many people. They are committed to the road to hell. They are on it and it seems impossible that they should ever be delivered. You hear people expressing it in terms such as these: 'I was born a Roman Catholic'; 'I've always gone to that church'; 'This is my philosophy'; 'This is my way of life'; 'I'm too old to change now.' But there is a way out:

> **... do this, my son** [says the father]**, to free yourself,**
>   **since you have fallen into your neighbour's hands:**
> **Go and humble yourself;**
>   **press your plea with your neighbour!**
>
> (6:3).

You are trapped. What began as a handshake, as you **'struck hands in pledge'** (6:1) becomes falling **'into your neighbour's hands'** (6:3) and will end up as being in **'the hand of the hunter'** (6:5). All you can do is **'humble yourself'** (literally, 'trample on yourself') and beg for mercy. Remember Jesus' words: 'Settle matters quickly with your adversary who is taking you to court. Do it while you are still with him on the way, or he may hand you over to the judge, and the judge may hand you over to the officer, and you may be thrown into prison. I tell you the truth, you will not get out until you have paid the last penny' (Matt. 5:25-26).

Plead now; otherwise you will end up in hell. You may say, 'But if I go to the priest, or some other religious leader, or to my friends or family or whoever, they will not let me go.' Then go higher. Go to the top. It is said of one American president that he had a sign on his desk saying, 'The buck stops here.' But the buck stops higher than that. Go to God himself. Humble yourself before God and say, 'I'm trapped in my ways, trapped in my commitments … but let me go, you alone can set me free.'

'Allow no sleep to your eyes, no slumber to your eyelids' (6:4). We must not rest until it is sorted out. Keep going to God until there is a release.

My mother's father always kept pigeons in the backyard. Sometimes he would have trouble persuading a new bird into the pigeon loft he had constructed and so he made a little trapdoor for getting them in. Various snares and traps are used to catch birds and other animals for different reasons. Some can be very dangerous. There have even been mantraps, intended to give would-be poachers a cruel surprise. If you are in your sins, hell is like a terrible mantrap about to close its jaws on you. You must **free yourself, like a gazelle from the hand of the hunter, like a bird from the snare of the fowler'** (6:5). Do whatever you need to in order to get free: humble yourself; plead. Remember the first part of Jesus' parable in Matthew 18:23-35, which speaks of 'a king who wanted to settle accounts with his servants'. A man owing what in today's terms would be millions of pounds is brought to him and, as he is unable to pay, the king orders that he and his family should be sold into slavery to pay off the debt. Then we read that 'The servant fell on his knees before him. "Be patient with me," he begged, "and I will pay back everything."' We also read that 'The servant's master took pity on him, cancelled the debt and let him go.' That is the prospect for us if we will only go to God and plead the name of Christ. Indeed, there is no other way out.

The route of laziness (6:6-11)

In verse 4 we are urged: 'Allow no sleep to your eyes, no slumber to your eyelids,' and in verses 6-8 the sluggard is exhorted to emulate the ant and start working now. Here is a favourite theme in the book. It comes out in several proverbs (e.g., 10:4; 13:4).

There are apparently various species of ant and most of them are characterized by the wise habit of storing up **'provisions in summer'** in preparation for the winter months when food will be scarce, even though 'It **has no commander, no overseer or ruler'**. There is irony in the very choice of comparison here as the ant is so tiny compared with man. Further, even without leadership it recognizes the need to prepare for days ahead.

The application is in verse 9, where the son is depicted as having become a sluggard: **'How long will you lie there, you sluggard? When will you get up from your sleep?'** Judgement Day is fast approaching; why are you unwilling to prepare? It is often said that the road to hell is paved with good intentions. Good intentions are not enough to save anyone. Too often sheer laziness keeps us from doing what we ought to do. It can lead to terrible accidents. Jobs are left half finished, doors are left open, or items are not properly secured, and the consequence is sometimes disastrous. Spiritual laziness can have even greater consequences. That is why Jesus urges us, as we have said before, to 'Make every effort to enter through the narrow door' that leads to eternal life 'because many, I tell you, will try to enter and will not be able to'

(Luke 13:24). Heaven is not won by effort; however, without effort — striving in prayer, studying the Word, etc. — there will be no heaven.

This lesson is one that applies to many aspects of this life. The child who spends all his pocket money on sweets will never save up for the special thing he wants; the slothful farmer will have no harvest for market; the indolent student will fail his examinations; the lazy athlete will not win the gold medal. What is true in these areas is true also in the spiritual realm.

The warning continues:

A little sleep, a little slumber,
**   a little folding of the hands to rest —**
and poverty will come on you like a bandit
**   and scarcity like an armed man**

                                                    (6:10-11).

Not all people, but many people are poor because they are lazy, or those on whom they depend are lazy. Spiritual poverty is also often due to spiritual laziness. Some of us need a loud wake-up call to spiritual realities. We need to learn to make the most of every opportunity in these evil days (see Eph. 5:14-16). Those who profess faith in Christ must not be complacent but see that 'The hour has come for you to wake up from your slumber, because our salvation is nearer now than when we first believed. The night is nearly over; the day is almost here. So let us put aside the deeds of darkness and put on the armour of light. Let us behave decently, as in the daytime, not in orgies and drunkenness, not in sexual immorality and debauchery, not in dissension and jealousy. Rather, clothe yourselves with the Lord Jesus Christ, and do not think about how to gratify the desires of the sinful nature' (Rom.13:11-14).

Commentator David Hubbard argues that hard work ought to be routine for those who profess to serve a carpenter-Christ, admire a tentmaker-apostle and 'who call ourselves children of a Father who is still working (John 5:17)'.

C. H. Spurgeon used to say that he did not want 'drones' in the church he pastored. He wanted every member to be a worker. The devil finds work for idle hands to do and we need to take steps to avoid laziness. Early rising and careful planning are old-fashioned virtues that we must keep alive. The nineteenth-century American preacher J. W. Alexander wrote somewhere of how as a young man he made it a practice never not to do a thing simply because it was too much trouble. If he wanted to play his flute but it was up in the attic, he would make a point of going to get it. Such practices will do us a great deal of good. When we are lazy, we are robbing ourselves.

Hell is the worst kind of poverty and we must avoid that place at all costs. Do not get waylaid by hell or mugged by Hades. Spurgeon once said that 'The most likely man to go to hell is the man who has nothing to do on earth. Idle people tempt the devil to tempt them.' His contemporary, the American evangelist D. L. Moody, often remarked that though he often saw drunks and prostitutes converted, he rarely saw a lazy person profess faith. We pity tramps, beggars and drunkards, but we shall end up in the gutter of hell if we do not take care and wake up ourselves.

The route of corruption (6:12-15)

How is a person saved from hell? Only by faith in the atoning work of Christ. Salvation is by faith, not good deeds. However, we must turn from sin, from anything and everything displeasing to God. There is no place in heaven for scoundrels and villains. Remember Paul's words: 'Do you not know that the wicked will not inherit the kingdom of God? Do not be deceived: Neither the sexually immoral nor idolaters nor adulterers nor male prostitutes nor homosexual offenders nor thieves nor the greedy nor drunkards nor slanderers nor swindlers will inherit the kingdom of God' (1 Cor. 6:9-10).

To indulge any sin is to take a step further on the road to hell. In verses 12-15 a man is described who is, in many ways, the very opposite of the sluggard. He is very active — but only in the cause of sin. His 'body language' gives him away. Every part is given over to deceit and depravity: he **'goes about with a corrupt mouth'**; he **'winks'** maliciously **'with his eye'** and uses **'his feet'** and **'his fingers'** to signal and motion for **'evil'**. He has **'deceit in his heart'** and so **'plots evil'**. **'He always stirs up dissension.'** The latter word is found only in Proverbs. This man constantly stirs it up.

How do you use your mouth? Do you lie and swear and gossip? What about the rest of your body? How is it used? Is it in a way that is glorifying to God? What about your heart? What is going on there? What are you scheming and plotting?

The Lord knows all about such a person. He is **'a scoundrel and villain'**, worthless and wicked. **'Therefore disaster will overtake him in an instant; he will suddenly be destroyed — without remedy.'** He schemes against man and God, but God will bring judgement on him. He cannot survive. Such a person does not know how soon things will change for him. It can happen 'in an instant … suddenly'.

These verses also warn us against the flamboyant and self-confident hucksters to be found in every generation and in all walks of life, including the religious. These wheeler-dealers use various dishonest means to promote harm and cause division. They are eventually found out and brought to book, but meanwhile the uninitiated are liable to be taken advantage of, not recognizing the various subtle moves of such people for what they are. We need to be as wise as snakes. We can so easily be corrupted.

Conclusion

Here are three routes that lead to hell. Each alone or all three together can cut you off from God for ever. Be wise and turn from such paths now, while there is still time to repent.

In 1877 Fanny Crosby's hymn 'Too late, too late' was published. She wrote:

His mercy lengthens out thy days,
His love to thee is great;
Oh, do not tempt that love too far,
Or it may be too late.

Further back, in 1863, in similar vein, 'Jesus of Nazareth passeth by' appeared. The work of American schoolteacher Etta Campbell, it closes with a solemn warning:

Ho! all ye heavy laden, come!
Here's pardon, comfort, rest and home:
Ye wand'rers from a Father's face,
Return, accept his proffered grace;
Ye tempted ones, there's refuge nigh:
Jesus of Nazareth passeth by.

But if you still his call refuse,
And all his wondrous love abuse,
Soon will he sadly from you turn,
Your bitter prayer for pardon spurn,
'Too late! Too late!' will be the cry —
Jesus of Nazareth has passed by.

13.
An eighth fatherly talk concluded: Seven things God hates

Please read Proverbs 6:16-19

Our subject is sin. That comes as no surprise, to be sure. This is a commentary on a book of the Bible and so you probably expected to read something about sin. And it may be you are not too bothered about that. In fact, maybe you could read page after page about sin and not find it too difficult. You could read that all people are sinners and not be too put out. You could even read that sinners go to hell and perhaps that would not unduly worry you.

It is a little like jokes about people of different nationalities. You may not be a fan of such humour but probably you do not mind it too much. If, for example, you are English and I remind you of the two Englishmen on the proverbial desert island who never speak a word to each other simply because there is no one to introduce them, perhaps you just smile. But what if you found your own name here and I included a joke that made fun of you personally? 'Have you heard the one about John Smith, or Joe Bloggs, or whoever?' That would be different. In a similar way, to read about sinners in general is not too much of a problem. However, to read that you yourself are a sinner is another matter entirely.

I cannot know into whose hands this book may fall. I probably do not know you personally. I do not know what your particular sins are. However, here in Proverbs 6 we find a list of sins. It is by no means exhaustive. The Bible tells us that men invent ways of doing evil. This list merely gives us some examples of sin. It is one of many such lists of vices and virtues found in the Bible (e.g., Ps. 15; Gal. 5:19-23). Such lists remind us that sin is not something vague, nebulous or indistinct. It is something that is concrete, real. You may not be guilty of all seven sins listed in these verses. The purpose of the list, however, is to convict or convince us that we are sinners. It is easy to suppose that we are not sinners, and so to think we are not in any great trouble. We convince ourselves that we are not serious sinners and so we feel that, with a little effort, all will be well. Or we may be tempted to say, defensively, 'I'm a sinner   so what?'

Making lists of things has become very popular in recent years. All sorts of strange, and sometimes interesting, lists have been composed. Before we look at the list here in a little detail, I want to say four things about it:

1. It is not my list. I did not make it up. It is from the Bible.

2. It is a list of hates, not of a great man, nor even of a holy man, but of God himself.

3. These are sins that God does not simply dislike, or have a mild aversion to. These are things that he hates. He detests and abhors them.

4. When we speak about 'God' we are not talking of some vague idea of God, but the true God who created this world, the God revealed in the Bible.

'There are six things the Lord hates, seven that are detestable to him' (6:16). The quoting of a number plus one is a typical way of presenting material found in many ancient sources, as well as in the Bible. In Proverbs 30 there are four instances of a number plus one being given

(30:15-16,18-19,21-23,29-30) and in the opening chapters of Amos a similar construction is used (Amos 1:3,6,9,11,13; 2:1,4,6).

The first five things mentioned here are related to a specific part of the body. That takes us back to our little check-up at the end of Proverbs 4 (see chapter 10) and the passage we have just been looking at in verses 12-15, with its references to 'a corrupt mouth', a winking 'eye', 'feet' that give signals, and to a person motioning with his 'fingers' and having deceit in his 'heart'. We are talking about something tangible when we talk about sin.

Seven things the Lord hates

1. Pride (6:17)

First on the list are **'haughty eyes'**. Looking down on others is the sin here. Pride, arrogance, smugness, presumption, haughtiness, conceit, self-confidence — those are the kinds of attitude that we are talking about here. Are you conceited? Are you a snob? Are you boastful and proud? It comes out in different ways in different people. If we are haughty about our looks, that is vanity; if we are wrongly proud of our people and culture, that is perverted nationalism or racism; if we are chauvinistic about our gender, that is sexism. We can have a wrong attitude about our family, our achievements, our religion — almost anything to do with ourselves or those connected with us. Each is a form of pride and God opposes them all. Pride is what brought Satan down. How can I know if I am proud? Easy! If you think you have no problems in that area, you most surely do! Spurgeon compares pride to the flies of Egypt — all Pharaoh's soldiers could not keep them out. Only a strong wind of the Holy Spirit will do it. Pray for that.

God hates pride.

2. *Lying* (6:17)

Next comes **'a lying tongue'**. Do you tell lies? Do you say or think what is not true? Do you bend the truth? Are you sometimes economical with it? What about exaggeration? (No never!) Do you use overstatement or understatement to distort the truth? Satan was not only proud, but Jesus calls him 'the father of lies'. Do not be like him, but be like the Lord himself, who is the truth, and live according to the truth.

The American founding father Thomas Jefferson spoke of honesty as 'the first chapter in the book of wisdom'. That may not seem quite to square with what we have in Proverbs, but to tell a lie is to fear man and disregard God.

God hates lying.

3. *Hatred* (6:17)

Thirdly, God hates **'hands that shed innocent blood'**. 'Ah, not me!' you say, relieved at last, 'I'm not guilty of murder.' But, surely, it is not only murder that sheds innocent blood. What about unbiblical abortion and euthanasia? And are not the hatred and neglect that lead to such sins and others like them also of the same species? Hatred is a sin. Jesus makes it clear in the Sermon on the Mount that even if we become angry with someone, we are in danger of breaking the command not to murder. Love is the Christian's watchword. Compassion, care, kindness and mercy should mark us, not hatred. The thing we should hate is hatred itself.

God hates hatred.

4. *Evil scheming* (6:18)

Next is **'a heart that devises wicked schemes'**. What lurks in your heart? Much of it may never come to pass, but God knows what is going on in there — plans to hurt and to harm, to steal and to take, to cheat and to lie, to be mean or spiteful. The Lord knows all about your plans. Rather than thinking on such evil schemes we should plan what is good and meditate on what is right. As Sinclair Ferguson once remarked, 'How we think is one of the great determining factors in how we live.'

God hates evil scheming.

5. Evil inclinations (6:18)

Then come **'feet that are quick to rush into evil'**. What sort of a person are you? Are you likely to do what is wrong? Are you easily led into sin? Do you say of some sins, 'I just can't help myself; I can't stop doing it.' Do some sins draw you like a magnet? You may never initiate any evil, but do you join in with others once they have made the first move? Is their influence spoiling and corrupting you? Are you following others into sin? Are you quick to follow the bad lead of others? Do you sometimes excuse yourself by saying, 'But everyone does it'? Perhaps you say that about petty pilfering, tax evasion, fiddling expenses, or flirting with the opposite sex. As a boy I used to try that excuse on my parents: 'Everyone else is doing it.' It never worked. Who else had done a thing was, understandably, irrelevant to them. Are you like a moth drawn to a flame? Is your life being marred by a proclivity to sin? We must resist temptation, turn round and run from sin.

God hates evil proclivities.

6. False witness (6:19)

The penultimate horror is **'a false witness who pours out lies'**. God detests lying of all sorts, as we have already seen. He also hates the sins of gossip and slander and libelling others. When we blame the innocent, God is not pleased. To let the blame fall on the innocent is not only a sin against them, but also against God himself. We must tell the truth, the whole truth and nothing but the truth.

God hates the bearing of false witness.

7. *Divisiveness* (6:19)

Finally, God hates **'a man who stirs up dissension among brothers'**. We may think this is not so bad a sin, but God hates those who sow discord and cause strife, who create conflict or promote friction. They are inimical to the God of love and order. The argumentative and the divisive are wicked. Warmongers, turncoats and troublemakers who divide nations; adulterers who break up families; contentious people who split churches; gossips who destroy friendships — all these are anathema to God. Instead he wants us to be reconcilers, peacemakers, facilitators of harmony. Paul warns Titus, 'Avoid foolish controversies and genealogies and arguments and quarrels about the law, because these are unprofitable and useless. Warn a divisive person once, and then warn him a second time. After that, have nothing to do with him. You may be sure that such a man is warped and sinful; he is self-condemned' (Titus 3:9-11).

God hates divisiveness.

The nature of sin

These verses remind us too that sin is not just a matter of what we do, such as having 'hands that shed innocent blood'. It is also a matter of:

1. What we *say*, such as having 'a lying tongue', or being 'a false witness who pours out lies';

2. What we *think*, as in 'a heart that devises wicked schemes';

3. Our *attitudes*, as displayed in 'haughty eyes' or 'feet that are quick to rush into evil';

4. The *effect we have on others*, as when a man 'stirs up dissension among brothers'.

This affects the whole of the body ('eyes', 'tongue', 'hands', 'heart' and 'feet', as well as the inner man).

Such sins are not simply wrong but God *hates* them. If we are guilty of any or all of these sins, or any like them, then we need to see that God hates those sins.

He loves humility, truthfulness and honesty, unity and harmony. He wants us to spend our time loving our neighbours. He wants our heads to be full of thoughts of what good we might do. He wants us to be on the lookout for something good that we can do. Is that you? To the extent that it is not, God hates it. The covenant Lord loathes and abhors such thoughts and ways.

A message of hope

Even in these few verses, it becomes clear that we are sinners and that God hates our sins. We have no right to go to him on our own terms. We do not deserve heaven. We are cut off from happiness and blessing. This seems a rather hopeless and gloomy message but, in fact, it serves to prepare us for the glorious message that through Christ all our sins can be forgiven. He never did anything that God hated — he was the dearly loved Son with whom the Father was always pleased. He was never proud but always humble. He never lied but is the truth. Far from shedding innocent blood, he allowed his own innocent blood to be shed. He brought good news; he did not lay evil plans. He went about doing good. False witnesses spoke against him but he said nothing false against anyone; rather, he exposed the truth. He has broken down the dividing wall between peoples by destroying 'the barrier, the dividing wall of hostility'. He did it by 'abolishing in his flesh the law with its commandments and regulations', and so he has created 'in himself one new man out of the two, thus making peace' (see Eph. 2:14-16). He suffered and died to pay the penalty for all such sins as those we have been talking about in this chapter. God's hatred burned itself out in him, as it were, there on the hill called Golgotha. He did it so that by faith in him we may know all our sins forgiven and our lives transformed so that they at least begin to resemble the glory and goodness of Jesus Christ. Trust in Christ and then use your eyes, tongue, heart, feet and every part to his glory.

14.
A ninth fatherly talk:
How not to waste your life

Please read Proverbs 6:20-35

I began my primary education in the 1960s. At the time there was much emphasis in British schools on letting children work at their own pace. Some revision of thought has gone on among educators since then, partly because of children like Dean Webb and myself. I distinctly remember the moment when, to Miss Martin's horror, she discovered that, after a whole morning, Dean had managed to finish just two sums and I had completed only one 'clock' (the Herculean task of drawing hands on a clock face ink-stamped into my exercise book and then writing the time underneath). Other children had worked well but we, I recall, had somehow wasted the whole morning.

Time is precious and we ought to be horrified at wasting it at any age. Have you ever spent half an hour queuing for something only to discover that you were waiting in the wrong line? How frustrating when you are putting together self-assembly furniture and after all your efforts to screw part A to part B, you find that you should have fitted them together the other way round! How many hours have we wasted in front of the television, or a computer monitor playing games, or reading nonsense in the newspapers? How easy, as Bing Crosby sang so long ago, to be 'busy doing nothing, working the whole day through, trying to find lots of things not to do'! Are you 'busy going nowhere'? Hours wasted are hours that need to be repented of. Otherwise, we shall wander into the frightful situation where we find we have wasted, not hours or days or weeks or months, but a whole lifetime. It is a real possibility. We may regret lost time very much in this life, but how much worse may we feel in eternity?

We can look at Proverbs 6:20-35 in this light and see here an exhortation and a warning.

An exhortation (6:20-23)

What you need to avoid wasting your life

'Listen', comes the cry from father to the son yet again, 'pay attention'. What you need more than anything else is the Word of God. It is vital. It is indispensable. We can think of God's commands as being like a map, a compass, a torch and provisions for the journey of life, all rolled into one. Without some insight into what God teaches, your whole life will be wasted. Every day that goes by without paying at least some attention to what God says in his Word is a day that is wasted. Each year that goes by without a genuine attempt to get to grips with its teaching is another year wasted. The Bible itself will not save anyone. It is not a lucky charm or talisman, although some treat it in that way. Rather it is as the Word is let loose, as it is applied to life and lived out, that it makes its impact. This is because it is in the Word, in its **'commands'** and **'teaching'**, that we are corrected and disciplined and shown how to live.

What the Word says can be summarized very simply:

1. God created this world perfect, but it is now a fallen world of sin and trouble.

2. We are all born sinners and we will not and cannot come to God as we are.

3. Nevertheless, God has done something to remedy the situation. He has sent his Son Jesus Christ who has lived and died to save a people for himself.

4. By trusting in Jesus Christ and repenting from sin we can know forgiveness, holiness and heaven.

What to do to avoid wasting your life

It is quite clear. We must read, mark and learn the Scriptures. To fail to acknowledge such things is akin to disobeying **'your father's commands'** and forsaking **'your mother's teaching'** (the mother is mentioned here again as in 1:8). To **'keep'** your father's commands is to hold on to them and obey them. Not to **'forsake'** your mother's teaching is never to turn from it (see 3:3; 4:6).

Further, we are told, **'Bind them upon your heart for ever; fasten them around your neck'** (6:21). These truths must be dearer to us than life itself. The words remind us of 1:9, and especially of the exhortation in 3:3 to 'Bind them around your neck.'

The blessings guaranteed

If we do this then many blessings will follow. The picture of life as a journey is used yet again (see 2:8,9,12-15,18-20; 3:6,17,23-26; 4:11,14-15,18-19,26-27). The traveller walks, sleeps, wakes again and also uses a lamp and something to keep him on the right track. We learn that in the Scriptures we have the following items that we need for life's journey:

A guiding star

'**When you walk, they will guide you**' (6:22). God's commands and his teaching show us how to live, what he requires from us. They are a sure guide to heaven. As we go up and down in this life, we are led.

A guarding eye

'**When you sleep, they will watch over you**' (6:22). There are dangers all around in this world but, with God's Word, even as we sleep we shall be guarded — not by magic but by the Spirit, as we trust in his Word.

A guardian mentor

'**When you awake, they will speak to you**' (6:22). The Scriptures fill our minds with wisdom and with discernment. They speak to us. Our first thought each day should be of God and his Word.

A glowing light

'**For these commands are a lamp, this teaching is a light**' (6:23). Found here for the first of six times in Proverbs, '**a lamp**' is a favourite image for the Word: 'Your word is a lamp to my feet and a light for my path' (Ps. 119:105); 'The commands of the LORD are radiant, giving light to the eyes' (Ps. 19:8). In the New Testament Peter writes, 'And we have the word of the prophets made more certain, and you will do well to pay attention to it, as to a light shining in a dark place, until the day dawns and the morning star rises in your hearts' (2 Peter 1:19). Once we see our own sin and Christ's righteousness, we are delivered from the darkness of ignorance.

A gateway to life

'And the corrections of discipline are the way to life' (6:23).
As noted before, light and life are often linked in Scripture:
'For with you is the fountain of life; in your light we see light'
(Ps. 36:9). As the Word corrects our wrong notions and ideas,
so we come to faith in Christ and we find the one who spoke
of himself in these terms: 'I am the light of the world. Whoever follows me will never walk in darkness, but will have the
light of life' (John 8:12); 'I am the way and the truth and the
life. No one comes to the Father except through me' (John
14:6). Repeatedly this theme is hammered out in Proverbs (e.g.,
4:22; 5:6).

A warning (6:24-35)

The exhortation leads into a warning, from verse 24 onwards.
It reminds us of Proverbs 5:5-6, which warns that the feet of
the adulteress 'go down to death; her steps lead straight to the
grave', and that 'she gives no thought to the way of life'.

What you need to avoid wasting your life

What has been said above may sound simple, but in this world
such things are seldom simple. There are many out there who
are determined to deceive us and to cheat us. Therefore, we
need to take heed. Here, then, is another warning against the
adulteress and against adultery.

It is important to get into our minds the picture of God and
ourselves as being, at least potentially, in a marriage covenant
one with the other. When we read of an adulteress, therefore,
we should think of anyone or anything that would lure us from
God and from his Word. All adultery is wrong, whether it is
physical adultery or adultery of a more spiritual nature — to

break faith, to abandon covenant promises, to play fast and loose with the faith and loyalty of another is a disaster on any level.

The evil nature of the adulteress

Five different phrases are used to describe the adulteress. Each brings out one aspect of the wickedness of adultery.

1. The immoral woman (6:24)

Here we picture a woman whose life is not ordered by God's commands. She is immoral, unrestrained by the dictates of Scripture. She is corrupt and debauched. Such a person will lure you away from morality and from the Word itself.

2. The wayward wife (6:24)

The 'strange woman' (AV) has abandoned faithfulness to her husband despite her promises. She wants you to roam too and to go astray, to abandon your commitment to God.

3. The prostitute (6:26)

Not all adulteresses are prostitutes as such, it may be argued, but they often share the mercenary attitude of the prostitute. Regardless of any promises they have made to anyone else, they want something more and are willing to use those who are unprepared for their ways and wiles. Verse 26 is very graphic: **'For the prostitute reduces you to a loaf of bread.'** There are people who are not concerned about you for yourself. They see you as a meal ticket, a means to an end, and so they give you their favours, not from motives of love and commitment but out of greed. Beware!

4. The adulteress (6:26)

The second half of this verse speaks of a man's wife, **'the adulteress'** who **'preys upon your very life'**. She cheats on her covenant with her husband; she cheats on God's law and she entices you to do the same. Do not follow her.

5. Another man's wife (6:29)

This epithet emphasizes that this is a woman who makes promises that offer what is not hers to give. She cannot be yours, whatever she may say, for she is already promised to someone else. She is spoken for. You would not listen to someone who tried to sell you stolen goods, I trust, so why listen to an adulteress?

The attractions the adulteress offers

So what is the attraction? Why do so many fall for the lies of the adulteress?

1. The smooth tongue (6:24)

This refers to sweet-talking, soft-soaping, human rhetoric designed to butter you up. All sorts of devices are employed to draw in the unwary and seduce them. Beware of such sales patter.

2. Her beauty (6:25)

There is no need to deny the attraction of the adulteress. Her seductive looks and her undoubted allure are not in doubt, whether it is straightforward physical beauty and charm, or something less tangible, such as the ideals of supposed freedom or brotherhood.

3. Her eyes (6:25)

The adulteress may concentrate on making one feature particularly attractive. She may boast of wonderful insights and flutter her eyelids in an irresistible way. But she must be resisted. Stand firm!

Mike Oldfield's song 'Family man' evokes her well:

> She had a sulky smile,
> She took a standard pose as she presented herself.
> She had sultry eyes,
> She made it perfectly plain that she was his for a price.

What to do to avoid wasting your life

This is surely obvious: **'Do not lust in your heart after'** the adulteress, **'or let her captivate you with'** her wiles (6:25). Do not sleep with the enemy. Do not commit adultery. Do not go near such a person.

Further, do not be captivated by her eyes, or lust after her beauty. That is where the problem starts. Like a fish on a hook, once we are caught there is unlikely to be an escape.

Keep away from danger. Do not even go near. Only by holding on to the Word are you safe.

A popular song from the seventies puts it this way:

> Stay awake!
> Look out, if you're out on a moonlit night. Be careful of
>   the neighbourhood strays,
> Of a lady with long black hair trying to win you with her
>   feminine ways...
> You'd better get out of there fast.
> She's just a devil woman, with evil on her mind ... Beware the devil woman...

The curses pronounced

Those who do succumb to temptation and commit either physical or spiritual adultery face the following curses:

1. Indignity (6:26)

You are debased. You are reduced **'to a loaf of bread'**. All you are is one more conquest; another trick, one more fool hooked in.

2. The danger of eternal death (6:26)

> **... the adulteress preys upon your very life.**
> **Can a man scoop fire into his lap**
>   **without his clothes being burned?**
> **Can a man walk on hot coals**
>   **without his feet being scorched?**
>
>   (6:26-28).

To flirt with such danger is to play with fire. You will be badly burned — literally, even.

Of course, some may read this and think they can get away with adultery, just as some people think they can walk over hot coals without scorching their feet. There are certainly many reports of the latter happening. On closer investigation, however, we find that so-called fire-walkers merely walk briskly over wooden coals (poor heat conductors) that have been alight for some time. Many sceptics will tell you just how easy it is to perform this trick. The *Leidenfrost* effect and the role of endorphins may or may not be important, but those who believe it is all a question of mind over matter need to think again. In July 1998 there was a widely reported case where trainee sales staff from a large insurance company on a 'motivational' weekend course suffered burns after walking on hot coals. Two had to be taken to hospital. If you really do walk on hot coals your feet will almost certainly be scorched, just as surely as scooping fire into your lap will burn your clothes.

Adulterers go to hell.

3. Punishment (6:29,33-35)

'No one who touches her will go unpunished' (6:29). This is proverbial. Many think they can get away with adultery entirely but it is a very rare thing when anyone does, even in this life. The more obvious dangers are spelled out here:

> **Blows and disgrace are his lot,**
> **and his shame will never be wiped away;**
> **for jealousy arouses a husband's fury,**
> **and he will show no mercy when he takes revenge.**
> **He will not accept any compensation;**
> **he will refuse the bribe, however great it is**
> (6:33-35).

The prospect for the adulterer is suffering with no escape. No amount of money will rescue him. Let me quote two modern examples culled from press reports.

One article told the story of a fifty-five-year-old Texan who fatally shot his wife and the man he suspected was her lover outside a hospital emergency room in Houston. Pete Brewer had suspected for about a week that his wife, Lee, was having an affair. Lee, aged sixty, had gone to visit a family member at a local hospital. She arrived there with another man, not her husband, where Brewer confronted the two. She told her husband she intended leaving him for the other man. After a brief conversation, Brewer pulled out a handgun, shot his wife, the other man and then himself.

Another story, this time from Britain, is similar. Here a jealous husband battered his estranged wife's lover to death in front of her. Hotel worker Steve Veal died in a welter of blows to the head with a hammer after the demented husband had lain in wait. The unnamed husband then left his shocked wife at the murder scene and killed himself. He had pounced on Mr Veal, aged fifty, as he tried to get out of his car at the hotel where he worked. His wife screamed in terror as her lover was beaten to death at the hotel in Effingham Park, Sussex. A barman at the hotel said of Mr Veal, 'He was a really popular chap — very likeable. No one had any idea he was having an affair. We are all really shocked.'

Such examples graphically illustrate the dangers people court when they leave behind the certainties of Scripture and a close walk with the Saviour for the dubious advantages of a supposedly more enlightened creed.

4. Shame (6:33)

Shame will especially be yours if you fall into this sin and waste your life. **'Disgrace'** will be your **'lot'** and your **'shame will never be wiped away'**. Humiliation and disgrace are inevitable. Think of the way satirists dealt with a man like Bill Clinton when his adultery became so widely known. I know of a minister who fell into adultery. He has repented earnestly but still, some years after the event, he feels ashamed even to show his face at large meetings.

It is clear, then, how easy it is to waste a whole life, simply by being taken in by the adulteress. Do not make that mistake. Run from indignity, danger, punishment and shame. Listen to

God's Word and be saved through faith in Christ. As this passage strikingly argues:

> **Men do not despise a thief if he steals**
> **to satisfy his hunger when he is starving.**
> **Yet if he is caught, he must pay sevenfold,**
> **though it costs him all the wealth of his house**
> (6:30-31).

Stealing brings grave dangers. Do not be a thief. But how much worse is it to be someone who commits adultery! Many an adulterer will look down on a thief. **'But a man who commits adultery lacks judgement; whoever does so destroys himself'** (6:32). Literally, the adulterer is 'heartless'. As the apostle Paul puts it in the New Testament, 'Flee from sexual immorality. All other sins a man commits are outside his body, but he who sins sexually sins against his own body' (1 Cor. 6:18).

All sin is evil, but adultery of any sort, spiritual or physical, is not only wickedness but madness too. If we have discovered the wisdom that is found in Christ, we are crazy to turn anywhere else. This is the way to everlasting punishment and shame. This is the way to death. Flee every allurement to sinful thought and sinful actions. Cling to wisdom. Run to Christ.

15.
A tenth fatherly talk:
Choose wisdom; flee adultery; choose life

Please read Proverbs 7:1-27

Some parents get embarrassed when it comes to fatherly talks with their children about certain subjects. Your experience may have been that on some matters no advice at all was given, or when an attempt was made, it was rather badly handled. Here in Proverbs we have a perfect example of how to go about such things. We all have something to learn.

Here in Proverbs 7 we have the familiar beginning, **'My son...'** (7:1). How to divide the text is debatable but this is perhaps the tenth and final fatherly talk (see 1:8; 2:1; 3:1). It is a parallel warning to that in Proverbs 5 (just as in chapters 2 and 4 we have had parallel descriptions of the benefits of wisdom). Here are exhortations, but not just exhortations. There is a story too. As American TV sitcom writers well know, a good pep talk ought to have a memorable and appropriate story somewhere along the line. The pattern here is a prologue in verses 1-5, followed by a story, or drama, in verses 6-23 and then a warning epilogue in the closing verses.

The prologue (7:1-5)

The subject

The prologue concerns again the father's words, commands and teachings — what is most often referred to in this book as wisdom or understanding.

His words

Here in Proverbs, as in the rest of Scripture, we have God's **'words'**. 'They are only words,' you may say, but they are precious words. The words of a loving father to his son can have a powerful effect. Because these are God's own words, they have a power of their own. It is by his word that God created this whole world, and with his word he will judge it. Ultimately Jesus Christ is his Word — the one and only Saviour. He is the living Word of God and there our thoughts must focus.

His commands

The prologue also speaks of God's **'commands'**, for these are not words that can simply be forgotten, but commands that must be obeyed. The commands of a parent, or your boss at work, or a righteous ruler, ought to be obeyed — how much more the very words of God! He must be heard; he must be obeyed. In the armed forces refusal to obey a command leads to a court martial, to dismissal, or even to death in some cases. How fearful we ought to be of disobeying God himself!

His teachings

God's Word is also his law, his instruction or teaching. If you want an education, you go to a teacher in order to learn. Of course, if you do not listen in class, that is your fault. We all need to go to the greatest Teacher, God himself, and we need to listen well. His lessons may sometimes be difficult, but they are free and they are always worth hearing.

Wisdom, understanding

In verse 4 the speaker talks about **'wisdom'**. Practical knowledge for this life and the life to come is found in God's Word. Here is the book of wisdom par excellence. Paralleled with wisdom is **'understanding'**, insight or discernment. To get to the real heart of what is true and right we must go to God. Ultimately, it is the gospel that is true understanding for it brings us to Christ, the Word of God and the wisdom of God.

The command

The thing to do with these words, commands, teachings, this wisdom or understanding, is to keep them, store them up, guard them and become intimate with them. This is what the father commands his son.

Keep God's words and commands

'My son, keep my words,' he begins. **'Keep my commands'** (7:1,2). To **'keep'** means 'to regard, give heed to, pay attention to'. Do you know the gospel? Do you care about it? Keeping also involves watching over and caring for. Do you see how important the wisdom found in God's Word is? It also means guarding. The Word of God ought to be precious to us. If a close friend says, 'Keep this for me,' you would surely guard whatever it was with your life. Are we keeping God's Word in that way?

Store up his commands within

'And store up my commands within you. Keep my commands...' (7:1-2). God's commands ought to be hidden in our hearts and treasured up as precious. If you have something valuable, you put it in a safe place — jewels in a jewel box, important documents in a locked file. Are you doing that with the good news about Christ? Are you like Mary who, we read, 'treasured up all these things and pondered them in her heart'? (Luke 2:19). Learning the Word and meditating on it are vital.

Guard his teachings

'Guard my teachings as the apple of your eye' (7:2). In ancient times some supposed that the pupil of the eye was solid like an apple. We instinctively blink or raise our hands to protect our eyes, as the pupil is a most sensitive and precious part. The same instinct for protection that we show towards our eyes ought to be manifested towards God's teachings. We must allow nothing to spoil or hinder them, even for a moment. The Hebrew idiom refers to the eye's 'little man'. Even more evocative is the thought of the father being reflected in the son's eye. That vision of him instructing his son must, as it were, be carefully guarded.

Bind them on your fingers

In Deuteronomy 6:8 the Jews are told regarding God's commandments, 'Tie them as symbols on your hands and bind them on your foreheads,' and down the years many Jews have taken that command quite literally.

Interestingly, in the light of the context of this command to **'Bind them on your fingers'** (7:3), the previous verse in

Deuteronomy says, 'Impress them on your children.' Later in the same passage we read, 'Do not follow other gods, the gods of the peoples around you' (Deut. 6:7,14). A similar connection is observable in Deuteronomy 11: 'Be careful, or you will be enticed to turn away and worship other gods and bow down to them... Fix these words of mine in your hearts and minds; tie them as symbols on your hands and bind them on your foreheads. Teach them to your children, talking about them when you sit at home and when you walk along the road, when you lie down and when you get up' (Deut. 11:16-20).

I suppose the nearest equivalent in everyday life would be the wedding ring — a constant reminder of one's marriage vows. Perhaps we could put it this way: 'Have these laws at your fingertips.' Always live in the light of the cross and the teachings of Scripture (see also 3:3).

Write them on your heart

It is usually an aid to memory, and often to understanding, to write a thing down; hence the use of notebooks and shopping lists and prayer reminders. Here the command is to **'Write them on the tablet of your heart'** (7:3) — a graphic picture of using memory and mind and conscience and affections together to deeply impress these things within. The phrase has been used already in 3:3 (see also 6:21). In the New Covenant believers have God's law engraved on the fleshy tables of their hearts. How do our hearts read? If all we find there is sin, a few vague ideas of what God's law requires and mere good intentions, we are doomed. The Spirit must write the Word itself there so that we will be eager to do all that God requires.

Get closely related to wisdom

From time to time we have to fill in forms that ask, 'Who is your next of kin?' This is the legal term for the member of your family who is closest to you. Who is your next of kin? Whoever it is, you should be at least as near to wisdom as you are to that person. Just as you speak to your close relatives, help them, pray for them and are willing to do whatever is necessary for them, so it should be with wisdom. **'Say to wisdom, "You are my sister," and call understanding your kinsman'** (7:4). Jesus, the Wisdom of God, spoke in similar terms when he said that his closest relatives were those who obeyed God's Word and that anyone who loved parents, spouse or children more than him was not worthy of him. If you want a real beauty to be yours, ignore the adulteress and embrace wisdom.

The promise

Finally, consider the promise concerning these commands and teachings: **'They will keep you from the adulteress, from the wayward wife with her seductive words'** (7:5). Back in verse 2 there is also the simpler **'... you will live'** (contrast with 7:23,27). Here is the way to abundant life, true life, eternal life, that has so often been spoken of already. Here again is the way of escape from the adulteress. If you forget God's words, or cast aside his commands, or disregard his teachings, it will lead only to death and to disaster and misery. A man who has a perfect wife at home will not cast a second glance at the adulteress. The man who has wisdom as his wife and is faithful to her will avoid all forms of adultery.

The drama (7:6-23)

To reinforce all of this we have a well-told story, realistic yet timeless, full of atmosphere, yet clear in its teaching. It is like a series of snapshots taken as events unfold. The observer is unnamed. As we have said before, these warnings are not

simply against the physical act of adultery, but have much wider
implications. The cults, false religions and philosophies, the
worldly lifestyle, materialism and nominalism are all wicked
temptresses whose siren voices will lead the unwary to their
death as they make shipwreck on the ocean's hidden rocks.

The story can be divided into four parts.

1. The victim (7:6-9)

The narrator looks out of what Peter Masters calls 'the most
extraordinary window in the Bible', for through it one 'can
see in pitch darkness, and also round corners and into houses'.
Unseen himself, through the lattice he is able to watch what
goes on (7:6). He sees some simple ones gathered, young men,
not yet mature, hanging about on a street-corner. His eye fas-
tens on one, **'a youth who lacked judgement'** (7:7). It is
'twilight ... the day [is] fading' and **'the dark of night'**
setting in. The young man would not dream of doing this in
broad daylight, but with darkness coming on he has separated
himself from his companions and is walking down the street
near the corner where a prostitute lives. He is in the red-light
district. The Bible speaks of 'the fruitless deeds of darkness'
(Eph. 5:11) and of how 'Men loved darkness instead of light
because their deeds were evil' (John 3:19).

> There are those who rebel against the light,
>   who do not know its ways
>   or stay in its paths.
> When daylight is gone, the murderer rises up
>   and kills the poor and needy;
>   in the night he steals forth like a thief.
> The eye of the adulterer watches for dusk;
>   he thinks, 'No eye will see me,'
>   and he keeps his face concealed
>
>   (Job 24:13-15).

At what point the youth determines to go to the prostitute is not clear, but to have gone to that part of the town at all showed foolishness. It epitomizes the shallowness and naïveté of the natural man with his vague and empty notions. The darkness also emphasizes the gathering gloom. 'People fall into the traps of sin and unbelief over time,' says Dr Masters. 'The aimlessness of early evening eventually becomes the secret perversion of midnight.' The narrator sees him **'walking along in the direction of her house'** (7:8). There is no mistake; he is deliberately heading for trouble. He lacks judgement. He is immature, simple, easily taken in. He is in the wrong place at the wrong time.

Do you go to the wrong places? Do you flirt with danger? Do you mix with the wrong kind of people? Take care! Are you dallying with anti-biblical ideas? Are you finding worldly ways attractive and experimenting with that lifestyle? Watch out! You would not light a match while refuelling your car, or jump into the lion enclosure at the zoo, so why go anywhere near sin?

2. The huntress (7:10-12)

Next, we meet the huntress. The young man is vaguely looking for her, it is true, but she does not wait for him to make all the moves. Out she comes to meet him, **'dressed like a prostitute'** (7:10). No detail is given, but she dresses as seductively as she can. Such things vary from culture to culture.

She has a **'crafty intent'**. Like a hunter, she wants to lure her prey. By nature:

> **She is loud and defiant,**
> > **her feet never stay at home;**
> **now in the street, now in the squares,**
> > **at every corner she lurks**

(7:11-12).

There is something brazen and rebellious about this woman. At every corner and on every street she appears in one form or another, eager to trap her victims. Today she is on the television and in the cinema and can be called up on the internet. You see her face in magazines and newspapers and hear her voice on the radio. She is all the rage in colleges and universities. She is involved in politics and is to the forefront in fashion, sport, the media and the arts. She makes her presence felt in temples, mosques, churches and chapels. In public places her face gazes at you from billboards, and in a thousand different ways she lets what she has to offer be known. Prostitution itself is only one form of a hideous game of mousetrap designed to ensnare the unwary in all sorts of evil.

3. Her tactics (7:13-21)

Despite elements of subtlety in her approach, she can at times be totally shameless in her invitation to sin. We read how **'She took hold of him and kissed him'** (7:13). She knows when to strike and can easily catch a person off guard. The narrator continues:

> **... with a brazen face she said:**
> **'I have fellowship offerings at home;**
> **today I fulfilled my vows'**
>
> (7:13-14).

She does not balk at using religion, or telling any untruth, to lure her victim in. Attempts are often made to sanitize sin: 'It's Christmas'; 'Just this once'; 'In the interests of science...'; 'Think of the good it will do.' Flattery is also in her armoury: **'So I came out to meet you; I looked for you and have found you!'** (7:15). The appeal is so often sensuous. She says:

I have covered my bed
   with coloured linens from Egypt.
I have perfumed my bed
   with myrrh, aloes and cinnamon.
Come, let's drink deep of love till morning;
   let's enjoy ourselves with love!

(7:16-18).

She is playing on his sense of sight and smell and his desire to love and be loved, and to know the pleasures of love. Satan will use any device available to draw us away from Christ — what John Bode referred to as '… the sights that dazzle, the tempting sounds'.

The youth seems hesitant perhaps. By now all he cares about is being caught. What about her husband? But she reassures him:

My husband is not at home;
   he has gone on a long journey.
He took his purse filled with money
   and will not be home till full moon

(7:19-20).

If only the young man had responded as Joseph had: 'How then could I do such a wicked thing and sin against God?' (Gen. 39:9). Instead, there is a guilty silence. Any lingering doubts are dulled by flattery: **'With persuasive words she led him astray; she seduced him with her smooth talk'** (7:21).

4. The kill (7:22-23)

The pace has been slow and seductive so far but in verses 22-23 it accelerates and speed and suddenness are emphasized:

> **All at once he followed her**
>   **like an ox going to the slaughter,**
> **like a deer stepping into a noose**
>   **till an arrow pierces his liver,**
> **like a bird darting into a snare,**
>   **little knowing it will cost him his life.**

The picture of an ox being taken to slaughter, or of a deer or a bird being trapped, is used to convey what goes on. For the ox, the day of slaughter begins like any other except that the animal is taken on a journey. The journey itself is not unpleasant but it leads to death. Picture the deer ambling through the forest as it has done in the past, the bird flying free. Then suddenly a trap closes — a noose or snare — and the creature is captured. That is what sin is like if we could only see it as it is.

The epilogue (7:24-27)

Finally, there is the epilogue given by the father figure. He gives three simple instructions.

1. Follow wisdom (7:24)

'Now then, my sons, listen to me; pay attention to what I say' (This is the penultimate reference to **'sons'** in the plural). Above all, listen to God. We must pay attention to Scripture.

2. Avoid the adulteress (7:25)

This is the particular stress at this point: **'Do not let your heart turn to her ways or stray into her paths.'** If the child had switched the tap off before the basin had become so full, the bathroom would not have been flooded.

3. Be warned and see where that way leads (7:26-27)

These verses act as a form of epitaph at the close of the chapter:

Many are the victims she has brought down;
her slain are a mighty throng.
Her house is a highway to the grave,
leading down to the chambers of death.

Take warning from the sufferings of others — the wretchedness of alcoholics and drug addicts; the remorse of adulterers, fornicators and perverts; the misery of murderers and thieves. These people were just like us at one time.

Think of hell at this moment, full of souls in agony because of their regrets. Think of people who thought that it was enough to be a nominal Christian, or who were drawn into heresy or a cult or false religion, or who thought that to live a respectable life was enough. The way of disobedience is one that leads down — down **'to the grave ... down to the chambers of death'**. Millions are already in hell — Make sure that you do not end up joining them. Rather, run to Christ and embrace him in faith. He is meek and gentle and is willing to receive sinners.

Once again, 'I call heaven and earth as witnesses against you that I have set before you life and death, blessings and curses. Now choose life, so that you and your children may live' (Deut. 30:19). 'See, I am setting before you today a blessing and a curse — the blessing if you obey the commands of the LORD your God that I am giving you today; the curse if you disobey the commands of the LORD your God and turn from the way that I command you today by following other gods, which you have not known' (Deut. 11:26-28).

In January 1992 American Aileen Wuornos was convicted of the murder of Richard Mallory. A prostitute, she had been working in Florida and had probably shot and robbed six, possibly seven, men between December 1989 and her eventual arrest in January 1991. Wuornos claimed that the men that she killed had first attacked her and that she had acted only in self-defence. Whatever the full truth behind these terrible incidents, a series of men — Richard, David, Charles, Peter (probably), Troy, Dick and Walter — all came to this woman, drawn by whatever charm they thought she possessed. They came expecting, perhaps finding for a moment, some sort of satisfaction from her. However, they were like oxen going to slaughter; each was 'like a deer stepping into a noose till an arrow pierces his liver, like a bird darting into a snare'. They little knew it would cost them their very lives. She brought down many victims, her slain — what a throng! Her house was 'a highway to the grave, leading down to the chambers of death'. Her story stands as a warning to all who are tempted to leave the highway of holiness. A moment's unguardedness and we can be on the road to making this world our absorbing passion. Jesus warned Peter and the other disciples: 'Simon, Simon, Satan has asked to sift you as wheat' (Luke 22:31). Perhaps that prompted Peter's later word of caution when he wrote, 'Be self-controlled and alert. Your enemy the devil prowls around like a roaring lion looking for someone to devour' (1 Peter 5:8).

16.
A talk from wisdom itself:
Listen to Wisdom's call

Please read Proverbs 8:1-21

The theme of the whole book of Proverbs is wisdom, but chapter 8 is unique in that here wisdom itself speaks. One writer speaks of the chapter reaching 'the high water mark' of the series of lessons on wisdom. Another describes it as 'the core course in the teacher's curriculum'. Yet another sees the preceding chapters as rough sketches or cartoons leading up to the full-colour portrait that we find here.

This is one of the greatest chapters of the Old Testament — we could compare it to an Alpine or Himalayan peak. Similar material is found back in Proverbs 1 (it parallels the call in 1:20-33) and in other places, but here especially we meet Wisdom face to face. Here is Wisdom personified. It is no longer the teacher calling out, but Wisdom herself. The NIV uses the appropriate heading: 'Wisdom's call'.

Before we look at the chapter in detail it may be useful to consider again the question of just what or who Wisdom is? To what, or to whom, is the author pointing? It is clear that what is being advocated here is not some worldly form of wisdom but a distinctly heavenly one. From the earliest Christian centuries many have gone further and asserted that this chapter refers not simply to God's wisdom in the abstract, but to the Lord Jesus Christ, the Word of God, who, as Paul says, is 'the wisdom of God', the one 'who has become for us wisdom from God' and 'in whom are hidden all the treasures of wisdom and knowledge' (1 Cor. 1:24,30; Col. 2:3). Augustine used it against the Arians in the fourth century and Calvin against Servetus in the fifteenth century. In 1710 Matthew Henry wrote in his commentary, 'That it is an intelligent and divine person that here speaks seems very plain ... and that intelligent divine person can be no other than the Son of God himself.' In the nineteenth century William Arnot went as far as to say that 'If the terms are not applied to Christ, they must be strained at every turn.' For Edward Payson, 'He who is styled the Word of God in the New Testament calls himself the Wisdom of God in the Old.' T. T. Perowne wrote, 'The vivid and august personification falters not on its way, till it presents to us rather than predicts, him who is *the Word of God, the only begotten of the Father, the Son of his love, who became flesh and dwelt among us* because from all eternity his delights had been with the sons of men.'

While we recognize that much that can be said about a divine attribute is also applicable to a divine person, surely it is right for us to see here a foreshadowing of the doctrine of the divine Word. Certainly we shall never understand wisdom unless we come to see that it is personified in Christ. The message of this chapter is: 'Listen to Wisdom's call.' Ultimately that means to listen not only to God's wisdom in a general sense, but more particularly to listen to Christ calling to you so that you trust in him with all your heart. In verses 1-21 we are given several reasons why we ought to listen to Christ.

1. Because his call is comprehensive and fervent (8:1-5)

Wisdom — that is, the wisdom found in Christ — is hidden in the sense of being hidden from the proud. On the other hand,

when on earth, Jesus himself stressed that 'I have spoken openly
to the world... I always taught in synagogues or at the temple,
where all the Jews come together. I said nothing in secret'
(John 18:20; cf. Matt. 9:35; Mark 14:49; Luke 13:26; John
7:37). Wisdom, like Christ, takes the initiative. Both show great
earnestness and perseverance too: **'She takes her stand'** (8:2).
They tend to **'call out'** (8:1), to raise the voice in every public
place: **'She cries aloud'** (8:3). Wisdom cannot be hidden but
calls out to everyone: **'I raise my voice to all mankind'** (8:4).
It is not 'O Jews,' or 'O gentlemen,' or 'O scholars,' says
Matthew Henry, but 'O men' — that is, every human being.
Beyond ignorance, no qualification is necessary to hear that
cry. **'You who are simple, gain prudence'** (an unusual word
for wisdom, emphasizing its practical side); **'you who are foolish, gain understanding'** (8:5).

The public places referred to can perhaps be understood
further as referring to certain times in life, thus:

> **'On the heights along the way'** (8:2) — at impor-
> tant and significant points on the road of life.
> **'Where the paths meet'** (8:2) — at times when a
> decision has to be arrived at, a choice made between
> alternatives.
> **'Beside the gates leading into the city, at the en-
> trances'** (8:3) — at times when a judgement needs to
> be made, a message considered, or a transaction engaged
> in (such things went on in the city gate).

It is important to grasp this. We may think that wisdom
must be a totally hidden thing, a private thing. Surely it can
only be available to a very select few. It cannot be available to
all. As we have noted, there is certainly a sense in which that is
true, but not absolutely by any means. Wisdom is open and
accessible to all. On one level, the streets really are paved with

gold! Man's wisdom tends to be hidden away in dusty tomes, behind cloistered walls, within ivory towers, in files marked 'top secret'. The norm is for human wisdom to be available only to a select few, and then only after a long and difficult initiation and when certain demanding qualifications and attainments have been realized. It is typical of the devil to try to dupe people in this way. This was his approach with Eve: 'This is the tree you need to eat from, the forbidden tree. This is the one that will make you wise. Just listen to me; I'll get you in.'

In the light of this we can say, as a rule of thumb, that *the Christian should immediately be suspicious of any form of supposed wisdom that is secretive or exclusive*: for example, exclusive orders, secret societies, clandestine meetings, anything to do with the occult (the very word means 'hidden') and the cults that, to varying degrees, are marked by secrecy and suspicion.

The eighteenth-century Swedish scientist Emanuel Swedenborg was typical when he announced in 1757 that he had discovered 'heavenly secrets contained in the Holy Scriptures' and began to unfold them with wonderful things he claimed to have seen 'in the world of spirits and in the heaven of angels'. 'Swedenborgian' views exist to this day.

Kabbalists of various sorts, especially among the Jews, similarly claim to have found secret wisdom in the Bible from time immemorial. One of the most recent popular eruptions of that kind of thing was in 1997 when the best-selling book *The Bible Code* by Michael Drosnin appeared. The secrecy that sometimes surrounds Freemasonry is another example of this approach, as is the old Roman Catholic idea of depriving people of the Bible because of their ignorance. Christians should shun such supposed wisdom. Jesus says, 'So if anyone [speaks of Messiah and] tells you, "There he is, out in the desert," do not go out; or, "Here he is, in the inner rooms," do not believe it. For as lightning that comes from the east is visible even in the west, so will be the coming of the Son of Man' (Matt. 24:26-27). In Revelation he speaks with undisguised contempt of 'Satan's so-called deep secrets' (Rev. 2:24).

Christ and true wisdom, this chapter makes clear, *is found everywhere*. This is seen both in God's special revelation, preserved in Scripture, and in God's general revelation where 'Through all his mighty works amazing wisdom shines'. Christ 'is not far from each one of us' (Acts 17:27). Paul writes to the Romans that '… the righteousness that is by faith says: "Do not say in your heart, 'Who will ascend into heaven?' " (that is, to bring Christ down) "or 'Who will descend into the deep?' " (that is, to bring Christ up from the dead). But what does it say? "The word is near you; it is in your mouth and in your heart," that is, the word of faith we are proclaiming' (Rom.10:6-8).

Christ and true wisdom are preached in all the world. This is true of creation, where, to quote Isaac Watts, 'in every star thy wisdom shines'. Apart from creation itself this is true only of the gospel. The Bible, let us not forget, continues to be the best-selling book ever. It is available in over 2,000 different languages. Regular Christian broadcasts go out to more than 260 countries of the world and hundreds of thousands of cross-cultural missionaries labour to share the gospel in an increasing number of places.

You do not have to be anyone special, in worldly terms, to hear Christ and God's wisdom. *It is something that is open to all.* However simple or foolish we are, we are all invited to come to Christ and gain prudence and understanding. Wisdom does not take from us. Its characteristic, rather, is to bestow spiritual wealth and to make our treasuries full (8:21). It is all grace, as Paul reminds believers: 'It is by grace you have been saved, through faith — and this not from yourselves, it is the gift of God — not by works, so that no one can boast' (Eph. 2:8-9).

As we saw earlier, *true gospel preaching*, preaching Christ, *must not be confined to certain select groups, or to certain clearly defined places*, whatever laws governments may pass or traditions may dictate. Like the sower of the parable, we must scatter the seed widely and cast our bread on the waters. Into the highways and byways we must go (see Luke 14:15-24) promiscuously and indiscriminately preaching Christ. We must be ready to face the rough and tumble, the cut and thrust, of going out into the market place of ideas and presenting our wares.

Christ is searching for his own more than they are searching for him. In truth, there are no real seekers or searchers after God: 'There is no one who understands, no one who seeks God' (Rom. 3:11). We only see this properly when we come to faith, but that is the truth. The nineteenth-century Congregationalist Josiah Conder put it well:

> 'Tis not that I did choose thee,
> For, Lord, that could not be;
> This heart would still refuse thee
> Hadst thou not chosen me.

2. Because he is pre-eminently worth listening to (8:6-16)

Wisdom urges us to **'listen'** (8:6) to her and to **'choose'** her (8:10). A number of things are said to show that Christ the wisdom of God is pre-eminently worth listening to and choosing.

His moral worth (8:6-9)

Wisdom has **'worthy things to say'** (literally 'princes' or 'nobles' — thus 'high things' or 'noble things'):

I open my lips to speak what is right.
My mouth speaks what is true,
   for my lips detest wickedness

                                             (8:6-7).

How unlike the adulteress! Think of Jesus saying, 'I am the truth.'

All the words of my mouth are just;
   none of them is crooked or perverse.
To the discerning all of them are right;
   they are faultless to those who have knowledge
                                             (8:8-9).

Of course, they are 'foolishness to those who are perishing, but to those who are being saved' they are right, faultless and powerful (see 1 Cor. 1:18).

Wisdom concludes: 'I walk in the way of righteousness, along the paths of justice' (8:20). As we have noted already, any supposed wisdom that is not righteous and just is unworthy of the name. No one is more worthy, no one more true, no one more just than Jesus 'the Righteous One'. He is 'holy, blameless, pure, set apart from sinners' (Heb. 7:26), the Prince of Peace, worthy of all honour. For believers he is our wisdom and our righteousness, he 'has become for us wisdom from God — that is, our righteousness, holiness and redemption' (1 Cor. 1:30; cf. 1:24).

2. His incomparable nature (8:10-11)

True wisdom is superior to **'silver'** or **'choice gold ... more precious than rubies ... nothing you desire can compare with her'** (8:10,11; cf. 8:19; 3:14). Like these things Christ is God-given, rare, precious, useful, hard to gain, lasting, valuable.

Moreover, he is higher, older, more necessary and more likely to do us good than these things. That is why we must choose Christ first. Nothing begins to compare with knowing him. Remember how Jesus brings this out in the parables of the treasure and the pearl of great price. He also asks what a man can give in exchange for his soul.

Hymn-writers have tried to express it. Professor Bobi Jones translates William Williams thus:

> Jesus, Jesus all-sufficient,
> Beyond telling is thy worth.
> In thy name lie greater treasures
> Than the richest found on earth.
> Such abundance is my portion with my God.

He is a glorious Saviour. He is 'chosen by God and precious to him … a chosen and precious cornerstone, and the one who trusts in him will never be put to shame' (1 Peter 2:4-6; cf. Isa. 28:16). Let nothing distract you from setting your heart on him. As one writer put it, if silver were being handed out you would not hesitate to take it — so why refuse wisdom, worth so much more?

3. His matchless character (8:12-16)

You can tell a great deal about a person from the company he keeps and the things he possesses. Verse 12 lies at the heart of the chapter. Here wisdom says, **'I, wisdom, dwell together with prudence; I possess knowledge and discretion.'** Such things were found in Christ while he walked on earth. They appear to be part of conventional wisdom, but on closer inspection they are found to be absent. True wisdom, on the other hand, begins with the fear of the Lord (1:7). This leads to a hatred for evil. It never encourages **'pride and arrogance, evil behaviour'** or **'perverse speech'** (8:13). If you know the wisdom that is in Christ you will be prudent, discreet, judicious and will be one who turns away from sin. It is by trusting in Christ that we are able to flee from such things.

Wisdom continues:

> **Counsel and sound judgement are mine;**
> **I have understanding and power.**
> **By me kings reign**
> **and rulers make laws that are just;**
> **by me princes govern,**
> **and all nobles who rule on earth**
> (8:14-16).

All rule is ultimately in Christ's hands. There is no other true power or wisdom. All forms of power and wisdom find their perfection in him. As we have already seen, in him 'are hidden all the treasures of wisdom and knowledge' (Col. 2:3). Remember how he answered Pilate when Pilate asked him, 'Don't you realize I have power either to free you or to crucify you?' He replied, 'You would have no power over me if it were not given to you from above' (John 19:10,11). All wisdom and power is ultimately God's. Following his resurrection, Jesus said, 'All authority in heaven and on earth has been given to me' (Matt. 28:18). The Father has committed it all to the Son. 'All things have been committed to me by my Father... Come to me, all you who are weary and burdened, and I will give you rest. Take my yoke upon you and learn from me, for I am gentle and humble in heart, and you will find rest for your souls' (Matt. 11:27-29). 'For he "has put everything under his feet"' (1 Cor. 15:27, quoting Ps. 8:6).

3. Because of the rewards he gives to all those who do (8:17-21)

The third argument is in verses 17-21 and concerns the rewards Christ gives to those who listen to his call. Jesus says to his disciples, 'Whoever has my commands and obeys them, he is the one who loves me. He who loves me will be loved by my Father, and I too will love him and show myself to him' (John 14:21). Perhaps he was drawing on Proverbs 8:17 for that statement. It begins with the words: **'I love those who love me.'** The words 'know' and 'love' often have a connection in the Bible and certainly if you know wisdom you will love it. Do you love Jesus Christ? Do you know him? If you knew him, you would love him. It is only those who do not know him who do not love him. And he loves all those who love him. Of course, as John reminds us, 'We love because he first loved us' (1 John 4:19), but whatever love we show to him is always reciprocated many times over.

Wisdom continues, **'and those who seek me find me'** (8:17). Some translations have 'seek early' as the Hebrew word translated 'seek' is an intense one. Probably, however, the meaning is more on the lines of to 'seek earnestly'. Those who reject God find that when they eventually do seek him it is too late and they do not find him. Those who lovingly seek him now will find him. This sentiment forms the basis of what Jesus says in the Sermon on the Mount: 'Ask and it will be given to you; seek and you will find; knock and the door will be opened to you. For everyone who asks receives; he who seeks finds; and to him who knocks, the door will be opened.' He goes on: 'Which of you, if his son asks for bread, will give him a stone? Or if he asks for a fish, will give him a snake? If you, then, though you are evil, know how to give good gifts to your children, how much more will your Father in heaven give good gifts to those who ask him!' (Matt. 7:7-11).

If you seek the Lord, the wisdom of God, with all your heart you will find him. Christ is not far from any one of us, but we must seek to find him. The Syro-Phoenician woman of Matthew 15:21-28 is a great example of one who earnestly sought and found.

Proverbs 8:20, which we quoted earlier, reminds us that because Wisdom can say, **'I walk in the way of righteousness, along the paths of justice,'** we can be sure that following Christ will always lead into righteousness. Integrity brings its own rewards.

This passage also speaks of rewards: **'With me are riches and honour, enduring wealth and prosperity'** (8:18). In true, concrete, proverbial style the promise is of wealth, success and fame. Often the blessings are tangible even in terms of this world, but not always. The following verse raises our thoughts to a higher plane: **'My fruit is better than fine gold; what I yield surpasses choice silver'** (8:19). There are greater rewards than this world knows anything about. They are also in the gift of Christ, God's wisdom and ours.

The final verse we consider here pictures Wisdom **'bestowing wealth on those who love me and making their treasuries full'** (8:21). It is like a great king who has returned from the battlefield and shares the plunder with his favourites. The psalmist speaks of how Christ, when he 'ascended on high ... led captives in his train and gave gifts to men' (Eph. 4:8, quoting Ps. 68:18). Paul sees these gifts as including apostles, prophets, pastors and teachers — those who have taught and those who continue to teach the gospel. That is at the core, but much else is included. Go to Christ today and receive his many rich blessings. Matthew 6:33 summarizes the message of verses 20 and 21 very well: 'But seek first his kingdom and his righteousness, and all these things will be given to you as well.' None but Christ can truly satisfy.

Robert Murray M'Cheyne once preached on the text, 'To you, O men, I call out; I raise my voice to all mankind' (8:4). He spoke of Christ offering himself to mankind as Saviour — the most awakening, the most comforting and the most condemning truth in the entire Bible. If Christ is so offered, what will God do with those who refuse him?

17.
More words from Wisdom and a father's concluding call

Please read Proverbs 8:22-36

When in 1851 John Mason Neale published an adaptation of the ninth-century Latin hymn *Veni Immanuel* in his *Mediaeval Hymns*, he included a verse based on Proverbs 8:

Draw nigh, thou Wisdom from on high,
And order all things far and nigh;
To us the path of knowledge show
And cause us in her ways to go.

He thus confirmed his own acceptance of the widespread view that Proverbs 8 is about Messiah. Even if we have problems with that idea, we can at least sing the words above and see how appropriate it is (to use David Atkinson's words) 'to understand Jesus in the terms in which wisdom is described'.

In Proverbs 8:22-31, Wisdom continues to call out. On the basis of verses 1-21 we have already seen that Christ is worth listening to because of his comprehensive and fervent call, his pre-eminent worth and the rewards he gives. Here we consider Wisdom's concluding words and then (8:32-36) a father's concluding words.

Christ's ancient person and his sympathy towards man
(8:22-31)

We have already noted that Christians have often understood
this chapter as referring to Jesus Christ. What sometimes mo-
tivates those who oppose this view is the way that followers
of the ancient heresy of Arianism (which taught that the Son
of God was not an eternal being but had a beginning) seize on
the words, **'The LORD brought me forth as the first of his
works'** (8:22), and say, 'Surely this shows that Jesus had a
beginning.' One ancient Greek translation, the Septuagint, even
uses the word 'created' instead of 'brought forth' (although
another preferred 'possessed'). The Hebrew word means 'to
get' or 'to possess' (see the NIV footnote). The context decides the sense. So, for example, we *possess* goods by purchasing; we *have* children by begetting and giving birth; we
gain wisdom by learning. However, God did not need to learn
wisdom. He always possessed it. Similarly, Jesus is the eternally begotten Son of God. He was always God's Son.

He is **'the first of his works'** in the sense that he is the
greatest. Jesus certainly existed before Bethlehem. Even the
prophecy in Micah 5:2 points to this:

> But you, Bethlehem Ephrathah,
>   though you are small among the clans of Judah,
> out of you will come for me
>   one who will be ruler over Israel,
> whose origins are from of old,
>   from ancient times.

He was brought forth before God's **'deeds of old'**. He **was
'appointed'** (the same word is used in Ps. 2:6) **'from eternity, from the beginning, before the world began'**. The first

evidence of the Son of God's existence was not at Bethlehem but before the creation of the world. He says here:

> **... before the world began.**
> **When there were no oceans, I was given birth,**
> > **when there were no springs abounding with**
> > **water;**
> **before the mountains were settled in place,**
> > **before the hills ...**
> **before he made the earth or its fields**
> > **or any of the dust of the world**
>
> (8:24-26).

It is hard to imagine a time when there was no earth, when the Atlantic and the Pacific did not exist, when there were no Niagara Falls, and not even an intermittent spring at the bottom of someone's garden. But there was such a time, and the Son of God was around then. Before Mount Everest, or Kilimanjaro, or Snowdon, or the seven hills of Rome, he was there. Before fields of wheat or barley, or before even one grain of sand was made, he was there.

He testifies:

> **I was there when he set the heavens in place,**
> > **when he marked out the horizon on the face of**
> > **the deep,**
> **when he established the clouds above**
> > **and fixed securely the fountains of the deep,**
> **when he gave the sea its boundary**
> > **so that the waters would not overstep his com-**
> > **mand**
> **and when he marked out the foundations of the earth**
>
> (8:27-29).

Think of the Lord establishing the heavens, the horizon separating heaven and earth, the clouds above and the furthest recesses of the deep beneath, establishing the sea and the land and laying earth's foundations. **'Then'**, says Christ, **'I was the craftsman at his side. I was filled with delight day after day...'** There is some question over the translation **'craftsman'**, but it is likely to be correct.

The fact that the Second Person of the Trinity shared in the skilled work of creating the universe is declared in the New Testament in several places: 'In the beginning was the Word, and the Word was with God, and the Word was God. He was with God in the beginning. Through him all things were made; without him nothing was made that has been made' (John 1:1-3). 'He is the image of the invisible God, the firstborn over all creation. For by him all things were created: things in heaven and on earth, visible and invisible, whether thrones or powers or rulers or authorities; all things were created by him and for him. He is before all things, and in him all things hold together' (Col. 1:15-17). '...[God's] Son, whom he appointed heir of all things, and through whom he made the universe' (Heb. 1:2). These passages clearly draw on Proverbs 8.

In verse 31 his delight is specifically spelled out. We know from Job 38:7 that at creation 'the morning stars sang together and all the angels [literally, "the sons of God"] shouted for joy'. They were clearly not alone.

'Rejoicing always in his presence' (8:30). The delight could be that of the Father in the Son, or the Son's delight in the Father — probably the latter. Both are true.

'Rejoicing in his whole world' (8:31). Christ also delighted in the whole creation.

'And delighting in mankind' (8:31). He especially delighted in mankind, the children of Adam.

There are many things to learn about God's Son here then:

his essential unity with the Father;
his eternal nature;
his agency in the creation of the universe;
his joy in God's presence;
his joy in unfallen creation;
his joy in unfallen mankind.

Here we focus on three things: First, he is primary and indispensable. Second, he is older than the universe itself and fundamental to its existence. Third, he is filled with delight and joy whenever and wherever he sees his Father at work

Why must we all listen to Jesus Christ? We have already considered his universal call, his pre-eminent worth and the rewards he gives to all who turn to him, but here is a further argument — his ancient person and his sympathy with mankind.

Do you understand just who it was that lay in the manger in Bethlehem? Do you realize who it was who grew up in poverty in Nazareth? Do you see who it was who preached and healed in the streets of Galilee? Have you grasped who died on the cross at Golgotha? A man, yes, but more than a man. Like the disciples before us, however long it takes, we must come to see that the Lord Jesus Christ is God. Like Thomas we must bow down before him and worship him and say, 'My Lord and my God.' We must trust in him. There is no other way to wisdom. There is no other way to God.

Products are often sold on the strength of their long pedigree and their reputation for reliability. Certain firms will include the date the company was established in their advertising materials, or emphasize their durability in some other way to underline their reliability. Christ goes back beyond eternity, before the beginning of the world. He has sustained the world until now and will do so to the end.

There is more. He died on the cross in the place of sinners in order to please his Father and because of his joy and delight in saving this world. His joy and delight in man and in God's creation led to his dying to redeem man and the creation. If you trust in him, you will be saved by him.

A father's concluding words (8:32-36)

The final verses of the chapter are yet again the words of a father to his sons. Once more we have a rallying call to flee to Christ — on this occasion, chiefly because he is the one who is willing and able to bless all who come to him. Abraham was told, '… through your offspring [seed] all nations on earth will be blessed' (Gen. 22:18). The seed of Abraham is ultimately Jesus Christ: 'The Scripture does not say "and to seeds", meaning many people, but "and to your seed", meaning one person, who is Christ' (Gal. 3:16).

In verses 32-34 there are two parallel commands and two parallel promises.

The commands

Now then, my sons, listen to me…
Listen to my instruction and be wise;
   do not ignore it

(8:32,33).

What does the Lord Jesus require of us? As has been said many times before, we must **'listen to'** him and **'not ignore'** him. If we really are sons of wisdom, if we really belong to Christ, we will listen to him. 'He who has ears to hear, let him hear.'

The promises

> **Blessed are those who keep my ways...**
> **Blessed is the man who listens to me,**
>   **watching daily at my doors,**
>   **waiting at my doorway**
>
>   (8:32,34).

Blessedness is happiness in God. These final beatitudes of Proverbs 1-9 reveal that God's blessing is reserved for those who keep Christ's ways, who stick to the path of wisdom. They listen to Christ with great eagerness, **'watching daily at [his] doors, waiting at [his] doorway'**. The parents of a well-known actress live near our house and some years ago a man became so obsessed with this young woman that, until a court order banned him, he would constantly wait outside the door hoping for a glimpse of his object of devotion. People will go to extraordinary lengths, waiting outside someone's house just in the hope of catching a glimpse of their hero or heroine. How much effort have we expended in the pursuit of wisdom, in the pursuit of Christ? Do we really want to know him? What efforts are we making to pursue him? Do we truly love him? He is the only way to true blessing, true happiness. Every other way leads only to a curse. Fix your eyes then on him.

One old writer speaks of waiting at the gate like Uriah (2 Sam. 11) ready to serve; like Lazarus (Luke 16) in dependence, and like royal courtiers seeking justice and favour from the king. In such ways we ought to wait at the gate of wisdom for Christ.

The last two verses are again of a summary nature (cf. 1:32-33; 2:21-22, etc). They spell out the consequences, both positively and negatively, of finding or not finding Christ, who is wisdom. The theme of life and death is a constant one in Proverbs 1-9. The verses here have a complex pattern.

For whoever finds me	finds life
	and receives favour from the
	LORD.
But whoever fails to find me	harms himself
all who hate me	love death.

Positively: what it means to find Christ

'For whoever finds me finds life and receives favour from the LORD' (8:35). If you find Christ, if you trust in him; if you come to know him and love him, then you have found life and God's everlasting favour. 'For God so loved the world that he gave his one and only Son, that whoever believes in him shall not perish but have eternal life' (John 3:16). 'I tell you the truth, whoever hears my word and believes him who sent me has eternal life and will not be condemned; he has crossed over from death to life' (John 5:24). 'For my Father's will is that everyone who looks to the Son and believes in him shall have eternal life, and I will raise him up at the last day' (John 6:40; cf. 11:26). 'I am the way and the truth and the life. No one comes to the Father except through me' (John 14:6).

Negatively: what it means not to find Christ

'But whoever fails to find me harms himself; all who hate me love death' (8:36). There is no greater tragedy than to fail to find the Lord Jesus Christ. If a person suffers an injury at the hands of another it is tragic, but when his wound is self-inflicted it is doubly tragic. This is the fate of all who fail to find wisdom. They do themselves irreparable harm. This knowledge no doubts adds to the pangs of hell.

From time to time, I visit patients in St Mary's Hospital, Paddington. I often see the plaque there reminding us that it is where the Nobel-Prize-winner Sir Alexander Fleming discovered penicillin in 1928. I believe there is now a little museum there. I sometimes wonder how many lives have been saved because of that discovery (perhaps those of some reading this book). Not to have found it would have meant death for many; its discovery has meant life for many. In a far greater way the discovery of Christ means everlasting life, and not to find him means everlasting death. Once more, the book of Proverbs calls on us to choose. Do you love Christ? If you do not love him, you hate him. There can be no neutrality. To hate him is like loving death. It is to do great harm to yourself. Do not make that fatal mistake.

18.
Two pressing invitations: One from Wisdom, one from Folly

Please read Proverbs 9:1-18

Invitations to weddings, birthday parties, meals and get-togethers are usually a pleasure to receive. With five children in our family, we frequently receive them. A problem that arises from time to time is that there is a clash of dates. Often we find a way round it, but sometimes a decision has to be made as to which invitation to accept and which to decline. Sometimes deciding is straightforward, but at other times it is not. Usually we are happy with the final decision, but not always.

Proverbs 9 closes the 'grammar' section of the book, providing a transition between the lofty heights of chapter 8 and the practical 'vocabulary' that follows. David Hubbard says that its contents 'capture much of the mood of the wisdom speeches in a highly digested format'. It contains two invitations side by side — one from Queen Wisdom, the other from the woman Folly. John H. Stek has pointed to a parallel with 1:8-19, where we began with a brief invitation to wisdom and a much longer one to evil. Here both invitations come with an 'RSVP'. We must respond to them. We must all accept one invitation or the other. We cannot remain neutral. The choice is not the straightforward one of where to spend an afternoon or an evening, but where we shall spend eternity. It is between life and death. It is that stark. The purpose of this chapter is to persuade you to choose wisdom, and so to choose life, to accept God's invitation and to turn down flat that from the devil. It is as basic as that.

The wholesome invitation of Queen Wisdom (9:1-12)

The preparations she has made (9:1-2)

> **Wisdom** [as in 1:20 a plural of excellence is used] **has**
> **built her house;**
> **she has hewn out its seven pillars.**
> **She has prepared her meat and mixed her wine;**
> **she has also set her table.**

Her preparations are thorough and on a grand scale. She has prepared something large, solid, magnificent and meant to last. She has not simply prepared food and drink; she has built a palace. It is a perfect structure marked by symmetry, stability and beauty. True wisdom is not like the world's shambling, fragmented and contradictory systems. Costly and beautiful, Wisdom's house is solid and unmoveable. Perhaps the wide porch points to grace. An invitation to a banquet certainly does. The food is provided; the guests are simply invited to come and eat.

The use of the past tense points to the preparations that God made in eternity in order that there might be a banquet to which sinners could be invited. It was in eternity that the plans were laid that the Son of God should come from heaven to earth to establish a 'house of God', a temple, the church of God. There was no spontaneous 'Let's have a party tonight.' Preparations began before the world's creation and for long years were in the making as God took Noah, then Abraham, then Jacob and his twelve sons to form the nation of Israel. He brought them out of Egypt by a mighty hand, established them in the promised land and made David king so that, after many setbacks, Messiah might be born in Bethlehem and the gospel preached in all the earth. This was by no means a hastily thrown together affair. It was historic, grand, on a vast scale, the result of detailed planning and intended to be for ever. You cannot miss this. You must not.

The invitation she gives (9:3-6)

In verse 3 we read about the final part of the preparations: **'She has sent out her maids, and she calls from the highest point of the city.'**

First, her **'maids'**, her ladies-in-waiting, are sent out. The male equivalent is given in the more elaborate parable of the wedding banquet. The king 'sent his servants to those who had been invited to the banquet to tell them to come, but they refused to come. Then he sent some more servants and said, "Tell those who have been invited that I have prepared my dinner: My oxen and fattened cattle have been slaughtered, and everything is ready. Come to the wedding banquet… Go to the street corners and invite to the banquet anyone you find"' (Matt. 22:3-4,9). God's servants have gone out into the world as his ambassadors (see 2 Cor. 5:20). 'God in his wisdom said, "I will send them prophets and apostles…"' (Luke 11:49). To this day preachers continue to go out inviting sinners to come in.

The second part of the verse describes how Wisdom herself **'calls from the highest point of the city'**, inviting the simple in. The picture breaks down a little here in that someone who sends out maids does not need to call out herself. However, this is the reality. God's servants preach the message, but he is the one who speaks. Creation and providence are voices that say, 'Come to God.' His sending of Christ and of the Holy Spirit are further calls, as is the Word of God in Scripture. Every time the gospel is faithfully preached the invitation is given once again and God calls.

The message is for **'all who are simple'** and **'to those who lack judgement'** (9:4). In Joseph Hart's words, 'All the fitness he requireth, is to feel your need of him.' It says, **'Come in here! ... Come, eat my food and drink the wine I have mixed'** (9:4,5).All that you need, all that is good, all that will revive you and nourish you is here, ready and waiting. The gospel does not require us to do anything. Everything has been prepared already. There is variety and quality in gospel fare:

> Come, all you who are thirsty,
>   come to the waters;
> and you who have no money,
>   come, buy and eat!
> Come, buy wine and milk
>   without money and without cost.
> Why spend money on what is not bread,
>   and your labour on what does not satisfy?
> Listen, listen to me, and eat what is good,
>   and your soul will delight in the richest of fare
>
> (Isa. 55:1-2).

Jesus said, 'Whoever eats my flesh and drinks my blood has eternal life, and I will raise him up at the last day. For my flesh is real food and my blood is real drink' (John 6:54-55).

Eighteenth-century hymn-writer Anne Steele captures the mood well. She speaks of Mercy but could equally well have her sister Wisdom in mind:

> Ye wretched, hungry starving poor,
> Behold a royal feast! ...

O come and with his children taste
The blessings of his love;
While hope attends the sweet repast
Of nobler joys above.

Proverbs 9:6 has two parts: first, a negative with a promise, and then a positive command.

The negative with a promise

'**Leave your simple ways and you will live.**' We need to repent. We need to turn away from sin. Too long we have walked in simple, naïve, morally deficient ways. We must leave those broad paths that lead to destruction and get on the narrow road that leads to eternal life. Here is almost the final reiteration of this great and fundamental promise.

The positive command

'**Walk in the way of understanding.**' Wisdom calls us from ignorance to 'walk in the way of understanding'. We must trust in Christ and walk with him. We must follow where he leads.

What is your response?

There are only two possible responses to this invitation — rejection or acceptance.

Rejection (9:7-8)

Whoever corrects a mocker invites insult;
whoever rebukes a wicked man incurs abuse.
Do not rebuke a mocker or he will hate you.

I know that mockers, those who refuse to accept correction, who reject wisdom's invitation, will not thank me for writing this. Perhaps there will be complaints. If you refuse a wedding invitation you can write back an abusive letter, you can send a simple apology, or you can ignore it completely. So it is with Christ. We may hurl abuse at Christians, or mock and abuse the Bible. We may reject Christ in a much quieter way. We may try to simply ignore the issue. However, rejection is rejection.

Reception (9:9-12)

How different the wise man, the righteous person in Christ! I know that if I **'rebuke a wise man ... he will love'** me for it. Here is a rebuke — you are a sinner; you have broken God's law; you deserve hell. Some mock at such statements, but the wise accept it. Do you love me for writing such things? Then you are wise. You know you have broken God's law; you know you deserve death, but there is forgiveness through trusting in Christ. Here is wisdom. Come to Christ for it. My aim is to **'instruct a wise man'**, for then **'he will be wiser still'** and to **'teach a righteous man'**, for then **'he will add to his learning'**.

This leads us back to the vital question of what wisdom is. It is no accident that verse 10 (which is very similar to 1:7) comes at the very heart of the chapter: **'The fear of the LORD is the beginning of wisdom, and knowledge of the Holy One is understanding.'** True wisdom begins with **'the fear of the LORD'** — giving reverence, honour and respect to him. To be wise is to know **'the Holy One'** (a phrase used over thirty times in Isaiah but in Proverbs found only here and in 30:3). If we do not know God we cannot know ourselves, and if we do not even know ourselves how can we claim to be wise? To know God we must know the Lord Jesus Christ, who is 'the Holy One' (as Peter confesses in John 6:69; cf. Mark 1:24; Luke 1:35; 4:34; Acts 2:27; 13:35, 1 John 2:20; Rev. 16:5). It is to him we must go.

All who come to Christ receive the reward of everlasting life in him. This is expressed in very concrete terms: **'For through me your days will be many, and years will be added to your life'** (9:11; see the alternative in 9:18). The invitation concludes with a final antithetical summary: **'If you are wise, your wisdom will reward you; if you are a mocker, you alone will suffer'** (9:12).

The positive

Real Spirit-given wisdom brings with it its own rewards, as has been said before. These New Testament texts bring it out: 'To those who by persistence in doing good seek glory, honour and immortality, he will give eternal life' (Rom. 2:7). 'If by the Spirit you put to death the misdeeds of the body, you will live' (Rom. 8:13). 'The one who sows to please the Spirit, from the Spirit will reap eternal life' (Gal. 6:8).

The negative

Mockery will never harm God. It will only bring harm to those who oppose him. Compare the parallel New Testament statements: 'But for those who are self-seeking and who reject the truth and follow evil, there will be wrath and anger' (Rom. 2:8). 'For if you live according to the sinful nature, you will die' (Rom. 8:13). 'The one who sows to please his sinful nature, from that nature will reap destruction' (Gal. 6:8).

(The Greek and Syriac versions of Proverbs have additional material at this point but it does not appear to be authentic.)

The fatal invitation of the woman Folly (9:13-18)

'But what about the other invitation?' you may ask. 'What does Folly have to say?' There is no need for us to draw too much attention to what she says. It would be difficult to ignore it, however, as it is so loud. **'The woman Folly is loud; she is undisciplined and without knowledge'** (9:13). This is Folly — loud, flashy, bold, brassy; rude, impudent, full of cheek; easy-going, unrestrained, disorganized; simplistic, superficial, cheap.

Unlike Queen Wisdom, the woman Folly makes no preparations for the future. She just goes out there and shouts. She does not even bother to stand up. She has a house, but it is unremarkable:

She sits at the door of her house,
   on a seat at the highest point of the city,
calling out to those who pass by,
   who go straight on their way

(9:14-15).

She calls to the same people as Wisdom. You do not have to make a beeline for Dame Folly's house to find her calling you in. She calls from exactly the same place as Queen Wisdom. Daniel Defoe wryly observed that:

Wherever God erects a house of prayer,
The devil surely builds a chapel there
And it is found, upon examination,
The latter has the larger congregation.

Verses 4 and 16 are exactly the same. Both Wisdom and Folly say **'to those who lack judgement'**, **'Let all who are simple come in here!'**

Folly's only problem is that she has nothing to offer. In Christ there is forgiveness, 'love, joy, peace, patience, kindness, goodness, faithfulness, gentleness and self-control' — every blessing. The meat is prepared, the wine is mixed, the table is set. Because Folly has nothing she has to make it all sound very interesting and exciting. She says, **'Stolen water is sweet; food eaten in secret is delicious!'** This is a total lie. There is clearly no wine. Water is free and does not have to be stolen. How could stealing it make it taste any sweeter anyway? (Perhaps there is an allusion to chapter 5). Probably in reality there is no food. That is one reason for wanting you to eat it in secret. If it makes a difference, food is surely more delicious eaten openly with friends rather than in secret. The world always wants to make what it has to offer sound exciting. Hence the lies about the joys of a promiscuous and perverted sex life; the extolling of the supposed joys of the so-called freedom of atheism and humanism; the constant talking up of illicit drugs, alcohol and the thrills of petty and organized crime. The truth is that there is nothing glamorous about serial adulterers, atheists, junkies, drunks and criminals. Sooner or later they end up miserable. (I have never met a genuinely happy atheist.) Liars and the greedy, idlers and those who have 'no time' for God lead increasingly depressing, empty and worthless lives, and to suggest anything different is to fly in the face of the truth. Puritan John Trapp wrote pithily, 'Many eat that on earth that they digest in hell.'

Do not be a fool. Despite the enticing 'come on' there is nothing worth having in the House of Folly. **'But little do they know that the dead are there, that her guests are in the depths of the grave'** (9:18). Every one who accepts her invitation goes to their death.

Not far from where I sit to write this is 195 Melrose Avenue, Cricklewood. In the late 1970s and early 1980s it was the home of Scots-born Dennis Andrew Nilsen, a man who was eventually to have a wax figure of himself in Madame Tussaud's famous chamber of horrors. Over the years that Nilsen lived in Cricklewood many people accepted his invitation to come round to the house. They expected to drink some 'stolen water' and to 'eat in secret'. At least twelve men who accepted his invitation never came out alive. To get rid of the corpses, Nilsen would cut them up on the kitchen floor. Sometimes he would boil flesh off the heads in a pot. He would hide the organs in plastic bags under the floorboards until he could dispose of them. Men would come back there never suspecting that corpses were stowed away in various places. Nilsen would spray the rooms twice a day to be rid of the flies that hatched. Another tenant complained about the smell, but she was assured that the bad odour was a problem with the building decaying.

Martyn Duffey, a homeless sixteen-year-old, accepted Nilsen's invitation to spend the night on 13 May 1980. Nilsen strangled him half dead, then pushed his head into a sink of water. He kept the body in a cupboard for two weeks before putting him under the floorboards. When Duffey entered that house little did he know that the dead were there, that previous guests like him had been killed. If only he had realized!

Some did escape in the nick of time, however. On 11 August 1980 Douglas Stewart was at the house. He later described waking in an armchair to find his feet tied and Nilsen putting a noose round his neck. He fought back, knocking Nilsen over. He was ordered to leave. He escaped by the skin of his teeth.

What a solemn note to end on! Maybe you have been drawn to the house of Folly. Wake up! Realize that you are in mortal danger. Get out before it is too late. Run from folly. Go to the palace of Wisdom. Find safety for ever in Christ.

The vocabulary
Proverbs collected by Solomon (10:1 – 22:16)

The arrangement and classification of the proverbs

With Proverbs 10 we begin on the 'vocabulary' of the book of Proverbs, the proverbs proper. Language vocabularies are presented in various ways — alphabetically, topically, or according to frequency of use. When we learn our mother tongue, however, things are rather less systematic. We do not know how Solomon gathered his material, or why it is in its present order. One imagines him noting down, say, one a day over a period of time, and then rearranging them to some extent. (Alison Le Cornu pictures sages taking pupils 'on a walk around the city' commenting 'on features of life as they occur'.) How many were original? How many were from Israel? How many were from elsewhere? Did he use previous collections? There is no way to be sure of the answers to such questions.

Arrangement

At first, the proverbs seem unrelated, random and in no particular order, but there often seems to be a method at work. It has been claimed that in fact there are about forty groups of proverbs arranged according to general subject matter. Whether or not this is so, sometimes a proverb does appear to relate to a preceding or following one, and at times there are clearly logical sequences over several verses. Certainly, where identical or very similar proverbs are reproduced — which happens at least once within the first collection (10:1 – 22:16) and at least five more times when we include later collections too — this is not evidence of sloppiness, but it is a case of the same proverb, or a similar one, being given a different application.

As everywhere else in Scripture, attention to context is important. For example, the proverb, 'There is a way that seems right to a man, but in the end it leads to death,' appears both in 14:12 and 16:25. In the first case the context is that of being deceived by appearances. In the second, it is that of imparting wisdom to others. Similar differences of context can be seen when we compare 12:11 with 28:19; 18:8 with 26:22; 19:24 with 26:15; 21:9 with 25:24; and 22:3 with 27:12.

Together the proverbs create a picture of what it is to be wise. It is a little like the composition of certain paintings or musical works. At first notes or colours seem haphazard, but slowly certain themes or colours dominate and the work starts to take shape. This arrangement reflects something of the way we acquire wisdom in life. As with the acquisition of language, there is a certain randomness. We then endeavour to systematize. One day we learn a big lesson, the next a few small ones and then, a little later, an old lesson is repeated, or comes home to us in a different way. (Sitting under faithful preaching is similar. However methodical a preacher may aim to be, various factors mean that the systematic learning possible with, say, a beginner's course in woodwork, cannot easily be duplicated in church.) Solomon appears to be artificially recreating life's experience for us, using God-breathed proverbs.

Various attempts have been made to set out the biblical material more systematically. Often helpful in many ways, these efforts tend to be either incomplete, or to sink under a welter of cross-references. This is because true wisdom often defies neat categorization. Solomon's method is far better didactically. It holds the reader's interest well. He is able to hammer away unrelentingly on certain vital themes, but because we never know what is coming next, interest is sustained. Sometimes he is especially 'giving prudence to the simple and knowledge and discretion to the young'. At other times, he helps us in 'understanding words of insight'. At yet other times, he chiefly wants to set us thinking (see the opening verses of Proverbs 1). The chosen method also encourages the drawing together of various threads to form a coherent whole, one of the crucial tasks of wisdom.

Our method in this section of the book will be to present the vocabulary divided, slightly arbitrarily, into more than twenty blocks. In each case we list the vocabulary first with notes, then present it 'conversationally', as it were, to show something of how to use it. At the head of each chapter, I have placed brief reminders of the chief topics in the section.

Classification

To some extent the form of the proverbs is amenable to classification.

Murphy, Alden and others note that in Proverbs 10:1 – 15:33 we have mostly antithetical or *contrasting* proverbs ('on one hand ... but on the other ...'): for example, 'A wise son brings joy to his father, but a foolish son grief to his mother' (10:1).

In 16:1 – 22:16 we find mostly synonymous and synthetic proverbs. In *synonymous* proverbs the first line is repeated in different words: for example, 'A generous man will prosper; he who refreshes others will himself be refreshed' (11:25). 'Honest scales and balances are from the LORD; all the weights in the bag are of his making' (16:11). In *synthetic* proverbs the first line is added to: for example, 'The blessing of the Lord brings wealth, and he adds no trouble to it' (10:22); 'Commit to the Lord whatever you do, and your plans will succeed' (16:3)

We shall note whether a proverb is contrasting, synonymous, or synthetic.

Some are straight *similes*. There are many of these in Proverbs 25-27 but one or two appear earlier: for example, 'As vinegar to the teeth and smoke to the eyes, so is a sluggard to those who send him' (10:26).

With *contrasting* ones we shall usually note the contrast first. Some are simple. For example, 'A wise son brings joy to his father, but a foolish son grief to his mother' (10:1), but others are *complex* (where the antithesis is suppressed in one half and has to be inferred from the other half of the proverb). An example is: 'The wise in heart accept commands, but a chattering fool comes to ruin' (10:8). I have tried to note these.

Some proverbs defy neat categorization and even within categories there can be variation.

A number of entries in the section 10:1 – 22:16 are introduced by an attempt to convey the proverb's meaning succinctly, often using alliteration or rhyme. These are set in a different font for easy identification.

Other notations used are:

A fortiori	Proverbs that use an argument from the greater to the lesser.
Beatitude	Proverbs that contain beatitudes.
Contrast (better than)	Proverbs that employ a contrast using a phrase such as 'better than'.
Command	Proverbs that are in command form. These are in turn designated as either:

(negative)	Proverbial commands framed in a negative way; or,
(positive)	Proverbial commands framed in a positive way.
Lord detests	Proverbs describing what the Lord detests or abhors.

In the Hebrew text the section covering Proverbs 10:1 – 22:16 is headed: 'The proverbs of Solomon'. Some 375 proverbs follow. Interestingly the four letters of the Hebrew name Solomon, taken as a number, add up to 375.

19.
The righteous wise man and the wicked fool

Please read Proverbs 10:1-14

Parents' joy, stolen goods, God's provision, laziness, diligence, blessing, reputation, submissiveness, integrity, guile, righteous speech, hatred, wise speech, increasing wisdom

Proverbs of Solomon

There is an argument for dividing the chapter after verses 9 and 21, but we shall take the first fourteen or fifteen proverbs together.

'A wise son brings joy to his father, but a foolish son grief to his mother' (10:1).
   Contrast: **'wise son' / 'foolish son'**
   Delighted dads; mourning mothers.

The first proverb is appropriate, bearing in mind Solomon's desire to make the simple wise and to enlighten the young. It also relates back to chapters 1-9. Related proverbs are: 'A wise son brings joy to his father, but a foolish man despises his mother' (15:20); and 'The father of a righteous man has great joy; he who has a wise son delights in him' (23:24-25; see also 17:21,25; 19:13; 23:15-16; 29:3).

Here the overall outcome of the son's upbringing is in mind. Positive and negative results are contemplated. If the son proves wise, his father rejoices (his mother too, no doubt!). If he turns out to be a fool, it means grief — a weight of sorrow for his mother (and father!). The contrast focuses on the parents' reactions — joy or grief. It is illustrated in the faces of a proud, smiling father or a tearful, sad mother. A weeping father and smiling mother would make the same point but probably not as well.

Picture the prodigal's father longing for his son's return, Eli remonstrating with his wayward sons, David weeping for Absalom. Or, better still, think of Rebekah's tears over Esau, or Monica weeping for an unconverted Augustine. Similarly, picture Hannah's joy when greeting Samuel at Shiloh and hearing good reports from Eli, Bathsheba's delighting in Solomon at the height of his glory, or Mrs Spurgeon's joy at learning of her son Charles' conversion. Better still, think of Jacob being presented to Pharaoh by Joseph, of the prodigal's father as he receives his son back; and even, to take the supreme example, of the Father looking on the Son with complacency and declaring, 'This is my Son, whom I love; with him I am well pleased.'

The appeal is chiefly to a young person's love for his (or her) parents. Do you really want to grieve your mother? Do you want to make your father glad? Then be wise. Take heed of this book. For the Christian, the question is: 'Do we want to grieve the Spirit, or give joy to the Lord?'

There is a word for parents too: what sort of child do you want? We smile at the foolish antics of toddlers and teenagers, but do we want our children to grow up to be fools? Have we contemplated the grief ahead if our offspring make moral shipwreck? Are we ready, then, to take steps to teach them wisdom?

No man is an island. Each affects the other. Do you long to see young people attaining wisdom and rejecting foolishness? Parents, teachers, ministers, politicians, those in the public eye — all have an impact. Are we cultivating wisdom?

The proverbs that immediately follow urge the son to choose righteousness over wickedness, diligence over laziness, wisdom over foolishness.

'Ill-gotten treasures are of no value, but righteousness delivers from death' (10:2).
Contrast: **'ill-gotten treasures'** / **'righteousness'**
Tawdry treasure; delivered from death.

This is like Proverbs 11:4 (see also 12:28; 23:5). There is a related proverb in Jeremiah:

> Like a partridge that hatches eggs it did not lay
>   is the man who gains riches by unjust means.
> When his life is half gone, they will desert him,
>   and in the end he will prove to be a fool
>   (Jer. 17:11).

Here **'ill-gotten'** wealth is in mind. Despite appearances, it is **'of no value'**, but, on the other hand, **'righteousness delivers from death'**. **'Treasures'** include anything this world values — money, possessions and less tangible things, such as fame or influence. If the treasure is of a wicked sort, the result of sin ('ill-gotten') even though it may appear to be worth having, it is in fact valueless and cannot benefit anyone. Think of an imprisoned bank-robber unable to enjoy the proceeds of his crime, of a boy suffering an upset stomach as a result of eating stolen crab apples, or of an actor at the height of fame but with no friends. Scriptural examples are Achan, whose covetousness brings disaster (Josh. 7); Ahab who, on taking possession of Naboth's field, is told that, in the same place where dogs licked up Naboth's blood, they will lick up his own blood (1 Kings 21:19); Gehazi who is struck with leprosy (2 Kings 5:20-27); Judas Iscariot, filled with remorse, throwing away his reward in disgust.

The contrast is with **'righteousness'**, a key term in Proverbs and throughout Scripture. It encompasses justice and goodness, and in the final analysis refers to being right with God. To be 'righteous' is to keep his law. Ultimately, this is possible only through faith in Christ. Only by trusting in him is justification, or legal righteousness, possible. Only by faith in him is sanctification, or actual righteousness, possible too. No sort of worldly wealth can save. Only righteousness **'delivers from death'**. When the building is burning around you, money in the bank or in your hand is useless. The only hope is to find the escape route. So, in this world, the only escape is to 'be found in him, not having a righteousness of my own that comes from the law, but that which is through faith in Christ' (Phil. 3:9). It was Christ's righteousness that kept him from decay in the grave: 'But God raised him from the dead, freeing him from the agony of death, because it was impossible for death to keep its hold on him' (Acts 2:24). And it is trust in him that saves us: 'I tell you the truth, if anyone keeps my word, he will never see death' (John 8:51).

The prophets underline these truths. Amos warns those 'who hoard plunder and loot in their fortresses' that 'An enemy ... will pull down your strongholds and plunder your fortresses' (Amos 3:10,11), which is what happened.

> Woe to him who builds his palace by unrighteousness,
>   his upper rooms by injustice,
> making his countrymen work for nothing,
>   not paying them for their labour
>
> (Jer. 22:13).

Such things were happening in Jeremiah's day, in contrast to the attitude of the previous generation. The latter 'did what was right and just, so all went well'. In faith, they 'defended the cause of the poor and needy, and so all went well' (Jer. 22:15,16).

Habakkuk says, 'The righteous will live by his faith' (Hab. 2:4). A well-known verse, it comes in the context of warnings to greedy Babylonians that woe comes 'to him who piles up stolen goods and makes himself wealthy by extortion'. Those he has plundered will 'suddenly arise' and the tables will be turned (Hab. 2:6-8).

In James 5:1-4 rich unbelievers are berated and told to 'weep and wail because of the misery that is coming upon you'.

'The LORD does not let the [literally, 'the soul of the'] **righteous go hungry but he thwarts the craving of the wicked'** (10:3).
> *Contrast:* **'righteous' / 'wicked'**
> The righteous rewarded; wrongdoers repulsed.

Righteous and wicked are constantly contrasted in Proverbs. For example, 'When calamity comes, the wicked are brought down, but even in death the righteous have a refuge' (14:32). The same kind of thing is found in the Psalms:

> Better the little that the righteous have
> > than the wealth of many wicked;
> for the power of the wicked will be broken,
> > but the LORD upholds the righteous
> > > > > (Ps. 37:16-17).

Some suggest taking verses 2 and 3 together to form a chiastic couplet, in which line 1 matches line 4 and line 2 parallels line 3:

Ill-gotten treasures	are of no value.
The craving of the wicked	he thwarts.
Righteousness	delivers from death.
The righteous	the LORD does not let go hungry.

There are definitely parallels and the verses amplify each other. The wicked gain their treasure unlawfully and end up with a mouth full of dust because the Lord thwarts their cravings. The righteous are delivered from death because he feeds them with the finest of wheat. The second proverb is more personal, speaking of **'the wicked'** rather than 'ill-gotten treasures', and of **'the righteous'** rather than 'righteousness'.

Here is the first reference in this section to **'the LORD'**, Israel's covenant God. It is no impersonal law that makes 'ill-gotten treasures … of no value' and 'righteousness' a deliverer 'from death'. It is the Lord who **'does not let the righteous go hungry'** and **'thwarts the craving of the wicked'**.

So here is a promise, or encouragement, and a warning, or censure. The promise is for **'the righteous'**. These, we have suggested, are those with faith in Christ and who show it in obedience to God. The Lord will not let them hunger; he satisfies them. The Bible is full of such wonderful promises. For example:

> … the eyes of the LORD are on those who fear him,
>   on those whose hope is in his unfailing love,
> to deliver them from death
>   and keep them alive in famine
>
> (Ps. 33:18-19).

> Fear the LORD, you his saints,
>   for those who fear him lack nothing.
> The lions may grow weak and hungry,
>   but those who seek the LORD lack no good thing
>
> (Ps. 34:9-10).

I was young and now I am old,
　yet I have never seen the righteous forsaken
　or their children begging bread
　　　　　(Ps. 37:25; cf. 37:18-19; Isa. 33:16).

In the New Testament we read, 'Blessed are those who hunger and thirst for righteousness, for they will be filled' (Matt. 5:6); 'Do not worry, saying, "What shall we eat?" or "What shall we drink?" or "What shall we wear?"... But seek first [God's] kingdom and his righteousness, and all these things will be given to you as well' (Matt. 6:31-33); 'My God will meet all your needs according to his glorious riches in Christ Jesus' (Phil. 4:19; cf. Heb. 13:5-6).

Temporally, Christians may lack at times, but never in real terms, for Christ their Shepherd leads them to green pastures and they feed on him, the Bread of life. Mature believers testify to having 'learned the secret of being content in any and every situation, whether well fed or hungry, whether living in plenty or in want'. They 'can do everything through him who gives [them] strength' (Phil. 4:12,13). Perhaps one of the most outstanding demonstrations of this truth is the story of the nineteenth-century orphanage founder George Müller. Again and again Müller found God providing in the most desperate of circumstances.

The warning is directed at **'the wicked'** who are without faith or regard for God's law. Their desires, their wicked **'craving'**, the Lord will thwart. He will thrust it out. It will all come to nothing. Having said that, we must not make the mistake of Job's friends and suppose that the wicked are always thwarted immediately. However, what is said here is always true spiritually and eternally, and is often seen even in this life.

Lazy hands make a man poor,
**   but diligent hands bring wealth.**

He who gathers crops in summer is a wise son,
   but he who sleeps during harvest is a disgraceful
   son

   (10:4-5).

Contrast: **'Lazy hands'** / **'diligent hands'**; **'wise son'** /
'disgraceful son'
Laziness leads to loss; diligence delivers delight;
Reapers and sleepers.

Here are the first of several proverbs on laziness and diligence.
It is a double proverb, or a pair of proverbs. First, there is a
warning: negatively, laziness (slackness) is likely to lead to
poverty. Positively, diligence (being keen, sharp) is likely to
lead to wealth. **'Lazy'** can be translated 'deceitful'. The two
go together. People try to hide their lazy ways, even from
themselves. Laziness itself also brings a false sense of security. **'A wise son'**, one who succeeds, is one **'who gathers
crops'** at the right time, **'in summer'**, while **'a disgraceful
son'** misses his opportunity and **'sleeps during harvest'**. This
second proverb takes us from the general point (diligence brings
its own rewards) to a narrower one: make the most of every
opportunity. We need not only to work hard, but also to do so
at the right time. Ecclesiastes 9:10 puts it bluntly: 'Whatever
your hand finds to do, do it with all your might, for in the
grave, where you are going, there is neither working nor planning nor knowledge nor wisdom.'

Already the call has gone out: 'Go to the ant … consider
its ways and be wise!' (6:6) The warning in that passage is the
same as here:

A little sleep, a little slumber,
   a little folding of the hands to rest —
and poverty will come on you…

   (6:10-11).

Part of the point of this imagery is that, as Proverbs 30:25 reminds us, ants, though 'creatures of little strength ... store up their food in the summer' — when they have the opportunity. The more general principle is repeated, word for word, in 24:30-34 (for similar proverbs to 10:4 see 12:24; 13:4; 20:13; cf. 18:9; 19:15; 20:4). A particularly vivid description is found in Ecclesiastes 10:18: 'If a man is lazy, the rafters sag; if his hands are idle, the house leaks.'

If verse 3 (like 10:22) emphasizes God's sovereignty, these verses are just as clear on human responsibility. People can be poor for various reasons, but if you are lazy, do not be surprised at your poverty. At times people use 'spiritual' arguments to excuse laziness. In Thessalonica in Paul's day some were saying, 'Christ is coming, so there's no point working. We'll live off what rich members provide.' Paul would have none of it. He commanded the others to steer clear of idle Christians and reminded them all of his own example — how hard he and his companions had worked so as not to be a burden. This was done 'in order to make ourselves a model for you to follow'. He had given a simple rule: 'If a man will not work, he shall not eat.' He concludes: 'We hear that some among you are idle. They are not busy; they are busybodies. Such people we command and urge in the Lord Jesus Christ to settle down and earn the bread they eat' (2 Thess. 3:6-12). This is in line with Ephesians 4:28.

As so often, these proverbs speak in terms of this world but have a clear spiritual application. Ancient Israelites were more aware of their dependence on the changing seasons than many of us are today, but there are still seasons in life. In the summertime of life especially, we need to seize opportunities. 'Remember your Creator in the days of your youth' (Eccles. 12:1). More generally:

Seek the LORD while he may be found;
    call on him while he is near.

> Let the wicked forsake his way
> and the evil man his thoughts…
>
> (Isa. 55:6-7).

Paul strikes the same note when he writes, 'Now is the time of God's favour, now is the day of salvation' (2 Cor. 6:2). How tragic to have to say:

> The harvest is past,
> the summer has ended,
> and we are not saved
>
> (Jer. 8:20).

The call to 'gather crops', rather than sleeping, has a definite gospel thrust. Becoming a Christian is very much a matter of reaping what has been sown. Effort is involved, but the work itself is complete. It is a matter of reaping. How tragic to let laziness rob you of what Christ gave! How slow we all are to take what God has already given!

Remember that it is written of Christ that 'Zeal for your house will consume me' (John 2:17, quoting Ps. 69:9).

Blessings crown the head of the righteous,
but violence overwhelms the mouth of the wicked.
The memory of the righteous will be a blessing,
but the name of the wicked will rot

(10:6-7).

Contrast: **'head of the righteous'** / **'mouth of the wicked'**;
'memory of the righteous' / **'name of the wicked'**
Beatitude
Righteous heads blessed, wicked mouths blasted;
Marvellous memories; rotten reminders.

Some translate the second line of verses 6 and 11: 'but the mouth of the wicked conceals violence'. This is possible but less likely. So the point is that the **'righteous'** have their heads crowned with blessings now and their memory will be a blessing in the future. The **'wicked'** have their mouths overwhelmed with violence now and their name will rot in the future.

'Blessings crown the head of the righteous.' This is the first of some ten beatitudes in the proverbs proper (see 11:26; 14:21; 16:20; 20:7; 22:9; 24:25; 28:14,20; 29:18; cf., in the earlier chapters, 3:13,18,33; 5:18; 8:32,34). It is the just and generous man who fears the Lord and trusts in him who is blessed.

The blessings are unspecified but must include (to use this world's terms) honour, respect, love, devotion, influence, success and wealth. In terms of Deuteronomy 28 it is being 'blessed in the city and blessed in the country', being 'blessed when you come in and blessed when you go out'. We are thinking of thriving families, abundant crops, plenty of livestock, a surplus to eat, victory over enemies leading to peace, enough to lend to others; being 'the head, not the tail'. Those who are righteous also leave behind their good example and any material goods accrued. Those who follow have something to be proud of, something to live up to: 'A righteous man will be remembered for ever' (Ps. 112:6).

In spiritual terms, the righteous know God's blessing in this life (as Deuteronomy says) by being God's holy people. Their sins are forgiven; they enjoy peace with God, communion with him as sons, answers to prayer and the joy of walking with him. These blessings go on beyond death as they meet with Christ and enter heaven itself to enjoy its delights. Their godly influence also continues to work itself out as their prayers, witness and other godly labours bear fruit in the rising generations. Think of the impact some who are long dead still have to this day through their writings, or through institutions they have helped to found. Obvious biblical examples include Mary, Jesus' mother, who said, 'From now on all generations will call me blessed' (Luke 1:48); and the woman who anointed Jesus at Bethany, of whom he prophesied, 'I tell you the truth, wherever the gospel is preached throughout the world, what she has done will also be told, in memory of her' (Mark 14:9). Supremely there is Christ himself, who was made 'a little lower than the angels' but God 'crowned him with glory and honour' (Heb. 2:7).

As for the wicked, whose lies and curses do so much damage, eventually all turns against them and their mouths are covered with shame. Think of Haman's face being covered as he was taken to be executed (Esth. 7:8). The wicked are eventually silenced and blaspheme no more. Like the builders of the Tower of Babel, who tried hard to make a name for themselves, even the names of the wicked are forgotten, or remembered only with horror, after they die — just as they themselves rot in hell.

Of course, these are generalizations and one can think of wicked people who apparently do well in this life, and of righteous people who know what it is to be persecuted, marginalized and forgotten. There is also a perverse fondness in some quarters for the memory of a Hitler or a Marquis de Sade, while heroes of the faith are largely forgotten. How many walk along London's Shaftesbury Avenue to the statue of Eros in Piccadilly Circus but know nothing of the godly earl whose name both statue and street recall? What do we know of those who first evangelized the British Isles? No one knows the name of the Primitive Methodist through whom Spurgeon was converted, or the preacher used to bring the great Puritan John Owen to assurance. We comfort ourselves, however, with the realization that the names of the faithful are written in heaven — in the Lamb's book of life. That matters more than anything else. None is missing. Is your name there?

'The wise in heart accept commands, but a chattering fool comes to ruin' (10:8).

Contrast (complex): **'the wise in heart'** / **'a chattering fool'**

It does not say, 'The wise in heart accept commands, but a chattering fool *does not*', or 'The wise in heart *will know success* but a chattering fool comes to ruin.' Rather the two thoughts are combined in a proverb that, like others, reminds us that things are not always what they seem. Here, to quote F. C. Cook, 'Inward self-contained wisdom is contrasted with self-exposed folly.' The silent but wise one is willing to listen. Like Isaiah's Messianic Servant he can say:

> The Sovereign LORD has given me an instructed tongue,
>   to know the word that sustains the weary.
> He wakens me morning by morning,
>   wakens my ear to listen like one being taught
>
>   (Isa. 50:4).

He accepts God's commands, whether direct or indirect. Picture an obedient child, a submissive wife, an uncomplicated Bible believer.

Then there is the **'chattering fool'**. Picture in your imagination Jack, a boy who cheekily answers back; Nora, who is a nagging wife; Ted, an unbeliever never stuck for a retort; or a so-called 'expert' called Piers who has a hundred reasons for not believing the Bible. They are too full of themselves to listen to anyone. We can sometimes find the first group unattractive and be drawn to the second, but the chattering fool is all talk. He **'comes to ruin'** in the end — sometimes in this life, though not always. In the life to come, the wise will certainly be rewarded and moral fools will be beaten down. Proverbs 18:6-7 makes a similar point. What matters is not how much you have to say for yourself, but a submissive heart that understands and accepts God's commands. A teachable spirit is vital if we are ever to be wise. Real Christianity is not a matter of talk, but obedience to God's commands (see 1 John). With Charles Bridges I must 'look at this picture as a beacon against the folly of my own heart'.

'The man of integrity walks securely, but he who takes crooked paths will be found out' (10:9).
Contrast: **'man of integrity'** / **'he who takes crooked paths'**
Integrity means security; deviance, discovery.

The former **'walks securely'**, but whether the latter feels secure or not, he **'will be found out'** (this is similar to 28:18). This proverb can be rendered: 'He who walks uprightly walks securely, but he who deviates from the road will be discovered.' The figure is a favourite — that of a journey, one that involves taking a specific route.

Here is a man who takes the straightforward route. It may be dangerous, but he is not afraid. Though he walks through the darkest valley, he fears no evil, for God is with him; his encouragements and chastisements comfort him and keep him going to the end. He is sure he will be safe. Christ as ever is the supreme example. He 'resolutely set out for Jerusalem' (Luke 9:51).

Here, on the other hand, is a man who knows a short cut, a winding path that seems quicker but is unauthorized. At some point on the journey his deception is discovered and he is disqualified.

Isaiah says something very similar:

He who walks righteously
    and speaks what is right …
this is the man who will dwell on the heights,

    whose refuge will be the mountain fortress.
His bread will be supplied,
    and water will not fail him

                            (Isa. 33:15-16).

Real security is found in sticking to the right path — the narrow road to life eternal. Those who follow crooked paths are eventually found out. Think of a child whose mother finds a half-eaten cake; a bigamist when wife number one realizes; an embezzler when someone discovers the figures do not add up. 'You may be sure that your sin will find you out' (Num. 32:23*)*. Even if we get away with it in this life, 'There is nothing concealed that will not be disclosed, or hidden that will not be made known' (Luke 12:2). 'The Lord ... will bring to light what is hidden in darkness and will expose the motives of men's hearts. At that time each will receive his praise [or condemnation] from God' (1 Cor. 4:5).

'He who winks maliciously causes grief, and a chattering fool comes to ruin' (10:10).
    Synthetic: **'winks maliciously'** / **'chattering fool'**
    Here are Winky and Prattly.

The second part of verse 10 reproduces that of verse 8. It has been suggested that this is due to dittography — a copyist supplying what he thought was missing from verse 10. The Septuagint supplies its own conclusion: 'He who winks the eye causes trouble, but he who boldly reproves makes peace' (see RSV). The idea, if correct, is that overlooking evil may seem the easy option, but it leads to trouble in the end, whereas taking the bull by the horns and boldly reproving sin leads ultimately to lasting peace.

    If we follow the NIV translation the verse is a warning that, while it is true that the chattering fool comes to ruin, not all silent types are men of integrity. There are people out there who, though they do not chatter like fools, are not only ruining themselves but will do us harm too if we are not careful. Matthew Henry warns, 'The dog that bites is not always the dog that barks.' We have already been warned about this sort of scoundrel in Proverbs 6:13. He is a man who may not appear to be evil at first sight. He certainly says nothing incriminating. Indeed, he says very little. A malicious wink is all he needs to see his evil deeds carried out. It is a frightening and sinister picture, one we have perhaps seen portrayed in gangster movies. The godfather nods to his henchmen and, off screen, the offender is brutally liquidated. It is a reminder that much grief in this world is caused by a largely silent minority who carry on their nefarious lives with a nod and a wink and little else to give them away. The **'chattering fool'** is noisier than the one who **'winks maliciously'**, but both are wicked. Like the psalmist we should pray that the Lord would not let such enemies gloat over us, or let 'those who hate [us] without reason maliciously wink the eye' (Ps. 35:19).

'The mouth of the righteous is a fountain of life, but violence overwhelms the mouth of the wicked'(10:11).
> *Contrast (complex):* **'righteous'** / **'wicked'**
> Vitality and violence.

The second part of this verse again reproduces that of an earlier one (10:6). That verse draws a contrast between the 'head' of the righteous and the 'mouth' of the wicked. Here it is closer still — between the **'mouth'** of each. One is **'a fountain of life'**; the other is overwhelmed by **'violence'**. A 'fountain of life' suggests a gushing spring, both lively and life-giving. In a land where water could be scarce, springs or fountains were especially appreciated. Fresh, bubbling water is much more refreshing than stale, stagnant water.

The same idea surfaces at several points and in different forms in Proverbs (see 16:22; 18:4). In 14:27 we are taken a step further back: 'The fear of the LORD is a fountain of life, turning a man from the snares of death.' Other Scriptures take us right back to the source: 'For with you is the fountain of life; in your light we see light' (Ps. 36:9). Jeremiah refers to God as 'the spring of living water'. He talks of the shame coming on those who forsake 'the LORD, the spring of living water' (Jer. 17:13). Elsewhere God speaks of Israel's 'two sins':

> They have forsaken me,
>   the spring of living water,
> and have dug their own cisterns,
>   broken cisterns that cannot hold water
>
> (Jer. 2:13).

This, then, is the background to verses such as Proverbs 10:11 or 13:14. Using different pictures, other proverbs convey a similar idea: 'The lips of the righteous nourish many' (10:21); 'The lips of the wise spread knowledge' (15:7).

Ezekiel 47 has a wonderful vision of a river flowing from God's throne, and in Revelation 22 it is 'the river of the water of life' that flows through paradise. Life and peace flow from God to all, and through all, who are righteous in Christ. This comes about, we know from elsewhere in Scripture, through the Spirit's work.

It may be Scriptures like those quoted above that Jesus has in mind when he says, 'Whoever believes in me, as the Scripture has said, streams of living water will flow from within him.' John explains that this was a reference to the Spirit whom believers were to receive after Jesus was glorified (John 7:38,39). In an earlier passage Jesus says, 'Whoever drinks the water I give him will never thirst. Indeed, the water I give him will become in him a spring of water welling up to eternal life' (John 4:14). It is the Spirit within who enables the righteous to speak words of life and peace.

To be 'overwhelmed' by **'violence'** suggests a mouth full of violent speech that eventually sinks under its own weight. The wicked preach violence of one sort or another and often in this life suffer the violence they themselves promote. Jesus reminds us, 'All who draw the sword will die by the sword' (Matt. 26:52). Eventually, such violent men will be silenced at the judgement and driven out. The violence of the mouths of many is tempered by common grace but, at times, frighteningly, it breaks out.

The words of the righteous, on the other hand, promote life — not only earthly life, as they speak up for the vulnerable and neglected, but also eternal life, as they declare the good news about Christ. In line with this, New Testament believers have the straightforward command: 'Do not let any unwholesome talk come out of your mouths, but only what is helpful for building others up according to their needs, that it may benefit those who listen' (Eph. 4:29). We must never underestimate the power of words to do harm or good.

'I tell you that men will have to give account on the day of judgement for every careless word they have spoken. For by your words you will be acquitted, and by your words you will be condemned' (Matt. 12:36-37). 'For out of the overflow of the heart the mouth speaks. The good man brings good things out of the good stored up in him, and the evil man brings evil things out of the evil stored up in him' (Matt. 12:34-35).

James's warnings about the tongue are well known.

'Hatred stirs up dissension, but love covers over all wrongs' (10:12).

Contrast: **'hatred'** / **'love'**

Hate reveals; love conceals.

One **'stirs up dissension'**; the other **'covers over all wrongs'**. One is a troublemaker; the other a peacemaker. Where there is hatred trouble is bound to ensue, but where there is love wrongs can be covered over — not in the sense of perverting justice but as in 17:9. Peter takes up this side of it (probably quoting this verse): 'Above all, love each other deeply, because love covers over a multitude of sins' (1 Peter 4:8).

Here are two characters. One is filled with hate. Because of that he always criticizes others, harps on their failures, picks them up on the slightest thing. Dissension and strife are inevitable. The other is full of love. As far as his own sins are concerned, no doubt he accepts that 'He who conceals his sins does not prosper, but whoever confesses and renounces them finds mercy' (28:13). In the case of others, he does not look for faults. Where there is failure he draws no attention to it. He does not keep reminding people of it. As soon as ever he can, he forgives and forgets (see 1 Cor. 13). This is part of wisdom (see 19:11 on overlooking offences). Think of Joseph speaking to his treacherous brothers after Jacob's death. They expected revenge but he says, ' "You intended to harm me, but God intended it for good to accomplish what is now being done, the saving of many lives. So then, don't be afraid. I will provide for you and your children." And he reassured them and spoke kindly to them' (Gen. 50:20-21).

This is the New Testament attitude: love your enemies; forgive all; live at peace with others as far as possible; there is to be no vengeance; overcome evil with good; show kindness and compassion to all (Matt. 5:44; Rom. 12:9-21; Eph. 4:32). If we know anything of love and forgiveness in Christ, then we will want to put an end to all hatred and do all we legitimately can to cover sin.

Wisdom is found on the lips of the discerning,
    but a rod is for the back of him who lacks judgement.

**Wise men store up knowledge,
but the mouth of a fool invites ruin**

(10:13-14).

Contrast (complex): **'the discerning'** (one with understanding) / **'him who lacks judgement'** (literally, 'him who lacks a heart', i.e. understanding); **'wise men'** / **'a fool'**
Retentive or rash?

The book of Proverbs makes many references to speech (the nearest to this is 10:21). Not pedestrian, this verse considers the **'lips'** of the one and the **'back'** of the other. On **'the lips of the discerning'** one finds **'wisdom'**; on **'the back of him who lacks judgement'** one finds **'a rod'**! In other words, find someone discerning and you will hear wisdom; listen to someone who lacks judgement and you will gain nothing. Such a person deserves a beating. (If you lack judgement that means you!) Derek Kidner sums up pithily: 'man — God's mouthpiece or God's mule'. He reminds us of the passage in the Psalms which says:

> I will instruct you and teach you in the way you should
>   go;
> I will counsel you and watch over you.
> Do not be like the horse or the mule,
>   which have no understanding
> but must be controlled by bit and bridle
>   or they will not come to you
>
> (Ps. 32:8-9).

Wise men **'store up knowledge'**; a fool **'invites ruin'**, or draws near to it. This proverb does not make the obvious comparison: 'Wise men store up knowledge, but *fools do not*'; or *'Unlike the mouth of the wise man*, the mouth of a fool invites ruin.' Rather, the two thoughts are combined. We see, on the one hand, a wise man gathering information and hoarding it so that his knowledge database grows and what he says is increasingly wise; and, on the other, a fool neglecting knowledge, and so saying what is foolish and courting ruin. We have already quoted Matthew 12:34-35. Proverbs 21:20 tells us, 'In the house of the wise are stores of choice food and oil, but a foolish man devours all he has.' This prior difference is what leads to the contrast between the way that the two speak.

What these fourteen, or fifteen, proverbs teach us

What God desires from us

It is the wise, righteous, diligent and loving who are spoken of favourably here. God wants us to be all those things.

Wise

The wise son brings joy to his father (10:1). The wise in heart are willing to accept commands (10:8). The discerning escape the rod (10:13). Wise men store up knowledge and escape ruin (10:14).

Righteous

It is righteousness that delivers from death (10:2). It is the righteous whom the Lord does not leave hungry (10:3). Blessings crown their heads and their memory will be a blessing (10:6-7). The man of integrity walks securely (10:9), and by means of what he says the righteous man is a fountain of life (10:11).

Diligent

Diligent hands bring wealth (10:4). He who gathers crops in summer is a wise son (10:5).

Loving

Love covers over all wrongs (10:12). Love is a vital Christian virtue alongside wisdom, righteousness and diligence.

What God opposes in us

Negatively, it is equally clear that God opposes those who are foolish, wicked, lazy and hateful.

Foolish

The foolish son is a grief to his mother (10:1). A chattering fool comes to ruin (10:8,10). He who lacks judgement is likely to be beaten (10:13). The mouth of a fool invites ruin (10:14).

Wicked

God thwarts the craving of the wicked (10:3). Violence overwhelms the wicked man's man mouth (10:6,11). His name will rot (10:7). He takes crooked paths but will be found out (10:9).

Lazy

Lazy hands make a man poor (10:4). If you sleep during harvest you are a disgraceful son (10:5).

Hateful

Those who are hateful stir up dissension (10:12).

The character of unbelief

The wicked fool sleeps during harvest, has ill-gotten treasures which are of no real value, invites poverty and ruin by his actions, and stirs up dissension. He brings grief to others and a rod to his own back. His craving will be thwarted; his crooked ways found out. Violence will overwhelm him and his name will rot.

The character of belief

The righteous wise man brings joy to his father, takes his opportunities by working hard, accepts God's commands, stores up knowledge within, speaks wisely, hides the mistakes made by others, always prospers. He will walk securely and be a fountain of life through his words. He will never hunger, but will be delivered from death and crowned with blessings. Even the memory of him will be a blessing.

20.
Life or punishment — which will be your pay?

Please read Proverbs 10:15-32

Security, income, obedience, hatred, verbose speech, pure speech, edifying speech, God's blessing, pleasures, dreads and desires, after the storm, sluggards, God-fearers, prospects, God's way, durability, wise speech, fitting speech

Here another eighteen proverbs touch on themes already broached, such as the tongue, and several new ones.

'The wealth of the rich is their fortified city, but poverty is the ruin of the poor' (10:15).
> *Contrast:* **'wealth'** / **'poverty'**
> Riches protect; poverty ruins.

For **'the rich'**, **'wealth … is their fortified city'**; for **'the poor'**, **'poverty'** is their **'ruin'**. One of several proverbs on wealth and poverty (see especially 22:7), this is the first of a number of observational proverbs, describing life as it is without overt moral teaching or guidance. The teaching in such proverbs comes from spiritually applying the pictures they paint.

Heavenly wisdom

The reality of life is that if you are rich you have a certain amount of protection against some of life's troubles: you can eat better, live more comfortably, give generously and worry less about certain things. If you are poor, it is different. Food and comforts are scarcer; you may be tempted to steal; you have greater everyday worries. Away with romantic notions of poverty! To a large degree, we do not decide how rich or poor we are, but the observation is that poverty ruins the poor and wealth is like a fortified city. It is a proverb designed to set us thinking, one of the book's set purposes.

On one hand, the danger for the wealthy is to rely on riches. That is implied more strongly in a similar proverb (18:11). The psalmist speaks of God's judgement on 'the man who did not make God his stronghold but trusted in his great wealth and grew strong by destroying others' (Ps. 52:7-8). Jeremiah 9:23-24 is apposite:

Let not the wise man boast of his wisdom
    or the strong man boast of his strength
    or the rich man boast of his riches,
but let him who boasts boast about this:
    that he understands and knows me,
that I am the LORD ....

We must not be like the rich farmer who told himself, 'You have plenty of good things laid up for many years. Take life easy; eat, drink and be merry' (Luke 12:19). Judgement Day will come sooner than we expect. The New Testament teaches that 'those who are rich in this present world' must 'not ... be arrogant nor ... put their hope in wealth, which is so uncertain, but ... put their hope in God, who richly provides us with everything for our enjoyment' (1 Tim. 6:17).

On the other hand, it is important to recognize that what **'ruins the poor'** is **'poverty'**, not necessarily any other defect.

It is wrong to assume that all poor people are lazy, wicked in some way, or under God's judgement. No, it is their poverty that brings them down. If that could be relieved things might be very different. The poor have no protection. It is the duty of the strong to defend and care for them. To despise the poor because they are poor is wicked (see 17:5; 22:22-23). James 2:5 says that God has 'chosen those who are poor in the eyes of the world to be rich in faith and to inherit the kingdom he promised those who love him'. James 1:9-10 urges 'the brother in humble circumstances ... to take pride in his high position. But the one who is rich should take pride in his low position, because he will pass away like a wild flower.'

Of course, if we have treasure in heaven then we have an impregnable source of safety there. In coming to this earth Christ left the fortified city of heaven and, for the sake of his people, 'became poor, so that [they] through his poverty might become rich' (2 Cor. 8:9).

'The wages of the righteous bring them life, but the income of the wicked brings them punishment' (10:16).

Contrast: **'wages of the righteous'** / **'income of the wicked'**

Righteous wages mean preservation; wicked receipts mean punishment.

This proverb balances the previous one by emphasizing that the income that really matters is not material. **'The righteous'** receive **'life'**; **'the wicked ... punishment'** (rather than sin) in return. This is a straightforward reminder that, although the wicked think that they are gaining all sorts of good things, they only gain 'punishment' in the end. The righteous, however materially poor they may be, receive wages far greater than any earthly ones — life itself. In practical terms, the wicked gain income by various, often dubious, means, such as cheating, stealing and gambling. They then squander their wealth in various self-indulgent ways that deserve punishment. The righteous earn their wages honestly and use them to forward life by helping their family, God's people, the needy, etc.

Paul's statement in Romans 6:23 that 'The wages of sin is death, but the gift of God is eternal life in Christ Jesus our Lord' clearly relies on this proverb (see also 9:10-12; 11:18). 'Wages' in the first part becomes 'gift' in the second to emphasize God's grace — removing any suggestion that salvation is earned. Jesus was quite willing to speak in terms of work at times: 'Do not work for food that spoils, but for food that endures to eternal life'; but he does add, 'which the Son of Man will *give* you' (John 6:27). The implication of the proverb is that the issue is not how much money we have, but, rather, what we do with it. Are we using what we have for righteous ends? Paul touches on this in Galatians 6:7-9: 'Do not be deceived: God cannot be mocked. A man reaps what he sows. The one who sows to please his sinful nature, from that nature will reap destruction; the one who sows to please the Spirit, from the Spirit will reap eternal life.' He concludes, 'Let us not become weary in doing good, for at the proper time we will reap a harvest if we do not give up.'

'He who heeds discipline shows the way to life, but whoever ignores correction leads others astray' (10:17).

Contrast: **'he who heeds discipline'** / **'whoever ignores correction'**

The focus is on the effect that such attitudes have on others. The former **'shows the way to life'**; the latter **'leads others astray'**. Later similar proverbs are either more general or focus on the harm inflicted on oneself by the failure to heed correction (see 12:1; 15:10; 29:1).

It is not easy to accept correction, but by doing so we not only help ourselves but others too. St Basil recommended receiving a rebuke like medicine — with the desire to get better. Most obviously, if we go wrong because we do not listen, then others are likely to go wrong too. If the teacher ignores the textbook, the whole class is misled. Further, the benefit in accepting discipline from others is not only found in the needful correction of our own ideas, but also in the humility that comes from realizing that we do not have all the answers. If we give the impression that we know it all, we tempt others to take the same attitude. A teacher who professes to know it all, a parent or preacher who thinks he never makes mistakes and a Christian who can learn nothing new are dangerous people! How different was the Lord Jesus who, though perfect, always showed a humble, even teachable spirit, especially as a boy but also as a man! He himself is indeed the way to life. If we give the impression that the road to heaven is easy, we do others a great disservice.

> **He who conceals his hatred has lying lips,**
> **and whoever spreads slander is a fool.**
> **When words are many, sin is not absent,**
> **but he who holds his tongue is wise.**
> **The tongue of the righteous is choice silver,**
> **but the heart of the wicked is of little value.**
> **The lips of the righteous nourish many,**
> **but fools die for lack of judgement**
>
> (10:18-21).

In this series of proverbs each deals directly or indirectly with the tongue — a favourite subject.

Contrast (complex): **'conceals ... hatred' / 'spreads slander'**
Hiders of hatred are liars; spreaders of slander are fools.

In verse 18 we do not find the usual kind of contrast. The proverb concerns sins of speech springing from hatred: first, misrepresentation or humbug; secondly, slander or defamation. In both cases the speaker does not tell the person concerned what he thinks of him. In the first instance he keeps quiet about it and says nice things instead. This is identified for what it is — lying. In the second case the speaker slanders the person he hates before others. The slanderer is here labelled 'a fool'. Some translations apply the description 'fool' to both sins.

The proverb acts chiefly as a warning against hatred and malice and, secondarily, as a warning about what goes on in the world. If you hate someone and decide to conceal it, you end up telling lies somewhere along the line. If you are more honest, you may slander the person to others. To spread malicious lies is to be 'a fool' — one who is without wisdom. Better to be done with your hatred. Such things go on, however, and we ought to be aware. Not every apparently kind word is what it appears to be. Slander is driven by malicious motives. Hatred explains many things that go on in this world. Scripture gives examples especially of the smooth but lying tongue. Believers must endeavour to be rid of all malice, hatred and slander: 'At one time we too were foolish, disobedient, deceived and enslaved by all kinds of passions and pleasures. We lived in malice and envy, being hated and hating one another' (Titus 3:3). 'But now you must rid yourselves of all such things as these: anger, rage, malice, slander...' (Col. 3:8; cf. 1 Cor. 5:8, Eph. 4:31, 1 Peter 2:1).

Contrast (complex): **'When words are many'** / **'he who holds his tongue'**
Sin is there when words are many; often the wise don't use any.

More directly to do with the tongue, verse 19 warns against talking too much. Proverbs 17:27 begins similarly: 'A man of knowledge uses words with restraint...' James 1:19 echoes the point: 'My dear brothers, take note of this: Everyone should be quick to listen, slow to speak and slow to become angry.' As a non-biblical proverb says, 'Speech is silver; silence is golden.'

As sinners, the more we talk, the more likely we are to sin. You say something for a joke; it goes well, so you try something else but it is not funny and hurts people. You are talking late at night, but start to gossip maliciously. You decide you must speak to someone about his actions, but you go too far and say what is untrue. You say something that you hope will provoke a reaction; it falls flat; so you try something more extreme, something wicked. Examples are legion.

Moreover, the more we say about ourselves, the more likely we are to boast. It was once said of a long-winded preacher that he preached the congregation into a good spiritual frame and then preached them out of it again. Long prayers can have the same effect. It is possible to talk for hours and say nothing worthwhile — just switch on your radio if you want evidence. This is a proverb, of course, and it would be wrong to assume we can solve the problem by clamming up. That is not the point. Rather, the more we say, the more care is needed so that our conversation is 'always full of grace, seasoned with salt' (Col. 4:6). If it is not, we sin. For such sins Jesus bled and died. Pray, 'Set a guard over my mouth, O LORD; keep watch over the door of my lips' (Ps.141:3).

Contrast (complex): **'tongue of the righteous'** / **'heart of the wicked'**
Silver tongues and nickel hearts.

There is a similarity between verse 20 and the pair of proverbs found in 25:11-12. Metaphorically, the **'tongue of the righteous'** is **'choice silver'**, while the heart of the wicked **'is of**

little value'. The Hebrew words translated 'of little value' may refer to filings of base metal, or scrapings of unrefined ore. In other words, a righteous man's words are worth a great deal, but even the deepest understanding of the wicked is worth very little. Better to hear a few words from a righteous man than to gain deep insight into 'the heart of the wicked'. The psalmist describes God's words as 'flawless, like silver refined in a furnace of clay, purified seven times' (Ps. 12:6).

Worldlings sometimes make the joke that a certain person is outwardly shallow, tasteless and heartless but if you scratch beneath the surface you will find he is ... shallow, tasteless and heartless! Too often it is true. Five minutes' conversation with a godly man can be immensely more rewarding than hours spent with some unbelievers. Unbelievers spend Sunday morning reading newspapers and gain little of any worth. At the same time believers hear God's Word and gain so much. Once again we see an illustration of the truth that 'The good man brings good things out of the good stored up in him, and the evil man brings evil things out of the evil stored up in him' (Matt. 12:35).

Contrast (complex): **'Lips of the righteous' / 'fools'**

In verse 21 we reach something of a climax. Words are a matter of life and death. The focus is again on the effect we may have on others. The contrast is not a simple one between the righteous and the wicked, or the wise and the foolish. The wicked are fools; the wise are righteous. Specifically it is righteous **'lips'** that **'nourish many'**, while **'Fools die for lack of judgement'**. The godly speak in such a way that they **'nourish'**, or impart life, to those to whom they speak. Interestingly, the word is used for a shepherd feeding, or caring for, sheep. A good shepherd provides for the flock. **'Fools'**, on the other hand, not only fail to impart life, but themselves **'die for lack of judgement'** — on account of their failure to discriminate accurately. I once read of a man who drowned trying to rescue a dog in a canal. Surely he manifested a lack of discernment. Picture, on the one hand, a doctor telling his patients how to get better and, on the other, a drunkard destroying himself by alcohol poisoning. Think of a mother providing for her child, and then of a girl with many problems who does not even know how to look after herself. Believers have wonderful words of life for all; unbelievers are doomed themselves and drag others down with them.

Perhaps we can summarize verses 19-21 thus:

Don't speak just because you can.
If you use your tongue, use it well.
A right heart leads to a right tongue.
Use your tongue to build others up.
Say the right thing at the right time.

'The blessing of the Lord brings wealth, and he adds no trouble to it' (10:22).

Synthetic: **'wealth' / 'no trouble'**
A blessing without a catch.

This is the second direct reference to **'the Lord'** in the proverbs proper. The basic idea is: **'The blessing of the Lord brings wealth.'** Added to that attractive thought is: **'... he adds no trouble to it'**.

It is true that 'Diligent hands bring wealth' (10:4), but God is sovereign, both as to whom he makes rich and whom he enables to enjoy that wealth. We must be both diligent and expectant. God's people are reminded not to say to themselves, 'My power and the strength of my hands have produced this wealth for me,' but rather to 'remember the Lord your God, for it is he who gives you the ability to produce wealth, and so confirms his covenant' (Deut. 8:17,18).

Hannah realized that:

[It is] the LORD [who] sends poverty and wealth;
   he humbles and he exalts.
He raises the poor from the dust
   and lifts the needy from the ash heap;
he seats them with princes
   and has them inherit a throne of honour
                        (1 Sam. 2:7-8).

Anyone who has observed the effect of wealth on people will realize that it can often lead to **'trouble'** of various sorts. What did Achan, Ahab, Gehazi or Judas gain from their covetousness? (See 20:21; 28:22). The great thing the Lord can do for believers is to bring them wealth without trouble.

It is important to remember that this is both a proverb and a verse in the Old Testament, where God's blessing was often of a more obviously material sort. There is no argument for saying, 'Every believer a wealthy believer,' or that 'Every blessed believer is blessed with wealth.' If we read carefully we shall see that wealth can be either a curse or a blessing. Rather, the point is that when God brings a blessing it is not superficial but worth having. Truly it can be said of those in Christ, 'All things are yours' (1 Cor. 3:21).

'A fool finds pleasure in evil conduct, but a man of understanding delights in wisdom' (10:23).
   Contrast: **'fool'** / **'man of understanding'**
   Passing pleasure; eternal enjoyment.

Here, for the first time, the wise man is called **'a man of understanding'**. The subject is what pleases these two men. A fool **'finds pleasure in evil conduct'**; a wise man, it is implied, **'delights in wisdom'**. What pleases us is a good test of our standing before God. What do you enjoy? The tragedy of unbelievers is not simply that they are not going to heaven, but also that they have no genuine desire to be there. Their idea of fun is to be involved in all that is evil. Some modern comedians try to make a joke of this and say they have no wish to be in heaven but want to be where the fun is, in hell. In such ways they reveal their ignorance and depravity. The wise man sees that sin is a serious thing with serious consequences. He is no kill-joy, but he seeks pleasure elsewhere. He understands the warning which tells him:

> Be happy, young man, while you are young,
>> and let your heart give you joy in the days of your youth.
> Follow the ways of your heart
>> and whatever your eyes see,
> but know that for all these things
>> God will bring you to judgement
>
> (Eccles. 11:9).

He seeks pleasure in the wisdom of the Bible. He looks to Christ, God's Wisdom. His motto is: 'Whatever is true, whatever is noble, whatever is right, whatever is pure, whatever is lovely, whatever is admirable — if anything is excellent or praiseworthy — think about such things' (Phil. 4:8).

> **What the wicked dreads will overtake him;**
>> **what the righteous desire will be granted.**
> **When the storm has swept by, the wicked are gone,**
>> **but the righteous stand firm for ever**
>
> (10:24-25).

Contrast: **'What the wicked dreads'** / **'what the righteous desire'** and, more simply,

Contrast: **'wicked'** / **'righteous'**
Dreads; desires.
Swept away; standing always.

These verses are about judgement. Both again concern **'the wicked'** and **'the righteous'**. The first describes their internal thinking; the second is more objective. **'The wicked'** dread judgement. Such fears may be intermittent and are often concealed, but there are things they dread. **'What the wicked dreads will overtake him.'** On the other hand, **'the righteous'** have certain desires — desires for God's blessing. Such desires will be granted. It does not say that every desire is granted, or suggest *when* such desires will be granted, but God will grant their desires as surely as he will judge the wicked.

Matthew 5:6 echoes the latter promise: 'Blessed are those who hunger and thirst for righteousness, for they will be filled.' The builders of the Tower of Babel feared ignominy and dispersal. In the end it came on them. Belshazzar was confronted by the thing he feared most — his overthrow. Ultimately, **'what the wicked dreads'** and **'what the righteous desire'** are the same — God himself. We all have to face him. Be it your dread or your desire, it will come to pass.

Verse 25 speaks of a **'storm'**, a judgement from heaven. **'When the storm has swept by'** you look and you find that **'the wicked are gone'**. On the other hand, **'The righteous stand firm for ever.'** Whatever storms come, they do not fall. They go on **'for ever'**. This has reference to both temporal and final judgement. It is not suggested that the righteous escape judgement. Rather, they will be able to stand even then. Jesus' story of wise and foolish builders grows straight out of this proverb. Verse 30 is similar. The righteous stand firm by holding on to Messiah (the one who calmed the raging Sea of Galilee and the storm of the cross itself) by being rooted and grounded in him. That is how to survive stormy weather.

'As vinegar to the teeth and smoke to the eyes, so is a sluggard to those who send him' (10:26).

Simile: **'vinegar to the teeth … smoke to the eyes'** / **'a sluggard'**

Sending sluggards stings.

We met the sluggard in Proverbs 6. Here is the first of a dozen proverbs in which he features. Several others refer to laziness and its deleterious effects. This observational one acts as a warning not only against laziness on our part, but also against relying on sluggards. If you want that item urgently, do not send a sluggard to fetch it! If the parcel simply must get there, avoid using the sluggard to take it! The similes are vivid. Many enjoy vinegar on chips but if you get a mouthful when you are expecting wine its acidic effect on the teeth is hardly pleasant. Smoke from a bonfire has a similar effect on the eyes. Further, if these experiences are prolonged, teeth and eyes can be damaged. To adapt Jerome Kern, who famously took up the latter image to describe the effects of a broken love affair:

> If you decide to send a sluggard, in the end
> You are bound to find, you will realize,
> Smoke gets in your eyes.

For Christians an obvious application is to preaching. Preachers are sent by God. If they are lazy they may do great, possibly permanent, harm. All believers are bound to share the gospel with others. None of us must be sluggards in this. The corollary is :

> Like the coolness of snow at harvest time
>   is a trustworthy messenger to those who send him;
>   he refreshes the spirit of his masters
>
>   (25:13).

Christ, who was sent from heaven, was no sluggard. Zeal for God's house consumed him.

'The fear of the Lord adds length to life, but the years of the wicked are cut short' (10:27).
Contrast (complex): **'fear of the Lord'** / **'years of the wicked'**
Fears that add years.

Earlier we learned that 'The fear of the Lord is the beginning of wisdom, and knowledge of the Holy One is understanding' (9:10; cf. 1:7; 2:5). Here is the first of several promises that this **'fear of the Lord adds length to life'** (cf. 14:27; 19:23; 22:4; see also 3:2). We have also been told that 'Long life is in [Wisdom's] right hand' (3:16); 'For through me your days will be many, and years will be added to your life' (9:11). And the psalmist says:

Come, my children, listen to me;
　　I will teach you the fear of the Lord.
Whoever of you loves life
　　and desires to see many good days,
keep your tongue from evil
　　and your lips from speaking lies

(Ps. 34:11-13).

The proverb continues: **'but the years of the wicked are cut short'**. Life is never long enough for the wicked. His view is epitomized in the popular Victorian gravestone — a sheared-off perpendicular column.

The secret of eternal youth has exercised many minds. Here it is. Not that this proverb is a copper-bottomed guarantee of old age for every God-fearer and early death for all who are wicked. Rather it is a general and spiritual truth. In general, just as obeying your parents in childhood prolongs life, so fearing God 'adds length to life'. One thinks most obviously of how youngsters can destroy themselves with alcohol and drugs, or by indulging a passion for dangerous sports or similar reckless exploits. Each time we hear of such a death it recalls the New Testament truth that godliness has 'promise for both the present life and the life to come' (1 Tim. 4:8). Further, even when a believer dies young he has known, and will know, the abundant life that Jesus speaks of — 'life ... to the full' (John 10:10). However long the unbeliever lives, it is a mere shrivelled existence, not worthy of being prolonged.

'The prospect of the righteous is joy, but the hopes of the wicked come to nothing' (10:28).
    Contrast: **'prospect of the righteous' / 'hopes of the wicked'**
    Fulsome future; hopeless hopes.

This harks back to 10:24-25. **'The prospect'** (or hope) **'of the righteous is joy'** because they are bound for heaven. **'The wicked'** may have many **'hopes'**, but they all **'come to nothing'** in hell. Despite apparently favourable indicators, their situation is hopeless, without God and without hope. As we read elsewhere, 'When a wicked man dies, his hope perishes; all he expected from his power comes to nothing' (11:7); 'When calamity comes, the wicked are brought down' (14:32). The latter verse makes the positive point too: 'but even in death the righteous have a refuge'. What Jesus has to say about the rich man and Lazarus in Luke 16 vividly depicts the contrast. Unlike the unbeliever, the Christian rejoices 'in the hope of the glory of God', a hope that 'does not disappoint' (Rom. 5:2,5). He has 'this hope as an anchor for the soul, firm and secure. It enters the inner sanctuary behind the curtain where Jesus, who went before us, has entered on our behalf' (Heb.

6:19). It is this hopeful prospect that leads to 'inexpressible and glorious joy' (1 Peter 1:8).

'The way of the LORD is a refuge for the righteous, but it is the ruin of those who do evil' (10:29).
   Contrast: **'righteous'** / **'those who do evil'**
   Refuge of the righteous; destruction of the depraved.

The subject is **'the way of the LORD'**. 'The way' is two-edged. On one hand, it is a refuge; on the other, to mix metaphors, it means ruin. This is reminiscent of what is said of Jesus under the figure of the capstone: 'Now to you who believe, this stone is precious. But to those who do not believe, "The stone the builders rejected has become the capstone" and, "A stone that causes men to stumble and a rock that makes them fall." They stumble because they disobey the message — which is also what they were destined for' (1 Peter 2:7-8, quoting Ps. 118:22; Isa. 8:14).

Jesus is also 'the way' (John 14:6), the only way to God. Those he makes righteous find him a refuge. Those who persist in evil know only ruin. He is the Saviour who saves his own; the Judge who damns the wicked. He is the one who sustains the life of every man. To some he will be an eternal refuge; others he preserves only for ruin. They may cry, 'Lord! Lord!' on that day but he does not know them.

'The righteous will never be uprooted, but the wicked will not remain in the land' (10:30).
   Contrast: **'righteous'** / **'wicked'**
   Rooted; removed.

This is like verse 25. Psalm 1 uses similar ideas. The 'blessed' man, the one 'who does not walk in the counsel of the wicked or stand in the way of sinners or sit in the seat of mockers', but who delights 'in the law of the LORD', and meditates on it, 'is like a tree planted by streams of water'. He will not be uprooted in the storms of life and death. 'The wicked', on the other hand, 'are like chaff that the wind blows away'. They 'will not stand in the judgement, nor ... in the assembly of the righteous... For ... the way of the wicked will perish.' Both in the psalm and the proverbs, 'the blessed man' or **'the righteous'** refers ultimately to Messiah. It is by holding on to him, by being rooted and grounded in him, that we can survive. Because of God's covenant the wicked Canaanites were not allowed to remain in the land and his own people took root there. They in turn were driven out because of sin. This illustrates the stable and sure hope of true believers and the hopelessness of rootless, wandering unbelievers with no resting-place.

> **The mouth of the righteous brings forth wisdom,**
> **but a perverse tongue will be cut out.**
> **The lips of the righteous know what is fitting,**
> **but the mouth of the wicked only what is perverse**
> (10:31-32).

Contrast (complex): **'mouth of the righteous'** / **'a perverse tongue'**
Contrast: **'lips of the righteous'** / **'mouth of the wicked'**
The righteous say what's proper; wrongdoers what's perverse.

Finally, there are two more proverbs regarding speech.

Verse 31 does not say, 'The mouth of the righteous brings forth wisdom, but a perverse tongue *does not.*' The latter fact is assumed. Rather, it states that such a tongue **'will be cut out'**. It will no longer be allowed to be used. A striking example of this is the way, in 1943, Australian heretic Samuel Angus, who denied Christ's deity, virgin birth, atoning death and resurrection, died from cancer of the mouth. God's judgements are seldom so dramatic in this life, but all who use their tongues perversely will lose their power to do so. Those who, on the other hand, are righteous in Christ will continue to bring forth wisdom.

Verse 32 is a contrast of the more obvious sort. On one hand, righteous lips **'know what is fitting'**; on the other, **'the mouth of the wicked'** knows **'only what is perverse'**. Part of the wisdom of the righteous is to be able to speak what is appropriate, pleasant and right. The wicked can say only what is perverse and twisted. The righteous give time to considering how they can best declare the good news of Christ, share words of comfort with those who suffer, strengthen and encourage the Christian community and strip from their speech anything that hurts others or does not glorify God. They are epitomized in great preachers such as Jonathan Edwards, C. H. Spurgeon and D. Martyn Lloyd-Jones, to whose sermons believers turn to this day. The wicked vie with each other to go further and further in depraved subjects — talking of inappropriate matters in public; making jokes about things private and sacred; endeavouring to stir up hatred by their words; using their mouths to do as much harm as they can. They are epitomized by the shock jocks and foul-mouthed comedians who believe that what is vile is funny.

What we learn from these eighteen proverbs

The nature of true wealth

The Bible never denies the advantages of wealth: 'The wealth of the rich is their fortified city, but poverty is the ruin of the poor' (10:15). However, what we need most is God's blessing. That brings spiritual wealth without the troubles involved in earthly wealth (10:22). There are more important things than worldly wealth, things truly worth having, such as a righteous man's tongue, which is like choice silver — unlike the heart of the wicked, which is of little value (10:20). The wages that ultimately matter are those of righteousness in Christ, for they bring life, while those of wickedness bring punishment (10:16).

The nature of wickedness

You can tell a wicked man by what he says. The righteous know how to say what is fitting, but the wicked can only speak perversely (10:32). Similarly, the righteous edify many by speaking wisely (10:21,31). Wicked fools commit various sins with their lips, such as fraud and slander (10:18). More generally, we need to be warned that when words are many, sin is not absent. The wise hold their tongues (10:19).

Laziness is another characteristic of the wicked and we are warned that to employ a sluggard is to court trouble (10:26).

We are also reminded of the contrast between the wise, upright man and the wicked fool: 'A fool finds pleasure in evil conduct, but a man of understanding delights in wisdom' (10:23).

The end for the wicked and the righteous

This theme is prominent in several proverbs here. Besides verse 16 we have a number of promises and warnings in verses 24-30. We are also told that fools die for lack of judgement (10:21) and that a perverse tongue will be cut out (10:31). On this basis we can say that if you heed discipline you show the way to life, but to ignore correction not only harms yourself, but also leads others astray (10:17).

21.
Forsake wickedness and be righteous — in Christ

Please read Proverbs 11:1-13

Honesty, pride, integrity, wealth, guidance, deliverance, expectation, trouble, knowledge, urban joy, urban prosperity, mockery, gossip

No one knows why chapters 10-29 of Proverbs are divided up as they are. There are no obvious reasons for the chapter-breaks beyond organizing the material in sections of roughly equal length. In a similarly arbitrary way we here consider the next thirteen proverbs. While the first two seem to have been inserted at random, we see clear connections between successive proverbs in verses 3-8, 9-11 and 12-13.

'The LORD abhors dishonest scales, but accurate weights are his delight' (11:1).
Lord detests
Contrast: **'dishonest scales' / 'accurate weights'**
Dishonesty appals; accuracy delights.

More than one proverb deals with this (see 16:11; 20:10,23). The law says the same: 'Do not have two differing weights in your bag — one heavy, one light. Do not have two differing measures in your house — one large, one small. You must have accurate and honest weights and measures, so that you may live long in the land the LORD your God is giving you. For the LORD your God detests anyone who does these things, anyone who deals dishonestly' (Deut. 25:13-15; cf. Lev. 19:35-36).

The prophets railed against those who perverted such laws. Amos decries skimping the measure, boosting the price and cheating with dishonest scales (Amos 8:5; cf. Hosea 12:7). The Lord asks:

> Am I still to forget, O wicked house,
> > your ill-gotten treasures
> > and the short ephah, which is accursed?
> Shall I acquit a man with dishonest scales,
> > with a bag of false weights?
>
> > > (Micah 6:10-11).

Such dishonesty not only brings chaos to society, but the Lord himself detests it. This applies not only to weights and measures, but to all dishonesty in business and commerce, including selling shoddy goods, dishonest or misleading labelling or advertising, hidden costs, pressure-selling, etc. Even where trading-standards officers, ombudsmen and trades associations are active, dishonesty frequently occurs. No Christian should knowingly be involved in such things. In business and commerce, as in every other sphere, we ought to be above reproach. This goes for all our dealings. Our Saviour paid the full price of our redemption, not holding back a mite. He must be our example in every area of life.

'When pride comes, then comes disgrace, but with humility comes wisdom' (11:2).
   Contrast: **'pride'** / **'humility'**
   Haughtiness brings shame; humility makes shrewd.

From outward righteousness we move to more inward righteousness. In Proverbs 3:34-35 we read that:

> [God] mocks proud mockers
>   but gives grace to the humble.
> The wise inherit honour,
>   but fools he holds up to shame.

In 16:18 we have the famous warning that 'Pride goes before
destruction, a haughty spirit before a fall' (16:19 and 18:12
cover similar ground).

The word used here for **'pride'** is rooted in the idea of
boiling up, and is used of people who are arrogant, presump-
tuous and who insist on having their own way. There are many
examples in Scripture — the builders of the Tower of Babel
(Gen. 11), Pharaoh (Exod. 1-12), Miriam (Num. 12), Haman
(Esth. 5-7), Nebuchadnezzar (Dan. 4.30), Herod Agrippa (Acts
12:19-23). All were disgraced because of pride. King Saul is
another. One of his last acts before Samuel announced his rejection as king was to erect a monument to himself (1 Sam.
15:12). Pride brought about the fall of Satan and of man. God
resists the proud and shames them — if not in this life then in
that to come.

The word for **'humility'** is rare and is found only here and
in Micah 6:8 in the exhortation to 'walk humbly with your
God'.

Pride, we are told, leads to **'disgrace'**, or shame; humility
to **'wisdom'**. The full sequence implied is:

> Pride leads to folly; folly to disgrace.
> Humility leads to wisdom; wisdom to honour.

A rabbinic paraphrase of the latter part has: 'Humble souls
become full of wisdom just as low-lying places become full of

water.' We must especially guard against religious pride, as Jesus' parable of the Pharisee and tax collector warns (Luke 18:9-14). He concludes: 'For everyone who exalts himself will be humbled, and he who humbles himself will be exalted.' He says the same thing after warning against taking 'the place of honour' at a wedding feast and risking being humiliated when someone else claims the seat. Rather, we should 'take the lowest place' (Luke 14:7-11). Jesus himself, who washed his disciples' feet, is the supreme example of such wisdom. That is why his honour is so great (see Phil. 2).

> **The integrity of the upright guides them,**
> **but the unfaithful are destroyed by their duplicity.**
> **Wealth is worthless in the day of wrath,**
> **but righteousness delivers from death.**
> **The righteousness of the blameless makes a straight**
> **way for them,**
> **but the wicked are brought down by their own**
> **wickedness.**
> **The righteousness of the upright delivers them,**
> **but the unfaithful are trapped by evil desires.**
> **When a wicked man dies, his hope perishes;**
> **all he expected from his power comes to nothing.**
> **The righteous man is rescued from trouble,**
> **and it comes on the wicked instead**
>
> (11:3-8).

These six proverbs have similar themes. Verses 3, 5 and 6 are very similar and all have the same pattern.

Contrast: **'the integrity of the upright' / 'the unfaithful … their duplicity'**
Goodness guides; duplicity destroys.

'**The upright**' will be led, or guided, by their '**integrity**' (11:3). '**The unfaithful**', on the other hand, will be '**destroyed by their duplicity**', or perversity (13:6 is similar). This is another call to think of the future. Where is your lifestyle leading? If you persist in crooked ways, they will eventually destroy you, but if you persevere in maintaining moral rectitude you have hope both now and for the future. Problems of guidance often turn out to be matters of integrity; with greater integrity we should have fewer problems over guidance. Joseph is the great Old Testament example of this principle. Not for a moment does he give in to the temptation to do anything less than what is righteous. Job is another example. They point us, of course, to the supreme example, Christ himself. Bridges comments: 'The single desire to know the will of God, only that we may do it, will always bring light upon our path.'

> *Contrast:* '**Wealth**' / '**righteousness**'
> Wealth worthless on the day of wrath;
> Righteousness rescues in the day of death.

In verse 4 the spotlight is again on the final outcome. Today wealth can seem so important, so attractive, but on '**the day of wrath**' it will be seen to be worthless. On the other hand, '**Righteousness delivers from death.**' That is what we need. 'In the way of righteousness there is life; along that path is immortality' (12:28; cf. 10:2; see 1 Tim. 4:8 again). In the Day of Judgement, it is not my bank balance that will be scrutinized, but whether I have the righteousness found only in Christ. This realization should be a motivating factor in everything we do in this life.

The psalmist speaks of 'those who trust in their wealth and boast of their great riches', thinking these will save them. However:

No man can redeem the life of another
    or give to God a ransom for him —
the ransom for a life is costly…

(Ps. 49:6-9).

Isaiah asks:

What will you do on the day of reckoning,
    when disaster comes from afar?
To whom will you run for help?
    Where will you leave your riches?

(Isa. 10:3; cf. Zeph. 1:18).

Jesus takes up the theme in the parable of the rich farmer who 'stores up things for himself but is not rich towards God'(Luke 12:15-21). It begins: 'Watch out! Be on your guard against all kinds of greed; a man's life does not consist in the abundance of his possessions.' Jesus speaks elsewhere of the importance of 'treasures in heaven' and of the rich man in agony in hell (Matt. 6:19-24; Luke 16:19-31). The man who stores up ill-gotten treasures is 'storing up wrath against [himself] for the day of God's wrath, when his righteous judgement will be revealed' (Rom. 2:5).

As Paul points out to believers, 'When you were slaves to sin, you were free from the control of righteousness. What benefit did you reap at that time from the things you are now ashamed of? Those things result in death!' (Rom. 6:20-21).

Writing to Timothy, he warns how 'People who want to get rich fall into temptation and a trap… For the love of money is a root of all kinds of evil…' (1 Tim. 6:9-10). In contrast Timothy must 'flee from all this, and pursue righteousness, godliness, faith', etc.

One old writer says that although righteousness cannot deliver from the day, it does deliver from the wrath of the day, and although it cannot deliver from death, it does deliver from the death of the wicked.

Verses 5 and 6 follow the same pattern as verse 3. This can be seen when we set them out thus:

The *integrity* of	the *upright*
guides	them,
but	the *unfaithful*
are destroyed	by their *duplicity.*

The *righteousness* of	the *blameless*
makes a straight way for	them,
but	*the wicked*
are brought down	by their own *wickedness.*

The *righteousness* of	the *upright*
delivers	them,
but	the *unfaithful*
are trapped	by *evil desires.*

Contrast: **'blameless' / 'wicked'; 'upright' / 'unfaithful'**

'Integrity' (11:3) becomes **'righteousness'** in verses 5 and 6, and in verse 5 'the upright' (11:3,6) are referred to as **'blameless'**. More interestingly, the phrase 'guides them' (11:3) is replaced by **'makes a straight way for them'** in verse 5 and **'delivers them'** in verse 6. This, no doubt, clarifies the sort of guidance intended. They are able to go forward in a straight line and are delivered from any troubles they might incur.

As for 'the unfaithful' (11:3,6), they become **'the wicked'** in verse 5. They **'are brought down by their own wickedness'** — a very similar idea to verse 3's 'destroyed by their duplicity'. Similarly, in verse 6 they do not know the deliverance enjoyed by the upright but **'are trapped by evil desires'**.

Honesty is the only policy. Imagine two men faced by a moral dilemma. Their boss wants them to do something illegal and offers a reward for it. The righteous man knows what to do, although it means no reward and the employer's disfavour. He will come through, nevertheless. The wicked man performs the illicit action and receives the reward but finds he is now little more than a doormat. Every day the boss seems to want him to take new risks! Life will not always be easy for the believer but it will at least be straightforward. Questions such as, 'Shall I skip going to school or work?'; 'Shall I tell the shopkeeper he has given me too much change?' or 'Shall I tell a lie to save my skin?' are easy to answer. One writer quotes a rabbinical saying: 'If you don't tell lies you don't have to remember what you said.' As Peter says, 'Who is going to harm you if you are eager to do good?' (1 Peter 3:13).

Verse 7 concentrates on the wicked man and his end:

Synonymous: **'wicked man dies'; '... power comes to nothing'**

When he dies **'his hope'** — what little hope he had — **'perishes'**. It is seen to be false. **'All he expected from his power comes to nothing.'** He thought that his money or influence, his family or his successful business would somehow win him a place in the sun, but it will be of no use whatsoever when he dies.

Jules Mazarin (1602-1661) was Richelieu's successor as first minister of France. On his deathbed he lamented: 'O my poor soul, what will become of you! Where will you go? Oh, were I permitted to live again, I would sooner be the humblest wretch in the ranks of mendicants than a courtier!' The final sad entry in the diary of twentieth-century comic actor Kenneth Williams was: 'What's the point?' Be warned.

Contrast: **'the righteous man' / 'the wicked'**
The righteous rescued; the wicked weakened.

The focus in verse 8 is primarily on **'the righteous man'**. As has already been intimated (11:6), he will be **'rescued from trouble'**. We have also learned that **'the wicked'** have nothing to look forward to. Here there is a new juxtaposition. The **'trouble'** from which the righteous man is rescued **'comes on the wicked instead'**. The tables will be turned. Being good is good for you; being bad is the opposite. The trouble towards which the righteous seemed to be heading, the trouble intended for them by the wicked, will in fact come upon the wicked themselves instead. What a great reversal is coming — a reversal often anticipated in Scripture, such as when Haman is hung on the gallows that he intended for Mordecai, or when Daniel's accusers die in the lions' den to which they had condemned him.

'With his mouth the godless destroys his neighbour, but through knowledge the righteous escape' (11:9).
Contrast (complex): **'mouth [of] the godless' / 'knowledge [of] the righteous'**
Godlessness destroys; knowledge delivers.

And so we come back to that perennial theme, the tongue. This time it is **'the godless'** who are mentioned first, then **'the righteous'**. It is another composite comparison — not between the 'mouth' of each, but between **'mouth'** on the one hand and **'knowledge'** on the other; it is not between one being destroyed and the other escaping, but between one escaping and the other destroying his neighbour. Several ideas are packed into one sentence.

Negatively, not only do the things 'the godless' man says cause harm to the man himself, but he **'destroys his**

neighbour'. By means of lies, slander, harsh speaking, gossip and false teaching, the godless bring those around them to destruction — temporal and eternal. Biblical examples are Ziba (2 Sam. 16) and the lying prophet (1 Kings 13).

Positively, the knowledge of 'the righteous' enables them to escape from all sorts of evil, both in this life and, especially, in the life to come. The idea of escaping has already featured in verse 6, which itself matches verses 3 and 5. This time it is **'knowledge'** that is seen as the essential requirement — knowledge of God's will and the need to do it. Wisdom and righteousness are frequently linked in this book.

> **When the righteous prosper, the city rejoices;**
> **when the wicked perish, there are shouts of joy.**
> **Through the blessing of the upright a city is exalted,**
> **but by the mouth of the wicked it is destroyed**
> (11:10-11).

Here we have two proverbs that, for the first time, speak of the city. For Solomon **'the city'** was, no doubt, Jerusalem but what he says applies to all cities, indeed all communities. We must remember that righteousness is not simply a matter of private morality. What an individual does can affect the whole community.

Synonymous: **'city rejoices'** / **'there are shouts of joy'**
Contrast: **'righteous prosper'** / **' wicked perish'**
Righteousness rallies — rejoice;
Wickedness weakens — whoops of delight.

Although presented in contrasting form, verse 10 is a synonymous proverb. The contrast **'When the righteous prosper'** / **'when the wicked perish'** is complementary. We see a city rejoicing. There are **'shouts of joy'**. Why? Because 'the righteous prosper' and 'the wicked perish'. If you come to a place and the people are generally happy and contented, it is usually because righteousness is prevailing there to some degree. Where evil men are in power and the wicked thrive, rejoicing and happiness are rare. This in itself should teach us the wisdom of righteousness. It benefits not only individuals, but the whole of society. In some parts of Britain people recall a time when there was no need to lock the door at night because stealing was so uncommon, but things have changed. If better times return there will be great rejoicing.

Contrast (complex): **'through the blessing of the upright'** / **'by the mouth of the wicked'**
Up with the upright; down with the depraved!

Verse 11 concludes that it is **'through the blessing of the upright'** that a city is exalted. On the other hand, **'by the mouth of the wicked it is destroyed'**. This takes us back to the damaging power of the tongue. A wicked man's mouth can destroy, not just his neighbour, but a whole community. When lying, slander, blasphemy and uncouth speech become endemic, communities fall apart. No man is an island. Righteousness lifts up a community; wickedness brings it down. The saying, 'All that is necessary for evil to triumph is for good men to do nothing,' comes to mind, as do the comments of the anti-Nazi pastor Martin Niemöller. The words of the latter, originally given in German, have been quoted in several different forms but the most accurate version is probably as follows: 'When Hitler attacked the Jews I was not a Jew, therefore I was not concerned. And when Hitler attacked the Catholics, I was not a Catholic, and therefore, I was not concerned. And when Hitler attacked the unions and the industrialists, I was not a member of the unions and I was not concerned. Then Hitler attacked me and the Protestant church — and there was nobody left to be concerned.'

> **A man who lacks judgement derides his neighbour,**
> **but a man of understanding holds his tongue.**
> **A gossip betrays a confidence,**
> **but a trustworthy man keeps a secret**
>
> (11:12-13).

Contrast: **'man who lacks judgement' / 'man of understanding'; 'gossip' / 'trustworthy man'**

Verses 12, 13 and 14 all have references to 'the mouth' and to expressing one's thoughts with it. These two proverbs also concern the tongue and its control. The way the proverbs keep returning to this subject underlines its vital nature. As James says, 'If anyone considers himself religious and yet does not keep a tight rein on his tongue, he deceives himself and his religion is worthless' (James 1:26). Again he writes, 'We all stumble in many ways. If anyone is never at fault in what he says, he is a perfect man, able to keep his whole body in check' (James 3:2).

In these two proverbs two temptations are considered: first, to give someone a piece of your mind, to let them know just what you think of them; and secondly, to gossip, to betray a confidence.

In both cases self-control is implicitly commended. The man who **'derides his neighbour'** is one who **'lacks judgement'**. The man who **'betrays a confidence'** is simply **'a gossip'**. On the other hand, the one who **'holds his tongue'**, despite the temptation to let the other man 'have it with both barrels blazing', is **'a man of understanding'**, and the one who **'keeps a secret'** is **'a trustworthy man'**. Letting fly at someone who has offended you, or who has done something foolish or wrong, is always a mistake. You are hardly likely to win a person over by such means. Something more thoughtful is required.

As the mother of Bambi's friend Thumper would say (according to the Disney film), 'If you can't say something nice, don't say nothing at all.' Parents who bawl at children, bosses who love to give their staff a public dressing down, car drivers who shout obscenities, those who laugh aloud at the mistakes of others — all need to remember this. They show a lack of judgement. It is best to avoid such people. A man who can keep a secret, however, is a man you can trust, a man worth knowing. He will not gossip because he knows that gossip is hateful, dispiriting, belligerent, judgemental, spiteful, mean, disloyal, self-congratulatory and slack — the very opposite of spirituality (see Gal. 5:22-23).

What these thirteen proverbs teach us

Here, as elsewhere, there is a sharp distinction between the righteous and the wicked. This is the distinction that matters. Whether you are male or female, rich or poor, clever or slow, what really matters is whether you are righteous in Christ, or still in the unrighteous state in which you were born. We are all either believers or unbelievers, missionaries or mission-fields. Consider what we learn of these two contrasting types. How do you match up?

Characteristics of the wicked

Dishonest (11:1)

All sorts of frauds and swindles are worked by the wicked: tax fiddles, false accounting, back-handers, fare-dodging, inflated expense claims, deceitful insurance claims, cheating in examinations, cutting corners, sweeping dirt under the carpet, putting one's hand in the till, falsifying mileage on cars, petty pilfering. The list is almost endless. The righteous can have nothing to do with anything of this sort (11:1,3).

Disdainful (11:2)

Just as prevalent are pride, arrogance and presumption. Perhaps the biggest mistake the proud make is to assume that God will save them despite their sins. On what basis?

Degenerate in speech (11:9-13)

Here again there is almost endless opportunity for sin, and many take it up with abandon. This is why 'When the wicked perish, there are shouts of joy' (11:10). Such people are 'trapped by evil desires' (11:6). They are headed for disgrace, destruction and demotion (11:2,3,5). 'When a wicked man dies, his hope perishes; all he expected from his power comes to nothing... [Trouble] comes on the wicked' (11:7-8). 'In the day of wrath' he realizes that 'Wealth is worthless'(11:4).

Characteristics of the righteous

Aerodynamic

Because of their integrity, the upright know what to do. The righteousness of the blameless makes a straight way for them (11:3,5). The road to eternal life is narrow but straightforward.

Accident-free

The narrow, straightforward road of righteousness leads to life. Righteousness delivers from death. It delivers the upright so that they are not trapped by their evil desires (11:4,6). 'The righteous man is rescued from trouble, and it comes on the wicked instead' (11:8). Through what they know, the righteous escape (11:9). Because he has life, the righteous man has a freedom that the wicked can only dream about.

Advantageous

The advantages of the righteous are not confined to themselves. While the godless destroy their neighbours, the righteous use their mouths to do good to all (11:9-11).

Astute

They know when to speak and when not to speak.

This is why 'the city rejoices' whenever 'the righteous prosper' (11:10). 'Righteousness delivers from death.' This point
is made repeatedly (11:4,6,8,9).

22.
How to succeed in business and in life

Please read Proverbs 11:14-31

*Advice (on a national level), pledges, kindness, cruelty,
contrasting rewards, life, what God delights in, justice,
discretion, desires, giving, generosity, hoarding, quests for good
or evil, confidence, grief brought on the family, soul-winning,
just deserts*

Proverbs 11:14 recommends many advisers. Here we have what
we can think of as seventeen excellent advisers, all of them
with something good to say. If we are wise, we shall take
notice of their advice and learn how to conduct ourselves,
both in business and in life in general.

**'For lack of guidance a nation falls, but many advisers
make victory sure'** (11:14).
  Contrast: **'lack of guidance'** / **'many advisers'**
  No guides — vanquished; many guides — victorious.

Here we have one of only a few proverbs that refer directly to
national concerns (cf. 14:28,34; 28:15,28; 29:2,18). The wisdom of Proverbs applies to individuals, families and communities, such as cities and nations. The wisdom contained in this

proverb is expressed later in terms of the individual (12:15; 13:10; 15:22; 19:20; 20:18). The closest parallel is: 'For waging war you need guidance, and for victory many advisers' (24:6).

Apparently the word used here for **'guidance'** is, at root, a naval term. It conjures up the picture of a ship sailing on the sea. One thinks of the *Titanic* crashing into the iceberg — a microcosm of society brought to disaster. Pride keeps us from taking advice. If we would only listen, what a difference it could make! A teachable spirit is vital if we are ever to be wise. Only God has no need to consult others. A nation, a church or an individual that will not be guided by the Word must fall.

Nations that pursue inward-looking, isolationist policies invariably end up in trouble. The lone dictator rarely does his nation lasting good. When power is concentrated in the hands of one man, it is bad news. Developed countries have learned the value of checks and balances, advisory bodies, consultation, think-tanks, research and debate, indeed of democracy itself. If we seek advice from only one source that may not help us, but if we look to many advisers and wisely sort the good from the bad, we shall be blessed. These things apply to nations, communities, churches, families — to any grouping. Acts 15 is an example of the principle in action in church life.

'He who puts up security for another will surely suffer, but whoever refuses to strike hands in pledge is safe' (11:15).
    Contrast: **'He who puts up security for another'** / **'whoever refuses to strike hands in pledge'**
    Shake and you suffer; stop and you're safe.

Balancing the previous one in part, this proverb warns against the dangers of entering into agreements, especially where they involve relying on other people, as in putting up security for them. Although its form might suggest otherwise, the point is not that we should never do this for anyone, but that if we do it we must realize the danger we court. The proverb's chief concern, as everywhere in the book, is a spiritual one. We dare not commit ourselves to helping evil people. Wisdom, therefore, dictates that commitments will be limited. The direction given here is found at length in Proverbs 6:1-5 (cf. 17:18; 20:16; 22:26-27; 27:13).

It is a temptation to those who seek righteousness to stand surety for anyone who asks. But to expose ourselves to the danger of losing our good name, to bankruptcy and poverty in that way may well show a lack of wisdom. More generally, it is important to realize that each of us can do only a limited amount to help others. If you fail to realize this, you yourself may end up being in need of help. Saying 'No' to the needy should never come easily, but sometimes it is what wisdom dictates. On the other hand, a willingness to suffer loss is part of the Christian life. Christ himself became a surety for his people even when they were still far off and strangers. He did it because of God's oath: 'Because of this oath, Jesus has become the guarantee of a better covenant' (Heb. 7:22). How he suffered because he was willing to act in such a way! Of course, he drew on the infinite resources of the bank of heaven but, nevertheless, he suffered cruelly.

A further application is the one we made in regard to chapter 6. If you raise the subject of religion with some, their response is: 'I've always been a Catholic,' or 'I've always gone to this church,' or 'I'm Jewish,' or 'I've never been religious.' People can show fierce loyalty to systems they sometimes barely understand. Rather, regardless of our background, it behoves us all to weigh up our commitments carefully. Consider Jesus and commitment to him. As we have said, he willingly went to the cross as a surety for his people. His death is unquestionably at least worth giving thought to.

> **A kind-hearted woman gains respect,**
> **but ruthless men gain only wealth.**
> **A kind man benefits himself,**
> **but a cruel man brings trouble on himself**
>   (11:16-17).

Contrast: **'A kind-hearted woman' / 'ruthless men'; 'kind man' / 'cruel man'**
Reach out, gain respect; be ruthless, gain riches.
Kindness brings blessing; cruelty brings bother.

We come next, appropriately enough, to the broader matter of kindness. Both verses are in favour of kindness and the rewards it brings. They are the first of several such proverbs (the closest in meaning is 19:17).

Unusually, verse 16 speaks of a woman rather than a man. Think of women such as Dorcas, 'who was always doing good and helping the poor', or the persuasively hospitable Lydia, or Phoebe, who Paul says had been 'a great help to many people, including me' (Acts 9:36; 16:15; Rom. 16:2). By speaking of the feminine singular, **'a kind-hearted woman'**, and the male plural **'ruthless men'**, the contrast is heightened. The former gains **'respect'**; the latter also gain something — but **'only wealth'**, which we know from previous proverbs is of limited value.

Some interpret this proverb in a different way and see it as a call for balance: 'A charming woman gains respect and a strong man gains wealth,' so, 'Be resolute but kind-hearted, compassionate but strong.' This would follow on well from verse 15.

Verse 17 has the more obvious contrast expressed in terms of the male: kindness benefits; cruelty brings trouble.

Again, the kind man **'benefits himself'**. With respect come other things, such as a quiet conscience, the gratefulness of others, etc. We think perhaps of the widow of Zarephath (1 Kings 17), the Shunammite (2 Kings 4), or Cornelius (Acts 10:2-4). The golden rule is: 'In everything, do to others what you would have them do to you, for this sums up the Law and the Prophets' (Matt. 7:12).

The cruel man **'brings trouble on himself'**. No wonder if he is disliked and people are never kind to him! The cruel are slow to see it, however. This comes out in 1 Kings 18:17-18. Ahab says to Elijah, 'Is that you, you troubler of Israel?' Elijah has to correct him: 'I have not made trouble for Israel... But you and your father's family have.'

Kindness is one aspect of the fruit of the Spirit and should be seen in all Christians. It brings its own rewards, even in this life.

> **The wicked man earns deceptive wages,**
> **but he who sows righteousness reaps a sure**
> **reward.**
> **The truly righteous man attains life,**
> **but he who pursues evil goes to his death**
>
> (11:18-19).

Contrast: **'wicked man'** / **'he who sows righteousness'**;
'truly righteous man' / **'he who pursues evil'**
Depravity deceives; righteousness receives.
(In Hebrew, there is apparently a play on the sound of the words for **'deceptive wages'** and **'reward'**).
Right — you live; evil — you die.

These proverbs, like others, both concern the outcome for the **'wicked'** and the **'righteous'**. Both are reminiscent of Proverbs 10:16. A consideration of the end is often a feature of biblical wisdom. That was Asaph's discovery in Psalm 73:

When I tried to understand all this,
    it was oppressive to me
till I entered the sanctuary of God;
    then I understood their final destiny

                                    (Ps. 73:16-17).

'The wicked' certainly earn, but the wages they receive
are **'deceptive'** (11:18). They think they have something worth
having but, in fact, as verse 19 points out, 'The wages of sin is
death' (Rom. 6:23). Paul argues, 'What benefit did you reap
at that time from the things you are now ashamed of? Those
things result in death!' (Rom. 6:21). The one who patiently
'sows righteousness', on the other hand, **'reaps a sure reward'**, one that will last through eternity.

Verse 19 states the truth more baldly, this time beginning
with the positive: **'The truly righteous man attains life'** —
this is the 'sure reward' that he reaps. He has abundant life
now and for ever through Christ. See Jesus' promise that
'Whoever follows me will never walk in darkness, but will
have the light of life' (John 8:12). On the other hand, **'He who
pursues evil goes to his death.'** He will die in the agony of
hell for eternity.

One writer points out that there is also a chiastic connection between verses 17 and 18. Thus

A kind man
benefits himself,

                                    but a cruel man
                        brings trouble on himself.

                                    The wicked man
                        earns deceptive wages,
but he who sows righteousness
reaps a sure reward.

'The LORD detests men of perverse heart but he delights in those whose ways are blameless' (11:20).

Lord detests

Contrast: **'men of perverse heart'** / **'those whose ways are blameless'**

Perversity detested; perfection delighted in.

If we are tempted to think the preceding proverbs are simply observing a natural law of life, as some argue, this one makes clear that it is in fact all to do with the Lord, the covenant God. The phrase, **'The LORD detests'**, or 'abhors', occurs in ten proverbs and also in 3:32, which is parallel to this verse, and 6:16 (where the NIV uses 'hates'). Other things God detests are lying lips (12:22); the sacrifice, the way and the thoughts of the wicked (15:8-9,26); the proud of heart (16:5); differing weights and measures (11:1; 20:10,23); and injustice (17:15; cf. 16:11; 21:27; 24:9; 26:25; 28:9; 29:27). In each case, it is dishonesty that is the focus.

Here the Lord detests a **'perverse heart'** but **'delights in those'** with blameless ways. His delight comes out at the beginning of the book of Job where he boasts to Satan of his blameless servant: 'Have you considered my servant Job? There is no one on earth like him; he is blameless and upright, a man who fears God and shuns evil' (Job 1:8; 2:3). It is not an easy concept in some ways, but the Creator of all things takes delight in the blamelessness of those created in his image. On the other hand, he detests those with perverse hearts. What is even more amazing is that part of his delight in the Lord Jesus is his blameless life: 'This is my Son, whom I love; with him I am well pleased' (Matt. 3:17; 17:5).

'Be sure of this: the wicked will not go unpunished, but those who are righteous will go free' (11:21).

Contrast: **'Wicked'** / **'righteous'**

The perverse punished; the righteous released.

The opening expression refers to hands and either concerns the *lex talionis* (an eye for an eye, etc), or means something like, 'You can shake on it.' An American might say, 'You can bet your bottom dollar on it.' An English gentleman might prefer, 'I give you my word,' and shake your hand.

There are two things to note here: **'the wicked'** and, literally, **'the seed of the righteous'**. The word **'seed'** is an important Bible word standing often for descendants, especially spiritual descendants. The promises are that the wicked **'will not go unpunished'**. It may not seem like that at times but the fact is that God's justice will seek them out, however far they appear to have gone from punishment. Similarly, on the other hand, the righteous, or their seed, will be delivered or **'go free'**. No one will get away with anything. God gives us his Word on this, his oath. We can be sure about it.

'Like a gold ring in a pig's snout is a beautiful woman who shows no discretion' (11:22)

Simile: **'gold ring in a pig's snout'** / **'beautiful woman who shows no discretion'**

You can't make a silk purse out of a sow's ear.

'Like' has been added here; the original is more condensed. The theme is incongruity. Derek Kidner calls such a proverb a 'jarring absurdity'. Others occur, for example:

> Under three things the earth trembles,
>   under four it cannot bear up:
> a servant who becomes king,
>   a fool who is full of food,
> an unloved woman who is married,
>   and a maidservant who displaces her mistress
>   (30:21-23; see also 17:7; 19:10; 26:1).

We consider the pig to be a rather dirty animal and, of course, for the Jews it was ceremonially unclean. The idea of putting a precious gold ring into a pig's snout is, therefore, somewhat ridiculous — an iron ring, yes, but not a gold one. It is as incongruous as a woman with natural outward beauty, **'who shows no discretion'** — literally, 'who departs from taste'. One envisages a pretty but shameless, heavily made-up, gum-chewing, cigarette-smoking 'moll' who always says the wrong thing. Sometimes the incongruity is less obvious, but anyone who has a natural grace should beware of this danger. Beauty is a gift from God and should not be despised, but if it is only skin-deep, a mere promise of good with no depth, how disappointing! That is why Peter tells women, 'Your beauty should not come from outward adornment, such as braided hair and the wearing of gold jewellery and fine clothes. Instead, it should be that of your inner self, the unfading beauty of a gentle and quiet spirit, which is of great worth in God's sight' (1 Peter 3:3-4).

This proverb is not only for women, however. Older commentators rightly saw in it a picture of the church of Rome, and no doubt there are other applications too.

'The desire of the righteous ends only in good, but the hope of the wicked only in wrath' (11:23).
> *Contrast:* **'desire of the righteous'** / **'hope of the wicked'**
> Great expectations; hope and anger.

The prominent theme from verses 2-9 and 18-21, as well as chapter 10, resurfaces here — the ultimate end for **'the righteous'** and **'the wicked'**. The book of Proverbs is far from being concerned simply with this life. The desire of the former **'ends only in good'**; the hope of the latter **'only in wrath'**. Some consider desires and hopes to be inconsequential, but

God sees our hearts and he reveals here that the righteous, who have their thoughts set on things above (see Col. 3:1), will know good — real and lasting good. Their desires are God-given and so must be good and will end only in good. Their motto is: 'For to me, to live is Christ and to die is gain' (Phil. 1:21). The Anglican Collect for Easter Day says, 'Thou didst put into my mind good desires; and thou wilt bring the same to good effect.'

Meanwhile, the futile hopes of the wicked lead only to wrath — real and lasting wrath. Not only will their hopes fail, but also God's wrath will come on them.

We need to consider these two outcomes carefully. What are you setting your heart on? Is your desire likely to be fulfilled? It is those who hope in the Lord who renew their strength and soar like eagles (Isa. 40:31). The psalmist says, 'Delight yourself in the LORD and he will give you the desires of your heart' (Ps. 37:4).

> **One man gives freely, yet gains even more;**
> > **another withholds unduly, but comes to poverty.**
> **A generous man will prosper;**
> > **he who refreshes others will himself be refreshed.**
> **People curse the man who hoards grain,**
> > **but blessing crowns him who is willing to sell**
> > > > > > (11:24-26).

These proverbs concern prosperity, giving and generosity. They remind us of what is in taught in verses 16-19. The subjects of wealth and giving arise in many places in Proverbs.

Contrast: **'one man gives freely'** / **'another withholds unduly'**

Give freely; you gain.
Withhold unduly; you wane.

Verse 24, like verse 18, is a warning that human logic often falls down. Human logic argues that if you are generous you will lose out. The paradoxical truth is that the more we give away, the more we gain. No wonder the Lord Jesus said, 'It is more blessed to give than to receive' (Acts 20:35). The proverb is not necessarily saying that the more money you give away with one hand, the more you will have in the other. That baldly materialistic view is very popular in some professedly Christian circles. Rather, the point is that although you may lose out financially or in other ways by being generous, what you gain is far greater. On the other hand, those who cling on to wealth come to poverty in the end — either in this life or the one to come. When you read of a formerly wealthy man becoming bankrupt, it is extremely unlikely that it is because he has been too generous to others.

What is scattered or withheld here is not necessarily money, we should note. The scattering principle, which certainly applies to seed and often to money, has a wide application, including kindness and care. A Christian doctor would sometimes leave a prescription with patients who only imagined they were unwell. It would read, 'Do something for somebody.' 'It is a powerful remedy,' he rightly added.

Synonymous: **'generous man'** / **'he who refreshes others'**
Generosity generates; refreshing refreshes.

Verse 25 is similar to the previous one, but focuses only on the generous man — one who is, literally, 'a soul of blessings'. It is like the first part of verse 17. The promise is of reciprocal prosperity (literally, 'fatness') and refreshment. This is something preachers and Sunday school teachers who prepare well certainly know, as do all who seek to help others in Christ's name.

The same principle is found in the law: 'Give generously to [your needy brother] and do so without a grudging heart; then because of this the LORD your God will bless you in all your work and in everything you put your hand to' (Deut. 15:10). It is also in the Gospels: 'Give, and it will be given to you. A good measure, pressed down, shaken together and running over, will be poured into your lap. For with the measure you use, it will be measured to you' (Luke 6:38).

Paul takes up the seed motif and says, 'Remember this: Whoever sows sparingly will also reap sparingly, and whoever sows generously will also reap generously. Each man should give what he has decided in his heart to give, not reluctantly or under compulsion, for God loves a cheerful giver' (2 Cor. 9:6-7).

What it must be to be the widow whom Jesus saw putting in the two mites at the temple! Her soul is in heaven, and here on earth we constantly commend her example!

Contrast: **'man who hoards grain' / 'him who is willing to sell'**

Accumulate; know hate.
Sell and all's well.

Verse 26 is slightly different and shows that generous attitudes must not be confined to giving to the needy. Islam has similar, much later, sayings (for example: 'If anyone keeps goods till the price rises, he is a sinner').

The picture in this proverb is from the world of commerce and involves two men — one who hoards grain, presumably in order to get a better price, and another who is willing to sell. People curse the first, but blessings crown the latter.

A legend from the Rhine area tells of a certain Count Graaf, a wicked and powerful chief, who made himself rich at the expense of others by erecting a toll house and by buying up grain. One year there was a famine and the count made a huge profit. However, according to the legend, an army of hungry rats invaded the toll house and slowly devoured him. In more recent years, there is evidence to say that Stalin's hoarding of grain in the 1930s exacerbated those famine years and is one more nail in the coffin of his reputation. Sometimes justice is even swifter. At least one Birmingham garage owner who sought to profit from the brief UK petrol crisis in 2000 by hiking up his prices was subsequently driven out of business by a local boycott.

There is no guarantee that people will thank you for being generous in the commercial world, but blessings will nevertheless follow, as many have found. Calculated greed is condemned here and generosity is praised and encouraged. Generosity is the thing. To be generous is to reflect the character of God himself, 'who gives generously to all without finding fault' (James 1:5). If you are a believer, 'you know the grace of our Lord Jesus Christ, that though he was rich, yet for your sakes he became poor, so that you through his poverty might become rich' (2 Cor. 8:9).

'Boosting the price' is condemned in Amos 8:5. All dishonesty and greed in business is condemned in Scripture.

'He who seeks good finds goodwill, but evil comes to him who searches for it' (11:27).
Contrast: **'he who seeks good' / 'him who searches for [evil]'**
Seekers finders, for good or ill.

This proverb sets out the principle that lies behind what has been observed in the previous three. The subject also came up back in Proverbs 1:18-19. The observation is made that a certain symmetry operates even in this life. The one **'who seeks good'** may not find wealth, but he will find what is more desirable — **'goodwill'**, from men or God or both. Others may seek wealth, but if they do so unlawfully they will find what is most undesirable — **'evil'**. It will backfire on them. The thought is somewhat similar to verse 17. There is also a resemblance between the second part and the words of the psalmist:

> He who digs a hole and scoops it out
>   falls into the pit he has made.
> The trouble he causes recoils on himself;
>   his violence comes down on his own head
>   (Ps. 7:15-16).

'Whoever trusts in his riches will fall, but the righteous will thrive like a green leaf' (11:28).
   Contrast: **'whoever trusts in his riches'** / **'righteous'**
   Simile: **'righteous … thrive like a green leaf'**
   Riches fail; righteousness flourishes.

This is another warning against the perils of relying on earthly riches. With it comes a promise that features a beautiful simile, picturing **'the righteous'** as thriving **'like a green leaf'**. The promise is for **'the righteous'** and the warning for **'whoever trusts in his riches'**. As one writer puts it, 'The first man is precariously propped up,' while the other is resilient, alive and growing. Eric Lane picks up the leaf imagery and speaks of riches as being like falling autumn leaves, while the believer is an evergreen shrub. Heavenly treasure is worth far more than earthly baubles. As John Newton wrote:

> Fading is the worldling's pleasure,
> All his boasted pomp and show.
> Solid joys and lasting treasure
> None but Zion's children know.

'He who brings trouble on his family will inherit only wind, and the fool will be servant to the wise' (11:29).
Synonymous: **'he who brings trouble on his family'** / **'fool'**
Contrast: **'fool'** / **'wise'**

The latter part of this proverb is typical enough. Whatever a fool may do, it serves ultimately only to advance the cause of the wise. How the first half is connected with it is not immediately clear, but losing an inheritance is the first step on the road to slavery. There is a warning against bringing trouble on one's family. It leads only to emptiness. When we do evil, we not only harm ourselves, but also those nearest to us. It is tempting at times to take it out on our nearest and dearest, or to take them for granted. Such actions lead at best to deep regrets, and in some cases to a family falling apart. Sons who go into life without remembering this end up in shame and servitude.

'The fruit of the righteous is a tree of life, and he who wins souls is wise' (11:30).
Synonymous: **'the** [fruit-bearing] **righteous'** / **'he who wins souls'**

In the concluding pair of proverbs, the first is famous. Following the Greek Septuagint, the RSV attempts to turn the personal evangelist's favourite verse into a more typical contrasting proverb: 'The fruit of the righteous is a tree of life, but lawlessness takes away lives.' However, it is more likely that the two halves are both positive, referring, firstly and unsurprisingly, to **'the righteous'**, and then to the one **'who wins souls'**. The former bears fruit that is a tree of life — a life-giving tree. The latter **'is wise'**. The thoughts are complementary. Thought of as a righteous man, the believer has a tremendous life-giving influence because of his teaching and life. Thought of as a wise man, by similar means, he wins, or captures, the souls of others so that they too walk in the ways of wisdom. If a wise doctor is one who heals, and a wise general is one who leads his men to victory, so a wise believer will heal the souls of others and win them for the Saviour. Supremely the tree of life is Christ's own cross. That tree of life was indeed the fruit of righteousness.

'If the righteous receive their due on earth, how much more the ungodly and the sinner!' (11:31).
 A fortiori

This proverb is the first of some six *a fortiori* arguments — that is, ones that argue from the greater to the lesser. It observes that, quite apart from any consideration of what happens after death, even here on earth rewards and punishments are often doled out in appropriate fashion. This is not always the case, of course, but often it is. Again following the Septuagint, the RSV makes it match 1 Peter 4:18: 'If the righteous man is scarcely saved, where will the impious and sinner appear?' The point then would be that even the sins of holy men receive a punishment.

What these eighteen proverbs teach us

In the light of verse 14 we see the other seventeen verses as a body of advisers eager to help in many areas, particularly in business and in life generally.

How to succeed in business

Several books have appeared that attempt to apply Proverbs to specific fields. Michael Zigarelli, for example, has a book called *Why manage by Proverbs?* In it, he apparently attempts to apply the teaching of the book to the modern business world. He cites 'stories of large and small companies that have implemented Proverbs' wisdom' and 'the academic literature to demonstrate that Proverbs' business directives have indeed been empirically tested three millennia after Solomon's ink dried'. Despite Proverbs' intensely spiritual nature, such principles can be extracted. A Christian headmaster in South Wales has attempted to base his educational philosophy on Proverbs.

Here the father is eager for his son to do well in the family business and the teaching has wide application.

The importance of discretion

Verse 22 warns against superficiality. We need to be discerning in the way we see others and in the way we conduct our own affairs.

The wisdom of generosity

It is a false deduction to suppose that giving freely will end in grief (see 11:24-25). Quite the opposite is true, even in business, where the power of the free gift, the introductory offer and 'two for the price of one' can be powerful tools. Often it is undue withholding that leads to poverty. Even the world knows that you have to speculate to accumulate and that 'You only get out what you put in'.

Remember that 'A kind man benefits himself, but a cruel man brings trouble on himself' (11:17). No one loses out by showing kindness. Often it has led to unexpected rewards even in this life.

'He who seeks good finds goodwill, but evil comes to him who searches for it' (11:27). We need to learn to be generous with time, compliments, encouragements, money and goodwill.

We should be generous towards God and our neighbours. Any expenditure will be handsomely repaid with interest for sure. Becoming a Christian is in many ways like throwing your life away, but Jesus insisted that 'Whoever wants to save his life will lose it, but whoever loses his life for me will save it' (Luke 9:24); and 'Whoever has will be given more; whoever does not have, even what he thinks he has will be taken from him' (Luke 8:18).

The evil of greed

This corollary to the previous point follows in the first part of verse 26. The man who is miserly, or who plays the market in a calculated manner, is not popular, especially with those whom he takes advantage of. Maximizing profit margins cannot be our only criterion in business. It is a bad move morally and unsound from a business point of view. Every business decision must consider the effect it is likely to have on individuals — customers, workers, other businesses. So-called market forces must not be allowed to dictate what will happen regardless of the cost in human terms. We must suppress our greed. Reject narrow ideas about what success in business means. The financial bottom line is not the true bottom line.

The importance of taking care over agreements and alliances

Verse 15 calls for care over entering into contracts, alliances, agreements and commitments. In every aspect of our lives, we need to take care over such things. Are you allied, even addicted, to someone or something that will drag you down to hell? Have you over-committed yourself in some area of life in a way that cannot work? Get out now, while you can.

The importance of refusing to trust in riches

This is the message of verse 28. True riches are found only in Christ, and to trust in anyone or anything else means disaster. It does not make good business sense to trust in riches, which are so fleeting.

The importance of God and the family

The leader of a major American corporation is said to have remarked that for him God came first, then his family, then his business. However, once through the door of his office the order was reversed. If that is true, the man showed poor business sense. Rather we should say, 'He who brings trouble on his family will inherit only wind, and the fool [the man who has no place for God] will be servant to the wise' (11:29). When my work becomes more important than God or my family then there is something seriously wrong. True success is then impossible.

How to succeed in life

On the broader matter of wisdom for life in general, this section, like previous ones, has a great deal to say for righteousness and against wickedness. The emphasis here is again on where they lead.

Advantages and disadvantages

At best 'Ruthless men gain only wealth' (11:16). 'A kind man benefits himself,' while 'a cruel man brings trouble on himself' (11:17). The advantages of the godly life are many, even on the earthly level. There are exceptions but, to some extent, you are less likely to be criminalized or to endanger life and limb. In general, people will be better disposed towards you. Some people seek to be outwardly good for these very reasons. They agree that 'Crime doesn't pay' and that 'Honesty is the best policy.' Ultimately skin-deep righteousness is not enough, however, as there is a world to come. Verse 31 must not be universalized, as has been said. If it were always the case, there would be little need for final judgement. It is a tragedy that so many see the advantages of an outwardly moral life but not the need for true righteousness in Christ.

Rewards and punishments

Some eschew such language, but it is perfectly biblical to say that sin leads to a fall into the punishment of death and wrath that is hell. Therefore you must repent and turn from sin. Positively, righteousness in Christ makes a person free so that he or she thrives and attains to life and the good and sure reward that is heaven. Therefore, trust only in Christ. There is nothing wrong with being straight like this. As we have already said, signs saying, 'No smoking — £50 fine,' are not just deterrents. If you smoke in those circumstances you really will be fined. Similarly, a good parent who promises a reward to a child for doing a certain thing will make sure he keeps that promise.

'Ruthless men gain only wealth' (11:16), and trusting in such wealth can only mean a fall, 'but the righteous will thrive like a green leaf' (11:28). 'One man gives freely, yet gains even more; another withholds unduly, but comes to poverty' (11:24) has an eternal dimension. We must not be fooled by mere outward appearances. The fact is that 'The wicked man earns deceptive wages.' On the other hand, 'He who sows righteousness reaps a sure reward' (11:18). 'The truly righteous man attains life, but he who pursues evil goes to his death' (11:19). Verse 21 is similar. The wicked seem to get away with it at times, but true freedom is found in Christ. God is just. He will root all evil out of his kingdom (see 11:23).

Delight and distaste

When considering how to succeed in life we must always first take into account what the Lord thinks. This is the ultimate question. All other considerations must be subordinate to it. In verse 20 we learn of those whom he detests and those in whom he delights. In which category am I? None of us is blameless by nature. Our hearts are perverse. All have sinned and fall short of God's glory. Our only hope, then, is to be declared blameless through faith in Jesus Christ.

Life and servitude

A final way to highlight the way to success in life is to consider what the godly, righteous and wise are like. 'The fruit of the righteous is a tree of life' (11:30). Such people win souls to the Lord. As they seek good, so they spread goodwill. Meanwhile, 'The fool will be servant to the wise' (11:29).

23.
Let fantasies go; righteousness is what counts

Please read Proverbs 12:1-12

Discipline, good men, stability, wives, plans, harmful speech, overthrow of the wicked, praise, making your mark, kindness, hard work, wicked desires

Here we consider the first twelve proverbs of the chapter. They are all of the contrasting type.

'Whoever loves discipline loves knowledge, but he who hates correction is stupid' (12:1).
Contrast: **'whoever loves discipline'** / **'he who hates correction'**

The Hebrew is terse. Literally, it reads: 'Loves discipline, loves knowledge; but hates correction, stupid.' The former **'loves knowledge'**; the latter **'is stupid'**. In verse 15 a similar point is made more positively.

Love of discipline is often commended. One of the hard things about gaining knowledge is that it involves discipline and being corrected. Arnot calls it 'a bitter but healthful morsel'. We naturally rebel against it, but to hate correction is to be 'stupid'. It is to be like a brute beast. A teachable spirit is vital. Obstinacy is senseless. To accept correction is wiser than pretending we do not need it. Bitter medicine can do much good. Adversity is the best university.

Is this not why big companies do market research and why successful athletes employ coaches who make them work hard? Remember how wisely David dealt with even the unfair cursing of Shimei and gained from it. My grandfather was sometimes obstinate. That obstinacy led him, so the stories go, on one occasion to put hair lotion on his grazed leg instead of antiseptic, and another time to smother the cabbages on his allotment in talcum powder instead of insecticide — stupid acts that could have been avoided if he had been willing to listen to others.

Much more serious is a refusal to listen to the gospel. Paul speaks of how the perishing are deceived. The reason they perish is that they 'refused to love the truth and so be saved' (2 Thess. 2:10). No progress can be made in the Christian life without discipline.

'A good man obtains favour from the Lord, but the Lord condemns a crafty man' (12:2).
  Contrast: **'good man' / 'crafty man'**
  God chooses the good but chides the guileful.

One **'obtains favour from the Lord'**; the other he **'condemns'**. What is a good man? A good man is one who is in covenant with the Lord, the covenant God. He resembles God himself and can expect the Lord's favour. Trapp mentions the boldness of Luther in prayer. At times, Luther was absolutely sure God would answer his bold prayers — and he did.

If a man is **'crafty'**, however, a wicked schemer who plots evil, the Lord will condemn him. He resembles his father the devil and cannot inherit the kingdom of God. In this life there may be temporary reversals — an Absalom will appear to

triumph over a David, a Jezebel over a Naboth. However, if
not now, then in the world to come, the Lord will show favour
to the good and condemn the crafty: 'For the LORD watches
over the way of the righteous, but the way of the wicked will
perish' (Ps. 1:6).

**'A man cannot be established through wickedness, but
the righteous cannot be uprooted'** (12:3).

Contrast (complex): **'man** [seeking to] **be established
through wickedness'** / **'righteous'**

This reminds us of 10:25. Under the image of two plants in
differing soils we have, rather than the more obvious, 'The
wicked will fall but the righteous will not,' a declaration that
wickedness cannot establish a person, while the righteous person will not be uprooted whatever comes. The wicked seek to
establish themselves by various evil schemes, but these are all
doomed to failure. Haman again comes to mind, as does Ahab,
seventy of whose sons died at one time and whose line was
wiped out. Caiaphas is a striking example of a man who thought
he could establish the nation by an act of gross wickedness but
served only to bring its life to an end.

Psalm 125 begins in similar vein to the second part of the
proverb:

> Those who trust in the LORD are like Mount Zion,
>   which cannot be shaken but endures for ever.
> As the mountains surround Jerusalem,
>   so the LORD surrounds his people
>   both now and for evermore.

In Isaiah the Lord tells his saints, 'No weapon forged against
you will prevail' (Isa. 54:17). Of his church Christ says, 'The
gates of Hades will not overcome it' (Matt. 16:18).

'A wife of noble character is her husband's crown, but a disgraceful wife is like decay in his bones' (12:4).
  Contrast: **'wife of noble character'** / **'disgraceful wife'**
  Noble or noxious?

We have had some comment on women's conduct in 11:16,22 but this is the first proverb to speak directly about wives. There are several others. The former is **'her husband's crown'**; the latter **'like decay in his bones'**. These powerful images declare what an important effect a wife can have on the life of her husband. The verse speaks to various people. To young men it says, 'Take care in choosing a life partner.' To wives it says, 'Do not forget what a powerful force you are for good or evil.' To husbands it says, 'If you have a noble wife' (as I do), 'then be thankful.' To everyone else it says, 'Never forget that although wives have a hidden role it is a very important one.' A successful marriage depends to a great extent on the wife's character. Arnot says, 'Man, though made for the throne of the world was found unfit for the final investiture until he got woman as a help.'

'Noble' means strong, controlled, dignified, demure perhaps, then able and reputable. Though the 'weaker partner', if she is a believer the wife is an heir with her husband 'of the gracious gift of life' (1 Peter 3:7), and so she must be 'noble'. If she is, she will be like a gold crown on his head. She will make her husband a king, or at least as happy as a king (as Matthew Henry puts it, drawing on the symbolism of crowns in Hebrew thinking).

If, however, she is **'disgraceful'** in some way it will be **'like decay in his bones'**, causing him to waste away from within.

In 1620 John Wing preached from this verse that a wife is a man's best outward blessing. As kings carefully choose their queens, so men must marry daughters of the King of kings. As his crown, a wife should be well respected by her husband and properly maintained. Further, as husbands are kings, wives should be both obedient and gracious.

Whenever we think about the marriage relationship we ought also to think of the relationship between Christ and his church that it pictures. Nobility in God's children reflects well on Christ and we 'crown him with many crowns, the Lamb upon his throne'. If we act disgracefully, we become like a cancer or gangrene in the bones, destroying the body of Christ.

'The plans of the righteous are just, but the advice of the wicked is deceitful' (12:5).
    Contrast: **'plans of the righteous'** / **'advice of the wicked'**

Literally it is the **'thoughts'** or 'calculations' of **'the righteous'** that are contrasted with the **'intentions'** or 'designs' of **'the wicked'**. The former plan what is **'just'**, and fair or straightforward, while the latter have **'deceitful'**, underhand, treacherous, devious designs. Think of Sanballat, who endeavoured to entice Nehemiah into his trap (Neh. 6). Think of Herod's lie that he wished to worship the newborn king, or the Jewish leaders who plotted against Jesus. The way we think determines our actions to a large extent, but one aspect of wisdom is not to rely on mere appearances, but to see that different people have different intentions. We must reckon with the fact that not all are as straightforward as we may endeavour to be. As Shakespeare's King Duncan observed, 'There's no art to find the mind's construction in the face.' Believers are sometimes tempted to be devious, but we must never give room to such thoughts, whatever others do. Like Paul, we must not make our plans in a worldly way, but must daily renounce 'secret and shameful ways', and 'not use deception, nor … distort the word of God. On the contrary, by setting forth the truth plainly', we must 'commend ourselves to every man's conscience in the sight of God' (2 Cor. 4:2).

We should be known for our straightforwardness; for our integrity, honesty, sincerity and incorruptibility. We must be upright, fair, men and women of principle, like Joseph, Nehemiah and Daniel, of whom it is written: 'They could find no corruption in him, because he was trustworthy and neither corrupt nor negligent' (Dan. 6:4).

'The words of the wicked lie in wait for blood, but the speech of the upright rescues them' (12:6).
  Contrast: **'words of the wicked'** / **'speech of the upright'**
  Wicked words waylay; righteous remarks rescue.

Next we come again to the prominent matter of speech. **'The words of the wicked'** are personified as lying **'in wait for blood'**. In contrast, **'The speech of the upright rescues them.'** By their words the wicked often set traps, or ambushes, for people. Think of Doeg the Edomite who spoke up and caused the death of the priests of Nob, or those who secured the death of Naboth. By means of defamation, denigration and deceit, evil men do great damage. This is a trial to the upright, but here they are told that their own upright words will rescue **'them'** from trouble. The reference could be to rescuing others, but is more likely to be to rescuing themselves. An example would be Mephibosheth's self-defence in 2 Samuel 19:25-30.

For a better example still, we read in the Gospels how 'The Pharisees went out and laid plans to trap [Jesus] in his words' (Matt. 22:15). They then asked him about paying taxes to Caesar and were told, 'Give to Caesar what is Caesar's, and to God what is God's.' We read that 'They were unable to trap him in what he had said there in public. And astonished by his answer, they became silent' (Luke 20:26).

We ought to remember the promise: 'But make up your mind not to worry beforehand how you will defend yourselves. For I will give you words and wisdom that none of your adversaries will be able to resist or contradict' (Luke 21:14-15). On the other hand, we must certainly learn to be like Paul, who could say, 'When we are cursed, we bless; when we are persecuted, we endure it; when we are slandered, we answer kindly' (1 Cor. 4:12-13).

What sort of speech characterizes you? Are you one who lies in ambush, trying to catch people out with your words, saying things that promote violence and strife? Or are you a rescuer, a healer, one who speaks words that promote harmony and peace, words that save both yourself and others from the snares of the wicked?

'Wicked men are overthrown and are no more, but the house of the righteous stands firm' (12:7).
   Contrast: **'wicked men'** / **'house of the righteous'**
   The wicked wither; the righteous remain.

We come back once more to the contrast between the **'wicked'** and the **'righteous'**, and to ideas similar to those we have encountered in verse 3 and in 10:25,30, etc. (cf. 3:33; 11:21). It also anticipates 14:11 (and 15:25). Each of these proverbs links with the picture of the wise and foolish builders referred to by Jesus at the close of the Sermon on the Mount.

We must never forget that the house of the wicked will be **'overthrown'**. Like Haman in the book of Esther, wicked men are overthrown never to rise again. So, soon they are **'no more'**. Meanwhile, **'The house of the righteous stands firm.'** Because it is built on Christ, it cannot fall. The word **'house'**, of course, speaks of more than bricks and mortar and stands for a household or dynasty. The story of Saul and David illustrates the proverb well. From David came Messiah, and soon

Satan's house will be no more, but Christ's kingdom will stand firm. It is only a matter of time.

'A man is praised according to his wisdom, but men with warped minds are despised' (12:8).

Contrast (complex): **'man ... according to his wisdom'** / **'men with warped minds'**

The wise we commend; the warped we condemn.

We have often remarked on the practical nature of true wisdom. It is this common-sense element that is to the fore here. The better we are at rightly apprising situations and acting on the information, the more likely we are to be praised by men as well as by God. If our thinking is warped, it should be no surprise that people despise us. Some Christians have mistaken the way people despise their warped minds for genuine persecution. We should remember that as Jesus grew up in Nazareth and his wisdom increased he grew in favour not only with God, but also with men. In the Old Testament, the wisdom of Joseph, Daniel, Nehemiah and others was obvious not just to believers but to unbelievers too.

If we are looking for a more spiritual application, we have only to turn to Jesus' parable of the shrewd manager. He notes how 'the people of this world are more shrewd in dealing with their own kind than are the people of the light'. Then he says, 'I tell you, use worldly wealth to gain friends for yourselves, so that when it is gone, you will be welcomed into eternal dwellings' (Luke 16:8,9)

In another relevant passage he says, 'Who then is the faithful and wise manager, whom the master puts in charge of his servants to give them their food allowance at the proper time? It will be good for that servant whom the master finds doing so when he returns' (Luke 12:42-43).

'Better to be a nobody and yet have a servant than pretend to be somebody and have no food' (12:9).

Contrast (better than): **'a nobody** [with] **a servant'** / **'pretend ... somebody** [with] **no food'**

Noble nobody or starving somebody?

The NIV seems to have the translation correct. This is the first of a series of some nineteen proverbs of comparison — a specific form of contrasting proverb (see, for example, 15:16,17; 16:8,16,19,32; 17:1,12; 19:1,22; 21:9,19). Still in a common-sense vein, like verse 11, it calls for a healthy dose of realism. It anticipates 13:7 and ties in with 24:27. Obsession with image is a curse. Substance must rule over image, content over style, reality over appearance. Here is someone who really thinks he is a **'somebody'**, yet he has no money even for food. Here is another who may be **'nobody'**, but at least he employs a servant to take care of his needs — providing work for others and comfort for himself.

Many young people find this hard to grasp and are unimpressed by parents who talk of hard work, job security and getting priorities right in ways that drive them to distraction. It is possible to err in either direction but realism is important. At school my plan was to leave as soon as possible, go to Bible College, then become a minister. I was rather disappointed when my pastor recommended the sixth form and university first. I ended up spending eight years preparing for the ministry! From this vantage-point, I have no regrets and only wonder if four or five more years of preparation might have been better. When a young person says, 'I want to be a missionary,' he needs to be encouraged, but in realistic terms.

Fantasy football and similar games have become popular in some newspapers in recent years. Some people play fantasy Christianity. They look like believers on the outside, but there is no reality. Jesus warns that 'Everyone who exalts himself will be humbled, and he who humbles himself will be exalted.'

'A righteous man cares for the needs of his animal, but the kindest acts of the wicked are cruel' (12:10).
   Contrast: **'righteous man'** / **'wicked'**
   Kind care; cruel kindness.

How can you tell if someone is righteous? There are all sorts of give-away signs. In the days when everyone had them, a simple way was to see how he dealt with his animals: **'A righteous man cares for the needs of his animal.'** The law was clear that animals must be given due rest (Exod. 23:12) and shown kindness (Deut. 25:4). It is no surprise to find that the moving spirit behind the founding of the Royal Society for the Prevention of Cruelty to Animals in 1824 was a Christian minister, Rev. Arthur Broome. S. T. Coleridge wrote:

He prayeth best who loveth best
All things both great and small;
For the dear God that loveth us,
He made and loveth all.

Having noted this, we must see that this is not the thrust of the proverb, however. A transculturized version might be: 'A righteous man looks after his car or his DIY tools.' This is not an infallible test. Some are kinder to their animals and their tools than to their fellow human beings. It is often a clue, however.

The contrast is that **'The kindest acts of the wicked are cruel.'** This last is a sort of oxymoron. Yes, you may see a wicked man doing a kind act, but you can be sure he has a cruel end in view. He opens the door for you, but only to make a face behind your back, or to make you think he is kind; he

helps an old lady across the street, but only to steal from her
or to impress his girlfriend. A biblical example is Judah's arguing against killing Joseph because they would gain more by
selling him (Gen. 37:26-27). Another would be when Nahash
the Ammonite agrees to make a treaty with the people of Jabesh
Gilead, but 'only on the condition that I gouge out the right
eye of every one of you and so bring disgrace on all Israel'
(1 Sam. 11:2).

In the New Testament, 'The Jews did not want the bodies'
of Christ and the thieves 'left on the crosses during the Sab-
bath', so 'they asked Pilate to have the legs broken and the
bodies taken down' (John 19:31). Paul speaks of those who
preached Christ but from very dubious motives indeed (Phil.
1:15-17). James talks of a man who says to 'a brother or sister
[who] is without clothes and daily food … "Go, I wish you
well; keep warm and well fed," but does nothing about his
physical needs' (James 2:15-16).

What truths are betrayed by apparently insignificant elements in my life?

**'He who works his land will have abundant food, but he
who chases fantasies lacks judgement'** (12:11).

Contrast: **'he who works his land'** / **'he who chases
fantasies'**
Labour and have food; fantasize and you'll lack.

I remember at school asking a friend why he spent the whole
of the mathematics lesson drawing cars. 'Oh, I'm going to be
a car designer when I grow up,' he replied. To be fair I also
whiled away plenty of time fondly dreaming of a future perfect weekend where I played first-class rugby on Saturday afternoon, thrilled the audience on stage with my own musical
compositions on Saturday night and then preached a soul-
saving, Christ-exalting sermon on Sunday morning!

Whereas verse 9 was in a sense about spending money this verse is more about earning it. This proverb warns us that chasing fantasies shows a lack of judgement. Working your land may not be glamorous, but it means **'abundant food'**, or as we might put it in a more urban culture, 'Concentrate on your studies and you'll get your qualifications,' or 'Get on with your work or your pay may be docked.' Dreaming about a win on the national lottery is counter-productive in many ways. Daydreaming is a subtle form of the laziness condemned elsewhere in the book. The trouble with fantasies is not only that the thoughts themselves are often impure, but that they lead nowhere anyway. Too often our dreams of Christian usefulness are just that — unrealistic fantasies.

We should note in passing that 28:19 preserves an almost identical proverb.

'The wicked desire the plunder of evil men, but the root of the righteous flourishes' (12:12).
Contrast (complex): **'wicked'** / **'root of the righteous'**
The wicked, they want the evil's winnings; the root of the righteous keeps on growing.

Here we begin again with the thought life. **'The wicked desire the plunder** [literally, "the net"] **of evil men.'** They hear of a raid, a robbery, a 'job' coming up or done. They would love to get some of the booty regardless of the risk. When I was a boy, clothing made by the Wrangler company was very popular. While still unconverted I remember going on a school holiday and learning that some in the party had found an outlet selling Wrangler goods and had purloined several items undetected. Although I did not steal (chiefly due to fear), to my shame I still desired some of the haul they had amassed.

Of **'the righteous'**, it is asserted not simply that they do not desire loot, but that their **'root ... flourishes'**. The wicked,

then, see the plunder that evil men get and desire it. The righteous not only have no desire for such things, but they 'flourish' from their 'root'. They see that the way to wealth and
material well-being is gradual, not sudden, more like the growth
of a tree than the sweep of a fishing net. They understand this
proverb and later proverbs such as 13:11 and 20:21 (see also
10:2).

What these twelve proverbs teach us

Taking these proverbs together we learn about some nine contrasts that we need to recognize and keep in mind.

The Lord's attitude to the good and to the crafty

He shows favour to 'a good man' but condemns 'a crafty man'
(12:2).

Human attitudes to the wise and to the warped

If a man has wisdom he is 'praised according to his wisdom,
but men with warped minds are despised' (12:8)

Reality for nobodies and for somebodies

Verse 9 argues indisputably that it is 'better to be a nobody
and yet have a servant than pretend to be somebody and have
no food'.

Discipline loved and hated

If you love discipline you love knowledge, and if you work
your land you will have abundant food, but if you hate

correction you are stupid and to chase fantasies shows a lack of judgement (12:1,11).

Wives noble and nasty

'A wife of noble character is her husband's crown, but a disgraceful wife is like decay in his bones' (12:4).

Schemes of the righteous and of the wicked

The righteous make plans that are 'just', but the wicked give 'deceitful' advice (12:5).

The speech of the wicked and of the upright

'The words of the wicked lie in wait for blood, but the speech of the upright rescues them' (12:6).

The stability of the wicked and of the righteous

'A man cannot be established through wickedness'; 'Wicked men are overthrown and are no more'; but 'The righteous cannot be uprooted,' and 'The house of the righteous stands firm' (12:3,7).

Kind acts of the righteous and of the wicked

'A righteous man cares for the needs of his animal, but the kindest acts of the wicked are cruel' (12:10).

The destiny of the wicked and of the righteous

'The wicked desire the plunder of evil men, but the root of the righteous flourishes' (12:12).

24.
Attitudes and utterances under the microscope

Please read Proverbs 12:13-28

Sinful speech, satisfying speech, teachability, provocation, honest speech, wise speech, truthful speech, plotting evil, troubles, lying, discretion, diligence, kind speech, choosing friends, laziness, the way to life

Here we deal with the sixteen proverbs in the second part of Proverbs 12.

> **An evil man is trapped by his sinful talk,**
> **but a righteous man escapes trouble.**
> **From the fruit of his lips a man is filled with good**
> **things**
> **as surely as the work of his hands rewards him**
> **(12:13-14).**

In these two verses we have two further proverbs regarding how we speak, and especially the results of what we say.

Contrast: **'evil man'** / **'righteous man'**

The former **'is trapped by his sinful talk'**, while the latter **'escapes trouble'**. Evil men often say things that lead them into trouble — they tell lies and are found out; they boast of non-existent skills which are then put to the test; they make rash promises and find themselves held to them; they slander others and so create enemies. A biblical example would be Adonijah's request for Abishag as his wife (see 1 Kings 2).

'**A righteous man**', however, will either say nothing, avoid such sins, or speak with such sweetness that he will not only avoid falling into a trap of his own making, but will also escape traps set by others.

In this life, the things we say can trap us and, unless God is gracious, we have no hope. When endangered by their own tongues Abraham, Isaac and David in turn escaped danger in Philistine country simply because of God's grace. Think too of Daniel escaping the lions' den and his three friends coming through the fiery furnace. Their accusers were liars and ended up in the very predicament they wished to inflict upon others. When Christ died, the Jews sinfully cried out, 'Let his blood be on us and on our children!' (Matt. 27:25), and so it was.

On the other hand, a gentle answer can turn away wrath (15:1), as Gideon proved with the Ephraimites (Judg. 8:1-3), and Abigail with David (1 Sam. 25:20-35). The way our Lord dealt with the question about taxes to Caesar is a startling outworking of the second part of the proverb. He sided neither with the rebels nor with the Romans.

The first part of the proverb is similar to 18:6-7; the second to 11:8 (see also Ps. 34:19). As Peter writes, 'The Lord knows how to rescue godly men from trials and to hold the unrighteous for the day of judgement' (2 Peter 2:9).

Simile: '**fruit of his lips**' / '**work of his hands**'

Verse 14 observes that when we speak well — in truth and love and humility — good things will come our way as surely as hard work with one's hands leads to its own rewards (13:2 and 18:20 are similar). It is through wise words that sinners are converted and believers encouraged. By such words the weak are strengthened, the ignorant informed and the wayward corrected. Words are powerful.

'The way of a fool seems right to him, but a wise man listens to advice' (12:15).
   Contrast: **'fool'** / **'wise man'**
   Fools are cocksure; wise men consider.

'Fools rush in where angels fear to tread,' goes the saying. From speaking we move, appropriately, to hearing. A fool's way **'seems right to him'**. What does he need advice for? We recognize him in the lines:

> Habit with him was all the test of truth:
> 'It must be right; I've done it from my youth.'

'But a wise man listens to advice' (this is similar to 12:1). It is the spirit of the disastrous age of the judges when every one does what is right in his own eyes.

   I remember my father sometimes becoming exasperated when I was a teenager and saying, 'You can't tell him.' Sadly, on many things you could not. Tongue in cheek, Mark Twain once commented on how when he was fourteen his father seemed to know nothing, but seven years later seemed to have learned a great deal indeed!

   Arrogant self-confidence is not confined to teenagers. There are people who simply never listen to what others have to say, however old they get. They are like the old sailor who thought he knew more than his compass. He wanted to go north, but it seemed to him that as hard as he tried to make the needle aim in that direction, it just kept on pointing south-west!

   It takes humility to accept advice, but what a blessing it can be! Moses (Exod. 18) and David (1 Sam. 25) are examples of men who were willing to listen to others. Even the boy Jesus in the temple asked questions as well as answering them.

When I first heard the gospel, it was hard to believe that these people had found the truth and I was in ignorance, but by God's grace I listened to their advice and was saved. Millions have done the same and gone to the Wonderful Counsellor, the all-wise Messiah, and found the best advice of all.

Of course, not all advice is good advice. We must be discerning, but a teachable spirit is an invaluable asset. Remember Cromwell's words: 'I beseech you, in the bowels of Christ, think it possible you may be wrong.'

'A fool shows his annoyance at once, but a prudent man overlooks an insult' (12:16)

Contrast: **'fool'** / **'prudent man'**

Fools — they're distressed immediately; wise men — they disregard insults.

A theme in Proverbs is how to spot a fool. A characteristic highlighted here is that he **'shows his annoyance at once'**. The **'prudent'** overlook insults. Skin like a rhinoceros hide and a readily turned cheek are vital for Christians, who must 'not repay anyone evil for evil' (Rom. 12:17). Fools, on the other hand, have never learned to count to ten. They are pots that quickly boil. (For similar proverbs, see 16:32; 19:11; 29:11; 14:17,29; 15:18; 17:14,27-28; 19:19; 25:28.)

Biblical examples of hot-tempered outbursts are found not only in Saul (e.g. 1 Sam. 20:30) and Nabal (1 Sam. 25:10), but also on one occasion in the meekest man of his day, Moses (see Num. 20:10-12). We all need to take care. Insults will always hurt, but we do not have to show that they do. Holding one's temper is not an easy virtue to attain but it is one we all ought to seek. In the seventeenth century George Herbert advised:

Command thyself in chief. He life's war knows
Whom all his passions *follow* as he goes.

Augustine said that to conquer ourselves is to conquer the
world. Even the pagan Pythagoras recognized that no man is
free while he cannot control himself.

An attitude of love will prevent us from slamming the door
in the face of an adversary. It will enable us to keep the door
open in hope of change. It is part of God's character to overlook insults. He sends the rain and sunshine on righteous and
unrighteous alike. Slowness to anger is one of his great characteristics (see Exod. 34:6). 'He is patient ... not wanting anyone to perish, but everyone to come to repentance' (2 Peter
3:9). It is often overlooked, but we see this in Jesus when he
'drove all from the temple area, both sheep and cattle; he scattered the coins of the money-changers and overturned their
tables'. This was not done in a burst of temper. Before doing
it, he carefully 'made a whip out of cords' (John 2:15; cf.
Matt. 21:12-13; Mark 11:15-17; Luke 19:45-46). Peter reminds us that this was typical: 'When they hurled their insults
at him, he did not retaliate; when he suffered, he made no
threats. Instead, he entrusted himself to him who judges
justly'(1 Peter 2:23).

A truthful witness gives honest testimony,
but a false witness tells lies.
Reckless words pierce like a sword,
but the tongue of the wise brings healing.
Truthful lips endure for ever,
but a lying tongue lasts only a moment

                                          (12:17-19).

In these verses we are back to sins of the tongue. Two of the
proverbs are the first of several about honesty. Proverbs 14:5

is very similar to verse 17. It says, 'A truthful witness does not deceive, but a false witness pours out lies.' The subject arises again in 12:22. In verse 18 we are dealing with thoughtfulness, or lack of it, when we speak.

Contrast: **'truthful witness'** / **'false witness'**

The ninth commandment condemns giving false testimony. In verse 17 this is underlined with what appears at first sight to be a truism, or tautology. The point, however, is that our character determines how we act. Truthfulness leads to **'honest testimony'**, but a false witness **'tells lies'**. When we read of someone who is morally corrupt being caught out in a deception, it is no surprise. Usually those who are morally upright tell the truth. This is one of the internal witnesses to the truth of Christianity. Is it likely that apostles who preached, 'Do not lie to each other, since you have taken off your old self with its practices and have put on the new self, which is being renewed in knowledge in the image of its Creator' (Col. 3:9-10), would nevertheless promote a falsehood when they preached that Jesus had risen from the dead? What a mess a society is in when its citizens cannot be trusted to tell the truth! False witnesses told lies about our Lord. He calls on all who trust in him today to bear faithful witness to him.

Simile: **'reckless words'** / **'sword'**
Contrast: **'reckless words'** / **'tongue of the wise'**
Reckless words wreck; hale tongues heal.

Verse 18 is similar to verse 6 and turns our attention again to the power of words to harm or to heal. Using words recklessly is like thrusting a person through with a sword. Failing to engage the clutch of the mind before putting our mouths into gear can lead to embarrassment, pain, and worse, for

others. 'I simply couldn't cope without my wife,' says Dominic
— but Jed's wife died six months ago! 'Everyone knows that,'
says Mick — but Angela didn't! 'Everyone was told weeks
ago,' says Jackie. 'I wasn't!' says Dick. Whenever we have in
mind to criticize or praise someone; to reveal a truth to or
about a person; to give people our opinion, or to tell them
what to do — we need to think carefully about the effect our
words will have. It is sheer recklessness not to do this.

We must speak the truth — but in love. In witness we do
not have to tell everyone all that we believe about hell on first
meeting them! We do not say to Muslims or Hindus, 'Now
you believe…' Rather, we listen first.

Wardlaw warns against reckless jesting too: 'The man of
wit *must* have his joke, cost what it may. The point may be
piercing in the extreme; but if it *glitters* it is enough; to the
heart it will go.'

There is hope in verse 18 too. **'The tongue of the wise'**
will be active in healing wounds. Words which give praise and
comfort, information and explanation, and which are marked
by honesty and tact, can do great good. The Lord himself spoke
such healing words and his followers should do the same.

Contrast: **'truthful lips'** / **'lying tongue'**
Truthful tongues triumph; lying lips languish.

One endures for ever; the other lasts only a moment. Like
truth itself, **'truthful lips'** will endure (12:19). **'A lying
tongue'** may appear to be unstoppable but it will soon come
to an end, as do lies themselves. Sophocles said, 'No lie reaches
old age.' Archbishop Tillotson wrote, 'Truth is always con-
sistent with itself, and needs nothing to help it out; it is always
near at hand, and sits upon our lips, and is ready to drop before
we are aware; whereas a lie is troublesome, and sets a man's
invention upon the rack and one trick needs a good many more
to make it good. It is like building upon a false foundation

which constantly needs props to shore it up, and proves at last more chargeable than to have raised a substantial building at first upon a true and solid foundation.'

The first part of the proverb finds its fulfilment ultimately in Christ, who said, 'Heaven and earth will pass away, but my words will never pass away' (Matt. 24:35).

'There is deceit in the hearts of those who plot evil, but joy for those who promote peace' (12:20).

Contrast (complex): **'hearts of those who plot evil'** / **'those who promote peace'**

Plotters of perversity deceive; promoters of peace delight.

The theme of dishonesty carries over into the first part of verse 20. These evil plotters and promoters of peace are no doubt the same characters as those who, on the one hand, use reckless words, or, on the other, whose tongues bring healing. Here the focus is on their hearts. The former are marked by deceit, while the latter know joy.

There is a little complexity, since it does not say, 'There is deceit in the hearts of those who plot evil; *honesty in* the hearts of those who promote peace,' nor '*There is no joy for* those who plot evil but there is for those who promote peace.' Rather the thoughts are combined.

What we seek for others and the way we seek it leaves its mark on us. Those who seek evil for others usually employ deception. When we seek to deceive others we deceive ourselves by thinking that we shall be happier if evil comes on someone else, but the deceit creates a tension that precludes joy. When we seek to live at peace with others and see them prosper, however, it brings joy to our own hearts. Remember Jesus' own words: 'Blessed are the peacemakers, for they will be called sons of God' (Matt. 5:9). Those who plot evil, on the other hand, are children of the devil and will suffer as he does. What joy lies in seeking blessing for others!

'No harm befalls the righteous, but the wicked have their fill of trouble' (12:21).
   Contrast: **'righteous'** / **'wicked'**
   Righteous? Expect healing. Wicked? Expect harm.

This is one of those great generalizing proverbs that we come across from time to time. If we are **'righteous'** in Christ then ultimately **'no harm befalls'** us. If we are **'wicked'**, we shall have our **'fill of trouble'**. The theology behind such proverbs can easily be mishandled if applied in a rigid way, as in the case of Job's so-called comforters. Rightly understood, however, this is a proverb full of encouragement for the righteous, an Old Testament equivalent of Romans 8:28. It is also a warning to the wicked. It sums up the story of Joseph and Daniel, and of Christ himself and all who follow him. Theirs is heaven, not hell; everlasting blessing, not everlasting damnation, though the contrary may seem to be the case at times. Such apparent reversals are there to test the righteous.

'The LORD detests lying lips, but he delights in men who are truthful' (12:22).
   Lord detests
   Contrast: **'lying lips'** / **'men who are truthful'**
   Lying lips he loathes; truthful types he trusts.

Here we come back to the matter of honesty. **'The LORD detests'** lies. **'Men who are truthful'** are those in whom he delights. (This we may have gleaned from 11:1,20, both of which use the formula: 'The Lord abhors / detests …') Ultimately, in the matter of honesty, what matters is not what works best, but what the Lord thinks. Here it is made very plain. The God of truth **'detests lying lips, but … delights in men who are truthful'**. These are strong words. Honesty is therefore not only the best policy, but also the only policy open to the man who fears the Lord. We must be honest in speech and honest in deeds. We 'must put off falsehood and speak truthfully' (Eph. 4:25). Here is a little reminder that, although the book of Proverbs may at times sound just like some of the common sense advocated by humanists, it looks beyond that. Do you?

George Herbert wisely wrote:

Dare to be true, nothing can need a lie;
A fault which needs it most grows two thereby.

'A prudent man keeps his knowledge to himself, but the heart of fools blurts out folly' (12:23).
Contrast: **'prudent man'** / **'heart of fools'**
Pacific Prudence and Big Blurter.

An interesting proverb, this one has a double contrast. **'A prudent man'** has **'knowledge'**, but is willing to keep it to himself. **'The heart of fools'**, on the other hand, **'blurts out'** what he thinks is knowledge but is in fact **'folly'**. In later proverbs, we learn that, in contrast to the knowledge of the wise, 'a fool exposes his folly' (13:16) and his mouth 'gushes folly' (15:2). The difference between the wise and foolish is not only in content but also in style. It is a little like the difference between a child emptying the toy-box across the floor and a craftsman carefully choosing the right tool from his toolbox. The fool is eager to speak first and show how clever he is, and so he does not wait until he has his facts right or his understanding clear, but **'blurts out folly'**. There is an English proverb which says, 'Empty vessels make the most noise.' Certainly fools are often the loudest in proclaiming their folly. Wisdom recognizes this and is careful to ignore the hullabaloo surrounding the big noises in this world's clamour and seek knowledge from the less publicity-conscious.

The prudent are willing to take time investigating, weighing things up, considering the various angles, even though that may mean remaining silent for some time. They avoid throwing pearls to pigs or what is sacred to dogs. They recognize that some displays of knowledge are mere self-promotion, and that to reveal certain things too early does more harm than good. Sex education would be an obvious area where prudence and folly are at loggerheads today.

Bridges comments that 'Nothing can justify speaking contrary to the truth. But we are not always obliged to tell the whole truth.' Abraham's dealings with Isaac, Joseph's with his brothers in Egypt and Esther's with her king come to mind. In the case of Joseph, perhaps he learned by experience not to blurt out his knowledge as he had as a teenager.

Think too how often fools have rushed into print to say that Christianity is finished and the Bible has been proved wrong. The prudent have been willing to wait and have been proved right many times. So it will be at the very end. Our Lord himself showed this aspect of wisdom in his early attempts to secure silence regarding his Messiahship and in the way he gradually revealed truth to his disciples (see John 16:12).

'Diligent hands will rule, but laziness ends in slave labour' (12:24).

Contrast: **'diligent hands'** / **'laziness'**
The diligent direct; sluggards slave.

Next (and again in verse 27) we return to the subject of diligence and laziness and where they lead. Several comments on this topic were made in the commentary on Proverbs 10:4-5. Here the focus is not simply on poverty or wealth, but on ruling or being a slave. If we are diligent (intelligently focused and persistent in a given task), we shall normally be given increasing responsibility in whatever sphere we labour at. If, on the other hand, we are lazy (laid back, unfocused and easily diverted) it will lead to bondage. Leaders are for the most part well-motivated, persevering individuals. Some never rise in their chosen field simply out of laziness. They are not interested.

Solomon, of course, knew all about **'slave labour'**. He also 'saw how well the young man' Jeroboam 'did his work' and 'put him in charge of the whole labour force of the house of Joseph' (1 Kings 11:28). Could he have guessed where that would lead?

We must not suppose from this proverb that diligence guarantees promotion. Even the most diligent are sometimes made redundant. However, like cream and hot air, speaking metaphorically, and like Joseph and Daniel, speaking biblically, it is the diligent who rise to the top. Certainly it is the saints who will rule in the world to come because they have been diligent today in the things that really matter. Those who are lazy about the things of God are slaves to sin and death.

'An anxious heart weighs a man down, but a kind word cheers him up' (12:25)
> *Contrast:* **'anxious heart'** / **'kind word'**
> An anxious weight lifted by cheer.

The practical theologian Professor Jay Adams tells a joke about a man who found someone willing, for a fee, to do all his worrying for him. He explains the arrangement to a friend and the friend thinks it is an excellent idea. He then spots a snag. 'How are you going to pay for this?' 'Oh,' says the man, 'that's his worry'! It makes a pleasant change to find some humour in what is normally no joke. **'An anxious heart weighs a man down.'** Sometimes even a little joke can make a worrier smile, though, and **'A kind word cheers him up.'**

Like others, this contrasting proverb raises the subject of heartache and happiness (One thinks especially of 15:13,15; 17:22; 18:14). When we are anxious we become downcast and depressed and our spirits sink. The solution is not necessarily to resolve the problem that triggers the anxiety but to replace the negative thinking with something more positive. It has staggered me on occasions to find myself in a thunderous mood, only for it to be dispelled by a mere smile or a pleasantry from someone. There can be no doubt that although kind words will not solve the world's problems, they will make life more bearable. With a little effort they can be given. What we need is not more 'trauma counselling' but more kind words (and kind acts).

As I write, I have just come back from counselling someone going through a period of depression. Besides several negative statements she also told me with joy how she had read in Mrs Cowman's *Streams in the Desert* some words of encouragement from Spurgeon that had lifted her spirits no end. If we are believers, we have good words to speak (and deeds to do). Through Christ we have come to 'know the word that sustains the weary' (Isa. 50:4). We must speak it as and when we can.

'A righteous man is cautious in friendship, but the way of the wicked leads them astray' (12:26).
> *Contrast (complex):* **'righteous man'** / **'way of the wicked'**
> The righteous man to caution tends
> When looking out for friends;
> Those who are on the wicked way
> Are always led astray.

There is some disagreement about the translation of the first half of this proverb. Some translate it as: 'A righteous man is a guide to his friend.' The verb used means 'to investigate' or 'make reconnaissance'. It seems likely, then, that careful research is being recommended before entering into a friendship. Proverbs has plenty to say about friendship or neighbourliness, but here caution is urged at the beginning. One of the ways that the wicked are led astray is by their lack of caution in this area.

Jesus recommends caution regarding the gospel in a passage we have quoted before: 'Suppose one of you wants to build a tower. Will he not first sit down and estimate the cost to see if he has enough money to complete it? For if he lays the foundation and is not able to finish it, everyone who sees it will ridicule him, saying, "This fellow began to build and was not able to finish." Or suppose a king is about to go to war against another king. Will he not first sit down and consider whether he is able with ten thousand men to oppose the one coming against him with twenty thousand? If he is not able, he will send a delegation while the other is still a long way off and will ask for terms of peace' (Luke 14:28-32).

Easily led, the wicked soon fall into evil ways, not because they are particularly wicked themselves but chiefly because they have fallen in with the wrong sort. Often in reports on criminal trials, one reads of how an evil man has drawn in someone else to take part with him in his evil deeds. This subject can be a contentious one between parents and children, but the effort to steer younger ones in the right direction early on will be rewarded. As we come to years of maturity some latitude is in order provided we still exercise care. We must remember that on earth Christ himself was a friend of sinners. He was no doubt cautious, but he was loving also.

'The lazy man does not roast his game, but the diligent man prizes his possessions' (12:27).
   Contrast: **'lazy man'** / **'diligent man'**
   Rotting roast; prized possessions.

Here diligence and laziness are contrasted again — to the groans of the lazy, no doubt (this is like 19:24). Lazy people do show some signs of activity. Here is one who has gone hunting and either cornered or caught an animal. The burst of energy is not sustained, however. He is too lazy to finish the job and snare it, or roast it. The lazy man leaves half-completed jobs wherever he goes — evidenced in partly decorated rooms, unfinished building projects, abandoned tools and toys, half-read books, incomplete manuscripts. Some approach Christianity like that. The seed is sown in their hearts but, being rootless, it all comes to nothing. Even among the saved there are those who seem to leave too much half done.

In contrast, **'The diligent man prizes his possessions'** (if the NIV has this difficult line right. It could be: 'The diligent man is a prize possession,' or 'Diligence is man's prized possession'). Wisely the proverb does not state that he 'gets everything finished'! There are sometimes good reasons why things remain unfinished. A diligent man does prize his possessions, however. Because he prizes them, he makes good use of them.

One of the great characteristics of God is his care for his creatures. When he begins to work salvation in a man's heart, he always brings the work to completion in the end. One of Christ's seven words from the cross was: 'It is finished!'

'In the way of righteousness there is life; along that path is immortality' (12:28).
Synonymous: **'way of righteousness'** / **'that path'**
The righteous route regenerates.

The chapter ends with another great generalizing proverb. Wholly positive with no antithesis, it asserts, in a way that some people think the Old Testament did not grasp (hence the various translations), that righteousness is good not only for this life, but leads to immortality. This is the narrow road that

Jesus spoke about and contrasted with the broad road (Matt. 7:13-14).

What we learn from these sixteen proverbs

As a general principle, 'No harm befalls the righteous, but the wicked have their fill of trouble' (12:21). Even when that is not so obvious in this life it is true that 'In the way of righteousness there is life; along that path is immortality' (12:28). Righteousness comes through faith in Christ but expresses itself in the lives of true believers. It is seen in their attitudes and their utterances.

Right attitudes

Certain characteristics mentioned here are seen in the wise and righteous.

Caution
This is especially manifested in making new friends. Such people are not easily led (12:26).

Teachability

They are willing to take advice. Such people are not headstrong or arrogant (12:15).

Peaceableness

They are willing to overlook an insult and not be annoyed too easily (12:16). They are characterized by peacemaking, not plotting evil (12:20).

Diligence and natural leadership

Such people get the job done (12:24,27).

Diligence is not confined to the righteous and the wise. Evil men are often diligent to do evil. The English Reformer and martyr Hugh Latimer once preached a sermon about the most diligent bishop in England — the devil! We must be diligent to do good.

Right utterances

Jesus said, 'But I tell you that men will have to give account on the day of judgement for every careless word they have spoken. For by your words you will be acquitted, and by your words you will be condemned' (Matt. 12:36-37).

In particular here, we are reminded that the speech of the righteous is marked by truthfulness and thoughtfulness.

Truthfulness

These proverbs remind us that 'Truthful lips endure for ever, but a lying tongue lasts only a moment' (12:19); and 'The LORD detests lying lips, but he delights in men who are truthful' (12:22). We must be truthful witnesses who give honest testimony, not false witnesses who tell lies (12:17).

Thoughtfulness

There are many ways of sinning, or of doing good, with your mouth. The wise often keep their knowledge to themselves and use their tongues to bring healing, rather than using 'reckless words' that 'pierce like a sword' (12:18), or blurting out 'folly' (12:23). They are always ready with 'a kind word' to cheer up someone weighed down with 'an anxious heart' (12:25).

Verses 13 and 14 remind us that truthful and thoughtful speech not only please God and lead to life, but when we speak rightly we ourselves are 'filled with good things'. 'An evil man is trapped by his sinful talk, but a righteous man escapes trouble.'

25.
Righteousness and wisdom, not riches and wealth

Please read Proverbs 13:1-14

Teachability, beneficial speech, careful speech, cravings of the sluggard, righteous hatred, integrity, false appearances, pros and cons of wealth and poverty, radiance, pride, increasing wealth, hope deferred, teachability, wisdom a fountain of life

Here we consider the initial fourteen proverbs of Proverbs 13.

'A wise son heeds his father's instruction, but a mocker does not listen to rebuke' (13:1).
  Contrast: **'wise son'** / **'mocker'**

Here we return to the theme of who is a wise son (see the early chapters), using a new word for **'rebuke'**. This proverb teaches similar truths to 15:5. Listening to rebuke and taking advice is often commended in Proverbs (see 1:25,30; 3:11; 9:7-8; 17:10; 25:12. Note especially 13:10; 19:20). So here teachability is again underlined. Pride and the hatred of rebuke are so prevalent and ingrained that we have to be reminded often of this fundamental need.

Christians think of the perfect son, the Son of God who 'although he was a son … learned obedience' (Heb. 5:8), so providing a perfect salvation and a perfect example. True sons of God receive his salvation and follow his example.

> **From the fruit of his lips a man enjoys good things,**
> **but the unfaithful have a craving for violence.**
> **He who guards his lips guards his life,**
> **but he who speaks rashly will come to ruin**
>   (13:2-3).

Again in these verses we have proverbs regarding speech.

Contrast (complex): **'From the fruit of his lips'** / **'unfaithful'**

The first line of verse 2 repeats the first part of Proverbs 12:14 and is very similar to 18:20. Here the proverb is contrasting, though not of a regular type. It is matched with **'but the unfaithful have a craving for violence'**. There is complexity, then: it is not, 'From the fruit of his lips a man enjoys good things *or bad things*,' or 'Some *have no craving for violence* / do only good, but the unfaithful have a craving for violence.' Rather we picture a man enjoying the benefits of godly speech, while the unfaithful crave violence and (it is implied) get it. Churchill wisely said that 'Jaw jaw is better than war war.' The benefits of godly speech vary — anything from a civil reply to a congregation full of thanksgiving to the Lord for your faithful preaching. The unfaithful often have a low view of 'mere words' and prefer to use their fists or their boots. Such an attitude is never welcomed.

Contrast: **'he who guards his lips'** / **'he who speaks rashly'**
Guard and gain; be rash and be ruined.

Verse 3 is a warning against rash speech (other proverbs on the same theme include 10:19; 12:13; 21:23). Some do struggle

to speak up, but the real battle for most of us is not to speak.
Yet once a thing is said it is too late to retrieve it. It may even
cost you your life, so guard your lips. Those who speak rashly
will come to ruin. Armed guards are posted at the gates of a
castle. We need guards at eye gate, ear gate and especially
mouth gate.

During World War II there was a slogan: 'Loose lips sink
ships.' They can do more than that. The advice given out to
American soldiers is worth pondering: 'Silence means security... Protect your conversation as you do your letters, and be
even more careful. A harmful letter can be nullified by censor-
ship; loose talk is direct delivery to the enemy ... your lips
must remain sealed... This takes guts. Have you got them or
do you want your buddies and your country to pay the price ...?'

> Oh, be careful, little tongue, what you say!
> For the Father up above
> Is looking down in love.
> So be careful, little tongue, what you say.

**'The sluggard craves and gets nothing, but the desires of
the diligent are fully satisfied'** (13:4).
  Contrast: **'sluggard'** / **'diligent'**
  Desires denied; appetites appeased.

In another contrast between the sluggard and the diligent man,
this proverb reminds us that cravings or **'desires'** are not fulfilled without hard work. Proverbially, the one who does the
hard work is the one who gains the rewards. We have already
been warned against chasing mere fantasies in 12:11 (cf. 6:6-11;
10:4-5,26; 14:23). No one owes us a living. Far from encouraging unrealistic fantasies, the truth is hard-nosed and places
full emphasis on human responsibility. 'The road to hell,' as

we have noted previously, 'is paved with good intentions.' Trapp says, 'The sluggard would and he would not. He would have the end but would not use the means.'

'The righteous hate what is false, but the wicked bring shame and disgrace' (13:5).
  Contrast: **'righteous'** / **'wicked'**

The proverb seems complex, but it is probably right to understand it as saying that while the former speak the truth, the latter are willing to bring **'shame'** (literally, 'a stink') **'and disgrace'** on others (although some understand it to mean that they bring such troubles on themselves). It is a warning against gossip, slander and all forms of deceit. We must not countenance such things and we must be aware that the wicked do introduce such things. The righteous are so loath to speak falsehood that they hate the very idea of it. Matthew Henry sums up succinctly: 'Where grace reigns, sin is loathsome; where sin reigns, the man is loathsome.'

'Righteousness guards the man of integrity, but wickedness overthrows the sinner' (13:6).
  Contrast: **'righteousness'** / **'wickedness'**
  Righteousness safeguards the righteous; wickedness supplants the wicked.

Bodyguards and wrestlers are common enough characters in this modern world. If you are a **'man of integrity'**, then **'righteousness'** will act as an effective bodyguard for you; and if you are a confirmed **'sinner'**, then expect to be overthrown by that heavyweight **'wickedness'**.

What makes an effective bodyguard? One called Henrik writes, 'My job is not to walk around and look tough, or to drink dry martinis at cocktail parties, telling stories about who I protected last month. No, my job is to make sure that my client is safe, and that he remains that way.' Training, experience and intelligence, plus mental toughness, emotional stability and physical fitness are all vital. True righteousness shares such characteristics.

As for wrestling, although there are various styles (Japanese Sumo and Jujitsu, Turkish Pehlivan, Swiss Schwingen, Icelandic Glima, British Cumberland-Westmoreland style, Central Asian Kuresh, Olympian Greco-Roman and freestyle), the object is always (to quote an encyclopaedia definition) 'to secure a fall'. So wickedness aims to 'cause the opponent to lose balance and fall to the floor, and ultimately to pin the supine opponent's shoulders to the floor'. It often succeeds, so beware.

Or think of **'righteousness'** as a strong tower that will not fall, and **'wickedness'** as a tottering structure that cannot stand. The thought chimes in with what is found in Proverbs 10:9 and 11:3-9. One old writer speaks of the way wickedness exhausts a man's property, takes his reputation and health, hastens death and destroys his soul.

> **One man pretends to be rich, yet has nothing;**
> **another pretends to be poor, yet has great wealth.**
> **A man's riches may ransom his life,**
> **but a poor man hears no threat**
>
> (13:7-8).

Here are two observational proverbs referring to wealth and poverty. Both warn us against making a superficial assessment.

Contrast: **'One man pretends to be rich'** / **'another pretends to be poor'**
Feigning fortune; pretending poverty.

The first contrast is not direct, but more a reminder that things are not always quite what they may seem. 'None can guess the jewel by the casket.' 'Not all clouds bring rain.' 'He that looks in a man's face knows not what money is in his purse.' I knew a man who worked in a hotel one summer and he told me that the people who gave the most generous tips were the less well off — probably because they were trying harder to impress. It is often not poverty that hurts, but the attempt to keep up appearances.

The attitudes referred to here are well exemplified, on the one hand, by conmen who, for their own advantage, have passed themselves off as wealthy dukes and maharajahs when in fact they had nothing and, on the other hand, by people who have lived frugal, even destitute, lives, only to be discovered at their death to be in possession of a huge fortune.

An example of the former would be the case of Evelyn Burton and Lyla Andre. An example of the latter would be that of Christine van Gulik. In 2001 British newspapers reported the convictions of two ruthless Australians whose elaborate fraud 'duped the cream of British equestrian high society'. Burton and Andre conned victims out of over £500,000. On the run from Australian police, they arrived in Britain in 1996. Staying at an exclusive hotel in Knightsbridge, they eventually ran up a bill for £35,000. Burton posed as a fabulously wealthy international bond-dealer. This enabled her to persuade investors to part with hundreds of thousands of pounds for bogus schemes promising astonishing profits. At their trial the judge described how they had 'indulged in a lifestyle of considerable luxury' to create the image of 'fabulously wealthy business tycoons' with access to enormous sums. Among their eight main victims was a former equerry of the queen. At the Royal Windsor Show, they even met the queen herself, having talked of offering hundreds of thousands in sponsorship money.

A little while later the same newspapers reported how spin-ster Christine Gulik had lived 'a pauper's life relying on hand-outs from her friends' in a tiny flat in Malvern, England. All the while she had sat on a £12,000,000 fortune which, when she died aged ninety-five, she left almost entirely to ten chari-ties. Only then did the secret of her fortune emerge.

People pretend to be rich or poor from various motives. The proverb is a warning against being deceived. More seri-ously, too many cast a passing glance at the gospel and as-sume it has nothing to offer. They choose rather to follow the superficially attractive crowd headed for hell.

This very compact proverb can be taken in a slightly differ-ent way to mean that 'One man makes himself rich, yet is nothing; another makes himself poor, yet has great wealth' or, better, 'is a great treasure'.

Contrast: **'man's riches'** / **'poor man'**
Riches ransom; poverty prevents.

Verse 8 provides a balance to Proverbs 10:15. It is easy to envy others, and there are many who wish they were rich. 'All the things I could do if I had a little money. It's a rich man's world,' wrote Björn Ulvaeus.

Here rich and poor are contrasted in such a way that the advantages of poverty are magnified. The rich man has the money to pay for, say, a kidnap ransom. Of course, the very statement reminds us that those who are poor are not even subject to such harrowing possibilities. Every situation has two sides and it is naïve to suppose that all the advantages lie on one side or another. When you become rich, you can easily make enemies. That particular problem does not arise if you are poor. 'A horn spoon holds no poison' (though a silver one may). Riches bring security but also threats, envy and many a begging letter. Poverty has at least some advantages. Which would you rather be when walking down a dark alley at night?

'The light of the righteous shines brightly, but the lamp of the wicked is snuffed out' (13:9).
  Contrast: **'light of the righteous'** / **'lamp of the wicked'**
  The right are bright; the wicked have no wick.

This proverb is similar to the thought in Proverbs 4:18. The sentiments in the first part are similarly expressed in Psalms 97:11 and 112:4 and those in the latter part in Proverbs 24:20 (see also 20:20; Job 18:5-6; 21:17). If our lamps are filled with the oil of joy, representative of the Holy Spirit, then we shall shine brightly (literally, 'rejoicing') for the glory of God. 'Give me oil in my lamp, keep me burning to the break of day,' is our prayer. If, like the foolish virgins, we have no oil, our flickering lamps will soon be snuffed out and we shall suffer the consequences.

'Pride only breeds quarrels, but wisdom is found in those who take advice' (13:10).
  Contrast: **'pride'** / **'those who take advice'**
  The arrogant awaken arguments; the cognoscenti court counsel.

This is the second of several warnings against pride (see 11:2). Here pride is personified. Pride is inimical to wisdom. It is an astute observation that pride, rather than honour or right, fuels many quarrels. If there were less pride there would be less quarrelling in churches, families and nations: 'What causes fights and quarrels among you? Don't they come from your desires that battle within you?' (James 4:1).

Teachability, humility, a willingness to take advice, are often commended to us (see 13:1,13; 12:15, with the comments there). Thus *negatively*, pride leads to quarrels and, *positively*, the wisdom that is humility leads to learning from others.

'Dishonest money dwindles away, but he who gathers money little by little makes it grow' (13:11).

Contrast: **'dishonest money'** / **'he who gathers money
little by little'**
Dishonest dollars dwindle; gradual gain grows.

Here is another proverb referring to money. It is, of course,
possible to gain money little by little dishonestly, or honestly
all in one go (the latter is dealt with in 20:21). Money gained
by dishonest means, such as blackmail, stealing, frauds and
scams, pyramid-selling, or dubious speculation, usually comes
in quickly. That is one of its attractions. Proverbially, such
money soon dwindles away. It is either stolen by others (according to a recent statistic one burglar in six himself becomes
a victim of burglary), legally confiscated, foolishly squandered,
or becomes a snare of some sort. 'Easy come, easy go,' is the
saying. The way to gain money that lasts is usually to gather it
'little by little'. There are many advantages in this method of
accumulation. It gives us time to think about how we will
spend our money. It gives us time to adjust to a better standard of living. Having worked hard to gain it, we will be more
careful how we spend it. If it is gained honestly it is also less
likely to be lost.

The 'little by little' principle has many applications. Most
benefits and skills are best acquired by this method. Bert
Weedon famously claimed to be able to have pupils playing
the guitar in a day, and there are plenty of books that claim
you can play the piano, or speak Spanish, in three weeks, but
in reality such things take much longer. It is possible to prepare certain foods and drinks in a fraction of the normal time
required, but only after a fashion. The idea of reading a single
book, attending one conference, or hearing one sermon that
will make us spiritually mature is very attractive. In all these
areas and many more (decorating the kitchen, bringing up children and mastering the book of Proverbs come immediately
to mind!) we need to see that this is the way forward. 'Get
rich quick' schemes seldom give us what they promise. In a

fast-moving 'instant' culture we need to recapture the values of bygone ages that recognized the advantages of taking time to do things.

'Hope deferred makes the heart sick, but a longing fulfilled is a tree of life' (13:12).
   Contrast: **'hope deferred'** / **'longing fulfilled'**
   Hope deferred, heart is diseased; longing fulfilled, life is full.

This is a beautifully poignant observational proverb. The first part provides a balancing warning to the 'little by little' principle of the previous verse. The proverb itself is balanced, strikingly describing the sadness of disappointment and the joy of **'a longing fulfilled'**.

It is Christmas and Jack, a poor orphan boy who had hoped against hope that there would be a real football this year despite so many disappointments, is holding back the tears. On the other side of town Ned, who is the same age, is jumping around the room for joy after tearing the paper from the football kit he has plagued his parents about since the previous September. In the same street lives Arthur. He has not had a visit from his son in Scotland for twenty years now. There was a card saying he would come if he was not too busy with work, but he has not arrived. Arthur is sick at heart. At the local hospital Karl and Melanie hug each other with tears of joy as after sixteen long years they have finally been blessed with a little girl, even though doctors had given up hope of their ever conceiving. And in the church, Ted and Rachel have mixed feelings. Their hearts are sick because Tim, their eldest son, now at university, has still made no profession of faith, yet they have found their teenage daughter Beth's recent baptism like **'a tree of life'** to them.

The **'hope deferred'** is not necessarily one that will not be fulfilled, but its drawn-out nature makes the heart sick with longing. Abraham and Sarah knew most about the 'hope deferred', but also something of the **'longing fulfilled'** with the miraculous birth of Isaac. If we are believers, we know that in the new Jerusalem the tree of life is there for us. Meanwhile as we wait we are often sick at heart.

'He who scorns instruction will pay for it, but he who respects a command is rewarded' (13:13).
    Contrast: **'he who scorns instruction'** / **'he who respects a command'**
    Rebellion reaps ruin; respect reaps reward.

This proverb links with verses 1 and 10. Here the emphasis, as so often, is on the end result (see, for example the end of Proverbs 1). Obedience, hard as it is sometimes, does bring rewards. Many of us can look back on life and see areas where if we had been more willing to accept instruction we would have avoided at least some of the heartaches. Foolish deeds have their consequences. There is no excuse for them when we have been taught otherwise.

    Felicity did not listen to her piano teacher and so she failed her examination. Joe refused to do what his financial adviser said and was left with a hefty tax bill. Those who ignore what faithful preachers say will one day **'pay for it'** in hell.

    Jeremy did what his violin teacher told him to and he passed the examination with merit. Geraldine took her bank manager's advice and saved herself money. Those who heed faithful preaching with the obedience of faith will be **'rewarded'** one day in heaven.

'The teaching of the wise is a fountain of life, turning a man from the snares of death' (13:14).
    Synthetic: **'teaching of the wise'** / **'life'**

Here is a generalizing proverb describing **'the teaching'** (that is, *torah,* or law) **'of the wise'** and what it does. Because it is '**a fountain of life**' (a phrase used back in 10:11), a spring welling up to eternal life, it can turn '**a man from the snares of death**'.

If we listen to the wise words here and in the rest of Scripture that are able to make us wise to salvation, then we shall find life. We shall avoid '**the snares of death**' that lie round and about us at every turn. The Word of God, the work of the Holy Spirit, is like a bubbling brook that refreshes us and gives us life, and a guide on the pathway to heaven leading us away from death and protecting from its snares. As we pass through the desert of this life, it nourishes and protects, refreshes and guards.

What these fourteen proverbs teach us about our real need

What it is not

In verses 7, 8 and 11 the topic is wealth. Few are prepared to argue seriously that life's purpose is making money, or that the more money we have, the happier we are. Many live on this basis, however. The most important thing about you is not whether you are rich or poor. Who knows who is really rich and who is really poor anyway?

Our great need is not more money, but new hearts. The classic line uttered by those who won large sums on the football pools was: 'The money won't change me.' That is both false and true. Wealth can alter a great deal in a person's life. Ultimately, however, it cannot change the heart. There is no essential difference between rich sinners and poor ones.

Meanwhile, it is worth bearing in mind that it is not 'always sunny in the rich man's world', and that the best way to grow wealthy is to do so 'little by little'. Another advantage of that method is that we are less likely to misplace our confidence in wealth.

What it is — wisdom

The book's constant message is that we need wisdom. In these verses we learn how to gain it.

Listen and take advice

See verses 1 and 10 (3:34 is on the same lines). 'Humble yourselves, therefore, under God's mighty hand, that he may lift you up in due time' (1 Peter 5:6).

Respect God's commands

'He who scorns instruction will pay for it, but he who respects a command is rewarded' (13:13). In Noah's day those who scorned his instruction paid dearly. It will be the same when Christ returns. God says:

> This is the one I esteem:
>> he who is humble and contrite in spirit,
>> and trembles at my word
>
> (Isa. 66:2).

Recognize that it is a matter of life and death. Have you realized that 'The teaching of the wise is a fountain of life, turning a man from the snares of death'? (13:14). The unbeliever's hope will always be deferred but the believer's longing will one day be fulfilled (13:12). Today he drinks from 'the fountain of life', and in that day he will eat from the 'tree of life'.

What it is — righteousness

Similarly, we can say that our great need is to be right with God. This comes through faith in Christ, who made atonement for sinners on the cross. Righteousness and wickedness are contrasted here, as elsewhere in the book (13:5,6,9).

Righteousness leads to honesty, integrity and joy. Wickedness leads to shame, overthrow and misery.

If we are truly justified through faith, it will lead to a life of righteousness. It will lead, for example, to diligence and guarding our speech.

Diligence

If we are righteous we will be diligent, not lazy. Then we shall not be victims of unrealistic cravings, but our desires will be 'fully satisfied' (13:4)

Careful speech

To guard your lips is to guard your life. Speaking rashly leads to ruin. Our speaking will bring its own rewards, while the 'unfaithful' crave only 'violence' (13:2-3).

Jesus warns us to 'Watch out! Be on your guard against all kinds of greed.' Why? 'A man's life does not consist in the abundance of his possessions' (Luke 12:15). He also said, 'It is written: Man does not live on bread alone, but on every word that comes from the mouth of God' (Matt. 4:4, quoting Deut. 8:3).

26.
Wisdom and righteousness —
the way and the rewards

Please read Proverbs 13:15-25

*Good understanding, prudent actions, messengers, discipline,
longings fulfilled, influence of others, misfortune, inheritances,
injustice, chastising children, satisfaction for the righteous*

Here we consider the remaining eleven proverbs of chapter
13. All are of the contrasting type.

**'Good understanding wins favour, but the way of the un-
faithful is hard'** (13:15).
  Contrast (complex): **'good understanding'** / **'way of the
unfaithful'**

The text does not say, 'Good understanding wins favour, but
bad understanding *is ill-favoured,*' or '*The way of the faithful
is a pleasant path,* but the way of the unfaithful is hard'. Instead it says that **'good understanding'** is agreeable and so
'wins favour', while **'the way of the unfaithful'** is both
'hard', or callous, and ill-favoured. Proverbs often points out
that, quite apart from anything else, 'the way of the unfaithful'
is not easy. The way of faith is demanding, but the way of
unbelief even more so. Satan is a hard taskmaster and many of

his servants tend to be miserable much of the time. However, the word 'hard' here probably does not mean that such people have a hard life, but that they are cantankerous and make things hard for others. 'Good understanding' wins favour from men, chiefly because it endeavours to be congenial. 'Let's take Peter,' they say. 'Let's choose Jack. He'll know what to do.' Daniel's demeanour in taking his stand in Babylon is an excellent example (Dan. 1). It was the Lord's congeniality that caused people to listen 'to him with delight' (Mark 12:37). The **'unfaithful'** are often prickly and unco-operative: 'Warn a divisive person once, and then warn him a second time. After that, have nothing to do with him' (Titus 3:10).

It is no part of a Christian's calling to be disagreeable for no reason: 'Make every effort to live in peace with all men' (Heb. 12:14); 'If it is possible, as far as it depends on you, live at peace with everyone' (Rom. 12:18).

'Every prudent man acts out of knowledge, but a fool exposes his folly' (13:16).
Contrast: **'prudent man'** / **'fool'**

Here is another apparent truism designed to remind us that there is a close connection between how we think and how we act. The **'prudent man acts out of knowledge'**, and it shows in his actions. Fools expose their **'folly'** in their actions. When we see people doing foolish things it is important that we recognize that more often than not they are acting according to a kind of ignorance. When a child ignores parental warnings and rushes into the road, or mixes with a crowd that get into trouble with the police, he 'exposes his folly'. When someone gets drunk, or is addicted to cocaine, he 'exposes his folly'. When people laugh at the Bible or reject biblical morality they do the same. 'The Bible is full of contradictions,' they say. Where? 'Evolution is a fact.' Since when? 'Christians think they're better than everyone else.' Not so. 'Jesus never claimed to be God.' No? On the other hand, an obedient child, a sober man and a Bible-believing Christian act 'out of knowledge'. Believers see the need to get the facts straight before speaking. Paul warns of those who 'want to be teachers of the law, but … do not know what they are talking about or what they so confidently affirm' (1 Tim. 1:7). The contrast is strikingly seen when the Sadducees ask Jesus their question about the woman who married seven brothers (see Matt. 22:23-33).

'A wicked messenger falls into trouble, but a trustworthy envoy brings healing' (13:17)

Contrast: **'wicked messenger' / 'trustworthy envoy'**
Wicked messengers reel; trustworthy envoys heal.

This proverb is about messengers. The former **'falls into trouble'**; the latter **'brings healing'**. The first, then, not only fails to do any good to others, but harms himself. The second not only does no harm to himself, but 'brings healing' to others. We think for example, of, on the one hand, various messengers of Satan in nightclubs and universities, brothels and churches who bring trouble on themselves as well as on others. On the other hand, we think, for example, of faithful Christian preachers whose message brings healing to many. Above all, we think of that faithful Servant and Apostle Christ himself, 'the apostle and high priest whom we confess', who 'was faithful to the one who appointed him' (Heb. 3:1,2). He came 'down from heaven', he says, 'not to do my will but to do the will of him who sent me' (John 6:38).

'He who ignores discipline comes to poverty and shame, but whoever heeds correction is honoured' (13:18).

Contrast: **'he who ignores discipline' / 'whoever heeds correction'**

Omit chastisement, be humiliated;
Observe correction and you will be honoured.

Old equestrians say, 'It's the bridle and spur that makes a good horse.' Here is yet another proverb extolling discipline and humility. Here the emphasis is on the way that ignoring discipline is likely to lead **'to poverty and shame'**, while heeding correction leads to honour (riches are not mentioned specifically).

Steve Redgrave is Britain's best-known oarsman, especially since his record-breaking fourth gold medal at the Sydney Olympics. From interviews, it is clear that his secret of success is simple discipline. One thinks, on the other hand, of someone like former footballer George Best as an example of great talent that eventually spoiled, chiefly through ill-discipline off the field.

The drunken poet Dylan Thomas is another negative example, as was the earlier poet Coleridge. The latter has been described as 'the supreme tragedy of indiscipline'. 'Never did so great a mind produce so little.' He joined the army after dropping out of university, but left because he could not rub down a horse. He then went to Oxford but left without a degree. He started a newspaper but after ten issues it closed. Another writer wrote that 'He lost himself in visions of work to be done, that always remained to be done. Coleridge had every poetic gift but one — the gift of sustained and concentrated effort.' His head was full of books to be written, but they were never printed because he lacked the discipline to sit down and write.

Seeing that we are wrong and accepting correction is never easy, but sometimes it is the only way forward. Our Lord himself 'humbled himself and became obedient to the point of death — even death on a cross. Therefore God also exalted him to the highest place and gave him the name that is above every name...' (Phil. 2:8-9). The same mind should be in us.

'A longing fulfilled is sweet to the soul, but fools detest turning from evil' (13:19).

Contrast (complex): **'a longing fulfilled'** / **'fools'**

Again we read about **'a longing fulfilled'**. Here it **'is sweet to the soul'**; in verse 12 it was 'a tree of life'. There we were told that 'Hope deferred makes the heart sick.' Here the real problem is highlighted: **'Fools detest turning from evil.'** This is why their longings are not fulfilled, or if they are fulfilled give no real satisfaction.

Here is a man who wants to be happy but he keeps plunging into sin — his marriage is being ruined by his adultery; his other relationships by his hatred and dishonesty; his relationship with God by his refusal to follow his instructions or worship him at all. Everything he touches is spoiled because of his hatred of repentance.

Here is someone else, with many dreams fulfilled and yet they do not satisfy. As with the Israelites in the desert, of whom the psalmist says, 'So he gave them what they asked for, but sent a wasting disease upon them' (Ps. 106:15), so this man seems to have what he wants, but still he craves for more. For most unbelievers, the idea of self-denial now in order that we may know greater blessing in the future does not come into their thinking. They will not turn from evil with the hope of future reward. They want instant gratification.

Believers, on the other hand, have the example of Christ himself, 'who for the joy set before him endured the cross, scorning its shame, and sat down at the right hand of the throne of God' (Heb. 12:2). He said to the disciples, 'I have eagerly desired to eat this Passover with you before I suffer' (Luke 22:15). How often he denied himself to be up before dawn or to pray late into the night!

'He who walks with the wise grows wise, but a companion of fools suffers harm' (13:20).

Contrast: **'he who walks with the wise'** / **'companion of fools'**

Walk with the wise — be wise; fellowship with fools and fail.

'Like breeds like,' says an English proverb. Here is another lesson on how to be wise. Habit, assimilation and transformation often conspire together to change us, for good or ill. Therefore, choose your friends carefully.

Have you ever found your accent changing? What caused it? Being with certain people. Some have detected the increasing presence of a rising intonation, or 'upspeak', in the speech of younger people, especially young women, in Britain: 'It, like, wants to know if you agree?' This is said to be due to the influence of Australian TV soap operas (although it is also a feature of certain regional accents, such as those of Belfast and Bristol).

We are affected by those who are close to us and so we need to choose friends whose influence will be positive. If we spend time speaking with wise friends, reading wise books, listening to wise sermons, we are much more likely to become wise than if we consort with foolish friends, read foolish books and listen to foolish sermons that do not extol Christ. Too easily we forget the power of the influence of others over us.

I remember a minister describing his reaction when his brother began to shake uncontrollably due to religious excitement. Despite himself and to his mystification he began to do the same. A Christian psychiatrist agreed that it was probably a sympathetic reaction to the phenomenon affecting his brother.

Or to use a different illustration — the girls working in a nineteenth-century perfume factory were relatively poor, but how beautifully they smelled as they daily came into contact with the product they were preparing!

'Misfortune pursues the sinner, but prosperity is the reward of the righteous' (13:21).

Contrast: **'misfortune'** / **'prosperity'**

Trespassers tracked hard by tragedy; righteous ones rewarded with riches.

Here we consider again the end for the sinner and for the righteous. **'Misfortune pursues'** the former, but **'prosperity'** will be **'the reward'** of the latter. The very way in which sinners conduct themselves means that they cannot escape from misfortune. Personified here, it is like a skilful football player determined to mark the opposing forward, a good policeman tailing a suspect, a determined huntsman chasing a hare or a fox. It is only a matter of time before misfortune catches up with the sinner. In contrast, **'the righteous'** will be rewarded with prosperity. As with other proverbs, too rigid an application of this proverb would lead us astray with Job's friends, who interpreted his misfortune as proof of his guilt. However, we do see the pattern unfolding in this life to some extent, and in the world to come this is exactly how it will be.

'A good man leaves an inheritance for his children's children, but a sinner's wealth is stored up for the righteous' (13:22).

Contrast : **'good man['s] inheritance'** / **'sinner's wealth'**

Goodness has effects beyond one's own generation. A truly good man will bring blessings on his children and grandchildren too. I can testify to it in the case of my wife and our own children. Although the same can be said for sin, its effects can be dissipated. The general rule is that the sinner's apparent gains are simply saved up until the righteous can use them.

A striking example of this, often referred to, concerns Voltaire's chateau in Ferney-Voltaire, on the French border, near Geneva, Switzerland. It was the French philosopher's home for the last twenty years of his life, from 1758. Here he wrote *Candide* and other works. Educated by Jesuits, his later anti-religious outlook led him to predict Christianity's demise. From 1846, the chateau and its grounds were owned by the Lambert family, however, and in the 1890s it was used by the Geneva Bible Society as a Bible depot. It is even said that Voltaire's old printing-press was used to print Bibles. Over the door of the chapel is the inscription *Deo erexit Voltaire* (Built by Voltaire for God).

Another example comes from 1888 when a certain W. C. Van Meter had large numbers of copies of John's Gospel in Italian printed in Rome. The room where the printing took place was a former torture chamber used by the Inquisition. An iron ring in the ceiling of the borrowed building drew the attention of the printer. On enquiry he learned of its past.

Or take the example of the Monte Carlo radio station, from where many Christian broadcasts have gone out in recent years. It was built by Hitler as a base for his own intended broadcasts. The extremely powerful short-wave transmitter used there was originally made for Major General Suharto, who led an abortive Communist coup in Indonesia in 1965.

More generally, advances in technology (radio, cassette tapes and the internet spring readily to mind) may be made by unbelievers but their chief role is in advancing the kingdom of God.

'A poor man's field may produce abundant food, but injustice sweeps it away' (13:23).
  Contrast (complex): **'abundant food'** / **'[swept] away'**
  A field of food and an unjust injury.

The NIV translation is similar to that of other modern versions. Older Bible versions tend to translate the second part more like the AV: 'but there is that is destroyed for want of judgement'. Is this a warning proverb or one that sounds a note of pessimism? Perhaps it is best to see it as a sad but realistic observation regarding poverty. It acts as a counterpoint to the previous two verses by reminding us that escaping from poverty is not simply a matter of pulling yourself up by your own bootstraps. A bumper harvest will not guarantee wealth while injustice remains. The Bible is never slow to point to injustices in this world. How we deal with these injustices is a more difficult question, but pretending that they do not exist is never encouraged in Scripture.

'He who spares the rod hates his son, but he who loves him is careful to discipline him' (13:24).
   Contrast: **'he who spares the rod'** / **'he who loves'**
   To spare the rod is to spite your son; if you're devoted, you'll discipline.

'Rule youth well, and age will rule itself,' and 'The kick of the dam hurts not the colt,' are English sayings.
   This is the first of several proverbs recommending corporal punishment in order to discipline children. In typically antithetical Hebrew style sparing the rod is said to be a form of hatred towards your son, while real love will result in careful discipline. Corporal punishment is currently unpopular in many parts of the world, largely due to an overreaction to cases of child abuse. Reasonable parents who love the Word of God will be willing to exercise corporal punishment at times and also discipline their children in other ways as appropriate. Physical punishment is not a panacea for all ills (children can quickly become inured to most punishments). A Scots proverb says, 'Never take the tawse [or strap] when a word will do the turn.' However, the cane is a useful instrument in a parent's toolbox, greatly superior to psychological abuse and depriving a child

of privileges or 'grounding', a currently popular means of discipline that simply prolongs tension and unhappiness. Many questions are left to common sense (e.g., At what age should physical punishment begin and end? Should girls be hit? Is an implement important?) Certainly, the idea of hitting a child in temper, hitting on the head, or causing permanent physical harm is never countenanced in Scripture.

'The rod' here stands ultimately for all legitimate punishment, not just beating. To spend too long arguing over the precise meaning is to forget that this is a proverb. By way of illustration, William Arnot helpfully describes the careful crafting of the famous Koh-i-noor diamond from a 'misshapen lump'. Slowly the hard but precious gem was 'polished into shape without cracking it in the process' to be a thing of beauty. 'Those who possess these diamonds in the rough,' he says, 'should neither strike them unskilfully nor let them be uncut.'

'The righteous eat to their hearts' content, but the stomach of the wicked goes hungry' (13:25).
Contrast: **'righteous'** / **'wicked'**
Righteous and replete; wicked and wasted.

Picture first Charles, a well-fed man who has enjoyed an excellent meal, and then Abi, a starving child, whose belly is swollen with hunger. No, it is not an advertisement encouraging giving to some crisis overseas; it is a picture of the righteous and the wicked. The problem, of course, is that you cannot produce photographs to show spiritual deprivation, and so it is always easier to arouse compassion for the physically starving than for the spiritually starving who are lost in wickedness. Here is another reminder of the tremendous blessing involved in being righteous in Christ and the curse that the wicked are under even now. The righteous read their Bibles and their souls are contented. The wicked will not read or, if they do, cannot take it in. A spiritual malnutrition puts them off it and so their souls starve. That is how it is.

What these eleven proverbs teach us

Taking comfort from verse 17, 'A wicked messenger falls into trouble, but a trustworthy envoy brings healing,' I hope I am being trustworthy in drawing together lessons here. May these words bring healing. Consider, firstly, the way of wisdom and, secondly, the rewards of righteousness.

The way of wisdom

The wise man co-operates

'Good understanding wins favour, but the way of the unfaithful is hard' (13:15).

The wise man proceeds from knowledge

'Every prudent man acts out of knowledge, but a fool exposes his folly' (13:16).

The wise man sets his heart on the right thing

'A longing fulfilled is sweet to the soul, but fools detest turning from evil' (13:19)

The wise man walks with the wise

'He who walks with the wise grows wise, but a companion of fools suffers harm' (13:20). If we spend our time with foolish people we are unlikely to grow wise. Rather, doing so will harm us. When we rub shoulders with the wise, it is almost bound to do us good. So seek out the wise — in churches, in books, on tape, on the internet, or wherever.

The wise man sees the whole picture

'A poor man's field may produce abundant food, but injustice sweeps it away' (13:23). Too often people refuse to see the whole picture. 'I'm happy as I am.' Yes, but what of the future? 'You can be happy without being a Christian.' Yes, in the present you may. Pray for deliverance from spiritual myopia.

The wise man is disciplined

'He who ignores discipline comes to poverty and shame, but whoever heeds correction is honoured' (13:18). That is why 'He who spares the rod hates his son, but he who loves him is careful to discipline him' (13:24). We are by nature creatures of habit. It is said that if you do a thing regularly for six weeks it is a habit. We must discipline ourselves to cultivate good habits, not bad ones.

The rewards of righteousness

Prosperity not misfortune

'Misfortune pursues the sinner, but prosperity is the reward of the righteous' (13:21).

A future not emptiness

'A good man leaves an inheritance for his children's children, but a sinner's wealth is stored up for the righteous' (13:22).

Contentment not hunger

'The righteous eat to their hearts' content, but the stomach of the wicked goes hungry' (13:25).

27.
How to be a wicked fool

Please read Proverbs 14:1-19

Wise and foolish women, uprightness, speech, pros and cons of technology, truthfulness, importance of attitudes, bad influences, reflection on one's ways, goodwill, secrets of the heart, future judgement, wrong roads, laughter, just deserts, gullibility, recklessness, hotheads and knaves, simpletons, triumph of the righteous

These nineteen proverbs are mostly contrasting ones. Some are very striking.

'The wise woman builds her house, but with her own hands the foolish one tears hers down' (14:1).
Contrast: **'wise woman'** / **'foolish one'**
Wise women win; foolish females fail.

Unusually, the characters here are female. Most proverbs apply equally to men and women. Is the approach here just for variety, or to emphasize that women have an important role in society, especially in the home? It is most likely that here Wisdom and Folly are personified. As we have noted before, they are always depicted as female. The word **'house'**, as so often in Scripture, stands for the household, or family. The wise woman works in such a way that her family is built up (with commitment, enthusiasm, contentment, submission, humility); the foolish one's antics (adultery, laziness, grumbling, rebellion, pride) serve only to tear hers down. More generally, wisdom builds you up; folly tears you down.

'He whose walk is upright fears the LORD, but he whose ways are devious despises him' (14:2).

Contrast: **'he whose walk is upright'** / **'he whose ways are devious'**
Faithful fearers; devious despisers.

Another apparent truism, this proverb re-emphasizes the close connection, established at the beginning, between upright behaviour and the fear of the Lord. The one **'whose ways are devious'** really despises God, whether he realizes it or not. There is something of a chicken-and-egg situation here. Does he despise the Lord because of his deviousness, or is he devious because he despises the Lord? The two go hand in hand. Hatred for God is a mark of the sinner left to himself (Rom. 1:30).

'A fool's talk brings a rod to his back, but the lips of the wise protect them' (14:3).
Contrast: **'fool's talk'** / **'lips of the wise'**

Here we are back to a favourite subject — right speech. There are two difficulties in this verse. Does the first part warn that **'a fool's talk brings'** trouble on himself — **'a rod to his back'** — or that he 'brings a rod of pride' on others, as he lashes out with his tongue? Does the second part say that the speech of the wise protects themselves, or others?

If we take the view on the first question that he brings trouble on himself, this proverb is similar to 10:13 and 18:6; see also 26:3 and the many references to the need to use the rod (though a different word is used here) in disciplining children (e.g., 13:24; 22:15). The view that the fool here brings trouble on others fits with 12:18. What misery fools bring on themselves and others by their foolish talk!

On the other hand, what good the wise do to themselves and others by saying what is right! One thinks of wise advice given in private ('Don't waste your money on that'; 'Don't take revenge as you plan'); in public speeches that lead to good laws (defending the elderly, the unborn, the poor and those easily led); and, especially, the faithful preaching of the gospel that saves so many from themselves ('Don't trust in yourself, but in Christ').

One of the ironies of our Lord's passion was that he was beaten as though he were a fool, even though he is the source of all wisdom. Today his wise lips speak up on behalf of those who deserve punishment.

'Where there are no oxen, the manger is empty, but from the strength of an ox comes an abundant harvest' (14:4).
Contrast: **'no oxen'** / **'strength of an ox'**

This proverb is somewhat observational, noting the advantages of technology and urging willingness to accept the untidiness that comes with progress. An ox may sound rather non-technological to some, but we must not underestimate the transforming impact of harnessing the strength of such beasts, especially for ploughing. It can mean an abundant harvest. You need to speculate to accumulate. Do not fall for a false economy. Of course, like any technology, oxen make demands — the manger needs to be filled to feed them. 'You can't make an omelette without breaking eggs.' 'No convenience without its inconvenience.' If you want everything neat and tidy, you will find progress difficult. We must not be like the cat that wanted fish without getting its feet wet, or the librarian who hated books being taken down from the tidy shelves.

As one commentator suggests, in church life especially, we must think like working farmers and get away from the 'museum curator' mindset. Reaching outsiders will confront us with all sorts of difficulties, but we should choose struggles and conversions over an easy time and no conversions. The unperturbed mystic in his prayer cell may seem very holy, but the man who goes out and seeks to help the needy will surely reap more abundantly. Bearing in mind the way Paul draws an analogy between oxen and Christian ministers, perhaps there is a warning here to churches that make no effort to call a minister — chiefly because they find life easier that way.

'A truthful witness does not deceive, but a false witness pours out lies' (14:5).
  Contrast: **'truthful witness'** / **'false witness'**

Like Proverbs 12:17, this is not a truism. The point here, as before, is that the character of truthful witnesses is that they do not deceive, while **'a false witness'** inevitably pours out lies (see also 14:25). Those who speak of Jesus Christ speak the truth indeed but, just as at his earthly trial, many false witnesses pour out lies. For an Old Testament example, consider Micaiah and the false prophets in 1 Kings 22.

'The mocker seeks wisdom and finds none, but knowledge comes easily to the discerning' (14:6).
  Contrast (complex): **'mocker'** / **'discerning'**
  Mockers seek for wisdom but they will find none;
  Knowledge to the discerning will quickly come.

Attitude is very important when it comes to seeking wisdom. Wisdom can be coy, and it is as well to know the right approach. **'The mocker'** believes he is seeking wisdom but, because of his attitude, he will not find it. He thinks he knows it all already, or simply desires a name for wisdom for his own ends. Often mockers ask questions that are red herrings — they are intended merely to confuse the hounds of heaven. Herod wanted to see Jesus perform a miracle simply for his own gratification. His wish was denied (Luke 23:8). The contrast is not a simple one, but adds that **'the discerning'** easily gain knowledge because they have the right attitude.

Cynicism abounds in Western thought, often to the detriment of real wisdom. An English proverb says, 'The wise seek wisdom; a fool has found it.' What about you? Is a bad attitude causing you to miss out on heavenly wisdom? Are you in danger of being like those Paul described as 'always learning but never able to acknowledge the truth'? (2 Tim. 3:7). He also spoke of how many claim to be wise but become fools (Rom. 1:22). Jesus praised God that he had hidden vital truths 'from the wise and learned, and revealed them to little children' (Matt. 11:25).

'Stay away from a foolish man, for you will not find knowledge on his lips' (14:7).
Synthetic command (negative): **'stay away'** / **' for you will not find'**

Here we have a straightforward command, although it could be read as an observation: 'When you go away from a foolish man you will ...' We have already learned that one way to acquire wisdom is to spend time with the wise (see 13:20). The corollary also holds good. **'You will not find knowledge'** on the lips of a fool, and so the less time you spend reading his books, watching his films, or sharing his conversation, the better for you. There are times when it is the Christian's duty not to stand and fight, but to run. Rather than casting pearls before pigs, or throwing sacred meat to dogs, we are usually wisest to give the fool a wide berth.

'The wisdom of the prudent is to give thought to their ways, but the folly of fools is deception' (14:8)
   Contrast (complex): **'wisdom of the prudent'** / **'folly of fools'**
   Prudence ponders; dullness deludes.

It is a mark of **'the prudent'** that, rather than rushing thoughtlessly through life, they **'give thought to their ways'**. They ask questions such as, 'Why do I do what I do? Where is this leading me? What does God think of this? Is there a better way?' Rather than the straight contrast, 'The wisdom of the prudent is to give thought to their ways, but the folly of fools *is to rush through life without thinking*,' or even, 'The wisdom of the prudent *is true*, but the folly of fools is deception,' we have the proverb as it stands. Fools believe a lie. Because they never stop to think, they never see how deluded they are. Success is surely not a matter of making money. There must be more to life, undoubtedly.

Arnot describes the madness of a man who worked in the reptile house at London Zoo. One day he began to play around with the snakes, trying to frighten his companions. Though he was warned how dangerous a bite from one of them could be, he carried on regardless and was eventually bitten. The fool died. One can think of similar incidents where people have done foolish things and lost their lives or come very close to it. Shortly before writing this, I read about a man who lost his life bungee jumping. Every time we hear of such a thing it is a reminder to give thought to our own ways.

'Fools mock at making amends for sin, but goodwill is found among the upright' (14:9).
Contrast: **'fools'** / **'upright'**

Following on from the previous verses, another contrast between wicked **'fools'** and the wise, or **'upright'**, is seen in the way that they deal with their guilt. For the fool the idea of **'making amends for sin'** is scoffed at. 'The upright', however, show **'goodwill'**. We see this in everyday life. Bump into a fool and, whether it is your fault or his, he will let you know what he thinks of you. Bump into an upright person and he is willing to take his share of the blame and more. There is a callousness about the fool. He refuses to put right his mistakes. The upright are ready to accept where they are in the wrong.

We are so used to this phenomenon that perhaps we are not struck by the irony of it. Whereas, from one point of view, fools should be more ready to make amends as they are so wicked, and the upright less so because they are so good, the opposite is true. Fools have no shame. One test of how upright and wise we are is our goodwill. Are we ready to admit that we are in the wrong? Or are we always defending ourselves? The godly are not yet made perfect, but at least they desire to be changed.

'Each heart knows its own bitterness, and no one else can share its joy' (14:10).
Synthetic: **'its own bitterness'** / **'its joy'**

Although joy and bitterness form something of a contrast, this is not a contrasting proverb as such. It is a poignant and moving reminder of how superficial we are at times. We can be so wrapped up in our own problems that we forget that **'Each heart knows its own bitterness.'** We sometimes envy others, forgetting the sadness that each knows. Grief for lost loved ones, fears about the future, regrets about the past, concern for family members, unrequited love, worries over health and finance — it all lies there just below the surface. Sometimes it shows itself in part; more often not at all. Sorrow is never easy to express; sympathy is even more difficult. We must not forget the sorrow that exists. It is easy to say, 'I know what you are going through,' but we seldom do. What a wonder that as believers we have a High Priest who fully sympathizes and understands as no other can!

Perhaps even more poignant is the second part of the proverb. **'No one else can share its joy,'** is an extreme statement, but it is a fact that sometimes we are so happy that it is impossible fully to share with others what we experience. As I go over this chapter an album of songs by Enya plays in the background. Much of it is in a mournful vein. 'Evacuee' begins:

Each time on my leaving home
I run back to my mother's arms,
One last hold and then it's over.

M. W. Balfe's operatic 'Marble Halls' describes a dream of a palace, but repeats the rueful lines:

But I also dreamt,
which charmed me most,
that you loved me still the same.

The music helps us enter the worlds of an evacuee and of a jilted lover, but only a little.

With a happier track 'Caribbean Blue', we can rejoice with writer Roma Ryan in our imagination — but only to a degree.

Then there is a track in Gaelic ('Ebudae') that says:

> Look, women working by day and late at night,
> They sing of bright days that were,
> A long way back and forth for ever.

and then a Shaker hymn beginning:

> My life goes on in endless song
> Above earth's lamentations.

It contains the refrain: 'How can I keep from singing?' Even a Highland woman or a Shaker believer could only enter so far into sympathy with the joys expressed here.

One commentator rightly says, 'Some things cannot be communicated and we must learn to know what they are.' Nevertheless it is the duty of the believer to his fellow believers to seek, as far as he can, to 'rejoice with those who rejoice' and 'mourn with those who mourn' (Rom. 12:15). Christ has done so and continues to do so perfectly. He is our model.

'The house of the wicked will be destroyed, but the tent of the upright will flourish' (14:11).
Contrast: **'house of the wicked'** / **'tent of the upright'**
The house of the vile ones, it will fall; the home of the virtuous flourish.

And so to another straightforward declaration regarding the contrasting futures of **'the wicked'** and **'the upright'**, focusing here on their **'house'** or **'tent'**, which possibly stands for the body, but more likely for the family. Its truth is reflected in the rise and fall of various dynasties in the history of the ten tribes and the flourishing of David's house, despite several anxious moments, down to the coming of Messiah. (This proverb is most like 12:7 but see also 10:25.) The future for 'the wicked' is destruction. The foolish man's house on the sand cannot stand. Its construction is too flimsy. The future for 'the upright' is rosy. His tent **'will flourish'** like a tree blossoming. Though storms come, the wise man's house will stand. Ahead lie resurrection and glory. Just as Christ rose, so will all who are upright in him.

The choice of **'tent'** for the upright, rather than 'house', perhaps stresses the pilgrim nature of life in Christ (see Heb. 11:8-10).

> **There is a way that seems right to a man,**
> **but in the end it leads to death.**
> **Even in laughter the heart may ache,**
> **and joy may end in grief**

                                                                    (14:12-13).

We take these proverbs together as both speak of an unexpected and unpleasant end.

Contrast: **'way'** / **'end'**
Right route; wrong result.

Verse 12 is another warning about being deceived by appearances. Again there is a poignancy to this striking proverb (which is repeated in Proverbs 16:25). It is widely believed that sincerity is enough. As long as your heart is in the right place, that is enough. This proverb reminds us that that is nonsense.

If I eat poisonous fungi, sincerely believing that I am eating edible mushrooms, that will not save me from death. One day, sincerely believing that an electric cable was not connected to the electricity supply, I decided to cut it with a pair of scissors. I soon discovered my mistake! It could have been fatal.

Or take a more striking example that did end in death. Consider what happened on Saturday, 3 October 1998. Certain

Pentecostal groups, especially in the southern Appalachian region of the USA, practise 'snake-handling' in their religious services, believing that some believers have the power to take up poisonous snakes and remain unharmed. A leading practitioner, 'Punkin' Brown, was handling a three-feet-long timber rattler. The snake bit him on the finger and within minutes he was dead. He was only thirty-four and the father of five children. Tragically, the children had lost their mother, Melinda Brown, three years earlier when she was bitten by a rattler in the 'Full Gospel Tabernacle in Jesus Name' church in Middlesboro, Kentucky.

Eve sincerely believed the devil's lie. She was deceived. In Noah's day people sincerely believed there would be no flood. They were wrong. Remember how Lot's sons-in-law laughed at him when he told them Sodom was to be destroyed? When the Egyptians followed the Israelites down into the bed of the Red Sea, they sincerely thought they could cross to the other side. They were sincerely wrong.

Professing Christians have burned people to death sincerely believing they were right to do so. Atheists sincerely believe there is no God. Others believe that they will go to heaven because of their good deeds, or because everyone goes to heaven. Such sincerity is not enough. It is misplaced faith. The popular way, the easy way, the familiar way is not necessarily the right way. The broad road leads to destruction.

Double contrast: **'laughter'** / **'heart … ache'**; **'joy'** / **'grief'**

Like verse 10, verse 13 is a poignant observation containing a contrast but not in the usual contrasting form. The story is often told of how a certain man went to the doctor complaining that he felt depressed. The doctor took him to the window and pointed to a circus in the distance. He recommended it to the man, especially the clowns, and one clown in particular who he thought was extremely funny. 'Go and see that clown,' he told the depressed man, 'and I guarantee that you will never be depressed again!' The punch line comes when the patient turns and with sad eyes says, 'But doctor, I am that clown!' The clown is sometimes said to be Joe Grimaldi or George L. Fox, who did suffer from depression, but it is more likely to be based on Leoncavallo's nineteenth-century opera *I Pagliacci* and its lead character, the broken-hearted clown Canio. He makes audiences laugh but behind his painted smile he weeps to the point of madness because his wife has betrayed him.

You have, perhaps, experienced what it is to be in the midst of great hilarity or joy, only to be suddenly overcome by a wave of sadness. And how often has a conversation, or a journey, or a visit begun with great joy, only to end for some reason in tears! I remember reading a tragic story about a businessman arriving home in a helicopter and being greeted by his young daughter running to him. In his joy at seeing her, he lifted her up high, forgetting that the helicopter blades were still rotating. Happiness and sadness live cheek by jowl in this world, as when a sports match is won and lost, a bus crashes at Christmas, a man dies on holiday, or a mother dies in childbirth. Shakespeare was well aware of this and there can be few of his tragedies without comic interludes, or comedies without their silvery undertones of sadness. Successful modern comedy writers have recognized this and the best always have a moment of pathos in the half hour. The 1970s American series *MASH* (an acronym for Mobile Army Surgical Hospital), with its backdrop of the Korean War, is an extreme example. The 1980s British series of historical comedies *Blackadder* is another. The latter ends with First World War soldiers marching to death on the battlefield.

What this proverb teaches us:

1. Again, *not to be superficial.* There is such a thing as insincere, hollow laughter. Do not be fooled.

2. *To be sensitive.* Think about what may be felt inwardly by someone, even when outwardly all seems well.

3. There is also *a warning* here. We can be laughing at death one moment and in hell the next.

'The faithless will be fully repaid for their ways, and the good man rewarded for his' (14:14).

Contrast: **'faithless repaid'** / **'good man rewarded'**
The faithless repaid; the faithful rewarded.

Here is yet another exhortation to consider the end (cf. 14:11), and the fact that a man reaps what he sows.

First, *a warning:* **'The faithless will be fully repaid.'** They will not get away with anything. Some versions speak of 'the backslider in heart' as the one repaid. The idea of turning back is certainly here. All of us must beware of 'a sinful, unbelieving heart that turns away from the living God' (Heb. 3:12).

Second, there is *an encouragement.* The faithful will certainly be **'rewarded for his [ways]'.** In Revelation 22:12 the Lord says, 'Behold, I am coming soon! My reward is with me, and I will give to everyone according to what he has done.' How we behave is vitally important. It has eternal consequences. Moses says of Israel:

> They are a nation without sense,
> there is no discernment in them.
> If only they were wise and would understand this
> and discern what their end will be!
>
> (Deut. 32:28-29).

**A simple man believes anything,
but a prudent man gives thought to his steps.**

A wise man fears the L**ORD**** and shuns evil,**
    but a fool is hot-headed and reckless.
A quick-tempered man does foolish things,
    and a crafty man is hated

(14:15-17).

Perhaps we can take these proverbs together as they speak of thinking carefully about how you live and then of hot-headedness and a quick temper.

Contrast: **'simple man' / 'prudent man'**
Gullibility, responsibility.

'They say that the word "gullible" has not appeared in English dictionaries since 1975.' If you believe that then you are definitely gullible! It is a mark of **'a simple man'** that he believes anything he is told (14:15). If you tell him the sky is falling, or that red traffic lights now mean 'Go', he will believe you. He is prepared to believe in fairies at the bottom of the garden, Martians landing, the Bible being full of errors, man's evolution over millions of years, or that committing adultery is not a sin that God judges.

'A prudent man', on the other hand, is not a cynic but he **'gives thought to his steps'**, and so he reckons with what the Scripture says. He believes that God created the world in six days and that he will be judged one day in accordance with the Ten Commandments.

The last part of this proverb is very similar to verse 8. We all laugh about the 1950s radio audience convinced by Orson Welles' production of *War of the Worlds* that Martians had landed in America, but gullibility is very common. We need God's grace to avoid it.

Gullibility is believing every word of man. Faith is believing every word of God.

The noble Bereans are a good model here — they did not take Paul's word for anything, but examined the Scriptures to see if what he said was true (Acts 17:11).

Contrast: **'wise man' / 'fool'**
God-fearer or hot-head?

As we have noted before, a mark of the wise man is his fear of the Lord. Because of this, he **'shuns evil'** (14:16). The **'fool'**, however, **'is hot-headed and reckless'**. Rather than fearing the Lord, he rushes headlong into sin without a thought.

The human body is characterized by certain reflex actions. It would seem that these automatic responses protect us from danger and help us adjust to our surroundings. Coughing, for example, is designed to expel an irritant from the windpipe. Sneezing similarly clears the nasal air passages of irritants and allergens. Yawning occurs when the brain finds there is too much carbon dioxide in the blood. Muscles in the mouth and throat contract and force the mouth open, allowing carbon dioxide to be expelled and replaced with a large amount of oxygen-rich air. Blinking occurs when we need to moisten and clean the cornea or when danger threatens (This reflex apparently occurs 900 times an hour!). Without these reflex actions, we would be unable to survive. It would seem that we also have an instinct for self-preservation that is genetically programmed so that we are naturally wary about heights and water, for example. These natural reflexes and instincts illustrate the way the wise person will automatically shun evil from fear of the Lord. Just as, with effort, our reflexes can to a large extent be overridden and our fear instincts conquered by desensitization, so we can fall into hot-headed and reckless ways that endanger our very souls. Just as some people will run into a burning building, or skydive from an aeroplane with little thought, so there are people who plunge into all sorts of sin, not thinking for a moment of the dangers they court.

Synthetic: **'quick-tempered man'** / **'crafty man'**

The third proverb just concentrates on the fool. Once again we have an apparent contrast, but this is not a contrasting proverb. He is called **'a quick-tempered man'** (14:17). Because he acts without thinking, he **'does foolish things'**. As one writer puts it, the smoke of his anger puts out the light of his judgement. If he would stop and consider, like the wise man, much of this could be avoided. He is not like gold that can be heated to a very high temperature without melting, or flint that has to be knocked very hard before sparks fly. Rather he is like an inflammable gas that will easily flare up, or very fine glass that will shatter with just a touch. There are other fools, of course, who have learned to control their tempers to a degree. They are **'crafty'** people. They are **'hated'** because all their self-control is used not for good ends, but for bad.

> **The simple inherit folly,**
> **but the prudent are crowned with knowledge.**
> **Evil men will bow down in the presence of the good,**
> **and the wicked at the gates of the righteous**
> (14:18-19).

We close this chapter with two more proverbs considering the destiny of **'the simple'** and **'the prudent'**.

Contrast: **'simple'** / **'prudent'**
Inheriting folly, invested with knowledge.

What will **'the simple'** inherit? **'Folly.'** What will happen to **'the prudent'**? They **'are crowned with knowledge'** (14:18). This is built into the very way that the simple and the prudent operate. Just as the good tree bears good fruit and the bad tree bad, so simpletons produce folly, while the prudent go on to rule in splendour by means of their knowledge. Here is a king with two sons — one foolish, one prudent. At his death the old man leaves the former a fool's cap as an emblem of his folly, but the latter inherits his crown.

Double contrast: **'evil men'** / **'good'** ; ' **wicked'** / **'righteous'** (cf. 14:11,14)

Verse 19 contrasts the different ends of **'evil men'** or **'the wicked'** with the end of **'the good'** or **'the righteous'**. (The latter picture describes the wicked as bowing down **'at the gates of the righteous'**.) The emphasis is on the triumph of the righteous over the wicked. They will be victorious over evil men. Such verses are there to encourage the righteous to persevere in the right way and to warn the wicked of their coming judgement. Sometimes it happens in this life. Think of Joseph and Pharaoh, Daniel and Nebuchadnezzar, and Elisha in his dealings with more than one king.

What these nineteen proverbs teach us

How to be a fool

It is important that these proverbs go to our hearts. Because of our perversity, teaching sometimes has more impact if we are told the very opposite of what we need to hear. When my children fail to respond to 'Put the toys away,' or 'Come to the table,' I sometimes try, 'Don't put the toys away,' or 'Don't come to the table.' It can be more successful. To the end of driving these lessons home, therefore, I thought we might take an unusual approach and consider how to be a wicked fool. Here are some useful ingredients.

Despise the Lord; do not fear him

Fundamental to foolishness is despising the Lord. Devious ways and a refusal to fear him go hand in hand (14:2).

Do all you can to destroy your family life

There is a lot that can be done here (see 14:1). Ideally, make no marriage covenant with your partner, but if one is made, do all you can to undermine it and break it. Cheat, deceive, be selfish. Spend little time at home, giving all your attention to outside interests such as your career. Wives, rebel; children, disobey; husbands, show no love or respect.

Speak harshly, not lovingly

In your conversation, think, not of how you can protect others, but how you can sting them with your criticism and wit (14:3).

Neglect the use of means

Do not think of the advantages of expending energy on development or progress in any area of life. Be a Luddite. Why go to church when the preacher makes you feel bad? Why read the Bible when it is such an effort? Why pray, when doing nothing is easier? Why change your opinions and be inconsistent? (14:4).

Commit yourself to being dishonest

It is not enough to tell a lie now and again. Everyone does that. The real fool 'pours out lies' (14:5). The more lies you tell, the more you will feel the need to tell.

Never give thought to your ways

Deceive yourself into thinking all is well. Never let the thought, 'Maybe I've sinned,' cross your mind. Never think of death or judgement or listen to your conscience. Keep things superficial. Certainly never let the thought of Proverbs 14:12 haunt you. If you do seek wisdom, assume that it is easy to find because you are a natural for it (14:6).

Treat sin and repentance as a joke

If you hear of someone breaking the law, or doing wrong, try to make a joke of it. Think of adultery, fornication, theft, envy and pride as topics for humour. If you hear a preacher telling you to repent, assume he cannot mean you. As for restitution, do not even think of trying to right wrongs! Mock those who do want to repent and make restitution (14:9).

Assume that there is no Day of Judgement

Ignore the warnings of Proverbs 14:11,14.

Believe anything

You might find it difficult to believe everything you hear, but try using phrases like 'Experts say ...', 'Science has proved ...', 'Modern thought accepts ...', or alternatively, 'The ancient Incas believed ...' and 'According to my horoscope...' It can help you to believe even the most outlandish nonsense (14:15; cf. 14:8).

Be hot-headed and reckless

Go as near to the knuckle, as close to the bone, as you dare. Sail close to the wind. Give no thought to your own safety or that of others. Drive crazily, drink madly, live like a lunatic. 'Love 'em and leave 'em.' Take a devil-may-care attitude. You will soon be dead (14:16).

Whatever you do, do what is wicked

The chief thing is to do foolish things, whatever they are. Say things that you do not mean and that you will probably regret. Do things that you will be sorry for and that upset others. Like a bored lumberjack, go about with a little chip of wood on your shoulder. As soon as anyone knocks it off, challenge him to a fight. If you cannot manage that sort of thing, concentrate on being sly and crafty. Plot intrigue and evil. Use cold calculation to cause as much harm in the long term as the hot-headed man with his rash bursts of temper does in the short term (14:17).

How to be wise

When, in the light of this, we consider the character of the foolish man, we see the point of the warning: 'Stay away from a foolish man, for you will not find knowledge on his lips' (14:7).

We must remember too that 'There is a way that seems right to a man, but in the end it leads to death' (14:12). If we pursue foolishness, we must realize where it leads: 'The faithless will be fully repaid for their ways… The simple inherit folly' (14:14,18).

Meanwhile 'the good man' is 'rewarded' for his ways and 'the prudent' are 'crowned with knowledge'. 'Evil men will bow down in the presence of the good, and the wicked at the gates of the righteous' (14:14,18,19).

Remembering that 'The mocker seeks wisdom and finds none, but knowledge comes easily to the discerning' (14:6), our first step is to look to Jesus, who:

feared God and did not despise him;
was a model of submissiveness and obedience;
spoke wonderful words of life and truth;
made it his custom to attend the synagogue;
knew the Scriptures and was a man of prayer;
is the Truth personified;
was thoughtful and careful in all he did or said;
was certainly no one's fool;
always did the Father's will;
was always serious about sin and repentance;
was always pure, holy and blameless.

28.
How a nation can be great

Please read Proverbs 14:20-35

*Poverty, response to need, plotting evil, benefits of labour,
wisdom, truthfulness, safety of God-fearers, life for God-fearers,
population growth, patience, envy, oppression, calamity,
wisdom, national righteousness, kings and their servants*

These sixteen proverbs cover a variety of subjects. Directly or
less directly, several are to do with affairs of state.

> **The poor are shunned even by their neighbours,**
> **but the rich have many friends.**
> **He who despises his neighbour sins,**
> **but blessed is he who is kind to the needy**
> $\qquad\qquad\qquad\qquad\qquad\qquad$ (14:20-21).

It is helpful to consider these proverbs together as they begin
with a reference to **'the poor'** and end with one to **'the needy'**.
The first observes or regards; the second imposes an obligation
or requirement.

Contrast: **'poor'** / **'rich'**
The poor rejected; the rich received.

Like Proverbs 10:15, this proverb is observational, realistically reminding us of disadvantages in being poor and advantages in being rich (13:8 gives the balance by highlighting the disadvantages of riches). It also reminds us that many friends are only fair-weather ones. One great problem for the rich and famous is to know who their true friends really are. The parable of the prodigal son seems to suggest that once the boy's money ran out, so did his friends. An English proverbial couplet says:

> In time of prosperity friends will be plenty,
> In time of adversity, not one in twenty.

Fortunately, not all 'friends' operate on that basis, as the stories of Ruth and Naomi and Jonathan and David demonstrate. The irony is that the poor are the ones who most need friendship, and the proverb subtly condemns choosing our friends on the basis of their wealth. Jesus deliberately sought out the poor as his friends. He does not shun even the poorest of people. What James says in his letter is relevant here (James 1:9-11; 2:1-6,15-16). 'Wealth brings many friends, but a poor man's friend deserts him' (19:4; cf. 19:6-7). Good questions for us are: 'Why am I that person's friend, and why is he mine?' The Lord, of course, never befriends us for anything we can give him, although we may be tempted to try to get something from him, as if his favour can be curried.

Contrast: **'he who despises his neighbour'** / **'he who is kind to the needy'**
Beatitude
Despising your neighbours will bring badness;
Devotion to the needy ends sadness.

This proverb takes up the theme of the previous verses, a common one in Proverbs. It warns against despising one's neighbour (because he is poor, for example) and urges kindness towards the needy (cf. 14:31). To despise one's neighbour is sin — literally, 'to fall short'. When we fall short of God's standards, we miss out on his blessings. To show kindness to the needy guarantees God's blessing in Christ — if not in this life, then certainly in the next.

'Do not those who plot evil go astray? But those who plan what is good find love and faithfulness' (14:22).
    Contrast: **'those who plot evil'** / **'those who plan what is good'**
    Wicked plots or worthy plans?

There is a measure of connection between this proverb and the last two. Despising one's neighbour can lead to plotting against him. But, it says, **'Those who plot evil go astray.'** They go astray not simply in the sense that they do wrong, but they also miscalculate the results of their plotting, not realizing it can do them no good. Alternatively, **'those who plan what is good'** will **'find'** (or possibly just 'show') **'love and faithfulness'** (some translations prefer 'mercy and truth'). It takes planning to do good. Such planning will be well rewarded. Evil and good do not come from nowhere; they are the result of plotting or planning. To plot evil is plainly wrong from every point of view and should expect no reward. Planning what is good leads to love and faithfulness, not only from those we help but, by grace, from God himself. Our intentions shape our character; our character shapes our destiny.

'All hard work brings a profit, but mere talk leads only to poverty' (14:23).
    Contrast: **'hard work'** / **'mere talk'**
    Toil brings profit; talk brings poverty.

Here is another proverb to go with several we have had on laziness (e.g., 10:4-5,26). This one is in a more positive form. Proverbially **'all hard work'** will bring **'a profit'** of some kind, **'but mere talk'**, boasting without doing, pursuing pure fantasy, or merely chatting instead of working, **'leads only to poverty'**. No pain, no gain; no sweat, no sweet. An English proverb says that nothing is to be gained without pains but poverty. Others point out that to get the fruit you must climb the tree; to get the kernel you must crack the nut; and ninety per cent of inspiration is actually perspiration. So we are back to the subject of poverty again (although using a different word).

What is true on the physical level is true also on the spiritual. Salvation is by grace, but we must work out our salvation with fear and trembling. The devil finds work for idle hands. As one writer once put it, the devil tempts us all, but if you are idle you tempt the devil.

'The wealth of the wise is their crown, but the folly of fools yields folly' (14:24).
Contrast (complex): **'wealth of the wise'** / **'folly of fools'**
Wise men are wealthy in wisdom, while fools are by their folly fooled.

Staying with poverty and wealth, **'the wise'** are once more contrasted with **'fools'** in a slightly complex way that some have tried to smooth out (see RSV). It is similar to verse 18. The contrast is drawn, not between 'wealth' and 'poverty', or 'wisdom' and 'folly', not between 'crown' and 'shame' or 'wisdom' and 'folly', but between **'wealth'** that **'is their crown'** and **'folly'** that **'yields folly'**.

We learn first, then, that **'the wealth of the wise'** is their wisdom, not mere material goods. They may not be kings in any other sense, but they wear the crown of wisdom — worth more than the crowns of many nations.

As for **'fools'**, whatever other advantages they may have, to their shame, their folly inevitably **'yields'** — don't expect something too profound! — **'folly'**. The latter observation is like the modern retort to those who blame the computer for their mistakes: 'Garbage in, garbage out.'

It is because of their wisdom that wealth can be useful to the wise. It is because their real crown is their wisdom that they can cope with earthly loss.

'A truthful witness saves lives, but a false witness is deceitful' (14:25).

> *Contrast:* **'truthful witness'** / **'false witness'**
> Truth saves; lies deceive.

Truthfulness is again commended here, as in verse 5 (see also 12:17). That **'a false witness'** causes death is implied rather than stated. Even where that does not happen, there is deceit. **'A truthful witness'**, on the other hand, **'saves lives.'** 'A career or a life may hang on a word,' says Kidner.

One thinks once again of Naboth and how false testimony condemned him. We remember, especially, the trial of the Lord Jesus and the desperate attempts made there to deceive. Honesty is a fine jewel, as one Puritan observed, 'but much out of fashion'. It is certainly a rare one. Today believers are called upon to bear faithful witness to Christ. In so doing they can save souls.

> **He who fears the LORD has a secure fortress,**
> **and for his children it will be a refuge.**
> **The fear of the LORD is a fountain of life,**
> **turning a man from the snares of death**
> > (14:26-27).

Similes: **'secure fortress'**; **'refuge'**; **'fountain of life'**; **'fear of the LORD'**

Fear of the Lord is one of the great themes of this book. Here are two straightforward proverbs that picture it for us in vivid terms.

Firstly, it is likened to **'a secure fortress'**, or **'a refuge'**. It is commended both to individuals and their children. We ought never to underestimate the immense privilege of growing up in a Christian home. Godly fear protects from all harm. It leads to confidence and security, assurance and safety. Fear of the Lord will keep you safer than any human wealth can.

Secondly, it is pictured in exactly the same way as 'the teaching of the wise' in Proverbs 13:14. It is **'a fountain of life'** — a life-giving spring of water. Changing the metaphor slightly, it is said to be like a signpost, or something more active, **'turning a man from the snares of death'**. Fear of the Lord — the very first step to wisdom — is a source of eternal life to all who have it. It will deliver from certain death in hell. Godly fear not only protects, it gives life. It leads to deliverance and life, salvation and vitality.

'A large population is a king's glory, but without subjects a prince is ruined' (14:28).

Contrast: **'large population'** / **'without subjects'**

Here is the first of several proverbs referring to kingship (cf. 14:35; 16:10,14-15). The book is not only the work of one or more kings, but teaches the wisdom that declares:

> By me kings reign
>   and rulers make laws that are just;
> by me princes govern,
>   and all nobles who rule on earth
>
> (8:15-16).

Here we are reminded that one of the chief glories of a king is not his palace or his crown, but **'a large population'**. On the other hand, **'a prince'** who is **'without subjects'** is **'ruined'**.

King Harald V became King of Norway on the death of his father King Olaf V in January 1991. Norway is a constitutional and parliamentary monarchy. Since 1814, executive power has nominally been in the king's hands. He makes all governmental appointments on the recommendation of the democratically elected party in power. Harald rules over some four and a half million people. They are his glory. Constantine Oldenburg, on the other hand, succeeded his father Paul as King Constantine II (XIII according to some) of Greece in 1964. Three years later a military junta seized political power and he and his family were forced to flee into exile. He was formally deposed in June 1973, when Greece became a republic. In 1994 he was even stripped of Greek citizenship. He is in the unenviable position of being a king with no subjects. His glory is gone.

Solitary splendour is self-extinguishing. What good is a king with no subjects, a chief with no braves, a teacher with no pupils, a pastor with no church, a father with no children? When the King of the Jews hung on the cross, many thought him a king with no kingdom and no subjects. The soldiers delighted in hailing him king with great mockery. Yet since that time his kingdom has grown and grown. Starting as a grain of mustard seed, it has become a great tree. Originally a small stone, now it is a mountain that fills the whole earth. The subjects of God's kingdom live for his glory.

'A patient man has great understanding, but a quick-tempered man displays folly' (14:29).
Contrast: **'patient man'** / **'quick-tempered man'**

Here is another reminder of the importance of patience (cf. 14:17). One way to know who is wise and who is foolish is to watch how they react to setbacks. The patient man shows he **'has great understanding'**; the **'quick-tempered man'** is revealing his folly.

As I write a senior British politician with a notoriously short fuse has disgraced himself by punching someone who threw an egg at him. For many observers his understandable but quick-tempered reaction has displayed his folly. How few even approach the perfect self-composure of our Lord Jesus, who was treated so shamefully by wicked men: 'When they hurled their insults at him, he did not retaliate; when he suffered, he made no threats. Instead, he entrusted himself to him who judges justly' (1 Peter 2:23).

'A heart at peace gives life to the body, but envy rots the bones' (14:30).
> *Contrast:* **'heart at peace'** / **'envy'**
> Ease energizes; envy erodes.

This proverb commends a heart at peace, or in good health, and condemns envy. The contrast here is between health and the rotting of the bones. Envy is one of those sins that actually gives no real pleasure at any point in its career. It 'shoots at others and wounds itself'. In recent years, the medical profession has become increasingly aware of psychosomatic effects. Emotional turmoil can have a direct effect on the body. A similar observation is made in Proverbs 17:22 (see also 15:13,30). This also takes us back to the promise in 3:7-8. To say that every faithful believer is guaranteed good health in this life is heresy, but it is also short-sighted to fail to see the undoubted physical benefits that come to those who live a life free from envy and whose hearts are at peace in Christ. Nursing resentment can do you physical harm as well as spiritual.

'He who oppresses the poor shows contempt for their Maker, but whoever is kind to the needy honours God' (14:31).

Contrast: **'he who oppresses the poor' / 'whoever is kind to the needy'**

Oppress the poor, oppose the Omnipotent; be kind to the needy and you honour him.

Here we are back to the repeated refrain regarding the poor, which was touched on in verses 20-21 and will be returned to, especially in Proverbs 22. The poor and needy spoken of here are those who are poor through no fault of their own. To oppress them is to show **'contempt for their Maker'**. It is the attitude that wrongly says, 'God doesn't care about them and neither do I.' Kindness to the needy is, on the other hand, honouring to God. This is a theme in many places in Scripture.

Here are a few which spring to mind: 'The King will reply, "I tell you the truth, whatever you did for one of the least of these brothers of mine, you did for me"' (Matt. 25:40 — here the nation of Israel gives way to the new-covenant community). 'If anyone has material possessions and sees his brother in need but has no pity on him, how can the love of God be in him? Dear children, let us not love with words or tongue but with actions and in truth. This then is how we know that we belong to the truth, and how we set our hearts at rest in his presence whenever our hearts condemn us. For God is greater than our hearts, and he knows everything. Dear friends, if our hearts do not condemn us, we have confidence before God' (1 John 3:17-21). 'If anyone says, "I love God," yet hates his brother, he is a liar. For anyone who does not love his brother, whom he has seen, cannot love God, whom he has not seen. And he has given us this command: Whoever loves God must also love his brother' (1 John 4:20-21).

God is not 'biased to the poor' as such, but he is the Creator of both 'the rich man in his castle' and 'the poor man at his gate'. Though fallen, both are in God's image and merit kindness and compassion for his sake. What are you doing to express kindness to the needy — particularly believers in need? In recent years our church has determined to give five per cent of general giving to support work among the homeless, but we are aware that such giving is only a beginning and we are eager to do more.

'When calamity comes, the wicked are brought down, but even in death the righteous have a refuge' (14:32).
   Contrast: **'wicked' / 'righteous'**
   The corrupt collapse in calamities; the decent defy death.

Yet again we look to the end. The Greek Septuagint deviates from the Hebrew (see RSV) and different versions attempt different translations. However, the NIV rendering given above seems right. **'The wicked'** may survive for some time but **'when calamity comes'**, down they go. They will be defeated. **'The righteous'**, in contrast, **'have a refuge'** even in death. They will be victorious. The believer does not look forward to death — the final enemy — but he does face it with confidence, knowing that in that great crisis he has a refuge in Christ — a safe place to hide. Are you hiding in him? Can you say with Job, 'Though he slay me, yet will I hope in him...'? (Job 13:15). He could declare:

I know that my Redeemer lives,
    and that in the end he will stand upon the earth.
And after my skin has been destroyed,
    yet in my flesh I will see God;
I myself will see him
    with my own eyes — I, and not another.
How my heart yearns within me!

                                                    (19:25-27).

Or can you say with Paul, 'The Lord will rescue me from every evil attack and will bring me safely to his heavenly kingdom. To him be glory for ever and ever. Amen'? (2 Tim. 4:18). 'Yes,' says the Spirit, of those who die in the Lord, 'they will rest from their labour, for their deeds will follow them' (Rev. 14:13).

'Wisdom reposes in the heart of the discerning and even among fools she lets herself be known' (14:33).
   Synthetic: **'in the heart of the discerning' / 'among fools'**

The NIV footnote (following the Greek and Syriac) gives as an alternative reading the more obvious contrast: 'but in the heart of fools she is not known'. Knowing the book's power to surprise, the synonymous option seems more likely. It does us no good to suppose that fools have no wisdom whatsoever. Even among them, wisdom **'lets herself be known'** to some extent. That is what makes the whole battle so difficult. If it was obvious that moral fools are fools indeed, who would follow them? Sadly, things are more complicated and the evil genius is not just a stock character in fiction. It is painstaking work, as it is so easy to fall into the same sins as they do, but we must do all we can to 'plunder the Egyptians' and take note of wisdom wherever it is found. This is the approach that the book of Proverbs itself takes, apparently making use of wisdom from a variety of sources.

'Righteousness exalts a nation, but sin is a disgrace to any people' (14:34).
   Contrast: **'righteousness' / 'sin'**
   Righteousness raises up; depravity disgraces.

This famous verse starkly contrasts the way that righteousness lifts up a nation and sin is a disgrace to any group of people. The nature of the exaltation or disgrace is not specified, but we know from Ezekiel 16 that the theocratic arrangement in which Israel was deprived of fruitfulness if she sinned (see Deut. 28) operates to a certain extent in all nations (cf. Amos 1:1 – 2:3; Jer. 18:7-10). A nation, therefore, that sells itself to sin should expect to suffer the consequences — disaster, dissension, declension and decay.

'A king delights in a wise servant, but a shameful servant incurs his wrath' (14:35).

Contrast: **'wise servant'** / **'shameful servant'**

Shrewd servants satisfy a king; shameful servants, they make him seethe.

Finally we return to the king (cf. 14:28). He delights in **'a wise servant'**, and a shameful one incurs his wrath. When we fail to attain to what we had hoped, it is easy to make excuses, but the fact is that a good ruler favours the wise and will be angry with those who act shamefully. If you are like the latter then you can expect wrath and even dismissal. This holds, in different ways, all the way from your boss at work to God himself, the Great King who **'delights in a wise servant'** but is angry with those who are shameful. This comes out in Jesus' parable of the talents (Matt. 25:14-30).

What these sixteen proverbs teach us

Verse 34 is often quoted. Most proverbs deal with life on the individual level, but not all — 11:14 is another good example where that is not so. Many proverbs can be applied not just to individuals but to nations too. I want to do that here.

It is less common now, but politicians used to talk about putting the 'Great' back into Great Britain. (The name is actually geographical — Great(er) Britain, as opposed to Britain or Brittany, the smaller area to the south in France.) What makes a nation great? How do we recognize a great nation? What should countries do to attain greatness? Is it a matter of empire, economy or emancipation? Verse 34 is clear: it is *righteousness* that exalts a nation. More lessons are found in the other proverbs. We can focus on four areas.

Leaders

Verses 28 and 35 both refer to kingship. Here we learn something about leadership. As a general rule we can say that good leaders will want to see population growth. Stalin and Mao are notorious examples of leaders who did the very opposite — decimating the population by harsh and cruel means. In China today, great efforts are made to limit families to one child each. When a nation is favourable towards abortion and euthanasia, when its immigration policy is wholly negative, when it sees material goods as being more important than its people, then it cannot be great.

Verse 35 reminds us that there is no point in blaming all a country's problems on its leaders. Leaders are significant; however, if, as in the days of Moses, the leader is faithful, but those below him are not, there can be little blessing.

Perhaps it is appropriate to mention verse 33 here. There certainly seem to be some leaders who are morally bankrupt in their personal lives, yet are good leaders in many other respects. What we do about the fact is another question, but simply denying that it is so is not an option.

Citizens

This brings us to the point that a nation's greatness lies in the character of its inhabitants — people like you and me. As ever, there is a stress on being righteous. As we have said, this can be found ultimately only by trusting in Christ, the Righteous One. Those who truly know God's will also have power to do that will — to be upright, holy and godly. It is the righteous who will triumph in the end, and even in a land where there is much unrighteousness God always leaves a remnant who will eventually be vindicated. This comes out in the promise: 'Do not those who plot evil go astray? But those who plan what is good find love and faithfulness' (14:22; see also 14:19). Even if they do not see God's work revived in this life there is still hope: 'When calamity comes, the wicked are brought down, but even in death the righteous have a refuge' (14:32). If a nation's people are not righteous, the nation cannot be righteous.

Righteousness is not something nebulous. It is quite specific. Three particular examples are highlighted in these verses.

Honesty

'A truthful witness saves lives, but a false witness is deceitful' (14:25). The story is told of golfer Robert Tyre Jones hitting his ball into the woods. Entering alone, he accidentally touched the ball while practising his shot. He emerged confessing his fault and so forfeited the championship. Praised for his sportsmanship, he replied, 'You might as well praise a man for not robbing a bank.' Writing at a time when cricket has become so riddled with cheating that it is fast losing credibility, one realizes how far we have come since the 1920s.

When a nation is marked by dishonesty and distrust, everything is spoiled. At present, some nations are so corrupt that bribery and dishonesty are commonplace. I remember being overseas once and hearing that the local students were on strike because cheating had been banned in the forthcoming examinations! In Britain teachers, police and others are snowed under by paperwork. Much of the reason for this is a basic mistrust. It is felt that professionals cannot be left alone to deal with the needs as they see fit.

Patience

'A patient man has great understanding, but a quick-tempered man displays folly' (14:29). In days of road rage, air rage and supermarket-trolley rage, and when even public figures are known to lose their cool from time to time and strike out, we know that Britain, to quote only one nation, has many problems. When my grandfather served in the First World War, he once watched a man on duty being stung several times by a wasp. The man did not flinch but patiently waited to be relieved of his duty. It was a rare act in those days; today perhaps such things are even rarer.

Contentment

'A heart at peace gives life to the body, but envy rots the bones' (14:30). Just as families and churches can be torn apart by the forces of jealousy and envy, so a nation can be similarly destroyed. In too many cases calls for better care towards the needy, for policies that favour the native-born over immigrants, and taxation that favours one part of a community over another spring from envy rather than any more noble source.

Attitudes to wealth and poverty

Some five verses in this section touch on wealth and poverty. Again, the question of a nation's attitude to these issues betrays whether it is great or otherwise.

A government that encourages avarice creates many troubles for its people. Rather it ought to be promoting wisdom

(14:24). The leaders ought to do all that they can to encourage hard work and a fair return for such hard work (14:23). If they encourage gambling and other get-rich-quick schemes over settled hard work, they do people no favours. On the other hand, they will recognize that there is nothing particularly advantageous in poverty and so will do all they can to help the poor. Even if no one else cares, at least a nation's leaders should care for the poor (14:20). The sentiments of verses 21 and 31 ought often to be heard in the corridors of power.

The fear of the Lord

Finally we underline verses 26 and 27 once again. Without genuine fear of the Lord in the land, a nation truly is sinking fast. The only hope of recovery is for God to be merciful in his wrath.

29.
Hearts and tongues and lives

Please read Proverbs 15:1-15

Gentle words, wise speech, God's omniscience, healing and deceiving tongues, heeding correction, treasure and income, lips and hearts, worship, the way of the wicked and the way of the righteous, deserters condemned, God's omniscience, teachability, emotions of the heart, hearts and mouths, wretchedness

These fifteen proverbs cover various subjects. Several are about the tongue and the heart.

> **A gentle answer turns away wrath,**
> **but a harsh word stirs up anger.**
> **The tongue of the wise commends knowledge,**
> **but the mouth of the fool gushes folly**
>
> (15:1-2).

Both of these proverbs refer to speech, although the first is as much about self-control.

Contrast: **'gentle answer'** / **'harsh word'**
Gentleness pacifies; gruffness provokes.

(This is a little like Proverbs 25:15.)

'Why didn't you wake me?' screams Max, late again. 'You need the rest, dear,' replies Martha. 'I'll put the shower on for you; there's coffee on the table. I'll take you to the station.'

'Why are you so stupid?' enquires Bob, appalled at the mess. 'I'm sorry,' says Kevin, 'I'll clear it up right away.'

'Why don't you make the coffee for a change, instead of me all the time?' says Sue. 'Okay,' says Sonia. 'I really ought to make it more often.'

It is not difficult to see how **'a gentle answer'** can turn away wrath. On the other hand, sometimes we would rather tell Max, Bob and Sue where to get off. Such an attitude will only exacerbate the situation. Good scriptural examples are found in the way that Gideon dealt with the Ephraimites in Judges 8:1-3 and Abigail's appeasement of David in 1 Samuel 25. On a higher plane, we remember the gentle words of Christ from the cross, especially when seeking forgiveness for his enemies, epitomizing the atonement that turned away the wrath of God.

Contrast: **'tongue of the wise'** / **'mouth of the fool'**

The second proverb focuses on the fundamental contrast between **'the wise'** and **'the fool'**. When they speak, they reveal themselves, either commending knowledge or gushing folly (15:28 is similar; cf. 12:23; 13:16). Chiefly we think of the Saviour who had 'an instructed tongue, to know the word that sustains the weary' (Isa. 50:4). What a contrast with the nonsense that gushes from the mouths of fools!

'The eyes of the LORD are everywhere, keeping watch on the wicked and the good' (15:3).

Synthetic: **'The eyes of the LORD are everywhere'** / **'keeping watch on ...'**

Here is our twelfth reference to the covenant God, **'the Lord'**, since Proverbs 10:3. As in 5:21, his omniscience is declared. Here a conclusion is drawn: his eyes **'are everywhere'**. In particular, he is **'keeping watch on the wicked and the good'**. If you do good, he knows; if you do evil, he knows too, even if no one else on earth does: 'Nothing in all creation is hidden from God's sight. Everything is uncovered and laid bare before the eyes of him to whom we must give account' (Heb. 4:13).

This is a word of encouragement to the good and a word of warning to the wicked. Wicked man, God knows all about your wicked schemes. Be sure your sins will find you out. As Elihu said:

> [God's] eyes are on the ways of men;
>   he sees their every step.
> There is no dark place, no deep shadow,
>   where evildoers can hide
>   (Job 34:21-22; cf. Jer. 16:17; 23:24, 32:19).

Or as Isaac Watts put it:

> Almighty God, thy piercing eye
> Strikes through the shades of night;
> And our most secret actions lie
> All open to thy sight.
>
> There's not a sin that we commit,
> Nor wicked word we say,
> But in thy dreadful book 'tis writ,
> Against the judgement day.

You who do good, you will certainly not lose your reward. The Lord will not forget you: 'The eyes of the Lord range throughout the earth to strengthen those whose hearts are fully committed to him' (2 Chr. 16:9).

'The tongue that brings healing is a tree of life, but a deceitful tongue crushes the spirit' (15:4).
> *Contrast:* **'tongue that brings healing'** / **'deceitful tongue'**
> Healing tongues heal; hypocritical tongues harm.

With the contrast in verse 4 we are back to the tongue. One **'brings healing'** through gentle, loving, right, helpful, appropriate, accurate speech and **'is a tree of life'**. We think especially of how faithful witness leads sinners to eternal life. **'A deceitful tongue crushes the spirit.'** Nothing compares with the disappointment of finding we have been misled. My dad loved to tease us as children. When my sister was quite young, she asked why my parents had given me (their first-born) two forenames while she only had one. My father said that when she was born, four years after me, there was less money and so they could only afford one name! At five she could accept this explanation but when, aged eleven, she repeated it to a friend, she was rather crushed to find that she had been deceived. A similar thing sometimes happens when children find out the truth about Father Christmas, the tooth fairy, or other make-believe characters. Much more serious is the crushing realization that we have been deceived about someone's character, as in adultery, fraud or theft, or when we find that something we thought insignificant — a small lump, a slight pain — turns out to be something much worse — cancer or some other life-threatening disease. Many false prophets deceitfully calm people's fears with a 'Peace! Peace!' when they ought to be declaring the painful but vital truths that could lead to healing.

'A fool spurns his father's discipline, but whoever heeds correction shows prudence' (15:5).
    Contrast: **'fool'** / **'whoever heeds correction'**

The relationship between father and son is prominent in Proverbs. Here **'a fool'** is said to be one who **'spurns his father's discipline'**. In contrast, it is a mark of the prudent that they heed correction. This affirms what we have already seen in Proverbs 13:1,18 (note the references given in the commentary on 13:1). If even the Lord Jesus obeyed both his heavenly Father and his earthly one, should we not be willing to follow his example and bear the yoke when young? (see Lam. 3:27). Pride is what keeps us from heeding correction.

'The house of the righteous contains great treasure, but the income of the wicked brings them trouble' (15:6).
    Contrast (complex): **'house of the righteous'** / **'income of the wicked'**
A house of treasure or a harvest of trouble.

The contrast between the **'righteous'** and the **'wicked'** is ubiquitous. Here the righteous man is pictured as having a house that **'contains great treasure'**, while the wicked have an **'income'** that **'brings them trouble'**. This picture of **'the income of the wicked'** has been used before (see 10:16). The picture of a house filled with treasure is found again later (24:3-4). The lesson is once more driven home that, despite appearances at times, righteousness brings excellent rewards and wickedness leads to trouble. The reason for this is, first, the sovereignty of God that issues in mercy to the righteous, and, secondly, the wise way in which, proverbially, the righteous manage the resources God puts at their disposal. The application is not just to money but to every resource. What great treasures fill the lives of those who are righteous in Christ!

**The lips of the wise spread knowledge;
not so the hearts of fools**

(15:7).

Contrast (complex): **'lips of the wise'** / **'hearts of fools'**

Next we are back with the **'lips'** and also with the **'heart'**. The complexity is similar to that in 15:14 and 10:20. It is because the hearts **'of the wise'** are full of knowledge that their **'lips ... spread knowledge'**. The ignorant words **'of fools'** evidence their wicked hearts. We are reminded of Jesus' statement that 'Out of the overflow of the heart the mouth speaks' (Matt. 12:34). The wise preach faithful sermons, teach in Sunday school, speak words of encouragement, give good advice, etc. Fools do not.

**The Lord detests the sacrifice of the wicked,
but the prayer of the upright pleases him.
The Lord detests the way of the wicked
but he loves those who pursue righteousness**

(15:8-9).

Lord detests

Both proverbs describe what **'the Lord detests'**, and then what it is that pleases him and who it is that he loves. The first proverb deals with a specific act; the second with lifestyle. Verse 26 tells us that the Lord detests 'the thoughts of the wicked'.

Contrast: **'sacrifice of the wicked'** / **'prayer of the upright'**

God scorns the sacrifices of sinners, but is pleased by the prayers of the pure.

Proverbs 21:27 is similar to the first part of verse 8 (see also 28:9). God's hatred of **'the sacrifice of the wicked'** has been known since the time of Cain. The mere act of sacrifice cannot make up for the fact that a man has no faith and acts from corrupt motives. Some religions are not concerned about this matter of motive provided things are fine on the outside. The true religion has never been like that (see Isa. 1:10-15). God sees through all hypocrisy. On the other hand, **'the prayer of the upright pleases'** the Lord. Because it is given in faith and comes from a pure heart (through Christ) it is acceptable and pleasing to God.

Contrast: **'way of the wicked'** / **'those who pursue righteousness'**
The wicked way he detests; the righteous route is his delight.

The Lord also hates **'the way of the wicked'** (15:9). Everything they do is detestable to him. They are incapable of doing anything truly good, anything that he loves, for they do not seek righteousness. On the other hand, **'He loves those who pursue righteousness'** — those who trust in Christ and who seek to live lives compatible with that faith. Such a statement acts once again as a warning to the wicked and an encouragement to righteousness for all who serve him.

'Stern discipline awaits him who leaves the path; he who hates correction will die' (15:10).
Synonymous: **'him who leaves the path'** / **'he who hates correction'**

This is another of several proverbs stressing the need for discipline (see also 15:12; 12:1; 13:1; and, especially, 5:12). The familiar picture of life as a road is used. We must walk the narrow path. Sin is deviation from that path. If we are unwilling to accept such truths and will not be disciplined, it will lead inexorably to death — physical and spiritual, temporal and eternal.

When someone is travelling through a rain forest there can be many dangers — snakes, crocodiles, poisonous plants and insects. Sticking to the right path is vital. In the armed forces soldiers are drilled in taking care of their guns and keeping them clean. A man who appears on parade with a dirty gun will find himself up on a charge. Why? Because in time of war it could be a matter of life and death.

The import of the first part of the proverb is that those who refuse self-discipline will be disciplined by other means. In Bunyan's *Pilgrim's Progress* Christian and Hopeful left the path for By-path Meadow. At first the wayside seemed pleasant, but then 'The night came on, and it grew very dark' and '... it began to rain, and thunder, and lighten in a very dreadful manner; and the water rose amain. Then Hopeful groaned in himself, saying, "Oh, that I had kept on my way!"' They ended up in the grounds of Giant Despair, who imprisoned them in Doubting Castle, 'a very dark dungeon, nasty and stinking', where they lay some days 'without one bit of bread, or drop of drink, or light, or any to ask how they did; they were, therefore, here in evil case, and were far from friends and acquaintance'. There they were severely beaten and strongly urged to commit suicide until they finally escaped by the skin of their teeth. In the course of recounting this episode Bunyan refers to one he dubs Vain-confidence who, 'not seeing the way before him, fell into a deep pit ... and was dashed in pieces with his fall'. He is reflecting on the dire consequences for those who leave the path of righteousness — discipline for believers and death for apostates.

'Death and Destruction lie open before the Lord — how much more the hearts of men!' (15:11).

A fortiori

This proverb takes us to the reason behind the truth that we can be sure of God's discipline, referring us back to verse 3 and the omniscience of God. If God knows all about the hidden facts of death and destruction (literally, 'Sheol and Abaddon'), then nothing is, or can be, hidden from him. He knows what is hidden in the hearts of men.

One afternoon in 1868 Henry Twells was invigilating an examination for just one scholar. As evening came on he wrote his hymn, 'At even ere the sun was set', which includes the lines:

> His kind but searching glance can scan
> The very wounds that shame would hide.

God is the great examiner of men's hearts. He watches as we work. Whether we go to heaven or hell, here or the other side of the world, in darkness or in light, he sees it all (Ps. 139). The light of his glory uncovers every hidden corner. The Puritan William Secker observed that 'God looks most where man looks least.'

'A mocker resents correction; he will not consult the wise' (15:12).

Synonymous: **'resents correction' / 'will not consult the wise'**

Here are two faults of fools, or mockers, that often go together. On one hand, the **'mocker'** hates being corrected. On the other, even when he knows in himself that he is in need of help or advice, pride keeps him from consulting **'the wise'**. So we return to the ever-recurring theme of teachability, or submissiveness.

Perhaps this is a good place to introduce the forgotten Middle English word, 'mumpsimus'. The story goes that an illiterate fifteenth-century priest was once taken up for using this word, which is a misspelling of the Latin *sumpsimus*. On being shown his error, he obstinately replied, 'I will not change my old mumpsimus for your new *sumpsimus*.' Such a man was also sometimes referred to as a 'foolosopher'. If he was in the legal profession he could be a 'jurisprude'. How will any of us ever be wise if we refuse to take advice or seek it out? We have already noted that even the Lord Jesus as a boy in the temple consulted with the wise. No doubt he also listened to his earthly parents even though he was not in need of correction. How different we can be when we refuse to accept good advice when offered, or to seek it even though we know we need it! One of the purposes of God's Word is to correct us. Sometimes we foolishly resent its corrections. At other times, we will not even consult it. That way lies foolishness.

> **A happy heart makes the face cheerful,**
> **but heartache crushes the spirit.**
> **The discerning heart seeks knowledge,**
> **but the mouth of a fool feeds on folly.**
> **All the days of the oppressed are wretched,**
> **but the cheerful heart has a continual feast**
> (15:13-15).

Like verses 7 and 11, these three proverbs all refer to the **'heart'** — here the unseen, inner man. Again and again the Bible draws us back to contemplating the state of the inner man.

Contrast: **'happy heart'** / **'heartache'**
A glad heart cheers; a glum heart crushes.

Verse 13 is a straightforward proverb reminding us that the state of the heart can often be read in the face and that temperament affects us all. (It has affinities with 14:30 and 17:22.) Our morale often makes a difference to the very way we look. That is why we use phrases such as 'What's up with you? Why so sad?' or 'What are you looking so cheerful about?'

The world's philosophy is to 'put on a happy face':

> Pick out a pleasant outlook,
> Stick out that noble chin,
> Wipe off that 'full of doubt' look,
> Slap on a happy grin.

Indeed, some Christians have taken up that approach and attempted to make more of it than is warranted, but this is to make the mistake of reversing what is noted here. It is the **'happy heart'** that will make for a cheerful face, not the other way round (although see verse 30, where the opposite point is made). Anticipating verse 30, it would be good for young preachers to consider how confusing it is for the hearers when a joyful message is intoned with a gloomy face. Congregations also ought, when singing words of joy, at least to attempt to express that joy in their demeanour. Temperaments vary but a cheerful face can do a great deal of good. If you have a bad conscience or are full of envy and discontent, it is no wonder that you never smile.

Contrast (complex): **'discerning heart'** / **'mouth of a fool'**
Searching souls seek for sagacity; fools feed their faces on folly.

Once more, heart and mouth are spoken of together in verse 14 (see 15:7). If our hearts are wise and **'discerning'** we will seek knowledge. The Queen of Sheba wisely sought out Solomon. Mary and Nicodemus were among those who sought out the one who is greater than Solomon. The Bereans are commended because they not only 'received' the gospel 'with great eagerness', but also 'examined the Scriptures every day to see if what Paul said was true' (Acts 17:11).

The heart of the fool is not mentioned, for the very way he speaks betrays his foolishness. He **'feeds on folly'**. That is his delight and the unproductive source of any nourishment he can find. There is a 'moreish' quality then, even an addictive one, about both wisdom and foolishness — the more you have, the more you want.

Contrast (complex): **'oppressed'** / **'cheerful heart'**

Verse 15 speaks of the power of the inner man to overcome outward circumstances. We all probably know something of this — triumphing over circumstances, mind over matter. If we do not we are the hopeless prisoners of our circumstances. Ultimately, it is the believer who knows this best because, although he is often oppressed by adversity and persecution, he nevertheless knows **'a continual feast'**. Unlike the fool, he is not feeding on folly, but has a cheerful heart that has been transformed by God. He has heard Jesus' voice, opened the door and Jesus has come in and eats with him. With David he can say:

> You have filled my heart with greater joy
>> than when their grain and new wine abound.
> I will lie down and sleep in peace,
>> for you alone, O Lord,
>> make me dwell in safety
>
> (Ps. 4:7-8).

Or he can say with Habbakuk:

Though the fig-tree does not bud
　　and there are no grapes on the vines,
though the olive crop fails
　　and the fields produce no food,
though there are no sheep in the pen
　　and no cattle in the stalls,
yet I will rejoice in the LORD,
　　I will be joyful in God my Saviour
                                    (Hab. 3:17-18).

Like Paul and Silas in prison in Philippi he sings. The writer of
the epistle to the Hebrews epitomizes the right outlook when
he says, 'Sometimes you were publicly exposed to insult and
persecution; at other times you stood side by side with those
who were so treated. You sympathized with those in prison
and joyfully accepted the confiscation of your property, because you knew that you yourselves had better and lasting
possessions' (Heb. 10:33-34).

What these fifteen proverbs teach us

The fifteen proverbs in this section can be grouped under the
following four headings

The heart

Because our inner thoughts and attitudes are largely unseen,
there is always the danger of neglecting them. The Bible often
draws us back to such matters, however. Several proverbs
refer to the heart (e.g. 14:30). In nearly every chapter of Proverbs there is at least one reference to it. In this section, we find
a little glut of them in verses 13-15 and others in verses 7 and
11. They speak of the inevitable connection between the inner

and outer man (15:13), the power of the inner man (15:15), the need to seek knowledge within (15:14) and the fact that God sees our hearts (15:11; cf. 15:3). Such considerations foster heart care (see 4:8).

Righteousness and wickedness

Verses 8 and 9 make clear God's attitude to righteousness and wickedness. The righteous are loved and please God, while he detests the wicked. That is why 'The house of the righteous contains great treasure, but the income of the wicked brings them trouble' (15:6).

Correction and conversion

The answer to wickedness is conversion. However, 'A mocker resents correction; he will not consult the wise' (15:12). Similarly, 'A fool spurns his father's discipline, but whoever heeds correction shows prudence' (15:5). Criticism is never pleasant, but if we listen and take heed to ourselves and repent there is hope. 'Stern discipline awaits him who leaves the path; he who hates correction will die' (15:10).

The tongue

One of the ways a true conversion manifests itself is in a person's speech. Several proverbs here deal with the tongue and its proper use (see especially 15:1-2,4,7). Here are pleas that we speak in a way that is 'gentle', not 'harsh', that brings 'healing' and 'life', as opposed to deceiving people and crushing their 'spirit', and that wisely commends and spreads 'knowledge', unlike those who foolishly gush 'folly'.

30.
How to fear the Lord

Please read Proverbs 15:16-33

God-fearing poverty, blessed poverty, patience, sluggards, wise sons, level-headedness, consultation, bons mots, the path of life, pride, wicked thoughts, greed, careful speech, God's presence, smiles, teachability, discipline, fear of the Lord

These eighteen proverbs cover a variety of subjects. They help us to understand the fear of the Lord that leads to wisdom, which is referred to in the first and the last of them.

> **Better a little with the fear of the LORD**
> **than great wealth with turmoil.**
> **Better a meal of vegetables where there is love**
> **than a fattened calf with hatred**
>
> (15:16-17).

Double contrast (better than): **'little with the fear of the LORD'** / **'great wealth with turmoil'; 'meal of vegetables where there is love'** / **'fattened calf with hatred'**

These first two proverbs are of the type which draw a contrast using the phrase 'better than'. The second is the more evocative of the two, using as it does the metaphor of a meal. The fact that **'love'** is placed as a parallel to fearing the Lord would suggest a vertical understanding of that word (i.e., love to God), rather than the more obvious horizontal one, although love to God should lead to love for men.

In the late 1940s or early 1950s Red Hayes wrote the following words. They capture something of what is said here:

> How many times have you heard someone say,
> 'If I had his money, I could do things my way'?
> But little they know, it's so hard to find
> One rich man in ten with a satisfied mind.
>
> Once I was living in fortune and fame,
> Everything that I dreamed of to get a start in life's game.
> Then suddenly it happened, I lost every dime.
> But I'm richer by far with a satisfied mind.

Also note the lines:

> The wealthiest person is a pauper at times,
> Compared to the man with a satisfied mind.

Despite such thoughts being almost commonplace, many still opt nevertheless for **'great wealth with turmoil'**. My mother-in-law's parents would use the phrase, 'Potes maip, melys cwsg', which means, 'Turnip soup, sweet sleep,' and succinctly expresses the thought here.

'A hot-tempered man stirs up dissension, but a patient man calms a quarrel' (15:18).
  Contrast: **'hot-tempered man'** / **'patient man'**
  Agitation aggravates; patience pacifies.

Patience has been commended before (14:17,29; see also 15:1). Here the emphasis, as in 20:3, is on the way the attitude of the **'hot-tempered man stirs up dissension'** and the ability of the **'patient man'**, not only to control his own temper, but also to calm **'a quarrel'** involving others. Instead of damping down the flames, the hot-tempered man wickedly stirs them up. Like fires, quarrels are often much more to do with people stirring things up than about combustible matter. Peacemakers, Christ says, are blessed and 'will be called sons of God' (Matt. 5:9). They let fires go out.

'The way of the sluggard is blocked with thorns, but the path of the upright is a highway' (15:19).
   Contrast: **'way of the sluggard'** / **'path of the upright'**

Here is **'the sluggard'** again, last seen in 13:4. The **'thorns'** that block his way are either in his mind, or are his own fault due to neglect. He is contrasted with **'the upright'**, whose **'path'** is **'a highway'**. This is not because the upright necessarily have an easier life, but because they know their destination and are determined to reach that goal through the Lord's enabling. Are you preventing your own progress by allowing the thorns of sin to grow unchecked? Are you making half-hearted attempts at dealing with things, and so doubling your work? On the other hand, it is thorns that block the way, not a wall. They must be removed, painful as that might prove. Be diligent to get back onto the highway of holiness, which alone leads to heaven.

'A wise son brings joy to his father, but a foolish man despises his mother' (15:20).
   Contrast: **'wise son'** / **'foolish man'**
   Dads delighted; mums mocked.

This is where we came in at 10:1. The development here is that the foolish bring grief because they despise their mothers. That is the inevitable conclusion when a person flies in the face of all the good things he has been taught. Of course, a foolish man despises his father as well as his mother, and a wise one also brings joy to his mother, but presenting the truth in this form is perhaps most likely to strike at the conscience.

'Folly delights a man who lacks judgement, but a man of understanding keeps a straight course' (15:21).
   Contrast: **'man who lacks judgement'** / **'man of understanding'**
   A man who lacks judgement finds folly a delight;
   And an understanding one will keep his course straight.

One is reminded of the fable about the hare and the tortoise. The hare has a thoroughly good time getting up to all sorts of foolish antics. The tortoise simply plods on. It is the latter who wins the race. US president Abraham Lincoln once said that the secret of his success was the fact that, although not a particularly fast walker, he kept on walking. William Carey, the pioneer missionary, similarly said that the one thing he was good at was plodding. Ill-discipline and a delight in folly can reneder a man unfit for any noble purpose. A resolute determination to forget 'what is behind' and strain 'towards what is ahead', pressing on 'towards the goal to win the prize for which God has called [us] heavenwards in Christ Jesus', transforms the situation, however much we may lack in other ways (see Phil. 3:14-15). Part of what is involved in getting to heaven is not being sidetracked by things that are vain.

'Plans fail for lack of counsel, but with many advisers they succeed' (15:22).

Contrast: **'lack of counsel' / 'many advisers'**
No counsel, failure; consult, you flourish.

This is reminiscent of 11:14 (see also 12:15; 13:10; 20:18). Given that not all advice is good advice, we must recognize, however, that it is pride that keeps us from asking for advice from others. If you listen to others you will avoid buying the lime-green suit, or the second-hand car that might kill you. Perhaps you will not marry the drunk, or retire to the country-side where no one will visit. Give up on self-reliance. Go first to God and also to his servants, to the experts in whatever field.

'A man finds joy in giving an apt reply — and how good is a timely word!' (15:23).
Synonymous: **'apt reply' / 'timely word'**

A double-bass player was lugging his instrument down some steps when a drunk asked him, 'How do you get that under you chin?' 'By keeping my mouth shut,' was the tart reply. This observational proverb describes the joy of being able to give an apt reply. Sometimes we hear a good reply and think, 'I wish I'd said that!' or we lie in bed thinking, 'That's what I should've said!' When I was a child I never knew anything clever to say when someone called me a pig. A few years ago, however, I heard my niece reply to someone:

> A pig is an animal.
> An animal is nature.
> Nature is beautiful.
> So thank you for the compliment!

Peter tells us, 'Always be prepared to give an answer to everyone who asks you to give the reason for the hope that you have' (1 Peter 3:15).

I remember Geoff Thomas saying that when a sceptic once said to him, 'Yes, but what do you mean by "God"?' he answered (using the catechism): 'God is a spirit infinite, eternal and unchangeable in his being, wisdom, holiness, etc.' I recall reading that to answer atheists you should say, 'Do you know everything then?' Of course, they will deny it and so you ask, 'Then how do you know that God's existence isn't simply one of the things you don't know?' I also like the answer to 'The Bible is full of contradictions,' which is: 'Which ones?' As for 'Where did Cain get his wife?' you should either say, 'I don't talk about other men's wives,' or 'If I tell you, will you agree to explore the Bible further with me?'

Someone told me of a well-known Bible teacher dealing with a woman at a public meeting who suggested that the apostle Paul was 'simply unclear' on the role of women in the church. After she had made her point, he replied that he had not understood what she was saying properly and so she had to go through it all again. He then said, to her consternation, that it was still unclear. This was a little cruel, but it made the point that, just as she did not like being told she was unclear, it is surely not acceptable to suggest that Paul is 'simply unclear'.

As for **'a timely word'**, the phrase has become a standard one among some evangelical Christians. It is most desirable that every time God's servants preach they should bring timely words for his people. We all need to speak the right words at the right time. We have a perfect model in Christ, who knew, for example, to speak in terms of regeneration when a Jewish religious leader came flattering him and about living water when a godless Samaritan woman approached.

'The path of life leads upward for the wise to keep him from going down to the grave' (15:24).
   Synthetic: **'leads upward ... to keep ... from ... grave'**
   Onward and upward, not downward and death-ward.

This sums up the Christian life very vividly using the familiar motif of a journey. Life is also a favourite picture for describing the godly way. So we see one road leading upwards to the joys of heaven and another leading down to the miseries of hell. Which road are you on? Wisdom means life. Avoid the path of the adulteress, which leads to death (see 2:18; 5:5; 7:27).

> **The LORD tears down the proud man's house**
> **but he keeps the widow's boundaries intact.**
> **The LORD detests the thoughts of the wicked,**
> **but those of the pure are pleasing to him**
>   (15:25-26).

Contrast: **'proud man's house'** / **'widow's boundaries'**
Lord detests
Contrast: **'thoughts of the wicked'** / **'those of the pure'**

Both these proverbs begin with **'the LORD'**, the name of the covenant God. In the first, he **'tears down'** a house; in the second, less concretely, he **'detests ... thoughts'**. In the first, his anger is directed at the **'proud'**; in the second, at **'the wicked'**. On the other hand, **'he keeps the widow's boundaries intact'** (despite, no doubt, the attacks of the proud) and finds the thoughts **'of the pure ... pleasing to him'**. If you are proud, expect disaster at God's hands, especially if you attempt to exploit the needy. On the other hand, those who are needy but who look to him can be confident about the future. If you are wicked and have wicked plans, they are loathsome to God. Rather think pure thoughts that please him.

'A greedy man brings trouble to his family, but he who hates bribes will live' (15:27).
   Contrast: **'greedy man'** / **'he who hates bribes'**

How little we may realize the potential for greed to bring trouble on us and on our families! The temptation to take a bribe, to grab a little extra, may be great, but think where it could lead — it could ruin both you and your family. If you do not care about yourself, at least think of your family — perturbed parents, worried wives, battered and grieving boys and girls. Many spouses and children can testify to the troubles that have come because a father or mother was always out working. Bribery is condemned in the law (Exod. 23:8; Deut. 16:19) and elsewhere. For example, 'Extortion turns a wise man into a fool, and a bribe corrupts the heart' (Eccles.7:7; cf. Ps 26:10; Prov. 17:23).

'The heart of the righteous weighs its answers, but the mouth of the wicked gushes evil' (15:28).
   Contrast: **'heart of the righteous'** / **'mouth of the wicked'**
   Righteous souls weigh replies; unrighteous mouths gush lies.

Here is a counterpart to verse 23. The way to find apt words is seldom to blurt out the first thing that comes into your head. I have heard it said of Professor John Murray that he would sometimes respond to a question by saying, 'I will have to think about that.' It might be some days before he gave an answer. Christ was again the perfect model. He knew just what to say when asked enthusiastically, 'What must I do to inherit eternal life?' and exactly how to respond to the question: 'Is it right to pay taxes to Caesar or not?' (Mark 10:17; 12:14). Would we have known? All of us can improve the way we speak if we give it a little more thought.

'The LORD is far from the wicked but he hears the prayer of the righteous' (15:29).
   Contrast: **'wicked'** / **'righteous'**
   Away from the wrong; alongside the right.

The wicked want to get away from God, and so when they are in need he does not come near. The righteous, however, are near him, as it were, and so he hears their prayer. A similar thought is found in Psalm 34:12-16. Peter quotes it in his first epistle:

> For the eyes of the Lord are on the righteous
>   and his ears are attentive to their prayer,
> but the face of the Lord is against those who do evil
>   (1 Peter 3:12).

'A cheerful look brings joy to the heart, and good news gives health to the bones' (15:30).
Synonymous: **'cheerful look' / 'good news'**

This proverb reminds us of verse 13, of which it is in part the corollary (it also anticipates 17:22 and 25:25). It reminds us of the power of a smile ('bright eyes') and of the effect of good news in general. A Chinese proverb says, 'Don't open a shop if you can't smile.' We all know what a difference a smile can make, or some good news. 'It's stopped raining.' 'Our team has won!' 'No school today.' Some have built whole philosophies on the fact that smiling and laughing can make such a big difference. Since Galen the therapeutic properties of happiness have been noted. There is an American Association for Therapeutic Humour based in St Louis. It is claimed that laughter can lower blood pressure, reduce stress, increase oxygen levels in the blood, promote endorphin activity so that we have a better sense of well-being, and even strengthen the immune system. *The American Medical Association Journal* for 14 February 2001 reported research in Japan showing how skin welts shrank in allergy patients who watched a Charlie Chaplin comedy, while those in the control group who watched a video on weather saw no such improvement. Another study of a group of 150 with heart disease showed them to be 40% less likely to laugh and much more likely to feel hostility and anger. A ten-year study published in the October 2000 issue of *The Archives of Internal Medicine* revealed that clinically depressed men are more than twice as likely to die of a heart attack as those who do not suffer from depression. While acknowledging such studies, the believer recognizes that those who accept the truly good news, the gospel, find not only bodily health but also everlasting life.

> **He who listens to a life-giving rebuke**
>   **will be at home among the wise.**
> **He who ignores discipline despises himself,**
>   **but whoever heeds correction gains understanding.**
> **The fear of the LORD teaches a man wisdom,**
>   **and humility comes before honour**
>
> (15:31-33).

All three of these proverbs emphasize yet again the strong element of teachability in true wisdom.

Synthetic: **'he who listens' / 'among the wise'**
He who a life-giving rebuke does not despise —
That man will find himself at home among the wise.

The first is a straightforward statement (15:31). The fact that the **'rebuke'** here is termed **'life-giving'** reminds us that a world can hang on such things. 'Don't do it,' is the message — you listen, you live; you ignore the advice, you die. The application to the gospel call is obvious, but there are wider applications too.

Contrast: **'He who ignores discipline' / 'whoever heeds correction'**

Verse 32 drives home the fact that to ignore discipline is a form of self-hatred. It is to hate your own soul. Heeding correction is the way to wisdom. So often those who are rebuked for their sins think that such rebukes will harm them. In fact, if they are heeded, they can do untold good. We are back to Proverbs 8:35-36 (see also 1:21-33; 5:11-13).

Synthetic: **'fear of the Lᴏʀᴅ' / 'humility'**
Fear leads from foolishness; humility to honour.

The two halves of verse 33 seem disconnected but are not. We are back with the root theme of fearing the Lord. This is paralleled with **'humility'**. These lead to **'wisdom'** and **'honour'**. Fear of the Lord is largely a matter of humility before him. It is not easy to humble ourselves, but it leads to great honour. Just as Christ humbled himself and so was lifted up, so all who humble themselves will be lifted up at the right time:

> If we died with him,
>   we will also live with him;
> if we endure,
>   we will also reign with him
>
>   (2 Tim. 2:11-12).

What these eighteen proverbs teach us

Taking these eighteen proverbs together, we are reminded firstly of just what an effect a little thing can have.

'A man finds joy in giving an apt reply — and how good is a timely word!' (15:23) 'A cheerful look brings joy to the heart, and good news gives health to the bones' (15:30). Such facts are hints that with little effort on our part a timely word, some good news, will fill us with joy. Sadly, we often do not know what is best for us. Sometimes not even a smile or an apt word will raise our spirits. We can even be perverse and refuse to believe there is any good news. If we were wise we would not act in such a way.

The fear of the Lord

So how can I be wise? Verse 33 brings us back to what has been stated already: 'The fear of the LORD teaches a man wisdom.' There has to be a humbling before God for there to be hope. 'Humility comes before honour.' See verses 31-32 on listening to rebukes and being disciplined. If only we can be wise, we shall see that, for the believer, 'The path of life leads upward' and will 'keep him from going down to the grave' (15:24). People think that money is the chief thing they need, but it is not (see 15:16-17). No, what we all need most is to fear the Lord.

Those who fear him are marked by the following characteristics:

Patient peacemaking

'A hot-tempered man stirs up dissension, but a patient man calms a quarrel' (15:18).

Honest hard work

'The way of the sluggard is blocked with thorns, but the path of the upright is a highway' (15:19).

Close concentration

'Folly delights a man who lacks judgement, but a man of understanding keeps a straight course' (15:21).

Listening learning

'Plans fail for lack of counsel, but with many advisers they succeed' (15:22).

Mild modesty

'The LORD tears down the proud man's house but he keeps the widow's boundaries intact' (15:25).

Immaculate intention

'The LORD detests the thoughts of the wicked, but those of the pure are pleasing to him' (15:26).

Selfless simplicity

'A greedy man brings trouble to his family, but he who hates bribes will live' (15:27).

Sober seriousness

'The heart of the righteous weighs its answers, but the mouth of the wicked gushes evil' (15:28).

Personal prayerfulness

'The LORD is far from the wicked but he hears the prayer of the righteous' (15:29).

31.
Serve your King and Judge with humble fear for ever

Please read Proverbs 16:1-9

God's sovereignty, motives, successful planning, God's omnipotence, arrogance, atonement, pleasing God, righteous poverty, God's sovereignty

As we observed earlier, from Proverbs 16:1 to 22:16 synonymous and synthetic proverbs begin to dominate. Two-thirds of the proverbs in chapter 16 are of the synonymous or synthetic sort. Here we shall look at just nine of them. They form a group because they are bounded by two declarations which are very much alike, and they have at their heart a similar sentiment expressed in verse 4. Nearly every one of these proverbs (all of them bar the one in verse 8) refer to 'the LORD'. This is one of the biggest concentrations in the book and perhaps reflects the more theological tone that some have detected in this section. The prominent doctrine here is God's sovereignty. Whenever we read of 'the LORD' in the Old Testament, we must remember that he is revealed in the New Testament as the Lord Jesus Christ.

'To man belong the plans of the heart, but from the LORD comes the reply of the tongue' (16:1).

Contrast: **'To man belong'** / **'from the LORD'**
Man applies; God replies.

Some translations present this as a synthetic proverb, but it is
probably a contrasting one like its counterpart in verse 9. It
proclaims God's sovereignty, as does the similar 19:21 (see
also 16:33; 20:24; 21:1). The emphasis is on the fact that,
with all his planning, man still has to recognize that what happens is always, ultimately, **'from the LORD'**.

How many times have people been fully resolved in their
minds what to say, only to change their minds at the last second, sometimes even surprising themselves with what comes
out! The phrase, 'I didn't mean it to come out that way,' bears
witness to this negatively; 'I felt as if it wasn't really me speaking,' bears positive witness to it. The latter has been the experience of preachers; the former that of those who have planned
to speak against them. Balaam is a classic example of the latter (Num. 22-24). The Lord always has the last word (see
GNB).

This does not mean that preparing what to say in a given
situation is pointless. Rather, we must always prepare in the
consciousness that we may end up saying something quite different. Spurgeon has a wonderful story of going to preach
somewhere and, as he opened the Bible, lighting on another
text, which he proceeded to read and preach. After he had
preached through two points and just as he was wondering
what to say next, the lights suddenly failed, and so he gave
some impromptu thoughts on Jesus, the Light of the World.
Apparently, people were converted by both parts of the address. As he notes, if he had proceeded with his original plan
things would have been very different.

Of course, the contrast between our plans and God's Word
is a major one. The following promise to the disciples comes
to mind: 'When you are brought before synagogues, rulers

and authorities, do not worry about how you will defend your-selves or what you will say, for the Holy Spirit will teach you at that time what you should say' (Luke 12:11-12). That seems to be a specific promise of inspiration, but Luke 21:14-15 is more general: 'But make up your mind not to worry before-hand how you will defend yourselves. For I will give you words and wisdom that none of your adversaries will be able to resist or contradict.'

'All a man's ways seem innocent to him, but motives are weighed by the LORD' (16:2).
Contrast: **'ways'** / **'motives'**
Man says that he is innocent, but God will look at his intent.

The sovereignty of God is again in the background, in particu-lar his omniscience. The proverb is like 21:2 (see also 24:12; 30:12). Perhaps this proverb reminded Solomon of similar but differently expressed words spoken to him by his own father David: 'And you, my son Solomon, acknowledge the God of your father, and serve him with wholehearted devotion and with a willing mind, for the LORD searches every heart and understands every motive behind the thoughts' (1 Chr. 28:9).

The world's religions are generally quiet on the subject of motives (the spirit in which we act), but true religion demands more than mere outward conformity. The very fact that God sees our hearts should highlight the need for a right spirit. God weighs motives to see whether our actions are vain and empty, or full of good intent. He is like a goldsmith weighing metals to distinguish real from counterfeit. As A. W. Tozer observed, what makes a work sacred is the reason why it is performed. God knows our motives, even when we are un-sure of them. They are always mixed, but the purer they are, the better they are. It is only when cleansed by Christ's blood that they can be acceptable to God.

Having the right motive is sometimes not easy. T. S. Eliot wrote:

The last temptation is the greatest treason,
To do the right deed for the wrong reason.

There are times when we suspect our own false motives but, as in the first part of the proverb, our instinctive reaction, apart from grace, is to defend ourselves, regarding all our motives as innocent. Although we must be charitable in our thoughts of others, we should be harder on ourselves.

'Commit to the Lord whatever you do, and your plans will succeed' (16:3).
　　Synthetic: **'commit'** / **'succeed'**
　　Trust to God in all you do,
　　And all your dreams will then come true.

This is one of the most frequently quoted proverbs. It is in the form of a conditional promise. The condition is that of committing all to the Lord — literally, rolling it all on to him (see 1 Peter 5:7). The promise is of success. It is another aspect of God's sovereignty. Because he is sovereign, we can trust him to enable us to succeed. It is similar to ceratain passages from the Psalms:

Delight yourself in the Lord
　　and he will give you the desires of your heart
　　　　　　　　　　　　　　　　　　　　(Ps. 37:4).

Cast your cares on the Lord
　　and he will sustain you;
　　he will never let the righteous fall
　　　　　　　　　　　　　　　　　　　　(Ps. 55:22).

Committing everything to the Lord does not mean saying a short prayer before doing what we have already decided to do, but endeavouring to do everything in line with what is revealed in his Word. Those who do this can be sure of his blessing ultimately. The success, as ever, ought not to be understood in merely worldly terms. Some translate more conservatively as 'Your purposes will be established,' in the sense that you will know what to do. Ultimately, however, such a believer cannot fail. We can think of it in terms of a map. If we follow the directions correctly, we shall reach our destination.

'The LORD works out everything for his own ends — even the wicked for a day of disaster' (16:4).
    Synthetic: **'works out'** / **'own ends'**

Again, the sovereignty of God is to the fore. Here is the reason for confidence in God. There is some disagreement about how to translate this potentially difficult verse, although it is certain that God is in control of all things and yet never the author of evil. He leaves no loose ends, but works everything together as part of his own divine purpose. Even rebellion and sin work together, ultimately, for his own good ends. We can seldom easily see how this can be so, but the Bible reassures us it is. The stories of Joseph and of Esther confirm it. Of course, the cross itself is the supreme example of this.

The LORD detests all the proud of heart.
    Be sure of this: They will not go unpunished
                               (16:5).

Lord detests
Synthetic: **'detests'** / **'not ... unpunished'**
God hates the proud;
They'll surely be cowed.

The sovereignty theme is not forgotten. As Thomas Manton points out, 'Other sins are against God's law but pride is against God's sovereignty.' That is why God hates it so much. It is the root of all other sins. This is another proverb which uses the formula, **'The LORD detests ...'**, and is one of many blasts against the sin of pride. In their pride, they do not realize it, but such people have no hope of being acquitted when God judges them. As D. L. Moody once put it, 'God sends no one away empty except those who are full of themselves.'

Not all versions translate the opening of the second line, **'Be sure of this'**; some have something on the lines of 'Even though they join together...' The Hebrew refers to putting hand to hand and can probably be paraphrased: 'You can shake on it.' In other words, 'This is certain.' The kingdom of heaven belongs to those who are poor in spirit, and the meek will inherit the earth. 'God opposes the proud but gives grace to the humble' (see 3:34; James 4:6; 1 Peter 5:5).

'Through love and faithfulness sin is atoned for; through the fear of the LORD a man avoids evil' (16:6).
> *Synonymous:* **'love and faithfulness'** / **'fear of the LORD'**
> Love and loyalty will atone;
> If you fear God, you'll leave sin alone.

'The fear of the LORD' is a familiar phrase in Proverbs. Here it is matched with **'love and faithfulness'**, which in the context must be man's love for God and faithfulness to him. Such attitudes both atone for sin and enable a man to avoid evil. Like other verses in Scripture, this sounds like an assertion of justification by works but is actually a reminder to the justified that they need to be sanctified. Enough time has been spent in sin, and so we must make the most of every opportunity to do right by loving God and being faithful to him. Fear of the Lord should lead us out of the paths of evil and into the ways of righteousness. This is possible for the man who has put his trust in Christ.

'When a man's ways are pleasing to the Lord, he makes even his enemies live at peace with him' (16:7).
> *Synthetic:* **'pleasing to the Lord' / 'enemies live at peace'**
> When your ways please the Lord, even foes are in accord.

Here is another encouraging promise. Being a proverb, it cannot guarantee peace, but we are being urged to concentrate on what really matters with the assurance that other things will fall into place. It is a little like Jesus' statement about seeking first the kingdom of God in the assurance that all our needs will be met. It may be this verse that prompted Peter to write, 'Be self-controlled and alert. Your enemy the devil prowls around like a roaring lion looking for someone to devour' (1 Peter 5:8 — see the references above to 1 Peter 5).

Self-control and alertness can mean peace, even from our greatest enemy. When our lives are truly righteous it is difficult for our enemies to do anything but be at peace with us, although they will try to spoil things, as Joseph and Daniel both discovered, in different ways.

'Better a little with righteousness than much gain with injustice' (16:8).
> *Contrast (better than):* **'a little with righteousness' / 'much gain with injustice'**
> Better righteous with a little than unrighteous with a lot.

This follows on from the previous verse and takes us back to Proverbs 15:16. There are more important things than what the world holds so dear. It is appropriate to quote Peter again: 'And the God of all grace, who called you to his eternal glory in Christ, after you have suffered a little while, will himself restore you and make you strong, firm and steadfast' (1 Peter 5:10).

'In his heart a man plans his course, but the LORD determines his steps' (16:10).
   Contrast: **'man plans' / 'LORD determines'**
   Man proposes; God disposes.
   Man devises; the Lord directs.

Echoing verse 1 but referring in the second line not to what is said with the mouth, but to where the feet travel, this proverb closely resembles the first part of 20:24: 'A man's steps are directed by the LORD.' Again and again we see this demonstrated in Scripture and in life. Once more, the purpose of the proverb is not to prohibit planning but to warn against opposing the Lord or worrying about the future.

What these nine proverbs teach us

God is our King and our Judge

As we have seen, the doctrine of God's sovereignty, his kingship, permeates these verses. God rules. Our lives are in his hands. He is not the celestial watchmaker of deism, but a God who continues to watch over his creation and work out his purposes in it. We may like to think that we do exactly as we wish, but it is not like that, as verses 1 and 9 make clear. It is our duty to submit to the King. With George Matheson we pray:

   Make me a captive, Lord,
   And then I shall be free;
   Force me to render up my sword,
   And I shall conqueror be.

He is not only our King but our Judge, too. Sometimes human courts try to judge motives. It is notoriously difficult. Because he is sovereign, God can do it with ease. 'All a man's ways seem innocent to him, but motives are weighed by the LORD' (16:2). We can only assume that people act with good intentions. God alone knows the true answer.

In verse 4, his role as both King and Judge comes out: 'The LORD works out everything for his own ends — even the wicked for a day of disaster.'

Therefore we should always serve him humbly with fear

In the light of this we must see the need to *serve* him (16:3) Even without the promise, the call to commit everything to him would still stand.

We must serve *humbly* (16:5) The note of judgement sounds again here.

We must serve *with fear* (16:6).

We must serve like this *always* (16:7) Like verse 3, this verse contains a great promise. Whatever happens, the believer can be confident. It is a proverb and so there is no guarantee of an easy life. However, 'Better a little with righteousness than much gain with injustice (16:8).

32.
The character and power of kings

Please read Proverbs 16:10-15

Kings' speech, weights, justice, favourites, a king's wrath, a king's favour

In Proverbs 16:10-15 five of the six proverbs refer directly to kings and how they should conduct themselves. The odd one out, which is to do with honest weights and measures, also has a bearing on government, as rulers are usually responsible for enforcing standards in that area.

This is not the only place in Proverbs that deals directly with kingship and the qualities required. Similar proverbs are found in a sequence at the beginning of chapter 25, where 'proverbs of Solomon, copied by the men of Hezekiah' begin, and in the early verses of chapter 31, where the advice of King Lemuel's mother is preserved. There are also isolated proverbs referring to kingship elsewhere — two earlier on (14:28,35), and several later ones (19:12; 20:2,8,26,28, etc.). No doubt Solomon, and later Hezekiah, had a great interest in such proverbs.

In the light of this we shall vary our approach here and consider these proverbs as a brief guide for leaders or rulers. They are of use to all in positions of civil authority — kings, queens, presidents, government ministers, local councillors, policemen, teachers. The principles set down here have relevance not only in the sphere of the state, but that of the family and of the church too. Further, each one of us is responsible to be king in his own sphere, ruling over our own souls at the very least.

The character and power of kings

They must be just

'The lips of a king speak as an oracle, and his mouth should not betray justice' (16:10).
> *Synthetic:* **'[kings] speak as an oracle'** / **'not betray justice'**
> Divine is what kings say;
> Justice they must not betray.

A king has great power, and so have lesser governors. Therefore it is vital that when they speak they speak justly. Like Romans 13:1-2, this verse appears to put the words of governors on a potential par with God's words. This is known as 'divination'. Not that kings are infallible. It is nothing short of tragic, however, when rulers are dishonest and unjust.

Justice is pictured here as an ally and friend, a wife even, who must not be betrayed. Pray that all in authority will be kept from such sins. If you have such power be determined, by God's grace, never to play fast and loose with justice. When any of us acts unjustly it is a sin, but the more power we have, the greater the consequences.

They must be fair

In the next verse we have a practical application. If civic authorities are just they will endeavour to see that fair play exists throughout their jurisdiction. One area where this will become apparent is that of commerce.

'Honest scales and balances are from the LORD; all the weights in the bag are of his making' (16:11).
  Synonymous: **'from the LORD' / 'of his making'**
  It's of the LORD when things are rightly weighed;
  All the weights by him are made.

(This reiterates Proverbs 11:1 and anticipates 20:10,23.) As we have seen, both the law and the prophets say the same thing.

The history and practice of weighing and measuring is fascinating, with surprising twists and turns. The earliest systems were rough and ready ones such as those based on body parts. An Egyptian cubit, for example, was the length of the arm from elbow to outstretched fingertips. By 2500 B.C. it had been standardized in a fifty-two-centimetre-long royal master cubit of black marble. In England, units such as the foot were for many years defined in terms of the measurements of the reigning monarch, not being properly standardized until the thirteenth century. Abuses and variations continued long after that. For example, until 1824 different gallons were used for ale, wine and corn. (A US gallon is still different to a UK one, as is a US ton.) The old UK system was originally defined by three standard measures — yard, pound and gallon. These were held in London. The US had a similar system. In 1963 the British Parliament passed a Weights and Measures Act defining yards and pounds in terms of metres and kilograms, as defined by the *Système International d'Unités* in October 1960. Thus a yard became 0.9144 metres and a pound 0.45359237 kilograms. (The act also abolished drachms, scruples, minims, rods, poles, perches, etc.) A 1985 act abolished more imperial measures for trade and defined a gallon as 4.54609 litres. The SI is based on seven principal units. A metre is defined as the distance light travels, in a vacuum, in 1/299792458[th] of a second. A second, the basic unit of time, is the length of time taken for 9,192,631,770 periods of vibration of the caesium-133 atom to occur. The kilogram is the only basic unit still defined in terms of a material object. It is the mass of an international prototype in the form of a platinum-iridium cylinder kept at Sèvres, France. Amperes, kelvins, moles and candelas are also closely defined. The system is rooted in the French metric system officially started in June 1799 with the intention of being 'for all people, for all time'. The metre was originally defined as being one ten-millionth part of a quarter of the earth's circumference. There is strong resistance to metrication in the UK for various reasons. Carpet salesmen, for example, found people more willing to pay £10 a square yard than £12 a square metre even though the two prices are almost the same.

What really matters is that there should be absolute honesty in this matter. Stealing a hundred pounds from a thousand people may not seem as wrong as stealing the same amount from an individual, but both acts are on a par morally. If we are privileged to live in a country where, under the enforcement of a careful system of laws and inspections, such cheating is comparatively rare, this is God's doing, as the proverb underlines. We ought therefore to give thanks and pray that it will continue to be the case.

They must be righteous

Verse 12 refers directly to kings, again continuing the theme: **'Kings detest wrongdoing, for a throne is established through righteousness.'**
   Synthetic: **'detest wrongdoing'** / **'throne is established'**
   Kings detest every misdeed;
   By doing right they will succeed.

A regime that is riddled with unrighteousness will not survive. Corruption means eventual collapse from within. For their own sake, then, rulers ought to eschew wrongdoing of every sort. But how can they know what is righteous? They must have recourse to God's Word. Failure to do this has been conspicuous in the recent history of the UK and other Western countries, as evidenced in laws regarding abortion, homosexuality and several other matters. There are bound to be consequences.

They must be honest

'Kings take pleasure in honest lips; they value a man who speaks the truth' (16:13).
> *Synonymous:* **'honest lips'** / **'man who speaks the truth'**
> Honest lips give kings great pleasure;
> A truthful man they'll always treasure.

The final piece of advice regards the counsel rulers take. They must never listen to those who are dishonest, but should seek out those who speak the truth. It is pleasant to be flattered. It is tempting to surround oneself with 'Yes' men, but it is a disastrous policy in the end. Integrity and a determination to arrive at the truth must characterize all who serve in civil government. It is very sad that so many politicians today have a reputation for dishonesty and deceit. An obsession with 'spin' has, if we may put it this way, spun out of control so that it is sometimes very unclear what is true and what is not.

Their power

In verses 14 and 15 we have two contrasting reminders of the power of kings. We are thinking of the power of ancient Eastern despots, a power that is rare today. Solomon himself had announced the execution of more than one man. There are still very powerful men in the world, nevertheless.

In negative terms

'A king's wrath is a messenger of death, but a wise man will appease it' (16:14).
  Contrast: **'king's wrath'** / **'wise man'**
  A king's wrath crucifies, but wisdom pacifies.

Even where a nation has rejected capital punishment, it retains the power of life and death. Decisions made at the top have ramifications that may mean a loss of life — for example, decisions about war, or about the provision that is made for the sick and the poor. Even where people do not lose their lives, they may lose their livelihoods, their property, their freedom. Those with any sort of power ought to remember this.

Here the emphasis is on the power of the wise to change the situation. Though the **'king's wrath'** can be **'a messenger of death'**, wisdom will find ways of appeasing it — most obviously in a plea for clemency when an execution is planned, but also by means of information, discussion and negotiation, as well as intercession to God and proclamation of his Word.

In positive terms

'When a king's face brightens, it means life; his favour is like a rain cloud in spring' (16:15).
  Synonymous: **'face brightens'** / **'favour'**
  Simile: **'[king's] favour'** / **'rain cloud in spring'**
  A king's smile means life for another day;
  His favour reveals there's rain on the way.

Here, as it were, is the result of pleading, of informing, discussing and negotiating, the result of prayer and preaching. We ought not to underestimate what a difference an enlightened ruler can make. According to Appendix 1 of the latest edition of *Operation World*, the CIA has a regularly updated

web site listing all the world's leaders. It also gives its own list
and urges prayer. What a difference it would make if that led
to the brightening of the face of some of those leaders towards Christianity! It would mean life. It would be **'like a
rain cloud in spring'** for some who are currently enduring
much trouble.

The character and power we all have

It is easy to criticize those who are in prominent positions but
before we go trying to remove specks of sawdust from the
eyes of others we will do well to remove planks from our
own. We too have responsibilities. Some are fathers and
mothers, or older siblings; some are pastors, deacons, Sunday
School teachers. We all have some responsibilities — at the
very least for our own selves. And so we ask the following
questions:

Are you just?

Do you speak honestly and justly? Especially in our dealings
with children, with employees, with anyone who depends on
us, we must be just.

Are you fair?

Jesus tells us that the measure we use for others will be the
measure used for us (Matt. 7:2). Just as we expect shopkeepers
to abide by legislation safeguarding the rights of consumers,
so we should be scrupulous in all our dealings with others too.
At home, in business, in every walk, believers must be totally
fair. If we are not, how can we possibly claim to belong to the
Lord?

Are you righteous?

Like kings we ought to 'detest wrongdoing'. If we do not, we are headed for disaster. It is ignoble, poor and mean to have any other attitude. In the Disney film the younger Lion King, Simba, has a vision of his dead father, Mufasa, who accuses Simba of having forgotten him. He goes on: 'You have forgotten who you are and so forgotten me... Remember who you are. You are my son, and the one true king.' We do not know whether the writer had anything in mind beyond the script itself, but one of the biggest problems facing Western man is his spiritual amnesia. He is busy trying to banish God from his mind and in the process he has forgotten that man was created to rule, to be king over creation and over his own life. Love of wrongdoing is not only rebellion against God, but a disregard for our once high position as vicegerents on God's earth.

Are you honest?

Again like kings, we should 'take pleasure in honest lips'; we should 'value a man who speaks the truth'. Listen to preachers who tell you the truth, not those who flatter and mollycoddle. Ask your friends to be straight with you about your sins and failures. There has been a trend among some evangelicals to set up 'accountability groups' because such straight talk is so hard to find. However we do it, we must seek honesty and steer well clear of all the so-called prevarication, misrepresentation, exaggeration, distortion and economy with the truth that are so prevalent today.

We must remember our responsibilities. We all have an impact on the lives of others. J. B. Priestley's mid-twentieth century drama *An inspector calls* about the death of a young woman is presented in the form of a detective drama but turns into an indictment of the middle-class family all of whose members, in some sense, bear a responsibility. It is fiction but the point is clear: the way we live has a bearing on the lives of others. The decisions we make can have important ramifications for others. Some see us as kings and wait on our words and actions. Our wrath can mean death, or at least disappointment; our smile can be 'like a rain cloud in spring'.

The character and power of Christ

Morality is never enough. We do need better civil, church, family and personal government, but passages like this one should also remind us that perfect government does exist in the person of the Lord Jesus Christ. He is the great King, God's anointed Head for his church. He is the one who is greater than Solomon. On earth, his only crown was a cruel crown of thorns. His only robe was a Roman soldier's cast-off. The only sceptre they offered him was a stick of hyssop with a sponge on it. Yet he rules over all the earth and what is only a counsel of perfection for earthly rulers is entirely true of him.

He is just

Every word he spoke is oracular. His mouth never betrayed justice. He is truly the Word of God and no man ever spoke as he did.

He is fair

Absolute fair play characterized his every action, even down to the very smallest of matters. He kept every jot and tittle of the law of God. For example, he was baptized and he paid the temple tax, even though morally he was not obliged to do either of those things. He is the one who weighs us in the balance, and where he finds us wanting he is able to make up the difference and make us full weight.

He is righteous

Like all good kings, he detests wrongdoing. On the contrary, he is 'holy, harmless and undefiled' and so is worthy of the eternal throne of heaven. His kingdom cannot be taken from him. His death on the cross makes this righteousness freely available to all who trust in him.

He is honest

Every word this king speaks is true and he takes pleasure in honest lips, delighting in men who speak the truth as he commands. Again, he is the truth. Those who do not know him are in ignorance and darkness.

If it is true that an Eastern despot had the power of life and death over his subjects, how much more is it so with Christ! He has the power to throw any one of us into hell. His 'wrath is a messenger of death'. However, 'A wise man will appease it.' How? Not by anything we do. It would be foolishness to think that was so. No, the wisdom revealed in God's Word teaches that God's wrath can be appeased only by faith in the Lord Jesus and his death on the cross.

To put it positively, when his face 'brightens', as it does when sinners put their faith in him, 'it means life; his favour is like a rain cloud in spring'. What blessings pour out on all who trust in him!

33.
Pleasant words on wisdom and righteousness

Please read Proverbs 16:16-33

*Wisdom, uprightness, pride, humility, faith, hearts and words,
understanding, instructive speech, pleasant words, wrong ways,
work, scoundrels, perverts and gossips, violence, plotters, grey
hairs, patience, God's sovereignty*

In this chapter we consider the remaining eighteen verses of Proverbs 16.

'How much better to get wisdom than gold, to choose understanding rather than silver' (16:16).
Double contrast (better than): **'wisdom'** / **'gold;** **'understanding'** / **'silver'**
Mental prowess beats precious metal.

Another proverb which uses the 'better than' formula, this verse again asserts the superiority of wisdom, as in Proverbs 3 and 8. The advantages of riches are never denied in the book, but wisdom is superior. Most people think that what they really need is more money, or more fame, or more time. In fact, what we all need is greater wisdom. Other things will then fall into their proper place. Solomon was in an excellent position to make this judgement. He knew that wisdom is harder to come by, more valuable, longer lasting, more satisfying and does more good.

Arnot pictures a captured warship full of gold. The captors, entranced by the gold, leave the ship in the hands of the captives. The latter quietly steer it home where their captors are themselves taken prisoner. If the original captors had paid more attention to sailing the ship, and less to the gold, they would not have lost both.

A lady once won £10,000. She asked John Newton, a man who knew something about the temptations of gambling, to congratulate her. 'Madam,' he replied, 'as for a friend under temptation, I will endeavour to pray for you.'

'The highway of the upright avoids evil; he who guards his way guards his life' (16:17).
Synthetic: **'avoids evil'** / **'guards his life'**
The honest highway from sin keeps away;
To guard your life, guard your way.

Here two pictures are used to describe the upright man, the one who is going to heaven. The favourite imagery of **'the highway'** (cf. 15:19) pictures an upright life as one that goes straight ahead, avoiding any kind of evil (that is, it avoids doing evil, not experiencing trouble). This is accompanied by the picture of a soldier guarding the way off that road. Such a person will not allow wandering. He stays on the road that, of course, leads to life, and so does himself much good. If we do not avoid evil, if we do not care about how we live, we shall surely die. An unguarded life is a sinful life, headed for death. Soldiers of Christ must:

Leave no unguarded place,
No weakness of the soul.

Instead they must:

> Take every virtue, every grace
> And fortify the whole.

Pride goes before destruction,
**   a haughty spirit before a fall.**
Better to be lowly in spirit and among the oppressed
**   than to share plunder with the proud**
(16:18-19).

These two proverbs can be taken together as, like verse 5, they both deal with pride.

> *Synonymous:* **'pride' / 'haughty spirit'**
> Pride leads to perdition, a fat head to a fall.
> The bigger they come, the harder they fall.

The first proverb is in the form of a warning. The proud have it coming to them. God will judge them. The story of King Nebuchadnezzar in Daniel 4 illustrates this well. It is said that Napoleon Bonaparte once had medals struck with his image and the superscription: 'London taken, 1804'. It was as a British prisoner that he eventually died in exile. The legend of Icarus, who flew too near the sun, is well known but its moral is often forgotten.

Whether we are proud of face, race, pace or grace, it must go, or we shall suffer the consequences. Spurgeon once said, 'Pride is most likely to meet destruction, because it is too tall to walk upright. It is most likely to tumble down, because it is always looking upward in its ambition, and never looks at its feet. There only needs to be a pitfall in the way, or even a stone, and down it goes.'

Contrast (better than): **'lowly in spirit and among the oppressed'** / **'to share plunder with the proud'**
Prefer prostration and persecution to plundering in pride.

The second of these proverbs recognizes that if you have a lowly spirit you will lack worldly ambition and so will end up among the oppressed. However, it is better to be in that position than to be more comfortably off financially as a result of sharing the **'plunder with the proud'**. To quote Spurgeon again, 'The gate of heaven, though it is so wide that the greatest sinner may enter, is nevertheless so low that pride can never pass through it.'

'Whoever gives heed to instruction prospers, and blessed is he who trusts in the LORD' (16:20).
Synthetic / beatitude: **'gives heed to instruction'** / **'trusts in the LORD'**
Listen and luxuriate; believe and be blessed.

Again the call goes out to listen. Listen to instruction, accept advice. Heed the Word (literally). With it is the promise that if we listen to the Lord and trust in him then we shall truly be blessed. The close of the Sermon on the Mount comes to mind again, where Jesus speaks of the wise way to listen.

'The wise in heart are called discerning, and pleasant words promote instruction' (16:21).
Synthetic: **'wise in heart'** / **'pleasant words'**

In the course of four verses (16:21-24), the two phrases used in the second line of this proverb are both repeated (**'promote instruction'** in verse 23 and **'pleasant words'** in verse 24), thus establishing some kind of link between these proverbs.

Verse 21 seems to point to the two ingredients necessary for learning.

On the one hand, we need to be **'wise in heart'** to receive instruction. Such people **'are called discerning'**. Sir Francis Bacon famously said that some books needed to be tasted, some swallowed and some thoroughly digested. It is the discerning who know which are which. We have noted this paradox before — the need to have wisdom in order to become wise.

The other side of the coin is that **'Pleasant** ["sweet" or "honeyed"] **words promote instruction'** ('persuasiveness', RSV). We all know what it is to hear or read one person on a subject and find ourselves confronted by a sea of mud, only to consult another who not only makes it clear, but entertaining too. Nowhere is it more vital than in the realm of preaching and teaching God's Word that this is kept in mind. We read of Jesus that 'All spoke well of him and were amazed at the gracious words that came from his lips' (Luke 4:22). With Jesus as our example how can we dare to be boring? Yet even the most wonderful truths can be made to sound uninteresting and turn people off. This does no good. Those who are 'wise in heart' will see the importance of 'pleasant words'.

Let us not forget, however, that sometimes the most beautiful jewels are kept in the drabbest of cases. We must not write off preachers too soon lest we miss some of those gems. We can also sometimes be mistaken in our initial assessment and the real problem may be our lack of discernment. Jesus did make a wonderful promise to his disciples: 'For I will give you words and wisdom that none of your adversaries will be able to resist or contradict' (Luke 21:15).

'Understanding is a fountain of life to those who have it, but folly brings punishment to fools' (16:22).

Contrast: **'understanding'** / **'folly'**
From understanding life will spring;
Folly to fools will punishment bring.

This is the fourth and final reference to **'a fountain of life'**.
This description is elsewhere attributed to 'the mouth of the
righteous' (10:11 — see our comments there); 'the teaching
of the wise' (13:14) and 'the fear of the LORD'(14:27), which,
of course, is the beginning of wisdom. Here it is **'understanding'** that is 'a fountain of life', which suggests liveliness and
life. Solomon and his first readers knew what it was for there
to be a shortage of water, and the picture of fresh, bubbling
water is a powerful one. Here the contrast is with **'folly'**, which
is all that fools have. It amuses them for a while (see 15:21)
but not for ever. We have already learned that folly leads astray
and is loud, deceitful, unproductive and quick-tempered (5:23;
9:13; 12:23; 13:16; 14:4,8,29). Here its power to bring **'punishment to fools'** is underlined.

**'A wise man's heart guides his mouth, and his lips pro-
mote instruction'** (16:23).
 Synthetic: **'wise man's heart'** / **'his lips'**

This brings us back to successful communication. Here the
importance of having a wise heart to guide your mouth is
stressed first. This is the other requirement for words that will
'promote instruction'. Pleasant words are important, of
course, but without good guidance from the heart they can be
merely pleasant words. Too many people speak without thinking first. Saying the first thing that comes into your mind is
seldom a good idea. The wise man says what is both wise and
edifying. This brings us again to the Servant Messiah of Isaiah's
prophecy:

The Sovereign LORD has given me an instructed tongue,
to know the word that sustains the weary.
He wakens me morning by morning,
wakens my ear to listen like one being taught
(Isa. 50:4).

'Pleasant words are a honeycomb, sweet to the soul and healing to the bones' (16:24).
Synthetic: **'sweet'** / **'healing'**
Simile: **'pleasant words'** / **'a honeycomb'**
Pleasant words are honey —
Sweet to the soul,
They make bones whole.

There is a saying that it costs nothing to be pleasant. Some find it difficult, nevertheless. Here the points made in the second half of verse 21 and in verse 23 are combined. This is done by highlighting two features which characterize honey — its sweetness and its healing properties. The **'pleasant words'** that are in mind here are those that are both **'sweet to the soul'** and likely to heal the bones. We instinctively think of pleasant words as being sweet to the body, rather than healing the soul, but this form of expression means that all aspects of the person are covered. The right words can heal relationships and restore well-being. Interestingly, the only other place that mentions **'a honeycomb'** is Psalm 19:10, where it illustrates the sweetness of God's Word. Think of the way the preaching of the gospel does such good to those who hear.

'There is a way that seems right to a man, but in the end it leads to death' (16:25).
Contrast: **'way'** / **'end'**
There's a way that seems right,
But it shuts out all light.

This is a repetition of Proverbs 14:12. Why is it repeated? It is not a mistake. Repetition is an important device for emphasizing certain truths. In 14:12 the context was being deceived by appearances. We saw there how sincerity is widely believed to be enough and quoted examples to show how ridiculous such a notion is. Here the context is that of imparting wisdom to others. How many times have people listened to a speaker who seemed so very sincere, only to find he was a charlatan? Jesus warns us to beware of wolves in sheep's clothing. Even where the sincerity is genuine, all sorts of lies have inadvertently been declared by many well-intentioned teachers. Not everyone who says he is a Christian really is. Many will cry, 'Lord, Lord,' on that day, only to be dismissed.

'The labourer's appetite works for him; his hunger drives him on' (16:26).
> *Synonymous:* **'appetite' / 'hunger'**
> Appetite toils; hunger energizes.

Here is a very practical proverb. Imagine two men going out to dig a field, or to build a wall. One is foolish; the other is wise. The foolish one starts on the job but after a while starts to feel hungry, and so downs tools and stops for something to eat. In fact every half-hour or so, he heads back to his sandwich box, or to the café, for another bite to eat. By the end of the morning his work is hardly started. The wise man, on the other hand, has practically finished because, although he has felt hunger pangs throughout most of the morning, he has carried on working until lunchtime. His appetite has worked for him. The nearer he got to lunchtime, the harder he worked. What seems like a disadvantage has been made to work to his advantage.

Of course, we ought to have higher goals in mind when we work, such as thinking of how we are going to help others with our wages and serving the Lord himself (see Eph. 4:28; 6:7). The Lord's words in John 6:27 are apposite: 'Do not work for food that spoils, but for food that endures to eternal life, which the Son of Man will give you.'

One minister mentioned in the book *More than notion* used to be ashamed of himself because he spent so much of his morning in the study thinking about dinner. He would sometimes punish himself by going without the meal. One sympathizes. However, with some tasks and on some days this is all the motivation we can muster. When we are dealing with children, too, we ought to remember that they need little encouragements to keep them going. Even the laziest can be coaxed in the right direction. In the world of boxing and beyond, the expression is sometimes heard that a person is 'not hungry enough'. Similarly, others are said to be 'driven'. Perhaps the saddest of situations is where the hunger drives on but the opportunities are very few. It is clear from Jesus' ministry that what drove him was a desire to do the Father's will. It was food and drink to him: '"My food," said Jesus, "is to do the will of him who sent me and to finish his work"' (John 4:34). If we had an appetite for serving God we would find that we accomplished many more useful things.

> **A scoundrel plots evil,**
> **and his speech is like a scorching fire.**
> **A perverse man stirs up dissension,**
> **and a gossip separates close friends.**
> **A violent man entices his neighbour**
> **and leads him down a path that is not good.**
> **He who winks with his eye is plotting perversity;**
> **he who purses his lips is bent on evil**
>
> (16:27-30).

These four proverbs introduce us to an odd set of characters
— **'a scoundrel'**, **'a perverse man'**, **'a gossip'**, **'a violent
man'** and one who plots **'perversity'**. In each case they are
briefly sketched and we are left to take warning. You would
not want to run into these fellows. Despite initial appearances,
these are all sins committed chiefly with the tongue — plotting, which occurs at the beginning and end of the sequence;
stirring up trouble, or gossiping, and enticing to evil. We are
far away from pleasant words here.

> *Synthetic:* **'plots evil'** / **'his speech'**
> *Simile:* **'[scoundrel's] speech'** / **'scorching fire'**
> Scoundrels evil plot;
> Their speech is piping hot.

There are scoundrels who are always plotting some evil scheme.
Their very words are like **'scorching fire'**, bringing the pot to
the boil (16:27). They bring ill-will, discontent and anarchy.

> *Synthetic:*   **'perverse man'** / **'gossip'**
> A wanderer strife creates;
> A gossip splits up mates.

Other proverbs deal with gossip (see 18:8; 26:20-22). The
subject was first raised in 11:13. Here, in verse 28, what is
primarily in mind is the sort of person who stirs up trouble and
always manages to cause a disagreement. He has an aptitude
for causing discord and conflict wherever he goes. People who
have been friends for years are at each other's throats in sec-
onds when someone like this is around.

> *Synthetic:* **'entices'** / **'leads him down'**
> The violent beguile
> Into a path that's vile.

There is a certain gregarious quality about some violent people: 'Let's go out for a punch-up.' They want others to join in with them, and so they entice them into violent ways (16:29). We met some of these characters in Proverbs 1.

Synonymous: **'winks with his eye'** / **'purses his lips'**
Eyes wink and plot perversity, lips purse set on sin.

Finally we meet the plotter again (16:30). With a wink of the eye and a pursing of the lips he conceals his plots from others and lets you in on his secret. He is plotting some sort of perversity. He is bent on doing what is evil.

'Grey hair is a crown of splendour; it is attained by a righteous life' (16:31).
Synthetic: **'grey hair'** / **'righteous life'**

Living as we do in the days of *Grecian 2000* and other products designed specifically to hide grey hair, and in a time when the cult of youth is so strong that the only thing a woman in her sixties can do to be commended is to look half her age, when the elderly are conspicuous only by their absence from the corridors of power — this verse looks a little out of place. As in Proverbs 20:29, it actually speaks positively about grey hairs. Throughout the Bible there is great respect for age, a respect that accompanies the realization that, all other things being equal, wisdom comes with it. Here the point is made that the most likely way to attain a good age is by being righteous. As the fifth command reminds us, a rebellious life is likely to be a short life.

The world of popular music, notorious for its idolatry of youth, has seen many artists fail to reach any great age because of its devotion to various evil practices such as drug abuse, recklessness and immorality. Of course, one can list godly men who have reached no great age either, but the proverbial truth still stands. Throughout Proverbs a long life is seen as one of wisdom's rewards (see especially 3:2,16,18,22; 9:11; 12:28; 28:16; see also 16:22 and the other verses which speak of the 'fountain of life'). The next time you see grey hair, perhaps in the mirror, think of it as a splendid crown. The grey heads may be a little dull at times, but they have experience and they know what is right.

'Better a patient man than a warrior, a man who controls his temper than one who takes a city' (16:32).
  Contrast (better than): **'patient man'** / **'warrior'**
  Victory over temper beats victory in war.

Bridges quotes Tsar Peter the Great as saying, 'I can govern my people, but how can I govern myself?' Patience and self-control are again commended (see 14:29; 15:18). This proverb, of the type introduced by the formula 'Better a ...', uses by way of contrast the simile of **'a warrior'** or **'one who takes a city'**. Great strength is needed for such a victory, but even greater strength — strength to control oneself — is necessary if we are going to be patient people who know how to control our tempers. The thought is similar to that of Proverbs 25:28, which says, 'Like a city whose walls are broken down is a man who lacks self-control.' For some this is easier than it is for others, but we all need well-honed fighting skills at times when we feel like losing our temper. A stringent training in strategic warfare is vital if we are to go through life without succumbing to the temptation to let off steam from time to time. James reminds us that 'Man's anger does not bring about the righteous life that God desires' (James 1:20). On reaching the age of thirty, Matthew Henry's father Philip wrote in his diary: 'So old and no older Alexander was when he conquered the great world; but I have not yet subdued the little world — myself.'

The proverb takes us back in part to the points made previously about kings. In the *Second book* of *Paradise Regained* Milton wrote:

> For therein stands the office of a king,
> His honour, virtue, merit, and chief praise,
> That for the public all this weight he bears.
> Yet he who reigns within himself, and rules
> Passions, desires and fears is more a king —
> Which every wise and virtuous man attains;
> And who attains not, ill aspires to rule
> Cities of men, or headstrong multitudes,
> Subject himself to anarchy within,
> Or lawless passions in him, which he serves.

'The lot is cast into the lap, but its every decision is from the LORD' (16:33).

Contrast: **'lot is cast'** / **'decision'**
The lot's in the lap, but Divinity decides.

Casting lots, also referred to in Proverbs 18:18, is apparently a generic term that can refer to various methods of decision-making. Sometimes straws or sticks were drawn from a container or thrown on the ground. The length or colour of the straw was decisive. The flipping of a small, flat stone could provide an answer, just as we toss a coin today. By shaking differently coloured or shaped stones from a pouch, directions could be made, depending on which came out first.

Here we return to the subject of God's sovereignty and the matter of providence. There is no such thing as chance or luck. Even the casting of lots into a lap is determined by God. When

twice a week numbered balls are drawn from a machine spe-
cially constructed for the purpose in the UK's national lottery,
many watch on television with bated breath, ignorant of what
the outcome will be. However, every time it happens we ought
to remember that God not only knows exactly what will happen, but has decided which balls should be drawn out. Once
we accept that this is so we must see that every apparently
random event is in fact part of God's overall purpose — even
the falling of a sparrow from the sky and the number of hairs
on our heads.

In the book of Esther the lot is prominent as it is by lot that
the evil Haman chooses the day for the destruction of the Jews.
However, God is in control and things turn out in the very
opposite way to that which Haman intended. Even a king's
sleepless night turns out to be a factor in the whole. The lot
features also in Jonah as the means for discovering Jonah's
guilt (Jonah 1:7). The book is one full of remarkable
providences, not least the great fish. In the book of Ruth we
are told that 'as it turned out' Ruth chose to glean in Boaz's
field (2:3) — the fact on which the whole story turns. Perhaps
the account most marked by 'chances and little contingen-
cies', however, is that of Joseph in Genesis.

We shall take just two examples from outside the Bible.
What else but providence explains how a hapless maid could
fail to introduce the young C. H. Spurgeon to Dr Angus who
was waiting in the other room? This nipped in the bud plans
for a theological education that might well have delayed and
even destroyed the phenomenal home-grown talents that made
him the greatest preacher of the nineteenth century, and perhaps of any century. Spurgeon himself recalled the story of the
north-country Puritan Bernard Gilpin. In the reign of 'Bloody
Mary' he was arrested and summoned to appear in London,
but fell from his horse and broke his leg. This delayed his journey. By the time they reached the capital the news was just

being proclaimed that Mary was dead. If he had not had that apparent mishap he would probably have died in the flames. We must never think any matter too small, too insignificant. With Almighty God superintending every detail, there can be no 'minor details'.

What these eighteen proverbs teach us

Taking these eighteen proverbs together then, I shall endeavour, guided by what I trust by grace is 'a wise man's heart', to 'promote instruction' (16:23). It is my hope that you too will be 'wise in heart' and 'called discerning' and that you will find these 'pleasant words' that can 'promote' your 'instruction' (16:21). We know that such 'pleasant words are a honeycomb, sweet to the soul and healing to the bones' (16:24) and that 'More flies are caught with honey than with vinegar.'

Wisdom or understanding

How vital it is

It is vital that we gain wisdom or understanding. It is the most important thing we can possess (16:16). It is also the best thing we can have, as 'Understanding is a fountain of life to those who have it,' whereas its opposite, folly, 'brings punishment to fools' (16:22).

How to gain it

The way to get it is to 'heed … instruction'. It is for the one who 'trusts in the LORD'. With it come prosperity and blessing (16:20).

A warning

Verse 25 acts as a solemn warning in this respect: 'There is a way that seems right to a man, but in the end it leads to death.'

Some examples

Wisdom can display itself in very practical ways, as in verse 26 or as an overarching principle, as in verse 33.

Righteousness or uprightness

If we are truly wise it will show itself in our lives. Examples given in this section include humility, patience and the avoidance of evil.

Humility

> Pride goes before destruction,
>   a haughty spirit before a fall.
> Better to be lowly in spirit and among the oppressed
>   than to share plunder with the proud
>
> (16:18-19).

Patience

'Better a patient man than a warrior, a man who controls his temper than one who takes a city' (16:32).

Avoidance of evil

We must not be scoundrels who plot evil, and whose 'speech is like a scorching fire' (16:27). We must not be perverse or gossips, stirring up 'dissension', or separating 'close friends' (16:28). We must not be 'violent', enticing neighbours and leading them 'down a path that is not good' (16:29). Nor must we plot perversity, winking and grimacing and 'bent on evil' (16:30). By the grace of Christ we must be the very opposite.

We must be determined to take 'the highway of the upright', which 'avoids evil'. We must guard our way. If we guard our way we shall guard our life (16:17). It is those who live a righteous life who gain the splendid crown of grey hair that marks old age and points to eternal life (16:31).

34.
Flee superficiality and injustice and seek wisdom

Please read Proverbs 17:1-28

Peace, wisdom, testing, wicked influences, mocking, grandchildren, arrogant and deceitful speech, bribery, discretion, teachability, rebellion, dangerous fools, ungratefulness, quarrels, injustice, money, friendship, pledges, quarrels, perversity and deceit, foolish sons, feelings, bribery, practical wisdom, foolish sons, integrity, reserve, silence

Here we consider all twenty-eight proverbs of chapter 17.

'Better a dry crust with peace and quiet than a house full of feasting, with strife' (17:1).
   Contrast (better than): **'dry crust with peace and quiet'** / **'house full of feasting, with strife'**
   Better a crust with quiet than a feast with fighting.

This proverb repeats the thought of Proverbs 15:17 and anticipates 21:9,19 (see also 16:8,19). Commenting on 15:17, we quoted a song. Another song ('Living in the love of the common people') by Hurley and Wilkins expresses allied thoughts, describing how abject poverty ('Living on free food tickets, water in the milk from the hole in the roof where the rain came through') can be negated with faith as a foundation, by prayer and family love so that:

> The closer the knit,
> the tighter the fit
> and the chills stay away.
> You can take them in stride,
> for family pride.

It is to be feared, however, that while many willingly own such sentiments in theory, in practice they too often opt for **'a house full of feasting, with strife'**. The last phrase of the verse could be translated 'strife offering' — a parody of 'fellowship' or 'peace offering' (Lev. 3:1, etc). The situation of Elkanah and his wives comes to mind (see 1 Sam. 1). Some families sit down to a sumptuous Christmas dinner, only to be at one another's throats before teatime. Better to have bread and cheese and no arguments than that. 'Godliness with contentment is great gain' (1 Tim. 6:6). Some churches pay a great deal of attention to the details of how holy communion is conducted, when their real concern should be the lack of unity among those who sit down together.

'A wise servant will rule over a disgraceful son, and will share the inheritance as one of the brothers' (17:2).
    Contrast: **'wise servant'** / **'disgraceful** [*not* 'disgraced'] **son'**
    Synthetic: **'will rule over'** / **'will share the inheritance'**
    Sagacious servants rule over shameful sons.

This synonymous proverb begins with a contrast. The emphasis, however, is all on the servant, who not only rules over the **'disgraceful son'**, but even shares in his master's inheritance as a son. The rewards of wisdom are in mind here.

In Solomon's own case, after his death, his able servant Jeroboam came to great power, while his disgraceful son Rehoboam lost out on a great deal. There are plenty of examples of foolish sons who either were, or should have been, disinherited, and able people with unpromising backgrounds who came to power. P. G .Wodehouse has an amusing take on this in the well-loved books featuring Jeeves and Wooster. Bertie Wooster may be rich and Jeeves only his butler, but there is little question as to who is the cleverer of the two. What is comical in fiction is often not so funny in real life. It is in the light of the truth of this proverb that many societies have attempted some sort of meritocracy where hereditary privilege is minimized and wisdom is rewarded regardless of background.

When we think of our Saviour, we know that he was both the Son of God and the faithful Servant. Believers who are faithful servants will know the blessing of being true sons as they sit down with Abraham and Isaac in God's kingdom. On the other hand, 'The subjects of the kingdom will be thrown outside, into the darkness, where there will be weeping and gnashing of teeth' (Matt. 8:11,12).

'The crucible for silver and the furnace for gold, but the LORD tests the heart' (17:3).
> *Simile:* **'crucible … furnace'** / **'the LORD tests'**
> Blazing hearth, agonizing heart.

The simile is that of a crucible or furnace burning out the ore to purify silver or gold. It is a picture of the way **'the LORD tests the heart'**. He turns up the heat, as it were, to burn off the dross, so that only what is precious remains. We are thinking here chiefly of various afflictions and troubles that come in life, but see Proverbs 27:21 for another example of a testing experience — praise from men.

The picture is common enough in Scripture. Peter speaks of sufferings as coming 'so that your faith — of greater worth than gold, which perishes even though refined by fire — may be proved genuine and may result in praise, glory and honour when Jesus Christ is revealed' (1 Peter 1:7). If our faith is real, we shall suffer no more lasting harm in afflictions than Daniel's three friends did when Nebuchadnezzar condemned them to the fiery furnace in Babylon. It is when we are pure in heart that we see God (Matt. 5:8).

Many inferences can be made from this hint. For example, our hearts are precious; they are impure in their natural state; a refining process is necessary; this involves intensity; the work is gradual; the work has to be carried out by someone and it will not happen naturally.

In *Rippon's Selection* of 1787 this famous paraphrase of comforting words spoken by God appeared:

When through fiery trials thy pathway shall lie,
My grace all-sufficient shall be thy supply;
The flame shall not hurt thee; I only design
Thy dross to consume, and thy gold to refine.

'A wicked man listens to evil lips; a liar pays attention to a malicious tongue' (17:4).
  Synonymous: **'wicked man listens'** / **'liar pays attention'**
  Birds of a feather flock together.
  It takes one to know one.
  Like breeds like.

These English proverbs make a similar point to the one that appears here. Another says that 'Great minds think alike,' but has the corollary that 'Fools seldom differ.' A rather obscure one says, 'Scabby donkeys scent each other over nine hills.'

The focus is not simply on **'evil lips'** and **'a malicious tongue'**, but on the **'wicked man'** who **'listens'**, the **'liar'** who **'pays attention'**. As with many other sins, sins of speech usually involve two parties — in this case, one to speak and one to listen. That is true not only of gossip and slander, but also of the sort of evil speech that seeks an audience to impress. It is only those who are wicked who are likely to listen to those who speak evil; it is liars who are most likely to be prepared to hear malicious things spoken. 'Those who forsake the law praise the wicked, but those who keep the law resist them' (28:4) is in the same territory. It is good to ask ourselves not only what we say and do, but what we are prepared to listen to or look at. Too often, even though we may refrain from gossiping ourselves, for example, we greatly enjoy the juicy morsels of hearsay that come our way. There should not be such a discrepancy. Dr Martyn Lloyd-Jones used to warn against lingering over the page of the newspaper containing the often lurid reports of court proceedings.

'He who mocks the poor shows contempt for their Maker; whoever gloats over disaster will not go unpunished' (17:5).
   Synthetic: **'shows contempt'** / **'will not go unpunished'**
   Oppress the poor, oppose the Omnipotent;
   Gloat over disaster; you'll suffer too.

This is similar to Proverbs 14:31 but has a different conclusion, one that points forward to 24:17-18. Here the needy are before us again, those who are poor through no fault of their own. To mock them is to show **'contempt for their Maker'**. Matthew 25:45 comes to mind. Christ says to sinners on the last day that they must depart, for 'I tell you the truth, whatever you did not do for one of the least of these [believers], you did not do for me.'

It is interesting that in the story that Jesus tells of Lazarus and the rich man it is the poor man who goes to heaven, while his oppressor goes to hell. All men are made in God's image and merit kindness and compassion for his sake. Whenever there is a disaster we must resist the urge to gloat, even if the victims are our mortal enemies. A phrase we have tried to ban in our house is: 'It serves you right.' Children instinctively mock those who suffer a setback. I remember how in the hall where we had our school dinners we would all laugh loudly whenever someone dropped and smashed a plate. Such childishness has no place in the Christian life.

What are we doing to express kindness to the needy — particularly believers in need? Think of the apostle Paul and how eager he was to remember the needs of the poor (Gal. 2:10). He wrote, 'Let us not become weary in doing good ... as we have opportunity, let us do good to all people, especially to those who belong to the family of believers' (Gal. 6:9-10).

'Children's children are a crown to the aged, and parents are the pride of their children' (17:6).

Contrast: **'children's children' / 'parents'**

Grandchildren their grandparents' grandeur; parents their progeny's pride.

This is a description of the ideal and will not come about without great effort. We have already learned that long life comes to the righteous (16:31). In Psalm 128 living 'to see your children's children' is seen to be a blessing that is granted to those who fear the Lord. Of course, grandchildren can be a thorn in the side, but ideally we shall so conduct ourselves towards them and towards our children that this will not be the case. Ideally, parents ought to be a source of pride to their children too. It is a great joy to be able to think of one's parents, as I can, with a measure of pride. Again, if parents fail to be what they ought to be that will not happen. We have responsibilities in both directions — to those older and those younger than ourselves. With both we expect to give and to receive.

The so-called 'generation gap' is not a modern phenomenon. It can easily creep into any society if there is not a determination to bridge it. When all the traffic is one way it is bound to happen. As far as they can, grandparents must see their grandchildren as a crown and children must think of their parents with pride. Godly grandparents have many good things to impart to their children and grandchildren. These in turn, where parents are godly, have a great deal to be proud of, if only both are awake to the possibilities. What is true here on the physical level is especially true on the spiritual level.

'Arrogant lips are unsuited to a fool — how much worse lying lips to a ruler!' (17:7).

A fortiori

Contrast: **'fool' / 'ruler'**

Fine talk from fools is foolish, as are lying lips on a leader.

This is another proverb that argues from the lesser to the greater. **'Arrogant lips'** could be translated 'eloquent lips'. The point is that there is something incongruous about a fool speaking in an apparently noble way. On the other hand, if you think of a ruler, how much worse if he should speak like a fool and tell lies! The idea is unfashionable today, but there is an expectation that those who lead will have a respect for the truth that we do not expect from those who are moral fools. This takes us back to 16:10. As we saw there, if believers forget who they are they will fall into all sorts of incongruities.

'A bribe is a charm to the one who gives it; wherever he turns, he succeeds' (17:8).

Synonymous:'**is a charm**' / '**he succeeds**'
A bribe works like magic;
It transforms what's tragic.

Unlike verse 23, which also deals with bribery, this is an observational proverb without moral comment — descriptive not
prescriptive. The observation regards how powerful bribery
can be. It is '**a charm**' (literally, 'a stone of grace'), acting as
an open sesame wherever he turns. It works like magic. It
guarantees success. So when we see someone being very successful we recognize that it may be that he has been bribing
people in some shape or form. There are countries in the world
where very little gets done unless there is some form of bribery. It is not easy for Christians to stand against such corruption. The law is clear about this, however: 'Do not accept a
bribe, for a bribe blinds those who see and twists the words of
the righteous' (Exod. 23:8). 'Do not pervert justice or show
partiality. Do not accept a bribe, for a bribe blinds the eyes of
the wise and twists the words of the righteous' (Deut. 16:19).

This has already been made clear in Proverbs 15:27. On the
other hand, it is true that the word for '**bribe**' also means
'gift'. The greatest gift from God is his Son. The phrase 'stone
of grace' is also evocative of Christ, 'the stone the builders
rejected' who 'has become the capstone' (1 Peter 2:7). Faith
in him indeed works wonders and guarantees success.

**'He who covers over an offence promotes love, but who-
ever repeats the matter separates close friends'** (17:9).
Contrast: '**he who covers over an offence**' / '**whoever
repeats the matter**'

This is like Proverbs 10:12 and is once more against retaliation and gossip. The verse could be perverted to advocate
covering up wrongdoing unjustly, but it is clearly intended to

teach that the loving thing to do with dirty laundry is to keep it out of the public eye. Peter says, 'Above all, love each other deeply, because love covers over a multitude of sins' (1 Peter 4:8). Love, of course, 'keeps no record of wrongs ... always protects, always trusts, always hopes' (1 Cor. 13:5,7). We are talking about the attitude displayed by the Lord Jesus towards the woman taken in adultery. **'Repeating a matter'** includes continually harping on it as well as gossiping (see 19:11).

'A rebuke impresses a man of discernment more than a hundred lashes a fool' (17:10).
> *A fortiori*
> *Contrast:* **'man of discernment'** / **'fool'**
> Wise? Rebuke's enough. Foolish? Rods are not.

Once again **'a fool'** is contrasted unflatteringly with a wise man, **'a man of discernment'**. Yet again the subject is teachability (cf. 13:1,10; 15:5). For a man of discernment a word of rebuke is enough. Just say the word and he will change. The fool, on the other hand, will not respond even if given a proverbial **'hundred lashes'**. Visible marks of the whip are contrasted with the invisible marks of a rebuke.

We see this every day. There are people who have seen the foolishness of drug abuse, or of immorality, or of neglecting the Bible or the Lord's Day. A rebuke or two has been enough to get them to see the error of their ways. There are others who, despite many setbacks and much suffering, persist in their foolish ways. A word is enough for a David or a Peter, while a Pharaoh or a Jeroboam disregards every rebuke. Bridges observes that 'A needle pierces deeper into flesh than a sword into stone.' He and others also see here a lesson for parents in how they deal with their children. They are not all the same. Pastors also need to take note.

'An evil man is bent only on rebellion; a merciless official will be sent against him' (17:11).

Synthetic: **'bent only on rebellion'** / **'merciless official … sent against him'**

This follows on from verse 10. It is perhaps better to read the first phrase in this proverb the other way round: 'A rebel is bent only on evil.' It is because of the nature of rebellion that the extreme measure spoken of in the second half is necessary. When rebels are active it is not time for mercy or for half measures. Ideally, **'a merciless official will be sent against'** such people. Similarly, in church life, rebels cannot be handled with kid gloves. They must be expelled from the congregation. Even in the family we sometimes have to think in these stern terms.

The principle underlying this, of course, is that a man reaps what he sows. Those who are bent on sowing evil will reap destruction. By nature, we are rebels against God and we deserve no mercy. However, verses like the following passage from the Psalms give us hope:

Some sat in darkness and the deepest gloom,
    prisoners suffering in iron chains,
for they had rebelled against the words of God
    and despised the counsel of the Most High.
So he subjected them to bitter labour;
    they stumbled, and there was no one to help.
Then they cried to the LORD in their trouble,
    and he saved them from their distress.
He brought them out of darkness and the deepest gloom
    and broke away their chains.
Let them give thanks to the LORD for his unfailing love
    and his wonderful deeds for men,

for he breaks down gates of bronze
    and cuts through bars of iron

(Ps. 107:10-16).

The nineteenth-century American preacher A. T. Pierson wrote these oft-sung words:

He maketh the rebel a priest and a king,
He hath bought us and taught us this new song to sing:
Unto him who hath loved us and washed us from sin,
Unto him be the glory for ever. Amen.

'Better to meet a bear robbed of her cubs than a fool in his folly' (17:12).
Simile (better than): **'bear robbed of her cubs'** / **'fool in his folly'**

Here is a proverb in simile form which employs the formula 'better than'. The picture is that of **'a bear robbed of her cubs'**. Bears are dangerous enough, but a mother bear robbed of her cubs is very dangerous indeed.

I read a report on some hikers in Lake Clark National Park and Preserve in Alaska, one of whom had to be flown to Anchorage for hospital treatment following an encounter with a bear. Gary Titus and Ellen Snoeyenbos, both aged forty-seven, were hiking in dense brush in the Twin Lakes area when a brown bear suddenly appeared. It apparently grabbed Titus' left leg, dragging him to the ground, and then lunged towards Ellen and grabbed her left boot. As she was dragged off, Titus hit the bear on the nose. It released the woman but bit the man's right hand, then ran off. Significantly it was then that Titus noticed the bear was with a cub. Park service spokeswoman Jane Tranel said that the bear was obviously just protecting her cub.

Such a scenario is compared here with that of meeting **'a fool in his folly'** — that is, a fool in action. Simply meeting a fool can be harmless enough, but if he has you in his sights, or if you get caught up in one of his schemes, then you need to realize just how dangerous that can be. Proverbially, you would be safer meeting a mother bear raging for her stolen cubs.

Fools ruin marriages. They corrupt young people. They can lose you untold millions. They split churches, denominations and Christian organizations. They can ruin whole countries. Think what a fool can do with a weapon or with a car. Bridges instances Jacob's sons reacting to the rape of their sister; Nebuchadnezzar heating up the furnace sevenfold; Herod in his fury over Bethlehem; Saul of Tarsus 'breathing out murderous threats against the Lord's disciples'. Be warned!

'If a man pays back evil for good, evil will never leave his house' (17:13).

Synthetic: **'man pays back evil for good'** / **'evil will never leave'**

Trapp says:

> To render good for evil is divine,
> good for good is human,
> evil for evil is brutish and
> evil for good is devilish.

To pay back evil for evil is certainly sinful, but to pay back evil for good is the strongest form of ingratitude. Even the world recognizes the wickedness of such an attitude. A person like that is courting evil and is inevitably heading for disaster. How can any good come to him or to his household? Any good he receives will only be returned as evil. Perhaps this is part of the solution to the problem of hell. The truly evil person will do no good, even though he is shown goodness. Evil will never leave such a person's house.

Of course, there is a sense in which we who are of the house of Adam are all under the guilt of having paid back evil for good. God has shown us nothing but goodness, yet we have returned evil for that good. Unless something radical happens our house of cards will fall. The answer lies in a new house, God's house, one over which 'Christ is faithful as a son', a house that we can be part of if we trust in Christ and 'if we hold on to our courage and the hope of which we boast' (Heb. 3:6).

'Starting a quarrel is like breaching a dam; so drop the matter before a dispute breaks out' (17:14).

    Synthetic: **'starting a quarrel'** / **'drop the matter'**
    Simile: **'starting a quarrel'** / **'breaching a dam'**
    Starting a quarrel is like breaching a dam;
    This is the moral — give up on your plan.

There are a few proverbs on quarrelling. This is the first. How easy it is to get into a quarrel! All right, then, it can be easy. It is like a little hole in a dam. It can be stopped with one finger at first, but if action is not taken quickly, or the quarrel is not dropped, things can escalate and a whole torrent can break through. We ought to have that thought in mind whenever we are tempted to become involved in an argument. Where will it end?

To use a different metaphor, we must nip it in the bud early on. Seneca observed that it is easier to abstain from a contest than to withdraw from one.

The instructive Dutch legend (actually a story spun by American writer Mary M. Dodge in 1865 in *Hans Brinker or The silver skates*) of the boy who put his finger in the hole in the dyke until it could be repaired is perhaps worth mentioning too. A little act of self-sacrifice early on in this area can save a great deal of trouble later on.

The context reminds us of Jesus' words when he said, 'Settle matters quickly with your adversary who is taking you to court. Do it while you are still with him on the way, or he may hand you over to the judge, and the judge may hand you over to the officer, and you may be thrown into prison. I tell you the truth, you will not get out until you have paid the last penny' (Matt. 5:25-26). Commentators are divided on whether to take these latter verses literally or metaphorically, but undoubtedly we are not wise to let our argument with God go on at any length at all.

**'Acquitting the guilty and condemning the innocent —
the LORD detests them both'** (17:15).
Synthetic / synonymous: **'acquitting the guilty'** / **'condemning the innocent'**
Lord detests
Incriminating the just, justifying criminals — God hates both.

Robert Alden's translation, 'incriminating the just and justifying the criminal' brings out the style of the Hebrew. Here we are in the law courts, and once again we learn about what the Lord detests. As ever, it is dishonesty and injustice. God is just and he loathes both **'acquitting the guilty and condemning the innocent'** in equal measure. Both liberal leniency and cruel conservatism are damned. He hates it both when a Barabbas goes free and when a Naboth is condemned. Such things have been rife at times and are condemned by Ezekiel (Ezek. 22:27-29) and by Amos, who condemns those who 'turn justice into bitterness and cast righteousness to the ground' (Amos 5:7). He says, 'You oppress the righteous and take bribes and you deprive the poor of justice in the courts'

(Amos 5:12). 'You have turned justice into poison and the fruit of righteousness into bitterness' (Amos 6:12).

We must be faithful and not be influenced by bribery of any sort. Being realistic, however, we must recognize that even the best judicial systems sometimes convict innocent men. In America the advent of DNA testing has seen the release of a large number of convicted criminals now deemed to have been innocent. One man had served eighteen years in a Louisiana prison for rape.

The proverb makes a New Testament phrase such as 'God who justifies the wicked' (Rom. 4:5) all the more startling. God never condemns the innocent (there are none) but, by his grace, he is able to justify the wicked if they put their faith in Christ.

'Of what use is money in the hand of a fool, since he has no desire to get wisdom?' (17:16). The NIV paraphrases here. More literally, it is: 'Why is there money in a fool's hand to get wisdom, seeing he has no heart for it?' Moffatt neatly translates the last phrase as 'when he has no mind to learn'. The picture may well be that of a fool who has the money to pay for an education but no desire to work. It is both a warning against investing in what are today known as underachievers and an uncovering of their real problem — a lack of wisdom, not of wealth. Throwing money at problems is a common enough reaction in times of affluence, but the real need is always for wisdom.

Examples of fools wasting money abound. Take these two stories of national lottery winners. Both went to prison. Reginald Tomlinson, aged forty-four, won £100,000 in 1997. A court heard how he had frittered away every penny. He had his cheque paid into his father's account, not wanting his ex-wife to know about it. He then splashed out on three expensive cars and a new house. His last £20,000 went on specialist equipment and the conversion of part of his home into a 'cannabis factory'. A policeman commented, 'It may sound a bizarre way to spend National Lottery winnings, but nothing surprises us.' Former RAF engineer Nigel Gardner-Hale won £3.4 million in January 2000. He gave up his job, bought a house back home in South Wales and threw a wild party where police found drugs were freely available. His defence counsel stated that 'Until his lottery win he had a remarkable career in the RAF… He was glad he was arrested as he knew he could have ended up becoming a problem drug user.' A friend commented, 'Nigel was never in any trouble until his lottery win.' These obvious examples underline the fact that the need of wisdom is always greater than the need for money. Churches and organizations need to learn this as well as individuals.

'A friend loves at all times, and a brother is born for adversity' (17:17).

Synonymous: **'friend' / 'brother'**

In 1942, King George VI's Christmas radio broadcast referred to a former US president who used to tell of a small boy who was carrying an even smaller child up a hill. Asked whether the burden was not too much, the boy answered, 'It's not a burden; it's my brother!'

The popular song from 1969, 'He ain't heavy — he's my brother', was apparently based on this story:

> So on we go, his welfare is my concern.
> No burden is he to bear; we'll get there,
> But I know he would not encumber me.
> He ain't heavy — he's my brother.
> If I'm laden at all, I'm laden with sadness
> That everyone's heart isn't filled with the gladness
> Of love for one another.

Verse 17 is one of several proverbs on friendship (see 12:26; 14:20; 16:28; 17:9, which we have already considered and, especially, 18:24; 27:6,9,10). True friends are there not only when times are good, but also when times are bad. Brothers are especially good to have when facing adversity.

The great biblical examples of friendship have adversity as their background. Think of Ruth and Naomi and David and Jonathan. In the case of Joseph we have one whose love for his brothers would not die despite their indifference, hostility, malice and fear.

One writer says that when a man born blind was asked what he thought the sun was like he said, 'Like friendship.'

Jesus himself, of course, is presented to us in Scripture as a friend and brother to believers. He is 'a friend of tax collectors and sinners' (Matt. 11:19), and calls us 'friends', not 'servants' (John 15:13-15). He goes further than that and is 'not ashamed to call [believers] brothers' (Heb. 2:11-13; cf. Matt. 28:10; Rom. 8:29). He says, 'Whoever does the will of my Father in heaven is my brother and sister and mother' (Matt. 12:50).

The commentator John Gill notes that 'The ancient Jews had a notion that this Scripture has some respect to the Messiah; for, to show that the Messiah, being God, would by his incarnation become a brother to men, they cite this passage of Scripture as a testimony of it.'

The theme of Christ's friendship has been a favourite with evangelical hymn-writers. Albert Midlane's hymn for children begins:

There's a Friend for little children
Above the bright blue sky,
A Friend who never changes,
Whose love will never die;
Our earthly friends may fail us,
And change with changing years,

This Friend is always worthy
Of that dear name he bears.

Think too of Peter Bilhorn's 'Oh, the best friend to have is
Jesus', C. Newman Hall's 'Friend of sinners, Lord of glory',
J. C. Ludgate's 'Friendship with Jesus' and Joseph Scriven's
'What a Friend we have in Jesus'. In 'I've found a Friend, O
such a friend!', James G Small speaks of him as:

So kind and true and tender,
So wise a Counsellor and Guide,
So mighty a Defender!

In the *Olney Hymns* John Newton wrote:

Poor, weak and worthless though I am,
I have a rich almighty Friend;
Jesus, the Saviour, is his name;
He freely loves, and without end.

**'A man lacking in judgement and puts up security for his
neighbour'** (17:18).
Synthetic: **'strikes hands in pledge' / 'puts up security'**

We have come across this subject before (6:1-5; 11:15). It is
not a contradiction of the friendship extolled in the previous
verse, but a warning that we cannot make blind guarantees or
hand out blank cheques. The words for 'friend' and 'neighbour' are the same in Hebrew but not all our acquaintances
can be put in the same category. (Interestingly, the Hebrew
idiom literally says that the man who strikes hands is 'heartless' — not the way we would put it.) Again we are confronted by the amazing fact that the Lord Jesus Christ stood
surety for us who believe. 'Jesus has become the guarantee

[surety] of a better covenant' (Heb. 7:22). It is 'the foolishness of God' and seems, in one sense, a very unwise thing to have done, but we know that, unlike us, he has the infinite resources to bring about his will.

'He who loves a quarrel loves sin; he who builds a high gate invites destruction' (17:19).
Synonymous: **'loves a quarrel'** / **'builds a high gate'**

Here we are back to quarrelling. Two sins seem to be in mind — contentiousness and pride. Some are argumentative by nature; they love controversy. They are deliberately cantankerous or belligerent. Such people need to realize that what they love is sin. Elders are specifically disqualified from holding office if they are given to this sin. Paul says, 'And the Lord's servant must not quarrel; instead, he must be kind to everyone, able to teach, not resentful' (2 Tim. 2:24).

Pride is often at the root of arguments at home, in church and in politics. The **'high gate'** here could be literal (burglars certainly take note of strong security), but is best taken as a figure for the superciliousness and arrogance that often foment quarrelling. A little more humility would go a long way towards preventing much of the division that is found in society. Without humility and an end to resistance to the gospel, we shall be destroyed.

'A man of perverse heart does not prosper; he whose tongue is deceitful falls into trouble' (17:20).
Synonymous: **'man of perverse heart'** / **'he whose tongue is deceitful'**

Here is a warning against those marked by perversity of heart and deceitfulness of tongue. Closely connected, hearts and tongues are often mentioned in the proverbs (see 16:23 for the last reference). The backfiring gun, or the message that you reap what you sow, is also constantly underlined. Not only do such people do harm, but there is trouble ahead for them.

'To have a fool for a son brings grief; there is no joy for the father of a fool' (17:21)
   Synonymous: **'fool for a son'** / **'father of a fool'**
   Foolish sons guarantee grief;
   A fool's father won't receive relief.

This is similar to 10:1; 15:20 and 17:25. Those verses refer to both parents; here only the father is mentioned. Perhaps this one should be read in terms of a warning to fathers. Even when you have done everything, your son may turn out to be a fool. If he is not a fool, there is still no place for bragging.

'A cheerful heart is good medicine, but a crushed spirit dries up the bones' (17: 22).
   Contrast: **'cheerful heart'** / **'crushed spirit'**

As we have noted previously, this proverb is of a piece with 12:25 and, especially, 15:13 (see also 18:14). When we looked at 15:30 we mentioned the physical benefits claimed for 'a cheerful heart'. Similarly, **'a crushed spirit'** can be detrimental to physical health and harmful in other ways too. The medical profession accepts that introspective, tense and depressed people are more likely to develop cancer than relaxed extroverts. There are few benefits in gloominess. Think often of heaven, believer, and you will be the better for it.

'A wicked man accepts a bribe in secret to pervert the course of justice' (17:23).
   Synthetic: **'accepts a bribe'** / **'to pervert ... justice'**

Bribery is mentioned in verse 8 and perverting the course of justice in verse 15. Here the proverb is unequivocal. It is **'a wicked man'** that **'accepts a bribe'**. Like many evil deeds, bribery is carried out in secret. The most common reason for it is to **'pervert the course of justice'**. It is never for any good end. Today it abounds. I keyed in the phrase 'Bribery scandal' to a computer search engine. It offered me 30,000 pages of text. Apart from Neil Hamilton and his plain brown envelopes in Britain, the highest-profile cases in recent years have concerned the Japanese government, the Olympic International Committee and the South African cricketer, Hansie Cronje. However, there have been many, many other cases in many different countries.

'A discerning man keeps wisdom in view, but a fool's eyes wander to the ends of the earth' (17:24).
Contrast: **'discerning man'** / **'fool'**
The discerning with wisdom feel at home,
But a dunce's eyes to earth's ends roam.

The first half of this proverb is like the first line of 15:14. Elsewhere chasing fantasies is contrasted with diligence (12:11; 28:19); here it is contrasted with keeping wisdom in view. The 'keeping in view' is twofold. Wisdom is both something to aim at and something that we shall gain if we do this. The temptation to daydream, to go wandering far and wide in the mind's eye, is a foolish temptation to some, especially the young. It is a temptation to be resisted.

Some years ago we had a man in the church here who lived on the opposite side of London and was consequently infrequent in attendance. He spent most of his money and spare time learning to fly aeroplanes. His reasoning was that he felt that God wanted him to be in our church and to one day spend two or three years working for Mission Aviation Fellowship.

Perhaps you have had, or still have, similar fantasies. The grass is always greener on the other side. Avoid having eyes that are bigger than your stomach, or biting off more than you can chew. There is something hard-headed and realistic about true wisdom.

'A foolish son brings grief to his father and bitterness to the one who bore him' (17:25).
 Synonymous: **'grief to his father'** / **'bitterness to the one who bore him'**
 Foolish sons make fathers forlorn; they make those who bore them bitter.

This proverb is similar to verse 21, but brings the mother back into the picture and also uses two words that are a little more intense in meaning than the grief mentioned there. It is a warning both to parents and their offspring, to believers and their spiritual counsellors.

'It is not good to punish an innocent man, or to flog officials for their integrity' (17:26).
 Synonymous (possibly *a fortiori*): **'punish an innocent man'** / **'flog ... for ... integrity'**

This may be a very terse example of a proverb which argues from the lesser to the greater. It begins with an 'also' or 'even'. Certainly punishing an innocent man is wrong and the warning has gone out in verse 15. When nobles, or anyone else in authority, stick their necks out and in their integrity either refuse to do something, or in some way take a strong stand for the right, it ill becomes those over them to have them punished. Yet it does happen that when a senior civil servant or a government minister attempts to make a stand for justice he can find himself the target of attack.

Think of how they reacted to Nicodemus in the Sanhedrin when he had the temerity to say, 'Does our law condemn a man without first hearing him to find out what he is doing?' They sneered at him: 'Are you from Galilee, too? Look into it, and you will find that a prophet does not come out of Galilee' (John 7:51,52). Such a reaction was unacceptable from any point of view. Christians should pray for leaders with integrity, and for those above them to respect that integrity.

> **A man of knowledge uses words with restraint,**
> **and a man of understanding is even-tempered.**
> **Even a fool is thought wise if he keeps silent,**
> **and discerning if he holds his tongue**
>
> (17:27-28).

Synonymous: **'man of knowledge'** / **'man of understanding'**
Synonymous: **'wise'** / **'discerning'**;
If you know and understand, you'll say little, you'll stay cool;
And if not, by staying silent, you'll at least not look a fool.

These two proverbs can be taken together. Both commend silence, or at least being slow to speak. We have already mentioned James 1:19 in connection with 10:19, which begins with a similar thought to that expressed in verse 27. Slowness to speak is a mark of the wise. This is because if we do not speak, then at least we cannot say anything foolish.

'A man of knowledge' is one who 'knows knowledge'. We are never very far from proverbs that remind us to be self-controlled. We must control our tongues, difficult though that is, or they will lead us into sin. A most obvious example here is what happens when a man loses his temper. The wise have learned to control their tempers. The phrase **'even-tempered'** is, literally, 'rare of spirit'. Sadly, it is a rare spirit that can keep his temper.

Alden says, 'It's one thing to be a fool, another to broadcast that fact to the world.' Although the advice in verse 28 is tongue in cheek, any fool who listens to the advice given will find himself growing wise simply by this expedient. He will have opportunity to employ the wisdom of a verse such as 18:17, for example.

What these twenty-eight proverbs teach us

We can look at these twenty-eight proverbs under three headings.

Desirables

We begin by asking what is desirable in life? What is really worth having?

Peace and quiet (17:1)

This is worth striving for at every level. A feast is desirable, of course, but cannot guarantee contentment.

Family (17:6)

This proverb presents an attractive picture of family life. Of course, some children and grandchildren never visit their grandparents, and children are abused. However, if you have a loving family, whether or not they are blood relations, what a blessing!

Friends (17:17)

A brother (or sister) is a great blessing, especially in adversity. If you have no siblings a friend can be as good or even better.

Again, friends can let us down, of course, but if you have a good friend or two, be thankful to God. Do not take them for granted.

A cheerful heart (17:22)

Even with no family or friends you can be cheerful. However, it is said that one in ten suffer depression at some point and there are many things to crush the spirit. If you have a cheerful heart it is from God. Do as James says: 'Is anyone happy? Let him sing songs of praise' (James 5:13).

Although these things are all desirable they are not the most important things in life. Verse 3 makes that clear: 'The crucible for silver and the furnace for gold, but the LORD tests the heart.' Here is another warning against superficiality.

There is a peace and quiet that is the quiet of spiritual death. What is the basis of your peace? There is a harmony of sorts in the world. What is the underlying basis of your fellowship with others? Many things can make one cheerful. Do you know the joy beyond understanding that is found only in Christ? We need to know the peace found only in friendship with Christ and the joy of being united to him.

Injustices

One way that God tests the heart is by allowing injustice. There are seven references to such things here.

Neglect of the disadvantaged (17:5)

God made the poor. We must champion their cause despite all temptations not to do so.

Dishonesty (17:7)

It is especially reprehensible when those in power deceitfully use that power for their own ends.

Bribery (17:8,23)

Many countries are crippled by this all too prevalent disease.

Rebellion (17:11)

Rebellion is not the answer to bribery and corruption. Where it occurs it will be stamped out.

Ungratefulness (17:13)

The ungrateful and the traitorous abound. There is no hope for them.

Favouritism (17:15)

Again this is common in many parts of the world.

High-handedness (17:26)

In many cases the just work of some is being hindered by the pettifogging and meddling of others, who try to tie the hands of those in power and hinder their efforts to do good.

Wisdom

Its importance

Wisdom is superior. It is more useful than money (17:16) We see the fool in action in verse 18. 'Yes,' he says without a moment's thought. 'I'll pay if you can't'; 'I bet you any money'; '£10 says it does'. These are his catchphrases. Wisdom is more important than privileges (17:2).

There is nothing desirable about being a fool. Fools are dangerous (17:12) and a source of shame and grief (17:21,25)

Its characteristics

It responds to rebuke (17:10).
It eschews daydreams (17:24).
It ignores lies and gossip (17:4).
Its speech is also distinctive, being modest, protective, agreeable, honest, restrained and temperate (17:7,9,14,19,20,27,28).

35.
Sin, misery, hell and mercy — an argument

Please read Proverbs 18:1-24

Unfriendliness, opinionated fools, wickedness, speech, prejudice, foolish speech (two proverbs), gossip, laziness, the Lord's name, wealth, pride, presumption, resilience, knowledge, bribery, cross-examination, decision-making, disputes, satisfying speech, the tongue, wives, poverty, friendship

We shall look at all twenty-four proverbs of the chapter together. Most of them refer to sin.

'An unfriendly man pursues selfish ends; he defies all sound judgement' (18:1).
   Synthetic: **'pursues selfish ends'** / **'defies all sound judgement'**
   A man who wants no friends is seeking selfish ends;
   From all sound judgement he descends.

There is some difficulty in translating the first part of this proverb, but the NIV is probably right. Here is a character we have not met in these pages before, although we may well have come across him in life. He 'separates himself' or is

'unfriendly'. He 'seeks according to his desire', or **'pursues selfish ends'**. When he states an opinion it is as likely that he does it to create attention as it is that he says it because he believes it. Selfishness drives him. Such a man 'meddles' (a rare word) 'with all wisdom' — **'he defies all sound judgement'**. We want to avoid such a person. He is the very opposite of the friend who sticks closer than a brother (18:24).

We must ask ourselves, however, whether we too are unfriendly in some of our attitudes. How much of what we say and do is a matter merely of selfishness? I can remember childhood acts of unfriendliness that shame me now — telling a nosy little boy to go away (I still remember his sad face), or acting unpleasantly towards Peter, a classmate who was rather better-spoken than the rest of us. Unfriendliness is a sin to repent of.

'A fool finds no pleasure in understanding but delights in airing his own opinions' (18:2).
    Contrast: **'understanding'** / **'airing his own opinions'**
    Understanding's no treasure;
    Showing off is his pleasure.

Fools are opinionated to such a degree that the very opportunity to air their opinions is stimulating and invigorating to them, regardless of how ill-founded those opinions may be. They have no interest in checking their facts, trying to understand, or comparing notes; they simply want to sound off, spouting their own ideas. Extraneous concepts and irrelevant arguments are given, oblivious to anyone else. The aim is to boost self, not to learn something new. Such an attitude is most dangerous and unhelpful. What a curse such people are! This is one reason why debating the gospel is seldom satisfactory. Far better to preach the Word.

'When wickedness comes, so does contempt, and with shame comes disgrace' (18:3).
   Synonymous: **'when wickedness comes'** / **'with shame'**
   With sin comes derision; with shame disgrace.

Here are the things that accompany sin — contempt, shame and disgrace. One follows the other. Sometimes we see it in this life, as when the evil deeds of someone in the public eye are exposed. One thinks of the media's utter contempt for disgraced pop-idol perverts Gary Glitter and Jonathan King. Even if a wicked man escapes such disgrace in this life, he will not in the next. There are many reasons to avoid sin, but at the very least we should recognize how it leads to scorn, derision, opprobrium, reproach and censure. It is because of sin that Christ suffered the ignominy he did. It is an unspeakably amazing fact that in him God has found a way to deliver sinners from contempt and disgrace.

'The words of a man's mouth are deep waters, but the fountain of wisdom is a bubbling brook' (18:4).
   Double simile: **'the words of a man's mouth'** / **'deep waters'**; **'wisdom'** / **'a babbling brook'**
   Words are buried water; wisdom a bubbling wadi.

This similitude is of deep waters and a bubbling brook. Man's speech is often like deep waters. This may refer to profundity or to obscurity (as Suzanne Vega put it, 'My words don't mean what I say'). A man who relies on his own resources is like one drinking stagnant water. In the case of the wise, their words are a fountain, or a brook of bubbling water — fresh and full of life. Their conversation sparkles with honesty and integrity. They are refreshing because they constantly draw on wisdom rather than their own limited resources. The latter phrase is similar to the first part of 10:11. Beyond the bubbling brook is the fear of the Lord (14:27) and the Lord himself. James says, 'Out of the same mouth come praise and cursing. My brothers, this should not be. Can both fresh water and salt water flow from the same spring? My brothers, can a fig tree bear olives, or a grapevine bear figs? Neither can a salt spring produce fresh water' (James 3:10-12).

'It is not good to be partial to the wicked or to deprive the innocent of justice' (18:5).

Synthetic: **'partial to the wicked'** / **'deprive the innocent of justice'**

Bias to the base and blaming the blameless — both are bad.

Here is another warning against favouritism (see 17:15). Either showing partiality to the wicked, for whatever reason, or depriving the innocent of justice is wrong. Such activity undermines the rule of law and creates great problems. Sometimes mistakes are made, but to deliberately be partial to the wicked or to deprive an innocent man of justice is unacceptable. Those in power must condemn the wicked and stand up for the innocent.

In January 2001, in California, a convicted murderer, Dwayne McKinney, was released after twenty years in prison. In a review of the evidence four witnesses confessed that they were mistaken about the identity of the person who fired the shot and now believe it was another man of similar appearance. A public defender commented, 'People make mistakes, and I know the witnesses acted in good faith originally. Every so often you have someone who is innocent and shouldn't be in prison. This was one of those cases.' McKinney, a former gang member, has a violent past but, interestingly, believed his release was an answer to prayer. Such injustices can occur in many spheres and we must all do what we can to root them out.

A fool's lips bring him strife,
   and his mouth invites a beating.
A fool's mouth is his undoing,
   and his lips are a snare to his soul

(18:6-7).

Synonymous: **'fool's lips'** / **'his mouth'**
Synonymous: **'a fool's mouth'** / **'his lips'**
Foolish talk brings strife and a beating, a snare and undoing.

And so we come back to the tongue yet again with two similar proverbs. These observations and warnings point out the connection between crime and punishment. If the fool would just be quiet he would avoid **'strife'** or **'a beating'**. His very words are so often what incriminate him. They are **'his undoing'** and a **'snare to his soul'**. The way the fool speaks is an invitation to be punished.

Sometimes if I have to discipline my sons, instead of being quiet, one of them will try to defend himself, or accuse another of wrongdoing. Often what he says does him no good and only incurs a more severe punishment. Silence is golden. Verse 7 may hint at a deeper level. The fool's whole way of speaking leads to death.

'The words of a gossip are like choice morsels; they go down to a man's inmost parts' (18:8).
   Synthetic: **'words of a gossip'** / **'go down to a man's inmost parts'**
   Simile: **'words of a gossip'** / **'choice morsels'**

Still on the topic of speech, here the subject of gossip is again in the frame (this proverb is repeated in 26:22). It is the sin of listening to gossip that is to the fore. Joseph Hall once commented that there would not be so many open mouths if there were not so many open ears. Just as some people enjoy a tasty meal, so others like nothing better than a juicy bit of gossip. What an appetite for chewing the fat or dishing the dirt we can have! Both giving out and listening to gossip are condemned in Scripture. It is one of the marks of depravity mentioned in Romans 1:29. Paul warns against the sins of 'younger widows' who 'get into the habit of being idle and going about from house to house. And not only do they become idlers, but also gossips and busybodies, saying things they ought not to' (1 Tim. 5:11-13).

'One who is slack in his work is brother to one who destroys' (18:9).

Synthetic: **'one who is slack' / 'one who destroys'**

Slackers and wreckers are brothers.

Couch potatoes are like lethal killers.

Here is another popular theme, that of laziness (see 10:4-5). In the starkest terms, the evil of laziness is here underlined. In the New Testament we read, 'Never be lacking in zeal, but keep your spiritual fervour, serving the Lord' (Rom. 12:11). 'We do not want you to become lazy, but to imitate those who through faith and patience inherit what has been promised' (Heb. 6:12).

Making the most of every opportunity, or redeeming the time, is emphasized in Ephesians 5:16 and Colossians 4:5. Writing to the Galatians, Paul makes the point with regard to doing good: 'Let us not become weary in doing good, for at the proper time we will reap a harvest if we do not give up. Therefore, as we have opportunity, let us do good to all people, especially to those who belong to the family of believers' (Gal. 6:9-10).

The name of the LORD **is a strong tower;**
   the righteous run to it and are safe.
The wealth of the rich is their fortified city;
   they imagine it an unscalable wall

(18:10-11).

Synthetic: **'name of the L**ORD**' / 'righteous run to it'**
Simile: **'name of the L**ORD**' / 'strong tower'**
Synonymous: **'wealth of the rich' / 'it'**
Simile: **'wealth' / 'fortified city … unscalable wall'**
The Lord's name's a strong tower;
There the good hide from sin's power.
The rich think they can't fall,
Wealth's an unscalable wall.

These two proverbs are best taken together as they use similar similes. The first speaks of the reality of the security found in the unseen God. The second (which is like 10:15) speaks of the imagined security that the wealthy have. The Lord's name can be thought of as a strong tower to which **'the righteous run'**. They put their faith in the Lord and seek his protection. They are safe. The temptation for the rich is to trust in their **'wealth'**. It becomes **'their fortified city; they imagine it an unscalable wall'**. Such trust is misplaced. A fortune can be lost in a moment and certainly will be of no use at death. How many build towers of Babel thinking they can get to heaven, when what they really need is to run to the covenant God! The image of running to the strong tower is powerful. It suggests danger and urgency. Run there now, before it is too late.

'Before his downfall a man's heart is proud, but humility comes before honour' (18:12).
   Contrast: **'proud' / 'humility'**

Man's heart's proud before he falls.
Humbled first, then honour calls.

Pride is a perennial theme in Proverbs (e.g., 11:2; 15:25; 16:5,18-19). The context points to the downfall coming to those whose pride means they refuse to work (like the nobles of Tekoa in Nehemiah 3:5), or to run to Christ, or who think that their riches will save them.

'He who answers before listening — that is his folly and his shame' (18:13).
Synthetic: **'answers before listening'** / **'folly and ... shame'**

Here is another way in which pride manifests itself, along with impatience, bias and sheer laziness (the proverb ties in with verse 17). To answer before hearing what the other person has to say is folly and shame. Good manners and common sense dictate the need to listen before answering. It is both unwise and unfair to do otherwise. There is nothing more frustrating than having people raise objections before you have had the chance to explain yourself. Too often so-called debate is a dialogue of the deaf where neither side stops to listen to what the other is saying. G. K. Chesterton famously spoke of Christianity as being not 'tried and found wanting', but 'not tried and not wanted'. People are so busy listening to the lies of false prophets that they have no time for the answers that believers are ready to give.

'A man's spirit sustains him in sickness, but a crushed spirit who can bear?' (18:14).
Contrast: **'man's spirit sustains'** / **'crushed spirit'**
Steady spirits sustain; shattered spirits strain.

Attitude is a very important factor in life. The medical world is increasingly aware of the power of mind over matter. Years ago Dr Martyn Lloyd-Jones told the story of an elderly woman who got him to promise that he would preach at her chapel annually for the rest of her life. Noticing how old she was, he did not think he was committing himself to many preaching engagements. She lived on for many years, however, seeming to flag at one point but being sustained by the thought of another opportunity to hear 'the Doctor' preach. We are speaking of the spirit inculcated by words such as this popular song by Wilson Phillips:

> Don't you know things can change?
> Things 'll go your way
> if you hold on for one more day.

On the other hand, when the spirit is crushed, living is not easy. It is the attitude summed up in the bleak humour of 'Forsyth's Second Corollary to Murphy's Laws' (Murphy's Laws warn that if things can go wrong they will!). It says, 'Just when you see the light at the end of the tunnel, the roof caves in.' Another corollary suggests that the light at the end of the tunnel is a train coming! It is not unusual to hear of elderly men or women losing their spouses and then dying themselves shortly afterwards on account of their broken hearts or crushed spirits. It is only through the gospel that a sustaining spirit can be found that will last into the world to come.

'The heart of the discerning acquires knowledge; the ears of the wise seek it out' (18:15).
Synonymous: **'discerning' / 'wise'**
Insightful hearts secure knowledge; intelligent ears seek knowledge.

Once more the paradoxical call to acquire knowledge, to seek it out, is sounded (cf. 10:14; 15:14). We need hearts and ears that are open to receive wisdom. 'He who has ears to hear, let him hear.' Be both inquisitive and acquisitive as far as knowledge is concerned.

'A gift opens the way for the giver and ushers him into the presence of the great' (18:16).
Synonymous: **'opens the way'** / **'ushers him into'**
Gifts open gates for givers, to the presence of the powerful
deliver.

This observational proverb is a little like 17:8. Some do buy their way into the presence of those in high places. They know how to hobnob with the great because their wealth and riches win them a place among such people. Many are yet to be disabused of the fact, but such bribery will not provide a passport to heaven.

'The first to present his case seems right, till another comes forward and questions him' (18:17).
Synthetic: **'first'** / **'another'**
When the first speaker speaks, he seems to say what's right;
But when a second speaks, there shines a different light.

I remember having to attend the Crown Court once as a potential witness in a case of drunken driving that led to a man's death. The defendant pleaded guilty in the end, but his lawyer sought to do what he could for the man by way of mitigation, and especially to reduce the severity of the punishment he was likely to receive by pleading the case of the man's children. Not being used to such places, I was beginning to feel some sympathy for the defendant's situation. When the judge came to pass sentence, however, he unsympathetically highlighted the irresponsible actions that had left a family bereaved and had no hesitation in imposing a six-month prison sentence and a stiff fine. Every day such things are seen in the law courts. A case is presented and looks watertight, but then a little cross-examination is employed and the situation appears in a very different light.

This observational proverb is a warning against jumping to conclusions. It is a reminder of the need for a careful and thorough consideration before making a decision. We must hear both sides of the argument before we decide. Not to do that is another example of the tendency to answer without listening referred to in verse 13 (cf. 18:2). Not just in court, but in many other situations, we need to hear both sides of the story before making up our minds. Sadly many an unbeliever has his head so full of anti-Christian arguments that he will not seek a second opinion. If he did, he would then see things presented from a very different perspective.

'Casting the lot settles disputes and keeps strong opponents apart' (18:18).

Synthetic: **'settles disputes'** / **'keeps strong opponents apart'**

Sometimes disputes cannot be settled and some sort of lottery has to settle the matter. When I was in school and international rugby matches were taking place in Cardiff a few tickets would be made available for sale. So many wanted them that it was necessary to draw lots for them. What fairer way could be found? Following verse 17, this proverb reminds us that even when we have heard both sides of a story, we may still be unable to decide which to favour. Christians know what it is to be confronted with weighty opinion on both sides and not to know whom to choose. Calvin says one thing; John Owen another. How will I decide? My wife advises this; my fellow deacon and friend that. What shall I do? Before Pentecost the lot was sometimes necessary and since then there have been Christians, like Wesley, who relied on it *in extremis*. Today we should rather look to the Spirit's leading to know what to do.

'An offended brother is more unyielding than a fortified city, and disputes are like the barred gates of a citadel' (18:19).

Synonymous: **'offended brother' / 'disputes'**
Simile: **'offended brother ... disputes' / 'fortified city ... barred gates'**

An offended brother's like a city fortified; disputes are like the gates cross-barred.

Other proverbs have spoken about arguments and disagreements. Here the warning is against falling into them. Once they start, the shutters go up and nothing passes in or out. People can be totally unreasonable at times if offended, or involved in a dispute. Barriers are easy to erect, but not so easy to bring down. As far as we can, we ought to avoid offending others or getting into disputes.

**From the fruit of his mouth a man's stomach is filled;
with the harvest from his lips he is satisfied.
The tongue has the power of life and death,
and those who love it will eat its fruit**

(18:20-21).

Synonymous: **'fruit of his mouth' / 'harvest from his lips'**
Synthetic: **'power of life and death' / 'will eat its fruit'**

The subject of speech is before us again. In verse 20 the picture is of words as being like food or grain. With the words we take into our mouths we fill our stomachs, as it were. We harvest what comes into our lips and so find food to sate our hunger. We need, therefore, to take care how we speak. It is very easy to be dismissive about words: 'Only words!' — but they are powerful things. They can mean the difference between life and death (18:21).

In Britain when the police arrest a person they formally caution him regarding his rights. The importance of what he says or does not say is emphasized. Even in everyday life words can have a life-or-death effect, as some know to their lifelong regret. 'If only I'd said something,' say some. 'If only I had kept quiet,' say others. Preaching especially is a life-or-death situation. Again care over what we say is commended. The second part of each proverb is a reminder that we reap what we sow as far as our speech is concerned.

'He who finds a wife finds what is good and receives favour from the Lord' (18:22).
> *Synthetic:* **'finds a wife' / 'receives favour'**
> Finding a wife will good afford;
> It leads to favour from the Lord.

This striking verse underlines the immense value of finding a wife. Its similarity to Proverbs 8:35 shows how important a good wife is. To find such a person, as many (including me) will testify, is a good thing and a favour from the Lord. Others are still seeking and need to keep praying and looking. It is a proverb, of course. Not all wives are a blessing (see 19:13,14), but this is the norm.

Bearing in mind the approach of Proverbs, there is undoubtedly a higher reference here — to the need to marry Wisdom. What a wonderful wife to find! It is the Lord's favour that leads to wisdom. As we have said many times, that wisdom is found in Christ.

'A poor man pleads for mercy, but a rich man answers harshly' (18:23).
   Contrast: **'poor man'** / **'rich man'**
   The poor plead for pity but the rich reply rudely.

Rich and poor are contrasted at various points in the book. Here they interact to the shame and the anguish of the poor man, who pleads in vain for mercy, and the moral reprehensibility of the rich man, who answers the poor man's plea harshly. One thinks of Lazarus and the rich man in Jesus' story recorded in Luke 16. 'Such detached reporting', says Derek Kidner, '... faces the reader with the ugliness of the world he lives in ... and reminds him to take its pains and prizes calmly.' Of course, not every poor man is oppressed, nor is every rich man an oppressor. These things are common, however, and are set out here to encourage the poor and warn the rich. God sees. The Lord abounds in riches, but he does not give a harsh answer to our pleas for mercy. Quite the opposite.

'A man of many companions may come to ruin, but there is a friend who sticks closer than a brother' (18:24).
   Contrast: **'many companions'** / **'friend who sticks closer than a brother'**
   Many mates may misuse, but a buddy who backs you is better than a brother.

Here is another proverb on friendship and brotherhood (see 17:17). The distinction is made here between **'companions'** and a truly good friend. It is often not until the chips are down that we know who our true friends are. Such a friend **'sticks closer than a brother'**. It is a great joy to know that there are such people in the world. I have no blood brothers but I have good lifelong friends, like Chris and Steve, who I know I can always depend on. After visiting Chris one time I did some reflecting on the ingredients in good friendship. I came up with six:

1. *Time.* Some friendships are made in a moment but usually they take time. In a busy world we must find time to make and keep friends.

2. *Shared experience.* This is probably essential.

3. *Mutual respect and admiration.* You know when someone respects you. It is one of the pleasures of friendship. Equally, it is good to look with some complacency on another human being. We get a glimpse of the Trinity in that.

4. *Tolerance and acceptance.* This is vital too. A difference of opinion should be a fairly matter-of-fact thing between friends. 'Wounds from a friend can be trusted, but an enemy multiplies kisses' (27:6).

5. *Openness.* A great thing about good friends is the chance to be at ease in their presence and, as appropriate, to talk openly and honestly with them. It is neither right nor feasible to do that with everyone. There is something akin to being in God's presence about it.

6. *It takes effort.* 'Do not forsake your friend and the friend of your father' (27:10). Without effort on one side or the other, friendships slide. What opportunities for doing good and receiving blessing are lost when this happens!

Inevitably, the believer thinks of the Lord Jesus Christ. We have already mentioned Matthew 12:48-50, where Jesus, having been told that his mother and brothers want to see him, replies, 'Who is my mother, and who are my brothers?' Pointing to his disciples he says, 'Here are my mother and my brothers.' His 'brother and sister and mother' are 'whoever does the will of my Father in heaven'. In Matthew 25 he describes the King at the judgement referring to what his disciples have done 'for one of the least of these brothers of mine' as being for him.

Paul writes, 'For those God foreknew he also predestined to be conformed to the likeness of his Son, that he might be the first-born among many brothers' (Rom. 8:29).

Again, we read, 'Both the one who makes men holy and those who are made holy are of the same family. So Jesus is not ashamed to call them brothers. He says, "I will declare your name to my brothers; in the presence of the congregation I will sing your praises"' (Heb. 2:11-12, quoting Ps. 22:22).

In Micah it is prophesied of Messiah that 'the rest of his brothers' will 'return to join the Israelites' (Micah 5:3).

Several hymns were mentioned in our consideration of Proverbs 17:17. John Newton's fullest exposition of this theme begins:

> One there is, above all others,
> Well deserves the name of Friend;
> His is love beyond a brother's,
> Costly, free, and knows no end:
> They who once his kindness prove,
> Find it everlasting love!

Another verse says:

> Could we bear from one another,
> What he daily bears from us?
> Yet this glorious Friend and Brother,
> Loves us though we treat him thus:
> Though for good we render ill,
> He accounts us brethren still.

Another, seldom sung these days, reads:

> Men, when raised to lofty stations,
> Often know their friends no more;
> Slight and scorn their poor relations
> Though they valued them before.
> But our Saviour always owns
> Those whom he redeemed with groans.

What these twenty-four proverbs teach us

This chapter, like others, is intended to persuade you, the reader, to a certain opinion. There is a debate here, a struggle even, a tug-of-war. You cannot decide what to think by tossing a coin or throwing a dice (as in 18:18). You need to think it through. The chapter gives three warnings about how to do this:

> 1. Do not be too quick to write off what is here (18:13).
> 2. Give it a fair hearing. Listen to argument and counter-argument (18:17).
> 3. Holding doggedly to your own opinions without trying to understand is foolish (18:2).

You may find yourself in deep water here as my words add either profundity or obscurity. I trust, however, that the 'fountain of wisdom' that is here will be 'a bubbling brook' of refreshment and life to you (18:4). I have preached on these verses in the past and it has given me satisfaction to do so. I am conscious of the life-or-death quality of such words. Again I say, choose life!

Sin is part of all our lives

This is something we are often slow to grasp. We tend to realize it first when we become guilty of specific sins. In this chapter some specific sins are highlighted.

Unfriendliness (18:1)

New Testament Christians are constantly encouraged to be hospitable and kind, yet I remember a personable and friendly minister describe a three-day ministers' conference at which no one spoke to him! Unfriendliness is selfish. It is not only sinful, but makes no sense. We all need friends.

Gossip (18:8)

Although not explicitly condemned here, we know this is another sin to be repented of.

Injustice (18:5)

Favouring the wicked and depriving the innocent of justice goes on in many areas. It is a sin knowingly to perpetrate such injustices.

Laziness (18:9)

Which is worse — a man who is given a car and smashes it up, or one who is given a car and leaves it to rust away? Apart from the time element, there is really little difference.

Pride (18:12)

It is easy to be proud now, but what about when everything goes wrong? What about in the face of death?

Sin is the cause of misery in this world

Although we love sin, it is the root of all our misery. Unfriendliness, gossip, injustice, laziness and pride cause much misery.
Two examples of the misery brought about as a result of sin
are found in verses 19 and 23.

Stand-offs (18:19)

Pride leads to disputes and to a siege situation as we try to
starve each other out. Until someone backs down the misery
goes on.

Oppression (18:23)

The Bible warns us that the poor will always be with us. Many,
nevertheless, believe in redistribution of wealth by some means.
The problem in this world, however, is not that there are rich
and poor, but that the rich oppress the poor and ignore their
cries for mercy.

Sin leads to disgrace and punishment

Verse 3 is a proverbial warning against going on in sin: 'When
wickedness comes, so does contempt, and with shame comes
disgrace.' We have not mentioned sins of the mouth here, but
we are told:

> A fool's lips bring him strife,
>   and his mouth invites a beating.
> A fool's mouth is his undoing,
>   and his lips are a snare to his soul

(18:6-7).

Sin and misery are not all there is in this world

Of course, this chapter and the gospel message have more to talk about than sin, misery and judgement. There is more to life than that. Christians must remember that. Despite man's fall, God, in his common grace, has filled this world with many good things. Some are mentioned here.

Family life (18:22)

What a blessing to have a wife! To have a family is a great thing. Give thanks every day for yours.

Friendship (18:24)

Even if we have no family, God may provide a boon companion, a good friend. What a blessing! One of the US's most successful comedy shows bears the name *Friends*. Part of its appeal is the delight of watching what appears to be a totally dedicated group of friends.

Wealth (18:11)

The rich may often be oppressors, but the Bible never denies the advantages of wealth.

A sustaining spirit (18:14)

Even those who have no family, friends or money are sometimes granted a sustaining spirit that pulls them through the crises they face.

Of course, there is a downside to all of this. Family life may be a trial. 'A man of many companions may come to ruin'

(18:24). We are tempted to put our trust in riches, and 'A crushed spirit who can bear?' (18:11,14).

Sin and misery have only one remedy — Jesus Christ

The use of the word 'spirit' in verse 14 points to the fact that the real battle is within, in the heart, or soul. Our great need is to be born from above. This is possible because of Jesus Christ. He is the archetypal 'friend who sticks closer than a brother' (18:24). He is 'a strong tower'. We must 'run to it' and find safety in him (18:10). Castles in the air are useless; only he can protect us and save us. If we go to God in his name he, who has opened the way to God, will usher us into the presence of the great King (18:16). 'The heart of the discerning acquires knowledge; the ears of the wise seek it out' (18:15). Keep seeking until you find.

36.
Wisdom and folly contrasted

Please read Proverbs 19:1-29

Blamelessness, zeal, responsibility, wealth, false witness, sycophancy, poverty, wisdom, false witness, incongruities, patience, kingly power, children and wives, parents and wives, laziness, obedience, kindness, parental discipline, temper, teachability, plans, desires, God-fearers, sluggards, deterrents, rebellion, a golden rule, corruption, punishment

We shall look at all twenty-nine proverbs of the chapter together.

'Better a poor man whose walk is blameless than a fool whose lips are perverse' (19:1).
    Contrast (better than): **'poor man whose walk is blameless'** / **'fool whose lips are perverse'**
    Better poor and faithful than perverse and foolish.

This is similar to Proverbs 28:6. The proverbs are constantly leading us to right priorities and sound values. We may find the perverse lips of the fool attractive, but the truth is that, whatever else he may lack, **'a poor man whose walk is blameless'** is far better off. Yet how many put up with all sorts of indignity and outrageousness from others just because they have wealth or other desirable commodities! Honesty is the best and only policy.

'It is not good to have zeal without knowledge, nor to be hasty and miss the way' (19:2).
Synonymous: **'zeal without knowledge'** / **'hasty and miss the way'**
To be zealous but ignorant is not okay,
Nor to be hasty and miss the way.

Even in school we learn that the first to finish is not always the best. Knowledge is more important than speed. Enthusiasm will not make up for a lack of knowledge, any more than money will. If I employ a tradesman or a professional, no amount of enthusiasm on his part will make up for any deficiencies he has in basic skills. Who would you rather removed your appendix — a competent surgeon, or an enthusiastic medical student?

Zeal without knowledge can be fatal. In the winter of 1994-95 calves were being flown in crates from Coventry in England to Holland and a number of protesters gathered at the airport gates. Among them was Jill Phipps. As a transporter came up to the gates, she and others would run up to it, banging on the doors with their fists and shouting at the drivers urging them to think what they were doing. The police would then manhandle the demonstrators out of the way. On one particular day, Jill and others eluded the police and reached a transporter. Instead of stopping until it was safe to continue, the driver, Stephen Yates, just drove on and Jill was crushed under the wheels. She died on the way to hospital. She had not thought such a thing could happen.

'Could my zeal no respite know,' observed Toplady, it could not atone for sin; 'Thou must save and thou alone.' He knew that only God could do it. It is easy to be so busy rushing along life's highway that we miss the important turnings and end up lost for ever. Paul observes concerning his fellow Jews that they were zealous for God (Rom. 10:2). Many religious people show a similarly admirable zeal, but as Paul says, when this zeal is not in accordance with knowledge it is useless. He himself had gone about persecuting Christians thinking he was doing God's will, as Jesus had predicted when he said, 'A time is coming when anyone who kills you will think he is offering a service to God' (John 16:2). What harm zealous but misguided people can do!

I minister in a largely Jewish area. Every summer young people come and give out tracts on the streets. Sadly, much of this literature ends up as litter on the pavement as people with more zeal than knowledge try to serve the Lord. From time to time London sees the advent of well-advertised evangelists, usually from America. They fill a stadium, get people to come forward and register large numbers of people as making professions of faith in Christ. Meanwhile the impact of Christianity visibly dwindles. D. L. Moody once said that he preferred his questionable way of evangelizing to the lack of evangelizing done by others. We can unfairly excuse lack of zeal at times but zeal must be according to knowledge or it will do more harm than good. Let's pray that our 'love may abound more and more in knowledge and depth of insight' (Phil. 1:9).

'A man's own folly ruins his life, yet his heart rages against the Lord' (19:3).

Synthetic: **'man's own folly'** / **'heart rages against the Lord'**

Your folly has ruined your life; forget your heart's rage at the Lord.

Whenever I read this proverb, I think of Bill Smith. Bill came regularly to the church where I grew up. I remember him once saying to me that he was very disappointed with the Lord because the Lord had not provided him with a wife. I can picture him now, holding his Bible in his hand, black dirt visible under every fingernail, wearing his scruffy suit and unpolished shoes. His hair was greasy and unkempt, his glasses needed a polish and his shirt was partly adrift to reveal a glimpse of dirty underwear. I was only a teenager but it did strike me that a lack of effort on his part in the hygiene and neatness departments may have had something to do with his problem! Not all our problems are caused by our own folly, but in many cases they can be traced back to just that.

As Job Orton once pointed out, too often men blame God for bad health when they have been intemperate; for difficult circumstances when they have made a bad choice; for rocky family relations when they have been neglectful; and for a lack of spiritual peace or progress when they have not made use of the means of grace. If we are believers, we can be sure that God is working everything together for our good. Sometimes we do not understand why we have to suffer certain things, but for anyone's heart to rage against God is foolish and sinful.

'Wealth brings many friends, but a poor man's friend deserts him' (19:4).

    Contrast: **'wealth'** / **'poor man'**

    The rich have many friends who vanish when distress descends.

Returning once more to the subject of friends, we see here the fair-weather variety (as in 14:20; 19:6-7; cf. 18:23-24). Again we see wisdom's hard-nosed realism as the spotlight is trained on the nature of true friendship.

'A false witness will not go unpunished, and he who pours out lies will not go free' (19:5).

    Synonymous: **'false witness'** / **'he who pours out lies'**

> False witnesses will punished be;
> Flagrant liars will not go free.

This proverb concerning perjury is repeated almost word for word in verse 9 (see there for comment; see also Deut. 19:16-19). The context here is bribery — one reason why false testimony is given. We must not give in to bribes or threats.

> **Many curry favour with a ruler,**
> > **and everyone is the friend of a man who gives gifts.**
> **A poor man is shunned by all his relatives —**
> > **how much more do his friends avoid him!**
> **Though he pursues them with pleading,**
> > **they are nowhere to be found**
>
> (19:6-7).

Synonymous: **'curry favour'** / **'friend'**
A fortiori
Synonymous: **'shunned by all his relatives'** / **'friends avoid'**
Synthetic: **'shunned'** / **'pursues'**

These two proverbs belong together and follow on from verse 4.

Verse 6 expands on the attractions of wealth to include the slightly different categories of power and generosity. It is important that we remember the danger of either trying to buy friendship, or of our friendship being bought by others. True friendship must go beyond that. Yet sadly sometimes when one partner goes up in the world a friendship can fail. When we think of the Lord Jesus Christ we know he was as much a friend to us who believe in his humiliation as he is now in his glory. Whether we are rich or poor, influential or not, makes no difference.

The temptation to **'curry favour with a ruler'** is one that Christians can fall into. Billy Graham's successful attempts to ingratiate himself with successive American presidents are well documented. One has little reason to question the motives, but the consequences have often been lamentable. Similar things could be said about evangelicalism's penchant for latching on to the rich and famous wherever it can.

Verse 7 is an oddity in that it is the only proverb of three (as opposed to two) lines in the whole section from Proverbs 10:1 – 22:16. It is either a corrupted text or unique. Whichever is the case, the sense is fairly clear. It brings out the harshness of some in this world. Family and friends are great assets, as we have said, but the poor are often neglected by their best potential allies because of their poverty. Despite his pleas, **'They are nowhere to be found.'** Jesus, on the other hand, had time for the poor and needy and did not neglect them. His followers should be like him.

'He who gets wisdom loves his own soul; he who cherishes understanding prospers' (19:8).
Synonymous: **'gets wisdom'** / **'cherishes understanding'**

Wisdom can do you nothing but good. Despite some good they may do, other things can have harmful side effects, but wisdom will always be a blessing. The blessing will not always be monetary or material, but it will always be substantial.

'A false witness will not go unpunished, and he who pours out lies will perish' (19:9).
Synonymous: **'false witness'** / **'he who pours out lies'**
False witnesses God punishes; the flagrant liar will soon expire.

Very similar to verse 5, this proverb is in line with Proverbs 12:17 and 14:5,25, but with the added warning of punishment.

One thinks of Jezebel, who engineered the death of Naboth and how it is recorded that, as she was thrown from an upper window, 'Some of her blood spattered the wall and the horses as they trampled her underfoot.' Jehu noted that this was a fulfilment of 'the word of the LORD that he spoke through his servant Elijah the Tishbite: "On the plot of ground at Jezreel dogs will devour Jezebel's flesh"' (2 Kings 9:33,36; cf. 1 Kings 21:23).

Similarly, in A.D. 70 Jerusalem, where the Messiah had been crucified some years before, was destroyed by the Romans. We do not always see such symmetry in this world but we shall in the next.

'It is not fitting for a fool to live in luxury — how much worse for a slave to rule over princes!' (19:10; see also 11:22; 17:7; 26:1; 30:21-23).

A fortiori: **'fool' / 'slave'**

It does happen, of course, that fools live in luxury and that slaves come to rule over princes. The writer of Ecclesiastes complains that 'I have seen slaves on horseback, while princes go on foot like slaves' (Eccles. 10:7). Proverbs 12:24 and 17:2 suggest that this happens because rulers are lazy or foolish in other ways. Sometimes other factors operate. Perhaps a modern manifestation of this is the way that entertainers such as sportsmen, musicians and actors, lawyers, non-executive directors and dealers on the stock market can sometimes earn phenomenal sums, while those in other worthy professions — nurses and pastors come readily to mind — are relatively low paid.

'A man's wisdom gives him patience; it is to his glory to overlook an offence' (19:11).

Synonymous: **'patience' / 'overlook an offence'**

Here is another proverb on the theme of patience. We have already learned that it is an aspect of wisdom (12:16; 14:29) and a useful gift to have (15:18; 17:14) which is commended in the following terms: 'Better a patient man than a warrior, a man who controls his temper than one who takes a city' (16:32). We have noted that it is a characteristic of God himself seen in the conduct of the Lord Jesus. When we are offended we tend to feel that our honour has in some way been diminished. In fact, the proverb points out, overlooking an offence adds to our glory.

To illustrate, which politician should be the more respected in the end — the one who ignores the people throwing rotten tomatoes and eggs, or the one who wades into the crowd with his fists flying?

'A king's rage is like the roar of a lion, but his favour is like dew on the grass' (19:12).
   Contrast: **'king's rage'** / **'his favour'**
   Double simile: **'king's rage'** / **'the roar of a lion'**; **'[king's] favour'** / **'dew on the grass'**
   A ruler's rage is like a roar; his goodwill is like green grass.

Here we are back to kings. (The verse is reminiscent of 16:14-15; see also 20:2, where the first part is identical to this proverb.) The context, following verse 11, reminds us that while it is right to overlook personal offences, the eye-for-an-eye principle is still appropriate in matters of civil government. The similes of **'the roar of a lion'** and **'dew on the grass'** are transparent. As well as the obvious reference to civil power, we must remember both our own power over others and Christ's power over us. When the Lion of Judah roars we must take notice (see Amos 3:4,8). His favour, however, is like the freshness of the early morning dew that nourishes plants. 'I will be like the dew to Israel; he will blossom like a lily' (Hosea 14:5). Just as the manna came to Israel with the morning dew, so Christ is the Bread of Heaven on whom we must feed (Exod. 16; John 6).

> **A foolish son is his father's ruin,**
> **and a quarrelsome wife is like a constant dripping**
> **Houses and wealth are inherited from parents,**
> **but a prudent wife is from the LORD**
>
> (19:13-14).

Both these verses refer to relationships with parents and also between husbands and wives. One is negative, the other positive.

Synonymous: **'foolish son' / 'quarrelsome wife'**
A foolish son is dad's mishap;
A nagging wife's a dripping tap.

Verse 13 begins with the familiar warning of what it is like to have a foolish son (e.g., 17:21,25), but goes on to provide a counterbalance to what was said in Proverbs 18:22 and what will be said in 19:14. Several other proverbs refer to this disturbing phenomenon, a standby of music-hall comedians that in reality is no joke (see 21:9,19; 25:24 and 27:15, which is almost identical).

The application here is, more narrowly, for the rising generation to avoid foolishness, for parents to be sober-minded, for bachelors to choose carefully and for wives not to nag. More broadly, the proverb warns against a false optimism about family life, which can be very demanding. An even more general point is that false religion involves partnerships and offspring that are less than desirable.

Contrast: **'houses and wealth'** / **'from the LORD'**
Houses, wealth — an inherited prize,
But from the Lord comes a wife who's wise.

This unexpected contrast follows on and reminds us again of the need for great care. The saying, 'You can choose your friends but not your relations,' is well known. I also like the advice concerning marriage that goes: 'Choose your love and love your choice.' Marriage choices have ramifications for generations to come, and so must not be entered into 'thoughtlessly or unadvisedly'. A great deal of prayer should mark every step of the way. We can inherit many good things from parents but not wisdom. That is God's gift. Money can't buy love — or wisdom either.

'Laziness brings on deep sleep, and the shiftless man goes hungry' (19:15).
Synonymous: **'laziness'** / **'shiftless man'**
Watch deep sleep creep as shiftless Simon starves.

In case we are tempted to forget this theme (last mentioned in 18:9) here it is again. The context this time is inheritance and obedience. Over-reliance on 'what turns up' and disobedience are often motivated by laziness. The **'deep sleep'** here is the stupor that comes on the indolent. Unlike the lazy person who does no work, laziness steadily works away at lulling the person to sleep and then stealing all the food. We must not give in to it:

Wake up, O sleeper,
    rise from the dead,
and Christ will shine on you

(Eph. 5:14).

'He who obeys instructions guards his life, but he who is contemptuous of his ways will die' (19:16).

Contrast (complex): **'obeys instructions'** / **'is contemptuous of his ways'**

Keep the law, keep your life; detest directions and duly die.

The words for **'obeys'** and **'guards'** are the same in Hebrew, meaning 'keep'. (We find similar pairings of verbs in 8:35; 18:22; 17:19; 21:23.) There is a little complexity here. It does not say, 'He who obeys instructions guards his life, but *he who does not* will die,' nor '*He who is careful about his ways* guards his life, but he who is contemptuous of his ways will die,' but combines those ideas. To fail to obey instructions is to be contemptuous of one's ways. This is true both on the everyday, mundane level and in more spiritual terms. 'Whoever has my commands and obeys them, he is the one who loves me,' says Jesus. 'He who loves me will be loved by my Father, and I too will love him and show myself to him' (John 14:21).

'He who is kind to the poor lends to the LORD, and he will reward him for what he has done' (19:17).

Synthetic: **'lends to the LORD'** / **'he will reward'**

This follows on from 14:31, but is even sharper and bolder. The wealth God has given us is for sharing with those in need. Such kindness is advocated throughout Scripture. 'To look after orphans and widows in their distress' is a mark of pure and faultless religion (James 1:27). Here is the root of what Jesus says about the sheep and the goats in Matthew 25. The figure of the Lord borrowing from us is a very daring one indeed. If only we really believed that being kind to the poor is lending to the Lord, we would give more often and more gladly. Do we honestly think he will default on paying us back, or that his interest rate will not be to our very great advantage?

'Discipline your son, for in that there is hope; do not be a willing party to his death' (19:18).

Synthetic command (positive): **'discipline'** / **'do not be a willing party to his death'**

This note has been sounded before, in 13:24, and will be again (see 22:15; 23:13-14; and, especially 29:15,17). Rather than the second line being an admonition against overdoing the discipline, the fifth commandment is probably in the background, with its promise of long life. To help children to honour their parents they need discipline. To fail here is to contribute to the likelihood of their early demise. Parents who say, 'We don't know where we're going wrong; we try to bring him up the right way — we give him everything he wants,' need to think again.

'A hot-tempered man must pay the penalty; if you rescue him, you will have to do it again' (19:19).

Synthetic: **'hot-tempered man'** / **'if you rescue him'**

Petulance pays penalties; rescues require repetition.

This is the counterpart to verse 11. If you lose your temper there are always disadvantages. You may break something, look foolish, say something regrettable, or lose the respect of others. There will certainly be a penalty, whatever it is. The man with a hot temper is not only a liability to himself but to others too. Here the warning is that **'if you rescue him'** by giving in to his raging demands you will be making things difficult for yourself. If flying into a rage has worked once he will try it again. This is seen in the temper tantrums of children and when adults with a short fuse regularly lose their temper.

As a toddler my sister would lie on the floor with her head back, only the whites of her eyes visible and her mouth wide open. The sound of her cry would disappear off the scale at a certain point, only to cut in again with renewed strength. When my mother approached a doctor about this, he gave her wise advice: 'Ignore it.' Every time we pander to the rages of others, young or old, we pay the penalty.

Something similar can be said for the more metaphorical temper tantrums threatened or carried out by those who want to manipulate us. If a child (or adult) who takes after Violet Elizabeth Bott threatens to 'thcweam and thcweam' until she's 'thick', let her do it. If a church member threatens to resign, a wise pastor will probably accept immediately, whether he believes in resignation or not. Governments who give in to terrorist demands will soon find that they are having to do so again.

'Listen to advice and accept instruction, and in the end you will be wise' (19:20).
> *Synthetic command (positive):* **'listen'** / **'in the end'**
> Listen and learn, and wisdom will be yours.

This wonderful proverb is the golden key to wisdom. It neatly summarizes the book's message. The older I grow, the more I see it is true. Will you come to the end of your life full of regret, thinking, 'If only I'd listened…!'?

'Many are the plans in a man's heart, but it is the LORD's purpose that prevails' (19:21).
> *Contrast:* **'plans in a man's heart'** / **'the LORD's purpose'**
> People prepare plans, but the purposes of Providence prevail.

Similar to 16:1,9, this verse reassures us that, although we are prone to fail, God's purpose prevails. Whether we work with God or try to work against him, it is his will that wins.

'What a man desires is unfailing love; better to be poor than a liar' (19:22).

   Synthetic (better than): **'what a man desires'** / **'better to be poor'**

The second half of this proverb is an abbreviated form of verse 1. Translations vary, as the Hebrew is difficult. The NRSV translates: 'What is desirable in a person is loyalty.' This makes more sense. The point then is that integrity is more important than wealth. In most situations what is wanted is your honest opinion, not your money.

'The fear of the Lord leads to life: then one rests content, untouched by trouble' (19:23).

   Synthetic: **'fear of the Lord'** / **'untouched by trouble'**
   Fear of God means life;
   One's at ease, set free from strife.

The eleventh of fourteen references in Proverbs to **'the fear of the Lord'**, this is the first since 16:6. (This one is most like 10:27 and 14:27.) Wisdom itself is often said to lead to life. The phrase, **'Then one rests content, untouched by trouble'**, paints a very attractive picture. It describes the calmness and decorum, the confidence and aplomb, the tranquillity and assurance of the man who fears the Lord. Because he fears the Lord, he is not afraid of anyone or anything else. Tate and Brady's psalm paraphrase says it well:

   Fear him, ye saints, and you will then
   Have nothing else to fear;
   Make you his service your delight;
   Your wants shall be his care.

   While hungry lions lack their prey,
   The Lord will food provide

For such as put their trust in him,
And see their needs supplied.

There is no suggestion that those who fear the Lord escape all troubles but, proverbially, they remain *untouched* by them. Unbelievers do sometimes say, 'I admire your faith and wish I had the same thing.' It is this contentment that they envy. Think of a Sunday for example. While you are making your way to church with your family to hear God's Word, they are, perhaps, just rising from bed, nursing a hangover, wondering where the rest of the family is and dreading the trip to the supermarket for the weekly shop. Being an unbeliever is no bed of roses. To quote another verse from the hymn above, we say:

O make but trial of his love;
Experience will decide
How blest are they, and only they,
Who in his truth confide.

'The sluggard buries his hand in the dish; he will not even bring it back to his mouth!' (19:24).
    Synthetic: **'buries his hand'** / **'will not even bring it back'**
    Submerged in a saucer, too tired to…

And so we come back to laziness (cf. 19:15), and a vivid picture of it (26:15 is almost exactly the same). Here we see that laziness is the height of stupidity and sloth. Having buried his hand in the dish, the sluggard cannot even be bothered to bring it back to his mouth so that he can eat! The picture is comical; the reality is not. There is a world of difference between resting content (19:23) and this.

'Flog a mocker, and the simple will learn prudence; rebuke a discerning man, and he will gain knowledge' (19:25).

Synonymous: **'flog a mocker'** / **'rebuke a discerning man'**

There are three people here. **'A mocker'** is an incorrigible
sinner. Flogging, or something similar, is the only thing he
understands. **'The simple'** are sinners still open to good impressions. Although they may not respond to a rebuke and
probably ought not to be dealt with too harshly, they will take
note of what happens to mockers. The deterrent element in
punishment is part of Scripture's overall understanding of
wrongdoing and how it is to be dealt with (see Deut. 13:11;
21:21). **'A discerning man'** is still a sinner but does not need
to be dealt with harshly. A rebuke is enough. So we have here
lessons for many situations regarding both our own willingness to toe the line, and how we get others to do so. It must
reflect God's own approach to crime and punishment.

**'He who robs his father and drives out his mother is a son
who brings shame and disgrace'** (19:26).
     Synthetic: **'robs … drives out'** / **'brings shame and dis-
grace'**

Here the foolish son of 10:1 and 17:25 is seen at his worst
(but see 20:20), robbing his father and driving out his mother.
What shame and disgrace such behaviour brings to all who
hear about it!

**'Stop listening to instruction, my son, and you will stray
from the words of knowledge'** (19:27).
     Synthetic: **'stop listening'** / **'you will stray'**
     Ignore instruction, stray from sagacity.

Here is a negative version of verse 20. Wisdom is not a level
you can reach and then leave off learning. We are leaky vessels that constantly need topping up. We are liable to stray.

Prone to wander, Lord I feel it,
Prone to leave the God I love.
Take my heart, O take and seal it,
Seal it from thy courts above.

And even the man who wrote those words in the eighteenth century, Robert Robinson, strayed far from the Lord.

'A corrupt witness mocks at justice, and the mouth of the wicked gulps down evil' (19:28).
  Synonymous: **'corrupt witness'** / **'mouth of the wicked'**

We see both outward and inward appearances here. Outwardly, the **'corrupt witness mocks at justice'**. You must not lie on oath, we say. Why not? He does not care about justice. Below the surface is a rapacious lust for sin. The picture of the wicked man greedily gulping down evil is a powerful one. Gourmands of evil exist.

'Penalties are prepared for mockers, and beatings for the backs of fools' (19:29).
  Synonymous: **'penalties'** / **'beatings'**
  Penalties are prepared for provokers; beatings for boobies' backs.

This warning echoes some that have gone before and others still to come (see 26:3). Anyone who does not listen to the warnings here will pay for it dearly.

What these twenty-one proverbs teach us

Taking these twenty-nine proverbs together we see a number of contrasts between wisdom and folly.

*Wisdom is good and leads to life and leisure; folly is bad
and leads to punishment and perdition*

Verse 8 tells us, 'He who gets wisdom loves his own soul; he
who cherishes understanding prospers.' On the other hand,
'Penalties are prepared for mockers, and beatings for the backs
of fools' (19:29). Of course, in this life this does not always
happen immediately. For example, justice is perverted (19:28).
There will be punishments for such people (19:5,9). This is
one reason why children must be properly disciplined (19:18)
and why self-imposed obedience is so important (19:16). It is
'the fear of the LORD' that 'leads to life: then one rests content, untouched by trouble' (19:23).

Wisdom acknowledges God; folly blames God

Verse 21 is a word of wisdom that must shape the thinking of
believers. Verse 14 affirms its truth in one specific direction.
The sovereignty of God is attacked from one side by the atheist who says there is no God, and on the other by the sort of
person who wants to twist the doctrine and blame God for his
problems (19:3). Wisdom is not a mere matter of knowledge,
but of rightly using knowledge. For example, someone who
knows a little bit about election may say, 'If I'm elect, I'm
elect, and if I'm not, I can't do anything about it anyway.'
Wisdom teaches us that we must trust in Christ whether we
think we are elect or not.

*Wisdom, not folly, has the right perspective on wealth and
poverty, zeal, family life and power*

Wealth and poverty

The fool believes money is the answer to everything. If you
are wealthy, all is well. The wise recognize that this is short-

sighted. They see the superficial nature of earthly wealth (as in 19:4,6-7). More than that, they see that there are things that money cannot buy (19:14) and that it is better to be poor and holy than rich and sinful (19:1,10,22). The wise are filled with compassion for the poor and do something about it (19:17).

Zeal (19:2)

Fools often believe that as long as you are enthusiastic that is all that matters. Commitment is all. A family member changes his religion. Worldly wisdom sometimes says, 'Well, if you're rejecting the faith you were brought up in at least be a good Christian, or Muslim, or whatever.' Such a view makes little sense. Also think what shame some enthusiasts bring on the gospel — people who bomb abortion centres, for example.

Family life

Wisdom recognizes the God-given blessing that family life is (19:14), but recognizes the problems that can so easily arise (19:13,26) and the hard work necessary to make it work (19:18).

Power

The wise recognize the power that kings and others have, and act accordingly. They bow down to God first and respect the authorities he has instituted (19:12).

Wisdom produces superior fruit to that produced by folly

Fools are often lazy (19:15,24) and hot-headed (15:19). The wise are kind (15:17) and patient (15:11) and know how to deal with the foolish (15:19). They are loyal and honest too (15:22).

Wise men listen; fools refuse to do so

This contrast is particularly important as it reveals the way to escape from foolishness and to gain wisdom. The key is in verses 20, 25 and 27. Fools talk too much. They do not listen. The wise are willing to listen to advice and even to rebukes.

37.
Forsake superficiality; seek wisdom and righteousness

Please read Proverbs 20:1-30

Drunkenness, a king's wrath, peaceableness, sluggards, hidden intentions, faithfulness, righteousness, justice, depravity, honest weights, children's actions, the Creator, laziness, bartering, wise speech, pledges, fraud, advice, gossips, rebellion, quickly gained riches, vengeance, honest weights, God's sovereignty, rash vows, justice, purity, faithfulness, youth and age, punishment

Here we consider all thirty proverbs in this chapter of Proverbs.

'Wine is a mocker and beer a brawler; whoever is led astray by them is not wise' (20:1).
> *Synthetic:* **'wine ... and beer'** / **'whoever is led astray by them'**
> Alcohol attacks; so I advise,
> 'Leave it out, or you won't be wise.'

Here is the book's first warning against alcohol abuse. A fuller treatment comes in 23:20-21,29-35. Here wine and beer are personified, the point being that alcohol can turn you into a **'mocker'** or a **'brawler'**. Acting as a depressant, alcohol slows down the body's normal functions and can lead to egotistic and aggressive attitudes that are not normally present. Just as drunks find difficulty walking in a straight line, so alcohol leads astray. Over-consumption is incompatible with wisdom. It is frightening to think what an effect excessive intake of alcohol has on people. All sorts of social ills can be traced to the abuse of this potentially good gift.

Among its '100 heroes of the 20th Century', *Time Magazine* included the self-effacing founder of self-help organization *Alcoholics Anonymous*, Bill Wilson, a man described by Aldous Huxley as 'the greatest social architect of our century'. Bill's problems began when, as a twenty-two-year-old second lieutenant in the army, he was offered his first drink. Although he had had a drunken father and as a child had been exposed to the temperance movement, he believed that he had 'found the elixir of life'. It was some seventeen years later, in 1934, that he finally quit drinking for good. By then he had destroyed his health and career and he and his wife were in great financial need. In custody for the fourth time at a Manhattan hospital, he had a religious experience that led to the founding, with Dr Robert Smith, of Alcoholics Anonymous and the introduction of its famous twelve-step programme the following year. Certain tenets of the organization are open to criticism. For example, the idea that there is a disease called alcoholism is highly questionable. However, the underlying notion that 'The key to sobriety was a change of heart' cannot be doubted. It is a foolish heart that is led astray by alcohol or other drugs.

Arnot gives the parable of a voracious, many-limbed creature sucking up an apparently excellent source of sustenance in the form of blood. When it is discovered that the creature is actually sucking the blood from one of its own limbs, the plan to put a stop to this is overruled by the money men, who argue, 'A third of the animal's sustenance comes from that opening; if you stop it, he will die!' Thus governments justify their high taxes on alcohol regardless of the cost in human misery.

What is said here of alcohol has an application to the abuse of other drugs also.

'A king's wrath is like the roar of a lion; he who angers him forfeits his life' (20:2).
Synonymous: **'wrath'** / **'angers'**
Simile: **'king's wrath'** / **'roar of a lion'**
A ruler's wrath is like a roar; raise his rage and relinquish all reserves.

The first half of this proverb reproduces the first line of a contrasting proverb in 19:12, but with a different word for anger. Here, instead of a contrast, the reality of arousing a king's wrath is followed through. In those days Eastern despots had absolute power, and arousing their wrath could easily mean death (see 16:14). Some who would not dare anger their boss or their friends seem to have no concern that God, the Great King, is angry with the wicked every day.

'It is to a man's honour to avoid strife, but every fool is quick to quarrel' (20:3).
Contrast: **'a man'** / **'every fool'**
It's to your honour if you avoid strife,
But fools are quick to go for a knife.

Many proverbs call for humility, patience and the avoidance of quarrelling (see 13:10; 14:17,29; 15:18; 16:32; and especially 17:14,19; 19:11. See also comments on 13:15). We can contrast Gideon favourably with Jephthah in this respect (Judg. 8:1-3; 12:1-6). Godly people are to be peaceable and peacemaking as far as possible. They do not go around looking for trouble. Paul tells Timothy, 'Don't have anything to do with foolish and stupid arguments, because you know they produce quarrels. And the Lord's servant must not quarrel; instead, he must be kind to everyone, able to teach, not resentful. Those who oppose him he must gently instruct, in the hope that God will grant them repentance leading them to a knowledge of the truth, and that they will come to their senses and escape from the trap of the devil, who has taken them captive to do his will' (2 Tim. 2:23-26).

Avoiding strife, resolving issues, reconciling enemies, bringing harmony — such activities mark an honourable man.

'A sluggard does not plough in season; so at harvest time he looks but finds nothing' (20:4).
Synthetic: **'in season'** / **'at harvest'**

Here is the sluggard again. It is particularly his failure to work when the time is right that is in mind, with its inevitable consequences (cf. 10:5). The word **'season'** could be translated 'cold season' explaining, perhaps, the sluggard's problem. Paul urges Timothy to 'Preach the Word; be prepared in season and out of season' (2 Tim. 4:2). The work of preparation is always demanding, but there can be no reaping without prior sowing. Ecclesiastes 10:10 makes a similar point in a different way:

If the axe is dull
    and its edge unsharpened,
more strength is needed
    but skill will bring success.

Students who fail to revise for examinations, decorators who fail to prepare walls before painting, preachers who preach without proper preparation — all are asking for trouble. Similarly, without falling into preparationism, we must say that telling people how to be saved when they do not even know they need saving is likely to produce only spurious converts if there is any response at all.

'The purposes of a man's heart are deep waters, but a man of understanding draws them out' (20:5).
> *Synthetic:* **'purposes of a man's heart'** / **'draws them out'**
> *Simile:* **'purposes of a man's heart'** / **'deep waters'**
> Desires dwell deep, but discerning delvers discover them.

The deep-water simile has already been used in Proverbs 18:4. Here we learn that one of the marks of wisdom is that it is able to draw out **'the purposes of a man's heart'**, like a bucket being cast into a deep well. (Every question is a turn of the windlass, says Plumptre). We have all been impressed with insights into human nature expressed by others wiser than ourselves. We too can have such abilities if we learn to be wise. The Master, of course, is the Lord Jesus himself. As we read of him talking to Nicodemus in John 3 and the Samaritan woman in John 4, and dealing with the rich young ruler in Matthew 19, we see an expert at work. Not everything deep in a man's heart ought to be drawn out, but sometimes the drawing out of his purpose can be a useful exercise.

'Many a man claims to have unfailing love, but a faithful man who can find?' (20:6).
> *Contrast:* **'man [who] claims to have unfailing love'** / **'faithful man'**
> Many say they're very kind,
> But constancy is hard to find.

The proverbs often alert us to the fact that things are not always what they seem. Sometimes it is obvious that a person's claims are false. The parody of the entertainer constantly talking of what he does for charity is a standing joke. Others are more subtle. Are we as faithful to others and to God as we claim to be, or as much as we imply? There are plenty of frauds out there, so beware. A naturally agreeable temperament is not the same as true faithfulness.

'The righteous man leads a blameless life; blessed are his children after him' (20:7).
   Synthetic / beatitude: **'righteous man'** / **'his children'**

Some children see little of their parents from day to day because their parents want money to give the children certain advantages in life. What all parents need to understand is that righteous living is the thing that is most likely to be an advantage to their children in the years to come. What Mum and Dad *do* before their closest critics is ultimately more important than anything they can say. What a glorious future there is for the righteous! (This proverb has affinities with 13:22 and 14:11.)

'When a king sits on his throne to judge, he winnows out all evil with his eyes' (20:8).
   Synthetic: **'king sits ... to judge'** / **'he winnows out all evil'**
   Simile: **'to judge'** / **'winnows'**

As in verse 2 and in Proverbs 16, the work of the king is before us again. Part of his work is to winnow out evil, just as a farmer winnows out chaff from his corn. Traditionally winnowing is done by lifting the threshed grain into the air and letting the wind scatter the chaff. The good remains; the bad is carried off on the breeze. The king can tell the difference between good and bad. He retains the good, but scatters the wicked. The idea of his doing it **'with his eyes'** indicates that he must be alert to what is going on in his kingdom. He will have his spies everywhere. The application is not only for civil government, but for family and church government too. Here spies are inappropriate, but open eyes and listening ears are vital. The idea is expanded in verse 26. A day is coming when the great King will sit on his throne to judge the world. After you are winnowed what will remain?

'Who can say, 'I have kept my heart pure; I am clean and without sin'? (20:9).
Synonymous: **'heart pure'** / **'clean and without sin'**

The answer to this question is clearly 'No one', especially in view of the king being on his throne. Human depravity is taught in many places in Scripture. See, for example, the Old Testament quotations in Romans 3. The observation here is more experiential than theological. Proverbs tends to concentrate on individual sins rather than on sin in general. It also shows how foolish sin is, rather than how wicked. Sandwiched between proverbs regarding winnowing out evil from a kingdom and honesty in business, the context suggests the need for fear and humility.

'Differing weights and differing measures — the LORD detests them both' (20:10).
Synonymous: **'differing weights'** / **'differing measures'**
Lord detests

Literally this proverb begins, 'A stone and a stone, an ephah and an ephah...' This verse and the very similar proverb in verse 23 are, in turn, very much like the first part of Proverbs 11:1. The addition here is the reference to **'measures'**. The proximity to verse 8 reminds us of the series in 16:10-12.

'Even a child is known by his actions, by whether his conduct is pure and right' (20:11).
Synonymous: **'actions'** / **'conduct'**
Kids are known by what they do,
Whether their actions are right and true.

As in verses 6 and 9, the fact that what people do does not necessarily match what they say is underlined here. With children, we pay less attention to what they say, and more to what they do. '**A child is known by his actions**' — good or bad. What is true of children is also true of adults. By the manner in which we live, we are all weaving a pattern that will one day reveal a complete picture.

'**Ears that hear and eyes that see — the** LORD **has made them both**' (20:12).
   Synthetic: '**ears ... eyes**' / '**the** LORD **has made**'

'**Ears that hear**' are obedient ears. '**Eyes that see**' are understanding eyes. Thus, beyond the obvious fact that our Creator gave us our eyes and ears is the equally important fact that it is he who enables us to be righteous and wise. Further, there is no excuse for disobedience or ignorance. We have only to use our senses to discover the truth. Too often we close our eyes and block our ears. It is only in Christ that this wilful deafness and blindness are removed. Hence Wesley's paradoxical invitation: 'Hear him, ye deaf ... ye blind, behold your Saviour come.'

'**Do not love sleep or you will grow poor; stay awake and you will have food to spare**' (20:13).
   Synonymous: '**do not love sleep**' / '**stay awake**'
   Command (negative)

Here the theme of laziness is given concrete form with a warning against loving sleep (it is like Proverbs 6:9-11). '**Stay awake**', is the promise, '**and you will have food to spare.**' This is the positive side of 6:11. It reminds one of English proverbs such as, 'Early to bed and early to rise makes a man healthy, wealthy and wise'; 'The early bird catches the worm,' or 'He who works before dawn will soon be his own master.' An interesting one says:

He that will thrive must rise at five,
He that has thriven may lie until seven,
But he that will never thrive may lie 'til eleven.

There are, of course, other factors involved in gaining wealth, but diligence is a major one.

' "It's no good, it's no good!" says the buyer; then off he goes and boasts about his purchase' (20:14).
   Synthetic: **'It's no good'** / **'off he goes and boasts'**

Now we are in the marketplace. The bargain-hunter is pointing out the faults of the item he wants to buy. He is apparently unimpressed with the salesman's claims. When he gets the item home, however, he boasts about his bargain buy. The retail system in modern Britain is not favourable to bartering, but I remember how my mother would always ask for something to be knocked off the price if she found a shop-soiled item, and there is a little leeway for barter even in the High Street. This is an observational proverb and so we are not given any firm help on where such shrewd practice becomes sinful. No doubt the seller is well aware of what is going on and has purposely set his original price high. The main lesson is again not to be superficial and not to take everything people say at face value.

Perhaps we can more specifically learn that criticisms are often made from envy. An English proverb says that 'He who speaks ill of the mare would buy her.' It is sometimes in a man's interest to downplay something in order to manoeuvre himself into a position to take it. It is not unknown for a company to talk down the share price of a rival company, only to swoop in and buy it. This is also one reason why unbelievers at one and the same time both oppose and desire Christian faith. From the other side there is the warning to professing

Christians: 'See that no one is sexually immoral, or is godless like Esau, who for a single meal sold his inheritance rights as the oldest son' (Heb. 12:16).

'Gold there is, and rubies in abundance, but lips that speak knowledge are a rare jewel' (20:15).
   Simile: **'gold ... rubies ... a rare jewel'** / **'lips that speak knowledge'**

Wise speech is frequently commended — here with a simile. What a rare and precious thing to hear someone speaking wisely! When you have opportunity to hear such language grab it with both hands. Think of Mary sitting at the Master's feet. Take time every day to read the Word of God. We also must cultivate the **'rare jewel'** of **'lips that speak knowledge'**. Pay more attention to how you sound and less to how you look!

'Take the garment of one who puts up security for a stranger; hold it in pledge if he does it for a wayward woman' (20:16).
   Synonymous: **'take the garment'** / **'hold it in pledge'**

Here we focus on a different role in the world of pledges — not putting up security for someone in need (which must not be entered into except with extreme caution — see, e.g., 6:1-5), but taking something from someone as security. Again the message is the same — be very cautious. With **'a stranger'**, someone you do not know, or **'a wayward woman'**, someone you cannot trust, make sure you get some security. This is a bad risk otherwise. Taking unnecessary risks is no part of doing good in this world (27:13 is very similar). Believers are to be as gentle as doves, but also as wise as snakes. It is frightening to see how willing some are to accept certain claims with no demand for evidence. Often great commitments are made to individuals whose authenticity is very dubious indeed.

'Food gained by fraud tastes sweet to a man, but he ends up with a mouth full of gravel' (20:17).
Contrast: **'tastes sweet' / 'mouth full of gravel'**
Food fraudulently obtained may taste great,
But it will turn to gravel once it's ate.

The devil presents sin to us as attractive and exciting, something to be desired. Sinners often go on believing this for the rest of their lives. However, sometimes even in this life they come to see that sin can offer nothing good. The aftertaste is too foul to warrant the experience. Here we picture someone involved in some sort of fraud in order to gain food. It tastes sweet at first, but in the end it is like gravel.

This reminds me of a story a preacher once told of watching a workman in his garden stealing fruit from a tree — a mixed plum and pear grafted onto the same rootstock. The look on the workman's face as he bit into the sour fruit was a picture. Think of a child accustomed to dipping a wet finger into what he thinks is the sugar and finding salt instead. Achan and Gehazi are obvious biblical examples.

A similar sequence of events unfolds in 5:3-4 and 9:17-18. Maybe the sexual arena is in mind here too. Certainly spiritual adultery is again the target. The delights of theological modernism, post-modern experientialism and other deviations soon leave a bad taste for those tempted by them.

'Make plans by seeking advice; if you wage war, obtain guidance' (20:18).
Synonymous command (positive): **'make plans' / 'if you wage war'**

Already in verse 4 we have been reminded of the importance of preparation. We are never very far from the subject of teachability either. The importance of seeking advice is underlined in Proverbs 12:15 and many other places (the nearest to this proverb is probably 11:14). It is our pride that keeps us from seeking advice. If there is a war, get help from every historian, military strategist, army commander and undercover agent you can! On the back of my copy of Sun Tzu's *The art of war*, a translation by Tao Hanzhang of a Chinese classic written some 2,500 years ago, a sobering observation is made: 'The western world might have been spared many of the horrors of the great wars of the 20th Century, if the central message of Sun Tzu's philosophy, in which means (warfare) and ends (political goals) are kept in balance, had been observed.' In the long war against Satan believers need all the advice they can get, both ancient and modern. A thorough study of church history should be a standard component in the preparation of ministers.

'A gossip betrays a confidence; so avoid a man who talks too much' (20:19).
  Synthetic command (negative): **'gossip betrays' / 'so avoid'**
  Gossips secrets will betray;
  So avoid a man with too much to say.

Gossip is in the sights again here. This time the advice is to avoid such people because, although you may get some pleasure from hearing what they have to say about others, their willingness to betray a confidence may have repercussions for you one day. A similar prohibition is made with regard to the hot-tempered in 22:24. In the New Testament Paul commands: 'Do not be yoked together with unbelievers. For what do righteousness and wickedness have in common? Or what fellowship can light have with darkness? What harmony is there between Christ and Belial? What does a believer have in common with an unbeliever? What agreement is there between the temple of God and idols? … "Therefore come out from them and be separate," says the Lord. "Touch no unclean thing, and I will receive you"' (2 Cor. 6:14-17).

We live in an age that recognizes the high value of confidentiality perhaps more than any other and scores of gadgets are available for covert surveillance of those determined secretly to take advantage of us. At the same time there seems to be a limitless supply of people with no regard for confidentiality or loyalty who are willing to sell their 'kiss-and-tell' stories to the highest bidder for publication in the newspapers. Such developments should alert us to the foolishness of supposing that off-the-record revelations and 'hush-hush' secrets will not be exposed to the cold light of day. We are wisest to share such things only with those whom we can definitely trust.

'If a man curses his father or mother, his lamp will be snuffed out in pitch darkness' (20:20).
Synthetic: **'curses' / 'lamp will be snuffed out'**

In Proverbs 19:26 the offence was robbing parents. Here a man **'curses his father or mother'**. A severe warning is made against such outrageous and ungrateful behaviour. We ought always to speak of our parents with the utmost respect, whether they are living or dead. This is what the law says, both in the Ten Commandments and, more specifically, in Exodus 21:17. A man's **'lamp'** is his life. Today the law may do nothing about such cursing but God will one day. The proverb has a wider application with regard to all who, literally or metaphorically, have borne us and nurtured us at their breasts.

'An inheritance quickly gained at the beginning will not be blessed at the end' (20:21).
Synthetic: **'at the beginning' / 'at the end'**

Money gained fast
Will never last.

Unlike Proverbs 13:11, which concerns money gained dishonestly, this proverb warns against **'an inheritance quickly
gained'** by any means. It is in the light of this factor that some
rich men have tried to bequeath their wealth in a controlled
manner, especially when those who will inherit have not yet
reached the age of majority. They want to avoid the 'too much
too young' syndrome that blights some young lives. This is
also one of the biblical arguments against the national lottery
(or Lotto) and similar enterprises. The idea of having a huge
influx of cash seems very attractive, but so often it does not
work. Such wealth can split families, lead to dangerous excess, or simply overwhelm. Even where none of those things
happens, the responsibility that such wealth suddenly brings is
so great in the light of the Judgement Day that what seems
like a blessing can easily become a curse. Jesus' parable of the
prodigal son is an acting out of the principle here, but with a
great word of hope for those who have already fallen.

**'Do not say, "I'll pay you back for this wrong!" Wait for
the LORD, and he will deliver you'** (20:22).
     Synthetic commands (negative/positive): **'I'll pay you back'**
/ **'Wait for the LORD'**

Personal revenge is condemned in Scripture. The law is against
it (Lev. 19:18), as is the Lord Jesus (Matt. 5:39-41) and the
rest of the New Testament: 'Do not repay anyone evil for evil...
Do not take revenge, my friends, but leave room for God's
wrath, for it is written: "It is mine to avenge; I will repay,"
says the Lord' (Rom. 12:17-19, quoting Deut. 32:35). 'Make
sure that nobody pays back wrong for wrong, but always try

to be kind to each other and to everyone else' (1 Thess. 5:15). 'Do not repay evil with evil or insult with insult, but with blessing, because to this you were called so that you may inherit a blessing' (1 Peter 3:9).

In Proverbs 17:13 we have a proverb about paying back evil for good; here it is a question of paying back evil for evil. Both are wrong. Rather we should **'wait for the Lord'** and not for vengeance, but for deliverance. The highest point in the series of proverbs on this theme is reached in 25:21.

'The Lord detests differing weights, and dishonest scales do not please him' (20:23).
>*Synonymous:* **'differing weights'** / **'dishonest scales'**
>Lord detests

This is similar to verse 10 and other proverbs on the same subject. Here the context is more that of personal responsibility than state legislation.

'A man's steps are directed by the Lord. How then can anyone understand his own way?' (20:24).
>*Synthetic:* **'directed by the Lord'** / **'understand'**

Again God's sovereignty is reiterated (see 16:1,9; 19:21). The lesson drawn with this rhetorical question is that we need constantly to depend on him. 'The arm of flesh will fail you; you dare not trust your own.'

'It is a trap for a man to dedicate something rashly and only later to consider his vows' (20:25).
>*Synthetic:* **'dedicate'** / **'later ... consider'**
>To devote thoughtlessly, and only later think,
>Is into a trap to slither and to sink.

The previous verse must not be made an excuse for rashness. The story of Jephthah (Judg. 11:30-39) is the most obvious one to illustrate this proverb. Impulsiveness is incompatible with wisdom. This is a species of the zeal without knowledge spoken of in Proverbs 19:2. It illustrates what is meant by saying, 'A fool's mouth is his undoing, and his lips are a snare to his soul' (18:7). As we are told in Ecclesiastes, 'When you make a vow to God, do not delay in fulfilling it. He has no pleasure in fools; fulfil your vow. It is better not to vow than to make a vow and not fulfil it. Do not let your mouth lead you into sin. And do not protest to the temple messenger, "My vow was a mistake." Why should God be angry at what you say and destroy the work of your hands?' (Eccles. 5:4-6).

Broken promises are ugly things. We should always take care when making promises. Vows made in storms are forgotten in times of calm. An acre of performance is worth twenty of the land of promise.

'A wise king winnows out the wicked; he drives the threshing wheel over them' (20:26).

Synonymous / similes: **'winnows'** / **'drives the threshing wheel over'**

The idea in verse 8 is expanded into a full-blown simile drawn from threshing and winnowing (assuming the NIV is right to add the word **'threshing'** before the word **'wheel'**). Threshing actually precedes winnowing. Threshing divides corn from husk; winnowing separates them. It shows us a man who is very serious about getting at the truth. He cannot be fooled. First, he works at distinguishing evil, then at removing it. Here is a model for us and a warning against trying to get away with evil deeds. We have moved from God's omnipotence to his omniscience.

'The lamp of the Lᴏʀᴅ searches the spirit of a man; it searches out his inmost being' (20:27).

> *Simile:* **'lamp of the Lᴏʀᴅ'** / **'searches out'**
> The Lord's lamp — it hunts down men's hearts;
> It penetrates their inmost parts.

What is hinted at in verse 26 is stated more plainly here. What is **'the lamp of the Lᴏʀᴅ'** that **'searches the spirit of a man'** and **'searches out his inmost being'**? This is debated. God himself is compared to a lamp in 2 Samuel 22:29: 'You are my lamp, O Lᴏʀᴅ; the Lᴏʀᴅ turns my darkness into light' (see also Rev. 21:23; 22:5). But how does he apply his light? The conscience is a favourite contender. The conscience is man's spirit, but it is man's spirit in the act of self-reflection. Perhaps the Word of God is a more likely candidate, although again for it to work the conscience must be properly informed. 'Your word is a lamp to my feet and a light for my path' (Ps. 119:105). In Proverbs 6:23 we are told, 'For these commands are a lamp, this teaching is a light.' In other words, this very book of Proverbs which we are studying has the power to search out our inmost beings. It deals with our souls.

'Love and faithfulness keep a king safe; through love his throne is made secure' (20:28).

> *Synonymous:* **'love and faithfulness'** / **'love'**

This verse opposes the idea that the key to success in leadership is a ruthless streak with regard to wickedness. With that there must be, as with the Lord himself, no shortage of **'love and faithfulness'** (the words are most often used in connection with God and his covenant). If those who depend on you, however young or few they be, think you are not devoted to them (in state, family or church) problems are inevitable.

'The glory of young men is their strength, grey hair the splendour of the old' (20:29).

Contrast: **'glory of young men'** / **'splendour of the old'**
A young man's glory is that he is strong;
His grey hair's splendour is the old man's song.

This beautiful proverb is designed to create understanding across the generation divide. The applications are many. They chiefly counter the envy, impatience and contempt that sometimes exist between old and young. There is also an implied encouragement to make a sensible assessment of your gifts, to be content with them and to use them. The young have no reason to covet the responsibilities of the grey heads; the old do not need to attempt to show off how strong they are. There is something disturbing about old men who wish they were seventeen again, or fourteen-year-old girls trying to look twenty-five. The young should not be layabouts; the old should be ready to share their experience.

Another lesson may be that of knowing where to turn for help. If you need help carrying furniture, look to the young; if you want advice on bringing up children, the grey heads have more experience. The truth is that in many areas we need a good mixture of old and young, of native strength and long experience. A church, or any organization for that matter, is blessed if it has a good age range.

'Blows and wounds cleanse away evil, and beatings purge the inmost being' (20:30).

Synonymous: **'blows and wounds'** / **'beatings'**
Blows cleanse sin; beatings cure souls.

The anti-corporal-punishment brigade are in the ascendancy in the West at the present time, but we need to recognize that, just as some stains in clothing will not budge without a good deal of rubbing, so sometimes physical punishment is necessary to remove evil. At times there has to be physical punishment, be it in war, criminal justice or family government. It is part of wisdom to know when such things are necessary.

Of course, if you are a Christian, you already know that 'Without the shedding of blood there is no remission of sins,' and you are trusting in the one who bled and died and suffered in your place. It is the **'blows and wounds'** that he suffered that can **'cleanse away evil'** from my soul. It is the **'beatings'** he suffered that can **'purge the inmost being'** of my person. It is that alone.

What these thirty proverbs teach us

Taking these proverbs together, we learn several things.

Verse 14 reminds us of the importance of *perspective*. The buyer says the item is no good; the seller that it is. They say this for their own reasons.

Both old and young have their assets (20:29). Sadly, many do not see this and try to pretend they are older (by smoking or drinking) or younger than they are (with dyed hair or face-lifts). Such pretence is common enough and *we cannot always take people at face value* (20:6). This is why *we must avoid being superficial* in our approach to things. 'The purposes of a man's heart are deep waters.' It is only 'a man of understanding' who draws them out (20:5).

More than that, *God's Word can actually shine into a person's very soul* (20:27). If 'Even a child is known by his actions, by whether his conduct is pure and right' (20:11), just a little shining of that lamp can reveal the true situation in our hearts. 'Who can say, "I have kept my heart pure; I am clean and without sin"?' (20:9). The truth is that we have all sinned and done many foolish things. The moment God's lamp shines in our hearts we know it.

Verse 15 reminds us, 'Gold there is, and rubies in abundance, but lips that speak knowledge are a rare jewel.'

Here *the foolishness of sin* is exposed once more. The focus is on a number of things:

Alcohol abuse. To abuse alcohol is foolish (20:1).

Argumentativeness. Eagerness to quarrel is a mark of the fool (20:3).

Laziness. The sluggard is a species of fool (20:4,13).

Dishonesty. God hates dishonesty (20:10,23).

Deceit. Those who seek advantages by deceit end up with nothing (20:17).

Self-confidence. Refusing to consult others is a form of pride (20:18).

Gossip. Contact with gossip in any form brings danger (20:19)

Eagerness for easy money. The warning in verse 21 needs to be heeded.

A vengeful spirit. Vengeance is God's work, not ours (20:22).

Making rash promises. Verse 16 advises care with pledges. Also, 'It is a trap for a man to dedicate something rashly and only later to consider his vows' (20:25).

Rebellion. He will judge those who are rebels (20:30).

In verse 7 we read, 'The righteous man leads a blameless life; blessed are his children after him.' But who is righteous? There are many claims to righteousness (20:6), but none have it (20:9) when a careful examination is made (20:8,26-27). On the Day of Judgement, there will be no hiding our deficiencies. If on earth, 'A king's wrath is like the roar of a lion,' and 'he who angers him forfeits his life' (20:2), what will it be to stand before God? Sin must be dealt with severely if evil is to be removed (20:30). However, the King is marked by 'love and faithfulness' and he has provided a way that, through 'blows and wounds' falling on his Son in place of sinners, all who trust in him can be cleansed from evil and purged within. All he requires is that we trust in him. He has given us ears to hear this message and eyes to see its truth (20:12). Our steps are all directed by him (20:24). All that we need to do is to bow down before him and accept his Word.

38.
How to escape eternal ruin

Please read Proverbs 21:1-31

*Kings' hearts, motives, obedience and sacrifice, pride, diligence,
fortunes made dishonestly, violence, deviousness, wives,
wickedness, punishment as a deterrent, the Righteous One,
charity, bribery, justice, deviation, wastefulness, wickedness and
righteousness, wives, wisdom and foolishness, righteousness and
love, wise men, speech, arrogance, sluggards, giving, hypocrisy,
false witness, wicked bravado, God's sovereign wisdom, God's
sovereign power*

Here we consider the whole of Proverbs 21.

**'The king's heart is in the hand of the LORD; he directs it
like a watercourse wherever he pleases'** (21:1).
 Synonymous: **'in the hand of the LORD'** / **'he directs it'**
 Simile: **'king's heart'** / **'watercourse'**
 Kings' hearts are in God's hands;
 By this means he waters his lands.

A **'watercourse'** is a man-made waterway, an irrigation canal,
as used in certain types of farming. By this means a man can

control the raising of his crops in a way that is not possible when simply relying on the rains. So here the sovereignty of the Lord is again asserted, as it is at the end of the chapter (cf. 19:21; 20:24). As one writer put it, 'Kings are more entirely in the hand of God than subjects are in the hands of kings.' If the Lord controls the highest, he also controls everyone else. The **'king's heart'** is in the first instance the heart of Solomon, but it is clear from elsewhere in Scripture that what is said here applies to foreign kings too. The heart of each is in God's hands and he directs it **'wherever he pleases'** in order to water his gardens. Tiglath-Pileser, Cyrus and Artaxerxes are obvious examples of the latter (see Isa. 10:6-7; 41:2-4; Ezra 7:21). Think too of the hardening of Pharaoh's heart and of the census decreed by Augustus. This is one reason why we can pray with confidence for rulers, even rulers hostile to the faith, as we are commanded to do. Pray for streams of good from all of them.

> **All a man's ways seem right to him,**
>   **but the LORD weighs the heart.**
> **To do what is right and just**
>   **is more acceptable to the LORD than sacrifice**
>   (21:2-3).

These two proverbs are on the same lines. They focus on what the Lord is looking at — the inner man, not the outer man, and mercy rather than sacrifice. David was one who well understood these things (see Ps. 51:6,16-17).

Contrast: **'a man's ways'** / **'heart'**
Men think they're right in every way,
But the heart is what the Lord will weigh.

Proverbs 16:2 is almost the same as the words here in verse 2 about God weighing motives. In both cases the proverb is preceded by one that speaks about God's sovereignty. Motives are what matter to God (see also 16:25; 20:6; 30:12). The problem with the wicked is that 'In his own eyes he flatters himself too much to detect or hate his sin' (Ps. 36:2). The Lord says to the Pharisees, 'You are the ones who justify yourselves in the eyes of men, but God knows your hearts. What is highly valued among men is detestable in God's sight' (Luke 16:15).

Paul understood this well. He says that he cares very little how the Corinthians judge him, or how 'any human court' decides. 'Indeed,' he says, 'I do not even judge myself. My conscience is clear, but that does not make me innocent. It is the Lord who judges me' (1 Cor. 4:3-4).

'To do what is right and just is more acceptable to the LORD than sacrifice' (21:3).
   Contrast (better than): **'to do what is right'** / **'sacrifice'**

The point of this verse has been made in a similar way in Proverbs 15:8. Jesus himself highlighted the saying from Hosea, 'For I desire mercy, not sacrifice' (Matt. 9:13; 12:7, quoting Hosea 6:6, which adds 'and acknowledgement of God rather than burnt offerings'). Isaiah 1:11-17 is a famous passage on this subject (see also 1 Sam. 15:22; Prov. 21:27).

'Haughty eyes and a proud heart, the lamp of the wicked, are sin!' (21:4).
   Synthetic: **'haughty eyes … proud heart'** / **'sin'**
   Simile: **'haughty eyes … proud heart'** / **'lamp of the wicked'**

The NIV follows the Greek version here and uses **'lamp'**. The Hebrew has 'ploughing'. There are several warnings in the book against pride (e.g., 6:17; 8:13). Often it is pride that is at the root of the self-confidence and hypocrisy that are spoken against in verses 2 and 3. There is something seriously wrong when a man's hope is mere pride. Jesus says, 'See to it, then, that the light within you is not darkness' (Luke 11:35). The Puritan Henry Smith addresses pride when he says, 'Many sins have done wickedly but thou surmountest them all.' His argument is that, whereas other sins are against oneself or others, 'The proud man sets himself against God.' Like Satan himself, pride sets itself up as equal to God, or greater than him.

'The plans of the diligent lead to profit as surely as haste leads to poverty' (21:5).

Contrast: **'plans of the diligent'** / **'haste'**

Diligent designs are to profit as hurried haste to poverty.

The note of 'diligence' is struck yet again. There is no lack of zeal in sounding out this message. Here we see that diligence is not the same as **'haste'**. The Bible's doctrine of providence is never fatalistic. It does not preclude our laying plans. The emphasis here is on planning ahead. 'More haste, less speed,' says the English proverb. 'Hasten slowly,' the Romans cautioned. The sort of haste in mind here is primarily the get-rich-quick variety — not so much slapdash, as ill thought out. This is why it leads, proverbially, to poverty. Sadly, so many will not even take the time to understand the gospel. If it cannot give them instant results, they do not want to know. And so they are doomed to eternal poverty.

'A fortune made by a lying tongue is a fleeting vapour and a deadly snare' (21:6).

Synthetic simile: **'fortune made by a lying tongue'** / **'vapour ... snare'**

Dishonest gold — disappearing air or a deadly snare.

A reference to Proverbs 13:11, which says, 'Dishonest money dwindles away, but he who gathers money little by little makes it grow,' shows how this proverb and the last are connected (in the reverse order). Here the getting rich quick is done by means of deceit, as in 10:2. This is as likely to fail as the previous scheme. The religion that some espouse is basically dishonest. It can bring them no good. Not only is it unsatisfactory in life, but it also leads to certain death. There are many in this world living a lie. They are building on sand. The NIV's **'deadly snare'** here could be 'a deadly seeking'.

'The violence of the wicked will drag them away, for they refuse to do what is right' (21:7).
Synthetic: **'will drag them away'** / **'refuse to do what is right'**

Another way of attempting to get rich quickly is the use of violence. As in verse 6, the note of judgement is sounded again here. The reciprocal nature of violence has been underscored previously (in 1:8-19 and other places). Jesus says that 'All who draw the sword will die by the sword' (Matt. 26:52). It is important that we remember such truths the moment we are tempted to resort to violence in order to bring about change. The violent think that their violence guarantees victory, but their very temper is dragging them away to hell.

'The way of the guilty is devious, but the conduct of the innocent is upright' (21:8).
Contrast: **'way of the guilty'** / **'conduct of the innocent'**
Guilty goings are crooked; blameless behaviour is correct.

As we have noted before, there is something crooked and perverse about the guilty, while the life of the innocent is straightforward. Amid their twists and turns and strange man-oeuvres, the devious get tied up in the rigging and make ship-wreck, while the righteous sail through, sometimes enduring storms, but always holding a straight course as best they can.

In his best Methodist style, Charles Wesley pleads with the devious:

> Weary souls, that wander wide
> From the central point of bliss,
> Turn to Jesus crucified,
> Fly to those dear wounds of his:
> Sink into the purple flood;
> Rise into the life of God.

'Better to live on a corner of the roof than share a house with a quarrelsome wife' (21:9).
Contrast (better than): **'to live on a corner of the roof'** / **'share a house'**
Better live at the top of the house,
Than sit downstairs with a quarrelsome spouse.

Translated into modern Western cultural terms, this proverb says that it would be better to be sleeping in the spare room (which is what the flat roofs of houses were used for at times) than to be downstairs sharing the house with a wife who is quarrelsome. This proverb is repeated in 25:24 and the senti-ment is similar to that of 21:19 and 12:4 (see also 19:13; 27:15-16.). Such a verse will give us no help on the question of divorce. Rather, while no doubt making clear how impor-tant a good match is, it illustrates the miseries of a false human wisdom that simply nags away with no ultimately satisfying answers. Arnot uses the illustration of two ships chained to-gether in stormy weather. More closely combined in some way, or completely apart, there is hope but chained together, 'They will rasp each other's sides off and tear open each other's heart and go down together.'

> **The wicked man craves evil;**
> **his neighbour gets no mercy from him.**
> **When a mocker is punished, the simple gain wisdom;**
> **when a wise man is instructed, he gets knowledge.**
> **The Righteous One takes note of the house of the**
> **wicked**
> **and brings the wicked to ruin.**
> **If a man shuts his ears to the cry of the poor,**
> **he too will cry out and not be answered.**
> **A gift given in secret soothes anger,**
> **and a bribe concealed in the cloak pacifies great**
> **wrath.**
> **When justice is done, it brings joy to the righteous**
> **but terror to evildoers**
>
> (21:10-15).

We can link all six of these proverbs together under the broad heading of justice. They deal with its dire necessity, deterrent value and sure triumph; the danger of neglecting it, its corruption and its effect on the righteous and evildoers.

Contrast: **'wicked man' / 'his neighbour'** (21:10)

Sin is the result, not only of weakness, but also of rapaciousness. The 'cravings of sinful man' constitute one of the three chief elements of worldliness (1 John 2:16). The wicked cannot go on without such sins. Although God's clear command is to love one's neighbour, the wicked refuse to show mercy. They see their neighbours only as obstacles to the fulfilment of their own selfish desires: 'What causes fights and quarrels

among you? Don't they come from your desires that battle
within you? You want something but don't get it. You kill and
covet, but you cannot have what you want. You quarrel and
fight' (James 4:1-2).

Such a proverb stands as a warning to us and shows why
justice must be firm and swift. It is a dire necessity.

Synonymous: **'when a mocker is punished' / 'when a
wise man is instructed'** (21:11)
Punish mockers — the simple in wisdom grow;
Give instruction to the wise and they will know.

Following on from verse 10, learning from mistakes is again
the subject. If justice prevails then three things will occur:

1. The mockers, with their closed minds, will be
punished.

2. The open-minded simple will be enlightened. If
not, they will assume they can get away with mockery.
Punishment has a deterrent value, as is made clear in
Deuteronomy 13:11 and elsewhere in the law.

3. The wise man, though he may not need such graphic
lessons, will still be instructed.

Knowing this is part of wisdom (A similar theme is found in
19:25).

Synthetic: **'takes note' / 'brings to ruin'** (21:12)
The house of the wicked the Righteous One's noting;
Soon down to ruin the wicked he'll bring.

'The Righteous One' could be someone less than God, but
here it is probably referring to God himself. He does two things:
he **'takes note of the house of the wicked'**; then he **'brings**

the wicked to ruin'. It is the gap between those two that gives the wicked a false sense of confidence about the future. It is misplaced. Again the lesson comes home that crime does not pay.

> *Synthetic:* **'if a man ...' / 'he too ...'** (21:13)
> Shut your ears to the cry of the poor
> And then when you cry out, God will ignore.

This is similar to other proverbs such as 19:17; 22:9; 28:27 (see also 14:31; 24:11-12). There is never any excuse for closing our ears to the cry of the poor. God does not, nor should those who follow him. The warning here is that if we do such a thing then we lose any moral right to have God hear us, for we too are poor and in need of his help. If we remember to keep this perspective, giving to the poor will become an obvious thing to do.

> *Synonymous:* **'a gift given in secret' / 'a bribe concealed in the cloak'** (21:14)

Bribery has been mentioned in 15:27; 17:8;23; 18:16 and 19:6. Although the proverb here in verse 14 is observational, its context points to the way that bribery corrupts justice. From another perspective there can be an innocent use of gifts honestly but quietly given that may be in mind here. The idea of pacifying God's wrath by a gift must surely be out of the question, however. Nothing will pacify his wrath but the blood of Christ.

> *Contrast:* **'joy to the righteous' / 'terror to evildoers'** (21:15)
> Justice — joy to the just; terror to the troublesome

This set of proverbs is rounded off with a brief summary of how justice affects both righteous and evildoer (21:15), which is similar to the proverbs about the city. More broadly, it is typical of the evildoer to be filled with terror at any idea of doing right, while the righteous find joy in such things. The innocent have nothing to fear where justice prevails. Graeme Goldsworthy comments: 'The assumption is that God preserves the order and that it is our task to perceive it and to live in harmony with it. At its centre is the covenant, and our faithful response to it is what is meant by the fear of the Lord.'

'A man who strays from the path of understanding comes to rest in the company of the dead' (21:16).
> *Synthetic:* **'man who strays'** / **'comes to rest'**
> From the prudent path don't ever bend,
> Or you will rest in a dead end.

This strikingly crafted proverb is another warning about the end ahead for those who forsake wisdom. Rebels long for freedom and for ease, but what they do not realize is that the path they are on ends in deadness and death. The same image is used in connection with the warnings against adultery earlier in the book. One of the many euphemisms used for death is that of being laid to rest. If the dead person is one who has trodden the path of understanding then he has entered the eternal rest of heaven. If he has strayed from the path, his resting-place is in everlasting death.

'He who loves pleasure will become poor; whoever loves wine and oil will never be rich' (21:17).
> *Synonymous:* **'loves pleasure'** / **'loves wine and oil'**
> Poverty's certain if you love pleasure;
> Love oil and wine and lose all your treasure.

The '**pleasure**' spoken of here is the same word as the 'joy' in verse 15. Paradoxically the pursuit of pleasure leads to poverty. It is the pursuit of righteousness that leads to true pleasure. It is the one who hungers and thirsts after righteousness who is filled. That is why Paul says of 'the widow who lives for pleasure' that she 'is dead even while she lives' (1 Tim. 5:6). A love of extravagance (what one writer calls 'champagne taste on a beer budget') will mean you will never be rich. Jesus puts it most starkly when he says, 'If anyone would come after me, he must deny himself and take up his cross and follow me. For whoever wants to save his life will lose it, but whoever loses his life for me will find it. What good will it be for a man if he gains the whole world, yet forfeits his soul? Or what can a man give in exchange for his soul?' (Matt. 16:24-26).

Paul notes that a mark of the last days (the days between Christ's first and second comings) will be that many will be 'lovers of pleasure rather than lovers of God' (2 Tim. 3:4).

'The wicked become a ransom for the righteous, and the unfaithful for the upright' (21:18).
   Double contrast: **'wicked'** / **'unfaithful'**; **'righteous'** / **'upright'**

This interesting proverb speaks of the way the death of **'the wicked'**, or **'unfaithful'**, provides a ransom for **'the righteous'**, or **'upright'**. In terms of a well-ordered society that is how it works. The wicked are expendable. They must die for the sake of the righteous. If they are allowed to live there will be no righteous left. It had become a commonplace in Jewish thinking no doubt, so that Caiaphas was able to say, as he did in reference to a man he thought of as expendable, 'It is better for you that one man die for the people than that the whole nation perish.' As John points out, 'He did not say this on his own, but as high priest that year he prophesied that Jesus would die for the Jewish nation, and not only for that nation but also for the scattered children of God, to bring them together and make them one' (John 11:50-52).

Paul goes so far as to say, 'God made him who had no sin to be sin for us, so that in him we might become the righteousness of God' (2 Cor. 5:21).

'Better to live in a desert than with a quarrelsome and ill-tempered wife' (21:19).

Contrast (better than): **'desert'** / **'with a quarrelsome and ill-tempered wife'**

Better desert heat
Than a wife who's not sweet.

Using a different picture, this proverb goes somewhat further than verse 9. In Scripture the desert is land that is not necessarily barren but is always uninhabited. It is a lonely, inhospitable place — the very opposite of what a family home should be. The man has now left the house. A mark of the false teacher is his tendency to be argumentative and his slow fuse. Get as far from him as possible. Better be the odd one out than follow the crowd and suffer.

Christian wives have, of course, often been very different from the woman portrayed here. Sarah Edwards, the wife of Jonathan, appears to have been an outstanding woman. The two would enjoy horse rides in the forest on some afternoons and they loved to discuss their activities and talk of things they were learning. They had nightly devotions and prayed together. Evangelist George Whitefield wrote of them, 'A sweeter couple I have not seen. Their children were not dressed in silks and satins, but plain, examples of Christian simplicity. Mrs Edwards is adorned with a meek, quiet spirit; she talked solidly of the things of God, and seemed to be such a helpmeet for her husband, that she caused me to renew those prayers, I

have put up to God, [for] a wife.' Jonathan's last words were:
'Give my love to my dear wife, and tell her that the uncommon union which has long subsisted between us has been of
such a nature as I trust is spiritual and therefore will continue
for ever.'

> **In the house of the wise are stores of choice food and**
> **oil,**
> **but a foolish man devours all he has.**
> **He who pursues righteousness and love**
> **finds life, prosperity and honour**
>
> (21:20-21).

Contrast: **'house of the wise'** / **'foolish man'**
Synthetic: **'pursues'** / **'finds'**
The house of the wise is full of choice food
But fools devour like a flood.
If love and righteousness you pursue,
Then life, wealth, honour will come to you.

These two proverbs give the positive side of what is taught in
verse 17. Although the pursuit of wisdom involves self-denial,
any loss is more than made up for. We lose out on earthly
delights, but heavenly ones are far superior. What the foolish
have is soon gone, but these are eternal delights. As Asaph
discovered, it is a contemplation of the future that puts it all
into perspective (see Ps. 73).

The pursuit of **'righteousness and love'** (God's mercy)
yields the familiar triad of **'life, prosperity and honour'** (cf.
3:16; 22:4). These are the things promised to Solomon by
God, along with wisdom, in 2 Chronicles 1. They also characterized his wise father David (1 Chr. 29:28). Paul may have
this verse in mind when he says that God will give eternal life

to 'those who by persistence in doing good seek glory, honour and immortality' (Rom. 2:7). Gregory the Great explained that spiritual riches are superior to earthly ones as the more they are expended, the more they bring in.

'A wise man attacks the city of the mighty and pulls down the stronghold in which they trust' (21:22).
Synonymous: **'attacks' / 'pulls down'**
Brain over brawn.

Paul's words in 2 Corinthians 10:4 spring to mind here: 'The weapons we fight with are not the weapons of the world. On the contrary, they have divine power to demolish strongholds.' We may lack brute strength, but if we have real wisdom we shall be able to demolish false arguments and false hypotheses and the false refuges in which those with influence and authority put their trust.

The theory of evolution is perhaps one of the strongholds most trusted in today by those in power. Yet a wise man like the lawyer Philip E. Johnson is able to pull down that stronghold with ease. In his book *Testing Darwinism* (published 1997), for example, in a chapter entitled, 'Tuning up your baloney detector', he notes how evolutionists make selective use of evidence, appeal to self-appointed authorities, use *ad hominem* arguments, raise up straw men, beg the question, assert things that cannot be tested, use vague terms and shifting definitions, and simply believe what they want to believe. John Blanchard has done similar work with regard to atheism in his work *Does God believe in atheists?* More generally, Josh MacDowell's *Evidence that demands a verdict* books are worth consulting, as are those of Francis Schaeffer and other apologists. Cornelius Van Til and those who have popularized his teaching have perhaps gone further still in showing just how weak the strong man's castle really is. What lies behind all this is the fact that 'The foolishness of God is wiser than man's wisdom, and the weakness of God is stronger than man's strength' (1 Cor. 1:25).

'He who guards his mouth and his tongue keeps himself from calamity' (21: 23).
Synthetic: **'he who guards'** / **'keeps himself from'**

When I was a teenager I remember my rugby-playing friends making trips to the dentist to be fitted with rubber gum-shields, once more familiar in the boxing ring. Sadly, in many cases it did nothing to curb the foul language that came out on the field. No dentist can deal with that problem; it is a matter of self-control and self-denial. In tune with other verses found here, this one on the subject of the tongue emphasizes the benefits of keeping a tight rein on it. Least said, soonest mended (13:2,3 are very similar).

In the fifth century Ambrose of Milan wrote a number of Latin hymns. There are several translations of his *Iam lucis orto sidere.* John Mason Neale renders the first six lines:

Now that the daylight fills the sky,
We lift our hearts to God on high,
That he, in all we do or say,
Would keep us free from harm today.
May he restrain our tongues from strife,
And shield from anger's din our life.

'The proud and arrogant man — "Mocker" is his name; he behaves with overweening pride' (21:24).
Synthetic: **'proud and arrogant man'** / **'behaves with overweening pride'**

Four terms are used here. The various Bible versions ring most of the changes on how to present them. The first and last terms are very similar and refer to pride or conceit. In the last instance, it is dubbed **'overweening pride'** or 'raging pride'. In between are references to arrogance or haughtiness and mocking or scoffing. There is a progression here, then: from pride and arrogance to being a mocker, and from being a mocker to an overweening pride, an insolent and unbending arrogance. The first risings of pride are dangerous and must be checked.

> **The sluggard's craving will be the death of him,**
> **because his hands refuse to work.**
> **All day long he craves for more,**
> **but the righteous give without sparing**
>
> (21:25-26).

Synthetic: **'craving'** / **'death'**
Contrast: **'sluggard'** / **'righteous'**

Verses 25 and 26 should be taken together. They begin with a synthetic description of the sluggard. Instead of working, he daydreams. He is full of desire, full of craving for delight. Instead of working all day, **'he craves for more'**. He is never satisfied. People talk of dying from overwork, but there is a death that comes from not working enough. This picture is then contrasted with **'the righteous'** who **'give without sparing'**. Instead of merely craving, they do 'something useful' so that they 'may have something to share with those in need' (Eph. 4:28). The sluggard is like the Dead Sea, where nothing can live. He is constantly taking in as he craves for more and more. Like the Sea of Galilee, full of life, the righteous **'give without sparing'**. Giving without sparing is sometimes illustrated by the contributions respectively made to a traditional

English breakfast by the pig and the chicken. The latter provides the egg, which involves a loss, but the former provides the bacon and so spares nothing.

Writing to the Romans, Paul reminds us how quickly life passes. We need to understand 'the present time. The hour has come for you to wake up from your slumber, because our salvation is nearer now than when we first believed. The night is nearly over; the day is almost here' (Rom. 13:11-12).

Charles Bridges mentions the need for diligent use of the Lord's Day, which the Puritans described as 'the market day of the soul'.

'The sacrifice of the wicked is detestable — how much more so when brought with evil intent!' (21: 27).
   A fortiori
   Synthetic: **'sacrifice'** / **'brought with evil intent'**

This takes us back to verse 3 and develops the first part of 15:8. If thoughtlessness is detestable to God, how much more the cynical attitude that disguises an evil intent in the worship! The passage from James 4 quoted earlier (see commentary on 21:10) goes on to say, 'You do not have, because you do not ask God. When you ask, you do not receive, because you ask with wrong motives, that you may spend what you get on your pleasures' (James 4:2-3).

'A false witness will perish, and whoever listens to him will be destroyed for ever' (21: 28).
   Synthetic: **'false witness'** / **'whoever listens'**

At this point we return to the theme of justice. False witness has implications not only for the witness himself, but also for anyone who takes his testimony seriously. He will die for his sin, but those who accept his lies will die because they listened to the false testimony that he gave. It is no wonder that Jesus spoke of false prophets as ferocious wolves. Whenever we consider false teachers, we must remember the harm they do both to themselves and to others (cf. 19:5,9).

'A wicked man puts up a bold front, but an upright man gives thought to his ways' (21:29).
   Contrast: **'wicked man'** / **'upright man'**
   A wicked man at boldness plays;
   The upright give thought to their ways.

The fact that the wise give thought to their ways has already been mentioned in 14:8. Here the reference to their ways is preceded by the observation that **'A wicked man puts up a bold front.'** He brazens it out; he acts as though all were well, even when he knows he is in the wrong. He claims to be fighting corruption when he is corrupt himself; he condemns sin in others but not in himself. It is frightening to think how many are living a lie. They put up a bold front and say that they know there is no God and they are not afraid to die, and so on. It is just a bluff. As the saying goes, there are no atheists in foxholes. If only more would give serious thought to their ways and the direction in which their lives are taking them!

> **There is no wisdom, no insight, no plan**
>   **that can succeed against the LORD.**
> **The horse is made ready for the day of battle,**
>   **but victory rests with the LORD**
>
> (21:30-31).

   Synthetic: **'no wisdom'** / **'can succeed'**
   Contrast: **'horse is made ready'** / **'victory'**
   The horse for battle has been dressed,
   But with God its success will rest.

The chapter ends, as it begins, with references to the Lord and especially to his sovereign power. Kidner sums them up as warnings not to fight against the Lord (21:30) or without the Lord (21:31).

Verse 30 is very striking with its triple negative. There is **'no wisdom'**, **'insight'** or **'plan'** that can beat the Lord. He cannot be outmanoeuvred, though many have tried. There have been football teams and boxers and grand masters of chess who have been labelled as unbeatable, but their day has come at last. The Titanic was famously thought to be unsinkable, but it sank. The Lord, however, is different. He is genuinely unbeatable and unsinkable. Nietzsche declared that God is dead. As someone facetiously put it after the death of Nietzsche: '"God is dead" — Nietzsche. "Nietzsche is dead" — God.' Mark Twain is said to have observed on one occasion that reports of his death had been greatly exaggerated. The same can be said of God, and will continue to be said. Despite all the best-laid schemes 'o' mice an' men', they have all, in the words of Burns, 'gang agley' and no future scheme can succeed either, despite the many boasts that atheists and others have so often made. He is sovereign and his will must be done.

The corollary here is that no one who opposes God is wise, bright or clever. The truth reaches its highest fulfilment at the cross: 'This man was handed over to you by God's set purpose and foreknowledge; and you, with the help of wicked men, put him to death by nailing him to the cross. But God raised him from the dead, freeing him from the agony of death, because it was impossible for death to keep its hold on him' (Acts 2:23-24).

In verse 31 we see the horse all ready for the day of battle. It is tempting to think that with such a fine knight victory is certain but the truth is that **'Victory rests with the LORD.'** One of the greatest illustrations of this, what happened to the

Egyptians at the Red Sea, is often referred to in Scripture. God determines who will win and who will lose, whatever the battle.

Erik Durschmied has made a study of the way this has worked out in history. In his first book, *The hinge factor* (subtitle, *How chance and stupidity have changed history*) he looks at various battles that have hinged on factors outside the expected run of battle. In a prologue he quotes Carl von Clausewitz as saying, 'Chance and uncertainty are two of the most common and important elements in warfare.' He himself comments: 'Many battles have been decided by the caprice of weather, bad (or good) intelligence, unexpected heroism or individual incompetence — in other words, the unpredictable.'

What is condemned here is not using earthly resources but relying on them. See the negative reference to King Asa in 2 Chronicles 16:12. Other scriptures draw the same conclusion:

> No king is saved by the size of his army;
>   no warrior escapes by his great strength.
> A horse is a vain hope for deliverance;
>   despite all its great strength it cannot save.
> But the eyes of the LORD are on those who fear him,
>   on those whose hope is in his unfailing love,
> to deliver them from death
>   and keep them alive in famine
>
> (Ps. 33:16-19).

Or, more briefly:

> Some trust in chariots and some in horses,
>   but we trust in the name of the LORD our God
>   (Ps. 20:7; cf. 147:10; Eccles. 9:11; Isa. 33:1).

What these thirty-one proverbs teach us

Taking these thirty-one proverbs together, there are a number of points we need to realize:

The power and priorities of the Righteous One

God is the Righteous One and his very holiness should make us tremble. Think of the things revealed about him here:

His power

This comes out in several proverbs, especially the first and the last two (21:1,30-31).

His priorities

He is more concerned with *the inner man* than the outer man (21:2). He is more concerned with *righteousness* than ritual (21:3).

He takes note of the house of the wicked

He knows that 'The way of the guilty is devious' (21:8). He recognizes that the wicked crave evil and refuse to show mercy. He takes note of all the sins here: pride (21:4), lying (21:6), violence (21:7), neglect of the poor (21:13) and any wandering from the path of understanding (21:16). Laziness and bearing false witness are also condemned here (21:25-26,28). The Lord sees it all and if you are guilty, he knows all about it.

He will bring the wicked to ruin but bless the righteous

This message is driven home again and again. It is there in verses 5 and 20, among other verses.

Negatively

Liars may make 'a fortune', but it is 'a fleeting vapour and a deadly snare' (21:6).

The refusal of the wicked to do right and their violence 'will drag them away' (21:7).

'A man who strays from the path of understanding comes to rest in the company of the dead' (21:16).

'The sluggard's craving will be the death of him' (21:25).

'A false witness will perish, and whoever listens to him will be destroyed for ever' (21:28)

Positively

'He who pursues righteousness and love finds life, prosperity and honour' (21:21).

'He who guards his mouth and his tongue keeps himself from calamity' (21:23).

How to make good use of this information

In view of verse 11, turn from being a mocker; if you are simple learn, and if you are wise be instructed by all that is above.

Judgement day is fast approaching. How does that thought strike you? Does it fill you with joy or terror? If you are righteous in Christ it can be the former; if not you ought to be terrified (21:15).

If you feel that your tottering tower is about to crumble, do not attempt to brave it out, pretending that all is well. Confess your wickedness and give thought to your ways (21:22,29).

It is clear that your greatest need is to be righteous. You think you are righteous, but you are not by nature, for God weighs the heart (21:2). A gift or a bribe cannot turn away his wrath against you (21:14) and no ritual or sacrifice can cleanse you (21:3), especially if you are merely trying to win favour for yourself (21:27). It is the atonement that Christ has won by becoming sin that alone can make you righteous and save you (21:18).

39.
Realize your danger; stop and take refuge in Christ

Please read Proverbs 22:1-16

Reputation, wealth and poverty, caution, humility and fear of the Lord, snares, raising children, economic hierarchies, requital, generosity, removing mockers, heart and speech, God's omniscience, a sluggard's excuses, the adulteress, child discipline, oppression and bribery

Here we have the final sixteen proverbs of this whole section.

'A good name is more desirable than great riches; to be esteemed is better than silver or gold' (22:1).
Double contrast (better than): **'good name'** / **'great riches'**; **'to be esteemed'** / **'silver or gold'**
Better poor but with a good name,
Better no wealth than to be in shame.

Back in Proverbs 3:4 there is a promise that those who are loving and faithful 'will win favour and a good name in the sight of God and man'. Here the desirability of such a blessing is stated. It is paralleled in Ecclesiastes 7:1, where we read, 'A good name is better than fine perfume.' Even in days when one can perhaps cover one's tracks more easily, the power of a good name is understood by many, from big businesses to young children. Of course, there are many evil men who endeavour to win a good name by devious means, as at Babel and Ephesus (see Gen. 11:4, Acts 19:27). The Lord gives the balance to this proverb by pointing out that fame is not always a good thing and that what matters far more than a good name on earth is a good name in heaven (Luke 6:26; 10:20). Daniel is a great example of a man who had experience of both and knew which was of the most value (see Dan. 6). Joseph is another.

'Rich and poor have this in common: the Lord is the Maker of them all' (22:2).

> *Synthetic:* **'rich and poor'** / **'the Lord is the Maker'**
> Every person, great or small —
> God is the Maker of them all.

Riches and poverty are prominent in this section (a similar idea is found in 29:13). The theme of God being the Maker of the poor has come up in 14:31 and 17:5. Hannah was another who understood that 'The Lord sends poverty and wealth' (1 Sam. 2:7). We often speak of death as the great leveller, but birth itself is also a leveller in one sense. No doubt the authors of the American Declaration of Independence were grasping for something of this sort when they wrote that all men are created equal. Various efforts are made by man to perpetuate distinctions between the wealthy and the destitute. Perhaps such differences are inevitable in a fallen world. We must always remember, however, that we all have the same Maker and a few pieces of material, a title, some extra money in the bank, or pounds of flesh on the body, cannot remove that fundamental equality. Especially in the church context we should remember to avoid the discrimination spoken of in James 2. Also, 'The eye cannot say to the hand, "I don't need you!" And the head cannot say to the feet, "I don't need you!"' (1 Cor. 12:21).

'A prudent man sees danger and takes refuge, but the simple keep going and suffer for it' (22:3).
    Contrast: **'prudent man' / 'simple'**
    The prudent see danger and so they flee;
    The simple keep on and know agony.

In Proverbs 14:16 we learn that the fool is 'hot-headed and reckless'. Here his recklessness is seen in an unwillingness to see danger and take refuge. (The proverb is repeated almost verbatim in 27:12. A similar point is also made in 29:1: 'A man who remains stiff-necked after many rebukes will suddenly be destroyed — without remedy.')

One thinks most obviously here of the habitual gambler or drunkard, the violent and those who become involved in the underworlds of drugs and sexual immorality. However, any sinner who misses the warning signs in life and keeps going is headed for danger. If you are on such a road, stop now before it is too late. Part of wisdom is to stop and consider where the road we are on is leading. If you continue living as you are doing, where will you be ten years from now, twenty years hence, and in eternity? Do not be like Pharaoh, who did not have the wisdom to give in. Rather be like those who, we are told, feared the word of the Lord and acted upon it (Exod. 9:20). Christ will return like a thief in the night. We must be ready.

'Humility and the fear of the Lord bring wealth and honour and life' (22:4).

Synthetic: **'humility and the fear of the LORD' / 'wealth and honour and life'**
Humility and fear, what do they give?
Wealth and honour and a life to live.

Alden rightly says that 'This verse encapsulates the whole book.' He likens it to an algebraic equation. We could put it thus:

$$h + fL = w + h^o + l$$

Similar promises are found in 3:16; 21:21 and elsewhere in the Old Testament:

Fear the LORD, you his saints,
    for those who fear him lack nothing.
The lions may grow weak and hungry,
    but those who seek the LORD lack no good thing
                                (Ps. 34:9-10; cf. 112:1-3).

He will be the sure foundation for your times,
    a rich store of salvation and wisdom and knowledge;
    the fear of the LORD is the key to this treasure
                                (Isa. 33:6).

In the New Testament the emphasis is more spiritual but the physical is not forgotten (see Matt. 6:33). Paul speaks of godliness 'holding promise for both the present life and the life to come' (1 Tim. 4:8). As we have seen previously, such verses cannot be taken to mean that all believers can expect to be wealthy, famous and live a long life. There are other factors at work and they must be considered too. However, in his time, God will bring such blessings to his own while denying them to fools.

'In the paths of the wicked lie thorns and snares, but he who guards his soul stays far from them' (22:5).
    Contrast: **'wicked'** / **'he who guards his soul'**

This is similar to 15:19, but here 'the sluggard' is replaced by the more general term, **'the wicked'**, and 'the upright' becomes **'he who guards his soul'**. Such parallels give us an insight into what wickedness and uprightness are. The thorns and snares on the path of the wicked are either in their minds, or real problems arising from neglect of their souls and from waywardness. The upright escape such dangers because they guard their souls. This does not mean such people necessarily have an easier life, but because they know their destination and are determined to reach that goal through the Lord's enabling, they avoid many thorns and snares. Are you preventing your own progress by allowing the thorns of sin to grow and failing to deal with them? Are you tempting the devil to lay snares in your path? The thorns and snares must be removed, painful though that may be. Do not neglect your soul.

'Train a child in the way he should go, and when he is old he will not turn from it' (22:6).
    Synthetic command (positive): **'train a child'** / **'he will not turn'**

We often turn to Proverbs for guidance on raising children. The word translated **'train'** is a rare one and includes the idea of inauguration or initiation. It could perhaps be translated: 'Dedicate a child.' The verse can be taken in different ways. It may be saying that if you train a child in the right way he will follow it when he is older. Alternatively, this could be taken as a warning that what children learn when they are young will shape their lives in the future. Less likely is the idea that we should train children to go where their interests lead. Whichever

way we take it, the practical point is that we need to devote
time and energy to wisely directing the young in right ways.
Where better to start than with this book of Proverbs? This
famous verse is missing from the Greek Septuagint for some
reason.

Preaching on this text, godly Bishop Ryle urged parents to
train their children 'in the way they *should*, not the way they
would go', doing it 'with all tenderness, affection and patience;
an abiding persuasion that much depends on you', and
'continually remembering to make your child's soul a priority'. He commends concentrating on training them in 'a knowledge of the Bible, a habit of prayer, habits of diligence and
regularity about the public means of grace and habits of faith,
obedience, truthfulness, redeeming the time and fear of over-
indulgence'. This is to be done 'remembering continually how
God trains his children, the influence of your own example,
the power of sin, the promises of Scripture' and 'in continual
prayer for a blessing on all you do'.

**'The rich rule over the poor, and the borrower is servant
to the lender'** (22:7).
  Double contrast: **'rich'** / **'poor'**; **'borrower'** / **'lender'**

This proverb is observational with an implied warning. Its construction is synonymous but involving two contrasting pairs:
'the rich' and **'the lender'** on the one hand, and **'the poor'**
and **'the borrower'** on the other. There may be little we can
do about whether we are rich or poor, but if we borrow from
others we ought to bear in mind that it is the lender who calls
the tune. At the time of writing, the newspapers are carrying
the sad story of a widow who borrowed a modest sum from
an unscrupulous moneylender some years ago and now owes
thousands of pounds. An extreme case, it illustrates the slavery to debt that many get themselves into. Mark Twain observed

the problem in his typically droll way: 'A banker is a fellow who loans you his umbrella when the sun is shining and wants it back the minute it begins to rain.' We should avoid borrowing if we possibly can. If we do borrow, we should look carefully into the interest arrangements.

On the other side, there are warnings to rich lenders not to lord it over those in debt to them. Amos in the Old Testament and James in the New both have strong words for those who take advantage of the poor.

True believers pray every day that the Lord will both forgive them their debts and strengthen them to forgive those who are debtors against them.

'He who sows wickedness reaps trouble, and the rod of his fury will be destroyed' (22:8).
    Synthetic: **'he who sows wickedness'** / **'rod of his fury'**

Here the frequent theme of reaping what you sow is expressed in those very terms (cf. Job 4:8, Hosea 8:7; 10:13; Gal. 6:7-8). To 'sow wickedness' is to go on in ways contrary to God's law. The inevitable consequence of such sowing is the reaping of trouble. **'The rod of his fury'** may be an image drawn from animal husbandry to go alongside that from arable farming. The man who used his rod so furiously on his animals will have his rod destroyed.

'A generous man will himself be blessed, for he shares his food with the poor' (22:9).
    Synthetic beatitude: **'generous man'** / **'shares'**
    The generous man we all adore,
    For he shares his food with those who are poor.

Here is the counterpart to the previous proverb. Wenceslas, the Czech patron saint, was a tenth-century Bohemian duke.

He was a keen, though not always wise, champion of the Christian religion. In 1853 John Mason Neale put a traditional story about him into verse and set it to a well-known melody. The hymn closes with an appropriate application:

> Therefore, Christian men, be sure,
> Wealth or rank possessing,
> You who now will bless the poor
> Shall yourselves find blessing.

The sentiments echo this verse. Here the **'generous man'** has, literally, a 'good eye'. The blessings of generosity are often commended in Proverbs (see 11:24-26; 14:31; 19:17; 28:27). Generosity is encouraged throughout Scripture (see Deut. 15:7-11; Ps. 41:1-3, Isa. 58:7-12; Matt. 25; 1 Tim. 6:18-19; Heb. 6:10). Perhaps the New Testament verses that best reflect this proverb are the following: 'Give, and it will be given to you. A good measure, pressed down, shaken together and running over, will be poured into your lap. For with the measure you use, it will be measured to you' (Luke 6:38); 'Remember this: Whoever sows sparingly will also reap sparingly, and whoever sows generously will also reap generously... God loves a cheerful giver' (2 Cor. 9:6-7).

We are to model ourselves on the Lord himself, who taught us that it is better to give than to receive. The eccentric eighteenth-century preacher John Berridge speaks of his 'bountiful, seeking, cheerfully merciful and unwearied eye'. We are poor, but he gives us the bread of life.

'Drive out the mocker, and out goes strife; quarrels and insults are ended' (22:10).
Synthetic: **'drive out'** / **'out goes'**

We have met **'the mocker'** many times in Proverbs. He has to be dealt with. Once this has been done, strife and arguments and name-calling are over. Alden quotes a pertinent rabbinical saying: 'When a fool leaves the room it seems as though a wise man entered.'

There are many applications here, especially to the importance of the state's dealing decisively with troublemakers and of churches' exercising good discipline. Parents and school-teachers also know the value of 'antiseptic bouncing', as it is referred to technically. The mocker can no longer make his clever remarks when he is out of the room. At the end of time we know that mockers will be shut out from the heavenly city for ever and Satan himself will be cast into the lowest parts of hell. Some people have an exaggerated view of what they consider to be 'toleration' that is totally unjustified.

'He who loves a pure heart and whose speech is gracious will have the king for his friend' (22:11).

Synthetic: **'he who loves a pure heart'** / **'king for his friend'**

There is some variation in the way this proverb is translated. The Greek version makes it a three-liner. The proverb seems to betray Solomon's influence. It is one of several that refer to kingship (14:28,35; 16:10,12-15; 20:8,26,28). Friendship with the king is a high prize. It comes to those who combine love for purity of heart on the inside with gracious speech on the outside. We have already been told that 'Kings take pleasure in honest lips; they value a man who speaks the truth' (16:13).

Wisdom is king and the true friend we need. References to kings also immediately alert us to the Great King and to friendship with him. Jesus says that it is the pure in heart who see God. We must also always take care over how we speak. His displeasure is not something we would ever want.

This is the third proverbial promise in this section (see 22:6,9) out of a total of twenty-five or so. Most chapters contain at least one (e.g., 10:7,24,30; 11:21,25,28).

'The eyes of the LORD keep watch over knowledge, but he
frustrates the words of the unfaithful' (22:12).
   Contrast: 'eyes of the LORD keep watch' / 'he frustrates'
   Watching wisdom, God frustrates faithless phrases.

God is the guardian of truth. Like a vigilant watchman he keeps
his eyes on it. He will not let it come to ultimate harm despite
the machinations of the wicked. He will frustrate the words of
the unfaithful so that what they say will do no final harm. The
father of lies himself will be cast into hell. The eyes of the
Lord are mentioned in 15:3 (cf. 20:8,27). Such thoughts should
give believers confidence.

'The sluggard says, "There is a lion outside!" or, "I will be
murdered in the streets!"' (22:13).
   Synonymous: 'There is a lion outside' / 'I will be murdered...'

Here the sluggard is making excuses. How can he possibly go
outside when there may be a lion out there, or some other
danger of death? (26:13 is similar). The humour and irony lie
in the fact that he was not much more likely to meet a lion on
the streets of ancient Israel than on the streets of modern
Britain.
   The story is told of the American statesman Daniel Webster
that as a boy he was set to mow his father's field. Being lazy,
he made a bad job of it but blamed the way the scythe was
hung. After various attempts to adjust it to his satisfaction, his
father told him he could hang it how he liked. He promptly put
it on a tree and declared it was just right. People can be very
adept at finding excuses for not doing what they simply do not
want to do. The sluggard may not do much, but he keeps busy
thinking up excuses as to why he should stay in bed. Such
discouragers are a curse on any society.

'The mouth of an adulteress is a deep pit; he who is under the LORD's wrath will fall into it' (22:14).
> *Synthetic:* **'mouth of an adulteress'** / **'will fall into it'**
> *Simile:* **'mouth'** / **'deep pit'**
> An adulteress's mouth is a great deep pit;
> One under God's wrath will fall into it.

Warnings against the adulteress abound in the first section of the book. In this second section, the 'strange woman' is referred to only here and in 23:26-28 (but see also 30:20). As we have seen earlier, the reference is much wider than physical adultery. Here she is likened to **'a deep pit'**. It is a mark of the Lord's wrath when anyone falls into spiritual or physical adultery. Such people have been given over to a great sin That road leads to hell. If the righteous are tempted to think that they are missing out, as they are constantly told today, they need to recall that in fact the Lord is saving them from calamity.

'Folly is bound up in the heart of a child, but the rod of discipline will drive it far from him' (22:15).
> *Contrast:* **'bound up in'** / **'drive it far from him'**
> Folly is found at the core of a child;
> A reforming rod whacks it into the wild.

Here is another reference to children (cf. 22:6) and to the use of the rod (cf. 13:24). Here the focus is on the fact that folly is bound up in their hearts. Experience confirms this.

'The rod of discipline' could be taken metaphorically, but in the light of other proverbs, the use of corporal punishment is clearly envisaged. Nothing but careful discipline will effectively remove folly. Children are to be beaten, not out of revenge, or because they irritate us, or to work off our anger, but as a matter of discipline. It is to be for their good. As

divinely appointed agents we endeavour to correct them and
turn them from the dangerous road of folly to which they turn
by nature.

Tedd Tripp's excellent *Shepherding a child's heart* deals
with five common objections to corporal punishment made by
parents:

1. 'I love them too much to spank them' — It is unpleasant but Proverbs 13:24 shows it is the loving thing
to do.

2. 'I'm afraid of hurting them' — Proverbs 23:13-14
comes in here. If we remain calm we shall not harm them.

3. 'I'm afraid of making them angry and rebellious'
— Keep the long term in view and see Proverbs 29:17.

4. 'It doesn't work' — Inconsistency, irresolution,
failure to hurt and hitting in rage are the real problems.

5. 'I'm afraid I'll be arrested' — Privacy and prudence are crucial factors here.

Another objection is that it teaches violence and getting
what you want by force, and that it will encourage violence
towards other children. Gary and Anne Marie Ezzo, who also
write on these matters, make a useful differentiation between
biblical chastisement and cultural spanking: *Cultural spanking* is 'done *to* the child; a reaction activated by frustration; a
last resort; meant to change outward behaviour; a punishment
of behaviour; frustrating for the child and without positive
long term effects'. *Biblical chastisement*, on the other hand,
is 'done *for* the child; a response activated by rebellion; an act
of love; used to change inward attitudes; intended to amend
behaviour; a means of clearing the child's guilty conscience
and mould lifelong character'. They say that the latter is rare.
They also believe it needs only to be carried on in the first five
years of a child's life.

Tedd Tripp is also rightly keen to stress (as this verse establishes) that it is the heart that needs to be disciplined.

'He who oppresses the poor to increase his wealth and he who gives gifts to the rich — both come to poverty' (22:16). *Synthetic:* **'he who oppresses'** / **'he who gives gifts'**

This verse is difficult to translate. Kidner writes of its 'cryptic brevity'. The NIV supplies the word **'both'** to make some sense of it. It could be saying, 'He who oppresses the poor increases his wealth and he who gives gifts to the rich comes to poverty.' The point then would be the observation that you will squeeze more money out of the poor by oppression than out of the rich by bribery. Taking the NIV's line we can say that by nature men tend to look down on the poor and look up to the rich. Despite its inherent absurdity we are more willing to give to the 'haves' than the 'have-nots'. This proverb underlines the fact that such worldly wisdom will eventually fail. Oppressing the poor foments rebellion and bribing the rich guarantees no future. Rather, we should generously give to the poor and humbly accept gifts from the rich. Many unbelievers simultaneously oppress poor believers and yet try to curry favour with God by giving to charity. This is a double-barrelled recipe for disaster.

What these last sixteen proverbs of Solomon teach us

At the end of a season, some footballers 'hang up their boots'. Others, though long in the tooth, decide to carry on and come to regret it. In sport, entertainment and many other fields a man can go on too long. This is true of preaching as it is of anything else. Some ministries have ended rather sadly because the man refused to retire. It is difficult to judge. The same is true, more mundanely, with eating food, drinking alcohol, climbing mountains, etc (22:3).

Of course, this truth can be perverted into an excuse for taking it easy (22:13). One way of hiding from hard work is under the cover of caution. People make excuses for not finding a job, not visiting, not fixing things. Unbelievers say, 'I'd like to be a Christian but...' They complain that there are 'too many hypocrites'; that 'Christianity is out of touch'; that they are not sure if the Bible is reliable, etc. The truth is often that they are simply afraid of putting self to death and taking up the cross. If you are determined to reject Christ, see the danger you are in. Better climb down now than go on to disaster. These issues can be developed further from other proverbs here.

Realize your danger

In general (22:5,8,10)

If you go down the path of sin, see the dangers (22:5). Some are obvious — drink, drugs, gambling, sexual promiscuity. We can say the same about living for money, possessions or popularity. It leads to unhappiness, pain, sorrow and hell. Think of the tragic Kennedy family in America.

Mockers inevitably cause strife, quarrels and insults (22:10). Remove them and trouble is at an end. This is clear in situations such as those in Ulster and the Middle East, or in matters such as football hooliganism. The problem with many unbelievers is an unwillingness to listen to truth because they are too busy mocking: 'Where did Cain get his wife?'; 'Why does God allow suffering?' and other less obvious jibes.

In verse 8 there is another warning: come the harvest, the truth will out. Are you sowing trouble for yourself?

Wealth and poverty (22:1-2,7,16)

Money is not the most important thing in life. Men like disgraced former British Conservative party chairman Jeffrey Archer will tell you that (22:1).

Bribery and oppression are common ways to seek riches. They seldom work in the end, even in this life. It is dangerous even to try (22:16).

There is a false view of riches and poverty. It is too easy to look up to the rich and down on the poor. However, as Kidner says, 'It is hard not to be guilty of some practical denial of this truth' (22:2). We need to be realistic. Realize the dangers of borrowing and of poverty too. This is an important message in our 'buy now pay later' instant-credit societies (22:7).

Children (22:6,15)

There is always the danger of going wrong, of taking the wrong path. Folly is bound up in their hearts. They are both foolish and stubborn, a bad combination (22:6,15).

Adultery (22:14)

See also Proverbs 2:16-22; 5; 7; 23:26-28.

Dishonesty (22:12)

It never works in the end.

Stop and run to Christ for refuge

Clearly, sin must come to an end. We must stop disobeying the Lord. More than that, there must be a definite turning to the Lord in faith and in holiness. This is the way to blessing.

We have already said that all mockery must go (22:10).

We are also warned of thorns and snares and positively called on to guard our souls. They are eternal. 'What will a man give in exchange for his soul?'

Humility and fear of the Lord are vital (22:4). Humble yourself before the Lord. Fear him — obey and serve him in Christ. That is the way to wealth, health and honour. 'Everyone who exalts himself will be humbled, and he who humbles himself will be exalted' (Luke 14:11).

Charm and purity are seldom found together. Usually the charming are not as pure as you expect. It comes out in what we learn of royalty, politicians and others. When they are, what blessings follow! (22:11).

God's true people are inevitably characterized by generosity. They freely receive and freely give. When a man is truly converted it will affect his wallet (22:9).

We must see the danger of sin, love of wealth, ill-discipline, adultery and dishonesty. Stop! Take refuge in Christ. Hide in him. Do not mock, but guard your soul by humbly fearing the Lord and finding inward and outward purity in him. Be generous, be disciplined in Christ and know God's blessings.

More vocabulary
Sayings of the wise (22:17 – 24:22)
More sayings of the wise (24:23-34)
More proverbs of Solomon (25:1 – 29:27)

40.
The perils of ambition

Please read Proverbs 22:17 – 23:8

*Oppression and divine retribution, bad company, bad deals,
cheating and defrauding, wrong priorities, needless pressures,
transience of riches, the snare of compromise*

Sayings of the wise

At this point, we come to the first of three new sections in
Proverbs. This one extends up to 24:22, where it is followed
by another similar but smaller collection (24:23-34). There is
a further collection in chapters 25-29.

Although this section largely contains proverbs proper of
various sorts, it seems to be a separate collection from that
found in 10:1 – 22:16 and shares some of the characteristics
of chapters 1-9. The father-son relationship is more prominent again, as are calls to wisdom. There are many commands.

Although they are far from agreement on the details, since
the 1920s many biblical scholars have been willing to see an
influence here from an incomplete Egyptian text referred to as
The teaching of Amenemope. It dates from the thirteenth or
twelfth century B.C. One Bible version even finds the name

Amenemope at the end of verse 19 (where the NIV has 'even you'). If the biblical writer has made use of a pagan source, this does not pose a problem for upholders of divine inspiration, unless they erroneously equate such a view with a divine dictation paradigm. Rather, the biblical writers selected and arranged their material, superintended by the Spirit, and so, if there is any borrowing from Egypt or another source here — and there is no proof of that — then we know that it must have been done under divine direction. As a result of common grace, or whatever term one uses, the world undoubtedly has a store of wisdom that is not opposed to biblical truth and indeed offers genuine insights into the human condition. For a divinely inspired author to take and adapt such material is perfectly congruent with the highest views of inspiration by the Spirit.

It is also perhaps worth saying that no Christian should ever be embarrassed about learning from an unbeliever. As a young undergraduate in university, I remember struggling with the whole question of how I could learn anything reliable from unbelieving lecturers in the English Department. I now see that there was a great deal to learn — more than I ever came to grips with. Of course, the teaching was often tainted with humanism and other false teachings, and not all of it could pass the litmus test of Scripture, but whatever does not contradict Scripture has something to teach us.

Verses 17-21 act as an introductory paragraph on how to approach these wise sayings and how to respond to them. The Greek extracts the phrase, **'the sayings of the wise'**, from this verse and uses it as a heading. The NIV translates the opening line of verse 20: **'Have I not written thirty sayings for you...?'** Although other translations differ, this is probably correct. The thirty are computed in various ways. Let us learn then, firstly, how to approach the wise sayings here or, for that matter, anywhere else in Scripture.

How to approach these wise sayings

1. Pay attention and listen

'Pay attention and listen to the sayings of the wise' (22:17). It is possible to take some things in, even when only half concentrating. However, these are words from God and any lack of attention or failure to listen on our part is unacceptable. They demand full and careful listening. 'He who has ears to hear, let him hear.' People who do not listen carefully to instructions end up making mistakes that could have been avoided. In examinations, students who do well are usually those who have listened well in class and who read the paper they are sitting carefully. To use another illustration, a man who is in love will read a letter from his beloved several times over, eager to catch every nuance.

2. Apply your heart to it

'Apply your heart to what I teach' (22:17). In the end, the only real way to benefit from these teachings is to learn them and keep them in our hearts. There is often an emphasis on the heart in Proverbs. These sayings must go deep into our psyche. In examinations, those who fail are usually those who have shown a lack of application. They have failed to be diligent and hard-working, and so they fail.

3. Keep them in your heart

'For it is pleasing when you keep them in your heart' (22:18). Think of examinations again and the great advantage of knowing things 'off by heart'. Although learning itself may be a painful process, knowing is a joy. As I write, I can hear my eldest son practising the clarinet. It has been a struggle, but he is now finishing with a piece that he has learned by heart and that gives him (and us) real pleasure. The way truly to benefit from Scripture is to keep it in your heart.

4. Have them all ready on your lips

'And have all of them ready on your lips' (22:18). Best of all is to know these wise sayings so well that you can teach them to others, either formally or informally. One test of whether we really know a thing is whether we are able to explain it clearly to others.

How to respond to these wise sayings

1. With faith

It is important that we remember that the purpose of Bible study is not to fill our heads with facts. The purpose of all this attention, application, retention and instruction is revealed in verse 19: **'So that your trust may be in the LORD, I teach you today, even you.'** This message is directly to *you*, and its fundamental purpose is to urge you to put your trust in the Lord. A man can spend a lifetime studying the Scriptures but if it does not lead him to faith in the Lord Jesus Christ, it can do him no good. The purpose of all this teaching is that you might trust in the Lord — yes, *you*!

2. With humility

'Have I not written thirty sayings for you, sayings of counsel and knowledge?' (22:20). Like all Scripture, the thirty sayings here are full of guidance and knowledge. It will be of no value to us, however, if we do not humbly make use of it.

By nature, we are slow to take advice. We think we can manage without help. Of course, we cannot. Sometimes when we do ask, we are given misleading advice and that makes us doubly unsure about asking for help. But here is guidance and knowledge that is guaranteed to be true. Humbly accept what is here and you will find the way to heaven and to every blessing.

3. With confidence

Verse 21 goes on to describe these sayings as **'teaching you true and reliable words, so that you can give sound answers to him who sent you'**. These 'true and reliable words' are words we can depend on, words we can be confident about. They are God's own words. Jesus spoke of building our lives on such words as being like being a wise man building his house on rock. To fail to build our lives on them is to be like a foolish man building on sand. Whatever the question is, we can be sure that the answer is to be found here in God's Word.

The one **'who sent you'** suggests the diplomatic role that some see here, but probably refers simply to the teacher of wisdom. Jesus is the one who sends his disciples out in his name.

The perils of ambition

In this chapter, we shall look at the first eight proverbs. They make various points and there is some disagreement about the thrust of certain of them, but perhaps they can best be brought together under the heading of 'the perils of ambition'. Ambition comes in various shapes and sizes. We see it everywhere — in sport and politics, education and entertainment, business and religion. In the twentieth century, many writers were aware of its dangerous tendency. John Cowper Powys called it 'the

grand enemy of all peace', and W. Savage Landor 'avarice on
stilts'. T. S. Eliot was of the opinion that 'Most of the trouble
in the world is caused by people wanting to be important.' In
earlier times the Puritan Thomas Brooks came up with a whole
series of epithets to conjure up the evil. It is a gilded misery, a
secret poison, a hidden plague, an engineer of deceit, the mother
of hypocrisy, the parent of envy, the origin of vices, the moth
of holiness, the blinder of hearts, turning medicine into mala-
dies and remedies into diseases.

Are you ambitious? Are you eager to get to the top? There
is such a thing as naked ambition, but sometimes it disguises
itself. For example, we can be ambitious for self-satisfaction
rather than fame or success, or we can have vicarious ambitions for others.

These proverbs contain eight principles outlining possible
perils of ambition. Seven of these eight are cast as negative
commands. There are over fifty commands in the book, most
of them in negative form. The previous couple are found in
20:13,22. Some twenty out of the 'thirty sayings' are either
negative commands, or contain an element of that.

1. Taking advantage of the needy

> **Do not exploit the poor because they are poor**
>   **and do not crush the needy in court,**
> **for the LORD will take up their case**
>   **and will plunder those who plunder them**
>
>   (22:22-23).

Synonymous command (negative) with reason: **'do not exploit' / 'do not crush'**

I saw once on a bumper-sticker: 'Even if you win the rat race,
that still makes you a rat.' One temptation that often comes to

the ambitious is that of getting ahead by treading on the heads of the defenceless. Exploiting the poor goes on all the time. They are forced to work for low wages, unable to find any-thing better. They are the ones most likely to fall for get-rich-quick schemes based on gambling or borrowing money. The poor and the weak are always open to exploitation by the rich and by those with power. The Lord himself, the proverb warns, will punish such ruthlessness. Poverty and oppression are themes in Proverbs (see, for example, 19:17; 21:13; 22:2,16).

2. Falling into bad company

Do not make friends with a hot-tempered man,
   do not associate with one easily angered,
or you may learn his ways
   and get yourself ensnared

(22:24-25).

Synonymous command (negative) with warning: **'do not make friends'** / **'do not associate'**

Another characteristic that often marks the ambitious man is his willingness to mix with all sorts of people, often unsavoury characters. The people we spend time with, either in real time or virtually through their books, films and magazines, will in-evitably have an effect on us. When I was at university, I made many new friends. I remember how in some cases I involun-tarily began to alter my language. I had always been 'tired' or 'whacked out', but now suddenly I found I was 'bushed'. Fool-ish friends had been 'twits' or 'dumbos'; now they were 'bricks'. We have noted elsewhere that this is part of the way that accents are formed.

This is a warning that is similar to Proverbs 20:19, which refers to gossips, and is the negative counterpart to 13:20 (see also the warnings in 1:10-19 and 12:26). Friendship itself is a theme in Proverbs.

3. Making bad deals

> **Do not be a man who strikes hands in pledge**
>   **or puts up security for debts;**
> **if you lack the means to pay,**
>   **your very bed will be snatched from under you**
>   (22:26-27).

Synonymous command (negative) with warning: **'do not be a man who strikes hands' / '... puts up security'**

This note has been struck several times before. People who are able to think and act fast are usually able to get on. However, ambitious desires can often lead a man to take risks that he ought not to. A few false moves and a fortune can be lost.

In 1894, the novelist Mark Twain had to file for bankruptcy. His problems arose from more than one source, but a major factor was his investment in the Paige Typesetter, a machine that was supposed to revolutionize the printing industry. Over a course of fourteen years, he spent hundreds of thousands of dollars on the invention, hoping to reap millions in return. He often dreamed of sudden wealth. In fact, what he came to was bankruptcy. The typesetting machine proved a failure on its first real test. Far more tragic is the commitment many make to false religion. The consequences will be woeful.

4. Cheating and defrauding

'Do not move an ancient boundary stone set up by your forefathers' (22:28).
    Synthetic command (negative): **'do not move...' / 'set up by your forefathers'**

Ancient Israel was divided between the different tribes from the time of Joshua. Each Israelite had his portion of land and although there was room for some change in circumstances, certain mechanisms were established in God's law to retain the status quo over the long haul. The story of Naboth's vineyard reflects how easily the ambitions even of a king could be thwarted while he was willing to act honestly. The temptation was there for the ambitious to cheat, either on the grand scale as Jezebel did, or more subtly by unlawfully altering boundaries. It was the opinion of the godless Lord Chesterfield that 'Without some dissimulation no business can be carried on at all,' and many since have shared his jaundiced opinion. The truth is that cheating and defrauding others is unacceptable on any level. Cutting corners, bending rules, dodgy dealing, white lies, fiddles, rackets and scams — the ambitious have their ways of getting ahead. But they forget that God sees it all and they will have to answer for it all on the Day of Judgement.

Many past writers have taken the ancient boundary stones as a metaphor of ancient doctrines and point to the way some have made a grab for prestige and power by shifting the boundaries of doctrine.

A very similar warning to this one comes in 23:10-11.

5. Getting priorities wrong

Do you see a man skilled in his work?
He will serve before kings;
he will not serve before obscure men

(22:29).

Synthetic: **'man skilled in his work'** / **'he will serve'**
Contrast: **'kings'** / **'obscure men'**

This is an observation, not a command. It notes that ambition does not always lead to success. There are many frustrated people around. In fact, many people pour so much energy into their ambitions that they have little time to develop any worthwhile skills or talents. On the other hand, there are many examples of those who were never seeking promotion or success and yet have achieved it. How? By concentrating on things that are more important. There are plenty of people today who are quite adept at pushing themselves or others forward. A phenomenon of the times is the PR company — wholly dedicated to promoting their client, whether he is worth promoting or not. Very often, it is the people with the real talent, the ones who really count, who are forgotten. Despite appearances, it is true that if all the top-flight footballers and pop singers of the world vanished over night, things would go on in much the same way as before. How different if we lost all our nurses or lorry drivers! The British honours system tries to recognize this. Most of the OBEs and CBEs and other honours go to people who are relatively unknown.

Integrity is a very important commodity, often in short supply. It is very easily lost in the pursuit of ambition. To take a secular example, think of the Beatles in the 1960s. Clearly men with some talent, they ended up playing concerts where their music could not be heard. They eventually saw through this and attempted to move in a different direction with their ill-fated Apple Corporation and other projects. They came to see, as we all must, that cultivating talent is far more important than merely attempting to be noticed. Horace Mann sought to capture the point with his maxim: 'Seek not greatness but seek truth and you will find both.'

By way of application, we remind ourselves that we must concentrate hard on what we do well and avoid acting like the overcautious man with one talent in Jesus' parable. Whether we are noticed for our skills is really in God's hands. Real talent may be missed at first, but it will one day be seen for what it is — if not in this life then certainly in the one to come.

6. Putting yourself under needless pressure

When you sit to dine with a ruler,
note well what is before you,
and put a knife to your throat
if you are given to gluttony.
Do not crave his delicacies,
for that food is deceptive

(23:1-3).

Synthetic command (negative): **'when you sit to dine'** / **'do not crave'**

Here the picture of the ambitious man reaches a climax. He has been invited to dine with the king! He is at Buckingham Palace, at one of the queen's famous garden parties or, more likely, he is an ambassador at court. Sadly, the ambitious man is not able to enjoy the moment. He knows he is going to see an array of delicacies and if he acts like a glutton — in the presence of the sovereign! — he is finished. And so he is constrained, tantalized even, in the very moment of his triumph as he remembers this warning.

This is typical of ambition and the poor wages it pays. We hear it repeatedly: 'Did you enjoy your moment of triumph?' 'Well no, I was thinking of the next thing.' Like the grave, ambition is never full (see 27:20; 30:15-16). Are you stuck on the misery-go-round of ambition? See where it leads. One of the qualities of wisdom is that it knows how to show restraint and understands what true greatness is all about. It notes well what is before it and sees that an invitation from a king to dine is not about food. These verses are more than a lesson in table manners or a warning against love of luxury. Rather, as Eric Lane puts it, this passage is a warning to social climbers that they are on a greasy pole and can easily fall.

7. Wearing yourself out for nothing

Do not wear yourself out to get rich;
   have the wisdom to show restraint.
Cast but a glance at riches, and they are gone,
   for they will surely sprout wings
   and fly off to the sky like an eagle

                                          (23:4-5).

Synonymous command (negative / positive) with warning: **'do not wear yourself out'** / **'show restraint'**

Similarly, we are warned once again against failing to show restraint and being deceived. There is something deceitful about wealth. It offers much, but gives little. It cannot satisfy and even when it appears to do so, that satisfaction soon evaporates. One who grasped at least something of this was the nineteenth-century Swiss palaeontologist Jean Louis Agassiz. Invited once to speak to a learned company, he complained that he could not afford to take time away from writing and research. When told what a lucrative opportunity he was passing up, he replied, 'I can't afford to waste my time making money.' Wisdom refuses to be obsessed with riches. It understands the importance of self-control and how easily wealth is lost. Do not let ambition rob you of true wealth.

8. Getting trapped in compromise

Do not eat the food of a stingy man,
   do not crave his delicacies;
for he is the kind of man
   who is always thinking about the cost.
'Eat and drink,' he says to you,
   but his heart is not with you.

**You will vomit up the little you have eaten
and will have wasted your compliments**

(23:6-7).

Synonymous command (negative) with reason and warning:
'do not eat' / 'do not crave'

This is the final picture we consider here. It is on similar lines
to the previous five verses. In the strange world of the ambitious, there are sometimes warm invitations from people who
hate the sight of them. Here we see the stingy man, if that
translation is correct. He begrudges you every mouthful from
his table. All your compliments are wasted on him. His insin-
cerity is nauseating. A meal should be an act of close fellowship, but such situations are typical for the ambitious. It is
often said in that world that there is no such thing as a free
lunch. Ambition can so spoil our lives that we are no longer
capable of acting altruistically because we are always thinking
about what advantage we may gain from such an action. Similarly, we cannot be sure that those who do us favours do not
have ulterior motives. One reason the rich and famous tend to
stick together is because they think they can trust each other
more, but even among them things are often not quite what
they seem.

Wisdom sees, then, that meals and other favours are laid
on for a variety of reasons. There are miserly, cynical and calculating people everywhere. The only way to escape them is
to run from selfish ambition itself. An enterprising preacher
once told King Richard I that God was angry with him for
not marrying off his daughters. When Richard protested
that he had none, the preacher told him their names —
ambition, avarice and affluence. Richard had an equally witty
reply (about giving his ambition to the Templars, his avarice to the monks and his affluence to the prelates) but the

thought was well aimed. Is ambition still there on the shelf in your house?

The way of ambition is a field of pitfalls. Its landmines are planted everywhere. Beware. We are all ambitious to some extent — if not for ourselves then for others. Avoid callousness, bad company, reckless commitments, cheating, wrong priorities, needless pressure, greed and compromise. In Philippians 2, Paul calls on believers to abandon selfish ambition and to follow the perfect example of Christ. Although he is equal with God, he did not consider that equality something to be held on to but humbled himself as a servant, even to the point of dying on a cross, a despised outcast. He now has the name that is above all names and one day every knee will bow to him and confess that he is Lord. As Michael Griffiths put it many years ago in a book calling for sacrificial service in God's kingdom, 'Give up your small ambitions.' Seek rather to serve the Lord and to please him.

41.
Five more perils to flee

Please read Proverbs 23:9-35

Addressing fools, taking advantage of others, application,
parental discipline, a wise son, envy and zeal, perseverance,
warning against indulgence, warning against the prostitute,
warning against alcohol

Here we consider a further series of sayings. Some of them
are just one short verse in length (between twelve and seventeen words in English). Others are longer, covering two or
three verses (twenty-five to thirty-five words). The saying in
verses 29-35 is over 120 words long. Eight are either negative
commands or contain some such element.

**'Do not speak to a fool, for he will scorn the wisdom of
your words'** (23:9).
Command (negative) with reason: **'do not speak ...'**

We begin with a negative command. It is similar to the warning back in 9:7 and ties in with 18:2. It also reminds us of
Jesus' later words in the Sermon on the Mount about not throwing pearls to pigs or what is sacred to dogs. My eldest son
reliably informs me that it is impossible to waste your breath,

but it certainly feels that way when you speak to a fool! You say, 'Say no to drugs'; 'Don't sleep around'; 'Repent from sin'; 'Trust in Jesus.' It appears to go in one ear and out of the other. We have a duty to speak to all and to neglect none. The practical lesson, however, is that we cannot waste time trying to convert people who simply do not want to listen to our message.

> **Do not move an ancient boundary stone**
> **or encroach on the fields of the fatherless,**
> **for their Defender is strong;**
> **he will take up their case against you**
>
> (23:10-11).

Synonymous command (negative) with reason: **'do not move'** / **'[do not] encroach'**

This repeats a similar proverb found shortly before in 22:28. The form is different, however. There are three differences:

1. In 22:28 the stone is said to have been 'set up by your forefathers'. Here what is in mind is not so much ignoring ancient rights as not taking advantage of the needy.
2. Here the sin of encroaching **'on the fields of the fatherless'** is added.
3. An argument against such sins is also given here: **'for their Defender is strong; he will take up their case against you'** (this is similar to 15:25).

The context is also different, with 22:28 coming in the context of relationships with people socially (it is preceded by the topics of striking deals, making friendships and exploiting the poor and followed by that of going up in the world socially).

Here the subject is more that of relationships in the context of teaching and learning. I would suggest that the point is less to do with ambition and more to do with the more basic matter of taking advantage of others. We ought not to put ourselves in a situation where we invite someone to take advantage of us (23:9), nor to take advantage of others (23:10-11). We should, on the other hand, profit by opportunities to learn (23:12) and to teach (23:13-14).

The reference to their **'Defender'**, or Kinsman-Redeemer, is ultimately to God, who takes up their case even when no one else will. He has never lost a case and never will. He will defend his own (see Lev. 25:25; the book of Ruth; Gen. 48:16; Exod. 6:6; Isa. 41-63). To oppose the poor is to oppose him.

'Apply your heart to instruction and your ears to words of knowledge' (23:12)

Synonymous command (positive): **'apply your heart'** / **'... your ears'**

Again a brief saying, this time we have a very positive exhortation, typical of the genre. The pattern is:

Apply your heart	to instruction
and your ears	to words of knowledge

It is a call to diligence, diligence in the pursuit of knowledge. Without it, we shall not get very far. We shall either lack inclination (as in 23:9) or be discouraged by the discipline (see 23:13-14). Do not get discouraged. Press on to wisdom! Pray for yourself and for others, in William Kingsbury's words:

Rouse us from sloth, our hearts inflame
With ardent zeal for Jesus' name.

Do not withhold discipline from a child;
    if you punish him with the rod, he will not die.
Punish him with the rod
    and save his soul from death

(23:13-14)

Commands (negative / positive) with reason: **'do not withhold discipline'** / **'punish'**

After a proverb about learning comes one about teaching. It
follows on from 22:6 and especially from 22:15 (see also
13:24). Eric Lane calls it 'the most powerful statement on the
subject in the whole book'. It is a negative command with a
negative promise, followed by a parallel positive command
with a positive promise.

Do not withhold discipline from a child;
        if you punish him with the rod, he will not die.
Punish him with the rod
                and save his soul from death.

As so often in Proverbs, there is a paradox. Causing physical
pain, which would seem detrimental to the body, is in fact a
means of saving the soul of the individual. Again, the fifth
commandment is in mind. **'He will not die'** could mean, 'Your
blows will not harm him,' or 'He will live long.' Perhaps both
are intended. The child will not only survive *despite* corporal
punishment, but he will survive *because of* it.

Little is said about this subject in the New Testament, although when divine discipline is discussed in Hebrews 12 it is
clear that the writer agrees with the Old Testament position.
Paul's emphasis when he speaks to parents is elsewhere. He
writes, 'Fathers, do not embitter your children, or they will

become discouraged' (Col. 3:21); 'Fathers, do not exasperate your children; instead, bring them up in the training and instruction of the Lord' (Eph. 6:4). In a sermon called 'Balanced Discipline' in his famous series on Ephesians, Dr Martyn Lloyd-Jones, having stressed the need to be filled with the Spirit, lays down seven principles regarding exercising discipline: it should never be exercised without self-control; in a capricious manner as regards temper or conduct; unreasonably or with an unwillingness to hear the child's case; in a selfish way; in a mechanical manner; too severely; or without recognizing growth and development in the child. He closes with exhortations never to try to 'foist our views upon our children', but to exercise discipline in love and in such a way that will lead children to respect their parents.

> **My son, if your heart is wise,**
> **then my heart will be glad;**
> **my inmost being will rejoice**
> **when your lips speak what is right**
>
> (23:15-16).

Synonymous: **'if your heart is wise'** / **'when your lips speak what is right'**

From the parents we turn to the children. These verses are like 10:1 and several others we have looked at already. The theme comes up again in verses 24 and 25. The father speaks and declares how very glad he will be if his son speaks **'what is right'**. This is the true joy of any teacher — to see his pupil doing, from the heart, what he has been taught. A lesson is learned when we can not only correctly repeat its leading themes, but we are affected inwardly by its import. The implication here is that we ought to seek wisdom. Real wisdom is not cold and intellectual; it strengthens relationships and causes heartfelt joy. There is a distinctive pattern here again:

> My son, if your heart is wise,
>   then my heart will be glad;
>   my inmost being will rejoice
> when your lips speak what is right.

> **Do not let your heart envy sinners,**
> **but always be zealous for the fear of the LORD.**
> **There is surely a future hope for you,**
> **and your hope will not be cut off**
>
>   (23:17-18).

Synthetic commands (negative / positive): **'do not let your heart envy'** / **'always be zealous'**
Synonymous: **'future hope'** / **'hope will not be cut off'**

The negative command here is matched by a positive one and a further positive word of encouragement. Envy can be taking pleasure in the downfall of others or desiring the good they have. Here the latter sin is in mind. (The theme is found in Psalm 37 and already in Proverbs in 3:31. We shall return to it in 24:1,19-20.) In the context, it is the father speaking to the son who warns against envying sinners. Instead, as Kidner puts it, we need to look up and ahead:

> *Look up.* The familiar idea of fearing the Lord is again present. If we look only at ourselves or at others, we are liable to be envious. If we look up we shall fear God.
> *Look ahead.* If we rely on mere human wisdom, we shall be in trouble. If we see beyond it though, there is hope. The eternal perspective is vital here, as Asaph discovered (see Ps. 73).

In June 1890 Spurgeon preached on this text. He prayed, 'God grant that this particular text may become proverbial in this church from this day forward.' He spoke firstly of the prescribed course for the believer. Rather than a religion of show, of spasms, or that is periodic in its flow, we need to be zealous for the fear of the Lord all day long. He goes through a typical day and illustrates what that means. He then gives excellent reasons for always fearing the Lord: God always sees us; sin is always equally evil; we always belong to Christ; we can never tell when Satan will attack; the Lord may come at any hour. What admirable results will follow if we are zealous for the fear of the Lord! It means safety, security, honour and usefulness. He then speaks of the probable interruption of seeing the evil prosper which can do serious harm. Finally, he closes with a helpful consideration. He recalls that there is 'an end to this life and to the worldling's prosperity. For believers there will be an end to their troubles but no end to their hope or expectation.'

> **Listen, my son, and be wise,**
> > **and keep your heart on the right path.**
> **Do not join those who drink too much wine**
> > **or gorge themselves on meat,**
> **for drunkards and gluttons become poor,**
> > **and drowsiness clothes them in rags**
>
> (23:19-21).

Synthetic commands (positive / negative) with warning: **'be wise'** / **'keep your heart on the right path'**; **'do not ... drink too much'** / **'... gorge themselves'**

This saying and the next begin with the command to **'Listen'**. The father again speaks to the son. Here he is quite specific.

The positive part calls for a hearing; the negative warns against joining in with drunkards and gluttons, for that way leads to poverty. Our word 'gluttony' is from a Latin word meaning 'to swallow' or 'gulp'. It can refer both to excess eating and drinking (or even over-indulgence in other ways), although we tend to use it mostly in regard to food.

The sins of drunkenness and gluttony are not exactly the same in that, unlike alcohol, most foods do not directly affect the brain. Excess intake of food has its dangers, however. Gluttony can mean loss for others, poor health, shortened usefulness and life-expectancy, and the diminution of time and desire for spiritual activity. Christ himself was accused of being a glutton and a drunkard (Matt. 11:19) and there is a line between asceticism and over-indulgence. Despite the accusations made against him, the Lord was able to tread that line and his followers should also be able to, by the grace of God.

The temptation to gluttony and drunkenness has been particularly strong at certain periods of history. Our modern situation is such that in some parts of the world it is always a possibility. Writing at the beginning of the twentieth century and dealing with the seven deadly sins, James Stalker felt that there was little need to say anything about the sin of gluttony. It is unlikely that he would write in the same vein today. At present, it is estimated that in the USA more than half of all adults are overweight or obese. Some 300,000 deaths per year are attributable to obesity and as much as six per cent of healthcare spending has to do with issues related to this matter. Indirect costs to businesses are also thought to be significant.

Similar things can be said about alcoholism. Believers must avoid these sins. Those who fall into them soon become impoverished, if not materially, then certainly spiritually.

Drunkenness comes up again in verses 29-35. Gluttony, along with sloth, envy (23:17) and lust (23:26-28), is one of the traditional 'deadly sins'. Appetite, specifically the desire to eat, is natural and unobjectionable although no one should be a slave to appetite. Overeating is a form of over-indulgence to be shunned by the believer. The spotlight has been on various eating disorders in recent years. Anorexia is in many ways the antithesis of gluttony, but another condition, bulimia, involves uncontrolled binge eating along with sporadic dieting and vomiting. These problems usually seem to have their roots in emotional disorders and that is probably true of gluttony too. Whatever the root cause of a sin, it is still a sin and must be repented of. In *The Screwtape Letters* C. S. Lewis suggests that being fussy over food is a form of gluttony — wanting things just the way we like them. It is also a form of gluttony to want more pleasure from food, or anything else, than it was intended to give. Paul speaks of those 'whose god is their stomach' (Phil. 3:19).

> **Listen to your father, who gave you life,**
> **and do not despise your mother when she is old.**
> **Buy the truth and do not sell it;**
> **get wisdom, discipline and understanding.**
> **The father of a righteous man has great joy;**
> **he who has a wise son delights in him.**
> **May your father and mother be glad;**
> **may she who gave you birth rejoice!**
>
> (23:22-25).

Commands (positive / negative): **'listen'** / **'do not despise'**
Commands (positive / negative): **'buy'** / **'do not sell'**
Double synonymous: **'father of a righteous man'** / **'he who has a wise son'**; **'be glad'** / **'rejoice'**

In order to keep to a total of no more than thirty sayings (22:20), we take these verses together although there is a good argument for seeing at least two separate sayings here. In verses 22-23 we have another command to **'Listen …'** followed by a further exhortation to acquire wisdom at all costs. In the light of the experience described in verses 24-25, the father is desperate for his son to grow up wise and disciplined. The reminders that your father **'gave you life'** and that your mother, who will grow **'old'**, was young when she gave you birth are designed to tug at the heartstrings and produce genuine affection and a consequent desire for wisdom.

In *Pilgrim's Progress* the pilgrims at one point pass through Vanity Fair, where all sorts of goods are on sale, representing the various philosophies and ideas, desires and pleasures of this life. Bunyan pictures the men in the market crying out to those passing to buy their goods. The answer the pilgrims give comes from verse 23: 'We buy the truth; we buy the truth.' The truth cannot literally be bought, but we must be willing to pay whatever price and make whatever sacrifices are necessary in order to get it, and then when we have it, we must make sure that we do not lose it.

Verses 24-25 remind us of 23:15-16 but are more objective in manner. They also refer to a grown-up child. A description is followed by a prayerful wish. The foolish sinner is reminded of what a disappointment he is to his parents by a positive description of the joy that parents have when their son does well. Again we are in the line from 10:1 to 15:20 that is also touched on in 17:21,25; 19:13 and 29:3. Too many parents are what one author has referred to as 'parents in pain'. Sometimes they have to confess that much of the failing was on their side. However, it can often be the other way round. This is one aspect of the burden of parenthood. Even the very best parents can be disappointed. In the sovereignty of God, whatever view we take of baptism and covenant children, we cannot guarantee how they will turn out. If we have foolish sons and daughters, who will not listen, all our efforts will not avail.

Preaching once on John 19:27, the Puritan John Flavel reminded his hearers of this verse saying, 'It may be you are vigorous and young, they [your parents] decayed and wrinkled with age: but, saith the Holy Ghost, "Despise not thy mother when she is old." Or when she is wrinkled, as the Hebrew signifies. It may be you are rich, they poor; own, and honour them in their poverty, and despise them not. God will requite it with his hand if you do.'

> **My son, give me your heart**
>   **and let your eyes keep to my ways,**
> **for a prostitute is a deep pit**
>   **and a wayward wife is a narrow well.**
> **Like a bandit she lies in wait,**
>   **and multiplies the unfaithful among men**
> (23:26-28).

Synthetic command (positive) with warning: **'give me your heart'** / **'let your eyes keep to my ways'**

Similes: **'a prostitute'**; **'a wayward wife'** / **'a deep pit'**; **'a narrow well'**

The father then gives another positive command, though it takes up the negative and oft-repeated theme of how the adulteress can lead astray. Here two similes are used to describe her. She is like a **'narrow well'**, which is similar to the **'deep pit'** here and in 22:14. If you fall down a narrow well, getting out again is virtually impossible. Perhaps some sort of animal trap is in mind. The second image is that of **'a bandit'**, a highway robber who lies in wait for his victims. Whereas bandits rob, she makes many unfaithful to their marriage covenants and so steals away the joy of unbroken homes.

Who has woe? Who has sorrow?
  Who has strife? Who has complaints?
  Who has needless bruises? Who has bloodshot
    eyes?
Those who linger over wine,
  who go to sample bowls of mixed wine.
Do not gaze at wine when it is red,
  when it sparkles in the cup,
  when it goes down smoothly!
In the end it bites like a snake
  and poisons like a viper.
Your eyes will see strange sights
  and your mind imagine confusing things.
You will be like one sleeping on the high seas,
  lying on top of the rigging.
'They hit me,' you will say, 'but I'm not hurt!
  They beat me, but I don't feel it!
When will I wake up
  so I can find another drink?'

                                                    (23:29-35).

Command (negative) with warning: **'do not gaze at wine'**

This famous set of verses gives an accurate description of
drunkenness. The question is raised whether the writer had
personal experience of what he portrays. What we find here
could just as easily be the result of close observation of others.
It begins with a series of three pairs of questions alerting us to
the affects of alcohol:

  1. *Woe and sorrow.* Alcohol is a depressant. It often
creates feelings of melancholy and sadness. It also frequently leads to more general unhappiness in a person's
life.

2. *Strife and complaints.* In some cases alcohol can make a person argumentative, aggressive and violent.

3. *Physical injury* as a result of falls and other strains. Drunks are liable to injure themselves, both by falling and hurting themselves when they are drunk, and because of the damage that excess alcohol can cause over the long term.

The answer to the six questions is given in verse 30. Wine is singled out as being the most common intoxicating drink of the time and place, but similar things can be said about beers and other drinks, and especially distilled spirits, not known until a later period.

Then comes the negative command, which is not simply to avoid alcohol, but rather not to be entranced by its initial desirability. Although its colour and look may be attractive, although it may go down very smoothly, the truth is that its after-effects (more and less remote) are sinister. Verses 33-35 describe a 'trip', or a session where all is unreal. The Hebrew of verse 34 is apparently evocative of a wobbling drunk. The Hebrews' general aversion to the sea also adds to the unease created by the picture. The top of the rigging is the least stable part of the ship. The description of the way the drunk feels inured to pain is accurate. One day when, as a boy, I was waiting for a bus with my father, he pointed out to me a flight of some twenty concrete steps. He remembered seeing a drunk falling from top to bottom of them. The man staggered to his feet apparently unharmed and went on his way. As my father remarked, he felt nothing then but it was no doubt a different story the next morning. The final remark also rings true. Referred to as 'the hair of the dog' (in view of the belief that the latter is the best antidote to a dog-bite), a commonly accepted 'cure' for a hangover is another drink. Of course, such a 'remedy' merely exacerbates the underlying problem.

Although they may work in different ways, what is said here about alcohol has an application in some measure to other drugs, legal or illegal. Many a pastor has also seen that all sorts of things can so drug and stupefy the unbeliever that he is intoxicated with the emptiness of this world. Here is the very opposite of what wisdom demands — positive relationships, self-control, thought about consequences, reality, not superficiality. The Bible does not say we must not drink alcohol or take other drugs, but it does warn very sternly against their abuse. James Stalker finishes his discussion of the deadly sin of 'Appetite' by saying helpfully that preachers must always insist on four things:

1. Drunkenness is a deadly sin.
2. Christians are not to associate with drunkards.
3. Christians are called to use the most effective means they know to put an end to all that is dishonouring to God.
4. The only perfect defence against drunkenness is a living, working and rejoicing religion.

He ends by quoting Ephesians 5:18: 'Do not get drunk on wine, which leads to debauchery. Instead, be filled with the Spirit.'

What these proverbs teach us

Taking the above sayings together, we are given a command and a warning.

Seek wisdom

This is a constant theme in Proverbs. Here we learn four things:

1. What you chiefly need (23:12)

'Instruction and … words of knowledge'. As we have already seen, what we need most is not money or possessions or power or fame, but wisdom.

2. How to get it (23:12)

Sometimes when I was young I would ask my mother for something and she would sarcastically recommend that I sit still and it would fly to me. It never happened. Wisdom certainly never comes that way. You must 'apply your heart … and your ears'. Wisdom is a gift, but it does not come automatically or by accident. You will not catch it like chickenpox.

3. Where it leads (23:15-16)

The pursuit of instruction and knowledge leads to a heart that is wise and to speaking what is right.

4. The advantages of wisdom (23:15-16)

It brings heartfelt joy to all who truly and rightly care for you. God himself speaks and he says:

> My son, if your heart is wise,
>   then my heart will be glad;
> my inmost being will rejoice
>   when your lips speak what is right.

Five perils to flee

If we run to wisdom, we shall find ourselves running *from* the following:

1. Rebellion (23:22-28)

These verses are really all about listening to your parents.

> *The temptation:* To ignore your parents and others in positions of authority — an attitude fostered in society today by broadcasters, journalists, advertisers and even some, paradoxically, in positions of authority. A society that ignores its elders is doomed.
> *The danger:* Great distress to those in authority (23:24-25). This is to say nothing of the early deaths and similar problems experienced by those who rebel.
> *The remedy:* Discipline (23:12-14).

2. Over-indulgence (23:19-21; 23:29-35)

> *The temptation:* Abuse of food or drink or drugs. It comes in different forms to young and old.
> *The danger:* Poverty and going astray from God.

> *The remedy:* Take great care with alcohol and other drugs. Be filled with the Spirit.

3. Adultery (23:27-28)

> *The temptation:* To leave God's way, literally or metaphorically, for a prostitute or another man's wife.
> *The danger:* Capture, loss and the end of all trust.
> *The remedy:* The only answer is either marriage or celibacy. Both demand self-control.

4. Oppression of the weak (23:10-11)

> *The temptation:* To cheat and take advantage of the needy.

The danger: Retribution from God.

The remedy: Do all you can to help the poor and needy, remembering who their Defender is.

5. Envying sinners (23:17-18)

The temptation: To envy the apparently easy life of the unbeliever.

The danger: A loss of zeal for the Lord.

The remedy: Look up to God and look ahead to the Judgement Day.

42.
Wisdom from heaven —
your vital need

Please read Proverbs 24:1-22

*Warning against envying or desiring the company of the wicked,
a house established and enhanced by wisdom, wisdom a source of
strength and guidance, fools, evil schemers, facing trouble, care
for the needy, a call to crave wisdom, plotting and persevering,
warning against gloating, against fretting, due respect*

Here we have the final 'sayings of the wise'. Again, a prominent theme is that of the blessings of wisdom and the perils of foolishness. The pattern seems to be a negative command, followed by six sayings that are more positive — three observations and three positive commands — and, finally, one positive and four negative commands. Each saying is full of interest and important to know.

**Do not envy wicked men,
do not desire their company;
for their hearts plot violence,
and their lips talk about making trouble**

(24:1-2).

Command (negative) with reason: **'do not envy'** / **'do not desire'**

The need to take care when choosing friends is a recurring theme in Proverbs and has been raised, for example, in this section (22:24-25). The warning against envying the wicked has been sounded in 23:17-18 and recurs in 24:19-20. In those other verses the usual biblical response is given — the need to keep the end in view. Here the other danger of desiring the company of the wicked is mentioned. We must neither injure ourselves struggling nor drift away. The reason given for careful separation from such people is the way that **'Their hearts plot violence, and their lips talk about making trouble.'** This takes us right back to the warnings of Proverbs 1. When all they think about is benefiting themselves and causing trouble for others, why would you wish to consort with them?

> **By wisdom a house is built,**
> **and through understanding it is established;**
> **through knowledge its rooms are filled**
> **with rare and beautiful treasures**
>
> (24:3-4).

Synonymous: **'wisdom'** / **'understanding'**
Synthetic: **'built'** / **'filled'**

This proverb on wisdom paints a very attractive picture, drawing a contrast with the wicked described in verse 1 and using the homely figure of a house and its furnishings. It again anticipates Jesus' parable at the close of the Sermon on the Mount. It can be taken literally or, metaphorically, as referring to a household or dynasty or, best of all, in reference to a life of wisdom.

There are two parts. First, there is the building and establishing of the house itself, then, secondly, filling it **'with rare and beautiful treasures'**. This powerfully illustrates how wisdom and understanding are gained. For example, growing wise is a long-term business. It demands hard work and skill.

Planning and careful thought are vital. Perhaps we can think of there being two aspects to the whole business. First, there is the work of constructing the house. Certain fundamental things must be understood and established if we are to begin to be wise. Educationists are aware of this. Beyond that, however, there is the filling of the house with treasures. If building a house is a work that takes some time, filling it with rare and beautiful treasures is the work of a lifetime. Further, it is implied that wisdom can provide not only shelter and protection, but also comfort and joy. The picture of the man, having built his house and having filled it with treasures, sitting back to enjoy them is very appealing. One can pursue the pictures almost endlessly. The thought of the rare and beautiful treasures being damaged because of some omission or neglect in the construction process comes to mind.

When you meet a person who is able to quote a great writer, tell you an illuminating story, or show you the best way of doing something, realize that such treasures were accumulated one by one with patience and proficiency.

In 1901, Flora Kirkland took up the theme of verse 3 in a hymn. These are some of the verses:

Building, daily building, while the moments fly,
We are ever building life-work for on high!
Character we're building, thoughts and actions free
Make for us a building for eternity.

Choosing, as we labour, what we wish to take,
Oh let us be careful for the Master's sake!
He will help our labour, he will strength bestow.
Let us choose for Jesus all we use below.

May the Lord approve us! 'Tis our earnest prayer.
Oh, to have our building tall and strong and fair!

Oh, to live for Jesus! Truly every hour,
Building, praying, trusting in his mighty power!

A wise man has great power,
**   and a man of knowledge increases strength;**
for waging war you need guidance,
**   and for victory many advisers**

(24:5-6).

Synonymous: **'wise man'** / **'man of knowledge'**
Synonymous: **'guidance'** / **'advisers'**

The words in each of these two verses will stand as sayings in
their own right. Perhaps we are right to follow the NIV, however, and combine them into a single saying. The sentiment of
verse 6 has already been expressed in 11:14 and 20:18. The
verses together ought to be compared with 21:22, which says,
'A wise man attacks the city of the mighty and pulls down the
stronghold in which they trust.' Here the context for consultation is the strength of wisdom, and so we have both the literal idea of consulting others and the metaphorical one of
consulting wisdom itself for help in the struggles of life. When
challenged, little boys will sometimes threaten to call on the
assistance of their older brothers. When we are under fire and
struggling we can lean on the wisdom of God's Word, the
wisdom of other believers and wisdom itself.

'Wisdom is too high for a fool; in the assembly at the gate
he has nothing to say' (24:7).
    Synonymous: **'wisdom ... too high'** / **'nothing to say'**

'The assembly at the gate' is, of course, where, in ancient
times, the town elders met to discuss important matters and
make judgements. The fool has nothing to say at such times

because he lacks wisdom. He can only deal with trifles, not anything that really matters. Like a high town wall, he finds wisdom an unscalable height. He cannot reach its top. Indeed, he does not even bother to make the attempt. This underlines both the uselessness of the fool and how to spot him.

> **He who plots evil**
> **will be known as a schemer.**
> **The schemes of folly are sin,**
> **and men detest a mocker**
>
> (24:8-9).

Synthetic: **'he who plots evil'** / **'men detest'**

In the same vein as verse 7, these verses refer to the worst kind of fool, the schemer or mocker — a fool who is both brazen and calculating in his foolish ways. Schemers are characterized by the way they plot evil. Their outrages, their **'schemes of folly'**, may be covered with a veneer of good but are unacceptable to God — they are sin. They are also often unacceptable to men when the latter become aware of them. People denounce those who plot evil as schemers and they **'detest a mocker'**. One thinks of the general attitude to fallen schemers of recent times such as Robert Maxwell and Lord Jeffrey Archer. The apparent humility and repentance of another who mocked, Jonathan Aitken, mitigates the sneering at him to some extent but his wickedness is still detested. Such words act as a warning to avoid descending to such sinful scheming. A bad reputation is a liability.

'If you falter in times of trouble, how small is your strength!' (24:10).
  Synthetic: **'if you falter ...'** / **'how small'**

This striking proverb is a rebuke to our pride and self-satisfaction. By nature, we are happy just to be coping with life from day to day. Most indeed do learn to cope with every-day problems at least. But then times of trouble come and someone who has been coping so well goes to pieces. The real test of a man and of his philosophy is how it stands up when he is under fire. One of the strengths of the gospel is that it is a religion for all circumstances. It is good to ask ourselves, whether we profess to be believers or not, how we cope with trouble. When we engage in self-examination, we should ask not only what we are like on the easy days, but also what we are like when times are tough. Jeremiah has a similar thought more poetically expressed:

> If you have raced with men on foot
> > and they have worn you out,
> > how can you compete with horses?
> If you stumble in safe country,
> > how will you manage in the thickets by the Jordan?
> > > > > (Jer. 12:5).

> **Rescue those being led away to death;**
> > **hold back those staggering towards slaughter.**
> **If you say, 'But we knew nothing about this,'**
> > **does not he who weighs the heart perceive it?**
> **Does not he who guards your life know it?**
> > **Will he not repay each person according to what**
> > **he has done?**
> > > > > **(24:11-12).**

Synonymous command (positive) with reason: **'rescue'** / **'hold back'**

This command is followed by a threefold question, designed to undercut any attempt at a superficial response. It rebukes the hireling and encourages the faithful shepherd. We are in the world of the Good Samaritan, the priest and the Levite. Again, the saying, 'All that is necessary for evil to triumph is for good men to do nothing,' comes to mind.

The command itself is a plea for us to rescue **'those being led away to death'** or **'staggering towards slaughter'**. This initially evokes fellow Israelites being attacked by enemies, but undoubtedly has a wider meaning. In these last forty years the pro-life movement has legitimately drawn a connection here with the slaughter of unborn babies that has been going on in the Western world. Operation Rescue has used the verse to justify blocking access to abortion clinics, which is much more questionable. As Walter Kaiser observes, these verses certainly do not teach that believers 'should become vigilantes, taking the law into their own hands, or opposing the state because they think it is evil'. Similarly, the lives of elderly people are undoubtedly in potential danger because of the so-called euthanasia lobby.

Of course, beyond this there is an application to all who are outside the kingdom of God. Apart from the grace of God, we are all **'staggering towards slaughter'**. Those of us who know the Lord have a duty to save as many as we can, to call them back to the Lord. The evangelist John Blanchard has used the illustration of motorway madness when multiple pile-ups occur in foggy weather. In that position one would urgently cry out to a driver approaching such a pile-up to stop. Basically, this is what evangelists do — they cry out to people headed for certain disaster to stop. Writing in 1869, Fanny Crosby urged us all to do the same in her hymn, 'Rescue the perishing':

Rescue the perishing, care for the dying,
Snatch them in pity from sin and the grave;
Weep o'er the erring one, lift up the fallen,
Tell them of Jesus, the mighty to save.

Rescue the perishing, duty demands it;
Strength for thy labour the Lord will provide;
Back to the narrow way patiently win them;
Tell the poor wand'rer a Saviour has died.

The attempts that we make to excuse ourselves by pleading ignorance are ruled out of court here as **'he who weighs the heart'** and **'guards your life'** knows the truth (see 21:2). A great Day of Judgement is fast approaching when everything will be out in the open. There will be no pretending then. We all know of people in trouble, near and far, in spiritual and physical need. Simply to ignore their plight is unacceptable.

> **Eat honey, my son, for it is good;**
> **honey from the comb is sweet to your taste.**
> **Know also that wisdom is sweet to your soul;**
> **if you find it, there is a future hope for you,**
> **and your hope will not be cut off**
>
> (24:13-14).

Synonymous command (positive) with reason: **'eat honey'** /
'... honey from the comb'
Simile: **'honey'** / **'wisdom'**

This saying is a father-to-son one and uses the picture of honey. Some people do not like honey, of course, but as the universal sweetener of the time it was, and is, a useful picture of what is both pleasant and profitable. Green vegetables are good for you but not sweet-tasting. Honey is both sweet and good for you. True wisdom is like that. The thing about it that is underlined here, as elsewhere, is that it is not only good for you, but pleasant too. In particular, to discover Christ, who is wisdom from above, is to know that you have **'a future hope'**, a hope that **'will not be cut off'**.

The sweetness of the life of wisdom, the Christian life, has been a theme touched on by many of the great hymn-writers. Newton wrote of 'How sweet the name of Jesus sounds' — soothing sorrows, healing wounds and driving away fear. Wesley exclaimed, 'O love divine, how sweet thou art!' and asked when his willing heart would be all taken up with it. Watts wrote:

> Sweet is the work, my God, my King,
> To praise thy Name, give thanks and sing...

and:

> How sweet and awful is the place
> With Christ within the doors,
> While everlasting love displays
> The choicest of her stores!

Other hymns on the theme include Louise Stead's 1882 hymn beginning:

> 'Tis so sweet to trust in Jesus,
> And to take him at his Word;
> Just to rest upon his promise,
> And to know, Thus says the Lord!

James Allen's hymn was reworked by Walter Shirley in 1770 and begins:

> Sweet the moments, rich in blessing,
> Which before the cross we spend,
> Life and health and peace possessing
> From the sinner's dying Friend.

Do not lie in wait like an outlaw against a righteous
　　man's house,
　do not raid his dwelling-place;
for though a righteous man falls seven times, he rises
　　again,
　but the wicked are brought down by calamity
　　　　　　　　　　　　　　　(24:15-16).

Synonymous command (negative) with reason: **'do not lie in
wait'** / **'do not raid'**

In a passage once again reminiscent of Proverbs 1, we have
here the first of three successive negative commands, each
accompanied by a reason for obedience. The lying in wait may
be literal, but must also be taken more metaphorically. There
are many ways of attacking the righteous — with the tongue,
through the printed page or some other medium, by means of
passing laws and regulations, by depriving them of certain
freedoms and opportunities. All these and more have been tried.

The warning, however, is that all such efforts are fruitless
as, no matter how many times **'a righteous man falls'**, he
nevertheless rises again. As we say today, 'You can't keep a
good man down.' Seven is a figurative number of complete-
ness (see Job 5:19). Such a man is ever resilient. The falls
envisaged are troubles, not sins, as is sometimes thought. The
verse is not dealing with that issue. The wicked, on the other
hand, are brought down by calamity. The supreme example of
this is the Lord Jesus himself, who literally rose from the dead
on the third day. There are also many examples of the righteous rising again. In Scripture, we think chiefly of Joseph, but
also of Daniel and of the Jewish people in general and the
constant opposition they received from their enemies. We see
the same thing in the New Testament, both in the case of the
people of God in general and in the lives of the apostles,

especially Paul. In church history, the same patterns are repeated. This is what prompted Tertullian to speak of the blood
of the martyrs as being the seed of the church. The more severe the pruning, the greater the growth, it seems (see John
15:2). To oppose God's people is to oppose God. It is a form
of madness.

> **Do not gloat when your enemy falls;**
> **when he stumbles, do not let your heart rejoice,**
> **or the LORD will see and disapprove**
> **and turn his wrath away from him**
>
> (24:17-18).

Synonymous command (negative) with reason: **'do not gloat'**
/ **'do not let your heart rejoice'**

Once more, we have a negative command with a reason attached. A superficial but illogical reading would suggest that
the point is that as a result of your not gloating over your
enemy's fall he will suffer more. However, the point is surely
that God's wrath will turn from him to you if you are guilty of
the sin of gloating. The desire for revenge on our enemies is
instinctive but must be resisted. God is the Avenger. When
our enemies are judged we may be grateful but we dare not
gloat. Rather, the spirit of the Sermon on the Mount should
grip us: 'But I tell you: Love your enemies and pray for those
who persecute you' (Matt. 5:44).

> **Do not fret because of evil men**
> **or be envious of the wicked,**
> **for the evil man has no future hope,**
> **and the lamp of the wicked will be snuffed out**
>
> (24:19-20).

Synonymous command (negative) with reason: **'do not fret'** / **'[do not] be envious'**

This third negative command with a reason takes us back to the problem of the prosperity of the wicked which we have touched on twice before in this section (23:17-18; 24:1-2). Fretting (literally, 'getting hot') is mentioned here along with envy (as in Ps. 37). The trio of sins attacked in verses 15-20 is: firstly, discouragement because of your enemies; secondly, gloating over your enemy's falls; and, thirdly, envying such evil people. None of these routes is an acceptable one for our thoughts to travel down.

On reflection, verses 7-12 cover similar ground and that is why the calls to wisdom are necessary. Verses 14 and 20 highlight the difference between the wise believer and the wicked man. Here the evil man is seen as a flickering lamp, whose light is soon to be extinguished. This vividly evokes his lack of a **'future hope'**. Bridges quotes the unbelieving philosopher Hobbes speaking of death as 'a leap in the dark' and notes that he spoke more truly than he realized.

> **Fear the LORD and the king, my son,**
>   **and do not join with the rebellious,**
> **for those two will send sudden destruction upon**
>   **them,**
>   **and who knows what calamities they can bring?**
>   (24:21-22).

Synthetic command (positive / negative) with warning: **'fear'** / **'join with the rebellious'**

The closing verses of the section begin with a call to that fundamental discipline that is at the root of all wisdom — fear of the Lord. Here the application is to submission to the powers that be. It is very like 1 Peter 2:17, where we read, 'Show proper respect to everyone: Love the brotherhood of believers, fear God, honour the king.' As Absalom and others learned, rebellion will be punished by men when and where they can and in due time always by God. Fear of the Lord is the best basis for a true and lasting respect for government.

What these proverbs teach us

Taking these sayings together, we can say something about the nature of wisdom and its demands.

The nature of wisdom

From this passage we can make two general observations about the nature of wisdom, followed by three that are more specific.

Wisdom is edifying (24:3-4)

Each day we either build up (or pull down) wisdom in our lives. Each day we fill our lives with what is good (or bad). If you fill your mind with the Word, with faith in Christ and with holy living you will be edified by true wisdom. Anything else will destroy and spoil. What are you feeding your mind with? Nothing can edify but true wisdom.

Wisdom is effective (24:5-6)

We are reminded in these verses that knowledge is power. Strategy is so important. The person who goes through life without heavenly wisdom is bound to be a loser. Defeat is inevitable. If you are following the wrong strategy you must look to Lord and learn the right strategy for life.

Folly is ultimately inadequate (24:7)

Fools get away with a lot. In many situations, it is easy to hide one's ignorance; in others, it is not. When things get serious, we find that the fool, despite his boasts, has nothing to say. It is easy to mock God's Word now and live for everything but the Lord, but what about on the Day of Judgement? Every mouth will be stopped then. What will you say? Will your folly be exposed? Only heavenly wisdom gives real hope.

Folly will ultimately be condemned (24:8-9)

In many cases the evil intents of fools can be hidden, but when the truth comes out everyone will condemn them. At the judgement the truth will out and all their evil schemes will be exposed. Religious hypocrisy especially will be uncovered. Not everyone who cries, 'Lord, Lord, did we not do this and that in your name?' will go to heaven.

Folly sometimes shows itself only when there is a real test, in times of trouble (24:10)

How do you cope in a crisis? The foolish man's house looks fine in the sunshine, but what about when a flood comes? The man in the dinghy looked safe enough before the storm came. The unbeliever can look at his Christian neighbour and think there is no difference, but the test needs to be carried out in adverse conditions. Then the truth comes out. There is no reason to think that because you feel you are coping with life you will cope with death too.

The demands of wisdom

There are a number of commands stated or implied here. Each
includes a reason. Most are negative but some are positive.
The wise person heeds such commands.

Don't long to be with the wicked (24:1-2)

The truly wise have no real desire to be with the wicked. If
you secretly want to be just like the unbeliever, there is
something seriously wrong. To mix with wicked people is to
mix with those set on violence and making trouble. Flee rather
to Christ.

Rescue those about to perish, and do not pretend ignorance
(24:10-12)

To walk by on the other side is a great sin. Have you ever
done it? Be in no doubt God will champion the needy.

Realize that wisdom from above is the only hope for your soul
(24:13-14)

Wisdom is what your soul really needs. This is chiefly because
heavenly wisdom means hope for the future. In Christ there is
a certain future in heaven. Outside him, there is no hope.

Don't try to oppose the righteous (24:15-16)

The history of the world is littered with those who have opposed God's people. Anyone who sets out on that road is
doomed to failure. However much they oppose the righteous,
the latter will survive. You can't keep a good man down.

Don't gloat when your enemy is in trouble (24:17-18)

It is tempting to do so, but it is a sin. It is always easier to see what others deserve than to see our own hell-deserving sins.

Don't fret because of the apparent success of the wicked (24:19-20)

One thing that keeps some from coming to Christ is that they think they will be at a disadvantage. They envy wicked people and fret because of their apparent success. This is unnecessary. We need an eschatological perspective.

Fear the Lord and don't join in with rebels (24:21-22)

Above all, fear the Lord. If we really fear God, it will show in our attitude to those he raises up to rule over us. If we are rebellious, we shall be destroyed.

43.
The judgement is coming, so get your priorities right

Please read Proverbs 24:23-34

*Favouritism, honesty, priority for essentials, honesty,
vengeance, diligence*

More sayings of the wise

Following the sayings of the wise, we have a very brief fourth
section to Proverbs — yet more sayings of the wise: **'These
also are sayings of the wise'** (24:23). As in the previous section, these sayings vary in length — in English, the one in
verse 26 consists of only ten words, the one in verses 23b-25
of forty-three, and the final one of eighty-one words. Also
similar is the fact that three of the sayings are commands, two
negative and one positive.

The unifying theme in the background here seems to be
judgement. Two sayings have a legal background. The first
talks about judging, guilt and innocence (24:23-25). The second (24:26) seems to follow on and go with the first. The
fourth (24:28) also refers to testifying (in a court?) and talks
of vengeance (a form of justice). The final saying (24:30-34)
refers us back to a character we have met before — the sluggard. Here we see his final end, his judgement.

In view of this it would seem that we ought to consider all these sayings in the light of the coming final judgement proclaimed throughout Scripture. Although the third saying (24:27) has no reference to judgement it is, like the others, a call to get one's priorities right, to put first things first. What best helps us to do this is to think about the coming judgement. The thought of hitting another car encourages drivers to give priority to traffic as directed; the thought of a coming examination helps students give priority to their studies; the thought of the consequences for us if we do not prepare properly helps us to get our priorities right.

Give priority to justice over favourItism

> **To show partiality in judging is not good:**
> **Whoever says to the guilty, 'You are innocent' —**
> **peoples will curse him and nations denounce him.**
> **But it will go well with those who convict the guilty,**
> **and rich blessing will come upon them**
> (24:23-25).

> *Contrast:* **'whoever says to the guilty, "You are innocent"' / 'those who convict the guilty'**
> *Beatitude*

We have had sayings like these before (17:15; 18:5; see also 28:21). In many places in the law warnings are given against partiality or favouritism, especially in the courts. The prophets also preached against it and it is condemned more than once in the New Testament. The reason is that it can so easily lead to dishonesty. Favouritism may spring from good motives, but if it leads to injustice and dishonesty, it is not good: 'Do not deny justice to your poor people in their lawsuits.

Have nothing to do with a false charge and do not put an innocent or honest person to death, for I will not acquit the guilty' (Exod. 23:6-7). 'Do not show favouritism to a poor man in his lawsuit' (Exod. 23:3). 'Do not pervert justice; do not show partiality to the poor or favouritism to the great, but judge your neighbour fairly' (Lev. 19:15; cf. Deut. 1:17; 16:19). It is never good to declare the guilty innocent. It is dishonest. Partiality and favouritism are condemned in 1 Timothy 5:21 and James 2:4-6. Impartiality is an aspect of God's character (2 Chr. 19:7). Peter speaks of him as 'a Father who judges each man's work impartially' (1 Peter 1:17).

Negatively, people rightly curse and denounce anyone who acts unjustly and shows partiality to the guilty. *Positively,* the one who convicts the guilty can expect things to go well with him and to receive rich blessing.

'An honest answer is like a kiss on the lips' (24:26).
   Simile: **'an honest answer'** / **'a kiss'**

A 'straight' answer is **'like a kiss on the lips'**. It is an act of kindness. It is like the most intimate expression of friendship. Of course, people try to pervert truth — they threaten truthful witnesses; they promote flattery and lying. However, God calls on us to make honesty a priority. As we have said, it is the *only* policy for those who respect God's Word. A godly man tells the truth even when it hurts (see Ps. 15:4). He also takes the truth as a kiss on the mouth, even when it hurts.

The paradox is that things will go better if we are honest than if we pervert the truth thinking that by doing so we are making things better (see 28:23).

Is justice a priority with you? It is with God. His justice cannot be perverted. Of course, one of the amazing ways this is seen is in the fact that God actually does justify the wicked.

That truth does not oppose this verse. He justly declares the wicked innocent in the Lord Jesus Christ. The idea that he simply saves his favourites (the Jews or whatever) is utterly repugnant. No, he saves justly at the cost of the death of his Son. We can be sure of the absolute justice of God. He will condemn all sin, either in us or in his Son (as seen on the cross). If he did not spare his own Son, I can be sure he will not spare me if I am still in my sins at the judgement.

Give priority to essentials over desirables

> **Finish your outdoor work**
> **   and get your fields ready;**
> **after that, build your house**
>
> (24:27).

Synthetic command (positive): **'finish ...'** / **'after that ...'**

The point here is not immediately clear, although the subject is certainly the importance of priorities. No doubt a rural setting is in mind. Certainly, it is no good to be putting all your energy into building yourself a fine house when there is work waiting to be done in the fields. What good is an impressive house when there is nothing to eat? David Hubbard describes being shown round the perimeter of a massive and elegant wall encircling an estate that was never built on owing to the cost of the wall!

'House' can refer to 'household' and one application here is to the matter of raising a family. Marriage and having children is something to be entered on when full preparation has been made. It is tragic when young people end up married and having children when they are not ready for it. To be fully prepared does not mean that you have a beautiful, fully equipped house to move into, but that you realize what a commitment marriage is. Again, patience and hard work are very important.

The application is more general than that. The point is that first things must be first, essentials before luxuries. Heaven and how to know God must be our first concern. Christ and serving him must be our number one priority: 'But seek first his kingdom and his righteousness, and all these things will be given to you as well' (Matt. 6:33). Remember what Jesus said to Martha when she complained of Mary: '... only one thing is needed. Mary has chosen what is better, and it will not be taken away from her' (Luke 10:42). Another relevant passage, using a different figure, is Luke 14:28-30.

We all like the idea of seeing our desires for this life fulfilled, but the priority must be the world to come. The judgement is coming very soon. Oh yes, building a house on earth is fine, but first be sure that there is something growing in your field to keep hunger at bay over the coming winter. Where are all your energy and effort going? Into this life? Get your priorities right; think ahead. Look to Christ.

Give priority to honesty over vengeance

> Do not testify against your neighbour without cause,
> or use your lips to deceive.
> Do not say, 'I'll do to him as he has done to me;
> I'll pay that man back for what he did'
>
> (24:28-29).

Commands (negative): '**do not testify against**' / '**... use your lips to deceive**'; '**Do not say, "I'll do to him as he has done ..."**' / ' ' **"... I'll pay that man back."**' '

We shall take the two commands together. If verses 23-26 are about failing to condemn the guilty, verses 28-29 are concerned with the opposite problem of condemning the innocent. We need to be very careful when feelings of vengeance or desire for retaliation begin to grow in us. 'It is mine to avenge; I will repay,' says the Lord (Deut. 32:35). Trust him for vindication. 'Do not take revenge, my friends,' says Paul, 'but leave room for God's wrath' (Rom. 12:19). He has just told his readers, 'Do not repay anyone evil for evil. Be careful to do what is right in the eyes of everybody. If it is possible, as far as it depends on you, live at peace with everyone' (Rom. 12:17-18). (The proverb here is like Proverbs 20:22. In 25:21 we go one step higher.)

It is no good trying to take justice into our own hands, especially if we end up perverting it: 'If a malicious witness takes the stand to accuse a man of a crime, the two men involved in the dispute must stand in the presence of the LORD before the priests and the judges who are in office at the time. The judges must make a thorough investigation, and if the witness proves to be a liar, giving false testimony against his brother, then do to him as he intended to do to his brother. You must purge the evil from among you' (Deut. 19:16-19).

Honesty and patience are vital. Are you patient and honest? Are you waiting for the judgement and God's vindication? There will be no anomalies then.

Give priority to diligence over ease

I went past the field of the sluggard,
   past the vineyard of the man who lacks judgement;
thorns had come up everywhere,
   the ground was covered with weeds,
   and the stone wall was in ruins.

I applied my heart to what I observed
   and learned a lesson from what I saw:
A little sleep, a little slumber,
   a little folding of the hands to rest —
and poverty will come on you like a bandit
   and scarcity like an armed man

(24:30-34).

Here we see the sluggard again, first introduced in 6:6-11. Some of the same material is used here. This time the end of the story is given. The writer saw this with his own eyes and wants us to learn from it and not make the same mistake. The only way to do so is by applying it to our hearts. Are you doing that? This man's vineyard was neglected, not because he was ill but because he was lazy. To be lazy is to lack judgement. The lesson is in verses 33-34. If we are lazy or neglectful, we can lose everything.

What is your life like? Are there thorns everywhere? Is your life full of bad habits, things that cause pain, hurtful acts?

Or is it full of weeds? Is your life cluttered up with all sorts of worldly concerns so that there is no room for spiritual ones? The best antidote to weeds is to have flowers everywhere. Are there any in your garden?

Is the stone wall in ruins? Do you lack self-control? If you are like that — or if you are headed in that direction — you are in big trouble. Like a bandit, poverty will soon carry you off. You will end up in hell. Oh, take to heart the lesson of the sluggard! Do not be one who lacks judgement. Get your priorities right now. Give yourself to seeking the Lord, to prayer, to reading the Word and hearing it preached. Seek the Lord with all your heart. It is still a day of grace. There is still hope. Look to Christ.

C. H. Spurgeon preached twice on these verses. In one sermon he closes with two lessons:

1. *Our poverty by nature.* Unaided nature will always produce thorns and nettles, nothing else.

2. *The little value of natural good intentions.* He notes that the sluggard always meant to work hard one fine day: 'Only a little doze, and then he would tuck up his sleeves and show his muscle. Probably the worst people in the world are those who have the best intentions, but never carry them out.'

In the course of the other sermon he makes three points about the 'Broken fence' (the sermon's title):

1. *The boundary has gone.* Those lines of separation that were kept up by the good principles instilled in him by religious habits, a bold profession and a firm resolve, have vanished. Now the question is: '*Is* he a Christian?'

2. *The original desire is gone.* When a man's heart has its wall broken, his thoughts all go astray. They wander on the mountains of vanity. Like sheep, thoughts need careful shepherding or they will be off in no time. The godly hate vain thoughts but slothful men are bound to have plenty of them, for you cannot keep your thoughts from emptiness without stopping every gap and shutting every gate. Holy thoughts, sweet reflections and devout longings will be off and gone if we sluggishly allow the wall to get out of repair. Further, as good things go out, so bad come in. With the wall gone, every passer-by sees, as it were, an invitation to enter. The door is open and in he comes. Are there fruits? He picks them, of course. He walks about as if in a public place and he peeks into everything.

3. *The land itself will go away.* When the walls fall, the soil slips, terrace upon terrace and vines and trees go down with it. Then the rain comes and washes the

soil away until nothing is left but barren crags that would starve a lark. In the same manner a man may so neglect himself, and so neglect the things of God, and become so careless and indifferent about doctrine and holy living, that his power to do good ceases and his mind, heart and energy seem to be gone.

We must take such warnings seriously.
We close with Isaac Watts' words for children:

I passed by his garden, and saw the wild brier,
The thorn and the thistle, grow broader and higher;
The clothes that hang on him are turning to rags;
And his money still wastes, till he starves or he begs.

I made him a visit, still hoping to find
He had took better care for improving his mind:
He told me his dreams, talked of eating and drinking;
But he scarce reads his Bible, and never loves thinking.

Said I then to my heart, 'Here's a lesson for me:
This man's but a picture of what I might be…'

44.
Wisdom for rulers and for subjects

Please read Proverbs 25:1-28

Seeking truth, avoiding superficiality, removing wickedness, humility, accusations, confidences, apt words, rebukes, faithful messengers, boasting, persuasive words, moderation, false testimony, unfaithfulness, need for tact, love for enemies, sly words, wives, good news, importance of resisting evil, seeking honour for oneself, self-control

More proverbs of Solomon

'These are more proverbs of Solomon, copied by the men of Hezekiah king of Judah' (25:1). Here we start on a new section, the fifth part of the book of Proverbs and the final collection of proverbs by Solomon. It is found in the five chapters 25-29. It consists of more proverbs of Solomon that for some reason were not included in the earlier collection, but were assembled more than two centuries after Solomon's death (*c*. 930 B.C.) in the reign of good King Hezekiah (*c*. 715-686 B.C.). The men who did it were probably wise men and teachers of the law who served in Hezekiah's civil service. Were the sayings perhaps found in the temple during its cleansing? (see 2 Chr. 29).

The proverbs contain a number of vivid images, many drawn from the natural world — 1 Kings 4:33 tells us that Solomon 'described plant life, from the cedar of Lebanon to the hyssop that grows out of walls' and 'taught about animals and birds, reptiles and fish'. As before, they seem to have been arranged in an apparently random way, although the grouping is more thematic in places, such as in Proverbs 25:1-7 with its series of references to kings.

Chapter 25 divides fairly easily into five separate sections, which we shall look at under five main headings. You will notice that similes dominate this section. Usually the presence of a simile is not marked in Hebrew by the use of the words 'as' or 'like'. These are most often inserted by the translator. Here I have drawn attention to the various pictures used at the beginning of our comments on each verse.

Wisdom for rulers

Imagine Hezekiah's delight when this collection was first brought to his attention. Think of the onerous task of shepherding Israel as king. 'Help!' Here is help. Hezekiah's predecessor, the wisest king who ever lived, has collected useful proverbs for him, some specifically on the subject of kingship. Of course, we have already had proverbs on this subject (see especially 16:10-15; 20:2,8,26,28; 21:1). Here there are more. The first three are specifically about being king.

As has been said previously, we ought not to think that these proverbs have no relevance to us because we are not kings, or rulers. We are all called to be kings in some sense. Man was made to rule creation. We all have kingly responsibilities of one sort or other — to our children, to our wives, to ourselves. Here is heavenly wisdom on this matter. Further, the proverbs are designed not only for kings, but also for those who instruct and influence them.

It is your noble task to diligently seek out truth

'It is the glory of God to conceal a matter; to search out a matter is the glory of kings' (25:2).

Contrast: **'glory of God'** / **'glory of kings'**

Picture: There are many things in this world that we do not understand now, or have failed to understand in the past. God knows all these things. He has, as it were, concealed them from us.

Kings should know what is going on. They need to grasp things so that they can make sound decisions. Part of God's glory, what makes him the King of kings, is the way he knows so much more than we do. 'Oh the depths…!' we declare with Paul. There are many mysteries. It is our duty, as kings, to delve into some of these. It is your duty to find out the truth. Do not stick your head in the sand. Search out the facts earnestly. Remember Jesus' promise: 'Seek and you will find.' Give attention to God's Word ('Your Word is truth,' said Jesus). Ignorance is ignoble and shameful. You need to learn how to live, what goes on in this world and to be aware of any plots against you. Satan is certainly active, and you ought to know this.

This is the common interpretation of the verse. In 1877, however, C. H. Spurgeon preached an interesting sermon in which he challenges this view. He argues that in fact the verse is saying that whereas it is to a king's glory to discover the guilty and bring them to justice, God's glory is seen most clearly in the way he actually covers over the guilt of sinners and makes atonement for them. This is a very appealing interpretation and one that well deserves consideration.

If we stay with the traditional view we must remember that there are many things that God does not need to conceal because they are beyond us, and even though concealing is part of his glory, so also is revealing.

It is your noble task to avoid superficiality

'As the heavens are high and the earth is deep, so the hearts of kings are unsearchable' (25:3).
 Simile: **'the heavens are high and the earth is deep'** / **'the hearts of kings are unsearchable'**

Picture: Earth's atmosphere has three parts (stratosphere, mesosphere and below these the troposphere). The troposphere varies in height according to season but in summer extends about five miles (eight kilometres) above the poles and eleven miles (seventeen and a half kilometres) above the equator. Above that is space and above that again the third heaven, where God's throne is. The deepest place on earth is probably the Marianas Trench, south-west of Guam in the Pacific Ocean. At a depth of 36,198 feet (almost 11,000 metres), it is deep enough to contain Mount Everest. Such heights and depths are unsearchable.

A terse proverb in the original, this is probably to be understood as the counterpart to the previous verse. Part of the nobility of kings is that, like God, there ought to be something mysterious about them: 'He performs wonders that cannot be fathomed' (Job 5:9; 9:10); 'His understanding no one can fathom' (Isa. 40:28). Kings are to be good diplomats. They should not wear their hearts on their sleeves. Nobility involves a certain reserve and caution in speech and manners.

They have secrets. In the 1930s, Frank Buchman led a popular movement, known as the Oxford Group, or Moral Rearmament. One of its principles was absolute honesty. This involved openly confessing any hard thoughts against another person. Today there is a secular trend which involves dragging all the dirty laundry out in public by confessing to the newspapers. Usually such things are best shared with as few people as possible.

A sad feature of modern society is the superficiality, the lack of depth all round. We constantly hear complaints of things undergoing 'dumbing down'. Another sad feature is the way some are quite happy to be gushing and ephemeral. Indeed, they revel in it. A love of irony is made the excuse for all sorts of superficial nonsense. Are you merely skimming the surface of life? You have a soul. You have been made to serve God. Do not throw your life away on baubles.

Sometimes a person's actions may seem inexplicable, especially in the case of those in authority. We do not always have the facts and must be slow to judge them. This theme recurs in verses 7 and 8. For example, when Harold Wilson suddenly resigned as British prime minister there was much speculation as to the reason for his action, some of it pejorative. It later transpired that it was his fear of premature senility that led him to give up the job so soon. Only when this became clear was it possible to assess his action properly.

It is your noble task to drive out wickedness

Remove the dross from the silver,
> **and out comes material for the silversmith;**
remove the wicked from the king's presence,
> **and his throne will be established through righteousness**

(25:4-5).

Synthetic command / simile: **'remove the dross from the silver ... material for the silversmith' / 'remove the wicked ... his throne will be established'**

Picture: the refining of silver, an image also found in 17:3 and several other places in Scripture. God himself is so pictured in Malachi 3:2-3. The heat is turned up so that the dross is burned up and only the silver remains.

This is one of the deep works a king must perform. He is to be a refiner of silver. The atmosphere in the good king's court is such that wicked courtiers cannot feel comfortable. It is too oppressive for them. If wicked advisers remain there is no hope of successful government. Is this how you deal with wickedness in your life? This is how God deals with wickedness in his kingdom.

These things were to some extent true of Solomon and Hezekiah, but supremely they are true of Christ. He studied the Word of God and he lived out every sentence of it. He was full of integrity and full of depth. One day, he will judge the world. Go to him to learn to be kingly.

Wisdom for subjects

Of course, we are not only kings but subjects too. We are to be subject to God in everything; to the authorities that exist at various levels in the state; to our parents as children and to our husbands as wives in the family; to each other in the life of the church. The sayings in verses 6-10 are chiefly intended for subjects.

Seek humility

> **Do not exalt yourself in the king's presence,**
> **and do not claim a place among great men;**
> **it is better for him to say to you, 'Come up here,'**
> **than for him to humiliate you before a nobleman**
> **(25:6-7).**

Command (negative) with reason: **'do not exalt yourself in the king's presence'** / **'do not claim a place among great men'**

Picture: demotion and promotion in a royal court.

The king is sovereign. He chooses who will serve in his court. Pushing ourselves forward and seeking great things for ourselves is never right. The humiliation of demotion is not easy to face.

Being in a largely sedentary calling, I sometimes go lane-swimming to keep fit. The local pools arrange it so that there are three lanes — fast, medium and slow. I can never forget the humiliation of being in the middle lane on one occasion and being asked by a lifeguard to move to the slow lane as I was slowing others down. Jesus makes the same point when he says, 'When someone invites you to a wedding feast, do not take the place of honour, for a person more distinguished than you may have been invited. If so, the host who invited both of you will come and say to you, "Give this man your seat." Then, humiliated, you will have to take the least important place. But when you are invited, take the lowest place, so that when your host comes, he will say to you, "Friend, move up to a better place." Then you will be honoured in the presence of all your fellow guests. For everyone who exalts himself will be humbled, and he who humbles himself will be exalted' (Luke 14:8-10).

Whenever I see Hampton Court, the story of Cardinal Thomas Wolsey and Henry VIII comes to mind. Built as Wolsey's own private residence, the palace was eventually given to the king in a vain attempt to stall the cardinal's demotion, following a meteoric rise to a point where he had even nursed ambitions of becoming pope.

We need to humble ourselves before God, the great King, and before men. The disciples found that lesson hard to learn, and so do we. Note Jesus' reply to the request that James and John be given special places of honour: 'You know that the rulers of the Gentiles lord it over them, and their high officials exercise authority over them. Not so with you. Instead,

whoever wants to become great among you must be your servant, and whoever wants to be first must be your slave — just
as the Son of Man did not come to be served, but to serve, and
to give his life as a ransom for many' (Matt. 20:25-28).

Another warning against ambition comes later, in verse 27.

Be slow to accuse others

> **What you have seen with your eyes**
> > **do not bring hastily to court,**
> **for what will you do in the end**
> > **if your neighbour puts you to shame?**
>
> > > > > (25:7-8).

Command (negative) with warning: **'do not bring hastily…'**

Picture: You think you see someone doing wrong and so you
rush into court to expose that man's crime.

It is said that in Britain we are growing increasingly liti-
gious. Some are caught out by this and fail to win the large
sums they expect. How many times have you turned to accuse
someone else, only to realize it was your own fault? Our instinct is to blame others. Think of Adam and Eve in the Garden of Eden (Gen. 3). We must accept our own guilt. We must
also be slow to judge or blame others. Paul's warning in 1 Timothy 5:19 is appropriate here: 'Do not entertain an accusation
against an elder unless it is brought by two or three witnesses.'

Do not betray confidences

> **If you argue your case with a neighbour,**
> > **do not betray another man's confidence,**
> **or he who hears it may shame you**
> > **and you will never lose your bad reputation**
>
> > > > > (25:9-10).

Command (negative) with warning: **'do not betray another man's confidence'**

Of course, there are more subtle ways of attacking others. We can 'accidentally' let something slip. We can repeat intimate conversations to others. If we do that we may get a name for being a gossip, something condemned more than once in Proverbs. Such things are common today. In the New Testament, every encouragement is given to try to keep things quiet, to cover over sin. See the way that in Matthew 18 the way to deal with difficulties does not begin with telling them to the church. Great efforts must be made to avoid that scenario if possible. We must always seek peace as far as it lies in our power to bring it about.

Wisdom in relation to the tongue

This last reference leads on to a whole series of proverbs regarding the tongue and especially its competence. It is a reminder of the importance of this small but powerful member.

Recognize the beauty of apt words

'A word aptly spoken is like apples of gold in settings of silver' (25:11).
Simile: **'word aptly spoken'** / **'apples of gold in settings of silver'**

Picture: golden jewels offset by a silver surround. They look very attractive.

This verse exemplifies its own desideratum. Kings often have to give speeches. We all have to speak to an audience at times. Eloquence and rhetoric are often despised today, but we ought not to underestimate the power of fitting words spoken in a pleasing manner. Sometimes even a very few words are fondly remembered long after the event. Think of some of the sermons you have heard, or words of counsel you have received.

I remember someone once saying that it is important in a depression not to do too much thinking. What a help that little gem has been! It is to be hoped that similar gems will be found in the settings of silver we have sought to create for them in this book.

Recognize the beauty of Scripture. Endeavour yourself both to be winning in the way you speak and to speak the right word at the right time. John Kitto says we should understand the text as referring to citrons rather than apples and, like others, sees them as golden fruits in a silver basket. He draws attention to the 'apples of gold' found in the writings of the Puritan Thomas Brooks. He refers to a volume of Brooks' sayings produced under that title. He urges us to place them in the silver baskets of our minds. Here are two of them: '*Now* is an atom that will puzzle the wisdom of a philosopher, the skill of an angel, to divide.' 'Two things make good Christians: good actions and good aims; and though a good aim does not make a bad action good (as in Uzzah), yet a bad aim makes a good action bad (as in Jehu).'

This proverb acts as an introduction to the six that follow, which also deal with speech.

Appreciate rebukes

'Like an earring of gold or an ornament of fine gold is a wise man's rebuke to a listening ear' (25:12).
   Simile: **'wise man's rebuke'** / **'earring of gold ... ornament of fine gold'**

Picture: an attractive golden earring or some similar piece of jewellery. Perhaps we can think of two items of matching gold jewellery — one standing for the rebuke and the other for the hearing of it.

If comforting a person with the right words is hard, to rebuke someone is even harder to do well. It is never easy. Somehow, we must try to avoid putting the person down and discouraging him or her. Much depends on the receiver. I remember with diffidence once approaching an experienced and well-respected preacher to point out his classic misinterpretation of a famous text. He was unwilling to listen properly to what I had to say. It was like trying to pass on an unwanted gift. If there is willingness to receive it, even a rebuke can be an asset, something attractive. We can learn from it. Jesus said, 'He who has ears to hear, let him hear.' Do you have a listening ear? Part of the purpose of this chapter is to rebuke you. Are you paying attention? Are you appreciating it?

Pass on messages faithfully

Like the coolness of snow at harvest time
   is a trustworthy messenger to those who send him;
   he refreshes the spirit of his masters

(25:13).

   Simile: **'coolness of snow at harvest time' / 'trustworthy messenger'**

Picture: in the only place where the comparison is made explicit we see a man sweating in the toil and heat of harvest (May-October) and being refreshed by snow from the mountains. Perhaps an iced wine-cup is in mind.

Whether one is sent with an answer or a question, faithfulness to the task is vital. Such faithful messengers refresh their masters' spirits like **'the coolness of snow at harvest time'**. Eloquence must never lead to dishonesty. We must be faithful messengers if we are to refresh others. Here is a word for preachers and for all who seek to share the gospel message. We can be refreshing to God if we are faithful. We must not be like the Laodiceans of whom Christ said, 'I know your deeds, that you are neither cold nor hot. I wish you were either one or the other! So, because you are lukewarm — neither hot nor cold — I am about to spit you out of my mouth' (Rev. 3:15-16).

Do not make empty boasts

'Like clouds and wind without rain is a man who boasts of gifts he does not give' (25:14).

Simile: **'clouds and wind without rain' / 'man who boasts of gifts he does not give'**

Picture: clouds and wind that threaten rain but in the end bring nothing.

Another temptation in speech is to hype up what we are saying. However, empty promises and boasts are useless. To brew up a storm about nothing is wrong. Watch out for false teachers who do this. It is all wind and fury, but the showers of real blessing never come. Peter and Jude speak of them in these terms: 'These men are springs without water and mists driven by a storm. Blackest darkness is reserved for them. For they mouth empty, boastful words and, by appealing to the lustful desires of sinful human nature, they entice people who are just escaping from those who live in error. They promise them freedom, while they themselves are slaves of depravity — for a man is a slave to whatever has mastered him' (2 Peter 2:17-19). 'These men are blemishes at your love feasts, eating with you without the slightest qualm — shepherds who feed only themselves. They are clouds without rain, blown along by the wind... These men are grumblers and fault-finders; they follow their own evil desires; they boast about themselves and flatter others for their own advantage' (Jude 12,16). Faithful preaching is not like this.

Recognize the power of persuasion

'Through patience a ruler can be persuaded, and a gentle tongue can break a bone' (25:15).

Simile: **'gentle tongue ... bone' / 'patience'**

Picture: a soft and fleshy tongue breaking a hard and solid bone. It is a striking image. Few tongues can literally break bones, although one might persuade a person to break a bone by something one says. Probably the thought is that of softening a hard bone with the soft tongue to the point where it can easily be broken.

Few people recognize the power of words. They speak of 'mere words' and claim that 'Words will never hurt me,' and so on. But think of the effect patient persuasion can have. Do not doubt the power of persistent false teaching on one hand, and of faithful daily witness and preaching on the other. While one brief tirade is likely to do little, patient and persistent persuasion may do much. Note how Paul urges gentle instruction for those who oppose God's servants, 'in the hope that God will grant them repentance leading them to a knowledge of the truth' as they come to their senses and escape the devil's trap (2 Tim. 2:25).

Know when to stop

> **If you find honey, eat just enough —**
> **too much of it, and you will vomit.**
> **Seldom set foot in your neighbour's house —**
> **too much of you, and he will hate you**
>
> (25:16-17).

Simile: **'honey ... eat ... too much ... you will vomit' / 'set foot in your neighbour's house — too much ... he will hate you'**

Picture: eating too much sweet honey and vomiting as a result.

In Proverbs 24:13 we were encouraged to eat honey. The trouble with honey, however, is that its sweetness makes it sickly if one takes too much. The picture can be applied to many things. I often think of it as we approach the final day of a ministers' conference. Moderation is necessary in most things. Only the gospel itself is exempt. Here it is applied to the pleasure of company and the danger of outstaying your welcome. This has a wider application than to speech itself, but it is a related topic. Matthew Henry quotes the well-known English proverb, 'Familiarity breeds contempt,' and the less familiar, 'After the third day fish and company become distasteful.' Part of the art of witnessing and preaching is knowing when to stop. It also applies to Christian friendship and fellowship.

Do not give false testimony

'Like a club or a sword or a sharp arrow is the man who gives false testimony against his neighbour' (25:18).
　　Simile: **'club'**; **'sword'**; **'sharp arrow'** / **'false testimony'**

Picture: using a wooden club, a metal sword or a sharpened arrow to inflict harm.

Here we are not thinking of simple unfaithfulness but of malicious witness. To bear false witness is like bringing out an instrument of murder and using it. There is little difference.

Wisdom in relation to others

The proverbs above lead on to the more general subject of relations with others.

Take care on whom you rely

'Like a bad tooth or a lame foot is reliance on the unfaithful in times of trouble' (25:19).

Simile: **'a bad tooth or a lame foot'** / **'reliance on the unfaithful'**

Picture: the imagery of the bad tooth and lame foot point to their uselessness rather than the pain they may cause. Rather than helping you to eat, a bad tooth gets in the way. A lame foot is an encumbrance, not an asset, on the road.

So it is with the unfaithful if we are tempted to rely on them in times of need. Take care to whom you look. Christ is the only one we can always rely on. Be thankful to him when he gives friends who can also be relied on in times of trouble. He himself had no such help in his time of greatest need. Can people rely on you at such times?

Avoid inappropriate cheer

> **Like one who takes away a garment on a cold day,**
> **or like vinegar poured on soda,**
> **is one who sings songs to a heavy heart**
>
> (25:20).

Simile: **'one who takes away a garment on a cold day ... vinegar poured on soda'** / **'one who sings songs to a heavy heart'**

Picture: Again we have strong imagery. Taking away someone's coat when it is cold is obvious. In the case of vinegar being poured on soda we are talking about something likely to cause a moment's fizz but that will spoil both ingredients.

The warning is against insensitive approaches to those with heavy hearts. Singing songs is also metaphoric. You certainly do not say, 'Let's have a sing-song,' to someone who is downcast. In practice, however, very similar approaches are made. Mourners are told, 'Life must go on,' and those who have been jilted that there are 'plenty more fish in the sea'. The depressed are urged to 'cheer up' and Christians with cancer are glibly told that 'all things are working together for their good'. Job's counsellors are perhaps the quintessential example of how not to comfort heavy hearts. It is often said that their finest hour was when they simply sat there and said nothing. Romans 12:15 tells us to weep with those who weep. Like our Good Samaritan Saviour, we should pour in oil and wine, not vinegar and cold air.

Love your enemies

**If your enemy is hungry, give him food to eat;
    if he is thirsty, give him water to drink.
In doing this, you will heap burning coals on his head,
    and the LORD will reward you**

                                                        (25:21-22).

Synonymous command (positive): **'give him food'** / **'give him water'**

Simile: **'if your enemy is hungry give him food; if he is thirsty ... water'** / **'you will heap burning coals on his head'**

Picture: finding your enemy in need of food to eat or water to drink.

These verses are quoted in Romans 12:20. A. W. Pink quotes one old writer as saying, 'The law of love is not expounded more spiritually in any single precept either by Christ or his apostles than in this exhortation.' It is the high point in the series beginning at Proverbs 17:13 and going on in 20:22, etc. The reference to heaping **'burning coals on his head'** is variously understood. Is it speaking of God's wrath, the man's own shame, a means of atonement (as with the censer of burning coals referred to in Leviticus 16:12), a provision for a need or the man's purification? The idea of stoking up greater judgement on him is the converse of what is suggested. The other options also create difficulties. In a little book on Romans 12:14-21 *(How to overcome evil)* Jay Adams argues that 'The coals are your good deeds heaped on him.' He reminds us that the allusion is to ancient warfare when hot coals would be poured out on enemy troops in order to repel them. In modern terms, he says, we need to use our good deeds like napalm. 'Your good deeds will so blunt his attack, disorient and discourage him that he'll be ineffective as an enemy.' This, he reminds us, is God's method in the cross.

However we understand the coals, it is clear that even if the person is our worst enemy our reaction when he is in trouble must be to do all we can to help him. My father-in-law travels often to the United States. He tells the story of a man in the Deep South, walking along the street with an African American brother, when they passed a typical 'redneck' who made some sneering remark about the black man. The latter then spoke about how he would like to get his own back on the white man. He described how he would like to find the man by the roadside one rainy night having to deal with a puncture in his car tyre. He would like to be driving past at that time. Why? So he could gloat? Oh no. He would like to be able to stop his car, get out and come and help the man who had been so insulting to put a fresh tyre on the car. That is a 'spirit of revenge' that all Christians should seek to nurture.

Do not be sly

'As a north wind brings rain, so a sly tongue brings angry looks' (25:23).

Simile: **'north wind brings rain' / 'sly tongue brings angry looks'**

Picture: the north wind bringing rain.

Again, do not simply pretend to be friendly to enemies. Those who slyly use their tongues to slander others deserve to meet with anger. When the north wind blows it often brings dark storm clouds. When we speak slyly, we should expect something similar. It is an act of love to respond to a sly tongue with angry looks. Bridges says that the sly tongue here wounds four at once — the speaker, the one he slanders, the hearer and God himself.

Beware the quarrelsome wife

'Better to live on a corner of the roof than share a house with a quarrelsome wife' (25:24).

Better than: **'corner of the roof' / 'share a house'**

Picture: living quietly in the spare room rather than downstairs with a quarrelsome wife.

This repeats 21:9 and reminds us again that marriage will not solve every problem. The context is the power of the tongue. There is nothing worse than someone near to you who always wants to quarrel about everything. At the time of writing, today's newspaper previews a television comedy drama that focuses on an Australian couple who have been married for forty years: 'The way she sees it, there are a million things to do around the house, and all Joe wants to do is sit around drinking beer and reading the obituary column. The way *he* sees it, Dossa is turning into the biggest nag in Australia.'

Like the proverb, the situation sounds comical but in reality, it is tragic. Yet quite apart from tragic marriage partnerships, there are also millions married to cults and false philosophies that can only make them miserable.

Recognize the power of good news

'Like cold water to a weary soul is good news from a distant land' (25:25).
   Simile: **'cold water'** / **'good news from a distant land'**

Picture: refreshing, cold water, straight from the spring.

Here is the very opposite of the previous picture. Like a refreshing cup of cold water is good news from far away. Solomon knew what it was like to wait for good news of his sailing ships (1 Kings 9:26-28). Think further back to Jacob receiving the wonderful news that Joseph was alive down in Egypt (Gen. 45:26). Or what about Paul waiting for news from Thessalonica? (1 Thess. 3:5-8). Communications are so much quicker today but good news from missionaries in other lands still refreshes us when we hear it.

When William Carey went to India in 1793 delays and losses meant that he received no letters for nearly two years. In his journal for the end of January 1795 he wrote, 'Much engaged in writing, having begun to write letters to Europe; but having received none, I feel that hope deferred makes the heart sick. However, I am so fully satisfied of the firmness of their friendship that I feel a sweet pleasure in writing to them, though rather of a forlorn kind; and having nothing but myself to write about, feel the awkwardness of being an egotist. I feel a social spirit though barred from society... I sometimes walk in my garden, and try to pray to God; and if I pray at all it is in the solitude of a walk. I thought my soul a little drawn out today, but soon gross darkness returned. Spoke a word or two to a Mohammedan upon the things of God, but I feel to be as bad as they.' Then on May 9 we have the following entry: 'Blessed be God, I have at last received letters and other articles from our friends in England ... from dear brethren Fuller, Morris, Pearce, and Rippon, but why not from others?'

The greatest good news is the good news from heaven that Christ saves sinners. That is more refreshing than anything. Jesus likens it to living water which when you drink you never thirst again (John 4:14).

In a sermon on this verse, Spurgeon speaks mainly on the good news from heaven for sinners and saints. For sinners the good news is that God remembers you with pity and has prepared the way by which you may come back to him. He has sent you his Word, and sent his servants to invite you to come back to him. Many have already returned and been welcomed. For them God has provided all the means needed to bring them back. Sinners can turn to Christ now.

He also speaks of good news from earth to heaven. He suggests that it flies there when a sinner repents, when Christians run well, when the kingdom advances and when saints come home. He says, 'I sometimes like to send a message home by some whose hands I grasp as they are in the last article of death. Rowland Hill, when he was very old, said to one aged Christian who was dying, "I hope they have not forgotten to send for old Rowley"; and then he added, "Take my love up to the three glorious Johns, the apostle John and John Bunyan and John Newton."'

Wisdom in relation to oneself

Do not give way to the wicked

'Like a muddied spring or a polluted well is a righteous man who gives way to the wicked' (25:26).

Simile: 'muddied spring ... polluted well' / 'righteous man who gives way to the wicked'

Picture: a spring or well producing contaminated water.

The word 'compromise' does have a good sense but when it is the compromise that means a good man has given way to the wicked, it is tragic. It is like coming parched to a spring or a well in that hot and dusty land, only to find that it has been polluted and the water cannot be drunk. In recent years the evangelical world has been hit hard by cases of godly men giving in to moral and doctrinal error. Each time the spring has been muddied or the well polluted we have grieved. It is the very opposite of the refreshment spoken of in the previous verse. The worst scenario occurs where men have attempted to carry on in the ministry and so the pollution has spread far and wide.

In a book originally published under the title *Can fallen pastors be restored?* John Armstrong lists eight things pastors need to do to avoid falling into sexual misconduct. They can be summarized as: understanding the nature of sexual temptation and of the seductive woman of Proverbs 6; guarding your mind and your own marriage; taking precautions as you minister; maintaining relationships with real accountability; cultivating all round well-being and often contemplating the consequences of sexual sin. Similar things could be said regarding other pollutants.

Do not seek your own honour

'It is not good to eat too much honey, nor is it honourable to seek one's own honour' (25:27).

Simile: 'to eat too much honey' / 'to seek one's own honour'

Picture: eating too much sweet and sickly honey.

Here the picture of eating too much honey is applied to ambition and self-seeking. The saying is otherwise similar to 27:2 and warns against getting intoxicated with thoughts of our own importance. Adlai Stevenson famously said, 'Flattery is all right as long as you don't inhale.' Fishing for compliments seems innocuous, but it is a dangerous sport where it is easy to be pulled in and to drown. We desire to be thought well of, of course (honey is sweet), but it cannot be allowed to become our *raison d'être* in life (too much honey is not good). The apostle Paul was scrupulous in this regard, as his letters to the Corinthians testify in many places. As for our Lord, even his enemies had to acknowledge that he paid no attention to the opinions of men (Matt. 22:16).

Be self-controlled

'Like a city whose walls are broken down is a man who lacks self-control' (25:28).

Simile: **'city whose walls are broken down'** / **'man who lacks self-control'**

Picture: a walled city with broken down walls due to war or neglect.

When the walls of Jericho tumbled down the Israelites were able to march in and take the city. What a delight it was to Israel's enemies when Jerusalem's walls lay broken down in the time of Nehemiah! When we lose our tempers the devil has similar opportunities. We shall make no spiritual progress without self-control. Tantrums are sometimes tolerated, even promoted in some situations, but can do no ultimate good.

Beethoven was once performing a new piano concerto in Vienna. Forgetting that he was the soloist, he began conducting and then threw out his arms with such force that he knocked the lights off the piano. He began again with two choirboys holding the lights. This time his hand hit one of the boys, who dropped the light. Enraged, he then struck the piano with such force that the first chord broke six strings. The audience was in fits of laughter despite the man's undoubted genius.

Paul reminds Timothy that 'God did not give us a spirit of timidity, but a spirit of power, of love and', last but not least, 'of self-discipline' (2 Tim. 1:7). Proverbs 16:32 interestingly makes a similar point by drawing a different illustration from the same situation.

45.
The fool, the sluggard and other troublemakers

Please read Proverbs 26:1-28

Honouring fools, undeserved curses, rods for fools, not answering fools, answering fools, sending messages by fools, proverbs and fools, honouring fools, proverbs and fools, messages carried by fools, repeated folly, sluggards' excuses, sluggards and sleep, sluggards and completing work, sluggards and conceit, meddling, practical jokes, gossiping and quarrelling, false enthusiasm, hidden malice, attacks that backfire, flattery

In Proverbs 26 we meet some rather unsavoury characters. In considering them three purposes are in view: firstly, to warn against such people; secondly, to warn against becoming like them; and, thirdly, to urge faith in Christ, who is nothing like these characters at all

The first two characters we have met before in Proverbs; the others we have not. Again, there are many similes here, which I have attempted to explain first.

The fool

Verses 1-11 are nearly all about the fool. The fool is mentioned over fifty times in the book of Proverbs. It is important always to remember that the word refers to moral deficiencies rather than mental ones. A fool is one who deliberately chooses what is wrong. Here we have a number of lessons on how to handle such people.

Do not honour a fool

'Like snow in summer or rain in harvest, honour is not fitting for a fool' (26:1).
    Simile: **'snow in summer or rain in harvest'** / **'honour ... for a fool'**

Picture: inappropriate weather. Both snow in summer and rain at harvest are unwanted and tend to spoil things.
    'The richest blessings lose their value when unsuitably bestowed,' says Bridges. Rain is a blessing but it is not appreciated when the harvest is being gathered in (also on this same theme is verse 8 below). To give honour to a fool is not only incongruous, but also potentially disastrous. It gives the fool a false idea of himself; it inevitably rebounds on the person who gives it, and is a bad influence on others. Yet today the opposite line is often taken. Fools, such as criminals and corrupters of morals, are fêted with publicity and awards, while the wise are despised. The Lord Jesus Christ is especially mocked and derided.

A ray of light

In verse 2, there is a ray of light amid the gloom cast by the fool, especially if he curses you.

'Like a fluttering sparrow or a darting swallow, an undeserved curse does not come to rest' (26:2).
    Simile: **'fluttering sparrow or ... darting swallow'** / **'undeserved curse'**

Picture: a sparrow or a swallow apparently not coming to rest at any point because there is no appropriate landing-place.

It is a little like: 'Sticks and stones may break my bones, but names can never hurt me.' Fools surround us and some of them imagine they can throw curses like thunderbolts but, in fact, a curse can never come to rest if it is undeserved. Remember how Balaam spoke: 'How can I curse those whom God has not cursed?' (Num. 23:8). Goliath's curse on David (1 Sam. 17:43) and Saul's curse on Jonathan (1 Sam. 14:28) similarly failed because they were undeserved. The Lord Jesus Christ is an anomaly in one sense. He hung on the cross under a curse even though he deserved no such treatment. On the other hand, his resurrection was his vindication.

If you desert a fool or decry him, he may well curse you for it. That can be unpleasant but such a curse can do you no harm if you are not a fool yourself. But that is the recurring question: 'How can I be wise?' The initial lesson is there again in verse 12: 'Do you see a man wise in his own eyes? There is more hope for a fool than for him.'

A fool deserves to be punished

'A whip for the horse, a halter for the donkey, and a rod for the backs of fools!' (26:3).
  Simile: **'whip'; 'halter' / 'rod'**

Picture: in order to get a response from a horse or a donkey whips and halters are sometimes necessary. The sound of the whip startles the animal and makes it move; a halter around its neck persuades it to move in the required direction.

Corporal punishment has been all but totally outlawed in the United Kingdom, yet it is the case that some fools respond to nothing else. There are children who will not respond to anything else. There are teenagers and young men who might respond to the birch or something similar in a way that they never will to 'community service' and other schemes.

Respond to him appropriately

> **Do not answer a fool according to his folly,**
>   **or you will be like him yourself.**
> **Answer a fool according to his folly,**
>   **or he will be wise in his own eyes**
>
>   (26:4-5).

   Commands (negative/positive) with reasons: **'do not answer'** / **'answer'**

Here is a classic case of what at first sight appears to be a contradiction. However, it is hardly credible that the writer would not have noticed it! Rather, these adjacent proverbs bring out, on the one hand, the limitations of any given proverb and, on the other, the dilemma we face when reasoning with the unreasonable. Sometimes it is better to veer towards the Scylla of simply saying nothing. At other times it is better, indeed necessary, to head towards the Charybdis of reasoning with such people. Part of wisdom is the skilful application of the right method at the right time. On one hand, we want to avoid becoming fools ourselves by answering foolish questions. A Jewish proverb says that when a wise man argues with a fool then two fools are arguing. On the other hand, sometimes the fool has to be taken on at his own game or he will never see his error.

    For example, when the so-called Jehovah's Witnesses knock at your door do you spend time speaking to them or not? Pray for wisdom. If we see something blasphemous on television or in the newspaper, should we always respond? How should we deal with people who appear to be wasting our time? Open-air workers are always wrestling with the problem of how to deal with hecklers. Like the Lord Jesus we must avoid using the fool's methods and repaying insult with insult (see 1 Peter 2:23; 3:9), and we must sometimes answer their foolish questions and accusations with great wisdom (see Matt. 12; 15; 21; 22).

Do not rely on him as he is useless

'Like cutting off one's feet or drinking violence is the sending of a message by the hand of a fool' (26:6).
   Simile: **'cutting off one's feet'** / **'sending a message by ... a fool'**

Picture: to cut off one's feet would be an example of madness. **'Drinking violence'** is a metaphor for encouraging violence to come down on one's own head — another example of madness.

'Like a lame man's legs that hang limp is a proverb in the mouth of a fool' (26:7).
   Simile: **'lame man's legs'** / **'proverb in the mouth of a fool'**

Picture: a man whose legs are paralysed cannot walk. If he is sat on a stool, his legs simply hang limp. He cannot move them.

   Verse 6 takes up the theme of 25:13,19. Spurgeon has a proverb that says positively, 'Your trust is worthy when you trust the trustworthy.' Verses 6 and 7 both remind us that fools are unreliable. Even if they start with the truth, they will mishandle and distort it at some point. This is one reason why hearing the gospel is so difficult. So few who claim to preach it get the message right — it is only the wise in Christ who truly understand it. When you hear an important message, bear in mind who is speaking. Does he have it right? Even the little wisdom that fools have is likely to be handled ineptly.

Wisdom is not simply a matter of reading up on a subject. Even if a fool spoke one of the inspired proverbs, he could make it sound lame. Think of how people will use any number of biblical phrases, or language similar to that used by Christians, such as, 'There's no rest for the wicked'; 'You've got to have faith'; of someone being 'the salt of the earth', 'a Good Samaritan', or 'back on the straight and narrow', or of ideas falling 'on stony ground', without their ever coming to grips with the real meaning of these expressions.

'Like tying a stone in a sling is the giving of honour to a fool' (26:8).
Simile: **'stone in a sling' / 'honour to a fool'**

Picture: some translations suggest that the image is simply that of a stone in a sling. A stone is placed in the leather pocket of a sling, swung round and propelled at the enemy. David famously killed Goliath by this deceptively simple means. Both in the past and to this day in the Middle East, the weapon has proved surprisingly effective. The NIV pictures it as tied down for some reason and so rendered ineffective.

This reinforces what we have said above on verse 3. One would think that giving a man authority would produce some effect. Do not be so sure if the man is a fool. It is like expecting a good shot from a spiked gun. Simply ordaining a man or making him a deacon guarantees nothing.

Do not depend on him as he is dangerous

'Like a thornbush in a drunkard's hand is a proverb in the mouth of a fool' (26:9).

Simile: **'thornbush in a drunkard's hand' / 'proverb in the mouth of a fool'**

Picture: Think of a drunkard. In his hand he has a thornbush. It is not clear which end of it he is holding — the safe or thorny end. In the former case if he is violent, or just careless, anyone who goes near him is in danger of being torn by thorns. In the latter case, the fool does himself no good with what wisdom he has. Like a drunkard, he is insensitive to the pain he inflicts.

'Like an archer who wounds at random is he who hires a fool or any passer-by' (26:10).
Simile: **'archer who wounds at random' / 'he who hires a fool ...'**

Picture: Here is an archer. He takes his bow and arrow and shoots randomly at anyone he sees. Probably the equivalent today would be a man with a gun shooting at anyone who happens to come in his sights. How dangerous!

The fool is not simply useless. He is positively dangerous. Think of how biblical proverbs are misused today. The fool will tell you that 'Money is the root of all evil,' and that 'Charity begins at home,' and 'God helps those who help themselves.' Biblical principles are undermined and distorted despite a patina of apparent wisdom. Watch out! Luther says, 'When a drunkard carries and brandishes in his hand a sweet briar, he scratches more with it than he allows the roses to be smelled; so a fool with the Scriptures or a judicial maxim oft causes more harm than profit.' Many wrest the Scriptures to their own destruction and that of others.

Or think of the way many people acquire their philosophies. They see a television programme, or a magazine article, or they read a book, or sometimes have their own idle thoughts. Soon these things are raised to the level of a creed and become guiding axioms. If you had an important errand to be run would you just rush out and ask anyone to do it? No, you would choose someone reliable. You would use the best person available. So why trust your soul to fools? Why trust in ideas you simply came across by chance? There are other applications. One has only to think how some churches choose their deacons and some places their politicians.

There is much dispute about the translation of this proverb owing to various problems. We have followed the NIV.

See that he is incorrigible

'As a dog returns to its vomit, so a fool repeats his folly'
(26:11)
   Simile: **'dog ... its vomit' / 'fool ... his folly'**

Picture: I will never forget the first time I saw a dog being sick and then eating its vomit. It turns the stomach. Human logic says, 'If it has caused me so much trouble once why even think about trying it again?' An animal does not use such logic.

Many people do not recognize a fool when they see one. One reason is that they look at the wrong thing. They say of a person, 'Look at the good he does ... the company he keeps ... the reforms he makes ... his potential...' But if he keeps going back to folly then he is a fool. Have nothing to do with him. Temporary repentance of the sort illustrated here is so common some make a joke of it. Giving up drugs, drink or a debauched sex life is easy, they say: 'I've done it loads of times!' What this hides is the way they are really disgusted at these sins but cannot stop going back to them. The apostle Peter takes up this proverb with an additional one from elsewhere to describe apostasy: 'If they have escaped the corruption of the world by knowing our Lord and Saviour Jesus Christ and are again entangled in it and overcome, they are worse off at the end than they were at the beginning. It would have been better for them not to have known the way of righteousness, than to have known it and then to turn their backs on the sacred command that was passed on to them. Of them the proverbs are true: "A dog returns to its vomit," and, "A sow that is washed goes back to her wallowing in the mud"' (2 Peter 2:22).

The sluggard

Here we come to a second sort of troublemaker. There is good reason to believe that the sluggard is in mind not only in verses 13-16 but also in verse 12. This becomes clear when we compare it with verse 16. Verse 12 applies not only to sluggards, however.

'Do you see a man wise in his own eyes? There is more hope for a fool than for him' (26:12).
   Synthetic: **'man wise in his own eyes'** / **'more hope for a fool'**

It is frightening to think that there is something worse than being a fool — being a fool but thinking you are wise. That is the very worst sort of fool. It is no good reading about fools and thinking, 'I'm glad I'm not like that.' Rather we should see how much we resemble the fool. We deserve judgement, not honour. We are unreliable, unskilled, reckless, incorrigible and at the mercy of every fool who comes along. That is our nature. Our only hope is Christ, the wisdom of God. He is worthy of all honour. He is reliable, skilful, wise, ever good and well able to overcome all his enemies. Run to him. Paul makes a similar point when he says, 'The man who thinks he knows something does not yet know as he ought to know' (1 Cor. 8:2; cf. 3:18).

Here, then, are some characteristics of the sluggard:

He always makes excuses

'The sluggard says, There is a lion in the road, a fierce lion roaming the streets!' (26:13).
   Synthetic: **'sluggard says, "There is a lion..."'**

Picture: a sluggard saying he cannot go out into the street because there is a lion there.

This is similar to 22:13 although it is suggested that possibly the sluggard now sees two lions rather than one — one to the right and one to the left. 'I'm not lazy,' says the sluggard; 'I'm a realist.' 'I'm just facing the facts,' he declares. People give endless excuses for not coming to Christ. They are too young or too old, too busy or not too sure. They cannot believe God exists; they cannot understand the Trinity, or election; they are concerned about evolution; they cannot accept miracles; they are unsure about the Bible's trustworthiness; and what about suffering? So often these are mere excuses.

Spurgeon pleads with sinners as he expounds this text: 'If thou desirest Christ truly, there is no effectual difficulty that can really block thee out from coming to him. You notice that Solomon does not say that there were any lions in the way: he only tells us that the sluggard said so. Well, you need not believe a lazy man. The sluggard said it twice; but it did not make it true. Everybody knew what a poor fool he was, and that it was only in his own imagination that there were any lions at all. Do not believe your sluggish self then, and do not believe the sluggish speeches of others. There are no lions except in your own imagination.'

He loves sleeping

'As a door turns on its hinges, so a sluggard turns on his bed' (26:14).
　　Simile: **'door ... on its hinges'** / **'sluggard ... on his bed'**

Picture: a door is attached to its frame on one side by its hinges. It can swing back and forth, but will not come away from its frame in the wall unless the hinges are unscrewed. So the sluggard seems to be umbilically connected to his bed. He can move in it but he cannot, it seems, get out of it. You see him rise a little and think he is about to get up but, no, he promptly flops back down again.

This typifies the sluggard's lack of ambition or drive. He cannot come to church, study the Bible, or discuss the gospel because he is 'too busy in the evenings', or 'not good in the mornings', or 'finds it difficult to follow'. In truth, he is simply lazy! He may have a fit body, but he has an undisciplined mind.

Isaac Watts wrote:

'Tis the voice of the sluggard; I heard him complain:
'You have waked me too soon, I must slumber again.'
As the door on its hinges, so he on his bed,
Turns his sides, and his shoulders, and his heavy head.

'A little more sleep, and a little more slumber;'
Thus he wastes half his days, and his hours without number:
And when he gets up, he sits folding his hands,
Or walks about saunt'ring, or trifling he stands.

He never completes anything he starts

'The sluggard buries his hand in the dish; he is too lazy to bring it back to his mouth' (26:15).

Synthetic: **'buries his hand'** / **'too lazy to bring it back'**

Picture: at a meal the sluggard gets his hand as far as the bowl of crisps, or whatever, but is somehow unable to bring it to his mouth. (19:24 is almost exactly the same.)

The sluggard does not like to be hassled. He shows interest in the gospel but it soon fades. Why? Because he is a sluggard. He would rather starve than make an effort. Yet Jesus says plainly, 'Make every effort to enter through the narrow door, because many, I tell you, will try to enter and will not be able to' (Luke 13:24).

The call to 'make every effort' is a recurring one in the New Testament: 'Let us ... make every effort to do what leads to peace and to mutual edification' (Rom. 14:19). 'Make every effort to keep the unity of the Spirit through the bond of peace' (Eph. 4:3). 'Let us ... make every effort to enter that rest, so that no one will fall' (Heb. 4:11). 'Make every effort to add to your faith goodness ... knowledge ... self-control... perseverance ... godliness ... brotherly kindness ... and ... love' (2 Peter 1:5). 'Make every effort to be found spotless, blameless and at peace with him' (2 Peter 3:14).

He is conceited

'The sluggard is wiser in his own eyes than seven men who answer discreetly' (26:16). Here is a straight comparison. The sluggard, of course, will not accept all this. He defends himself. He will argue over whose turn it is to make the tea, and who is going to run upstairs and fetch the book. These are not principled stands but symptoms of laziness.

It is true that many who say, 'I'm a Catholic,' or 'I'm Muslim,' or atheist, or whatever, are simply hiding behind an excuse. I remember a zealous Christian calling at our house to invite us to church when I was a boy. My mother, who was not then converted, said, 'But I'm Church of England.' 'Ah, I was brought up on the Thirty-nine Articles myself,' was his genuine reply. My mother had never heard of the Thirty-nine Articles. The 'Church of England' plea was really a smokescreen. In many ways the lazy person is worse off even than the fool.

Look to Christ, who has done all the work so that simply trusting in him is truly enough.

Other troublemakers

In verses 17-28 we have a whole string of other troublemakers. Most of these proverbs refer to sins of the tongue.

The meddler

'Like one who seizes a dog by the ears is a passer-by who meddles in a quarrel not his own' (26:17).
Simile: **'one who seizes a dog by the ears'** / **'one who meddles'**

Picture: seizing a dog by its ears is not a good idea. Dogs have sensitive hearing and most do not take kindly to having their ears touched, let alone squeezed. This is a reckless thing to do.

In the sixties a photograph of President Johnson lifting his pet beagle by the ears was circulated. Many people sent the president a copy of this proverb as they saw American policy in Vietnam as contravening the advice contained here. Certainly the legacy of that war has been a bitter one for the American people. When we wade into someone else's quarrel we need to realize what we are getting into. Jesus himself was careful in this area. He asked a man who wanted him to sort out a legal wrangle with his brother, 'Who appointed me a judge or an arbiter between you?' (Luke 12:14). 1 Peter 4:15 also warns Christians against being meddlers. Here is a warning to unbelievers too. Stop asking, 'What about those who never hear about Christ?' or, 'What about those of other religions?' Leave those questions for others. A heckler once asked the Welsh evangelist Seth Joshua, 'What about election?' In an example of answering a fool according to his folly, he replied to the effect that the man should not be reading other people's letters. Election is a subject that comes up in New Testament letters addressed to believers, not unbelievers!

The joker

Like a madman shooting
   firebrands or deadly arrows
is a man who deceives his neighbour
   and says, 'I was only joking!'

(26:18-19).

Simile: **'madman shooting firebrands or deadly arrows'** / **'man who … says, "I was only joking"'**

Picture: This time we have a man shooting not just arrows, but arrows tipped with flames, or with poison. He is not just shooting randomly; he is a madman shooting anywhere and everywhere.

A couple of years ago an Andrew Lumsden from Doncaster found himself in court. He had been on an aeroplane flying to Turkey when a stewardess asked him what the plastic tube around his neck was. He said it was a bomb! The jury agreed with the judge that it was 'daft, but not criminal' and found him 'not guilty', but he has no doubt learned his lesson. Further back still I remember reading about the death of a student in the midst of a supposed initiation ceremony where he was blindfolded and made to believe that his throat was being slit. Although it was in fact only the edge of an ice-cube that was applied to his throat, he believed what he was told and died from the shock. It is not unusual these days to read of the death or near-miss of a bridegroom on his 'stag night'.

The proverb does not ban all joking, or even all practical joking, but it warns against the 'I meant no harm' attitude that some jokers have. It urges us to think carefully about the likely consequences of our actions. When we come to the question of the soul, of eternity and of God, especially, it is a deadly serious business. There is no place for silly deceptions.

The gossip and the quarreller

Without wood a fire goes out;
**   without gossip a quarrel dies down.**
As charcoal to embers and as wood to fire,
**   so is a quarrelsome man for kindling strife**
                                            (26:20-21).

Simile: **'wood'** / **'gossip'**; **'fire'** / **'quarrel'**; **'charcoal ... wood'** / **'quarrelsome man'**

Picture: an open fire. If there is no wood in the grate, then the fire will die down to nothing. However, if charcoal is added to the embers or wood while it is still blazing, then the fire is not likely to go out. Fire consumes fuel. Deprived of fuel, the fire itself goes out.

'The words of a gossip are like choice morsels; they go down to a man's inmost parts' (26:22).
    Simile: **'words of a gossip'** / **'choice morsels'**

Picture: Eating is not only for keeping oneself alive. There is pleasure in eating choice morsels, even if they are not particularly good for you. Their taste, the very feel of them in your mouth sometimes, is delightful.

This proverb repeats the one found in 18:8.

An anonymously penned description reads thus: 'I am more deadly than the screaming shell of the cannon. I win without killing. I tear down homes, break hearts, wreck lives. I travel on the wings of the wind. No innocence is strong enough to intimidate me, no purity pure enough to daunt me. I have no regard for truth, no respect for justice, no mercy for the defenceless. My victims are as numerous as the sands of the sea and often as innocent. I never forget and seldom forgive. My name is Gossip.'

There are many anti-Christian rumours about, many specious arguments. In the early days, Christians were accused of cannibalism. Other similarly preposterous accusations can fly about today. It is amazing how accusations of anti-Semitism, a lack of intellectual credibility and the undoubted iniquities of the crusades are still raised to this day. Christians have done wrong things, but so often there is no real fire — only the kindlings of gossipmongers and divisive men.

The hypocrite

Christianity is often plagued by hypocrites. Hypocrites are characterized by two things:

False enthusiasm

'Like a coating of glaze over earthenware are fervent lips with an evil heart' (26:23).
  Simile: **'coating of glaze over earthenware'** / **'fervent lips with an evil heart'**

Picture: When earthenware has been fired it is often the practice to coat it with a glaze that gives the surface a hard, shiny exterior, which can be very attractive. (The idea here is perhaps that of using silver dross.) It covers up the naturally dull, lacklustre finish that pottery will normally have.

Is your apparent enthusiasm really hypocrisy? Spurgeon once said, 'Nothing is more to be despised than a mere painted fire, the simulation of earnestness. Sooner let us have an honest death than a counterfeit life.'

Hidden malice

A malicious man disguises himself with his lips,
  but in his heart he harbours deceit.
Though his speech is charming, do not believe him,
  for seven abominations fill his heart.
His malice may be concealed by deception,
  but his wickedness will be exposed in the assembly
                                                  (26:24-26).

Command (negative) with warning: **'do not believe'**

Picture: the lips are pictured as a disguise to cover the man's real identity.

There are such people about. Nehemiah knew of them (see Neh. 6). At times, the preached Word exposes their true nature; it will certainly be revealed on the Day of Judgement.

Another ray of light

In verse 27 there is a word of comfort to those who are being attacked, another ray of light: **'If a man digs a pit, he will fall into it; if a man rolls a stone, it will roll back on him.'**
  Synonymous / simile: **'if a man digs a pit, he will fall' / '...rolls a stone, it will roll back'**

Picture: This is very simple: a man digging a pit to catch someone else falls into it himself, or as he is trying to roll a stone onto someone else, it rolls back onto him.

Here we see the biter bit and the consequences of spitting at the wind. (This theme was first broached back in 1:18-19.) As well as the proverb about the biter being bit, there is in modern English an expression from Hamlet to be 'hoist with his own petard' — the petard being a notoriously unreliable war machine that used gunpowder. The evil man lights the fuse intending to kill others and 'Kaboom!' — he blows himself up!

Here is a warning, in context, particularly against hidden malice. For all their efforts, those who oppose Christ are self-defeating. The greatest example of this is the cross itself. Do not oppose Christ; instead flee to him. Otherwise, it will be your undoing. The picture of the rolling stone reminds one commentator of the Sisyphus myth in which the ancient King of Corinth was condemned to spend eternity rolling a stone to the top of a hill, only to have it roll down again. It is more reminiscent of those who thought that sealing and guarding a stone rolled into the groove of the entrance to a grave could prevent it from rolling back again to their hurt as it revealed the empty grave of the risen Christ.

The flatterer

'A lying tongue hates those it hurts, and a flattering mouth works ruin' (26:28).
   Synonymous: **'lying tongue'** / **'flattering mouth'**

The final character is the flatterer. 'Beware the flatterer: he feeds you with an empty spoon,' wrote Cosino de Gregorio. Another writer warns that 'Flattery looks like friendship, just like a wolf looks like a dog.' Philip Henry wrote that unjust praises can be as dangerous as unjust slanders. Another writer speaks of the most deadly wild beast being a backbiter and the most deadly tame one a flatterer. And yet how we love to be flattered! (That excludes you, of course, my better sort of reader — or does it?). Many secular writers are willing to see advantages in flattery, but this proverb assures us that flattery can do no one any lasting good.

In 1682 Henry Hurst noted how this verse condemns immoderate desire for praise, blind acceptance of what others say of us, valuing ourselves by human opinion, engineering opportunities for our praise ('fishing' for compliments), concurring with undue praise and choosing flatterers as friends (sycophants, toadies, yes-men). He also lists the best means for believers to cure themselves of a love of flattery. Consider its name, how it ill becomes others and the misery it can bring. Be 'suspicious' of praise and do not make friends with a flatterer. See that it is diametrically opposed to God's Word and judgement. Get such a strong love of good and hatred of evil that you do not need man's opinion to spur you to do good or restrain you from evil. Get a humble heart, a clear view of your future reward and always remember that to receive flattery is sacrilegiously to rob God. The **'ruin'**, or knocking down. spoken of at the end of the proverb will come not only to the flattered, but also to the flatterer. As an English proverb puts it, 'Make yourself all honey and the flies will devour you.'

46.
Be wise in relation to your outlook and in your outlook on relations

Please read Proverbs 27:1-27

Uncertain future, boasting, facing provocation, jealousy, rebuke, a surfeit, home life, friendly counsel, friendship, wise sons, prudence, cautious kindness, thoughtful kindness, quarrelsome wives, friendly debate, loyal service, the heart, insatiability, dealing with compliments, removing folly, wise use of resources.

Proverbs 27 contains a further series of proverbs designed to reveal heavenly wisdom. Here we consider two areas: generally, our outlook on life and, specifically, the matter of relationships.

In this chapter and the next two we deal with the material in a more thematic and less consecutive way.

Be wise in relation to your outlook
(27:1-2,7,11-12,19-20,22-27)

There are a number of proverbs here that teach a wise outlook on life in general. The basic point that is emphasized is the need to be cautious. Do not be reckless. Do not be thoughtless. Avoid irresponsibility. Care is necessary. Once you say that, it sounds obvious, but it is amazing how little such things are practised. There are a number of reasons why due caution is necessary.

The uncertain future is not something to boast about

'Do not boast about tomorrow, for you do not know what a day may bring forth' (27:1).
Command (negative) with reason: **'do not boast'**

Here is another command and again a reason is given. As soon as we say it, it is obvious. We can all see it, but most of the time the fact is forgotten. An elderly lady in the church I pastor, now with the Lord, hailed originally from Cardenden in Fife. She could remember how as a girl people spoke admiringly of a local boy from Bowhill called Johnny Thomson who played for the great Glasgow Celtic football club. The day of Friday, 4 September 1931 was no doubt much like any other Friday for the widely admired twenty-two-year-old, still living at home with his parents. It was the eve of a local derby against rivals Glasgow Rangers at the Ibrox Stadium. No one could have guessed it would be Thomson's last full day on earth. Five minutes into the second half of the Saturday game, the ball swung into the Celtic goal mouth and Thomson ran from his goal to dive for a fifty-fifty ball at the feet of opposing centre-forward, Sam English. Tragically, he never got up. He lay prone on the field until he was carried off. At 9.25 p.m. that night he died in Ward 5 of the Victoria Hospital. Thirty to forty thousand attended the funeral and to this day Celtic players still visit his grave when they play in Fife.

Other examples could be given, but the lesson is to realize that our future is in God's hands. James 4:13-16 brings it out very well. We must take care. Nothing is guaranteed. It is part of wisdom to see its own limitations. We simply have to trust that the God of miracles, by whom everything is planned, will guide us with his hand.

Jonathan Edwards once preached a sermon on this text called 'Procrastination, or the sin and folly of depending on future time'. We are not to boast about tomorrow. It does not yet belong to us and we are ignorant of it until it comes. This is not, of course, an absolute ban on any planning for the future. Some preparation for future days is wise and necessary. What is forbidden is depending on the future or assuming that it will come. We do this if we set our hearts on enjoyments in this life, become proud of our worldly circumstances, envy sinners, or refuse to live with the eternal state in view. Edwards follows these points with serious enquiries as to how his hearers are living and an explanation of how to live every day on earth.

Boasting is not good anyway

'Let another praise you, and not your own mouth; someone else, and not your own lips' (27:2).

Synomymous command (positive): **'let another praise ...'** / **'someone else'**

This follows on from the previous proverb. With the future so uncertain, it is best not to boast about it but to look to God. If praise is necessary, leave praise to others, chiefly to God, as Jesus did (see John 12:43). Receiving praise brings its own difficulties, as verse 21 makes clear. Self-praise is mere pride, however subtly we attempt to do it. As we have noted before, wisdom includes humility. Both John the Baptist and John the apostle are our examples here. The former wanted Christ to increase and himself to decrease. The latter would not so much as mention his own name when he wrote about the Saviour.

(Verses 3-6 go on to speak about some of the trials life brings — through provocation, jealousy and rebuke. As they are to do with relationships, we shall deal with them below.)

A surfeit can make things worse, not better

'He who is full loathes honey, but to the hungry even what is bitter tastes sweet' (27:7).
   Simile: **'... full loathes honey'** / **'hungry ... bitter tastes sweet'**

Picture: One man has just finished a big meal and is full; another is hungry. The first is offered honey and the second something bitter. The one refuses; to the other his meal is sweet.

This is not about life's inequalities. Rather it is an observation of how when an appetite (for food, sex, excitement, luxury, praise, or whatever) is sated then it becomes jaded (literally, the verse refers to trampling on the honeycomb). In our mad rage to accumulate, we can end up in a worse state than those who have very little. Less is more, as it is sometimes put. Many people are so surrounded by goods that they cannot appreciate any of them. We must seek what is essential. Jesus told Martha, who was distracted by many things, that one thing is needful — to listen to him.

In a sermon on this text, Spurgeon asks believers, 'What was it that first attracted us to God? Was it not the sweetness of Christ? What was it that banished all the bitterness of our fears? Was it not the sweetness of his pardoning love? What is it that holds us so that we cannot go, which enchains us, seals us, nails us to the cross, so that we can never leave it? Is it not that he is so sweet that we shall never find any to compare with him, and therefore must abide with him because there is nowhere else to go?'

Yet there are those who find Christ bitter to their taste because they are so full of other things. Those who find Christ sweet find that even bitter things, such as repentance, are sweet in him.

(Verses 8-10 all refer to relationships and so are dealt with below.)

Foolishness affects those who love you most

'Be wise, my son, and bring joy to my heart; then I can answer anyone who treats me with contempt' (27:11).
  Command (positive) with reason: **'be wise'**

From the beginning of the proverbs proper there have been several references to teachers and pupils (usually in terms of father and son — see, e.g., 10:1). The first half of verse 11 is familiar. The fresh thought here is that of the father being able to deal easily with any criticism because the son's wisdom is so evident. One thing that parents dread is to have someone come to their door making accusations against their children. It happened in my home once when I was a boy. Some neighbours told my parents that they had heard me swearing in the street. 'No, surely not our son,' was their response. But when I was confronted, I had to confess it was true. What shame I had brought on my parents! How much better, if a little affected, a young Polish prince who is said to have carried with him everywhere a picture of his father which he would take out at appropriate moments and say, 'Let me do nothing unbecoming so excellent a father.'

The idea puts one in mind of the Lord's rightly placed confidence in his servant Job despite Satan's insinuations. Supremely we think of the incarnate Son of God whom the Father audibly commended from heaven as his beloved Son on more than one occasion.

There is nothing better for a teacher of God's Word than to know that those whom he teaches are becoming wise. I can think of nothing better than to receive news of someone I have taught saying that person has shown evidence of being wise.

Merely pressing on can be counter-productive

'The prudent see danger and take refuge, but the simple keep going and suffer for it' (27:12).
   Contrast: **'prudent'** / **'simple'**

This contrasting proverb (which repeats 22:3 almost verbatim) compares the prudent, who see danger and flee, with the simple, who go on and end up in trouble. This is another call to caution. The prudent see the storm coming and head for shelter; they know disaster is looming and they take refuge, willing to hide from the danger ahead. I like the nineteenth-century story of a boy leading a donkey towards a Derbyshire pit when there was an explosion. When search was made the donkey was found dead but the boy had dived into a hole and so was saved. Too many today are like the donkey. They head down a road that is bound to lead to disaster, oblivious, it seems, to the danger. Especially see the danger that lies ahead for you outside of Christ and run to him. Do not keep going on in your sins.

(Verses 13-18 also refer to relationships and so are dealt with below.)

Outward appearances can be deceptive

'As water reflects a face, so a man's heart reflects the man' (27:19).

Simile: **'water' / 'man's heart'**

Picture: The way water in a pond or puddle reflects a person's face when he looks into it.

This verse is very compact and so difficult to follow. The NIV seems as reliable as any other rendering. When it comes to praising one another, it is good to remember this. Just as you can see your own reflection when you look in a pond, so in your heart you will see what you are really like, or possibly what others are like (by comparison). Whichever is the point, a true reflection is something deeper than the mere outward and not a matter of how a man looks in water or in a mirror. Again, this is something obvious but is often forgotten. Remember who you really are. Remember that it is your heart that God sees.

Man's earthly appetite is insatiable

'Death and Destruction are never satisfied, and neither are the eyes of man' (27:20).

Simile: **'Death and Destruction' / 'eyes of a man'**

Picture: Death and destruction (literally, 'Sheol and Abaddon') and the way they never come to a halt. People keep on dying; destruction continues.

Sheol and Abaddon are also mentioned in 15:11. The proverb is like two verses in Ecclesiastes: 'The eye never has enough of seeing, nor the ear its fill of hearing' (Eccles. 1:8); 'All man's efforts are for his mouth, yet his appetite is never satisfied' (Eccles. 6:7). Life here on earth is a constant search for satisfaction. Outside of Christ, we are doomed to disappointment and destruction. Alden says, 'Cemeteries are full of people who died still thinking wealth could bring them happiness.' It is foolish to suppose that our eyes can be satisfied in this life. Rather we must look to Jesus Christ. The man who was content with the 36-inch screen television will soon want a 48-inch one. A standard receiver will be fine, but only until he sees a digital flat screen. The history of art and photography is in part the story of man's attempts to satisfy the eye. There always seems to be something more to say with pictures. Much the same could be said about many forms of music. Part of the reason for this is the fact that we have not yet reached the perfection of heaven. As it was once famously (if ungrammatically) put, 'I can't get no satisfaction.' No, and outside of Christ you never will.

(Verse 21 is also about receiving praise and is one of the tests that relationships bring.)

Foolishness is deep-seated and ingrained

Though you grind a fool in a mortar,
grinding him like grain with a pestle,
you will not remove his folly from him

(27:22).

Simile: **'grinding ... grain with a pestle'** / **'remove his folly'**

Picture: A pestle and mortar, as used for grinding herbs or corn or other materials.

The point here is to remind us not to be superficial. Our foolishness is not easily removed and replaced with wisdom. We need the grace of God. We must not give up on people too easily but, sadly, some fools will never be redeemed. With children, there is hope; hence Proverbs 22:15. However, a man set in foolish ways may well be irredeemable. A Jewish proverb says that drunks can be sobered up but fools remain fools. A well-known verse says:

Can the Ethiopian change his skin
  or the leopard its spots?
Neither can you do good
  who are accustomed to doing evil

(Jer. 13.23).

Advantages do not remain automatically (27:23-27)

Similarly, the long proverb at the very end of the chapter makes a matching point. It is a beautiful rural saying (there are five different references to animals and in verse 25 three different types of hay are listed). It begins in the form of a command: **'Be sure you know the condition of your flocks, give careful attention to your herds.'** The reasoning behind this is: **'... for riches do not endure for ever, and a crown is not secure for all generations.'**

   Synonymous command (positive) with reason: **'be sure you know' / 'give careful attention'**

Neglect of one's assets can easily lead to material loss. Responsibility and diligence are often commended in Proverbs.

   The landowner's care in husbandry must be combined with care in the way the arable land is used. If you arrange things wisely, rotating crops and staggering planting, then:

**When the hay is removed and new growth appears
   and the grass from the hills is gathered in,
the lambs will provide you with clothing,
   and the goats with the price of a field.
You will have plenty of goats' milk
   to feed you and your family
   and to nourish your servant girls**

(27:25-27).

Good things do not appear out of thin air. If the animals are fed properly, however, then they will provide wool and milk, which will bring in money to take care of you and others. What these verses describe may hardly seem anything exciting, but attention to everyday duties is vital for kings and for everyone else. We dare not presume on God's providence — for our homes, our families, our jobs, or for God's mercy and willingness to forgive.

Perhaps these verses also have something to say about sustainable resources, as against get-rich-quick schemes that are not self-sustaining. If our setting is a more urban one we may need to be sure we know the condition of our cars and give careful attention to the state of our houses. We need to know where diligence at work will produce more free time, better wages and career opportunities. Wherever we are, we must be diligent and think ahead in the right way. This applies in the life of the church as much as anywhere else. The pastor or under-shepherd in particular ought to know the condition of his flock and give careful attention to all his work.

Be wise in your outlook on relations
(27:3,5-6,8-10,13-18,21)

It is easy to become self-centred in the search for wisdom and to forget that we are intended to live on earth along with everyone else. This is one reason why you can be sure that a man who claims to be wise but lives off on his own somewhere as a hermit is not truly wise. No, true heavenly wisdom is practical; it works in everyday life, in relation to others. True Wisdom himself, Jesus Christ, came down to earth and lived among us.

The blessings of relationships

If we are wise in our relationships, it will lead to many blessings. The proverbs here cover several areas:

Home life

'Like a bird that strays from its [literally, 'her'] **nest is a man who strays from his home'** (27:8).
    Simile: **'bird that strays from its nest' / 'man who strays from his home'**

Picture: a bird that leaves its nest and does not find its way back, and so is in danger.
    Lane argues that this is a verse about banishment and its ill-effects. Others see it as a warning against leaving home or abandoning your post. It condemns the quitter, the runaway, the wanderer, the rolling stone, the drifter, the rootless man. Again and again such a life is celebrated in literature and popular culture. Think of W. H. Davies's 'Supertramp', for example. The contemporary Hispanic American singer Nelly Furtado has an interesting song using the very image used here:

> I'm like a bird, I'll only fly away,
> I don't know where my soul is ... where my home is.

The picture of a bird flying is very attractive but here it expresses a young woman's inability to settle down in a relationship, although her partner is clearly ready for that. 'Your faith in me brings me to tears,' she sings. Such attitudes abound in a society where young people fly the nest before they are ready to set up on their own in a proper manner. Many are tempted to think that getting away from home is the answer to their problems — the teenager who argues with his parents, the young man looking for adventure, the spouse who has fallen out with his or her other half. Here, however, it is given the thumbs down. The truth is that such a supposed solution to a man's problems will seldom work.

The wider application relates to the unlikelihood of achieving much in any area if we do not settle to the task, if we are not at home with it. The ability to persevere is an important virtue. That applies to anything from finishing a task at your desk or workbench, or finishing a book (reading or writing it), to fathering a godly family, pastoring a church, or governing a country. Spurgeon says, 'The unrest of that man's mind, and the instability of his conduct who is constantly making a change of his position and purpose, augurs no success for any of his adventures.'

Friendship

A number of proverbs appear here on this important theme, one that we have considered previously.

'Perfume and incense bring joy to the heart, and the pleasantness of one's friend springs from his earnest counsel' (27:9).

Simile: **'perfume and incense' / 'pleasantness of one's friend'**

Picture: The enjoyment that perfume and incense give by means of their penetrating aroma, especially in a hot climate.

One of the advantages of friendship is that a friend can tell you your faults and passionately urge you in the right direction in a way that an enemy cannot, and in a way that even a family member cannot do so well. This is part of what is involved in friendship.

Do not forsake your friend and the friend of your father,

and do not go to your brother's house when disaster strikes you —

better a neighbour nearby than a brother far away

(27:10).

Synthetic command (negative): **'do not forsake'** / **'do not go to ...'**

Contrast (better than): **'a neighbour nearby'** / **'a brother far away'**

The first part of the verse is a command to take friendship seriously. It extends from generation to generation. Once again, the father is talking to his son. Further, blood may be thicker than water but a friend nearby is better than a relative who is either too far away or simply does not want to know. We all need friends. Friendship can sometimes be found even when we are away from the nest.

The greatest friend there can be is Christ. We have looked at that truth, for instance in considering 18:24. As a father myself, like other Christian fathers, I want to press on my five sons the need to avoid forsaking my great Friend, one who has always shown himself friendly to them. I know that if they trust in him, he will never forsake them. That could never be.

Being kind

Verses 13 and 14 follow the general principle expressed in verse 12:

Take the garment of one who puts up security for a stranger;

**hold it in pledge if he does it for a wayward
woman.**
**If a man loudly blesses his neighbour early in the
morning,**
it will be taken as a curse.

Synonymous command (positive): **'take the garment'** / **'hold
it in pledge'**
Synthetic: **'loudly blesses'** / **'curse'**

These apparently unrelated proverbs teach us two important
things about being kind to others.

1. Be kind but cautious. Verse 13 is very similar to
20:16. **'A stranger'** is someone you do not know, **'a
wayward woman'** someone you cannot trust. If standing surety for such a person, then make sure you get
some security. It is a bad risk otherwise. Taking unnecessary risks is no part of doing good in this world. We
must be as wise as snakes.

2. Be kind but thoughtful. It matters not only what
you say, but how and when too! Similarly, our efforts at
other sorts of kindness can often be unwanted. A relative of ours was away somewhere and mentioned our
family and the fact that we have five boys. The next
thing they knew they found themselves weighed down
with a pile of second-hand clothing most of which, we
must confess, was never worn.

Some see this proverb as chiefly warning against flattery, and others assume the 'blesser' has evil intentions.
Christ is the model of total approachability and wise
kindness. If we say we follow him, we ought to be like
him.

Friendly debate

Verses 15 and 16 warn that quarrelling is most undesirable. However, friendly debate can be a good thing: **'As iron sharpens iron, so one man sharpens another'** (27:17).

    Simile: **'iron sharpens iron'** / **'one man sharpens another'**

Picture: Sharpening a knife, which is often done by means of rubbing it up and down another piece of metal.

    Friendly debate can be tremendously stimulating. Scholars and artists and preachers well know the advantages of peer criticism. Loners can be very dull and boring. They can often lack penetration in a way that the man who has debated with others does not. In friendship the sparks sometimes fly, but that is all part of what is involved.

Loyal service

'He who tends a fig tree will eat its fruit, and he who looks after his master will be honoured' (27:18).

    Simile: **'he who tends a fig tree'** / **'he who looks after his master'**

Picture: Looking after a fig tree well (planting, watering, fertilizing, pruning and protecting it) and, in due time, eating its fruit.

    It is easy to look down on, even to sneer at, a loyal servant, but faithful service brings its own rewards. The Christian knows this better than any. He serves his Master Christ and he knows that his reward is sure. The paradox here is that the reward is not always obvious. Many things can be enjoyed, or at least we can tolerate them, whether there is a reward or not. When the element of reward is added, it means that every objection is overruled. On the other hand, we sometimes think we are engaged in a task that is not worthwhile and feel like giving up. The answer is always to consider the end in view. Where is this leading me? If it is a worthwhile job, we shall see why we must continue.

The testings of relations

We must not think of friendship, or any other relationship, as an automatic ticket to happiness. In relationships, we are also tested. This happens in all sorts of ways. Five examples are given here.

1. Provocation

'Stone is heavy and sand a burden, but provocation by a fool is heavier than both' (27:3).
  Simile: **'stone … sand'** / **'provocation by a fool'**

Picture: a heavy stone or a bag of sand, especially when these are being cleared from land to make it ready for planting. Lifting either is not easy. It is a two-handed man-size job.

Provocations can be deliberate or accidental. They can be major or minor. When they come from fools they are very heavy indeed. If we are goaded by fools we must be determined to be patient. Part of working closely with others is the danger that things they do will irritate and provoke us. That is why we should avoid fools if we can.

2. Jealousy

'Anger is cruel and fury overwhelming, but who can stand before jealousy?' (27:4).
  A fortiori

This is the other side of the coin. What if your wife is a jealous woman? Or what if you are riven with jealousy? Such a powerful emotion can tear things apart. It is even stronger than anger or fury. It has been called the raw material for murder. Shakespeare dubbed it 'the green-eyed monster which doth mock the meat it feeds on'. Jealousy can be a positive thing, of course. God himself is a jealous God and no jealousy is more powerful than his. However, sinful jealousy is the sort we are most likely to meet in human beings. We must beware of rousing it in ourselves or in others. It is a dangerous thing, as David found when he roused it in Saul, and as the Lord himself experienced when he opposed the religious establishment of his day.

Rebuke

Better is open rebuke
    than hidden love.
Wounds from a friend can be trusted,
    but an enemy multiplies kisses

                                                       (27:5-6).

Contrast (better than): **'open rebuke'** / **'hidden love'**
Simile: **'wounds'** / **'kisses'**

Picture: Someone wounding you, say with a knife, and another person kissing you.

I have a slightly unusual uncle. As a young man, he was walking up Stow Hill in Newport with his friend, known as Garth. They were discussing whether they would fight their own brothers. Then Garth said, 'But you wouldn't hit me, would you, John?' The next moment Garth was flat on the floor. He had received a wound from a friend. Had it been someone John did not like he would not have hit him.

Fortunately, not all friendships are that strange, but you see the point!

This 'better than' proverb contrasts **'open rebuke'** and **'hidden love'**. It carries on the war against flattery (see 9:8-9; 15:31). One of the marks of true friendship is willingness to give a rebuke when it is appropriate. It is the enemy who **'multiplies kisses'**. The picture is slightly different but one thinks of Judas' kiss and Peter's wild lunge with the sword at the arrest of Jesus. Rebukes are not easy to take but we know that, like bitter medicine, they are given for our good. This is true of the rebukes that come to us in God's Word and that fall to us in his providence.

A quarrelsome partner

A quarrelsome wife is like
  a constant dripping on a rainy day;
restraining her is like restraining the wind
  or grasping oil with the hand

                                               (27:15-16).

Double simile: **'quarrelsome wife'** / **'constant dripping on a rainy day'** ; **'restraining her'** / **'restraining the wind'**; **'grasping oil with the hand'**

Pictures: the constant drip, drip of water as it leaks out of some place in the rainy season. With that we have the double picture of trying to hold back the wind (as, for example, when putting up a tent in a high wind) or trying to grab a handful of oil.

Problems with quarrelsome wives have been mentioned before (see 19:13; 21:9,19; 25:24). As we said then, this is not evidence of chauvinism, but is down to the way the book is cast — a book of advice from father to son. There have been men who suffered because of quarrelsome wives. John Wesley is a well-known example. In 1751, he suffered a fall on an ice-coated London Bridge and was carried to the home of Mary Vazeille, the wealthy widow of a London merchant. Wesley had a history of falling for his nurses and within a week they were married. It was a disaster. The best construction we can put on some of Mrs Wesley's eccentric behaviour is that she was mentally ill. One of Wesley's preachers, John Hampson, described once finding her 'foaming with fury. Her husband was on the floor, where she had been trailing him by the hair of his head; and she was still holding in her hand the venerable locks which she had plucked by the roots. I felt as though I could have knocked the soul out of her.' The two spent little time together, and in 1771 we find a sad but matter-of-fact entry in Wesley's journal: 'I came to London, and was informed that my wife died on Monday. This evening she was buried, though I was not informed of it…'

The thrust of the proverb here is the impossibility of re-straining such a person. Wesley's best efforts — and he made many it seems — all failed. Even if you find a wife and show her great love, it may not be easy. Nothing is guaranteed. Hubbard relates the story of someone telephoning the architect Frank Lloyd Wright to complain that the roof of a house designed by the great man was leaking and the water was going all over a favourite chair. His response? 'Move the chair!' Sometimes there is little we can do about our situations but see them as sent by God to try us.

Praise

'The crucible for silver and the furnace for gold, but man is tested by the praise he receives' (27:21).
  Simile: **'crucible … furnace'** / **'praise'**

Picture: the familiar idea of precious metals such as silver and gold being separated from the ore by means of intense heat in a crucible or furnace.

This is not immediately obvious but when you are praised, you are facing a real test of character. It is so easy to believe everything that people say — even their exaggeration. It is easy to forget about the things in your life for which they would not praise you. The antidote then is to look at your heart and to ask yourself, 'What does God think of me?' Perhaps the verse is best understood as saying not simply that praise is a test but, more subtly, that the way to see a man's true state is to consider how he deals with praise. We remember what happened to the devil and how he fell from his high place. Others have gone the same way.

47.
Wisdom for government

Please read Proverbs 28:1-28

*Fear and confidence, national stability, oppressive leadership,
forsaking the law, understanding justice, innocence better than
wealth, keeping the law, usury, prayer and the law, corrupt
leadership, wisdom better than wealth, elation and fear,
repentance, fear of the Lord, folly of tyranny, evil of tyranny,
murder and conscience, falling and safety, diligence, faithfulness
rather than wealth, partiality, stinginess, rebuke, robbing
parents, greed, trust in self, giving, fear and blessing*

Here we have a further twenty-eight proverbs of King Solomon collected by the men of good King Hezekiah. More like those found in Proverbs 10-22 than those which immediately precede them, many of them are of the contrasting variety so common in chapters 10-15. Understandably, several have reference to the work and life of kings. In the chapter, three broad subjects are covered, all of them of interest to kings — leadership, law and justice, riches and poverty. All involved in civil government should be clear on these important subjects. We are all involved in government to some extent, whether it is in voting for local and national representatives, or as parents and guardians, in our places of work, or in governing our own lives. It is important that we receive this wisdom from God.

First, we briefly remind ourselves of a fundamental teaching found in verse 14. It is in the form of a beatitude accompanied by a warning: **'Blessed is the man who always fears the Lᴏʀᴅ, but he who hardens his heart falls into trouble.'**
Beatitude
Contrast: **'man who always fears' / 'he who hardens his heart'**

'The Lᴏʀᴅ' has been added by the translators, who have probably hit on the right meaning. The fear of the Lord is fundamental. Without this, there can be no blessing. The form is a contrasting one — the God-fearer is blessed; the man with a calloused heart **'falls into trouble'**. Pharaoh, in the early chapters of Exodus, is the classic example, but there have been many others since. The other verses provide us with a distillation of the true heavenly wisdom that begins with the fear of the Lord. They are to be heeded.

Leadership good and bad

Some seven proverbs here touch directly on the matter of leadership.

(Verse 1 is dealt with below under the heading of 'Justice and law'.)

A single wise leader is a blessing

'When a country is rebellious, it has many rulers, but a man of understanding and knowledge maintains order' (28:2).
Contrast (complex): **'many rulers' / 'man of understanding'**

This is another of a limited number of proverbs which have a national reference (others include 11:14; 14:28,34; 29:2,18). The contrast is between a country that keeps changing its ruler, which, it is implied, leads to chaos, and one with a wise leader who can keep order. Fragmentation is one of the things that marks a society in decline. Solomon was wise. He ruled over a great empire. Hezekiah was similarly a ruler over Judah, which was only ever ruled by a single dynasty. In contrast, the northern kingdom went through a series of nine different dynasties before its final and inevitable collapse. Frequently change is a mark of disarray. Think of the difficulties a relatively stable country such as Italy has had because of having so many different prime ministers between the last war and the present administration. The problem is that we need not just stability but wisdom too. Think of a church, a business, a family, an individual. Where the leadership is constantly changing, there is something wrong. It is often a mark of rebellion. Above all, in every area we need to submit to Christ as our leader. How we need his wise leadership every day of our lives! In his kingdom, order is always maintained.

An oppressive leader is a curse

'A ruler who oppresses the poor is like a driving rain that leaves no crops' (28:3).
Simile: **'ruler who oppresses the poor'** / **'driving rain that leaves no crops'**

We need not only wise leaders, but merciful ones. The word translated 'ruler' could perhaps mean 'poor' or 'evil man'. That is an even more tragic scenario. The picture used is of a driving rain destroying crops. Oppression is cruel and destroys whatever assets remain in a country. We shall always want to seek to escape such a thing. If we turn to Christ, ultimately we shall. In Matthew 11:28-30 he cries out: 'Come to me, all you who are weary and burdened, and I will give you rest. Take my yoke upon you … for I am gentle and humble in heart, and you will find rest for your souls. For my yoke is easy and my burden is light.'

(Verses 4-7 and 9 all touch on justice and law and verse 8 on the theme of riches and poverty, so all are dealt with below under the appropriate headings.)

A corrupt leader will be judged, a blameless leader blessed

> **He who leads the upright along an evil path**
> **will fall into his own trap,**
> **but the blameless will receive a good inheritance**
> **(28:10).**

Contrast (complex): **'he who leads the upright along an evil path' / 'blameless'**

The principle set out in the first part of the verse has already been declared in 26:27 and other places. Leadership brings great responsibilities. If they are corrupt, leaders will lead the upright astray by means of deception. They will be judged for that. The picture is that of a trap or snare. The blameless, on the other hand, will be blessed. We need to seek leaders who will not be corrupt. In our own leadership, we must always lead people in right paths. If we are blameless in Christ, we can be sure of **'a good inheritance'**.

(Verse 11 refers to wealth and poverty and is dealt with below.)

A righteous leader is a source of joy, a wicked leader a cause of terror

'When the righteous triumph, there is great elation; but when the wicked rise to power, men go into hiding' (28:12).
Contrast: **'when the righteous triumph'** / **'when the wicked rise to power'**

'When the wicked rise to power, people go into hiding; but when the wicked perish, the righteous thrive' (28:28).
Contrast: **'when the wicked rise to power'** / **'when the wicked perish'**

We can take these two proverbs together. They clearly match (they are similar to 11:10 and 29:2). When righteous leaders are in power and wicked ones perish there is great rejoicing, as the first part of verse 12 and the second part of verse 28 declare. On the other hand, they also teach that when wicked ones are in power men hide. However much the world may look down on virtue, it still wants it in its leaders. It wants a Joseph, a Daniel, an Alfred the Great, an Edward VI, a George Washington, not a Pharaoh, a Belshazzar, a Herod, a Bloody Mary, a Stalin or a Pol Pot. When people such as those in the latter group have arisen the wise have gone into hiding where they could. What relief when such reigns have ended and what elation there has been when people like the former have come to power!

(Verse 13 is dealt with below under the heading of 'Justice and law'; verse 14 has been dealt with above.)

A tyrannical leader is unbearable

> **Like a roaring lion or a charging bear**
> **is a wicked man ruling over a helpless people.**

A tyrannical ruler lacks judgement,
but he who hates ill-gotten gain will enjoy a long
life

(28:15-16).

Simile: **'roaring lion ... charging bear'** / **'wicked man**
ruling over a helpless people'
Contrast (complex): **'tyrannical ruler'** / **'he who hates ill-**
gotten gain'

The picture of wild beasts is used to evoke the tyrant in verse
15. Tyranny leads to danger and fear, to trouble and mistakes.
The best leaders are not selfish or greedy tyrants, but benevo-
lent and kind servants. They usually last longer than do the
tyrants. Think of Judah's good rulers as compared with Israel's
evil ones, or even of Queen Elizabeth II as compared with the
Communist leaders of the twentieth century. The greatest example of this is Christ himself, who gave himself up for his
people. Submit to him and follow his example.

(Verses 17-27 are dealt with below.)

Justice and law

Innocence leads to confidence, wickedness to fear

'The wicked man flees though no one pursues, but the
righteous are as bold as a lion' (28:1).
Contrast: **'wicked man'** / **'righteous'**
Simile: **'righteous'** / **'bold as a lion'**

God uses this image of fleeing without being pursued when he
warns his people against disobedience in Leviticus: 'I will set

my face against you so that you will be defeated by your enemies; those who hate you will rule over you, and you will flee even when no one is pursuing you' (Lev. 26:17). 'As for those of you who are left, I will make their hearts so fearful in the lands of their enemies that the sound of a wind-blown leaf will put them to flight. They will run as though fleeing from the sword, and they will fall, even though no one is pursuing them' (Lev. 26:36).

This is what literally happened to the Arameans in 2 Kings 7. Similarly, the psalmist writes of those who were 'overwhelmed with dread, where there was nothing to dread' (Ps. 53:5).

There is nothing quite like a clear conscience. English proverbs liken it to a soft pillow, an easy couch, a coat of mail and a continual feast. A striking contemporary example of this is the story of Denver-born Katherine Ann Power. At the end of the sixties she was a student in Boston caught up in the peace movement of the day. To raise funds the anti-war group she was in organized a bank raid, in which she was the driver of the getaway car. In the course of the crime William Schroeder, a police officer, was killed. Legally, Power was considered an accessory to murder. Although the others were soon captured she became a fugitive and evaded arrest. She took on a new name and identity, settling in Oregon under the name Alice Metzinger. She even married and had a son. In 1993, however, some twenty-three years after the murder, she finally turned herself in to the Massachusetts authorities and received a prison sentence which she has now served. Why did she give herself up? By that time it is highly unlikely that she would have been indicted. Being reunited with her original family no doubt played its part, but the chief motive for her action was the desire for peace of mind. Suffering from a deep depression, she came to accept, together with her therapist, that the underlying problem was her sense of guilt for her past crime.

She was being tormented by guilt. However skilful she had been at hiding from law-enforcement officers, she could not hide from herself and the knowledge of her crime.

Here the righteous man, the man with a clear conscience, is said to be like a lion. He is a legitimate tyrant over his own moral life. The righteous have no fear. Behind them is only God's goodness and mercy. Do you know this blessing? Think of how Daniel and his three friends faced the fiery furnace. This is what made Moses bold before Pharaoh, Elijah bold before Ahab, Paul bold before his Roman judges and Luther bold before the emperor. If we are wearing the breastplate of righteousness we can say with David:

> The LORD is my light and my salvation —
>   whom shall I fear?
> The LORD is the stronghold of my life —
>   of whom shall I be afraid?
>
> (Ps. 27:1).

(Verses 2 and 3 have been dealt with above.)

The law — the importance of having a high view of it

'Those who forsake the law praise the wicked, but those who keep the law resist them' (28:4).
    Contrast: **'those who forsake the law' / 'those who keep the law'**

This contrasting proverb compares lawbreakers and those who have a low view of the law, on the one hand, with law-keepers and those who have a high view of the law, on the other. When they forsake the law, the former are really commending the wicked, while by keeping the law the latter are resisting them.

Are you a law-breaker or a law-keeper, an upholder of God's law, or one who not only breaks his law but also encourages others to do the same? In these days of moral relativism, many have a low view of the law. We see the results of that all around us.

Justice — to understand it, seek the Lord

'Evil men do not understand justice, but those who seek the LORD understand it fully' (28:5).
   Contrast: **'evil men' / 'those who seek the LORD'**

There is much talk from politicians about justice. True justice is understood by looking to God and his Word. Many problems spring from a failure in this very area. For example, what is just about allowing unborn babies to be put to death? What is fair about locking a man in prison for the rest of his life? What is righteous about forcibly redistributing wealth? Justice is seen vividly at the cross. Even God's own Son was damned when sin was placed on him. Evil men do not understand the cross, or, for that matter, very much about justice in general. However, in contrast, **'those who seek the LORD understand it fully'**.

Innocence is more important than wealth

'Better a poor man whose walk is blameless than a rich man whose ways are perverse' (28:6).
   Contrast (better than): **'poor man whose walk is blameless' / 'rich man whose ways are perverse'**

This is very similar to 19:1. Of course, Solomon was both rich and upright for much of his life. In this 'better than' proverb, however, it is a poor man who is depicted as being good. This form is intended to show that integrity is more to be desired than riches, innocence more than wealth. We must walk the straight and narrow, not in wandering ways. Seek first and foremost to be right with God. Avoid perversity.

The law — the discerning seek to keep it

'He who keeps the law is a discerning son, but a companion of gluttons disgraces his father' (28:7).
    Contrast: **'he who keeps the law' / 'companion of gluttons'**

How can a person be innocent? Apart from anything else, wisdom says that a Christian must follow the law. Disgrace comes to his family when a man has gluttons as his companions. He soon becomes like them and disgraces his father. The next step is what we read of in verse 24.

(Verse 8 is dealt with below.)

The law — if we ignore it, our prayers will go unanswered

'If anyone turns a deaf ear to the law, even his prayers are detestable' (28:9).
    Synthetic: **'turns a deaf ear to the law' / 'prayers ... detestable'**

This is a warning. The evocative deaf ear is a disobedient ear. Many pray only in a tight spot, or think that their prayers will cover up their failures. This is a great miscalculation. No, we must be both obedient and prayerful. This is something the psalmist understood: 'If I had cherished sin in my heart, the

Lord would not have listened' (Ps. 66:18). And John wrote in his first epistle, 'Dear friends, if our hearts do not condemn us, we have confidence before God and receive from him anything we ask, because we obey his commands and do what pleases him' (1 John 3:21-22).

(Verses 10 and 12 have been dealt with above; verse 11 is dealt with below.)

Confess your sins rather than covering them up

'He who conceals his sins does not prosper, but whoever confesses and renounces them finds mercy' (28:13).
    Contrast: **'he who conceals his sins' / 'whoever confesses and renounces them'**

This contrasting proverb states the very opposite of what many people believe, although it is confirmed by cases such as those of Katherine Power, mentioned above. In recent years, American President Bill Clinton thought he could prosper by concealing his sin in connection with Monica Lewinsky. He was wrong. When he confessed and apparently renounced his sin he received a much better response. This proverb is not talking about covering sin in the good sense found in 10:12 and 17:9. Here are the roots of those wonderful words in 1 John 1:8-10: 'If we claim to be without sin, we deceive ourselves and the truth is not in us. If we confess our sins, he is faithful and just and will forgive us our sins and purify us from all unrighteousness. If we claim we have not sinned, we make him out to be a liar and his word has no place in our lives.'

(Verse 14 was dealt with in the introduction and verses 15 and 16 in the first section.)

The law (the sixth command) — we invite mental torture if we break it

> **A man tormented by the guilt of murder**
> **will be a fugitive till death;**
> **let no one support him**

$$(28:17).$$

> *Synthetic:* **'tormented by … guilt'** / **'fugitive'**
> *Command (negative):* **'let no one support'**

A story appeared a year or two ago about a house in Humberside being renovated where they found a suicide note dated 4 August 1901. It included a full confession of the murder of a housemaid. It is an example of the power of guilt, especially guilt for murder, to torment the perpetrator to death. When looking at verse 1 we noted there too the power of conscience. If we come across those who have committed murder, or even those who are guilty of the hatred that is the first step on that road, we must do nothing to support them in their sin. They must know that unless God sets a mark upon them, as he did with Cain, there will be no relief until they die, and not even then will there be any relief unless they repent now.

Innocence leads to safety, perversity to a sudden fall

'He whose walk is blameless is kept safe, but he whose ways are perverse will suddenly fall' (28:18).
    Contrast: **'he whose walk is blameless'** / **'he whose ways are perverse'**

It may seem to work out differently, but this is the truth. Governments of all sorts should reflect this in the way they administer justice. They ought to protect the innocent and bring down the perverse. Even where the perverse survive a while they will suddenly fall at a time of God's choosing.

These words are intended to encourage the blameless in Christ and warn the perverse.

(Verses 19 and 20 are dealt with below.)

However attractive, partiality is never good

'To show partiality is not good — yet a man will do wrong for a piece of bread' (28:21).
   Synthetic: **'partiality'** / **'wrong for a piece of bread'**

Favouritism is very common, but it flies in the face of all that is right and just. Judges are corrupted, politicians bought, policemen silenced, bosses compromised, preachers weakened and our consciences negated by partiality. It should not exist, but it does. Erasmus thought that the expression in the second half of the verse was an allusion to the way a dog will do anything for a piece of bread held out to it. It is often said that every man has his price. For some it is very low.

God never shows favouritism. The expectations of heaven that so many have, based on special treatment for some, are totally unreasonable. Bribery will not work with the Just One either.

(Verse 22 is dealt with below.)

Rebuke is better than flattery

'He who rebukes a man will in the end gain more favour than he who has a flattering tongue' (28:23).
   Contrast (better than): **'rebukes'** / **'flattering'**

This is the principle we are working on in this book. It should be the policy of all governments. It is a principle that God himself uses. As we have seen several times, the wise accept rebukes. This subject was last raised in Proverbs 27:5-6.

The law (the fifth and eighth commands) — it is wrong to break it

> **He who robs his father or mother and says,**
>   **'It's not wrong' —**
> **he is partner to him who destroys**
>
> (28:24).

Synthetic: **'robs'** / **'says, "It's not wrong"'**

This subject has been raised in 19:26. There are many things that are as bad as murder. They are not as rare as we may think (see 18:9). The example hinted at here is the practice of *corban*, condemned by Jesus in Mark 7. This was the practice of neglecting parents on the pretext that help they might otherwise have received was promised to temple funds. The sin is exacerbated by the claim of innocence. Are you guilty of such sins?

Riches and poverty

Riches are not the most important thing in life. Many people are willing to agree with that viewpoint but in practice they only pay lip-service to the sentiment.

Things that are more important than riches

Innocence

This has already been established in verse 6.

Wisdom

'A rich man may be wise in his own eyes, but a poor man who has discernment sees through him' (28:11).

 Contrast: **'rich man ... wise in his own eyes'** / **'poor man who has discernment'**

Picture here a proud rich man. He thinks he is wise. Maybe everyone in his own circle thinks the same. But here is a poor man. He may be poor, but he has the discernment to see through the other man. It is often easy to see through the pretentiousness of those who are outside our own circle. Think of Hans Christian Andersen's tale of the emperor's new clothes. We must never suppose that riches are equal to wisdom. Alden quotes a line from the musical *Fiddler on the roof*:

> It makes no difference if you're right or wrong;
> When you're rich they think you really know.

What our peers think of us should not weigh too heavily with us. Complacency is no proof of wisdom either. Of course, without discernment we shall assume that what everyone else believes is true.

Faithfulness

'A faithful man will be richly blessed, but one eager to get rich will not go unpunished' (28:20).

 Beatitude / contrast: **'faithful man'** / **'one eager to get rich'**

God looks for faith. Is it found in your heart? Eagerness to get rich is a snare and will be punished, if not in this life then certainly in the one to come.

How to find the right way to blessing

Finally, we consider a series of proverbs that show the right way to blessing.

Not by being stingy but by helping the poor

'He who increases his wealth by exorbitant interest amasses it for another, who will be kind to the poor' (28:8).
    Synthetic: **'increases his wealth by exorbitant interest'** / **'amasses it for another'**

'A stingy man is eager to get rich and is unaware that poverty awaits him' (28:22).
    Synthetic: **'eager to get rich'** / **'unaware that poverty awaits'**

'He who gives to the poor will lack nothing, but he who closes his eyes to them receives many curses' (28:27).
    Contrast: **'he who gives to the poor'** / **'he who closes his eyes to them'**

Again the prominent theme of generosity to the poor is evident (see 19: 7 and other verses).

In the first of these proverbs the stingy man **'increases his wealth by exorbitant interest'**. This is a lone reference to the subject in Proverbs. The law forbade most forms of usury: 'If you lend money to one of my people among you who is needy, do not be like a money-lender; charge him no interest' (Exod. 22:25). 'Do not take [excessive?] interest … from him, but fear your God, so that your countryman may continue to live among you. You must not lend him money at interest or sell him food at a profit' (Lev. 25:36-37). 'Do not charge your brother interest, whether on money or food or anything else that may earn interest. You may charge a foreigner interest, but not a brother Israelite, so that the LORD your God may bless you in everything you put your hand to in the land you are entering to possess' (Deut. 23:19-20).

This is a sin that Nehemiah had to oppose in his day (see Neh. 5). As Proverbs 13:22 notes, all that a greedy man is doing is amassing a fortune that will one day pass to someone who will use it to relieve the poor. There is a warning and an encouragement in this statement.

Verse 22 is very similar to the second part of verse 20. It warns the stingy man (the man with the evil eye) that his eagerness to get rich counts against him. He will one day end up in poverty — either here or in hell. Poverty of soul leads to poverty in every department.

Verse 27 reassures us that we lose nothing by giving to the poor. Closing our eyes to the poor will lead, however, to curses. This is taken up by Jesus in the New Testament when he pronounces the meek blessed, saying they will inherit the earth, and declares that it is better to give than receive (Matt. 5:5; Acts 20:35). Once again it is 'Reap what you sow' or, as an English proverb puts it into rhyme, 'Sow thin, mow thin.'

Not by chasing fantasies but by working hard

'He who works his land will have abundant food, but the one who chases fantasies will have his fill of poverty' (28:19).

Contrast: **'he who works his land'** / **'one who chases fantasies'**

This contrasting proverb, which is very similar to 12:11, speaks of two kinds of *fillings* — food and poverty. The emphasis is on making good use of resources. It is amazing how much fantasizing we can indulge in — dreams of leisure, power, success and happiness. It is incredible how many lives are taken up with pursuing impossible, unrealistic goals. Rather, we must work hard in the real world. This is how the kingdom of God advances. In the eighteenth century John Berridge wrote that 'Every man has a piece of land to till, which is the ground of the heart.' Taking his cue from Jesus' parable of the sower, he says that the heart must be broken up. The Word must enter it as the plough does the ground. Seed must be sown, weeds killed and clods of harshness broken. Are we diligently using the means of grace so that such things can happen?

Not by being greedy but by trusting in the Lord

'A greedy man stirs up dissension, but he who trusts in the LORD will prosper' (28:25).
   Contrast: **'greedy man' / 'he who trusts in the LORD'**

The contrast here is between a greedy man (some translate it as 'proud man') and one who trusts in the Lord. Greed, like pride, shows a lack of trust in the Lord. Jesus says, 'Seek first [God's] kingdom and his righteousness and all these things will be given to you as well' (Matt. 6:33).

A little complex, this proverb declares not only that those who trust the Lord prosper and the greedy do not, but also that the latter **'stir up dissension'** by their greed. Hatred, pride, mocking and anger do the same thing (see 10:12; 13:10; 15:18; 21:24; 22:10).

'He who trusts in himself is a fool, but he who walks in wisdom is kept safe' (28:26).
   Contrast (complex): **'he who trusts in himself' / 'he who walks in wisdom'**

This is a promise together with a warning. It is a negative version of the previous verse and of 3:5. If you are not trusting in the Lord, you are trusting in yourself, in your own heart, in some way. He who trusts in the Lord **'walks in wisdom'** and so will be **'kept safe'**. When you trust in yourself, you are **'a fool'**. This is because the heart is desperately wicked and beyond cure. Such advice flies in the face of much that is said today about the need to believe in ourselves and to increase our self-confidence. Rather, we say with the hymn-writer George Duffield:

> The arm of flesh will fail you,
> You dare not trust your own.

48.
Lessons in wise and righteous leadership

Please read Proverbs 29:1-27

Stubbornness, good government, love of wisdom, justice and bribery, flattery, the evil and the righteous, the righteous and justice, mockers, raging fools, bloodthirstiness, self-control, rulers and lies, oppression of the poor, justice and security, discipline imparting wisdom, downfall of the wicked, discipline leading to delight, revelation, perverse servants, hasty speech, pampered servants, hot tempers, pride and humility, honour among thieves, fear and trust, authority and justice, hostility between the righteous and the wicked

Here we have the last chapter containing proverbs of Solomon. Again, it is part of the collection assembled by Hezekiah's men. In general, we notice, firstly, that, like many of Solomon's proverbs, especially the earlier ones, several refer directly to the major themes of wisdom and righteousness. Once more, as in Proverbs 25-28, there is much here on leadership but many other matters are also covered. As we have seen earlier, even though we are not kings or those in positions of high authority, we all need to know about such things. We are responsible both for others and for ourselves.

Lessons in leadership, or wisdom and righteousness for leaders

(Verses 1, 2 and 3 are dealt with below.)

Lessons for kings

'By justice a king gives a country stability, but one who is greedy for bribes tears it down' (29:4).
    Contrast: **'a king** [who brings] **justice'** / **'one who is greedy for bribes'**

Stability comes to a nation when its leaders seek justice rather than financial gain. The evil of bribery has already been mentioned in 17:23. So many times in recent years countries in the second and third worlds have suffered because their leaders have been busy lining their own pockets rather than promoting justice — Amin, Bokassa, Ceausescu, Duvalier, etc. The list is long. Solomon himself knew well that this was the way forward. Did he ever talk over this proverb with Rehoboam? If he did, it seems to have been forgotten by that hapless son. The greedy man may not himself be a leader but an influential man who undermines and counteracts the stability provided by the leader.

(Verses 5-11 are dealt with below.)

'If a ruler listens to lies, all his officials become wicked' (29:12).
    Synthetic: **'listens to lies'** / **'officials become wicked'**

Once it is known that a leader is willing to listen to things that are not true, it is an invitation to all his officials to tell him what he wants to hear and to believe what they want to believe rather than what is true. Even if the trickle-down theory is not sound as far as a nation's economy is concerned, one can be sure that it holds good for integrity. If a country's leaders show integrity, it is likely to have a marked effect on those below them. If the leaders are corrupt, what is there to stop that corruption spreading like gangrene all the way through society?

Lawson argues that it was the corrupt attitude of Tiberius that contributed to Pilate's fears of being labelled a traitor which in turn led to the crucifixion of the innocent Christ. In terms of the church it was Geoffrey Chaucer's poor parson who loved that saying: 'That if gold ruste what shal iren do?' It is an interesting question as to whether a people ever rises above the standards set by their minister.

> **The poor man and the oppressor have this in**
> **   common:**
> **   The LORD gives sight to the eyes of both.**
> **If a king judges the poor with fairness,**
> **   his throne will always be secure**
>
> (29:13-14).

Synthetic: **'poor man' / 'oppressor'**
Synthetic: **'king' / 'his throne'**

In verse 13 we have another reminder of the true status of the poor (cf. 22:2). The poor man is fundamentally no different from the man who oppresses him. Both were created by God and in his image. Oppressors ought to think carefully, therefore, about how they deal with the poor. Rulers especially should be kind to the poor. Governments should always be concerned about the needy who are under their jurisdiction. This is likely to lead to stable government. There will certainly be no peasants' rebellion when this is the case.

(See below for verses 15, 16 and 17.)

A wise and righteous ruler recognizes that his people's greatest need is the Lord. See the famous but often misunderstood verse 18: **'Where there is no revelation, the people cast off restraint; but blessed is he who keeps the law.'**
   Beatitude / contrast: **'people [who] cast off restraint'** / **'he who keeps the law'**

The Old Testament revelation consists of law, prophecy and wisdom. Here wisdom commends prophecy (not vision in the sense of insight or foresight — see 1 Sam. 3:1), which itself commends keeping the law (3:1). This is every nation's greatest need, and yours and mine too. Preaching of the Word leads to holiness. That is wisdom. Without it, people go their own way and anarchy prevails. That is foolishness. Amos speaks of it in terms of a famine (Amos 8:11-12). Hosea also speaks of God's people suffering from such a lack of knowledge (Hosea 4:6). Ignorance is not the mother of devotion but of chaos.

(See below for verses 19-25.)

At such times, we must remember too that **'Many seek an audience with a ruler, but it is from the LORD that man gets justice'** (29:26).
   Contrast: **'ruler'** / **'the LORD'**

Although our leaders may fail us, we must look beyond them to the Lord for justice in Christ. When governments are unfavourable to the gospel, we understandably turn to a verse like this. The collapse of Communism is surely an illustration of how believers, who could gain no audience with their earthly leaders, prayed to the Lord and he sent them justice. We ought also to turn to this verse, however, when a government seems

favourable. It is never right to put our faith in princes rather
than in God:

> Do not put your trust in princes,
>> in mortal men who cannot save.
> When their spirit departs, they return to the ground;
>> on that very day their plans come to nothing
>>>>> (Ps. 146:3-4).

We must always remember that the final verdict in every case
will come from the highest court of all.

Lessons for parents

**'The rod of correction imparts wisdom, but a child left to
himself disgraces his mother'** (29:15).
　　Contrast: **'rod of correction'** (used) / **'child left to himself'**

**'Discipline your son, and he will give you peace; he will
bring delight to your soul'** (29:17).
　　Synthetic: **'discipline your son'** / **'he will bring delight'**

Here is a final reminder about corporal punishment for children, a topic last raised in Proverbs 23:13-14. When a **'rod of
correction'** is used, it is imparting wisdom, a helpful thought
to have in mind when exercising such discipline. Unlike the
previous passage on this theme, the emphasis here is on the
benefit to the parents rather than the child. The same is true of
verse 3, where a grown-up child is in mind. This is also a point
to remember: simply to leave a child to himself will lead in the
end to disgrace coming upon you. The disgrace to the mother
is especially highlighted. Discipline is the way to peace, a peace
that comes at a price. What a delight it is when a child grows
up to be a credit to his or her parents!

The context points to a wider application for the verses but they apply in the first place to parents. Or to put it another way, a well-governed country needs well-governed homes. Proverbs is famous for its commendation of strict discipline. This is the only way to wisdom and success. By nature, we are all foolish and perverse, and so strict discipline is vital.

It might be worth saying here that verses on corporal punishment are not necessarily confined to Proverbs. At the time of writing, a group of Christian schools are arguing their human right to exercise corporal punishment on the basis that it is a biblical doctrine. A professedly Christian academic is countering them in the courts. Dr Lloyd Pietersen has said, 'I cannot think of a single New Testament passage that supports the idea of corporal punishment.' He is aware of Ephesians 6:4, which speaks of bringing up children 'in the training and instruction' or 'nurture and admonition of the Lord'. Apparently, he is unaware of the argument that says that while the latter term refers to what is said to the child, the former refers to what is done to him. The first term could be rendered 'discipline'.

Lessons for masters

'A servant cannot be corrected by mere words; though he understands, he will not respond' (29:19).
Synthetic: **'mere words'** / **'he will not respond'**

'If a man pampers his servant from youth, he will bring grief in the end' (29:21).
Synthetic: **'pampers his servant'** / **'grief in the end'**

In the Old Testament period the permanent master / servant situation was common. Today it is a more transient thing. However, we are often on one side or the other of such a relationship, either at the office or factory; at the school or college; in a shop or restaurant; when something needs to be made or repaired; whenever we ask someone to do something for us, or are asked to do something for someone else. Of course, there is a sense in which all believers are servants to God. We should also not forget that the words 'minister' and 'deacon' both mean 'servant'. Further, the context again points to a wider application. The call is for strong leadership. Mere words are not enough; pampering servants is a recipe for disaster. Servants and workers have an inherent tendency to be 'unresponsive and irresponsible' (to quote Kidner) and will take advantage of a soft approach. This is a fact of life. Be prepared, therefore, not only to tell the waitress or workman what you want, but also to check whether it is done, or to provide some incentive or penalty. Without pomposity or nastiness, make quite clear that you expect a top-rate job with no slacking. Otherwise, it will only lead to grief in the end. Many times one has observed situations where arrangements are made on a friendly level instead of in a brisk and businesslike manner. So often there is misunderstanding and disappointment on one side or the other and the arrangement is a disaster. A certain amount of cynicism and sternness can be a great help.

At school, mathematics was never my strong point. It did not help that we had a succession of teachers who I felt were rather lax in their approach. I was then put into Mrs Matthews' class. She was very strict and would check to see if the homework had really been done! It was tough but I passed the vital 'O' level examination without which I could not have gone to university. Such strictness does not come easily to some of us. What a benefit it can be, however, in the context of the family, the church, the state, and many other spheres too! The other side of the coin is that when we are in a serving situation we should consider our masters 'worthy of full respect, so that God's name and our teaching will not be slandered'. This is doubly so where we are dealing with believers (1 Tim. 6:1-2).

Lessons in wisdom

'A man who loves wisdom brings joy to his father, but a companion of prostitutes squanders his wealth' (29:3).
 Contrast: **'man who loves wisdom'** / **'companion of prostitutes'**

The unexpected parallel points to the fact that the wayward son is not concerned about the effect on his father. He is happy to squander his hard-earned wealth on prostitutes. The proverbs are written chiefly in the form of advice that a father gives to a son. We have considered many proverbs like this one (10:1 is the first). The whole point of the book is to encourage us to love and seek wisdom. There is nothing better. Those who are profligate, who waste their strength, their effort and their wealth are often condemned. The true philosopher (which literally means 'lover of wisdom') avoids bad company and so does not waste money or sadden his father. Are you throwing your life away? Get heavenly wisdom.

 Four particular characteristics of the wise are highlighted here. (Verse 4 has been dealt with above, for 5-7 see below.)

They are a calming influence

'Mockers stir up a city, but wise men turn away anger' (29:8).
 Contrast: **'mockers'** / **'wise men'**

The ability to stir up a crowd is sometimes admired, but it is often a mark of those who mock the truth. A much more admirable power is that of being able to calm a situation. Think of Moses and Aaron at Sinai. If only this were true of some politicians! On a higher plane, we can think of the prayers of the people of Nineveh, which averted the wrath of God (see

Jonah 3). What an impact wise men can have on a city when they pray to God!

They realize that they cannot solve every problem

'If a wise man goes to court with a fool, the fool rages and scoffs, and there is no peace' (29:9).
   Contrast: **'wise man'** / **'fool'**

Here is the balance. Wisdom humbly recognizes its limitations and acts on it. Some matters are best dropped. The wise man knows when to take on authorities and when to run and hide. He knows where to take his stand. At times he will be like Nehemiah and expect a royal escort. At other times he will be like Ezra and realize that such a request will only be seen as expressing a lack of faith.

(Verse 10 is dealt with below.)

They practise self-control

'A fool gives full vent to his anger, but a wise man keeps himself under control' (29:11).
   Contrast: **'fool'** / **'wise man'**

Self-control has been commended many times (e.g. 25:28). A fool loses his temper but a wise man holds back. It is one of the give-away signs. Many things cause us dismay but we do not need to speak, or do anything, about all of them. Rather we must learn to control our emotions. I once saw a man with a large computer-keyboard 'control' button emblazoned on his T-shirt. It would make life easier if we were all fitted with a button that would give automatic control! The picture suggested to Eric Lane is that of taking a crying baby out of the room. That is what we will do with our tempers when they flare, if we are wise.

(Verses 12-15,17-19 have all been dealt with above)

They are especially slow to speak

'Do you see a man who speaks in haste? There is more hope for a fool than for him' (29:20).
  Contrast (better than): **'man who speaks in haste' / 'fool'**

This follows on from what has gone before. If we listened more and spoke less what a difference it would make! The scorn expressed here has been reserved previously only for the man who is wise in his own eyes (26:12). Both character- istics are species of the same pride and thoughtlessness. Here the context of the servant / master situation in the surrounding verses suggests that this relationship is an obvious area where we need to heed the proverb.

The kind of man who is commended, then, is a peacemaker, one who is humble, self-controlled and slow to speak. 'My dear brothers,' writes James, 'take note of this: Everyone should be quick to listen, slow to speak and slow to become angry, for man's anger does not bring about the righteous life that God desires. Therefore, get rid of all moral filth and the evil that is so prevalent, and humbly accept the word planted in you, which can save you' (James 1:19-21). Later he asks his readers, 'Who is wise and understanding among you? Let him show it by his good life, by deeds done in the humility that comes from wisdom. But if you harbour bitter envy and selfish ambition in your hearts, do not boast about it or deny the truth. Such "wisdom" does not come down from heaven but is earthly, unspiritual, of the devil. For where you have envy and selfish ambition, there you find disorder and every evil practice. But the wisdom that comes from heaven is first of all pure; then peace-loving, considerate, submissive, full of mercy and good fruit, impartial and sincere. Peacemakers who sow in peace raise a harvest of righteousness' (James 3:13-18).

Thus we must accept the Word and seek heavenly wisdom. Seek Christ both as Saviour and as the great exemplar of all this.

Lessons in righteousness

General remarks

(Verses 21 and 26 are dealt with above, verses 22-25 at the end.)

Righteousness is a mark of the truly wise and uprightness is commended just as often as being wise. We must all choose which way to go. We must go one way or the other: **'The righteous detest the dishonest; the wicked detest the upright'** (29:27).

Contrast: **'righteous'** / **'wicked'**

This verse ties up the whole section beginning at 28:1. In both verses the word for **'the righteous'** is plural and that for **'the wicked'** singular (in 29:10 this is reversed). Perhaps we can see some encouragement for the righteous in that fact, certainly as to how it will end. This sums up the outlook of Proverbs well. There is an implacable hatred between the righteous and the wicked. We are all on one side or the other. As Jesus said, 'He who is not for me is against me.' Which side are you on?

The wicked hate the very presence of the righteous, and so persecution is almost inevitable for the believer: **'Bloodthirsty men hate a man of integrity and seek to kill the upright'** (29: 10).

Contrast: **'bloodthirsty men'** / **'man of integrity'**

We are in many ways surrounded: 'Everyone who wants to lead a godly life in Christ Jesus will be persecuted' (2 Tim. 3:12). Are you willing to suffer? Think of Christ himself and how he was opposed. If you follow him, you will be persecuted too.

But it will inevitably lead to true joy. This is true on both a national and a personal level.

On a national level

'When the righteous thrive, the people rejoice; when the wicked rule, the people groan' (29:2).

Contrast: **'when the righteous thrive'** / **'when the wicked rule'**

Here once again is the key to a happy society — it will come about when the righteous thrive (cf. 28:12,28).

On a personal level

'An evil man is snared by his own sin, but a righteous one can sing and be glad' (29:6).

Contrast: **'evil man'** / **'righteous one'**

We have often noted how the evil man is his own worst enemy and seen the advantages of righteousness. 'The evil deeds of a wicked man ensnare him; the cords of his sin hold him fast' (5:22). Or again:

The righteousness of the blameless makes a straight way
      for them,
      but the wicked are brought down by their own
      wickedness.
The righteousness of the upright delivers them,
      but the unfaithful are trapped by evil desires
                                          (11:5-6; see also 12:13).

The wicked cannot escape their sins, for they hold them fast.
Here too is the opposite. Whatever happens to the righteous
man, he can still sing, like Paul and Silas in prison at Philippi
(Acts 16), and be glad. Hebrews 12:2 tells us how Christ faced
the cross conscious of the joy to follow.

Of course, joy is not always immediate but will win out in
end: **'When the wicked thrive, so does sin, but the righteous will see their downfall'** (29:16).
      Contrast: **'wicked'** / **'righteous'**.

It is this realization that sustains God's people in testing times.
The book of Proverbs often urges us to keep the end in view.

Further characteristics

Some come out negatively, some positively.

He responds to rebuke

**'A man who remains stiff-necked after many rebukes will
suddenly be destroyed — without remedy'** (29:1).
      Synthetic: **'man who remains stiff-necked'** / **'destroyed'**

This is the lesson of the flood in Noah's day and of Sodom in
later times. It is the situation now for all those who refuse to

repent and bow the knee to Christ. Paul says of the wicked: 'While people are saying, "Peace and safety," destruction will come on them suddenly, as labour pains on a pregnant woman, and they will not escape' (1 Thess. 5:3).

Are you responsive? This is the last of some five places in Proverbs where this theme arises. We are told that 'disaster will overtake' the scoundrel and villain 'in an instant; he will suddenly be destroyed — without remedy' (6:15). There is a warning to the wicked against rebellion towards God or the king, otherwise '... those two will send sudden destruction upon them, and who knows what calamities they can bring?' (24:22). In 28:18 we read, 'He whose walk is blameless is kept safe, but he whose ways are perverse will suddenly fall.' Back in chapter 3 there was a promise addressed to faithful sons:

> Have no fear of sudden disaster
>   or of the ruin that overtakes the wicked,
> for the LORD will be your confidence
>   and will keep your foot from being snared
>
> (3:25-26).

(Verses 2-4 have been dealt with above.)

He sees the danger of flattery

'Whoever flatters his neighbour is spreading a net for his feet' (29:5).

Synthetic / Simile: '**flatters**' / '**spreading a net**'

This subject was raised earlier:

> Like a coating of glaze over earthenware
>   are fervent lips with an evil heart.

A malicious man disguises himself with his lips,
    but in his heart he harbours deceit.
Though his speech is charming, do not believe him,
    for seven abominations fill his heart.
His malice may be concealed by deception,
    but his wickedness will be exposed in the assembly...
A lying tongue hates those it hurts,
    and a flattering mouth works ruin

                      (26:23-28).

The purpose of this book is not to make you feel good about
yourself. You should not aim to flatter others either. Neither
desire flattery nor give it.

    (Verse 6 has been dealt with above.)

He seeks justice for the poor

**'The righteous care about justice for the poor, but the
wicked have no such concern'** (29:7).
    Contrast: **'righteous' / 'wicked'**

Here we are reminded that it is a mark of the righteous that,
unlike the wicked, they **'care about justice for the poor'**
(literally the verse speaks in terms of wisdom — of knowledge and ignorance rather than care and concern). Job was
able to testify:

Whoever heard me spoke well of me,
    and those who saw me commended me,
because I rescued the poor who cried for help,
    and the fatherless who had none to assist him.
The man who was dying blessed me;
    I made the widow's heart sing.
I put on righteousness as my clothing;

> justice was my robe and my turban.
> I was eyes to the blind
>   and feet to the lame.
> I was a father to the needy;
>   I took up the case of the stranger.
> I broke the fangs of the wicked
>   and snatched the victims from their teeth
>   (Job 29:11-17).

What an example to us he is! How different those in Ezekiel's day of whom the prophet says, '… they have treated father and mother with contempt … they have oppressed the alien and ill-treated the fatherless and the widow… The people of the land practise extortion and commit robbery; they oppress the poor and needy and ill-treat the alien, denying them justice' (Ezek. 22:7,29).

(Verses 8-21 have been dealt with above.)

He stays calm

'An angry man stirs up dissension, and a hot-tempered one commits many sins' (29:22).
   Synonymous: **'angry man'** / **'hot-tempered one'**

Again we have a negative example set before us. Notice how this links with wisdom (see verses 8 and 11). This is similar to the first part of 15:18. There are many sins that a person would not have committed if he had not lost his temper.

He is humble

'A man's pride brings him low, but a man of lowly spirit gains honour' (29:23).
   Contrast: **'man's pride'** / **'man of lowly spirit'**

Pride is a great barrier to wisdom. It is often spoken against in Proverbs (e.g., 18:12). Humility is commended everywhere in Scripture. Here the warning is that pride actually leads downward and it is humility that brings honour.

He sees the folly of sin

'The accomplice of a thief is his own enemy; he is put under oath and dare not testify' (29:24).
   Synthetic: **'accomplice of a thief'** / **'under oath '**

Again we have a wise saying commending righteousness. The two are intertwined. The wicked often put themselves in impossible positions. The accomplice of a thief cannot testify without incriminating his partner. To do this will bring trouble from that man. On the other hand, to say nothing will only make him guilty of a further crime — that of perjury.

He recognizes that salvation comes through trusting in the Lord

'Fear of man will prove to be a snare, but whoever trusts in the LORD is kept safe' (29:25).
   Contrast: **'fear of man'** / **'whoever trusts in the LORD'**

Righteousness is not a matter of human effort but of faith. Do you have such faith? Give up living to please men. If we really trust in God, we will care little about what men think of us. Too often our first thought is of what others will say, rather than what God will say. This was the downfall of Abraham, Isaac, Aaron and Saul. Many have fallen at the same hurdle. Elijah and Peter also come to mind. The psalmist echoes the sentiment: 'It is better to take refuge in the LORD than to trust in man' (Ps. 118:8). Jesus says, 'Do not be afraid of those who kill the body but cannot kill the soul. Rather, be afraid of the One who can destroy both soul and body in hell' (Matt. 10:28).

Final lessons
Sayings of Agur (30:1-33)
Sayings of King Lemuel (31:1-9)
Epilogue: the wife of noble character (31:10-31)

49.
Learning from Agur about God, about man

Please read Proverbs 30:1-17

Sayings of Agur

The wisest man who ever lived was Solomon (see 1 Kings 4:29-34). He was not, however, the only wise man of his time. It is clear that he made a judicious use of the wisdom of others in assembling his proverbs. In chapter 30 we apparently have the wisdom of **'Agur son of Jakeh'**. This could, of course, be a pseudonym for Solomon, but that seems unlikely.

We do not know anything of this man Agur. It would seem that Solomon gained his information about him through a secondary source, namely the **'Ithiel'** and **'Ucal'** referred to in verse 1, although the Hebrew could be read another way to say, 'I am weary, O God, I am weary, O God, and faint.' Otherwise we do not know who these two were either. Agur could have been a contemporary unconverted pagan whose ideas Solomon has adapted. Alternatively, he may have been a contemporary converted pagan. It seems most likely, however, that he was a man of God from the period of Job (experts say the style of verses 4 and 5 suggests this). He seems to speak firstly of himself and God (looking inwards and upwards in verses 1-9) and then about others (as he looks around from verse 10 onwards). In this chapter we shall consider verses 1-17.

Looking upwards and inwards to learn about God and yourself

It is clear from what we read here that Agur was a humble man. It is possible to read his words as sarcasm but it is much more likely that this is a genuine confession of both ignorance and weakness.

You are ignorant and you need to study God's revelation of himself.

Humbly acknowledge your ignorance

'I am the most ignorant of men; I do not have a man's understanding' (30:2). Agur may seem to have gone over the top in his expressions but he wants to stress that he is not relying on his own wisdom at all. If we do not think we are ignorant that shows how ignorant we really are (see 26:12; 1 Cor. 8:2). Agur confesses his lack of knowledge, of wisdom (that is, wisdom about how to live) and the existence of the Holy One: **'I have not learned wisdom, nor have I knowledge of the Holy One'** (30:3).

In verse 4 he asks five vital questions. Have you ever asked them? It is the saddest thing that so many have never done so. The problem is not simply that people do not know the answer to these vital questions, but that there are many who do not even know that these are the questions they should be asking.

The answer to these questions begins to become clear, of course, from an examination of the rest of Scripture:

1. **'Who has gone up to heaven and come down?'**
John 3:13 tells us, 'No one has ever gone into heaven except the one who came from heaven — the Son of Man,' that is, the Lord Jesus himself.

2. **'Who has gathered up the wind in the hollow of his hands? Who has wrapped up the waters in his cloak?'** The answer is God himself, of course (see Job 38:4-41; Ps. 104:2-35; Isa. 40:12-31).

3. **'Who has established all the ends of the earth?'**

The earth is the LORD's, and everything in it,
    the world, and all who live in it;
for he founded it upon the seas
    and established it upon the waters

(Ps. 24:1-2).

4. **'What is his name, and the name of his son?'**
'Moses said to God, "Suppose I go to the Israelites and say to them, 'The God of your fathers has sent me to you,' and they ask me, 'What is his name?' Then what shall I tell them?" God said to Moses, "I AM WHO I AM. This is what you are to say to the Israelites: 'I AM has sent me to you'"'(Exod. 3:13-14).

In Luke 1:35 an angel tells Mary, 'The Holy Spirit will come upon you, and the power of the Most High will overshadow you. So the holy one to be born will be called the Son of God' (see also Mark 1:1; Luke 22:70; John 20:31).

However, Agur's point is that no one knows the answer to these questions exhaustively, or anywhere near as fully as they should, or as they could without divine aid. Even in this New Testament era we have to admit that there are many mysteries.

Humbly acknowledge the perfection of God's Word

Agur is not simply negative. He does not only acknowledge his own ignorance. This is a major step but we need more. He (or someone commenting on his words) humbly acknowledges the purity and sufficiency of God's Word.

The purity of God's Word

'Every word of God is flawless' (30:5). And so if I rely on God's words — that is, on God — then there is no need for me to be fearful. He can be fully trusted.

'He is a shield to those who take refuge in him' (30:5). We met this idea right back in Proverbs 2:

> For the LORD gives wisdom,
>   and from his mouth come knowledge and
>   understanding.
> He holds victory in store for the upright,
>   he is a shield to those whose walk is blameless,
> for he guards the course of the just
>   and protects the way of his faithful ones.
>   (2:6-8).

The same idea is also found almost verbatim in Psalm 18:30:

> As for God, his way is perfect;
>   the word of the LORD is flawless.
> He is a shield
>   for all who take refuge in him.

The New Testament speaks appropriately of the shield of faith. The purity of God's Word affirmed here is best spoken of today as the inerrancy of God's Word. In his *Systematic Theology* Wayne Grudem defines it thus: 'The inerrancy of Scripture means that Scripture in the original manuscripts does not affirm anything that is contrary to fact.'

The Bible is absolutely reliable. It contains no mistakes whatsoever. Whatever subject it addresses, it always tells the truth. As originally given it is flawless, immaculate, perfect, without error. That is why we can rely on it. Are you relying on God's Word?

The sufficiency of God's Word

'Do not add to his words, or he will rebuke you and prove you a liar' (30:6). To add to God's words shows gross ungratefulness and is a wicked sin. We must rely on God's Word alone. Similar warnings are found near the beginning and the end of the Bible. In the law God says to the people, 'Do not add to what I command you and do not subtract from it, but keep the commands of the LORD your God that I give you' (Deut. 4:2; cf. 12:32). In the last chapter of the Bible we read these solemn words: 'I warn everyone who hears the words of the prophecy of this book: If anyone adds anything to them, God will add to him the plagues described in this book. And if anyone takes words away from this book of prophecy, God will take away from him his share in the tree of life and in the holy city, which are described in this book' (Rev. 22:18-19).

In 1675 Puritan Matthew Sylvester preached on this verse. He spoke of additions that are not forbidden, such as words that explain the sense, force and usefulness of Scripture; pertinent and distinct applications of general rules and whatever may preserve, promote or quicken due purity, truth and order. On the other hand, we must not accept anything that is not God's as though it were; anything that vies with his revealed truths or laws; anything that seems to argue God's ignorance, imprudence or negligence; anything that destroys the end, or contradicts the purpose, or tends to weaken the Word's majesty or power; or that builds what God destroys, or destroys what he builds, or that wrongly construes the Word.

The reason why we have no need to add to Scripture is that Scripture is sufficient. In Wayne Grudem's *Systematic Theology* again there is a definition: 'The sufficiency of Scripture means that Scripture contained all the words of God that he intended his people to have at each stage of redemptive history, and that it now contains everything we need God to tell us for salvation, for trusting him perfectly and for obeying him perfectly.'

In the light of that, there is no room for additions that are likely to serve only to create confusion.

Pray to God for grace

You are weak and you need to pray for God's grace and providence.

The truly wise person — that is, the true believer — not only reads and believes God's Word but also seeks God's face in prayer. Here we have a model prayer for our use:

Two things I ask of you, O LORD;
    do not refuse me before I die:
Keep falsehood and lies far from me;
      give me neither poverty nor riches,
      but give me only my daily bread.
Otherwise, I may have too much and disown you
      and say, 'Who is the LORD?'
Or I may become poor and steal,
      and so dishonour the name of my God

                                                    (30:7-9).

From these words we draw four lessons:

    1. Recognize your own tendency to be dishonest and pray for grace to avoid that flaw.

    2. Pray that you may not dishonour God, at the same time recognizing that you are incapable of this in your own strength.

    3. Pray to be led out of temptation. See the dangers at either extreme — riches or poverty.

    4. As you pray have faith (**'I ask of you, O Lord'**), be fervent (**'do not refuse me'**) and persistent (**'before I die'**).

Do you pray? If so, good. Do you pray recognizing your own great weakness? Even better. Do you pray chiefly to honour God regardless of self? That is the grand goal of prayer. This is what we find in the Lord's Prayer. We are to pray, 'Lead us not into temptation, but deliver us from the evil one.' We are to begin with the petition, 'Our Father in heaven, hallowed be your name,' and to ask, 'Give us today our daily bread' (see Matt. 6:9-13). The same spirit manifested here is also found in Paul, who said, 'But godliness with contentment is great gain. For we brought nothing into the world, and we can take nothing out of it. But if we have food and clothing, we will be content with that' (1 Tim. 6:6-8).

In 1682 Puritan John Oakes preached on this text observing that 'A middle estate or condition in the world, upon rational and religious grounds, is most eligible for a man, as such, with respect to this life, or for a Christian, as such, designing the happiness of another life.' He then states that God is sovereign and decides our state in life as he chooses. He does this according to his infinite wisdom in a way that best suits his purposes — the glory of his name and the good of his people. Oakes also notes that no outward condition influences

God or can make a person more or less acceptable to him. Finally, he concludes that it is not equally desirable or appropriate for everyone to be in the same condition in the world under all circumstances, nor for a person to always retain the same status in all circumstances. Our situation can change. That too is in God's hands.

Looking around and learning about man

From verse 10 onwards we have a series of proverbs that arise out of observations of what is going on around the writer. We especially focus on sins observed in others. Again the links between wisdom and righteousness that we have seen in the rest of the book are shown to be very strong. In verses 10-17 we have four proverbs — two short, two long. Each one deals with a particular sin which we must avoid.

Tale-bearing

'Do not slander a servant to his master, or he will curse you, and you will pay for it' (30:10). The law also warns against the sin of slander, or tale-bearing: 'Do not go about spreading slander among your people' (Lev. 19:16). Here the warning against the sin is given with a concrete example containing a command and a warning.

The command

'Do not slander[a fellow-?] **servant to his master.'** To slander someone is to speak falsely and maliciously against that person. What we have in mind here is tale-bearing, informing on someone else.

The warning

'**... or he will curse you, and you will pay for it.**' This is proverbial but it is a reminder that slanderers can often come unstuck. From time to time well-known people in Britain have threatened to take newspapers to court and have been paid a great deal in damages, either out of court or by way of compensation. Are you guilty of slander or telling tales? It is a sin and you must repent from it.

Arrogance

In verses 11-14 we have a simple series of four snapshots of (growing?) arrogance, a sin often highlighted for disapprobation in Proverbs. Each verse begins with a reference to '**those who...**'

1. A child rebelling against his superiors

'**There are those who curse their fathers and do not bless their mothers**' (30:11). Even at the most tender age, pride can begin to raise its ugly head. If unchecked what a monster it can turn into! Some of the worst atrocities in man's history have been the temper tantrums of overgrown babies.

2. A young man who is self-deceived

'**Those who are pure in their own eyes and yet are not cleansed of their filth**' (30:12). Perhaps the most dangerous kind of arrogance is the sort that does not even recognize its own portrait, '... having a form of godliness but denying its power' (2 Tim. 3:5). It is exemplified by the Pharisee in Jesus' parable in Luke 18:9-14.

3. A middle-aged fool who looks down his nose at everyone

'Those whose eyes are ever so haughty, whose glances are so disdainful' (30:13). There are people whose very way of looking at others reveals their settled arrogance and superciliousness.

4. The full-grown tyrant who does not have a good word to say for those he supposes to be his inferiors

> **Those whose teeth are swords**
> **and whose jaws are set with knives**
> **to devour the poor from the earth,**
> **the needy from among mankind**
>
> (30:14).

Here is the hideous, full-grown monster (Similar imagery is used in Psalm 57:4 and the same sequence of slander and arrogance is found in Psalm 101:5).

It is easy to see such sins in others, but what about ourselves? Do pride and arrogance, haughtiness and conceit lurk in your breast or mine?

Greed

> **The leech has two daughters.**
> **'Give! Give!' they cry.**
> **There are three things that are never satisfied,**
> **four that never say, 'Enough!':**
> **the grave, the barren womb,**
> **land, which is never satisfied with water,**
> **and fire, which never says, 'Enough!'**
>
> (30:15-16).

Again this is a longer proverb. This time the details are enumerated, as in 6:16-19. It begins in a somewhat comical fashion but it soon takes up a more tragic theme. Here are two female leeches — twins perhaps, or maybe mother and daughter. Leeches are small blood-sucking creatures that live in water. There are over 300 different varieties altogether. They feed on other creatures by painlessly sucking blood from them. In verse 15, these two cry, **'Give! Give!'**

We meet people like that. John Fogerty describes them in his 1960s' protest song 'Fortunate son':

> Some folks are born silver spoon in hand, Lord, don't
>   they help themselves ...
> Some folks inherit star-spangled eyes. Ooh, they send
>   you down to war, Lord,
> And when you ask them, 'How much should we give?'
>   Ooh, they only answer, 'More! more! more!'

To this example from nature, Agur adds four examples of the insatiable in life.

1. The grave

It never comes to the point when the grave says, 'Okay, enough have died.' Death goes on, and will go on until the very end of time. We must never forget that fact.

2. The barren womb

It is a terrible thing for a woman to want children yet not to be able to have them, for whatever reason. It is foolish to say to such a woman, 'Well, you've been trying for a few years now. Best just give up on it,' or 'Why don't you just forget about the idea and concentrate on something else?' No, while such a woman has the possibility of bearing children she will long for that. Pray for women in that situation.

3. Land which is never satisfied with water

In recent years, the UK has had problems with the water table in some areas. When a period of water shortages was followed by some very wet weather, many of us were surprised to know that still more rain was needed to remedy the problem. Without regular rainfall, a land will be a desert. The desert of Judea is often referred to in Scripture.

4. Fire

The insatiable nature of fire is well known, especially to those who have seen its devastating effects.

No direct application is made here but in Proverbs 27:20 we read what may be the clue: 'Death and destruction are never satisfied, and neither are the eyes of man.' Beware of vaulting ambition and of greed of all sorts. Such desires can never be fully satisfied. Rather look to the Lord who alone can fully satisfy our deepest longings.

Rebellion

> **The eye that mocks a father,**
> **   that scorns obedience to a mother,**
> **will be pecked out by the ravens of the valley,**
> **   will be eaten by the vultures**
>
> (30:17).

Again we have a brief proverb to close. Once more, the pattern is command and warning. We have, first, a description of the sin and, second, of the punishment.

A description of the sin

Rebelling against one's parents is a breach of the fifth commandment. In particular the thought here is of a contemptuous look, what was once referred to in the armed forces as 'dumb insolence'.

A description of the punishment

This is very graphic, but remember that it is proverbial and comes from a desert culture. Imagine, for example, a Bedouin boy, or a child living in the Australian outback for that matter, mocking his father's warnings not to stray, disobeying his mother's instructions not to wander from the tent or from the house. Yet the boy is fascinated. He cannot resist exploring this forbidden domain. Perhaps he strays once or twice and is punished but he does it again. One time he strays too far and cannot be found. It is some weeks before they eventually locate the remains of his body. Ravens have plucked out his eyes and the vultures have consumed his flesh. With suffering comes disgrace — the body does not receive burial. The lesson is clear: do not rebel against the authorities that God has constituted.

Isaac Watts asks children:

Have you not heard what dreadful plagues
Are threatened by the Lord,
To him that breaks his father's laws,
Or mocks his mother's word?

He then versifies and concludes:

But those that worship God, and give
Their parents honour due,

Here on this earth they long shall live,
And live hereafter too.

A summary of what this passage teaches

Humble yourself before God

'All of you, clothe yourselves with humility towards one another, because, "God opposes the proud but gives grace to the humble." Humble yourselves, therefore, under God's mighty hand, that he may lift you up in due time' (1 Peter 5:5-6).

Study and believe his Word

'Let the word of Christ dwell in you richly...' (Col. 3:16). 'Continue in what you have learned and have become convinced of ... the holy Scriptures, which are able to make you wise for salvation' (2 Tim. 3:14-15).

Trust in the Lord Jesus Christ who is revealed here

Salvation is 'through faith in Christ Jesus' (2 Tim. 3:15).

Pray for God's grace

'Let us then approach the throne of grace with confidence, so that we may receive mercy and find grace to help us in our time of need' (Heb. 4:16).

Turn from sin — from tale-bearing, arrogance, greed, rebellion

'The Redeemer will come to Zion, to those in Jacob who repent of their sins' (Isa. 59:20).

'Brothers, do not slander one another. Anyone who speaks against his brother or judges him speaks against the law and judges it. When you judge the law, you are not keeping it, but sitting in judgement on it... As it is, you boast and brag. All such boasting is evil' (James 4:11,16).

'Put to death, therefore, whatever belongs to your earthly nature ... evil desires and greed, which is idolatry. Because of these, the wrath of God is coming. You used to walk in these ways, in the life you once lived. But now you must rid yourselves of all such things as these: anger, rage, malice, slander...' (Col. 3:5-8).

'Submit yourselves for the Lord's sake to every authority instituted among men: whether to the king, as the supreme authority, or to governors, who arc scnt by him to punish those who do wrong and to commend those who do right' (1 Peter 2:13-14).

'Obey your leaders and submit to their authority. They keep watch over you as men who must give an account. Obey them so that their work will be a joy, not a burden, for that would be of no advantage to you' (Heb. 13:17).

50.
Watch with Agur and grow in wisdom

Please read Proverbs 30:18-33

Here we continue to look at the proverbs in chapter 30, assembled presumably by Agur. Solomon gives us examples from
his wise sayings. Throughout the chapter, and especially in
verses 18-33, we see that Agur's wisdom is characterized by
certain attitudes. His wisdom is observant, gentle and
memorable.

> *Observant.* It is based on careful and thoughtful ob-
> servation of God's creation and of human activity.
> *Gentle.* His lessons are not driven home in an obvi-
> ously forceful way. Rather, he is subtle, as a wise man
> ought to be. He creates interest and then leaves thoughts
> to linger in our minds and do their own work. In one
> instance the lesson is not even stated.
> *Memorable.* Along with the use of striking pictures,
> Agur especially likes to use numerical reinforcers — '...
> three things ... or four things...' There is an earlier ex-
> ample of a similar approach in 6:16: 'There are six ...
> seven...'

The very way these lessons in wisdom are presented, then,
teaches us something about wisdom:

Be observant, especially when it comes to the creation all around you, and man in particular. Open your eyes and look.

Be gentle, subtle, not aggressive and insensitive. Such an approach is usually more effective.

Be busy working at ways to memorize what really counts.

More specifically, these verses warn against four dangers and then give a concluding summarizing proverb that we do well to ponder.

Watch out for when the difficult becomes easy

Four amazing, incomprehensible things pictured (30:18-19)

There are three things that are too amazing for me,
four that I do not understand:
The way of an eagle in the sky...

If you have ever seen an eagle, or any bird of prey, flying high up, either in life or on film, you will have been struck by the amazing ease with which it flies. Perfectly adapted to its home 'high in heaven', this 'bird of the broad and sweeping wing' has its throne 'on the mountain top' while its fields are 'the boundless air' (I am quoting John Gates Percival). Hang-gliding is the nearest man can get to it.

'The way of a snake on a rock...' A snake has no legs but it is able to move along quickly, even on rough ground. If you have ever walked across pebbles with bare feet you will appreciate the skill. Emily Dickinson's 'narrow fellow in the long grass' is one who 'likes a boggy acre, a floor too cool for corn'. She speaks of him and tells how:

… when a child, and barefoot,
I more than once at morn,
Have passed, I thought, a whiplash
Unbraiding in the sun, —
When, stooping to secure it,
It wrinkled, and was gone.

'The way of a ship on the high seas.' We know that by
Solomon's time navigation and shipping skills were quite
advanced. The Phoenicians were the most skilful sailors at
that time and Solomon made use of some of Hiram's men for
a fleet that was based at Elath, in the Gulf of Akabah on the
Red Sea. It brought gold from Ophir. Other trading ships
brought silver, ivory, apes and baboons. It is a majestic sight
— a sailing ship gliding through the high seas. Even landlubbers
can enter into John Masefield's enthusiasm for 'the wheel's
kick and the wind's song and the white sail's shaking'. What
can compare with a 'windy day with the white clouds flying,
and the flung spray and the blown spume, and the seagulls
crying'?

'And the way of a man with a maiden.' The last reference
is either to man's wooing of a maiden or the act of love itself.
The imagery of the Song of Solomon is evocative:

Listen! My lover!
    Look! Here he comes,
leaping across the mountains,
    bounding over the hills.
My lover is like a gazelle or a young stag.
    Look! There he stands behind our wall,
gazing through the windows,
    peering through the lattice…
Until the day breaks
    and the shadows flee,

turn, my lover,
> and be like a gazelle
or like a young stag
> on the rugged hills

(S. of S. 2:8-9,17).

The point of the comparison in each case

Some believe that the point of comparison here is the fact that in each case no trace is left. Probably it is rather that these are all mysterious things that seem hard, almost impossible to achieve — flying, moving smoothly over rough terrain, sailing on the sea, a man wooing a maiden.

An application

The application seems to be in verse 20, where the adulteress sees the act of adultery as just like having meal:

This is the way of an adulteress:
> **She eats and wipes her mouth**
> **and says, 'I've done nothing wrong.'**

You say, I hope, 'That is a terrible thing to think,' and ask, 'How can she live with herself?' Yet for her it is no big deal. Yes, the first time she did it, it was probably quite something (think of a fledgling eagle making its first flight, a young snake, a sailor on his maiden voyage), but no longer. Her conscience has been seared. What about you? Are you so used to some sins that you no longer think anything of them? What danger! Recognize this and repent. Because he had never sinned the Lord Jesus always saw sin in all its horror, in a way that we do not. We must endeavour to see sin through his eyes.

Watch out that success does not go to your head

Four almost unbearable things pictured (30:21-23)

> **Under three things the earth trembles,**
> **under four it cannot bear up:**
> **a servant who becomes king...**

At times those from very humble circumstances have risen to
great power. Often they have been filled with pride at their
sudden rise.

'A fool who is full of food.' The fool in Proverbs is not an
idiot but a wilful sinner, a man bent on doing evil. He is bad
enough at the best of times, but when he has stuffed his face
full he is even worse.

'An unloved woman who is married.' It may have been
her own fault — maybe it is not — but here is a woman who is
unmarried. She is 'on the shelf', a spinster. As the years go by
she has less and less chance of marrying. Then suddenly she
finds a suitor and he asks her for her hand in marriage. Unless
God's grace is very effective indeed, the temptation to be full
of herself will be difficult to resist. (This seems more likely
than the idea that this is a married woman whose husband
does not love her.)

'And a maidservant who displaces her mistress.' Before
her death but after her divorce there were several articles in
the press suggesting great rivalry between Princess Diana and
Tiggy Legg-Burke, the young princes' nanny employed by
Prince Charles. Much of this stemmed from the way Diana
had been partly displaced. The famous biblical example is Hagar
who bore Ishmael to Abraham as a surrogate for the barren
Sarah. Genesis 16:4 records how 'When she knew she was
pregnant, she began to despise her mistress.'

The point of the comparison in each case

These are all examples of situations where success can go to a person's head. Those not trained for national leadership often fail; a woman who suddenly finds herself in a position of influence can easily become proud.

An application

This is not spelt out, but there is a clear warning here against letting success go to our heads. It happens so very easily. I know how in my own experience I had a fairly low opinion of myself until I sat the old 11-plus examination and passed for the grammar school. This made me very cocky indeed. I remember the same feeling when I first began to attend church regularly. Are you becoming proud of your successes or of your achievements? You are rich — so? Clever — so? Religious — so? These are all danger points. The only hope for any one of us is the grace of God found in Christ.

Watch and learn how to overcome your limitations

Four small creatures pictured

'Four things on earth are small, yet they are extremely wise' (30:24). The following verses consider four small creatures that are wise in certain respects.

'Ants are creatures of little strength, yet they store up their food in the summer' (30:25). The ant is a small insect but hard-working (as was noted in Proverbs 6:6-8) and throughout the summer months it concentrates on building up stores of food for the winter. You may perhaps have observed how hard they work.

'Conies are creatures of little power, yet they make their home in the crags' (30:26). Perhaps the rock badger or hyrax is in mind. Certainly a coney is a small animal like a rabbit. Such creatures protect themselves by hiding in holes in rocks. Though they are small, when predators come they can safely hide without fear of danger.

'Locusts have no king, yet they advance together in ranks' (30:27). Here is another insect. Locusts are larger than most ants but are still small. However, together they can cause devastation on a vast scale. A million locusts can eat as much vegetation in a day as ten elephants and there can be up to eighty million of them in a single square kilometre.

In June 2001 the Republic of Dagestan in southern Russia was hit by a plaguc of locusts which devastated huge tracts of farmland. Russian television spoke of more than 70,000 acres of pasture being destroyed in a week. More than 200,000 acres were infested altogether as insects flew in from neighbouring regions. The authorities spent some two million dollars tackling the problem, mainly spraying the fields with pesticides. Georgia, Azerbaijan, Kazakhstan and ten provinces in China were hit at the same time.

'A lizard can be caught with the hand, yet it is found in kings' palaces' (30:28). The reference here is to a lizard, not a spider (as in some Bible versions). In India and other warm countries these small reptiles are often seen in houses. They can easily be caught but most people are not interested. They are often found indoors, even in palaces.

The point of the comparison in each case

In each case the stress is first on the limitation and then, secondly, on the wise way in which that limitation is overcome.

An application

Firstly, stop and think about the wonder of the one who made all these creatures, and thousands more. Secondly, do not despise the weak. Thirdly, do not make your limitations an excuse so that you regularly fail to overcome them.

We can also make a number of more specific points of application:

1. *Prepare for the coming judgement while you can.* In Haddon Robinson's words, 'Next time you see an ant, remember: winter is coming! The best time to prepare for tomorrow is today.' We must store up God's Word in our hearts that we might not sin against him (Ps. 119:11).

2. *Hide in Christ the Rock.* There is no other refuge. With Fanny Crosby we sing:

In thy cleft, O Rock of Ages, hide thou me!
When the fitful tempest rages, hide thou me!
Where no mortal arm can sever
From my heart thy love for ever,
Hide me, O thou Rock of Ages, safe in thee!

And we join with William Orcutt Cushing in singing:

Safe to the Rock that is higher than I,
My soul in its conflicts and sorrows would fly;
So sinful, so weary, thine, thine, would I be;
Thou blest 'Rock of Ages', I'm hiding in thee.

3. *Unite with fellow believers.* United we stand, divided we fall. If we neglect to gather with God's people and work alongside them what hope is there of success? We do have a King. He leads us in his service.

4. Despite your vulnerability, *be very bold to believe you can enter the palace* of the great King by God's grace. He will bring us into his glorious heaven if we look to him.

Watch and learn what is the nature of true dignity

'There are three things that are stately in their stride, four that move with stately bearing' (30:29). Three stately animals are pictured — a fearless **'lion, mighty among beasts, who retreats before nothing'**, **'a strutting cock'** (probably), **'a he-goat and a king with his army around him'**. You have no doubt seen the animals in life or on film and it is not difficult to picture a king in ancient times, Saul or David for example, leading out his army.

The point of the comparison

Nothing is spelled out, but it is likely that Agur wants us to think of the nature or variety of dignity.

An application

Recognize where true dignity lies — not in our own bravery, clothing, uniqueness or strength. Rather human dignity lies in being made in the image of God. This is especially seen in man's re-creation in the image of God through faith in Christ.

Summary

Watch out that pride and sin do not turn you into a trouble-maker:

> **If you have played the fool and exalted yourself,**
>   **or if you have planned evil,**
> **clap your hand over your mouth!**

(30:32).

The whole chapter is marked by a certain humility. Here it is again. When we recognize our stupidity and sin we need to clap our hands over our mouths. What nonsense we have spoken! What trouble we have caused! The same Hebrew word is used for 'churn', 'twist' and 'stir'. Just as **'churning the milk produces butter'** and **'twisting the nose produces blood'**, so **'stirring up anger produces strife'**, or so sin leads to trouble. Realize this and confess your sins. Give up using the oft-repeated line: 'I've never harmed anyone.' Rather confess your sins and repent from them all.

51.
Instructions for those dedicated to God

Please read Proverbs 31:1-9

Sayings of King Lemuel

The penultimate section of Proverbs is described as **'the sayings of King Lemuel'**. Once again, we do not know who Lemuel was, or when and where he lived. The name Lemuel is unusual today, even among Christians, although it has been more popular in the past. It means, 'belonging to God'. For that reason some have wondered if it is an alias for Solomon or another previous contributor. There is no King of Israel or Judah by the name of Lemuel. Indeed the name is found nowhere else in the Bible. He could have been an Edomite or Arabian but the name points to a king from the time of Job, from the period before the call of Abraham. The oracle preserved here was actually taught to him by his mother. It is **'an oracle his mother taught him'**. The role of the queen mother is often an important royal post. Wherever the oracle came from, it would have been of obvious interest to King Solomon.

As we have intimated before, such material should be of interest to all of us as there is a sense in which we all reign as kings — over families, over other dominions and over ourselves — and we must rule well. Any help we can gain should be valued. The oracle touches on familiar themes, but it is good to consider them again. Those who believe in baptizing infants dedicate their children to God in that act. Many who reject infant baptism will nevertheless hold an act of dedication for a newborn baby. All who have grown up in a Christian home have in one way or another been dedicated to God. Others have perhaps been involved in services or acts of dedication as Sunday school teachers, ministers and missionaries. Therefore, many reading these pages will have quite literally been dedicated to God. Perhaps, they are of especial interest to such; therefore, this chapter has been given the heading, 'Instructions for those dedicated to God'.

Like Samuel's mother, Lemuel's mother had clearly dedicated her son to God. This is clear from his very name and from her reference to him as **'son of my vows'** (possibly meaning 'answer to my prayers'). All children should be dedicated to the Lord. They are not our children but God's anyway. In the Bible, we think especially of Moses, Samuel, Samson and John the Baptist whose births and early days are described most fully. In Numbers 6 it is explained how an Israelite who wanted to dedicate himself to God for a certain period could do so by taking a Nazirite vow. Samson was under such a vow all his life and this is possibly true of Samuel and John too. We also read in the New Testament of Paul apparently taking a similar vow for a period (Acts 18:18).

There does not have to be a church service for a child to be dedicated to God. Some are wary of such things. I am a Baptist minister. Our church has never baptized an infant but I have been told quite categorically by at least one mother that, before my time, all her children were christened in the church I now pastor! The truth is that, whether our parents dedicated us or not, the purpose of life is to be given over to serving God.

The supreme example of all this, of course, is the Lord Jesus Christ. His whole life was dedicated to God. He is the supreme Nazirite, the supreme Lemuel. In fact, the only true way of dedicating oneself to God is in Christ. Are you dedicated to God? Is your whole life given up to serving him? That is how it must be for all of us.

Here are two major guiding rules for all who are. The first rule is negative; the second positive. This is by no means exhaustive teaching, but these principles, expressed in typically concrete Old Testament terms, are vital. We must get these principles clear.

Avoid sinful excess in indulging your appetites and desires

An obvious feature of kingship, especially in the case of an oriental despot, is the abundant opportunity it offers for excess. The stories of excess among royals are legion. In more recent times, a new royalty has emerged of actors, artists, entertainers and others whose excesses are also legendary. There are many forms of excess — excessive laziness, overeating, living only for the pleasures of art and entertainment, etc. Here the focus is on the obvious examples of sexual gratification and the over-consumption of alcohol.

Do not use up your energy seeking sexual gratification

This theme is dealt with very thoroughly in Proverbs 5. Here it is expressed with the negative command: **'Do not spend your strength on women, your vigour on those who ruin kings'** (31:3). The harem was a common feature of an oriental kingdom. Kings, like Solomon himself, often had many wives and many concubines. The temptation to sexual excess was very real. It is a temptation facing many people today, especially those in positions of privilege and responsibility. The whole problem has been exacerbated by the widespread availability of pornography in its various forms via magazines, television, video and the internet.

It is clear from the Bible that sexual desire is a good gift from God and is not to be despised. However, in a fallen world there is perversion and abuse. Sexual desire is intended by God to be exercised only within the marriage bond, and there with a measure of care and restraint. To plough our energies into expressing our sexual desires in any other way is to sin and to waste our God-given strength. Those of us who are married must confine our sexuality to the marriage bed. Those who continue to be single, or have become single again, must seek the utmost purity in thought and deed. The idea of diverting our energy elsewhere has often been mocked. However, you must exercise self-control, confident that without a marriage partner God will enable you to give undivided attention to the work of the kingdom as you focus on 'the Lord's affairs — how [you] can please the Lord' (1 Cor. 7:32).

Do not over-indulge in the consumption of alcohol or other drugs

Back in Proverbs 23:29-35 we have had a clear warning against the dangers of alcohol. Here a similar note is struck:

> **It is not for kings, O Lemuel —**
> **not for kings to drink wine,**
> **not for rulers to crave beer**

(31:4).

Another feature of oriental monarchy was the great banquets at which there was often excess. We think of what we learn of

Belshazzar in Daniel 5, or King Xerxes in Esther 1, and the dreadful night when Salome danced before Herod, culminating in the death of John the Baptist. Again we see this sort of thing in our own day, among many others. Drunkenness and the abuse of other drugs are an increasingly common feature of our society today.

Alcohol is sometimes referred to as 'the devil's brew'. The use of this expression is understandable but to ascribe it to the devil is to give him undue credit. We may want to debate the ethics of distilling spirits but alcohol itself is a good gift from God. However, as with sexual desire, those who are dedicated to God will handle it very carefully indeed. When an Israelite took a Nazirite vow he was not to let any alcohol pass his lips. Not even a raisin was permitted. The Rechabites of Jeremiah's day were under a similar vow. There are those today who have chosen never to drink alcohol, except at the communion table or for medical purposes. Others will not take alcohol at certain times. Like policemen, they 'do not drink on duty'. Certainly all who are dedicated to God must be very careful with every drug — from caffeine to morphine. It is definitely a sin to be drunk and so we need to take great care, especially in the present climate. To say, 'No drugs will ever pass my lips,' is an unnecessarily extreme position that may well prove unworkable but moderation is important.

Realize what will happen if you do

It will lead to ruin

We need to see that sexual excess leads to ruin. If all our energy goes into this, disaster will follow on many fronts. It wastes time, money and spiritual, mental and physical energy. It often leads to other sins too — for example, deceit, cruelty, selfishness, disrespect, idolatry, vile speech and covenant-breaking.

It also often causes jealousy, malice, bitterness and rage. Beware of sexual excess. Is this not one of the lessons to be learnt from the life of Samson? He was a great man of God ruined by his inability to control his passions, especially his sexual passions. Think too of David's fall and, indeed, of what happened to Solomon himself.

It will lead to injustice

'Lest they drink and forget what the law decrees, and deprive all the oppressed of their rights' (31:5). Overindulgence in alcohol or other drugs is likely to lead to injustice. Again it wastes time, money, and spiritual, mental and physical energy. If the king is often drunk, he is likely to be a bad ruler. Strict penalties rightly operate in many areas of responsibility where alcohol or other drugs are found to have been used. Alcohol in particular is a depressant and is well known for impairing judgement. The number of deaths and injuries on the roads due to excessive consumption of alcohol is a scandal. If a drunk is dangerous behind the wheel, how much more so at the head of a country! The full story of the former Russian premier Boris Yeltsin is not yet known but there can be no doubt that his thinly disguised struggles with the bottle did his country no good.

If you want to serve God faithfully let nothing impair your faculties, but be wholly devoted to God in Christ. Perhaps one of the saddest stories in the Bible is the story of Noah following his disembarkation from the ark. He had survived. Here was a new world, the opportunity for a new start, but what happened? In the midst of his celebrations he became inebriated and lay naked in his tent for all to see. What dire, unforeseen consequences followed! If someone as godly as Noah could fall in such a way let us take great care that we do not.

Seek to comfort the needy and defend their rights

In Proverbs 24:11-12 we read:

> Rescue those being led away to death;
>   hold back those staggering towards slaughter.
> If you say, 'But we knew nothing about this,'
>   does not he who weighs the heart perceive it?
> Does not he who guards your life know it?
>   Will he not repay each person according to what he
>   has done?

Those verses complement what is found here in Proverbs 31:6-9.

Many people think that if they do not sleep around or get drunk they are quite virtuous. But that is only the negative side. Without the positive element found here no great progress is really being made. The negative and the positive aspects are deliberately entwined here. The negative denial should lead to the positive acceptance. Two duties are outlined. Once more, we have general principles enshrined in concrete Old Testament terms.

Be concerned about the perishing and anguished and do something to comfort them

> **Give beer to those who are perishing,**
>   **wine to those who are in anguish;**
> **let them drink and forget their poverty**
>   **and remember their misery no more**
>
> (31:6-7).

Rather than taking beer or wine for himself, the king should use it to help others. To put it very graphically, Lemuel's mother says, 'Put a mug of beer to the mouth of the man who is dying of thirst; give a sip of wine to the man who is in anguish and needs to be calmed down. Instead of dulling your own mind with alcohol, you should be giving it to the poor to help them forget their poverty and their misery.' This is a text that mockers sometimes like to quote but it is not to be taken in a strictly literal sense, as if the best kings provide free beer and wine, or abolish all taxes on alcohol. Rather, the point is that instead of self-indulgence, kings, and all who are dedicated to God, should do all that they can to relieve the suffering of the needy and help them in their troubles. The medicinal use of beer and wine is probably uppermost in the thinking here. Compassion is certainly a must. Are you compassionate? Are you given to comforting the needy and the poor? What are you doing to encourage and to help the suffering and those in need?

Speak up for the downtrodden and needy and see that they get justice

Verses 8 and 9 expand on this further:

> **Speak up for those who cannot speak for themselves,**
> **for the rights of all who are destitute.**
> **Speak up and judge fairly;**
> **defend the rights of the poor and needy.**

Do not only give them comfort and relief, but do something positive to see that they get justice. We all have a part to play, especially those of us who live in a democracy where there is relative freedom. We must work on both fronts, of course — both caring and campaigning. As John Stott has famously put it, there is a duty not only to tend the wounds of the beaten man on the road between Jerusalem and Jericho, but also to do something if we can to make that road safer for travellers.

There are many vulnerable and needy people in every society — the elderly, the sick, the disabled, the poor, children, the unborn, victims of crime and persecution, refugees, aliens, etc.

We have already quoted Job 29:11-17 in the comments on Proverbs 29:7 (see pages 760-61). Job was prevented for a while from doing the kind of things he described in that passage, but, no doubt, when God restored him he did them again. What an example he is to us! Like the Lord Jesus himself, we must go about doing good to all who are in need. To quote Paul's words for the final time, 'Let us not become weary in doing good, for at the proper time we will reap a harvest if we do not give up. Therefore, as we have opportunity, let us do good to all people, especially to those who belong to the family of believers' (Gal. 6:9-10).

A crude reading of this passage, uninformed by the New Testament perspective, may understand it as saying no more than, 'No fornication or drunkenness but do lots for charity and social improvement and you will go to heaven.' But what it is really saying is that the person truly dedicated to God (that is the first step) will avoid excess and will devote him or herself to helping the needy by comforting them and speaking up for them.

As so often in Scripture this is a personal appeal — 'O my son, O son of my womb, O son of my vows' (31:2). God speaks to you believer, as his child, and he says, 'O my son, O temple of my Holy Spirit, one whom I have chosen, take care to turn from sin and to do good.'

It is not only kings who have great privileges and great responsibilities: 'From everyone who has been given much, much will be demanded; and from the one who has been entrusted with much, much more will be asked' (Luke 12:48).

52.
At home with Wisdom

Please read Proverbs 31:10-31

Epilogue: The wife of noble character

Finally, we come to the last section of this wonderful book of Proverbs. Bringing something to a close is almost as difficult as starting it. No one wants the finale to flop, but if jumping on to the big two-wheeler was difficult, how much more difficult to jump off again without crashing! This is why young preachers learning the craft of preaching are rightly told to take care over both their introductions and their conclusions. Equally, some older pastors, having started their ministry well, have great difficulty in bringing it to a satisfying conclusion.

How would you end a book like this? Probably the ending we have here is not what you would have expected. What we have is a separate concluding section, not by Lemuel or by his mother, but by an unknown hand. It is an acrostic poem.

In England in 1599, a certain Sir John Davies presented to Queen Elizabeth I a set of twenty-six poems, the first letter in each succeeding line of each one spelling out the words, *Elisabetha Regina*. Much later, when Queen Victoria was on the throne, Lewis Carroll did something similar at the close of

his *Through the looking glass*. Acrostic poems have been a
fascination in many ages and to this day acrostic puzzles are
loved by many. Among the Hebrews, the fashion was to use
the twenty-two successive letters of their alphabet. There are
as many as fourteen examples of this in the Old Testament.
Psalm 119 is the most famous. There in each octave of verses
the first word of every verse begins with the same Hebrew
letter. English Bibles traditionally print the successive Hebrew
letters over each set of verses to draw attention to this. Other
examples can be found in Psalms 9; 10; 25; 34; 37; 111; 112;
145; Lamentations chapters 1-4 and Nahum 1:2-10.

The poem here apparently describes the ideal woman, 'an
omni-competent woman' with 'no blemish other than her per-
ceived perfection' according to Alison Le Cornu. Surely an
unusual choice of subject for a conclusion! However we may
explain the choice, the emphasis has certainly been on men in
the previous parts of the book, with references to the son, the
shepherd, the farmer and other predominantly male preserves.
Although Wisdom has been presented as a woman, there have
been several potentially derogatory things said about the distaff side. Think of the adulteress, the nagging wife and so on.
This closing passage comes, perhaps, as a refreshingly different approach.

On the face of it, it is an idealized description of a well-to-
do woman of ancient times, what Le Cornu calls 'the epitome
of every man's conjugal dreams'. At first, it appears to be a
guide for men looking for such a wife, or for women wanting
to be all that they ought. It is common for evangelical commentators to take it that way. This is probably not its main
purpose, however. In Proverbs chapters 1 and 8, Wisdom is
personified as a woman. Again, in 9:1-6 we have Wisdom as a
welcoming hostess. In contrast, 9:13-18 introduces the woman
Folly. The various references to the adulteress, we have suggested, are not only to counter physical adultery, but also

spiritual adultery when people are attracted to false teaching. Such warnings are found in chapter 5 and in 6:20 – 7:27. In a similar way, 31:10-31 teaches not only principles of feminine godliness, but also principles of wisdom useful to all. Indeed, the main purpose of this passage is to give a final, memorable picture of Wisdom 'at home'. Here we take up the invitation offered in 9:4-6.

John H. Stek has said that this final section 'constitutes a subtle return to a central theme of the book found in the opening speeches and forms with them an envelope around the book of instruction as a whole. Hence, it appears to be a recommendation to marry Lady Wisdom.'

As for the deeper question of why wisdom (or its opposite) should so often be thought of in feminine terms:

Firstly, there is the fact that this book is framed in terms of a father speaking to his son.

Possibly, the idea that wisdom is often found where least expected is thus underlined.

Maybe it also has something to do with the fact that women are usually physically weaker than men ('the weaker vessel') and so are often more reliant on their native wit, the power of the mind and the subtle approach. We speak readily of feminine intuition, feminine wiles, etc. As a generalization, it is fair to say that there is something more delicate, gentle, quiet, subtle, tender and thoughtful about the feminine approach, as opposed to the often coarse, loud, rather gauche one we associate with males.

Greg Uttinger adds appropriately that 'It is in their wives that godly men find or should find the clearest and dearest personal representation of Jesus Christ.' If their wives even approximate to the dignity, skill, energy and well-doing exhibited here they will.

The wise woman is not an unusual character in the Old Testament. The wise woman of Tekoa (2 Sam. 14), Abigail (1 Sam. 25) and the woman from Abel Beth Maacah (2 Sam. 20:14-22) are obvious examples, along with Rahab, Ruth, Deborah and Esther; and even Tamar and Bathsheba display dignity and wisdom at least in some measure (see Gen. 38; 1 Kings 1). Such women, like their counterparts today, epitomize what is described here. Women who seek to be like them should take to heart the description given, but the chief purpose of the passage is to draw both men and women to embrace Wisdom.

Her desirability

Lee wants to be popular with his mates, or even a famous footballer one day. Jake would be happier to get on in his present job and build up a healthy bank balance. Edwina says that as long as she has her health and her peace of mind that is enough for her. Many people think that the great thing to have in this life is fame and popularity, wealth and success, or health and peace. These are fine things in their own way but, as the book of Proverbs sometimes reminds us, what we need more than anything else is wisdom from on high. Thousands of people in the United Kingdom play the national lottery, or Lotto, once or twice a week and expectantly check their numbers when the draw is announced. Why? Because they seriously believe that if they won the jackpot, all their problems would be over. In truth, money itself can solve nothing. A man who is a fool is a fool whether he is rich or poor. Money will not make him wise or happy, however many millions he may win. There is plenty of evidence for that. As Proverbs 17:16 asks, 'Of what use is money in the hand of a fool, since he has no desire to get wisdom?' That is the greatest need — wisdom.

At least three reasons are given here to explain the attractiveness and desirability of wisdom.

1. Her great rarity and innate worth

'She is worth far more than rubies' (31:10). There are plenty of healthy people around in this world. Probably 90% of people in this world are able-bodied. There are plenty of rich people too. This is more surprising perhaps but, apparently, one in every 5,000 people in the United Kingdom is a millionaire! There is no shortage of famous people either, even if it is only of the 'fifteen-minute' variety. But how many wise people are there in this world? They seem to be so very few. Try to think of someone who is wise. Names do not immediately spring to mind. In civil government, in law, in medicine, in science, in the churches, there seem to be very few wise ones. The thing we most need in every branch of learning and industry and religion is the rarest asset of all.

2. Her power to provide complete confidence and everything of value

'Her husband has full confidence in her and lacks nothing of value' (31:11). Once you find Wisdom and embrace her as your wife you can have complete confidence in her. Others may let you down, but Wisdom never will. You can put your full confidence in her. She will always do the best thing in every situation. You may lose your health, your money may disappear and your popularity may not last, but if you have wisdom, you lack nothing of real value.

3. Her power to be a constant source of good and not harm

'She brings him good, not harm, all the days of her life' (31:12). The person who has wisdom has a constant source of good. Wealth and fame are as likely to do us harm as to do us good. Not even health and peace can guarantee inevitable good.

We must recognize how desirable wisdom is. It is our greatest need. But where to find it? As we have often pointed out in this volume, it is clear from the Bible that true wisdom is found only in the Lord Jesus, who is the Word and wisdom of God. It is by trusting in him that we learn to be wise.

Her quality

A number of characteristics of true wisdom come out here. They have all been mentioned before. If we have wisdom, it will produce these same characteristics in us.

1. She is careful and caring

> **She selects wool and flax**
> **and works with eager hands.**
> **She is like the merchant ships,**
> **bringing her food from afar...**
> **She watches over the affairs of her household**
>   (31:13-14,27).

Careful selection of wool and flax is necessary to provide ample supplies for her needlework so that the family can be fed. Foodstuffs are needed to nourish them. Today the woman might be heading for the haberdashers and the supermarket but the point is the same — **'she selects'**. She does not stuff any old rubbish into the supermarket trolley. Wise people are careful people. They choose with care.

2. She is diligent and hardworking

What a hive of activity there is here!

She gets up while it is still dark;
   she provides food for her family
   and portions for her servant girls.
She considers a field and buys it;
   out of her earnings she plants a vineyard.
She sets about her work vigorously;
   her arms are strong for her tasks.
She sees that her trading is profitable,
   and her lamp does not go out at night.
In her hand she holds the distaff
   and grasps the spindle with her fingers
                                        (31:15-19).

She is not only up early but she works late too, if necessary. She is enterprising. In twenty-first-century Britain she may be dealing with household appliances and tradesmen rather than with servant girls, and a little business run from home may be more likely than buying fields and planting vineyards, but the principles of diligence and hard work do not change. Wisdom does not fly to you. You must be up and about working at gaining it and employing it. The distaff and spindle have also been superseded by purchases at the department store or the second-hand shop, but vigour and strength are still the way forward and there must be no idle moments. At the end of verse 27 it says she **'does not eat the bread of idleness'**. Nor does anyone who is wise, or who hopes to be wise.

3. She is giving and loving

She opens her arms to the poor
   and extends her hands to the needy.
When it snows, she has no fear for her household;
   for all of them are clothed in scarlet
                                        (31:20-21).

She works for the sake of her family, but not only her family
— also for the poor and needy. Anyone who lacks generosity
and love has not yet understood true wisdom.

4. She is attractive and creative

**'She makes coverings for her bed; she is clothed in fine
linen and purple'** (31:22). There is nothing dowdy about this
woman Wisdom. She has flair. She not only knows how to
provide for people but there is something aesthetically pleasing about her whole approach.

I will never forget the first visit to our local church of Mr
Michael Toogood who worked so faithfully planting the church
in the notorious Soho area of Central London. Among his set
of projected slides were 'before and after' shots of the first
family home in a block of flats there in notorious Soho. In the
first exterior shot, even a glance revealed the dirty and dilapi-
dated state of the residence. But the next shot was a burst of
colour as a clean, freshly painted flat shone out from behind
beautiful hanging baskets and standing pots of pretty flowers.

It has been argued that the power and beauty of seventeenth-
century paintings of Dutch interiors derive from the renais-
sance of Calvinism in that part of the world at that time. Certainly, wherever Christian people have gone in the way of wisdom there has been undoubted beauty in the artefacts they
have produced. We may not all be artistically gifted, but where
wisdom is at work then beauty will be found too.

5. She is valuable and honourable

**'Her husband is respected at the city gate, where he takes
his seat among the elders of the land'** (31:23). Inevitably,
wisdom brings both responsibility and honour. The city gate

was where the elders met in ancient Israel and where judgements were made. If Wisdom is your 'wife' you will be given responsibility, and while you remain true to her you will be accepted and respected by all who love justice and fair play.

6. She is enterprising and outgoing

'She makes linen garments and sells them, and supplies the merchants with sashes' (31:24). We have already alluded to Wisdom's enterprising nature. Here she is seen not only providing for her family and for the needy, but producing goods for sale at a profit both for her own retail and to supply others. Some take a narrow view and suppose that a woman's place is in the home and only in the home. That sounds more restrictive than the Bible. Wisdom certainly does not sit around waiting for things to happen. It sees where there is a demand and it supplies that demand. It is active in buying and selling. It is business-minded, commercial, enterprising, even adventurous.

7. She is dignified and assured

'She is clothed with strength and dignity; she can laugh at the days to come' (31:25). Wisdom gives a strength and dignity that cannot be bought. Some think physical exercise will secure their future. Others suppose the latest fashions will give them some sort of status. True wisdom recognizes that dignity and confidence come through Christ. He alone can give us absolute confidence for both time and eternity.

8. She is wise and true

'She speaks with wisdom, and faithful instruction is on her tongue' (31:26). She is committed to teaching others.

True wisdom always has an effect on others. Like the woman here who speaks wisely to others and faithfully teaches, so true wisdom imparts its fruit to others. It may be in a formal setting; more often, as here, it is not. Whatever the circumstances, true wisdom finds ways to share its discoveries with others.

Her glory

In verses 28-31, there is a description of the rewards that the woman Wisdom receives. This brings home to us the glories of wisdom. There are three things to notice in particular.

1. She is gratefully praised by those nearest to her

Her children arise and call her blessed;
**   her husband also, and he praises her:**
Many women do noble things,
**   but you surpass them all**

(31:28-29).

Those who have wisdom, who know Christ, will know gratefulness and glory, whether we think of it in terms of a husband's embraces or the praises of Wisdom's children. When you ask truly wise people the secret of their wisdom they do not say, 'Oh it's me. I'm just like that.' No, they acknowledge that any wisdom they have is a gift from God and they give glory to Christ. Their highest praise is reserved for the Lord. Many have done noble things, but the Lord Jesus Christ surpasses them all. He alone deserves the pre-eminence. Listen to this testimony from the wise. It is not wealth or fame, or even good health or education that you need, but Christ.

2. She shows that charm is deceptive, beauty fleeting and the fear of the Lord pre-eminent

'Charm is deceptive, and beauty is fleeting; but a woman who fears the LORD is to be praised' (31:30). Charm can take you a long way in this world but it is deceptive. 'Watch him — he's a real charmer,' people say. Beauty, of course, does not last, however much help it receives from bottles, tubes and even plastic surgeons! But what does last is the fear of the Lord — which, of course, is where wisdom begins and has been a theme throughout this book. In his first epistle Peter is so bold as to give the women of the church to whom he writes some beauty tips. What does he recommend? Not 'outward adornment, such as braided hair and the wearing of gold jewellery and fine clothes. Instead', he says, '[your beauty] should be that of your inner self, the unfading beauty of a gentle and quiet spirit, which is of great worth in God's sight' (1 Peter 3:3-4). How are you seeking to make yourself beautiful?

3. She is the source of many great works for which she should be praised

'Give her the reward she has earned, and let her works bring her praise at the city gate' (31:31). As with the neighbouring book of Ecclesiastes, Proverbs ends with a reference to the judgement. Here we are at the city gate, the place where we first heard Wisdom's voice (see 1:21) and the place of judgement. And who is before the court or, perhaps better, whose name is on everyone's lips? The name of this woman. And so it will be on the final Day of Judgement itself. The name on everyone's lips then will be the name of Christ, God's wisdom, for then it will be realized that every good work ever done has been done through him.

Will your good deeds be on display on that day? It is only possible to have any truly good deeds through the Lord Jesus Christ, the wisdom of God. Therefore, look always and only to him. That is the message of this book.

Select bibliography

The main commentaries consulted in preparing this present commentary (in chronological order of publication) are these:

Henry, Matthew. *Commentary on the whole Bible* (1710), MacDonald edition

Lawson, George. *Exposition of the Book of Proverbs* (1829), Kregel edition

Bridges, Charles. *A Commentary on Proverbs* (1846), Banner of Truth edition

Harris, W. *The Preachers' Homiletical Commentary* (1891), Baker edition

Kidner, Derek. *Proverbs — introduction and commentary* (1964), Tyndale Old Testament Commentary series (General editor: D. J. Wiseman), IVP.

Alden, Robert L. *Proverbs, a commentary on an ancient book of timeless advice* (1983), Baker Books

Hubbard, David A. *Proverbs* (1989), Word Communicator's Commentary series (General editor: Lloyd J. Ogilvie)

Goldsworthy, Graeme. *The Tree of Life, Reading Proverbs Today* (1993), Anglican Information Office

Atkinson, David. *The Message of Proverbs* (1996), Bible
Speaks Today series (Old Testament Editor: J. A. Motyer),
IVP
Murphy, R. *Proverbs, Ecclesiastes, Song of Songs* (1999), New
International Bible Commentary (Old Testament Editors:
R. L. Hubbard, R. K. Johnston)
Lane, Eric. *Proverbs, Everyday wisdom for everyone* (2000),
Focus on the Bible series, Christian Focus Publications

Among other volumes consulted were William Arnot's *Stud-
ies in Proverbs: Laws from heaven for life on earth* (1884,
Kregel edition) and Stephen Voorwinde's *Wisdom for today's
issues, a topical arrangement of the Proverbs* (published by P
& R). Help was also obtained from magazine articles by Peter
Masters (in *The Sword and Trowel*) and John H. Stek (in *The
Calvin Theological Journal*).